NAPOLEON'S INVASION OF RUSSIA

Napoleon's Invasion of Russia

George Nafziger

Foreword by David Chandler, Head of Department of War Studies,
The Royal Military Academy Sandhurst

★

PRESIDIO

To Robert Iannuzzelli
The seeds he planted bore this fruit.

American School of Paris
1963–1964

Published by Presidio Press
31 Pamaron Way, Novato CA 94949

Library of Congress Cataloging-in-Publication Data

Nafziger, George F.
 Napoleon's invasion of Russia.

 Bibliography: p. 641.
 Includes index.
 1. Napoleonic Wars, 1800–1814—Campaigns—Soviet Union. 2. France. Armée—History—Napoleonic Wars, 1800–1814. 3. Soviet Union. Armiîâ—History—19th century. I. Title.
 DC235.N24 1988   940.2′7   88–6029
 ISBN 0-89141-322-7

Printed in the United States of America

Contents

TERRAIN DIAGRAMS (following page 340)
Engagement at Romanov, 7 March
First Battle of Polotsk, 17 June
Engagement at Mir, 28 June
Battle of Saltanovka, 11 July
Battle of Ostrowno, 13/14 July
Battle of Jakobovo, 19 July
Battle of Loubino, 7 August
Battle of Smolensk, 7 August
Battle of Gorodetchna, 12 August
Battle of Borodino, 7 September
Battle of Trautino, 6 October
Battle of Polotsk, (second battle) 18 October
Battle at Malo-Jaroslavetz, 24 October
Battle of Smoliantsy, 1 November
Battle of Krasnoe, 5 November
Battle of Berezina, 16 November

Foreword

Apart from the Battle of Waterloo and the Campaign of the Hundred Days, no episode exerts a greater fascination over the military historian or general reader with an interest in the Napoleonic period than the Campaign in Russia, 1812. The subject has inspired Tchaikovsky's famous *Overture*, many memoirs by participants who survived the great cataclysm (Russian as well as French and their allies), historical analyses almost without number, numerous notable paintings, perhaps the greatest novel ever written (Leo Tolstoy's *War and Peace*), a number of films and television series, and at least half-a-dozen war games (boxed and video). Now George F. Nafziger has contributed this impressive volume as the latest—but doubtless not the last—serious study of this great and compulsive theme.

It is not 175 years since Napoleon launched his huge, ill-fated attack on Tsarist Russia. The subject still grips, confounds, horrifies, yet fascinates the reader—in my case, after all of a quarter-century of study of the Napoleonic era, without the least trace of diminution. Here, indeed, is a titanic struggle with few equals in scale and drama. It is a subject worthy of an ancient Greek tragedian—a compelling cause fought as much against climate and geography as between armies, presided over by gigantic historical figures in Napoleon, Kutusov, Ney, Davout, Barclay de Tolly, and Tsar Alexander I, towering over a joint military cast of a million or more, containing large battles, a myriad individual acts of heroism (and a few infamous acts) all leading up to cataclysmic disaster for *la Grande Armée de Russie* and to the *Götterdammerung*—the "Twilight of the Gods"—for undoubtedly the greatest "Grand Captain" of modern history, the Emperor Napoleon I.

Tolstoy was at pains to portray Napoleon and Kutusov as in the grip of superhuman forces, mere leaves blown to and fro by the winds of Fate, with scant if any power to affect the great issues at stake; but, as this book makes clear, this determinist interpretation is not sustainable. The history of the Campaign of 1812 is in fact an immense "passionate drama" involving the lives and deaths of hundreds of thousands of participants, exalted and humble, their individual destinies very much dependent on the calculated decisions and human foibles, strengths, and weaknesses of their chiefs. It was an age of giants.

It is hard to comprehend what is meant by casualty figures on the scale involved. The *Grande Armée's* central army group—perhaps 450,000-men strong at the outset—came out of Russia only some 25,000-strong. Of 250,000 horses, only 18,000 skeletal mounts and draught animals survived. Of more than 1,000 guns taken over the Niemen River frontier in June 1812, a mere 120 remained with the army in early January the next year. Possibly the most expensive day in world history, in terms of human loss of life and misery caused by conventional battle, was 7 September 1812—the battle of Borodino. By nightfall a joint total of at least 74,000 soldiers had become casualties, including in their number no fewer than 71 generals. These figures even outshadow those of the first day of the battle of the Somme, 1 July 1916, when 60,000 British troops were mown down by German machine-gun and artillery fire for minimal losses sustained by the defenders. At Borodino, 104 years earlier, it was as if a jumbo-jet loaded with passengers had crashed *every three minutes* from dawn to dusk in an area barely six square miles in extent—say central London or central New York. Small wonder Napoleon termed it "the most dreadful of my battles." But the same God of war could claim, a year afterwards, that he had "fought 60 battles and learnt nothing that I did not know at the beginning." Even if this was a cast-off remark intended for effect rather than literal accuracy, it is a pretty chilling pronouncement. If there was one date when Napoleon should have learnt a great deal, that was surely 7 September 1812.

For the student of military history, the events of 1812 are full of interest. Although overshadowed by events in Eastern Europe, it should also be recalled that the war in the Iberian Peninsula was reaching its first great climax, as Wellington secured control of the twin corridors linking Portugal and Spain (but not without such gory events as the storming of Badajoz) and then proceeded to commence the liberation of the latter country (aided by the reductions in French manpower ordered by Napoleon to build up his armament along the Polish frontier), leading to the battle of Salamanca (news of which only reached Napoleon on the eve of Borodino—a comment on the communication problems of the time), the joyous occupation of Madrid, and then the setback before Burgos which led to a rapid retreat back to Portugal, with everything to be recontested in 1813. The year 1812 also saw the Anglo-American war break out in the Western hemisphere, with its dramatic frigate actions at sea and its American setbacks on land. It was indeed a year of Destiny for a strife-torn world.

Some of the major areas of interest the Russian campaign offers are as follows: The causation of this great struggle between nations and alliances was many-sided, but was it inevitable? Or could the two power blocs have lived amicably side by side? These are matters with no little modern significance. The preparations for war by both sides and the differing natures of their respective armies also repay study. Were they effective? Could they have been improved? Were the war plans realistic and attainable, or were they rapid improvisations to meet an evershifting situation (particularly the Russian strategy of trading space for time)? The communication, command, and control systems on both sides were stretched to the limit. Could these have been improved? The roles of distance, climate, and local fertility within Russia posed the French with as daunting problems of supply, health, and exhaustion of resources as any faced by Hitler's Wehrmacht in 1941–1944. Did Napoleon take these factors properly into account? The importance of the peasant-partisans under General Davydov in harassing the French lines of communication and supply is much stressed by modern Soviet historians. Was this threat containable in 1812; and, if so, what are the possible implications for today? The French lost more animals—and nearly as many men—in the advance to Moscow as they did in the celebrated retreat, yet their morale remained high. That certainly cannot be said of the retreat to Poland. What psychological lessons about men under severe physical stress in a hostile environment are relevant to late 20th-century experience? The list could go on almost indefinitely— but George Nafziger's excellent treatment will suggest answers to many of the posed questions, and no doubt give rise to many more. For, as Professor Geyl of the Netherlands once percipiently remarked, "History is indeed an argument without end."

No two historians are ever likely to agree, therefore, over every detail. To my mind, however, three overriding questions require to be answered. First, did Napoleon's misreading of the character of Alexander I—the sometime admiring client and fellow-despot of Tilsit, 1807— enable the latter to call the Emperor's bluff in June 1812? It can be argued that Napoleon intended nothing more than a demonstration-in-force upon the western periphery of the Tsar's domains, or at the worst a rapid campaign in western Poland, to bring Alexander back into a compliant frame of mind over the Continental System and other issues. In the event, this proved one of the most costly miscalculations in history— if miscalculation, indeed, it was—and one that cost both sides very dearly in the course of the resolution of the daunting and continuing series of crises that resulted.

Secondly, given the need to invade Russia, was Napoleon correct in deciding to advance beyond Smolensk in 1812, or should he have wintered, rested, and regrouped around that city before resuming the campaign in the Spring of 1813? Again, this is a most complex question, much bedeviled by benefit of hindsight. However, it would seem that Napoleon's opportunistic tendencies as a gambler drove him on, overwhelming the sound dictates of caution. As the finance minister, Mollieu, trenchantly described it, ''Although Napoleon's common sense amounted to genius, he could never see where the possible left off.'' The results were Borodino, Moscow—and ultimate disaster.

Third and last, it can be argued that the greatest and most critical moment of decision for Napoleon came on 25 October 1812, in a stormy conference with six of his marshals in a peasant's hut at Gorodna, in the course of which Murat and Davout almost came to blows. It was one week after the evacuation of Moscow, and the day following the inconclusive battle of Maloyaroslavetcz, where the French had failed to break through the Russian forces holding a river line, thus blocking the French chosen line of retreat towards Poland by way of Kaluga and the unravaged countryside of the Ukraine. The question was, as brilliantly depicted in a fine picture by Vereschagin, ''Should we break through or should we retreat?'' Finally Napoleon, untypically, settled for what seemed the safer course—to retire—although it is now known that the Russians had abandoned all hope of holding him from Kaluga had he reopened the action. This critical decision, that doomed the *Grande Armée* to retire along the twice-ravaged route back to Smolensk by way of the ghastly charnel-house of the Borodino battlefield, led to disaster. What might have transpired had the bolder decision been taken? That is the great and unanswerable question.

"War," as General James Wolfe of Quebec fame once remarked, "is an option of difficulties." That is undoubtedly the case, but Napoleon made demonstrably the wrong decision for whatever final reason. Sometimes relatively small events can sway far greater issues. Earlier that same morning, the Emperor had been caught almost unescorted by a surprise attack on the French rear areas by a strong party of Cossacks. He had to draw his sword in self-defense before a rescue could be improvised. The incident—although eye-witnesses avow that the Emperor was at some pains to laugh it off at the time—in fact impressed him deeply. It probably was the issue that tipped the balance in favor of caution at the conference later that day. It certainly caused Napoleon from that day forward to wear poison in a small bag hung around his neck: the fear of possible capture and humiliation worried him more than the frequently encountered prospect of a violent death. But even this psychologically significant precaution let him down in the end. When, on the night of 12 April 1914, some days after his first abdication at Fontainebleau, Napoleon attempted to end his troubles by committing suicide, he swallowed the contents of the bag—but only succeeded in making himself violently sick. Since late October 1812, the poison's potency had diminished.

Russia has never fallen to direct invasion from the West—except, arguably, in 1917, but that debacle was due as much to internal revolution as to external factors. The Teutonic Knights attempted it in the 15th century, Charles XII of Sweden in 1708–1709, Napoleon in 1812, and Adolf Hitler in 1941. Each would-be conqueror in turn failed, defeated by distance and climate as much as by the sturdy defence of their Motherland, "Holy Russia," by the inhabitants. Each successive attacker might have done worse than to study the history of what had happened to his forebears and thus avoided some of the identical pitfalls each encountered and fell into in turn. Perhaps Field Marshal Lord Montgomery of Alamein, K.G., had a point when he wrote in the 1960s, "in my view one of the basic rules of war is—don't march on Moscow." The ancient state of Muscovy has only been conquered from the East.

"The Emperor's health has never been better." Thus ended the famous bulletin which broke the news to an already long-apprehensive French public of the climactic disaster that had befallen the army in Russia. Napoleon had indeed failed, but, as I remarked a fifth of a century ago in *The Campaigns of Napoleon,* it had been "the failure of a giant surrounded by pygmies." Still, the failure was probably not undeserved for all that. The reader must make up his or her mind on this, and many other issues, after reading this new book. Its author has chosen to replough a much-traversed furrow of 19th-century military and political history, but the task has rarely been done with more attention to facts and detail. Not everyone will agree with all of his arguments and interpretations—why, after all, should they?—but they should take them seriously. As the French philosopher Voltaire expressed it in the 18th century, "I may disagree wholeheartedly with what you say, but I will fight to the death for your right to express it." So may it be—now and always.

DAVID G. CHANDLER, Head, Department of War Studies, the Royal Military Academy Sandhurst,
Vice President of *La Commission Internationale d'Histoirie Militaire,*
author of *The Campaigns of Napoleon,* etc.
Sandhurst and Yateley
May Day, 1987.

Introduction _____

This work is intended to be an examination of the military aspects of the greatest campaign and undertaking of Napoleon's career. There is so much to be said and studied on this campaign that for the 170 years since its occurrence, authors and historians have filled countless volumes lining the shelves of libraries throughout the world.

Many of those works are directed at a cursory review of the military actions and dwell on the immense losses and misery of the disastrous retreat from Moscow. Other works concentrate on the strategic aspects of the campaign and those missed opportunities that might have turned the campaign in Napoleon's favor. Still other works concentrate on the politics and personalities of this dynamic period.

In contrast to those works, which tend to be broad-scoped studies, this work will address all the factors that comprise or impacted the military aspects of the campaign. In addition to a review of the military operations, ranging from the tactical to the strategic, it will address the political, economic, and supply considerations that were so important to the campaign.

Researching the tactical action revealed many excellent sources, but a number of instances were found where period accounts contradicted one another. De Segur's account of the battle of Ostrowno has the 8th Hussars attacking and defeating three Russian cavalry regiments that stood motionless as each was attacked and defeated in its turn, abandoning their artillery to be captured by the French. In contrast, General Wilson's account of the battle has two squadrons of Russian hussars and a half horse battery engaging and defeating the French Hussars, driving them back on their parent formation. It was then this larger formation, a division, that defeated the Russians and captured their artillery.

With such divergent accounts, it was often difficult to ascertain what was fact and what was the author's bias. When several sources were reviewed, the most commonly reported and plausible account was more heavily weighted when the account presented in this work was prepared. Such detail as regimental names and numbers were generally accepted from every source presenting such data. If none of the accounts agreed very closely in their detail, a composite account was developed and the most obvious nationalistic biases were removed.

A great diversity of spelling of Russian names was found in the various sources consulted. Most of the sources used were French and their transliterations vary significantly from those used by the Germans, the second principal linguistic source. Only one period English source was used, Wilson, and he provided a third spelling of many names. The selection of a consistent form for each name was, therefore, very difficult. An effort has been made to use as many common spellings as possible, and consistent, appropriate other spellings were used as needed.

In addition to the purely military aspects of the campaign, attention is also given to the military supply systems of the period. The phrase "an army marches on its stomach" was never truer than in this period. It was the source of victory and defeat for many armies. It was the driving force and principal consideration for many of the military decisions made. In this campaign, supply was one of the principal causes of Napoleon's eventual defeat, and supply cannot be ignored if justice is to be given to its significance.

With the intention of doing a thorough examination of the campaign, this volume traces its roots back to 1806, where the initial steps that eventually lead to the invasion are first found. The first chapter on the Continental System is not intended as a detailed discussion of the topic. Rather it is provided with the intention of explaining in broad terms the economic and political factors that lead to the eventual breaking of relations between Napoleon and Czar Alexander. It was this political rupture that lead to the 1812 campaign.

Chapter I

The Causes of the 1812 Campaign

The causes of the 1812 campaign can be said to have had their roots in the military rivalry between France and Russia and the economic rivalry between France and England, but the first shots of this campaign are found in a series of decrees issued in 1806 that gave birth to what was known as the "Continental System." England and France were fighting for the economic domination of Europe.

The term "Continental System" was coined by Napoleon to describe the system by which he intended to defeat England after his efforts to defeat the British navy on the high seas had failed. England was not a self-sufficient country and depended on both its imports of raw materials and its continental markets for its existence. Napoleon hoped that by cutting off these markets he could ruin the British economy and force the British to submit to his will. In addition, Napoleon had the second goal of forcing the Continental states into a total economic dependence on the industrial exports of France, which would give him an economical dominance to match his military dominance of Europe.

Napoleon hoped that he could pursue these goals with the cooperation and approval of his Continental allies. He spent much time condemning Britain's maritime policies, such as the exclusion of non-British products from Britain's colonies and Britain's seizure of the colonies of many of the Continental states. Napoleon postured and posed as the defender of the Continental interests against an unprincipled Britain.

The institution of the Continental System began with the British declaration that the entire coast of the Continent from Brest to the Elbe was in a state of blockade. This was instituted on 16 May 1806. In retaliation, Napoleon closed the entire north German coast of Friesland to British goods.

This situation remained unchanged until late 1806, when the Prussians were beaten by Napoleon. When Prussia ceased to be a military threat to Napoleon, he proceeded to seal off the major commercial cities of Hamburg, Bremen, and Lubeck. This provided a "hermetic seal" against British goods on the Atlantic coast of Germany. He also began the process of seizing all of the British goods that were to be found in those territories. The significance of this move was great because those cities were the principal conduits by which Britain shipped her goods into Europe.

The immediate result of these orders was the seizure of massive quantities of British goods and the enrichment of Napoleon's war treasury. Napoleon's next step was the issuance of the famous Berlin Decrees on 12 November 1806. The preamble of the decree denounced the British blockade of 16 May as a violation of recognized international law. The text of the decree stated that the British Isles were, themselves, in a state of blockade, forbade all trade in British goods, ordered the arrest of all British subjects in allied states, made all British goods liable to seizure, and refused port access to any vessel coming directly from Britain or any of her colonies, or that had called on one of those ports since the issuance of the decree.

The decree applied to all of France's allies and, in theory, formed a counterblockade against British financial incursion extending from northern Germany to Italy, excluding Portugal. Lacking a fleet, Napoleon was unable to actually enforce his blockade of Britain, so the results of this decree were felt principally by the neutrals engaged in commerce, who ran the risk of capture by French privateers.

Those Continental states that were not allies also felt pressure to comply with the decree. Napoleon's victorious armies provided a strong incentive, often stronger than the state's desire for British trade.

Napoleon's aim was to expand the economic isolation of Britain by eventually sealing off every Continental state. Napoleon knew this endeavor would result in serious economic privations for France and her allies, but he also knew that the impact would be even greater, fatal he hoped, on Britain.

Britain's only defense against this decree was to penetrate the blockade with as much commerce as possible. The first British reprisals were the Orders in Council of 7 January 1807. These orders forbade neutrals to trade between the ports of France and her allies, under pain of seizure and the confiscation of ship and cargo. This action, again, was felt primarily by the neutrals like America and Denmark. To these neutrals, these acts were more damaging than the Berlin Decree, as Britain had the navy to enforce its sanction. The impact of these orders on France was minimal.

Napoleon's seal on Continental trade was not complete. The War of the Fourth Coalition, the 1805–1807 campaigns, was terminated by the Treaty of Tilsit. It had several provisions that related to the Berlin Decree and it closed Prussian and Russian ports to Britain. After the signing of the treaty, only Austria, Portugal, Denmark, Sweden, and parts of Italy still traded with Britain.

Of these states, Denmark had special significance. Its geographical location at the mouth of the Baltic forced the British to act quickly. Britain offered Denmark a secret defense alliance. In return for this alliance, the Danes were to turn over their fleet to the British for safekeeping until peace was reestablished. Needless to say, the Danes refused to submit to those humiliating terms. Britain's response was to invade Denmark and seize its fleet on 5 September 1807. This action gave much credence to Napoleon's charges and resulted in the immediate conclusion of a military alliance between Denmark and France. Denmark was now in the Continental System.

As Napoleon began his plans for the invasion of Portugal, Czar Alexander of Russia declared war on Britain. Russia was unable to actively engage British forces, but chose to make military moves against Sweden, who still traded with Britain. Russia invaded and took Finland, which it had long coveted. The successful conquest of Finland left only Portugal as a major port of entry for British commerce to Europe, and Britain was faced with the need to devise other methods to penetrate the Continent.

Britain responded with a new set of Orders in Council that were to do to France's commerce what France was doing to Britain's commerce. All ports that were closed to British commerce were declared blockaded and subject to the same restrictions as if a British fleet were actually posted in their roads. All trade articles from states adhering to the Continental System or their colonies were declared lawful prizes, as were the vessels that carried them. This last move further penalized the neutral states.

However, in an effort to win over the neutrals, Britain permitted direct neutral trade between any British port and any enemy colonial port, other neutral port, or enemy colonial ports not actually blockaded by a British fleet. In addition, trade with Continental ports was permitted, but this could be done only if the neutral vessel put into a British port and paid charges that were essentially equal to the import duties into Britain, before proceeding to the enemy ports.

This system favored British products, since they did not require a reexport certificate, and especially favored sugar, coffee, and cotton carried in British bottoms. The principal thrust of this plan was to force all goods bound for the Continent through British ports.

The next move was Napoleon's. On 17 December 1807 he issued the Milan Decree. This declared that all ships that submitted to a search by the British on the high seas lost their national character, were "denationalized," and were declared lawful prizes if captured by a French or allied privateer. The decree went on to state that every vessel that put into a British port or a British colonial port was also a lawful prize.

The Milan Decree was the logical conclusion of the economic war that was building in intensity. It was declared that there were no more neutrals and forced a declaration of alliance by all states.

As a result, many neutrals now faced economic ruin. In response, the United States of America issued the Embargo Act of 1807. This resulted in so much self-inflicted punishment that it was repealed in March 1809. The Americans replaced it with the Non-Intercourse Act, which prohibited trade only with Britain, France, and their colonies. It was repealed in 1810, and new legislation was written which stated that if either belligerent repealed its decrees against American shipping, the Americans would reinstitute the sanctions of the Non-Intercourse Act against the other belligerent.

Napoleon's concern now became how to maintain his system's airtight seal against British trade and how to bring those few states outside of the Continental System into it. His next step was to invade Portugal in 1808.

The year 1808 saw broad advances for Napoleon's Continental System. Portugal was quickly overrun and Austria was forced to break with England and join the System. The Kingdom of Tuscany was annexed, as were Corsica and Elba. In Italy, only the Papal States were outside the System. This was quickly changed by a total occupation of the

Italian peninsula by the end of 1808. France also occupied the Adriatic island of Corfu, another point of entry.

During his negotiations at Tilsit, Napoleon had encouraged Alexander's hopes of taking Wallachia and Moldavia away from the Turks. Negotiations did not result in a ceding of this territory to Russia. Alexander then directed his minister in Paris to demand that France recognize the Russian occupation of those provinces as well as the French evacuation of occupied Prussia. Napoleon refused. This was the first crack in the Franco-Russian alliance. Napoleon stated that his occupation of Prussia was covered by a separate treaty, to which Russia was not privy. He stated that he was willing to recognize the Russian occupation of Wallachia and Moldavia only if they reciprocated by permitting France to receive compensation in Silesia at Prussian expense.

Accession to these demands would strengthen France's position in central Europe by enlarging the newly created Grand Duchy of Warsaw. Alexander could not countenance this and refused, keeping his troops on the Danube. This act permitted Napoleon to propose various military arrangements to the Turks, while posing as friend to both countries.

Napoleon realized that he and Alexander had conflicting goals in the east, but Napoleon knew that he could not afford to provoke the Russians until the Spanish problem was resolved. Napoleon felt that once this was accomplished, he could renew discussions regarding the fate of the Turkish Empire.

In the meantime, he required the active cooperation and support of Russia in his efforts against Britain. Napoleon sought to renew his influence over the czar by another personal interview. To gain time and tantalize the czar, he sent a letter to Caulaincourt, the French ambassador in Saint Petersburg, directing him to propose a joint Franco-Russian action against the Turks. The proposal suggested that after partitioning Turkey, France and Russia should invade India, which Britain had recently conquered.

These proposals were sufficient to entice Alexander to the interview, but the date was not fixed. Before the final arrangements could be made, Napoleon was obliged by political developments to go to Bayonne and ply his wiles on the Spanish royal family. The outcome of those negotiations was disastrous and led to serious problems in Spain, requiring his full attention. His plans for beguiling Alexander had to wait.

The Spanish blunder rapidly grew in magnitude. It was eventually to tie down major elements of Napoleon's armies, keeping them in Spain for the next six years, when their presence could have been decisive in central Europe.

The British government realized that Napoleon's Spanish blunder was a unique opportunity to open the Continent to British goods as well as to harass Napoleon. They immediately gave promises of aid to the Spanish juntas that arose and dispatched a small expeditionary force. This force defeated Junot's army and drove him out of Portugal. At the same time the French suffered another humiliating blow at Baylen, when the Spanish armies, the military joke of Europe, surrounded and captured a complete French division. Humiliation followed humiliation when the captive Spanish division under General La Romana, posted on the Danish coast, was spirited away by the British navy and returned to Spain, where it joined the fight against Napoleon.

These humiliations shook Napoleon's and France's prestige. This was positive evidence that the French were no longer invincible, encouraging Austria to push its rearming and attracting the attention of Prussia. Napoleon was forced to return his attention to central Europe before he could finish with the Spanish problem. Disturbed by the rising of nationalism in Prussia, Napoleon withdrew some of his troops from Spain and forced a new treaty on Prussia in September 1808. This set Prussia's war indemnity from the 1806 campaign at an impossibly high figure, forced the surrender of several Prussian garrisons on the Oder, and limited the Prussian army to 42,000 men.

In a small gesture to Alexander, Napoleon withdrew his remaining troops from Prussian territory. The immediate result of this was the convening of the delayed interview with Alexander. The interview was held on 27 September 1808 and lasted until 14 October.

The existence of friendly relations between France and Russia was critical to the peace in Europe. Napoleon strove to renew the alliance forged at Tilsit. The situation was quite different now. Napoleon was no longer flushed with the moral superiority of Jena-Auerstädt, and Friedland. Indeed, French military prowess had been damaged by the reverses in Spain.

Alexander had made up his mind to curtail his alliance with France. He had begun to recognize that the best foreign policy for Russia lay in an alliance with Austria, which would provide a counterbalance to Napoleon's growing hegemony over western Europe.

To this end, Alexander employed every diplomatic game he could.

He realized that if Napoleon were able to subjugate Austria, Russia would be next. Alexander realized that Russia was essential to Napoleon's plan and that he could use this to obtain his way with the Turks. With the possibility of realizing his goals in southern Europe so near at hand, Alexander feared that his plans might be upset by Austria's growing militarism and desire to avenge herself for Austerlitz.

Alexander directed his ambassador to attempt to persuade the Austrians to sit by quietly and allow Spain to sap Napoleon's strength. This effort proved fruitless.

The actual interview of the two emperors was unusual. Though a timid person, Alexander remained unmoved by Napoleon's entreaties. He avoided accepting any proposal that would engage Russia in a war with Prussia or Austria and other proposals that might require the withdrawal of his troops from the Danube. The interview ended with a superficial renewal of the Treaty of Tilsit.

Despite his resistance to becoming involved in a war, Alexander did agree that Russian troops would assist France, should she become engaged in war with Austria. At the successful conclusion of such a war, Napoleon promised to recognize Russia's possession of Wallachia and Moldavia in return for the Russian recognition of his conquests in Spain.

With this modest reassurance, Napoleon lead some 200,000 of his veterans into Spain and began a lightning campaign that smashed every Spanish army he encountered. The British, under Moore, were driven to Corunna, where they barely escaped under the guns of the British navy.

After Corunna, Napoleon returned to Paris to put down an anti-imperial intrigue. This arose because of rumors of Austria's warlike intentions. The news had reached Paris that the Austrian War Party had won the internal Austrian political struggle and was forcing Emperor Francis into renouncing the humiliating Treaty of Pressburg signed in 1805 after Austerlitz. This resurgence of pride was closely linked to the rising sense of German nationalism that had begun to appear in the German states along with a call for independence from French dominance. This sense of nationalism had, ironically, been spread by the conquering French armies, as the French had been the first Europeans to embrace the sentiment of nationhood.

An outspoken advocate of national war against France, Count Philip Stadion, was made chancellor of Austria. Archduke Charles, a military hero, was made commander-in-chief of the Austrian army. The Archduke's first actions were the institution of several structural reforms in the Austrian army and the firing of nationalistic fervor in the army. The size of the Austrian army was increased to 300,000 standing troops, and an additional 200,000 landwehr, or militia, were raised, drilled, and enrolled as the army's reserve.

A ferment had begun in Austria, and a report from the French ambassador in Vienna gives a perspective on the intensity of that emotional boil. He stated that "the newspapers contain nothing but tirades against France, and advertisements of patriotic works and accounts of the prowess of Austrian heros."

The Austrians knew of the agreement between Alexander and Napoleon vis-à-vis a war with Austria, but they also knew that Alexander would not make much effort to uphold his treaty obligations. The Austrians felt that Napoleon's entanglement in Spain and Alexander's unlikely involvement in a war with Austria would provide them with an opportunity to reclaim the territories they had lost. They began their 1809 military operations in Bavaria.

Napoleon's reaction was swift and decisive. He withdrew two infantry divisions and the Guard from Spain. This force moved rapidly through France, gathering strength, and headed for the battlefront. Napoleon called up conscripts before their classes were due to be called up and re-combed the previous draft classes for further soldiers.

His efforts produced 200,000 soldiers and a masterful campaign that pushed the Austrians back beyond the Danube. His troops were not the well disciplined and drilled troops he had had in 1805, however, and his first attempt to cross the Danube near Vienna proved disastrous. The Battle of Aspern-Essling was a major military setback and blow to Napoleon's personal prestige. This setback was to have long-range implications for Napoleon because it was his first personal setback and it seriously shook his image of invincibility. It began to enter the minds of the military men of Europe that Napoleon could be successfully opposed on the battlefield.

Russia did participate in the 1809 campaign against the Austrians, but Russian troops did little more than occupy some of Austria's eastern provinces.

Napoleon finally crossed the Danube in a brilliant feat of military engineering and inflicted a crushing defeat on the Austrians at Wagram. This defeat, coupled with other setbacks, forced Francis to sue for an armistice. A treaty was signed three months later.

Napoleon grew more and more worried about the loyalty of Prussia, his nominal ally, and about the chances of a British landing on the Baltic coast. The British did eventually land, but not on the Baltic. After the conclusion of the principal operations against the Austrians, the British landed in the Scheldt estuary, part of Holland. The operation was an endless series of bungled opportunities and bad military judgment. The French were able to seal off the British incursion, and they allowed malaria to finish off the British invasion force. Seeing their operation was lost, the survivors were picked up by the British navy and taken home.

The instability of Prussia was impressed on Napoleon by a number of insurrections and mutinies such as von Schill's raid. Prussia was being swept up by the same military and nationalistic feelings that had pushed Austria into the 1809 campaign.

The Treaty of Vienna, signed on 14 October 1809, further humiliated Austria. It severed 3,500,000 of Austria's citizens from her and gave a large piece of Austrian territory to Bavaria, France's ally. Triest and the strategic coastal area along the eastern bank of the Adriatic Sea were ceded to France to form the Illyrian provinces of France. This last action sealed off southern Europe from British trade from the border of Turkey westward.

The treaty also transferred Galacia to the Grand Duchy of Warsaw, which shocked Alexander, since it was a flagrant violation of Napoleon's verbal assurances that this would never be done. Alexander redoubled his efforts to have Napoleon sign an agreement stating that the Kingdom of Poland would not be restored. This fear was the next major crack in the Franco-Russian alliance.

In 1809 the few remaining portions of independent Italy came under French control. Much of the territories occupied by the French were formally annexed into metropolitan France, as Napoleon began recreating Charlemagne's "Holy Roman Empire." Napoleon's conflicts with the Pope grew, as such conflicts had with every European emperor before him. Napoleon proposed to the Pope that the college of cardinals not be recruited predominantly from Italy, but that a third of them come from the French Empire. Pius VII refused and retaliated by refusing to give his blessings to the bishop candidates proposed by Napoleon. In anticipation of the annexation of the Papal States, the Pope drew up a bull of excommunication against Napoleon. When Napoleon learned of this, he retaliated by arresting and imprisoning the Pope. Pius VII was imprisoned in Savona on the Riveria and proved a great embarrassment for Napoleon.

In 1810, Napoleon took action against his brother Louis, king of Holland. Because of Napoleon's long and deeply held belief that the Dutch were not assisting in the financing of his campaigns as much as he perceived they could, and because they had rather blatantly ignored the trade prohibitions with Britain, Napoleon deposed Louis and annexed Holland into metropolitan France.

Russia's bitterness over Poland continued to grow and new concerns grew about Napoleon's dealings with the Turks, with whom the Russians were now at war. Alexander began having serious doubts about Napoleon's designs and intentions for southeastern Europe. He had received reports about a proposed union of the Balkan states similar to the Confederation of the Rhine, Napoleon's collection of puppet German states.

Whatever Napoleon's intentions were, it became clear that it was never his intention to permit Russia to conquer Constantinople. This situation became more difficult as Napoleon began to insist on a more stringent enforcement in Russia of the articles of the Continental System. He urged the confiscation of neutral vessels in Russian ports, and the entire System, which was crippling Russia's economy, became even more unpopular.

Britain had been Russia's best market for wheat, timber, hemp, and tallow. The restrictions on trade were rapidly forcing Russia into desperate straits. The czar refused Napoleon's demands, alleging that Russia's prosperity depended on the trade and goodwill of the neutrals. It is probable that if Napoleon had made any concessions on the Balkan or Polish issues, Alexander would not have made an open issue of the Continental System. Alexander's refusal opened the Continent to British goods and served notice to the world of his decaying alliance with France.

On 31 December 1810 Alexander issued a decree which favored the entry of neutral ships into Russian ports and virtually excluded the imports of silks, wines, and brandy, which were principally exports of France.

During the next year and a half, both emperors engaged in massive preparations for the pending war. Many Prussian military men saw this growing rift and offered their professional services to Russia, who eagerly accepted them. Alexander's first plans were to carry the war into Germany as had been done in 1806, but the certainty of a hostile Warsaw in his rear made that impossible. These plans were dropped as soon as the

Polish intentions became clear. This development pleased Napoleon greatly, for it eliminated the likelihood of a Prussian or Austrian uprising to support the Russians.

On 24 February 1812 Napoleon concluded a treaty with Prussia which provided him with a contingent of 20,000 Prussian troops to join his growing Grande Armée. It also allowed the French to garrison the Silesian fortresses, and it permitted them to march through Prussian territory and to requisition supplies from Prussian territory.

A similar treaty was signed with Austria on 14 March 1812. That country agreed to provide 30,000 men on the understanding that Austria would recover part of the Illyrian provinces and some of the territory ceded to Bavaria. Austria was also guaranteed that it would receive part of the Prussian province of Silesia, taken from Austria by Frederick the Great during the Seven Years War.

Though successful on those two counts, Napoleon did not succeed with Turkey or Sweden. In Sweden, Napoleon had to deal with Bernadotte, a former French general, who had been elected to the Swedish throne on the death of the previous king. There was little love lost between Napoleon and Bernadotte, who had been feuding since the French Revolution, when only fate had raised Napoleon to the French imperial throne and not Bernadotte.

Bernadotte was elected to his throne, and if his popularity fell, he could be easily ousted. This fact played both economic and military roles as the wars progressed. At the moment, application of the embargo of British commerce would hurt the Swedish economy and cause Bernadotte's popularity to fall. He could not chance that decrease in popular support.

In April 1812 Bernadotte concluded an alliance with Russia and pledged the support of a Swedish corps in northern Germany in event of war. In return he was promised a free hand in Norway, currently part of France's ally, Denmark.

In April a second political reverse was suffered by Napoleon when Russia and Turkey signed a treaty, ending their hostilities over Wallachia and Moldavia. The Peace of Bucharest, signed on 12 May 1812, provided that Turkey would recover Wallachia and Moldavia in exchange for Bessarabia. The sultan had won a lenient peace for his country, and the czar had regained the use of his army for the pending campaign.

Tensions grew and Alexander issued an ultimatum. He stated that he would negotiate with France only if the French were to withdraw from Prussia. Napoleon responded by marching on the Vistula. The Grande Armée advanced into Polish Lithuania steadily from May until 23 June 1812, when the leading elements reached the Niemen River, separating the Grand Duchy of Warsaw and Russia. There was no formal declaration of war. For three days after the first units swam and marched across the Niemen, a steady stream of French, Prussians, Austrians, Dutch, Belgians, Swiss, Italians, Neapolitans, Egyptians, Croatians, Spaniards, Portuguese, Poles, Bavarians, Hessians, Württembergers, Saxons, Westphalians, and members of a number of other small German states marched into Russia. The 1812 campaign had begun.

Chapter II

The French Army: Its Organization, Training, and Equipment

The French Infantry

The army's infantry is its most essential component. Even today, no army can take and hold any ground without the use of infantry. The French army in 1812 was no exception, and infantry made up by far the greatest portion of that army. This force of infantry was organized into companies, battalions, and regiments, all of which had undergone a number of evolutionary changes during the twenty years since the French Revolution.

The basic administrative unit of the French army was the company. In combat it received a different designation that will be discussed later. In 1812 the standard infantry company had a theoretical strength of 140 men: 3 officers, 14 noncommissioned officers, 2 drummers, and 121 soldiers. The strength of these companies could run as few as 40 or as many as 160.

There were two basic types of infantry: line and light (henceforth referred to by the French term "légère"). As a result of the Decree of 18 February 1808, each battalion was reformed with six companies. These battalions had two elite companies and four center companies. In a line battalion there were four fusilier companies, one grenadier company, and one voltigeur company. In the légère battalions these companies were known as chasseurs, carabiniers, and voltigeurs respectively.

The grenadier and carabinier companies were the senior companies in the battalion. The next most senior company was the voltigeur company. The seniority of the fusilier companies was based on the company number.

In addition to the six infantry companies, each battalion had a staff which directed the efforts of the companies. This staff was formed with three officers, one medical officer, and five noncommissioned officers.

The battalions were the building blocks of the regiment. The Decree of 18 February 1808 set the strength of a regiment at four field battalions and one depot battalion. The depot battalion had a slightly different organization, consisting of four fusilier or chasseur companies.

The four field battalions were intended for combat in the field. The depot battalions had entirely different functions. The depot battalion was numbered as the 5th Battalion in every regiment. The depot battalions were stationed in garrisons and forbidden to leave them except on the explicit orders of the emperor. Each depot battalion had four companies of fusiliers and a staff. The companies had the same organization as the companies in the field battalions, but the battalion staff, under the command of a major, consisted of five officers, three noncommissioned officers, and a student drummer.

Each company had different specific duties. The fourth company of the battalion rarely if ever left the depot. It was charged with training recruits and included in its ranks the regiment's artisans, the "enfants de troupe" (soldiers' sons carried on the battalion payroll), and any veteran soldiers awaiting retirement, discharge, or pensioning. The first and third companies were responsible for transporting newly trained recruits to the field battalions. As a precaution, to prevent the new men from deserting, several such companies would be formed into a "bataillon de marche," and several of these battalions would be converged into "regiments de marche."

The second company of the battalion was generally assigned to act as guards for naval vessels as well as for the garrisons to man them. In addition to the duties of the companies, the depots generally had a cadre of recruiting officers—generally a captain, two lieutenants, and two sous-lieutenants.

An examination of the Order of Battle for I Corps of the Grande Armée in Appendix III will show that many of the regiments had five field battalions. This expansion was due to an effort on the part of Napoleon to fully utilize the number of recruits that were being drawn into his army. By 1813 at least one regiment had eight battalions.

This expansion began with the Decree of 23 April 1811, which directed the raising of a sixth battalion for the 12th, 17th, 21st, 30th, 33rd, 48th, 57th, 61st, 108th, and 111th Line Regiments. These battalions were formed around cadres drawn from the regiment's other battalions, new recruits, and detachments from the various penal regiments. A total of 750 men were to be drawn from these sources to complete these battalions. The sous-lieutenants were to come from the military school at St.-Cyr, the captains and lieutenants were to come from the Imperial Guard. These sixth battalions did not have elite companies. Instead they had a fifth and sixth fusilier company.

The results of the drafts of 1811 and 1812 were proving more success-ful than originally anticipated. Napoleon went on to consider raising a seventh battalion for many regiments. The history of these battalions was varied. None was organized or participated in the 1812 campaign. In 1813 many were torn apart to rebuild the first five field battalions, and others operated as a newly raised seventh battalion.

The National Guard

In addition to what might be called the "regular army," there was a second-line formation known as the Garde Nationale. The Senatus-Consulte of 13 March 1812 ordered the formation of an active National Guard consisting of eighty-eight cohorts. The National Guard was orga-nized in three "bans," or call-ups. The first ban was composed of men aged twenty to twenty-six and belonging to the last six draft classes. The second ban was all men between twenty-six and forty who were still in good health. The last, or "arrière ban," was composed of all fit men between forty and sixty.

Each of the eighty-eight cohorts was to be established with a strength of six fusilier companies, an artillery company, and a depot company. The staff was organized with a Chef du Cohort commanding two other officers and seven noncommissioned officers including four master arti-sans.

The six companies were organized in the same manner as those in the companies of a line infantry company. The cohort had no elite compa-nies. Their officers and noncommissioned officers were drawn from the ranks of officers and soldiers that had been retired because of age or wounds that were now considered'not to be too debilitating. Generally, these men retained their ranks when drawn into the National Guard. As a result, these National Guard battalions had a very sound cadre.

Penal Regiments

There was a third infantry formation in this period: the penal regiment. The French army consisted mainly of conscripts, for the levée en masse had long supplanted the volunteer forces of 1792. Like all armies, the French army was plagued by desertion, as shown by a letter from the duke of Feltre, French minister of war to Napoleon, who described the situation in the 12th Military Division. Of the 840 men being transported to l'Île de Ré, 88 men deserted between Surgères and Luisagnan. He reported another instance where a deserter was executed in front of his unit and, despite this, in the following month a further twenty-six men deserted.

In general, desertion was punishable by death. The Decree of 2 February 1811 superseded the Law of 21 Brumaire An V (12 November 1796) and all previous laws relating to desertion. It stated that the death penalty was mandatory for the leaders of desertion plots and under special circumstances was also applicable to the principal instigators. The Decree of 23 November 1811 had qualified the general death sentence, stating that those individuals who were pardoned for an earlier desertion and did not return to their units would be executed.

The Decree of 24 January 1811 had been issued to use the deserters that were being recovered. It directed the raising of the penal Régiments de Walcheren, de Belle-Île, and de l'Île de Ré. The Régiment de Belle-Île was a légère regiment, while the others were line regiments. None of their battalions had elite companies, though they were constituted in every other sense like those of the line infantry regiments. These regiments were assigned to form the garrisons of the islands whose names they bore. The Régiment de l'Île de Ré also maintained garrisons on the islands of Oléron and Aix.

When these penal regiments were raised, the minister of war presented the nomination for the senior regimental officers, the colonel, major, quartermaster, and adjutant-majors, and the officers of the first battalion, to Napoleon for his approval. After the first battalion had a strength of 600 men, the nominations for each successive battalion were presented. The sergeants and corporals were drawn from the fusiliers and tirailleurs of the Imperial Guard in the hope that they might instill some military discipline in the deserters.

Each of the penal regiments drew its men from specific military divisions. The men going to the Régiment de Walcheren came from the 15th, 16th, 17th, 24th, 25th, 26th, 31st, and 32nd Military Divisions. Those of Belle-Île came from the 11th, 12th, 19th, 20th, and 21st; and those of Méditerranée came from the 6th, 7th, 8th, 9th, 10th, 27th, 28th, 29th, and 30th Military Divisions.

The Decree of 11 March 1811 renamed the Régiment de la Méditerranée the 1er Régiment de la Méditerranée and ordered that it be increased to the full four field and one depot battalion organization. It was to be trained and equipped as a légère regiment. The same decree also authorized the raising of the 2eme Régiment de la Méditerranée, which was to be constituted as a line infantry regiment. Neither regiment was to have elite companies, but the decree stated, "When these regiments have two years of service, our Minister of War shall receive our orders for the formation of one or more companies of elites." These elite companies were eventually raised during the 1813 campaign.

The Decree of 12 March 1811 also addressed the penal regiments. The Régiment de Walcheren was ordered to raise a third battalion with Spanish prisoners of war. Each company was to have the standard 140 men. These men were to be volunteers, and if they served "well and faithfully for six years," they would be given a full pardon and allowed to return to their homeland, Spain. This battalion was formed on the Rhine and outfitted in Strasbourg.

The ultimate function of the penal regiments was not combat. Prior to the invasion of Russia they were to serve as manpower pools for other units, replacing losses and providing new drafts to fill out new units. The Régiment had a force of 4,000 men, but prior to 1812 it had sent 600 others to form the fifth battalions of the 29th and 112th Line Infantry Regiments, 840 to form the 7/6th Line Infantry Regiment, 500 to the 14th Légère, 860 to the 6th Line Infantry Regiment, 560 went to the 5/14th Line Infantry, and 360 were detached to form the 1st and 2nd Sapper Companies de l'Elbe. This indicates that a total of 8,590 men passed through the regiment and into the regular army. In addition, the 2eme Régiment de la Mediterranée processed 8,160, l'Île de Walcheren processed 10,831, Belle-Îsle processed 4,580, and l'Île de Ré processed 6,220 men. This means that the penal regiments salvaged and rehabilitated 38,351 deserters, returning them to the ranks. This number, which is equivalent to a full division, clearly indicates the importance of these regiments to Napoleon.

Tactics and Drill

In 1812 there was only one set of drill regulations in effect for the French, the Regulation of 1791. These regulations were founded on the linear tactics of the eighteenth century but had undergone major modifications during the wars since the French Revolution. The modifications were principally in the field of skirmish tactics (something not discussed in the regulation), a new form of the basic anticavalry formation known as the "square," and a few other tactics.

The French infantry company, when used as a tactical organization, was renamed and known as the "peloton." It was formed in three ranks spaced at thirteen-inch intervals. The first rank was composed of the tallest men and the second rank had the shortest men. During a campaign, if casualties were sufficiently great, the third rank would be fed into the first two ranks to maintain the peloton's frontage.

Each peloton was divided into two sections for drill purposes. Two pelotons operating together formed a "division," which should not be confused with the larger formation consisting of thousands of men. All maneuvers and tactics were performed with either the section, peloton, or division.

The tactics and linear evolutions employed by the armies of this period were extremely complicated and called for extensive schooling of both the soldiers and officers. The first step for a new recruit was the "école du soldat" or soldier's school. This school was divided into three parts. The first taught the recruit how to carry his weapon; the second taught him how to maintain, load, and fire it; the third taught the different marching cadences, the principals of marching, dressing of the ranks, formation conversions, and changes of direction. From there the soldier learned and relearned each maneuver in successively larger and larger formations.

The basic pace was twenty-six English inches (two French feet) in length. The French used this pace with five cadences: the "pas ordinaire" (76 paces per minute), the "pas de route" (85–90 paces per minute), the "pas acceleré" (100 paces per minute), the "pas de charge" (120 paces per minute), and the "pas de course" (200–250 paces per minute). The "pas de course" was used after 1792 to some advantage and was prescribed in the Exercise Regulation of 1769. However, Napoleon generally preferred the "pas acceleré."

Musketry

The system of fire used by the French prior to this period had been established by the Regulation of 1764. It was based on the three-rank peloton. The Regulation of 1791 had established a two-rank voluntary firing system to supplement it, because fire from the third rank had proven impractical when the troops were wearing backpacks. In this situation the third rank loaded muskets and passed them forward.

The French infantry were taught to fire by peloton, by demibattalion, and by battalion. They were taught an advancing fire where the battalion would advance alternate pelotons, which would fire when they halted. The nonfiring pelotons would then advance. Though the men were taught to fire with the front rank kneeling, in actual combat this was discouraged. It was found that the men were unwilling to stand up once permitted to kneel.

One of the principal forms of musketry was fire by ranks. During this evolution, the third rank stood six and one-half inches to the right and fired through the gaps in the two front ranks. In this system the third rank fired first, then the second rank fired and the first rank fired last. Since the ranks were never permitted to fire voluntarily, the peloton was always able to maintain a reserve firing capability. This was intended to protect it against a surprise cavalry attack. In comparison, the British two-rank system seems to have proven superior, but it should be remembered that the Prussians, and no doubt other armies, practiced a "swarm attack" with light cavalry that was designed to tease a line into firing. Once the line had fired and was struggling to reload, heavy cavalry, which had been masked by the light cavalry, would sweep down upon the now helpless infantry.

A musket ball if fired horizontally would carry about 400 paces. In order to hit a target at 800 or 900 paces it was necessary to aim three feet above the target. Formal guidance was provided for aiming, but in actual practice aimed shot was rare, and someone being hit by an aimed musket shot was even rarer. In combat situations, men would begin to load and fire automatically, ignoring target location or terrain. They were known to fire horizontally from parapets, and the shot would pass over the heads of their enemies.

Musketry in this period was inaccurate at best, even without considering the problems of the individual handling the weapon. The tolerances of the weapons were crude and as the ball passed down the barrel it bounced from one side of the barrel to the other, seldom going in the direction in which it was aimed. This inaccuracy led to the dependence on massed formations that fired generally unaimed weapons at another large target.

The Regulation of 1791 was exacting in its requirements for target fire. Marshal Davout further reiterated this ordinance and ordered on 16 August 1811 that "all soldiers shall exercise at 50 toises (108 yards = 100 meters), then at 100 toises (216 yards = 200 meters), and finally at 150 toises (324 yards = 300 meters). He added that at "50 toises the troops would see their shot falling low and at 150 toises their shot would fire higher''—that is to say above the point at which they had aimed.

The Prussians, as did others, performed a famous experiment to determine the accuracy of their weapons. They erected a canvas screen, 100 feet by 6 feet, roughly the shape of a formed infantry peloton. A grenadier company fired volleys at this target from ranges of 225, 150, and 75 yards. The hits registered on the target were 25 percent, 40 percent, and 60 percent respectively. The geometric increase in accuracy resulting from the decrease in target range had bloody ramifications if a trained unit held its fire to the last minute. Despite this, most battlefield casualties resulted from casual musketry fire and artillery fire, not from volleys exchanged between two infantry formations.

A good shot from a musket under combat situations could hit a man at 100 yards, despite the target practice prescribed. Rifles were more accurate than muskets, but were handicapped by a much lower rate of fire. While rifles were in use by the military during this period, they had generally disappeared from the French army. The Bavarian, Austrian, and Prussian light infantry were armed with rifles, but in the French army only the sergeants of the light infantry voltigeur companies carried them.

The musket of this day had several drawbacks besides the lack of accuracy. The principal charge in the musket was detonated by a spark produced by a flint hitting the steel frizzen. This spark ignited loose powder in the pan which, in turn, transmitted the fire into the musket via the touch hole. The flint was subject to wear and required adjustment or replacement after about twenty rounds. The powder in the pan was also known to ''flash'' without igniting the main charge (hence the phrase ''a flash in the pan''). This was dangerous because soldiers often did not realize that their musket had not fired. If they reloaded the musket and attempted to fire it a second time, the double or multiple charge in the barrel could detonate with disastrous results.

Assuming that everything went well and the piece fired, a rate of three to four rounds a minute could be attained. This rate of fire could not be maintained very long. The barrel would foul from the residue of the coarsely milled and refined powder. Accuracy would also diminish as repeated volleys fouled the barrels and filled the air with smoke that obscured the enemy.

Maneuvering and Formations

Upon completing this phase of training, the soldier advanced to the "école de bataillon." This school was divided into five sections. The first was concerned with the opening of ranks and firing in formation; the second dealt with formation changes to column from line; the third addressed long-distance marching and such diverse movements as changes of direction and countermarching; the fourth section taught the different methods of passing from column to line; and the fifth section taught the different methods of entering and exiting the battlefield, changes of front, the passage through line formations, the attack column, and how to rally and reform.

The linear evolutions in the field were little more than a regiment or brigade application of the lessons taught in the battalion school. This drill permitted the regiment or battalion to perform all that was necessary for it to operate in the field.

The Regulation of 1791 had directed that the square, an anticavalry formation, be formed in the shape of a dense, solid column if a single battalion was to form the square. The only hollow square discussed was a multibattalion formation. However, because of the reorganization of the battalion from the eight-company organization to a six-company organization by the Decree of 18 February 1808, this formation was not readily adaptable. In place of the dense column, the "carré d'Egypte" became far more commonly used. This formation was rectangular, formed with a one-peloton depth and a division (two-peloton) frontage. It was only three ranks deep. Since this formation had two different-sized faces, it could be arranged parallel or perpendicular to the battle, depending on where the greater fire was required.

In addition to battalion squares, the French also formed regimental squares. These were often massive formations formed with several battalions. They were arranged to maximize the fire that could be directed against the enemy cavalry. They were used at the battle of Borodino and many battles in 1813.

The three infantry schools produced a soldier capable of performing every maneuver necessary. The officers and noncommissioned officers attended these schools so that they might obtain a complete understanding of the maneuvers, but after they completed those schools they passed on to further training provided in "regimental schools" established for that specific purpose. Marshal Davout was the first to formally establish these schools, and he made them standard preparation for command. In February 1811, the regimental schools had the goal of training 200 students per infantry regiment (60 corporals and 140 soldiers) and 100 per cavalry regiment (30 brigadiers and 70 troopers), all chosen for their aptitude.

These regimental schools ran for two to three months. They were taught by officers and noncommissioned officers from a manual on the duties of an officer written by Marshal Davout. This manual, which presented everything in a practical manner, with an eye towards actual field considerations, concerned itself with every aspect of the regiment's functions. These included placing sentinels, going on patrols, making day and night reconnaissance, searching woods and villages, constructing field works, occupying defiles and bridgeheads, crossing ditches, serving guns, spiking and unspiking guns, and other necessary skills. In addition there was training in writing, mathematics, and bookkeeping.

During the Armistice of Schönbrunn, in 1809, General Mathieu Dumas was charged with drawing up a regulation on the service of troops on campaign. Unfortunately, this regulation was drawn up in too great haste and was little more than a compilation and revision of the old regulations. It proved to be an unworkable tangle that was of little use to the French army.

In 1812, General Preval undertook the same project and wrote "Projet de règlement de service pour les armées en campagne." Chapter X was particularly instructive. It addressed general tactics that were, in the author's words, "no stranger to any military man of the times," discussing the procedures for advanced guards, approaching the battlefield, dispositions to be used, and successful tactics. Part of this work stated:

> One may not write regulations on the manner for the disposition of one's forces that are fixed and inflexible, since situations and types of troops interact with the nature of war and terrain to make different demands upon a general.
>
> The advanced guard should be preceded during the march by a screen of skirmishers to protect it from attacks. These skirmishers are to occupy, fatigue and disconcert the enemy, containing his skirmishers, proving and examining enemy positions and prepare for the coming combat.
>
> After the advanced guard overthrows the enemy's advanced positions it is to occupy the important points and facilitate the

maneuvers of the main body. In addition, it is to engage in probing attacks and other diversions to confuse the enemy's maneuvers.

When in the proximity of the enemy, one should form several lines, if the number of troops permits. If this is not possible and only two lines can be formed, one should place several battalions behind the wings of either flank. These lines may be of troops in column or line, according to the terrain and the desires of the general, be it to demonstrate or attack. The forward guard, so as not to become confused with other troops, should be placed on the wings, in villages or in raised or broken terrain.

The reserve shall be behind and at the center or rear of important points. It shall be, as much as possible, composed of the elite corps, both infantry and cavalry. Its objective is to achieve the defeat of the enemy, reestablish a lost battle, or cover a retreat. Celerity should be one of the principal qualities of this reserve corps.

Cavalry should be placed in echelons on the wings, terrain permitting. One should recommend to it vigor and quickness, and the goal of turning the enemy. It should never accept an enemy charge standing. It should use the superiority of its formation and never go to the gallop closer than 100 yards from the enemy.

The artillery shall be employed to extinguish the enemy batteries, when one is disposed to attack a point. In defense they shall direct their fire upon the troops advancing on them. In these two cases, they should be massed as much as possible, since the effect of their fire is superior when concentrated.

In combat and other field operations, it was always desirable to take the offensive and to force the enemy over to the defense. The French strove to initiate attacks with a superior force as soon as possible, using false attacks to disguise the target of the main thrust. Advantage was taken of terrain to conceal the main striking force and permit the massing of superior forces without detection by the enemy. An excellent example of this was Napoleon's use of terrain and fog at Austerlitz.

The French considered it necessary for a general to be slow in making his plans and swift in executing them. It was important that he never hazard an attack without assuring his communications and lines of retreat, should it be necessary to break off the action and retreat.

Napoleon required that the army corps, the divisions, and even the brigades always operate in a mutually supporting manner. He was not pleased if a general ignored this procedure, no matter how great that general might win, if the other general and his forces were lost because of his failure to support them.

When successful, the French employed their light troops to pursue the beaten enemy. Other forces were not generally used in this function until order had been reestablished and they were formed into columns. Even in pursuit, the French would advance cautiously, moving from position to position, always ready to receive an attack if the enemy succeeded in reforming or if pockets of resistance were encountered.

Skirmishers

Further tactical advice was provided by Marshal Davout, who issued two instructions that went into effect during the last months of 1811. The instruction dated 16 October 1811 concerned itself with skirmishers. The second instruction, dated 3 November 1811, addressed the use of squares. In both instances, Davout's instructions were probably a reflection and codification of the general practices of the French army in this period. Davout wrote them down and formally distributed them to his generals because he felt some concern about the lack of training in his recently expanded regiments.

In the first instruction he acknowledged that it was always preferable to employ entire pelotons as skirmishers rather than sections or other smaller units. He directed that the skirmish line would operate about 200 paces in front of the column or line and was to be divided into three sections. The first and second ranks of the two wing sections would be deployed immediately by files and form a semicircle at intervals of fifteen paces between pairs of soldiers.

In each section, the third rank, the sergeant, the corporals, and a drummer or bugler were held in reserve with an officer, either a lieutenant or a sous-lieutenant. The peloton captain remained in the center of this formation with his sergeant major.

This reserve, generally no fewer than six men, was to furnish replacements for the line, reinforcing points where the skirmish line was attacked and providing escorts for the officers. They also served as rallying points and guided withdrawals. If a noncommissioned officer was detached to carry orders to the skirmishers, he was escorted by a fusilier drawn from the reserve. The skirmishers were trained to work in a mutually protective pair. One member of each pair always had his musket loaded and ready to fire in case they were attacked while the other member of the pair was reloading.

When protecting a retreating line, the skirmishers formed themselves parallel to the line and withdrew in such a manner that the captain could always maintain visual contact with the line he was charged with protecting. Communications were continuously maintained through the use of noncommissioned officers.

The skirmishers were trained to operate at the "pas ordinaire" and the "pas acceleré," but they often operated at the "pas de course" because they were obliged to move quickly when covering changes in direction or charges. In case of a cavalry attack on them, the skirmishers would retire to the parent unit at the "pas de course," but it would seem likely that they ignored a fixed cadence when executing this particular maneuver. If they did not return to the main body, they would find individual cover in holes, behind obstacles, or in other places of security from which they could continue to fire.

On a plain, the French skirmishers were to march forward silently, with calm sangfroid, holding the enemy at such a distance with their fire that his fire could not reach their parent unit. In broken terrain they were to search through any cover that might conceal an ambush. Davout's instructions went on to direct:

> If the skirmishers were to traverse a village, the captain was to march in the rear with his reserve and take an advantageous post with his reserve which would permit the occupation of the principal avenues as the skirmishers searched through the village and provide the skirmishers with a rallying point.

> If the skirmishers were marching through woods or through terrain broken by trenches, hedges, or ruins, etc., they must advance with the greatest caution and place themselves such that if they encounter the enemy, they are able to profit from the enemy's errors and force him to abandon his position.

> If the enemy is under cover or in ambush he must be turned. Some brave individuals must make themselves visible on a high point behind the enemy, which the enemy feels to be secure. This will always force him to abandon his positions and at a considerable loss.

> When advancing, the skirmishers and their officers should main-

tain their attention not only on the enemy, but also on their own troops. Even more so, their attention should be directed towards the terrain, seeking places of cover in case of a fire fight or retreat.

Davout's instructions for skirmishers were simple, functional, and of practical utility for the prosecution of war in this period. His instructions for attacks on villages and entrenchments were no less judicious:

Suppose a skirmish line, followed by reserves, is ordered to advance in an attack on an entrenchment, village, farm, forest, etc. It is probable that the enemy, when attacked along the length of his front will deploy as far as possible so as to offer an equal resistance. If the attacking commander holds a good reserve force and extends his skirmishers on the double to the extremities of the enemy, where they attack the enemy vigorously on his flanks, he is assured of a complete success if he then drives his reserve into the enemy's front.

The same attack can be executed with skirmishers vigorously engaging the front of the enemy's line as the reserve drives itself into the enemy's flank.

As mentioned above, Davout's letter of 3 November 1811 concerned the forming of squares. This letter was part of his almost continuous effort to refresh his corps in all the basic tactics of the day and to ensure a uniformity of procedure among its units.

Experience, Davout said, had shown the necessity of placing a reserve in the center of any square, but this reserve was never to be made more than one-twelfth of the total strength of the unit forming that square. The officer commanding a square was required to carefully observe the sustained enemy attacks and any disorder caused in the ranks due to artillery fire so that he could reinforce weakened spots.

In response to cavalry attacks, Davout recommended that the squares use only fire by rank or by file. Fire by file commenced at a maximum range of 150 paces and from the right. Each file was to fire with increasing rapidity as the cavalry closed. Fire by rank was only to be executed at 100 paces or less. The ranks fired successively: while one was firing, the other two ranks either reloaded or stood by with loaded weapons. This last form of fire, Davout stated, was the most effective against charging cavalry.

Davout specified that squares should generally be positioned in echelons so that they were mutually supporting, with the regimental artillery pieces posted at the outermost corners of the regimental-square checkerboard in an effort to provide greater firepower at the most vulnerable part of the square. The corners subject to the lowest threat were made impenetrable by placing caissons and other train equipage in them. These were then covered with small groups of skirmishers. The intervals between the squares (usually 120 paces) were filled with other caissons, forges, field baggage, and such equipment as could not be brought into the squares. Though this might seem to provide cover for the attacking cavalry it did not. It was intended that these obstacles would break up the cavalry's formation, which was its principal strength, and which gave it the ability to break infantry squares.

Rations

The infantryman was concerned with tactics, but his principal concern was the same in 1812 as it is today: his rations. The rations issued in 1812 were set by the Decree of 20 June 1810. The noncommissioned officers and soldiers received a daily bread or biscuit ration. This bread was three-quarters wheat and one-quarter rye or barley of good quality. On campaign the soldier received a biscuit ration (in place of the bread) which weighed 550 grams (1.2 ounces), a rice ration weighing 30 grams (1 ounce) or 60 grams (2.1 ounces) of dried vegetables, 240 grams (8.6 ounces) of fresh meat or 200 grams (7.1 ounces) of salted beef or lard, 16 grams (0.6 ounces) of salt, and a liquor ration. The latter, distributed by special orders from the commanding officer, consisted of a liter of wine for four men, a liter of brandy for six men, and in hot weather, a liter of vinegar for twenty men.

In addition to food, each soldier was authorized a wood ration of 2.4 kilograms (6.1 pounds) or 1.2 kilograms (3 pounds) of coal or peat during the winter. This ration was progressively diminished as the wars progressed. Each soldier was also authorized 15 kilograms (12½ pounds) of straw for bedding every fifteen days.

Officers received various numbers of the basic rations. Senior officers received several rations so that they might provide for their suites and for those whom they would entertain.

Infantry Weapons

After rations, the soldier was most concerned with his weapons. The most common infantry weapon in use in 1812 was the Charville 1777. This was issued to the fusiliers and grenadiers, while the voltigeurs were generally issued a lighter weapon, a "fusil de dragon." The sappers were issued musketoons.

The munitions issued with these weapons were in the form of cartridges. Thirty cartridges were carried in their "giberne" or bullet pouch. The weight of powder was usually equal to the weight of the ball. The balls varied from sixteen to twenty to the pound.

The French word for cartridge, "cartouche," is derived from the Italian word "cartocchio," which means a "large paper." This transition from the Italian to the French occurred because the cartridge was a small paper bag that contained both powder and shot.

The infantry generally did not carry munitions unless they were on campaign. On the day of battle the drum-major and his drummers were sent to the divisional artillery caissons to obtain cartridges for their regiments. The general practice, although not required by regulation, was to stack the cartridges behind the ranks.

The voltigeur sergeants carried rifles, the only rifled weapons in the French army in this period. The sergeants carried loose powder and shot instead of the cartridges issued the other infantrymen.

Infantry Equipment

Noncommissioned officers, grenadiers, drummers, hornists, musicians, and sappers were equipped with a "sabre-briquet" or short infantry sword. Each soldier carried a haversack divided into four compartments. The bottom compartment was separated into two compartments by a linen divider. The third compartment, a sack that hung on the side of the haversack, was for dirty linen. The fourth compartment was formed by a wooden palette.

The lowest compartment was for the soldier's personal effects. He placed his two rolled shirts, stockings, handkerchiefs, a collar, and clean gaiters here. Over the shirts he placed a pair of linen pants. The soldier's case was placed in a corner of the haversack.

The greatcoat was carried on the haversack and tied with two leather thongs. A pouch in the palette carried the soldier's extra pair of shoes, his brush, and his heelball.

A four-day ration of bread was carried in the front pocket of the haversack. Any additional bread was hung from the haversack on a cord. Although it was subject to spoilage from the sun and rain, as well as loss and theft, the soldiers never abandoned this traditional practice.

The meat ration was divided into two- or three-pound sections and placed in a handkerchief or hung in a sack from the haversack. If the meat was dried or salted it would be wrapped and placed in the haversack with the bread ration.

In addition to the thirty cartridges in his giberne, the soldier carried a number of tools in a small pine box. There was a sheepskin pouch that had a screwdriver, a bullet extractor, spare flints, some shot, some grease, a block of wood or horn, and a sheepskin apron called a "sous-palette," which kept the cartridges together and separated them from the other items in the giberne.

French Cavalry

Just as with the infantry, French cavalry was broken into two types: heavy and light. Unlike the infantry, there were other differentiations beyond these two basic groups.

In 1812 the heavy cavalry consisted of two carabinier regiments, fourteen cuirassier regiments, and thirty dragoon regiments. Although their origins, traditions, and original purposes were different, all three shared the primary function of shock or battle cavalry. As the main striking force of the Grande Armée, the heavy cavalry was designed to strike and rupture the enemy's line, thus causing the disintegration of the enemy army. In addition, the dragoons were often employed as vedettes, patrols, convoy escorts, and in antipartisan operations. These functions were a holdover from their historical roots as mounted infantry. These tasks were, as a result, not performed by the carabiniers or cuirassiers.

The light cavalry consisted of eleven hussar regiments, thirty-one chasseur à cheval regiments, and nine chevauléger-lancier regiments. The light cavalry was intended as a scouting and reconnaissance force or used to pursue the beaten enemy, but it was also used for shock actions on the battlefield.

All French line cavalry regiments were organized with four squadrons. Each squadron had two companies. Since a squadron generally had 125 horses when on a wartime footing, the theoretical strength of a regiment was 1,100 men and 1,000 horses. Before the invasion of Russia, Napoleon tried to ensure that each regiment would be able to present between 850 and 900 sabers on the battlefield, but as the campaign progressed, 500 men per regiment was a more common figure.

The Decree of 18 June 1811 ordered the conversion of six dragoon regiments and one chasseur regiment into chevauléger-lancier regiments. According to the Decree of 15 July 1811, each of these regiments was to have four squadrons of two companies each (the first company of the first squadron was designated as the elite company).

The Decree of 4 December 1811 increased the strengths of the other line cavalry regiments to a uniform 1,044 men in the field and 50 in the depot. This was further altered by the Decree of 10 January 1812, which ordered the raising of a fifth squadron in the two carabinier regiments, the fourteen cuirassier regiments, and the four dragoon regiments that were part of the Grande Armée. The chasseur à cheval, hussar, and chevauléger-lancier regiments were exempt from this order. Though the decree was issued, none of the fifth squadrons participated in the campaign.

The Men and the Horses

The recruiting standards for the cavalry prescribed maximum and minimum height standards for both the troopers and their mounts. Carabiniers and cuirassiers were to be 5 feet 10 inches and 5 feet 8 inches or taller respectively. The Decree of 21 April 1807 set the range of heights for hussars and chasseurs between 5 feet 3 inches and 5 feet 5 inches tall. Entry into the dragoons was less restrictive and men under 5 feet 4 inches were taken. This applied to the chevauléger-lancier regiments as well.

Standards for the horses were also stringent. Mounts had to be between five and eight years old and were subject to the following height restrictions: for carabiniers and cuirassiers, 5 feet 1 inch to 5 feet 3 inches tall (at the withers); for dragoons and horse artillery, 5 feet to 5 feet 3 inches tall; for chasseurs and hussars, 4 feet 10 inches to 5 feet; and for the chevauléger-lanciers, 4 feet 9.5 inches to 4 feet 11 inches. In any given cavalry unit, one-sixth of the horses were whole mares and the rest were geldings. A horse for a cuirassier or carabinier cost 520 francs, all the rest cost 380 francs.

In order to acclimate the horses to the noise of war, the French employed a very simple system. Initially the horses would be subjected to random pistol shots on their way to the stables or when they were feeding. Gradually the intervals between shots would be shortened until the horses were acclimated to a considerable din. Once this was done a number of troopers would form a line, armed with pistols and muskets. The young horses walked towards this line as the troopers fired their weapons. When the horses closed to 25 yards, the firing stopped. The horses continued to close, and once they reached the line they were caressed and fed. This process would be repeated several times until the horses were undisturbed by any of the battlefield noises.

Cavalry Drill and Tactics

French cavalry regulations prescribed three gaits for the cavalry: the pace, the trot, and the gallop. Since usual reckoning held that a horse's stride was 2 feet 9 inches at the pace, 4 feet at the trot, and 10 feet 8 inches at a gallop, a pacing horse could cover 120 yards in a minute, a trotting horse, 260 yards, and a galloping horse, 330 yards.

While infantry regulations prescribed the number of steps per minute for an infantryman, the cavalry regulations did not do the same for the horses. The regulations did, however, establish squadron schools where the officers learned to regulate the unit's speed and maintain formation. The officers were taught to judge and measure both distances and the time necessary to cover them at various gaits. They also learned how to estimate the frontage of a squadron or regiment in relation to the number of files it had.

The cavalry regulation used in 1812 was issued on 22 September 1804, though an unaltered second edition was published in 1810. This regulation established regimental schools in which both the horses and troopers learned their trade. The men's and horses' training began with a series of long marches in groups of four men on horseback. This progressed to full pelotons (squadrons) and finally divisions (two squadrons). During this training such evolutions as direct and oblique marches, conversions from fixed and moving pivots, flank marches, formation and column marching, the elongated column, the tight column, and finally the marching column were taught. The marching column was used solely to accommodate the march. It was formed by fours, but more commonly by twos, to allow the riders to select the easiest paths for their horses.

The cavalry was taught to form and use the various combat formations, column, line, and echelon. These were mass formations where the horses were closed in tight and the knees of the troopers touched, much as the elbows of the infantry touched.

The troopers in the first rank were taught to carry their sabers during a charge with the wrist twisted at one-third of the height of the eye, the arm half-extended, and the cutting edge of the saber to the right with the point somewhat lower than the hilt. The second rank was taught to hold their sabers elevated, the arm half-extended, the point a little below the head and higher than the hilt.

Among the various procedures taught the cavalry, the most significant and important was to rally quickly in the event of an unsuccessful charge. Blown cavalry milling about, out of formation, was highly vulnerable, and the sooner it could re-form the more likely it was to survive.

The cavalry was also taught to operate in skirmishing formation, by squad. The squad would deploy sixty paces in front of the squadron and spread out to cover its entire front.

In addition to the usual cavalry training, the dragoons also received infantry drill. This was a vestige from the days when dragoons were mounted infantry, not battle cavalry. Reflecting this heritage, the formation of dragoons remained identical, whether on foot or mounted. Each squadron constituted a foot division, each platoon a section, and the entire regiment an infantry battalion with four divisions. Each squadron also had sixteen men designated as the "peloton de flanquers," or skirmishing squad. The French dragoons did not generally operate on foot, but they did so occasionally when the terrain did not favor mounted cavalry action, such as at Corunna in Spain. In 1805, because of a lack of horses, several foot dragoon regiments operated with the Grande Armée.

Other regulations set the wartime forage rations for the cavalry. These rations were set by the Regulation of 30 June 1810. When the cavalry was on the march, the straw ration was not changed, but the hay ration was increased by five pounds.

Prior to the issuance of this regulation, the French cavalry lived principally off the land, and forage rations were modified to supplement the countryside's ability to support the cavalry. Even with the issuance of the Regulation of 1810, French cavalry often reverted to its old practice of living off the land.

Cavalry Weapons and Equipment

The weapons issued to the French cavalryman in 1812, with the exception of the chevauléger-lancier, consisted of a saber, a pair of pistols, and a musketoon. Heavy cavalry was armed, pursuant to the Decree of 25 December 1811, with a Year XI Musketoon that was 2 feet 6 inches long. The musketoon of the light cavalry was 3 feet 7.5 inches long. The saber of the light cavalry was half curved, that of the hussars was fully curved, and that of the heavy cavalry was straight.

The chevauléger-lanciers carried the chasseur's saber, a single pistol, and a lance that was 8 feet 10 inches long. Their "maréchaux des logis" (sergeants) and "fourriers" (quartermasters) did not carry lances. In their place they carried a second pistol and a musketoon. A total of 228 men in the regiment did not carry lances.

In the cuirassier and carabinier regiments, all ranks from private to general wore the cuirass. With front and back plate, the cuirass weighed sixteen pounds, so it is no surprise that an unhorsed cuirassier's first act was to divest himself of this encumbrance. Nonetheless, the cuirass was substantial enough to turn the blow of a saber or bayonet and reportedly could turn a musket shot at 45 paces. The cuirass was made of steel. The one worn by the carabiniers was copper plated, front and back, but the plating was not very good and did not weather well.

Unlike the infantry, the cavalry regiments all wore regimentally distinctive uniforms. They carried their extra uniforms and equipment in a portmanteau tied behind the saddle. The dragoons and cuirassiers kept their shirts spread out and laid lengthwise, with two pairs of breeches folded and placed over them, running in the opposite direction. The powdersack was on one side, the toilet kit on the other. The nightcap, handkerchiefs, feed bag, and watering bag were placed in the portmanteau. A pair of shoes, the garrison cap, and other small personal effects were placed on top of this.

The light cavalry spread their shirts and breeches the same as the cuirassiers. The waistcoat was folded in two and placed in the corners with the scarf and handkerchiefs. Other equipment was placed like that of the heavy cavalry as well.

In addition, the light cavalry carried two bags suspended from the pommels of their saddles. The left bag carried medical dressings, boxes of grease, brushes, and powder sacks. The right bag carried the horse's hay ration and the trooper's bread ration.

French Artillery

At the beginning of 1812, the French artillery establishment consisted of nine foot artillery regiments, each with twenty-two companies; six horse artillery regiments, each with seven companies, except the 6th Regiment, which had eight companies; fourteen principal and thirteen "bis" train battalions, each with six companies; two pontoon battalions, the first having eleven companies and the second six companies; eighteen artillery "ouvrier" or artisan repair companies; five armorer companies; and one train "ouvrier" company.

In 1805 the foot companies had a strength of 100 men each, and the horse artillery companies had a strength of 96 men. Changes were introduced by the Decree of 18 October 1811 which raised the strength of a foot company to 4 officers and 110 men and a horse company to 4 officers and 96 men.

Since an artillery company consisted only of the gunners and their guns, it was not capable of movement until merged with a train company to form a "division of artillery." The train company, drawn from a train battalion, provided the equipment and horses necessary to move and service the guns. The train companies had one officer and 140 soldiers.

The train battalions had an unusual practice. During peacetime only the principal battalions existed, but during wartime the train battalion divided into halves and each half was brought up to strength with drafts forming a "principal" and a "bis" battalion. The thirteen "bis" battalions were formed this way.

In peacetime the artillerymen were assigned to garrison duties, and their guns and equipment, except for enough to permit limited training, were stored in magazines and arsenals. In 1811, while preparing for the campaign, Napoleon had this equipment massed in Strasbourg, Wesel, and Mainz.

In the field, each gun limber, caisson, and field forge was drawn by six horses. All other wagons were drawn by four horses. The fully equipped "artillery division" was divided into three two-gun sections, each commanded by an officer. The 12pdr guns and the howitzers were serviced by three caissons, while the 6pdrs had only two. In 1812 Napoleon made arrangements for each gun to have 200 rounds of ammunition with it. More ammunition was carried in the various divisional, corps, and army parks.

Artillery Equipment

The artillery used by the French in 1812 was manufactured according to the System of the Year XI. This system, fathered by Marmont, succeeded the Gribeauval System of pre-Revolutionary days. The Gribeauval System had utilized 4pdr, 8pdr, and 12pdr cannons as well as 6-inch and 8-inch howitzers. The System of the Year XI replaced them with all-brass 6pdr and 12pdr cannons and 5.5-inch howitzers. The only unique part of the Gribeauval System that it retained was the ready ammunition box between the trails of the gun carriage.

This change of systems was made to minimize the number of different rounds of ammunition and to replace the 4pdr/8pdr system with a gun that did both tasks. The 4pdr lacked any real firepower and the 8pdr was too heavy. The 6pdr made an excellent compromise between the two cannons. In addition, it allowed captured 6pdr ammunition to be readily used.

The 5.5-inch howitzer was not, however, as successful a change. It was too light for many of the 6- or 8-inch howitzer's tasks, but its caisson could carry seventy-five 5.5-inch rounds vice the fifty 6-inch rounds.

Artillery fired three types of ammunition—ball, cannister, or case— and the howitzers fired an explosive shell. Cannister or case were so-called because they were a quantity of small metal balls contained in a metal cannister that would just fit down the gun's bore, which had the effect of a large-shot gunshell when fired. It had an effective range of 100 paces but would carry farther. When defending against charging cavalry, fire was held to fifty paces, and a single gun could keep its own frontage clear of attacking cavalry.

Ball shot consisted of just that, a large solid metal ball that acted much like a bowling ball, skipping across the battlefield until it came to a rest. This was used to engage targets at ranges from 300 to 1,200 yards.

The explosive howitzer shell, when fired, often combined the skipping action of the ball shot, but when the simple fuse reached the main charge it would explode, scattering fragments in a very haphazard manner. This shell could be used to set fires and was the best weapon for attacking fortified positions where ball shot would have problems penetrating.

The horses assigned to artillery units had to be fast enough to cover 800 yards in nine minutes at a pace, in five minutes at a trot, and in two minutes at a gallop. They had to be able to carry 180 pounds for twelve hours, 300 pounds for eight hours and 150 pounds while towing 750 pounds for 20 miles. In addition, they had to be able to pull 1,500 pounds on horizontal terrain and 1,100 pounds on uneven terrain.

Preparations for the Campaign

In preparation for the 1812 campaign, Napoleon assigned two pieces of regimental artillery to most of his infantry regiments and four to a few. Each division received one horse and one 6pdr foot battery. Each corps received a "double batterie de reserve" consisting of two 12pdr foot batteries. Each light cavalry division received one horse battery and each heavy cavalry division received two. This brought the total strength of artillery assigned to the French and Italian portions of the Grande Armée to fifty-one batteries: 60 12pdr cannons, 214 6pdr cannons, and 106 howitzers. The artillery attached to the Guard consisted of eight horse batteries, eight foot batteries, and four line batteries, bringing the total to 730 guns.

The 3pdr and 4pdr regimental guns were introduced to counteract the low degree of morale among the new recruits in the rapidly expanding infantry regiments. It was hoped that the reassuring boom of a pair of guns would both encourage them and supplement the volume of their fire. Regimental artillery first reappeared when Napoleon issued the Decree of 9 June 1809, reinstating regimental batteries in six of the regiments serving in the "Armée d'Allemagne." The Decree of 11 February 1811 increased the strength of the regimental batteries and their associated train to a total of forty-four noncommissioned officers and men serving the guns and fifty-six serving the caissons and other vehicles. The entire company was commanded by a lieutenant who had a sous-lieutenant, a sergeant-major, and a fourrier in his staff.

The implementation of the instructions to form regimental batteries was slow. The first guns did not reach their regiments until 1 May 1811, when the 33rd Légère received them. Davout reported to Napoleon on 20 April that the guns were available to equip six regiments, but the usual bureaucratic lethargy held up their dispatch to the regiments.

The Decree of 22 April 1811 ordered that the regiments destined to become part of the Corps d'Observation should expand their regimental batteries to four guns. It also ordered that the Corps d'Observation du Rhin and the Corps d'Observation d'Italie should organize their regimental batteries with two guns, a cartridge caisson, and a military transport caisson.

The French minister of war, the duke de Feltre, reported to Napoleon on 12 June 1811 that fifteen regiments in the Corps d'Observation de l'Elbe had formed their regimental batteries. Of the twenty-nine regiments in the Corps d'Observation du Rhin, only the 5th Légère, Joseph Napoleon Regiment, the Portuguese Legion, Tirailleurs Corsicans, Tirailleurs du Po, and the 2nd Swiss Regiment had not formed regimental batteries.

The train units also received the same attention during 1811. The Decree of 29 June 1811 began the process of increasing the strength of the train battalions. Nine battalions were raised to a total strength of 12 officers and men in the staff, 141 officers and men in each of the six companies, and a total of 1572 horses in the battalion. A series of decrees, on 2 February 1811, 10 April 1811, and 4 December 1811, reorganized, expanded, and assigned the various train companies to the various corps of the forming Grande Armée.

To support and maintain his artillery, Napoleon issued the Decree of 20 March 1812, which reorganized the artillery "ouvrier" (repairmen) companies. These battalions had 149 officers and men. The five squadrons varied in strength from twenty-nine to thirty-two men each. These men actively repaired artillery equipment, limbers, caissons, and other such equipment. They did not work on the gun tubes.

Napoleon also created armorer companies with the Decree of 20 March 1812. These companies had a total of sixty-eight officers and men. In contrast to the ouvriers, the armorers worked on the gun tubes.

Engineering Units

In addition to these units normally considered part of the artillery establishment, other units were assigned to the general parks and reserves. These units were the pontooniers, miners, sappers, and engineering train units.

The Grande Armée had thirteen companies of pontooniers in 1812, seven in the 1st Pontoonier Battalion and six in the 2nd Pontoonier Battalion. The battalion staff had eight officers and men. The companies had 100 officers and men. The staff attended to the administration of the battalion and never went into the field. Indeed, the companies were scattered individually throughout the French army and sometimes only detachments were assigned to various corps.

There were twelve miner companies in the French army. Each was organized with 100 officers and men. Six of these, four from the 1st Battalion and two from the 2nd Battalion, were destined to join the Grande Armée.

The sappers were a highly respected formation. Their duties consisted of clearing obstacles under fire and leading assaults in house-to-house fighting. They were highly trained and very professional—so much so that they vied with the Grenadiers à Pied of the Imperial Guard for superiority in morale and military bearing. The sappers were exceedingly proud of their heritage and uniform. When it was decreed that they were to surrender their bearskin bonnets, the badge of their office, they flagrantly disregarded the order. They would have sooner shaved their beards, which were as much a symbol of their office and status as the cherished bearskins.

There were two types of sappers, however. The "French" sappers are what were just described. The French sapper battalions were organized with nine 80-man companies and a staff of nine officers and men.

There were also a small number of labor battalions that bore the name "sappers" or "pionniers," but these had none of the military prowess or history. The first of these was the Sapeurs de l'Île d'Elbe. It was formed with four companies and totaled 731 men. It was raised from the French penal regiments by the Decree of 18 June 1811. The other was the Pionniers Espagnols. This battalion had four companies and a total of 800 men raised from Spanish prisoners of war. This unit was so unreliable it wasn't even armed. Its only weapons were spades.

Like the artillery, the engineers had no indigenous transportation, and there was a separate engineering train battalion. This battalion was organized from the diverse, unrelated train companies that existed throughout the French army by the Decree of 25 March 1811. The engineering train companies carried every sort of engineering tool, material, and explosive necessary for sieges and other engineering work. Because of the vast assortment of equipment, the companies were never used intact, but were broken up, and those portions required were attached to the corps where they were needed.

French Supply Train

In addition to the combat and combat support units, another formation existed for the sole purpose of providing provisions for the combat units. Napoleon was the first general to establish a military supply system which tended the needs of the entire army, instead of just specific regiments.

In a letter dated 24 January 1812, Napoleon discussed his plans for this train with the count de Cessac. Napoleon had selected eight "bataillons d'equipage militaire" with a total of 2,016 wagons for use in his pending campaign. A further four new military equipage battalions which were equipped with one-horse wagons, four newly raised oxen military equipage battalions, and the Italian oxen military equipage battalions rounded out the supply forces.

This force was to be the main supply organization for the Grande Armée, and Napoleon should not be condemned for its failure to meet the needs of his army. It is only since the Second World War and the advent of the gasoline engine that an army has been able to transport the supplies necessary to sustain itself. Napoleon's supply system was dependent on the capabilities of the horse, and the horse's ability to move material was further reduced by the limitations of the wagons and roads of the day.

In preparation for what he knew would be a gigantic undertaking, Napoleon issued a number of decrees that established the strengths of these battalions. The Decree of 2 February 1811 established a new organization for the 2nd, 9th, and 12th military equipage battalions with six companies. Their companies had 129 officers and men and 42 wagons. The battalion staff consisted of a captain, four other officers, and nine noncommissioned officers.

The same decree established the 1st Light Military Equipage Battalion. It had a staff of four officers and eight noncommissioned officers. It had six companies organized with sixty-three officers and men. Unlike the other equipage battalions, this unit was a pack battalion and had ninety-two mules per company.

The Decree of 25 April 1811 reorganized the 10th Military Equipage Battalion such that the first two companies were equipped with wagons and the last four had mules. The first two companies had 129 men, 12 wagons, and 206 horses. The other four had 76 men, 12 horses, and 102 mules. The unit was formed from units then serving in Portugal.

The Decree of 24 August 1811 created the Guard Military Equipage Battalion. It had a staff and five companies. It had a total of 17 officers, 775 men, 1,165 horses, and 183 wagons, forges, and caissons.

The Decree of 24 January 1812 raised the 14th and 15th Military Equipage Battalions. These two units were the first units "à la comtoise," that is, equipped with light, four-wheeled wagons drawn by a single horse. The battalions had six companies, each company having 100 wagons, an ammunition wagon, and a field forge. These battalions had paper strengths of 681 men, 135 mounts, and 690 draft horses.

This decree also raised the 20th and 21st Military Equipage Battalions. Both battalions had six companies with a total of 483 men, fifty wagons, each drawn by two oxen, a field forge drawn by four oxen, and an ammunition wagon drawn by four oxen. One soldier was assigned to each pair of oxen in the company, and there were an additional eight men and eight yokes of oxen, which gave the battalion a total strength of 62 horses and 744 oxen.

The Decree of 23 February 1812 modified the Decree of 24 January 1812 and set the strength of the "bataillon à la comtoise" (one-horse wagon battalion) such that the staff had 14 officers and men and the companies each had 145 officers and men. Each company had 100 wagons, an ammunition wagon, and a field forge.

The Imperial Guard

No discussion of the French Napoleonic army would be complete without a discussion of the Imperial Guard. This force, which was actually a small army in itself, had its origins in Napoleon's personal bodyguard during the revolutionary period. The guard began with a few hundred men, and by 1814 it was to consist of thirty infantry regiments, fourteen cavalry regiments, two artillery regiments, and a number of ancillary units such as pontooniers, a military train, sappers, and a fire brigade.

By 1812 the Imperial Guard had already earned the excellent reputation that still springs to mind nearly two centuries later. It was to take a significant role in the 1812 campaign. As an elite corps, it acted as a ready reserve of reliable soldiers who could either deliver the "coup de grace" or, by their élan and professionalism, save a desperate situation. In 1812 the role of the Guard was the latter.

In 1812 the Imperial Guard consisted of the following:

1st Grenadiers à Pied (Old Guard)
2nd Grenadiers à Pied (Old Guard)
3rd Grenadiers à Pied (Middle Guard) (Dutch)
1st Chasseurs à Pied (Old Guard)
2nd Chasseurs à Pied (Old Guard)
1st Veteran Company (Old Guard)
Fusilier Grenadier Regiment (Young Guard)
6 Tirailleur Regiments (Young Guard)
1 Fusilier Chasseur Regiment (Young Guard)
6 Voltigeur Regiments (Young Guard)
National Guard Regiment (Young Guard)
Flanquer-Chasseur Regiment (Young Guard)
Grenadier à Cheval Regiment (Old Guard)
Chasseur à Cheval Regiment (Old Guard)
Mameluke Squadron (Old Guard) (Egyptian)
1st Chevauléger-lancier Regiment (Old Guard) (Polish)
2nd Chevauléger-lancier Regiment (Old Guard) (Dutch)
Gendarmes d'Elite (Old Guard)
4 Horse Artillery Companies (Old Guard)

6 Foot Artillery Companies (Old Guard)
4 Conscrit-cannonier Artillery Companies (Young Guard)
1 Pontoonier Ouvrier Company (Old Guard)
2 Artillery Train Battalions (Old Guard)
1 Veteran Cannonier Company (Old Guard)
8 Marine Equipage Companies (Old Guard)
3 Ouvrier Companies (Old Guard)
6 Equipage Train Companies (Old Guard)

This listing of the Guard includes the Dutch Guard, which was incorporated into Napoleon's guard after Holland became part of metropolitan France. The Decree of 13 September 1810 redesignated the Dutch Guard and the 1st and 2nd companies of the Garde du Corps as the "2eme Grenadiers à Pied de la Garde Imperiale." The 3rd and 4th companies of the Garde du Corps were distributed to the 1st Grenadiers and 1st Chasseurs à Pied. The same decree converted the Dutch hussars into the 2nd Chevauléger-lancier Regiment. The Dutch horse battery and train were incorporated as well.

The Dutch grenadiers remained the 2nd Grenadier Regiment until the Decree of 18 May 1811, which raised a new French grenadier regiment, naming it the 2nd, and redesignating the Dutch as the 3rd Grenadiers. This decree also raised the "2e Régiment de Chasseurs à Pied de la Garde Imperiale" (2nd Chasseur Regiment). The cadre of the new grenadier regiment came from the 1st Tirailleur Regiment and the new chasseur regiment came from the 1st Voltigeur Regiment.

Prior to 1811, there were velites attached to all of the guard cavalry regiments. The Decree of 1 August 1811 terminated the admission of men to the velites, and on 1 January 1812 the velites were absorbed into the other squadrons, bringing them to 250 men each.

The Decree of 18 May 1811 raised the 5th Voltigeurs and 5th Tirailleurs. The Flanquer-Chasseurs were raised by the Decree of 4 September 1811.

Serving with the Guard was a very great honor and privilege. The requirements for entry into the Guard were five years of service and participation in two campaigns. This meant that the Guard was an elite force of experienced, battle-hardened troopers. In addition to the honor of being so designated, there were very real material rewards to belonging to the Guard. An ordinary Guard grenadier received the pay of a sergeant in a line regiment. Guard corporals received the pay of sergeant-majors.

In addition, the Guard always received special rations and equipment. If any unit ever had its needs looked after first, it was Napoleon's "favorite children," the Imperial Guard.

All Guard infantry was organized with two battalions. The chasseur battalions contained 800 men organized in four companies of 200 soldiers. The regimental staff consisted of ninety-four officers and men.

In 1810 the Guard cavalry consisted of a staff, the three cavalry regiments (the grenadiers, chasseurs, and dragoons), and the Mameluke company. Each regiment had four squadrons of cavalry and a fifth squadron of velites, the squadrons being organized with two companies each. The staff had fifty-one men. Each company was organized with 125 officers and men. The Mameluke company was organized with 159 officers and men.

On 2 March 1807 Napoleon ordered the raising of a pulk, or regiment, of light cavalry with four light squadrons. This was followed by the Decree of 6 April 1807, signed by Napoleon in the imperial camp at Finkenstein, which raised the "Régiment de chevaulégers polonaise de la garde." It was formed with four squadrons, and each squadron had two companies. Its staff had 34 officers and men. Each company was organized with 125 officers and men.

The 2nd Chevauléger-lanciers de la Garde (Hollondaise) was formed by the Decree of 13 September 1810, which incorporated the Dutch Guard into the French Imperial Guard. The Dutch Guard hussars were converted to lancers and organized into eight companies. On 21 September the regiment had a strength of 58 officers and 881 men.

On 1 October 1810 the regimental staff of the 2e Chevauléger-lanciers was reorganized. Its staff had twenty officers and men. The four squadrons were raised to five by the Decree of 11 March 1812. The regiment now had a total of 1,212 men, and each company had a strength of 118 men, in contrast to the 123 men of the other guard cavalry companies. The Dutch lancer companies were organized with 118 officers and men.

The Decree of 1 August 1811 raised a fifth squadron in the Grenadiers à Cheval, the Chasseurs à Cheval, and the Dragoon Regiments. In addition, it restated Napoleon's desire to stop the admission of velites into the guard cavalry. Those velites who remained were absorbed into the 2e Chevauléger-lanciers de la Garde. The squadrons of velites were to remain in three corps, but as of 1 January 1812 they were to be broken up and distributed amongst the other squadrons of the grenadiers, chasseurs, and dragoons in order to bring them up to a total of five squadrons of 250 men.

The decree went on to say that the 2e Chevauléger-lanciers were to be completed entirely from the velites. In addition, every cavalier sent from the line cavalry regiments who did not have ten years of service was to be incorporated into the 2e Chevauléger-lanciers until such time as he had the required time in service. The decree also made the 2e Chevauléger-lanciers part of the Middle Guard.

A report from the minister of war to Napoleon relating to the status of the various Guard units and their designations as Old, Middle, and Young Guard, dated 11 October 1811, indicates that only the 2e Chevauléger-lanciers were considered Middle Guard and that all of the other Guard cavalry units were Old Guard.

The Decree of 11 March 1812 added a fifth squadron to the 2e Chevauléger-lanciers de la Garde and the Decree of 12 March added a fifth squadron to the 1er Régiment de Chevauléger-lanciers de la Garde.

On 9 June 1809 three companies of conscripted gunners were established: the compagnie d'artillerie des conscrits de la Garde, the compagnie d'artillerie des tirailleurs de la Garde, and the compagnie d'artillerie des fusiliers. These companies were known as "Nouvelle Garde," the first of the "Young Guard" of later years. Each of these batteries had eight guns manned by 140 officers and men. These units formed the first Young Guard artillery companies to be attached to the Guard. To support these three artillery companies, three new artillery train companies were established by the Decree of 21 October 1809. They were known collectively as the "conscrits-cannoniers."

In preparation for the 1812 campaign, foot artillery companies were raised to 124 officers and men, but the horse artillery retained its 1808 organization of 84 officers and men per company.

The conscrits-cannoniers were not reorganized by this decree. The equipment assigned to the Guard was distributed as follows:

Horse Artillery Companies
    4 6pdrs
    2 Howitzers
Reserve Foot Companies
    6 12pdrs
    2 Howitzers

Foot Companies
   6 6pdrs
   2 Howitzers
Conscrits à pied
   8 3pdrs or 4pdrs
Total
   16 guns

By 16 December, the foot artillery had two 12pdr batteries and four 6pdr batteries, as well as four batteries of eight 4pdr guns.

The Decree of 12 December 1811 established a 4th Company of Young Guard Foot Artillery. It was organized with the same establishment as the first three companies. This decree also added two brigadiers and fourteen gunners to the establishments of the Guard horse artillery companies.

The Order of 26 December 1811 fixed the artillery served the line that was to operate with the Guard artillery. This auxiliary artillery was to consist of four horse companies and six foot companies equipped with 72 guns, which brought the total artillery operating with the Guard to 166. To this was joined the 32 pieces of Italian Guard artillery, which brought the total that was to operate with the Guard to 208 guns.

The Decree of 12 January 1812 raised the "compagnie de cannoniers veterans de la garde." This company had fifty-one officers and men. It was formed as an Old Guard unit with gunners with five years of service in the Guard. It was actually raised on 1 May 1812.

On 18 February 1812 the Guard artillery train companies received an augmentation of ten men to their establishments.

The Decree of 27 March 1809 which described this force as a "corps de Marines" directed that this force be reorganized as a single "equipage." Its establishment was set at 148 officers and men. Each of the five squads was to consist of twenty-nine officers and men. On 1 March 1810 the Guard Marines had a total of 152 men, which had resulted from the escape of many of the men from the Spanish prisoner of war camps.

As Napoleon traveled about France, visiting Flessingue (Flushing) and other port cities, he was always accompanied by the Guard Marines. He decided that the 171 men that then comprised the Guard Marines were not adequate, and on 16 September 1810 he issued a decree from the palace of Saint Cloud that reorganized the Guard Marines with a total of 1,136 men. It consisted of a staff and eight companies. The staff consisted of eight officers and men. Each of the eight companies consisted of 141 officers and men.

The Légion d'Élite de la Gendarmerie, which was raised by the Arrêté of 28 Ventôse Year X (19 March 1802) consisted of a staff, two squadrons of two companies and a demibattalion of two companies. The staff consisted of thirty-one officers and men. Each mounted corps consisted of eighty-nine officers and men. Each company of foot gendarmes consisted of 122 officers and men.

The Decree of 24 August 1811 stripped the regimental equipage from the various guard combat formations and organized the "Bataillon d' équipage de train de la garde." This single battalion was to take care of the needs of the entire Guard. It was to consist of 17 officers and 755 men. The battalion was organized with six companies and had a total of 1,165 horses, including 117 mounts.

Chapter III

The Armies of France's Allies

Nearly half of the Grande Armée that entered Russia was formed with the armies of France's allies. In order to understand the true nature of the forces that invaded Russia, it is necessary to consider them as well.

The Bavarian Army

The Bavarians were one of Napoleon's oldest and most reliable German allies. They had fought under his banner in many campaigns and their homeland had served as a battleground more than once.

During the period between the French Revolution and Napoleon's second abdication, the Bavarian army underwent a continuous evolution, and immediately before the 1812 campaign there was a major reorganization. The Army Order of 29 April 1811 directed that each of the 12 Bavarian infantry regiments was to have two field battalions and one reserve or depot battalion. Each battalion had four fusilier companies, one grenadier company, and a schützen company. The regimental staff consisted of 35 officers and men, while each company had 148 officers and men. The four light infantry, or jägers, existed only as independent battalions. These battalions had a staff of twenty-three officers and men. The companies had 151 officers and men.

The Bavarian army had six chevauxléger regiments. Each regiment was organized with four squadrons, each squadron with two companies. The regimental staff had eighteen officers and men. Each squadron had 149 officers and men.

The Bavarian artillery consisted of a single artillery regiment with four battalions. Each battalion had five companies. Four of these companies were foot companies, and the remaining one was a light, or wurst, battery. The wurst batteries served the same function as a horse battery, but were not given that specific name. Wurst is the German word for sausage, and for the padded seat between the trails of the gun carriage and atop the caissons. This seat, which was designed to provide the gunners with a method of riding into battle, looked like a sausage, hence the name.

The Bavarian foot and light artillery companies were organized with eight guns each. They had either six 6pdrs or 12pdrs and two 7pdr howitzers. These batteries each had 100 officers and men.

To support the artillery, there was a train and transport battalion which provided the same services as the French artillery train. It had a staff of twenty-one officers and men. Each of its eight companies had 150 officers and men. In addition, there was an artillery ouvrier company that had ninety-nine officers and men.

There was a small pontoonier corps with two companies. The staff had four officers and men, and each company had seventy-two officers and men.

The Army of Baden

The Grand Duchy of Baden formed an alliance with France in 1803 and supplied a small contingent to the French army during the 1805 campaign. Baden became part of the Confederation of the Rhine in 1806 and continued its affiliation and alliance with France until late 1813, when the allies overran its territories. When Baden joined the Confederation of the Rhine, its army underwent a reorganization, and its regimental structure was changed to conform with the French system.

The Baden infantry consisted of one jäger battalion and four line regiments, each with two battalions. The line infantry battalions had one grenadier, one voltigeur, and four fusilier battalions. The regimental staff had eighteen officers and men. Each company had 138 officers and men.

The Lingg Jäger Battalion had a smaller staff commanded by a major, but the battalion organization was identical to that of the line battalions.

Baden had two cavalry regiments, one hussar, and one light dragoon. Both regiments were organized identically. Their regimental staff had fourteen officers and men. Each of the five squadrons had two companies. Those companies had ninety-five officers and men each.

Baden had one foot and one horse artillery battery. These batteries had eight guns. The foot battery had six 12pdrs and two 5.5-inch howitzers. It was manned by 139 officers and men. The horse battery had eight 6pdrs and was manned by 134 officers and men. There was also a train company assigned to these batteries, which had two officers, eight sergeants, and about five hundred others.

The Army of Cleve-Berg

Prior to 1806, Cleve-Berg had been part of Bavaria. In that year there were some territorial realignments and exchanges which resulted in two smaller duchies being merged with Dusseldorf as their capital. The newly created principality was then presented to Joachim Murat, Napoleon's brother-in-law. In 1808, when Murat left Cleve-Berg to become king of Naples, the oldest son of Louis Bonaparte, then king of Holland, was given the duchy. The troops of Cleve-Berg fought with the French in 1806 and in every campaign until the duchy was dissolved in 1813.

When Cleve-Berg was handed over by the Bavarians, it came with the infantry regiment that had been raised in the province. After the institution of the conscription, this regiment was raised from the four battalions it had in 1808 to six battalions. In August 1808, it was divided into 2 three-battalion regiments that shared a common depot.

In October 1808 a third battalion was raised, and in 1811 a fourth battalion was raised with a single battalion taken from the first three regiments. This force was then massaged and each of the four regiments had only two battalions. These battalions had the French six-company organization. The regimental staff had nineteen officers and men. Each company had 140 officers and men.

Cleve-Berg had a single light cavalry regiment that was attached to the French Imperial Guard. In 1812 a cadre of fifty men returned to Cleve-Berg and began forming a second regiment. This new regiment did not become active until 1813.

Cleve-Berg had a single artillery battalion with two batteries: one horse and one foot battery. The foot battery had six 8pdrs and two 6-inch howitzers. The horse company had six 4pdrs. These two batteries were served by a train company. In addition, there was a company of engineers who encompassed the functions of sappers, pontooniers, and miners.

The Army of Hesse-Darmstadt

One of the smaller contingents to join the Grande Armée in Russia was the army of Hesse-Darmstadt, a member of the Confederation of the Rhine which had been elevated from a landgraviate to a grand duchy as a result of its alliance with France.

On 15 January 1809 the organization of the three infantry brigades or regiments was altered. The brigade staff consisted of thirteen officers and men. The four companies in each battalion had 3 officers and 165 noncommissioned officers and men. There were no elite companies. The number of wagons assigned to the regiments was increased to four wagons. Each battalion had four wagons and two pack horses.

Only the Gross und Erbprinz Regiment, which served in Spain, adopted the six-company "French" organization. It had the same regimental staff, and the companies had 140 officers and men. A provisional light infantry regiment was formed from the Garde-Fusilier-Bataillon and the Leib-Fusilier-Bataillon. During 1813 this became the Garde-Fusilier-Regiment.

In preparation for the 1812 campaign, the Hesse-Darmstadt chevaux-léger regiment was reinforced and brought up to a strength of 12 officers, 2 middle staff personnel, 40 unteroffizier, 10 trumpeters, 375 chevauxlégers, 16 train soldiers, and 3 squadron smiths. It was organized in four squadrons.

The regiment was assigned to the IX Corps of Marshal Victor. As such it remained in Germany and Poland during the beginning of the campaign. The Garde-Chevauxlégers were assigned to the light cavalry brigade with the Baden Hussars under the command of Fournier.

In preparation for the 1812 campaign, a single battery was prepared on 30 May 1812 and assigned to the Grande Armée. This battery consisted of 3 officers and 100 noncommissioned officers and artillerists. It had a train of ninety men.

Between these two forces there were 143 horses, two 7pdr howitzers, four 6pdr cannons, four 7pdr grenade caissons, eight 6pdr caissons, six infantry caissons, one cavalry caisson, four utility wagons, one baggage wagon, and one field forge.

The Army of the Kingdom of Italy

Of all Napoleon's allies, the Kingdom of Italy had the most interesting relationship with France. In 1802 Napoleon had become president of the Republic of Italy (formerly the Cisalpine Republic). In 1805, a year after he crowned himself emperor of France, he declared the republic a kingdom and himself its king, placing the Iron Crown of Lombardy on his head. To rule in his place, he appointed his stepson, Eugene Beauharnais (Josephine's son by a previous marriage), as viceroy. As such, Eugene devoted himself to the organization of the Italian army.

In 1809 the Italian army consisted of seven line infantry regiments, four light infantry regiments, the Dalmatian Legion, the Istrian Chasseur Battalion, two dragoon regiments, two chasseur à cheval regiments, twenty-six foot batteries, six horse batteries, one train battalion, two sapper battalions, and three regiments of gendarmes.

The organization of the infantry regiments, set on the French model, had four field battalions with six companies, a depot battalion with four fusilier companies, and a regimental artillery company equipped with two 3pdr cannons. The battalions had six companies: one grenadier, one voltigeur, and four fusilier. The staff had 45 officers and men, the companies had 140 officers and men, and the regimental battery had 70 officers and men.

Italy had two dragoon regiments and four chasseur à cheval regiments. All were organized uniformly with a staff and four squadrons, each with two companies. The staff had twenty-eight officers and men. The companies had ninety-one officers and men.

The Italian artillery establishment consisted of two field battalions with thirteen foot batteries and a depot battalion. The depot battalion provided a combination of services, including the four pontoonier companies and one ouvrier company. In addition, there was a single battalion of horse artillery that had six companies.

The foot companies were equipped with six 6pdrs or 12pdrs and two howitzers each. The horse batteries had either four 6pdrs and two howitzers or five 6pdrs and one howitzer each. The 12pdr companies had 130 officers and men, the 6pdr foot companies had 114 officers and men, and the horse companies had 88 officers and men.

There were two train battalions, each with six companies. These appear to have been organized identically to their French counterpart.

The Italian ouvrier company had 101 officers and men, and the pontoonier companies had a supervising staff of 3 officers and men and a force of 75 officers and men.

There was a single sapper-miner battalion that was raised in 1807. It had five sapper companies and two miner companies. In 1812 there was a single engineering train company to support the sapper-miner battalion. It had three officers, seventeen noncommissioned officers, and fifty-six drivers.

In addition, Italy had a very large guard. It consisted of the Guard Grenadier Regiment, the Guard Chasseur Regiment, the Royal Velite Regiment, the Guard Conscript Regiment, a "Line Velite Regiment," four companies of Gardes d'Honneur, a foot battery, a horse battery, and two squadrons of Guard Dragoons.

The Army of Naples

Naples was the continental portion of what had been the Kingdom of the Two Sicilies, which had been seized by the French in 1805. It was initially ruled by Joseph Bonaparte, Napoleon's eldest brother. He was an exceedingly popular king and instituted many reforms that endeared him to the populace. When Joseph ascended the throne of Spain, he was replaced by Joachim Murat, the Bonapartes' brother-in-law and a marshal in the French army.

The Neapolitan army was one of the weakest links in Napoleon's army of allies. In a letter to Joseph, Napoleon summed up his opinion in no uncertain terms: "You must be aware that . . . these troops are no better than none at all." Napoleon's negative opinion is well illustrated by the history of the Pionniers Noirs, a French unit raised from mulattos and negroes in Santo Domingo. Considered the worst unit in the French army, it was transferred to the Neapolitan army in August 1806. Here it became the Royal African Regiment, or the 7th Infantry Regiment. Despite their previous reputation, these troops turned out to be better disciplined and more military in bearing than any other regiment in the Neapolitan army.

The Neapolitan army's biggest problem resulted from the fact that the lines of military authority were crisscrossed by informal lines of authority established by the numerous secret societies to which the soldiers belonged. The second major problem was desertion, combined with the nasty tendency of the Neapolitan deserters to become brigands.

The Neapolitan regiments were organized along the lines of the French regiments. Each regiment had three battalions. Each battalion had one grenadier, one voltigeur, and four fusilier companies. The regimental staff had thirty-five officers and men. Each company had 139 officers and men.

Naples raised two chasseur à cheval regiments that were organized along the French model. Though there were attempts to bring them up to full strength, the combination of poor training and constant desertion made this impossible. The theoretical regimental staff strength was twenty officers and men. Each company theoretically had ninety-five officers and men.

By 1812 the Neapolitan artillery establishment consisted of a full battalion of twelve foot batteries and two horse batteries. The bulk of the guns were captured Austrian guns passed on to them by the French. The batteries were organized on the French model with the foot batteries having six 6pdrs or 12pdrs and two howitzers. A 12pdr foot company had 126 officers and men, and a 6pdr foot company had 110 officers and men. The horse batteries had six 4pdrs or 6pdrs and two howitzers. The horse batteries had sixty-one officers and men. Attached to each battery was a train company organized like the light cavalry companies.

In 1812 the Neapolitan Guard consisted of four infantry regiments, two of Grenatieri a Piedi and two Veliti della Guardia Reale, as well as two cavalry regiments, called the Guardia d'Onore, and a single horse battery. The infantry regiments had two battalions. The cavalry regiments had only two squadrons each. Otherwise, these units were organized like their line counterparts.

The Saxon Army

The Saxon army underwent an extensive reorganization in 1810. It abandoned the old ''inspectoriates'' and organized three standing divisions, two of infantry and one of cavalry. During this reorganization, four infantry regiments, one cavalry regiment, and the Royal Household Artillery Company were disbanded.

The infantry divisions were organized into two brigades. Each brigade had two regiments. The cavalry division had three heavy regiments, four light regiments, and the hussar regiment.

The eight Saxon infantry regiments consisted of two battalions, each with four companies, and two grenadier companies. The regiment staff consisted of thirty-eight officers and men. The two grenadier and eight musketeer companies of the regiment had a total of 2,043 officers and men.

The grenadier companies were stripped from their parent regiments and organized into independent battalions that acted as a reserve for the Saxon army.

With the reorganization of the Saxon army in 1810, the two light infantry battalions were expanded into full regiments on 1 May 1810. The 1st Light Infantry Regiment was known as the Le Coq Light Infantry and the 2nd Light Infantry was known as the von Sahr Light Infantry. The regimental staff consisted of seventeen officers and men. The regiment had eight companies with a total of 1,440 officers and men.

In 1812 the Saxon cavalry consisted of three cuirassier regiments, three chevauxléger regiments, an uhlan regiment that was a redesignated chevauxléger regiment, and a hussar regiment. The Saxon cavalry was its most famous arm. It was noted for its professionalism and valor. After the 1806 campaign the Saxon cavalry was stripped of its horses to provide the French with remounts. However, these horses proved too spirited for the French and, with the new alliance between the French and the Saxons, they were returned.

The cavalry regiments, except the hussars, had the same organization. Each regiment had a staff and four squadrons. Each squadron had two companies. The staff consisted of eighteen officers and men. The eight companies now consisted of 768 officers and men.

The hussar regiment staff consisted of nineteen officers and men. Instead of four squadrons it had eight. These sixteen companies consisted of 1,056 officers and men.

In 1810, with the reorganization of the Saxon army, the regimental artillery was disbanded and the guns were concentrated into the artillery regiment, giving it sixteen companies.

The horse artillery consisted of two batteries formed in a brigade. They consisted of a small staff of 2 officers and two batteries with 240 officers and men and 226 horses.

The foot artillery staff consisted of twenty-four officers and men. The sixteen companies each had 114 officers and men. However, portions of this regiment were then redistributed to the line regiments in the form of four-gun regimental batteries.

The artillery was the weakest link in the Saxon army. It was armed with 3pdrs, 4pdrs, 6pdrs, 8pdrs, and 12pdrs. This resulted in a tremendous logistical problem because of the multitude of different ammunition. In addition, historically the Saxon artillery did not have a very high reputation. To support the artillery there was an artillery train battalion that consisted of 330 officers and men and 134 horses.

The Saxons had a small engineering force known as the Ingenieur-Korps staff which consisted of twenty-six officers and men. In addition there was a pontoonier company which had 127 officers and men. This pontoonier company sent a detachment into Russia.

The Army of the Grand Duchy of Warsaw

After the French victory over the Prussians in 1806, the Grand Duchy of Warsaw was created from the territories that Prussia had annexed from the final partitioning of Poland, as well as from some additional Polish territories taken from Russia and Austria.

Units of Polish émigrés had been serving with the French for years. Though these units remained in French service, they provided a large number of trained and veteran troops for the new Polish army.

In June 1811 the army of the Grand Duchy consisted of seventeen infantry regiments (three serving in Spain). Each regiment consisted of three battalions. These battalions had six companies of 130 men, giving the army a total of 32,760 infantry. There were now three chasseur à cheval regiments, two hussar regiments, one cuirassier regiment, and ten uhlan regiments, each of which had four squadrons, with the exception of the cuirassier regiment, which initially had only two squadrons. A squadron had two companies of 100 men, giving the Poles a total of 12,400 cavalry.

There were two squadrons of horse artillery with a total of 340 men, twenty companies of foot artillery, each with a total of 180 men, and a sapper-miner unit with 756 men.

Each infantry regiment raised a depot battalion in 1811 that had four companies, and the cavalry raised depot squadrons consisting of two companies. All of the artillery's depot needs were attended to by a single depot battalion of six companies.

The 1st, 5th, and 6th Cavalry Regiments were chasseurs à cheval, the 10th and 13th were hussars, and the 14th was a cuirassier regiment, though some sources indicated that it was a dragoon regiment at this time. The other regiments, numbering up to the 16th Regiment, were uhlan or lancer regiments.

By 1812 the army of the Grand Duchy consisted of 75,000 men and 165 cannon. It provided the forces that formed the V Corps of the Grande Armée during the 1812 campaign. This force was joined by all the Poles serving in the French army at that time, including the Vistula Legion and the 4th, 7th, and 9th Polish Regiments, though they served in other corps. Unfortunately, of the 7,000 Poles who entered Russia in the V Corps, barely 1,500 returned.

During the invasion of Russia, Napoleon liberated portions of ancient Lithuania which had been part of Poland in the not-too-distant past. There was sufficient pro-Polish sentiment there to cause Napoleon to form a provincial government there on 1 July 1812 and to make it part of the Grand Duchy.

The Decree of 1 July raised the Vilna National Guard, which was slowly fleshed out with men drawn from the recently captured territories. To police the countryside, Napoleon raised a gendarmerie in the Vilna, Grodno, Minsk, and Bialystok districts. This force consisted of a single company posted in each district.

In addition, Lithuania was the recruiting grounds for the 18th to 22nd Infantry Regiments and the 17th to 20th Uhlan Regiments. On 13 July Napoleon named the colonels for these regiments. The army of Lithuania, as it was called, was placed under the direct command of Napoleon and not made part of the army of the Grand Duchy's field forces. It did not receive its orders from the Polish general staff.

Because the territory had been ravaged by the retreating Russians, it was impossible for the Lithuanian army to be raised without active French financial support. Napoleon provided financial support, but not sufficient to do the job completely. In order to fully provide the finances for the fledgling army, the regimental commanders were selected from the most eminent and wealthy families of the country. They were expected to provide a great deal of the funds necessary for the organization of their regiments. Money was not the only problem. There were insufficient weapons, uniforms were hard to acquire, and horses were quite scarce. Approximately 40,000 muskets were provided by the French, but the lack of organization and the shortness of time prevented a complete distribution of these arms.

On 24 August Napoleon named General Hogendorp as president of the Commission of the Lithuanian Government and charged him with completing the organization of the Lithuanian army. Hogendorp promised

Napoleon that he would have the army completed by the beginning of January, but the outcome of the campaign prevented this from happening.

In the beginning of August it was decided that an additional six battalions, all of light infantry, would be raised. These battalions were formed from foresters and other outdoorsmen who had experience with weapons. They were to act as scouts and to control the incursions of cossacks, apprehend vagabonds, and act as a police force. They were organized from volunteers and the expense of their outfitting was to be absorbed by the proprietors of the forests in which they had worked prior to their volunteering.

In September it was decided to incorporate these six battalions into the regular army. In November the government of Lithuania resolved to form these troops into two regiments of light infantry, each with three battalions. However, recruitment was very slow and only one regiment was actually formed, and it had only two battalions. It was commanded by Colonel Kossakowski.

The first two battalions were raised in the Minsk district. Eventually a third battalion was raised near Vilna, but it did not join the regiment. It remained as an independent body for the rest of its existence. There is some indication that a fourth light battalion was raised, but very little documentation was found to provide details of its service.

A total of 15,000 Lithuanians were brought into active service by the French administration. These men and their regiments were distributed throughout the province, and with the retreat of the French army from Moscow, they quickly found themselves in combat. Some units participated in the battles during the passage of the Berezina and, along with approximately 6,000 others, withdrew with the French into Germany. Others simply vanished.

In 1810 there was a reorganization of the internal structure of the Polish infantry. Each battalion now was reorganized such that it had six companies. Of these companies, one was a grenadier company, one was a voltigeur company, and four were fusilier companies. Each regiment was still organized with three battalions, though before 1812 some regiments raised a fourth battalion. The regimental staff now consisted of thirty-eight officers and men. Each company consisted of 140 officers and men.

The internal organization of the cavalry in 1812 was quite consistent. The chasseurs, hussars, and uhlans were all organized with a staff and four squadrons, each squadron having two companies. The staff consisted of twenty-one officers and men. Each of the eight companies had ninety-eight officers and men.

The staff of the cuirassier regiment, when it had only two squadrons, consisted of sixteen officers and men. When the cuirassier regiment was brought up to the full four-squadron strength, its staff was reinforced and brought into conformance with the other cavalry regiments.

The Poles had a sapper-miner battalion which consisted of 756 men and 180 horses.

The artillery regiment consisted of twelve field companies and four static companies. The staff of the foot regiment consisted of twenty-two. Each field company had 180 officers and men. The static companies consisted of 127 officers and men.

The field company manned a battery of two 6-inch howitzers and four 6pdr cannons. There appears to have been only one 12pdr battery in the army of the Grand Duchy, and it appears to have had six 12pdrs and no howitzers. Most of the equipment was either captured Prussian or Austrian equipment. The foot regiment had a total of 2,685 men and 1,803 horses.

There were four horse artillery companies, each with four 6pdr cannons and two 6-inch howitzers. The staff of the horse artillery regiment consisted of nineteen officers and men. As with the foot companies, the horse companies had always consisted of 181 officers and men.

In addition, after instructions sent to the king of Saxony and the duke of Warsaw, each infantry regiment had two 3pdr regimental guns manned by a crew consisting of seventy officers and men. The batteries were equipped with two 3pdr cannons, three caissons, one field forge, one ambulance caisson, one document caisson, two caissons for cartridges and bread, and ninety-five horses.

The supplementary artillery battalion, established by the Decree of 26 June 1811, had a staff and eight companies. The staff had eighteen officers and men. Each of the eight companies had 132 officers and men.

There were artillery artisan companies formed with 144 officers and men. The pontoonier company, attached to the sapper battalion, had eighty-two officers and men. The sapper-miner battalion had a staff and six companies of sapper/miners in addition to the pontoonier company. The staff consisted of eleven officers and men. The companies consisted of 149 officers and men.

The Army of Westphalia

Westphalia, one of the largest states belonging to the Confederation of the Rhine, was ruled by Jérôme Bonaparte, Napoleon's brother. The Westphalians were, as a result, very closely tied to France.

Since the Kingdom of Westphalia had been put together from a number of smaller states in 1807, it had no military tradition or organization of consequence—it was an entirely new creation. It was totally patterned on the French model as a result. It had a guard patterned on the French Imperial Guard which even operated under the French drill regulations.

In 1812 the Westphalian army had eight line infantry regiments and four light battalions; a cavalry force of two cuirassier regiments, two hussar regiments, and two gendarme squadrons; an artillery regiment with six batteries and a pontoonier detachment; and Jérôme's Guard, which consisted of the one squadron Garde-du-Corps, a chevauxléger-lancier regiment, and a Guard horse battery.

The Westphalian Guard infantry consisted of the Guard Grenadier Bataillon, Jäger-Karabinier Bataillon, and the Guard Jäger Bataillon. The Grenadier Bataillon had an upper staff of 8 officers and men, a lower staff of 23 officers and men, and four companies, each with 116 officers and men. The Jäger-Karabinier Bataillon had an upper staff of 6, a middle staff of 6, and four companies, each with 103 men. The Guard Jägers had an upper staff of 5, a lower staff of 5, and four companies with 118 men each.

The line infantry regiments had two battalions each, except for two which had three. Each battalion had one grenadier, one voltigeur, and four fusilier companies. Each regiment had an upper staff of 13, a lower staff of 31, and a company strength of 140. The light infantry battalions shared a common staff and had the same company organization as line battalions.

The regiments had regimental batteries equipped with two 6pdr cannons. They were manned by thirty-two officers and men. In addition they had a small train unit of thirty noncommissioned officers and men.

The Westphalian Guard cavalry was not consistently organized. The Garde du Corps was literally a personal bodyguard with an upper staff of 9 officers and men, a lower staff of 43 officers and men, and a single company with 154 officers and men.

The Chevauléger-lancier Regiment had an upper staff of fifteen men, a lower staff of eleven men, and eight companies, each with ninety-four men.

Both cuirassier regiments had an upper staff with thirteen, a lower staff of eleven, and eight companies, each with seventy-nine men. The two hussar regiments had an upper staff and company strength like the cuirassiers, while the middle staff only had eleven men.

The Westphalian army had a Guard artillery company, four foot companies, and two horse companies. The Guard company had a staff of nine officers and men and a company strength of ninety-two officers and men. The line batteries had a regimental staff of nineteen officers and men. The foot batteries had 107 officers and men, and the horse batteries had 90 officers and men. All Westphalian batteries, line or Guard, had six guns, four 6pdrs or 12pdrs and two 7pdr howitzers.

As in the French army, there were artillery train companies assigned to each company to provide it with mobility. These companies had a strength of 103 officers and men.

There were sapper and ouvrier companies that had the same strength as the line foot companies.

The Württemberg Army

The entry of Württemberg into the Confederation of the Rhine was accompanied by a major reorganization. It expanded its army to eight infantry regiments, two light infantry battalions, and two jäger battalions.

On 6 April 1811 the Württemberg infantry regiments were slightly reorganized. It was with this organization that they entered Russia. Their staff now consisted of six officers. Each company now had 3 officers and 163 noncommissioned officers and men.

The Württemberg army had two chevauxléger regiments, two jäger zu pferd regiment's, and a Leibgarde zu Pferd Regiment. All cavalry regiments had four squadrons, each with 102 officers and men. Their staff consisted of 20 officers.

The Leibgarde zu Pferd consisted of four independent squadrons that were never formed into a single unit except in time of war. Each squadron was responsible for its own administration and was commanded by a major and an appropriate staff. Aside from this, the squadrons were organized like line squadrons.

On 1 May 1810 the Württemberg artillery corps underwent a major reorganization and now consisted of a staff, three horse companies, a foot battalion consisting of four foot companies, and an arsenal/depot company. The staff consisted of 9 officers and men. The 1st (Guard) and 2nd Horse Artillery Companies consisted of four 6pdr cannons, two 7pdr howitzers, six munition caissons, one tool caisson, three officers, ninety-seven noncommissioned officers and artillerists, twenty-four train soldiers, six other attendants, thirty-two mounts, and forty-eight draft horses.

The 3rd Horse Artillery Company consisted of three 6pdr cannons, one 7pdr howitzer, four munition caissons, one tool caisson, two officers, sixty-six noncommissioned officers and artillerists, and five other men.

The 1st, 2nd, and 3rd Foot Batteries had six 6pdr cannons, two 7pdr howitzers, eight munition caissons, three officers, 118 noncommissioned officers and men, and three artisans.

The 4th Foot Battery or Park Company in fact consisted of two batteries which had five 12pdr cannons, two heavy howitzers, and three munition caissons. These two forces were manned by 2 unterlieutenants, 2 sergeants, 112 artilleristen, and 6 handwerksleute.

In January 1810 the 2nd Horse Artillery Company was reduced to the strength and structure of the 3rd Horse Artillery Company. That October the artillery corps was again reassigned. The Guard Horse Battery (1st) remained part of the "maison du roi," while the other two were attached to the cavalry brigade. The foot artillery battalion was split between two infantry divisions.

On 2 December 1810 four 3pdrs were organized and manned by the excess artillerists. Three of these guns were attached to the Infantry Regiment Prinz Friederich.

On 24 April 1811 an artillery commando was dispatched to the fortress of Danzig in preparation for the pending invasion of Russia. This commando had three officers, eighty-one noncommissioned officers and artillerists, fifteen trainsoldaten, seven other men, two 6pdr cannons, two reserve caissons, two infantry caissons, two mounts, and twenty-four draft horses.

On 30 June 1811 the foot artillery battalion was re-armed and the four companies now had two 12pdr cannons, two 6pdr cannons, and two 7pdr howitzers each. In addition, the battalion still had the reserve park company. These reequipped and reorganized foot companies now had three officers, twenty-one noncommissioned officers, two drummers, seventy-six artillerists, two wagonmasters, forty-three train soldiers, three mounts, and forty-four draft horses. The reserve company consisted of

5 officers, 26 noncommissioned officers, 126 artillerists, 1 oberwagen-meister (senior wagonmaster), 6 wagon masters, 243 train soldiers, 7 mounts, and 476 draft horses.

In 1812, when the Württemberg contingent joined the Grande Armée in the great invasion of Russia, it consisted of two horse, two foot, and one heavy foot batteries. The horse batteries had four 6pdr cannon and two 7pdr howitzers. These guns were manned by (from sergeant down) 149 men, 44 train soldiers, 54 mounts, and 76 draft horses. The light foot batteries had three 6pdrs and two 7pdr howitzers. They were crewed by (from sergeant down) 153 men, 44 train soldiers, 2 mounts, and 76 draft horses. The 12pdr foot battery had six cannons, a few more men than the 6pdr foot batteries, two mounts, and eighty-eight draft horses. The artillery corps had a total of 1,020 men, 119 mounts, and 617 draft horses.

The Contingents of the Smaller German States

Among the many states that provided soldiers for Napoleon's Grande Armée were a number of very small principalities that were also part of the Confederation of the Rhine. The contingents of some of these states were so small that they had to be combined with the contingents of other states to form viable units. These troops were organized into the "division princière," under the command of General Daendels, and eventually became part of the 34th Division under General Morand. Some of these troops served as garrisons in the German fortresses and cities while others were sent into Russia.

The 3rd Rhinbund Regiment consisted of two battalions from Frank-furt and was organized on the French model. The 4th Rhinbund Regiment had three battalions formed with troops from the five Saxon ducal houses of Saxe-Meiningen, Saxe-Coburg, Saxe-Gotha, Saxe-Weimar, and Saxe-Hildburghausen. The 5th Rhinbund Regiment had three battalions formed with troops from Lippe, Lippe-Detmold, Lippe-Schaumburg, Anhalt-Kothen, Anhalt-Dessau, and Anhalt-Bernberg. The 6th Rhinbund Regiment had two battalions formed with the troops from Reuss, Waldeck, Schwarzburg-Sonderhausen, and Schwarzburg-Rudolstadt. The 7th Rhinbund Regiment had three battalions and was raised in Wurzburg.

In addition, Wurzburg also provided a 6pdr foot battery and a squadron of chasseurs. The latter were quickly withdrawn from the Grande Armée because they were also the only police force in Wurzburg.

The 8th Rhinbund Regiment was formed with two battalions and drawn from the states of Mecklenburg-Schwerin and Mecklenburg-Stelitz.

The Austrian Army

In contrast to most of the armies, the Austrian army was not organized along the lines of the French army and did not follow French practice when operating in the field. It had a long military tradition of its own and was faithful to this tradition where its practice differed from that of the French.

Austria provided a contingent for the Grande Armée as a result of the Treaty of 14 March 1812. Napoleon's faith in this contingent was mixed. He had married Marie Louise, the daughter of the Austrian emperor, and this should have given him considerable assurance of any Austrian contingent. However the Austrians had been among France's fiercest enemies until that marriage, and the considerable anti-French sentiment that had led the Austrians to the tremendous military disasters of 1805 and 1809 still existed.

The Austrian army had four distinct types of infantry: "German" line infantry, "Hungarian" line infantry, "Grenz" infantry and "Jägers." The German and Hungarian line infantry regiments both had three battalions of six companies and two grenadier companies that were generally detached. They also had staffs with seventy-five officers and men, but that's where the similarities ended. The German infantry company consisted of 198 officers and men while the Hungarian infantry company consisted of 218 officers and men. The grenadier companies of both regiments had 144 officers and men.

The German infantry regiment had a total of 4,077 officers and men with 3,639 serving in the three field battalions. The Hungarian regiments had a total of 5,167 officers and men with 3,999 serving in the three field battalions.

The Grenz infantry regiments were raised from men serving on the southern frontiers of the Austrian empire. They were military colonists and designated as the border guards ("Grenz" is the German word for border). They constantly skirmished with the Turks and because of this were one of the principal light infantry formations in the Austrian army. Their internal organization was much like that of the line. They had, however, only two battalions per regiment. Their company structure was identical to that of the Hungarian regiments, but they had a staff of only sixty-one officers and men. In addition they had regimental batteries with fifty officers and men each. The regiments had a total of 2,727 men.

The last infantry formation, also a light infantry formation, was Austria's seven jäger battalions. Each battalion had a staff of 14 officers and men, and six companies, each with 137 officers and men. The battalions had a total of 762 men each.

The Austrians, having a long military tradition of their own, did many things in the mode of the day, which were similar to the French methods, and did other things after their own manner. The drill regulations used by the Austrians in 1812 were written by Archduke Charles in 1807. These regulations set each company with a three-rank formation, each rank being two feet from the next rank. The interval between companies was four feet. The soldiers in a rank stood elbow to elbow, as in the French army. They normally marched at 90 to 95 paces per minute with a charge pace of 120 paces per minute. The archduke also introduced a new "maneuver pace" of 105 to 108 paces per minute.

Though most of the formations and tactics used by the Austrians were, for all intents and purposes, identical to those used by the rest of Europe's armies, the Austrians did have two unique formations: the "bataillonmasse" and the "divisionmasse." These two formations were in essence dense blocks of infantry that were formed in lieu of a square. The "divisionmasse" consisted of two companies organized such that it had a front of a half company and was four half-companies thick. The rear three ranks and the three flank files all faced outwards, forming what amounted to a hedgehog. The "bataillonmasse" was a column of companies formed as densely as the "divisionmasse." In both instances the ranks were closed up so that the gap between all ranks, different companies not being a consideration, was two feet. This dense formation gave the attacking cavalry no opportunity to penetrate its ranks. It did have one serious weakness, however, which was recognized by the Austrians. That was that artillery, when firing on this formation, would wreak havoc on it. Other formations, being less dense, would survive artillery fire with fewer casualties.

There was yet another formation used by the Austrians. This was the "klumpen" or quick squares. This formation was used by any infantry formation caught out of square. A noncommissioned officer or officer would call to his men and direct them to form around him in a tight ball formation with everyone facing outwards. This formation had no ability to move and its fire was not very effective. However, it would keep its members from being ridden down by the attacking cavalry. In contrast, the "bataillonmasse" and "divisionmasse" could both maneuver and fire quite effectively.

The Austrians also had their version of the French "ordre mixte." In this instance a single battalion would form a line and the end divisions formed in "divisionmasse."

The Austrians also attempted to copy the French practice of employing light infantry as an integral part of the battalion. To this end the Austrian infantry regulations directed that two corporals and twelve soldiers from each company in the battalion be armed with rifles and twenty-five rounds of ammunition. When operating as skirmishers, these men operated at about 300 paces from their parent company.

The jägers operated with the same tactical formations as the line infantry, but they were also a skirmish formation. One third of the jägers were armed with rifles, which had the disadvantage of reducing their rate of fire to one round for every two fired by the musket-carrying jägers, but the range was about 350 yards, markedly superior to those muskets.

The Austrian cavalry consisted of heavy and light regiments. The heavy regiments—cuirassiers and dragoons—had six squadrons each. The light regiments—chevauxlégers, hussars, and uhlans—had eight squadrons each. The staff of the heavy regiments consisted of forty-two officers and men. Each squadron consisted of 169 officers and men. This gave a heavy regiment a total strength of 1,267 officers and men. The staff of the hussar and uhlan regiments had fifty-three officers and men, the chevauxléger regiments had fifty-one. Their squadrons had 177 officers and men. This gave a hussar or uhlan regiment a total strength of 1,477 officers and men. The chevauxléger had 1,475 officers and men.

Like the French cavalry, the Austrian cavalry formed in two lines. In contrast to the French, where the company was the smallest tactical formation, the Austrians used the squadron as their basic tactical unit. There were, however, few other significant differences between the Austrian and French cavalry.

The Austrian artillery establishment consisted of four regiments. Each regiment had four battalions and each battalion had sixteen companies. Each company had 184 officers and men.

The Austrians had both foot and "wurst" companies. The foot batteries were formed into either position or brigade batteries. The position batteries had either four 6pdrs or 12pdrs and two 7pdr howitzers. The brigade batteries had eight 3pdrs or 6pdrs.

The brigade batteries operated with the second regiment of the brigade to which they were attached, unless they were equipped with 6pdrs. In that case they operated in front of the brigade. The position batteries served as a reserve and were deployed as requirements dictated. These were, with the wurst guns, the only guns generally considered discretionary and intended for use in large batteries. It was, however, unusual to find more than twenty Austrian guns operating in a single battery.

The "wurst" batteries, the Austrian equivalent of a horse battery, had four 6pdrs and two 7pdr howitzers. These "wurst" guns, the pattern for the Bavarian light batteries, had a sausage-like leather seat on the trail of the guns and on the caissons for the artillerists to ride into battle. The German word for sausage is "wurst," hence the name.

The laborers attached to each battery came from "handlager" companies, which served the same function as the French artillery train companies. Generally speaking, these companies operated in pairs or "divisions." The peacetime establishment of a "handlager" battalion consisted of a staff and eight companies. However, in wartime the number of companies expanded to the number necessary for the job at hand. These companies consisted of 181 officers and men. Each company was slightly more than was necessary to man three batteries.

The Austrian army was always noted as having a very large baggage train. This had been reduced by the Archduke Charles, but it still remained large. The train attached to a line regiment was thirteen wagons and twenty-six pack animals. A Grenz regiment had nine wagons and an indefinite number of pack animals. The jägers had seven wagons and twelve horses and cavalry regiments had six wagons and no pack horses.

The Prussian Army

If the Austrians could be declared a dubious ally, the Prussians must, by all rights, be considered marginal at best. The Prussians were an outspokenly arrogant and brash enemy that Napoleon had humiliated in one day in 1806. The vaunted army of Frederick the Great had been smashed and scattered to the winds. Prussian pride smarted under the humiliating terms of the subsequent treaties forced on them. However, their king was a weak individual who lacked the courage to act overtly.

Indeed, when it came time for Prussia to change sides, it was his generals who forced his hand, leaving him little option.

The Prussian army had undergone a series of major reforms since the 1806 disaster of Jena-Auerstädt. On 15 July 1807 the king of Prussia appointed Graf Lottum and Generalmajor von Scharnhorst to head the new Military Reorganization Commission. Under the terms of the Treaty of Paris, which ended the hostilities of 1806, the Prussian army was limited to 36,000 men: 22,000 infantry, 8,000 cavalry, and 6,000 artillerists. A royal Guard of 6,000 men was also authorized, but militia, civil guards, and all other paramilitary organizations were forbidden.

Thanks to the efforts of Scharnhorst and his colleagues, the traumatic evisceration of the Prussian army by this treaty did not have totally negative results. Scharnhorst, Yorck, and Clausewitz began this reorganization by drafting a new training manual. The regulations they compiled, issued on 15 January 1812, included the use of both column and line, abolished regimental artillery, and made the cavalry arm subservient to the infantry—all concepts that were quite new to many members of the pre-1806 Prussian officer corps.

Among the many other provisions of the new regulations was the establishment of the "Krumper" System, an ingenious means of increasing the size of the Prussian army, despite treaty restrictions. Men from active units were furloughed after a year's training, and they were replaced by new recruits. This provided the Prussians with a mass of trained soldiers, but only the treaty limit number in uniform at any given time.

These army reforms also instituted a brigade system as well as a new system of officer selection and advancement. Officer selection was no longer restricted to the noble class. Artillery and engineering schools were established to teach the science of those arms, and cadet and military schools were established.

The size of the Prussian contingent that accompanied Napoleon into Russia and the conditions under which it was to operate were established by the treaty signed on 24 February 1812. The Prussians did not send complete units of their standing army into Russia, but instead took individual battalions or squadrons from several regiments and formed combined regiments. This permitted them to "blood" portions of several of their regiments and generate some battle-hardened veterans.

In 1812 the Prussian army had twelve infantry regiments, two jäger battalions, one schützen battalion, and a two-battalion Guard infantry regiment. The line infantry regiments had a three-battalion establishment consisting of one fusilier battalion, which was trained to operate as light infantry, two musketeer battalions, and two grenadier companies. As in the Austrian and Saxon armies, these grenadier companies were detached from their parent regiments and organized into converged grenadier battalions that acted as an army reserve. The battalions were organized with four companies. The regiment had a total of 4,129 officers and men. Each company had a total of 156 officers and men.

The independent schützen and jäger battalions also had four companies. These companies had 106 men each. The battalions had a total of 428 officers and men. The converged grenadier battalions had a total of 631 men. Each company had 156 officers and men.

In 1812 the Prussian cavalry had four cuirassier, six dragoon, seven hussar, and three uhlan regiments. In addition, there was a small Guard force that consisted of a normal dragoon, a normal hussar, and a normal uhlan squadron. All of the cavalry regiments, despite their type, had four 125-man squadrons. The regiments had a total of 536 officers and men.

In 1812 the Prussian artillery establishment had four foot regiments and one horse regiment. Each foot regiment had twelve companies, while the horse regiment had only nine. The foot regiments were divided into 3 four-company brigades, each of which had three 6pdr batteries, a 12pdr battery, and a fifth company organized as a "parkkolonne," or park company, in support. These park companies carried the infantry and artillery reserve ammunition.

The batteries were organized with eight guns. The 6pdr foot and horse batteries had six 6pdrs and two 7pdr howitzers. The 12pdr foot batteries had six 12pdrs and two 10pdr howitzers. In all instances, the foot companies had 137 officers and men, and the horse companies had 153 officers and men.

In addition to this, the Prussians had a small engineering force. There were two types of engineers. The Festung-Pionier-Kompagnien (fortress-pioneer companies) served as garrisons in the Prussian fortresses and took no part in the 1812 campaign. However, the Feld-Pionier-Kompagnien (field-pioneer companies) accompanied the field army. They served the same functions as the sappers and pioneers of any other country. These companies consisted of eighty-four officers and men.

Chapter IV

The Organization of the Russian Army

The Russian Infantry

Prior to 1812, the Russian line infantry had three different regimental formations: grenadiers, jagers, and infantry. The basic organization of the component battalions was the same, but the battalions had different names. The grenadier regiments were composed of two fusilier battalions and one grenadier battalion; the infantry regiments, of two infantry battalions and one grenadier battalion; and the jager regiments, of two jager battalions and one carabinier battalion.

During the period between 1804 and 1812, the regiments bore the name of the province in which they had been raised. This was referred to as the regiment's "inspection." There were no permanent military field organizations larger than the regiment, the inspection being a purely administrative structure that included regiments of all arms.

In 1806 most of the inspections were abolished and replaced with thirteen divisions. With this there appeared, for the first time in the Russian army, permanent standing field organizations on the "divisional" level. These divisions combined both the tactical and the administrative functions. By 1812 these divisions were, for the most part, organized with four line infantry regiments and two jager regiments. These regiments were organized into two-regiment brigades, with both of the jager regiments forming a single brigade.

Only the Caucasus, Orenburg, and Siberian Inspections survived the first change. In 1807 the Caucasus Inspection became the 19th and

20th Divisions. At the same time a 21st and 22nd Division were raised. In 1808 the Orenburg Inspection became the 23rd Division and the Siberian Inspection became the 24th Division. In 1809 the 25th Division was raised, but its third brigade was weaker than normal.

In early 1812 the regimental organization was altered. Although there were still grenadier, infantry, and jager regiments, each regiment was organized such that its 1st and 3rd Battalions served in the field and its 2nd Battalion was the depot battalion. In addition, an infantry regiment now consisted solely of infantry battalions, a jager regiment solely of jager battalions, and a grenadier regiment solely of grenadier battalions.

Each battalion still consisted of four companies, but now one company was designated as the "grenadier" company in the infantry regiments. In the jager regiments it was a "karabinier" company. The grenadier regiments also had one of the grenadier companies designated as the "elite" grenadier company. This elite company was divided into a "grenadier platoon" and a "tirailleur platoon." The remaining three companies were also broken into two platoons each, but they had no distinct title.

The nonelite companies in a grenadier battalion were known as "fusiliers." Those in an infantry battalion were known as "musketeers," and those in a jager battalion were known as "jagers."

Each infantry regiment had a total of 2,033 officers and men, each battalion had a total of 646 officers and men, and each company had a total of 159 officers and men. These regiments had a surprisingly large staff of "noncombatants" that ranged from the usual regimental musicians to a Russian Orthodox priest and two alterboys. The regiments had a train formation consisting of an officer and forty-one drivers. These men handled the regiment's compliment of 161 horses and 41 wagons.

As mentioned earlier, the 2nd Battalion was the depot battalion. It acted as the depot in the home province and was responsible for the training and equipping of new recruits. During the French invasion, rather than waste this manpower, the depots were either stripped of their grenadier companies which were then converged into battalions, or they were called up and formed into reserve divisions. These reserve divisions were extremely weak and rarely were a significant field force. The reserve divisions assigned to the Russian 1st Corps were so weak that they were lumped into "converged infantry regiments" in order to organize a viable military formation.

The Russian company structural organization was very similar to that of the Prussian organization. The companies were organized in a three-rank formation. The interval between each rank was an "archine" (approximately fourteen inches).

Tactics and Drill

The Russian musketry drill was not dissimilar to that used by the rest of Europe. The companies were taught to fire by "divisions," by platoon, by rank, and by file. Fire by file or by two ranks always started from the right and was executed by half-sections. During this evolution, the front two ranks fired and the third rank loaded muskets for the first two.

When loading their muskets, the Russian soldiers did not always use the blunted ends of their ramrods which were designed for that purpose. Instead, they used the portion that was inserted into the stock to push the load home. Though faster, as it eliminated having to turn the ramrod around, it caused a large number of accidents.

The Russians employed four march cadences. The first was the slow pace ("tchyi szag") of 60 to 70 paces per minute. The second was the quick pace ("skoryi szag") of 100 to 110 paces per minute. The third, introduced by the Grand Duke Constantine, was the redoubled pace ("udwonyi szag"), of 140 to 160 paces per minute. In the execution of this cadence, the soldiers were generally unable to maintain contact at their elbows, as prescribed by regulations. It was a very fatiguing pace, and if maintained for a long period, it would result in disorder in the ranks. The drummers beat their drums as long as the cadence was maintained.

The fourth cadence was the "rapid pace." This was faster than the redoubled pace. It was primarily used by skirmishers and rarely by formed infantry.

For purposes of maneuver, the Russians renamed their companies "divisions." These divisions consisted of two platoons, the platoon being the basic maneuvering element. Each platoon was divided into two half-platoons consisting of from twelve to fifteen files.

The Russians used a variety of tactical formations. Their attack column was in fact two separate columns of platoons marching side by side. They formed a square like the French, but also formed a dense anticavalry formation identical to the Austrian "Quarre auf der Mitte." In this formation the column closed up the intervals between the companies, and the center companies split into half-platoons, the central half-platoons pushing into the gaps between the flank half-companies and the front or back company. The flank of the battalion now gave the appearance of having six rather than the usual four companies, but the battalion was hollow in the middle.

Skirmishing tactics in the Russian army were exceedingly primitive. It has been suggested that the Russians used their jagers as just another line infantry formation, but this is in error. While the Russians frequently employed skirmish tactics, they were not as sophisticated in their use as other European nations. Moreover, skirmishing tactics were not solely the domain of the jager regiments. Evidence repeatedly shows both line and militia units being used as skirmishers or having some portion of their forces detached as skirmishers.

The jager regiments were taught to skirmish in battalion-sized formations. This was the primary distinction between them and the line infantry regiments. They operated under a cumbersome set of regulations derived from English, Prussian, and Austrian drill regulations. Since there was no firm, disciplined enforcement of regulations, skirmishing tactics were left to the discretion of the individual regimental commanders. This was further hindered by an almost absolute lack of peacetime exercises and some other, rather unfortunate habits of the Russian regimental commanders.

Historical evidence indicates that skirmishers were an integral part of line battalions in 1812, but the use and organization of these skirmishers has only been confirmed by documentation dating after 1812. Such documentation is of interest, but cannot be taken as an exact description of how it was done. In the late 1820s, it was standard practice for each section to provide skirmishers from its second and third ranks under the direction of an underofficer (NCO). This means that a battalion could field 104 skirmishers. They were dispatched and recalled with drum rolls, but, like the French skirmishers, they were directed with bugles.

The Russian Soldier

The Russian officer corps was composed of members of the upper classes, a good mixture of provincial gentry, and foreign career officers. According to tradition, the Russian officer was supposed to work his way up through the ranks, but very few actually did this. Barclay de Tolly was one of the few who did. Well-connected youths generally entered through the Page Corps, the Noble Land Cadet Corps, or one of the several cadet houses, where they pursued a general and military education while being promoted in absentia through the ranks. They were normally commissioned when they graduated at the age of twenty.

As in France, Russia conscripted its troops. Conscription was introduced in reaction to the growth of mass armies during the eighteenth century. In some years there was no draft, but in other years, like 1812, there were as many as three drafts, each taking up to five men per hundred souls.

The term of service for the Russian conscript was twenty-five years or life, the latter usually being shorter. Recruits were sent to the regimental depots for their training. There were between 50,000 and 60,000 recruits being trained in the regimental depots at any given time.

In 1810, when the elite companies were created in the infantry companies, the taller men became grenadiers and the smaller men became jagers. Barclay had decided that the elite companies would include only those whose skill and merit warranted the distinction. The slightest fault would deprive the jager and the grenadier of his distinction, and by 'fault' Barclay de Tolly meant not only carelessness in drill and similar mistakes, but any offense which might be inconsistent with good conduct and the honor of a crack soldier.

Barclay was applauded by many adherents of the Gatchina School, which advocated improved treatment of the soldiers. Prior to Barclay's banning its use, cruel and often barbaric punishment was inflicted for the slightest offense. Officers and noncommissioned officers carried canes and made frequent use of them, beating the soldiers for any fault. It was not uncommon for soldiers to be punished with long sessions in the drill square, and whole battalions often faded away on a diet consisting solely of bread.

Other innovations introduced in this period included the 110-pace-per-minute "quick pace" of Count Arakcheyev. Despite this modification, it was still executed in the stiff-legged goose-step. Barclay took much of the emphasis off rote drill and increased the attention to practical training. In prior years the Russian soldier had been taught by the school of Marshal Suvarov that the bayonet was "his friend and the musket was a lazy fellow." Barclay wrote on 10 September 1810 that "the main occupation of the soldier's training should be shooting at a target. The men can become good marksmen only when their officers avoid all compulsion and have a fundamental understanding of the mentality of the soldier." In 1811 Barclay issued his "Instructions for Target Practice."

Russian Weapons

In 1812 the Russians went to war with twenty-eight different calibers of infantry muskets and eleven different short rifles. The short rifles were issued to the flankers of the cavalry regiments. An additional twelve rifles were issued to the noncommissioned officers and the best shots in each jager company. In addition, as if to further complicate the number of calibers, the English provided 16,000 muskets. These were excellent weapons that were issued as rewards to the soldiers.

Despite the improved attitude towards musketry and marksmanship, the Russians were too deeply steeped in the doctrine of Suvarov and the bayonet for much change to occur.

Pre-War Developments

On 22 November 1811, most of the regiments raised a fourth battalion known as the reserve battalion. The internal organization of these battalions was distinctly different from the organization of the first three battalions, and they were formed from new drafts. On 14 March 1812, the second and fourth battalions of the regiments were drawn together and formed into the 30th through 47th Divisions. During the course of the campaign, these divisions were stripped and fragmented to fill out the first and third battalions in an effort to replace casualties.

Initially these reserve divisions were intended to operate in the rear of the main Russian lines. The 32nd Reserve Infantry Division, under Generalmajor Hamen, and the 33rd Reserve Infantry Division, under Generalmajor Villiaminov, formed the 1st Reserve Army under General-lieutenant Baron Müller-Zakomelski.

The 2nd Reserve Army, commanded by Generallieutenant Ertel, consisted of the 27th Line Division, under Generallieutenant Neverovski, and the 36th Reserve Division, under Generalmajor Sorokin. In addition, the 35th Reserve Division, under Generalmajor Zapolski, and the 34th Reserve Division under Generallieutenant Ertel, operated along the tributaries of the Dnieper for most of the campaign.

The 30th and 31st Reserve Divisions formed the garrison of Riga. The 36th Reserve Division joined Generallieutenant Sacken and took part in operations against the Austro-Saxon forces, while the 37th Reserve Division was delayed in its formation because its parent unit, the 27th Division, was itself newly formed.

The 6th and 21st Divisions, stationed in Finland, were reinforced by the 38th Recruit Division, formed from the depots in Kargopol and Olonets. The 39th and 42nd Recruit Divisions were destined to reinforce Müller-Zakomelski's 1st Reserve Army. The 43rd through 47th Recruit Divisions were to reinforce Tormassov's 3rd Army of the West, but the beginning of the campaign slowed the completion of these divisions, resulting in their battalions being deployed piecemeal, rather than as major reinforcements.

There was yet one other formation in the Russian army during this period—the converged grenadier divisions—which provided a means of more effectively utilizing the manpower tied up in the depots. The converged grenadier battalions consisted of three elite companies stripped out of the depot battalions. These battalions were then grouped in accordance with a system that retained their parent division integrity. That is, battalions from one division had their companies joined into two converged battalions and no companies from any other divisions were ever mixed with them. These converged grenadier divisions were then distributed between the field armies where they acted as a reserve force.

An examination of the Russian 1st Corps will show some converged infantry and cavalry regiments. These converged regiments were, in fact, various reserve divisions that had been reorganized into the most functional formation for their limited manpower. Generalmajor Hamen's 32nd Reserve Division was so understrength that it could best be employed as the two converged infantry regiments it became. The converged cuirassier regiment and the converged Guard regiments had similar origins.

Russian Cavalry

In 1807 there were six cuirassier regiments in the Russian army. Prior to 1812 these cuirassier regiments had five squadrons each, but by the end of 1812 a sixth and seventh squadron had been raised. During the campaign, the Pskof and Starodoub Dragoon Regiments were converted to cuirassiers, raising the total of such regiments to eight.

In 1809 there were eleven hussar regiments, each with ten squadrons and a reserve squadron which acted as a depot. During 1812 the Irkhoutsk Hussar Regiment was formed from the combined remnants of the dragoon regiment of the same name and the "opolochenie," or militia, horse regiment known as the Hussars of Count Slatikov.

In 1808 there were five uhlan regiments, organized the same as the hussar regiments. During the 1812 campaign the number of field squadrons was reduced to six. By the end of 1812 seven new uhlan regiments were organized by the result of the conversion of seven dragoon regiments to uhlan regiments.

There were thirty dragoon regiments in 1803. These had the same organization as the cuirassier regiments. During the 1812 campaign this number was reduced to twenty-one regiments as two were converted to cuirassiers and seven became uhlans. By the end of the 1812 campaign, the remaining dragoons raised a sixth field squadron.

The armament of the Russian cavalry regiments was not significantly different from that of their contemporaries, but a few differences evolved during the war with France. The most unusual difference was the equipping of the first rank of the first squadron of the hussar regiment with lances. The other change was necessitated by the heavy losses of material. The carbines were stripped from all of the cavalry regiments, and rifled carbines were issued to the sixteen men per squadron designated as flankers.

The cuirassier regiments had a total of 864 officers and men. Each squadron had 161 officers and men. The dragoon regiments had 897 officers and men. Each squadron had 166 officers and men. The hussar and uhlan regiments had 1,669 officers and men. Standards were carried only in the cuirassier, dragoon, and those light regiments which had distinguished themselves.

The structure of each regiment depended on its type, but was relatively consistent below the squadron level. Each squadron was organized into two half-squadrons. Each half-squadron had two platoons and each platoon had two half-platoons.

The Russian cavalry drill was primarily based on the Prussian drill of the period, but the Grand Duke Constantine made several changes which did not always have happy results. General Patapov produced a cavalry drill regulation based on Constantine's ideas, but it proved inexecutable on the battlefield.

The actual squadron school was decidedly different from that of the French army. Demiconversions were executed at the gallop, with an underofficer acting as a guide to control the movement in the same manner as in the British army. The Russians never deployed by platoons as did the French and Austrians, and the demiconversions were executed by threes because the number of files was evenly divisible by three. In a full conversion, the maneuver was executed in a different manner. A platoon of ten files was divided into three parts of four, three, and three files.

This conversion by threes forced the troopers to continually count their numbers and identify their position in the maneuvers. If there were casualties, the less-well-trained troopers often found it difficult to execute these maneuvers properly, and in consequence, the maneuvers would become sloppy. In contrast, under the French system, less-well-trained troops could be placed in the second rank and no problem would arise.

All Russian cavalry regiments, regardless of type, had a body of flankers whose function was skirmishing and scouting. In the dragoon and cuirassier regiments, where the entire regiments also received training in foot tactics like the French dragoons, these sixteen flankers were posted in the end files of each platoon. These were the men that were armed with rifled carbines.

A similar arrangement existed in the hussar and uhlan regiments, but this number was expanded considerably as the campaign went on. In the uhlan regiments, the extreme files of the first, second, and fourth platoons and the entire third platoon were designated as flankers. In the hussar regiments, all of the troopers were trained to function as skirmishers.

Russian Artillery

The artillery was probably the most important branch of the Russian army. The Russians were very partial to this arm, and as a result it was highly professional and very well trained, receiving special consideration and the finest horses available. Its weaponry included the licorne, a long-barreled howitzer designed and developed by Danilov and Martinov in 1757, that had a greater range and more accuracy than the howitzers used by the other European armies.

In 1805 the Russian artillery underwent a major material reorganization on a par with the introduction of the Gribeauval System in France. Count Alexei Arakcheyev standardized the calibers of the Russian guns to the 6pdr and 12pdr cannon and the 3pdr, 10pdr, and 20pdr licornes (the 3pdr was subsequently determined to be unsuitable and withdrawn from service in 1812). All of the Russian guns were made of highly polished brass, and after 1811 they were fitted with the "Karbanov System" of gunsights, which was among the best available at the time. Unlike the block system used by other European nations, this was an elevating wedge operated by screws. It gave the guns far greater accuracy.

In 1812 the Russian artillery consisted of position batteries, light batteries, and horse batteries. All three types of batteries had twelve guns each. Two guns were designated as a section, two sections formed a division, and three divisions formed a battery.

The position batteries consisted of four 20pdr licornes, four medium 12pdrs, and four short 12pdrs. The light and horse batteries had four

10pdr howitzers and eight 6pdr guns. The licornes were always posted in homogeneous divisions.

The Russian artillery was organized into twenty-seven brigades, each with one position and two light batteries. A brigade was assigned to each infantry division. There were also ten reserve brigades with four companies each and four depot brigades with eight companies each. In addition, the pontooniers and horse artillery were organized into independent formations that were distributed rather unequally throughout the army. There was also the garrison artillery and Guard Artillery Brigade. This gave the Russians a total of forty-five position batteries, fifty-eight light batteries, and twenty-two horse batteries.

In 1812 the "General Rules for Artillery in Field Action" was published by Generalmajor Kutisov, a student of Napoleon's concept of artillery. He advocated the use of massed artillery to knock holes in the enemy line or to stop attacks. In his work, Kutisov said that the main function of artillery was to engage in counterbattery fire and knock out the enemy's guns. He considered it worth checking the range at 1,000 yards because, though it would do little damage, it would discomfort the enemy's movements. At 450 yards, however, the fire would be murderous. He advocated that the artillery fire as rapidly as possible at the 450-yard range. He went on to advocate concealing as much of one's artillery as possible and slowly feeding it into the battle. This is what he intended to do at the Battle of Borodino, but he was killed before he had the opportunity to do so.

Other Line Units

In addition to the line infantry, there was also a small marine infantry organization. These four marine regiments had a three-battalion organization in 1803 and underwent the same reorganization as the rest of the line infantry in 1810. In 1811 they were incorporated into the army, and the first three were assigned to the 25th Division. The fourth went to the 28th Division. Only the Caspian Battalion was not changed by the 1810 reorganization. The marine regiments had a total of 1,968 officers and men. Each battalion had 633 officers and men, and each company had 158 officers and men.

The Russians had a long tradition of building field fortifications. In 1805 there were two regiments of pioneers, each with two battalions consisting of an elite company of sapper-miners and three companies of pioneers. In 1806 a third battalion was raised in both regiments. In 1812 two battalions of pioneers were organized from this force.

In 1812 the Sapper Regiment was formed by converging all of the existing engineering forces. It had a "Line Sapper Battalion" that had two companies of miners and two companies of sappers. The other battalion, the "Line Pioneer Battalion," had one company of sappers and three of miners.

The Russian Guard

The Russian Guard was formed in 1683 when Peter the Great organized the first two Guard infantry regiments, Preobragenski and Semenovski. The Guard infantry added a third regiment in 1730 with the raising of the Ismailov Guard Infantry Regiment. Prior to 1805 all three regiments were redesignated as grenadier regiments. Preobragenski had four battalions, while the others had three. When the Guard Jagers were raised by Paul I, they had only a single four-company battalion.

In 1806, when a second battalion was added, the Guard Jagers became a regiment. In the same year the Imperial Militia Battalion was raised from peasants in the imperial domains. In 1807 a second battalion was raised and this became the Finland Guard Infantry Regiment. In addition, the half-company of artillery attached to the guard passed into the Guard Artillery Brigade.

In 1811 the Guard infantry took on the same external organization as the line infantry. Each battalion had an elite company divided into two platoons, one of grenadiers and one of tirailleurs. In the Guard Jager Regiment they were known as carabiniers. In 1811 the Finland Guard Regiment became a light regiment.

During the last months of 1811 the Lithuania Guard Infantry Regiment was formed with two newly raised battalions and the fourth battalion of the Preobragenski Regiment. With the reorganization of the Russian army into standing divisions, the guard division had three brigades.

In 1812 the Guard Sapper Battalion and Guard Equipage Battalion were raised, mimicking Napoleon's Guard Marines.

The Guard infantry regiments had 2054 officers and men each. A Guard battalion had 644 officers and men each. A company had 153 officers and men each. The Guard Jagers had a slightly smaller organization. Each battalion had 444 officers and men. Instead of fifers they had buglers.

In 1805 the Guard cavalry consisted of the Chevalier Guards, Horse Guards, Guard Hussars, and Guard Cossacks. The organization of the first three regiments was identical. Each had a total of 872 officers and men organized into five squadrons. Each squadron had 160 officers and men.

In 1809 the Grand Duke Constantine Uhlans passed into the Guards and its ten squadrons were used to form the Guard Uhlans and the Guard Dragoons. These regiments had five squadrons each, but their organization was slightly larger. They had 917 officers and men each. Their squadrons had 164 officers and men each.

In 1812 there were three Guard cuirassier regiments. The Chevalier Guards and Horse Guards raised a sixth squadron. The Emperor Cuirassiers, who joined the Guard in very late 1812, had only five. The Guard Hussars, Uhlans, and Dragoons also raised a sixth squadron each.

The Guard artillery had a total of four foot batteries, two position and two light, and two horse batteries. The foot batteries had a total of 1,005 officers, artillerists, train, and other staff personnel. Each foot battery had 206 officers and men manning twelve guns. The batteries had the same mix of licornes and cannon as the line batteries. The two horse batteries had 358 officers and men. Each battery had 198 officers and men.

The Guard Equipage Battalion was a single battalion and an artillery section. The battalion was organized with 435 men. Each of its four companies had 104 officers and men. The artillery section had fifty-one officers and artillerists. The Guard Sapper Battalion had four companies, two of sappers and two of miners.

Russian Irregular Forces

The Russian army had two irregular formations of note. The most famous and glamorous of these were the cossacks, the border guards of the Russian Empire. They were posted on the frontiers where Russia contacted the wild eastern tribes and the ever-threatening Turks. The hostile nature of their territories, or "vioskos," resulted in their maintaining a continuous military organization always ready to engage the invader.

The size and composition of the cossack contingents from the various "vioskos" varied greatly. The famous Ataman Platov lead the Don Cossacks. This force consisted of many cossack "pulks," or regiments, and two cossack artillery batteries. There were also ten pulks of Black Sea Cossacks, four Crimean Tartar pulks, a single Orenburg Cossack regiment, ten Ural Cossack pulks, ten Siberian Cossack pulks and two horse batteries, three Bug Cossack pulks, and in 1812 the Ukraine raised four regiments. In addition there were two regiments of Bashkirs and two of Kalmucks. The organization of these regiments was quite irregular. The number of "sotnias," or squadrons, varied, as did the strength of those sotnias.

In 1811 the 1st and 2nd Ural Pulks were disbanded. On 5 June the Army of the Ukraine raised four new regiments. On 18 July 1812, fifteen Little Russia Cossack pulks were raised as a result of a draft, only to be disbanded in 1816. On 8 August 1812 the Orenburg Cossacks raised the Ataman Regiment, which had ten sotnias. In addition, twenty regiments of Bashkirs were raised, only to be disbanded in 1814 and 1815.

There were also two other regiments that had once been part of the cossack formations that were transferred to the regular army. These were the Tchougouiev Uhlan Regiment and the Tartar Horse Regiment. They had organizations that were roughly identical to those of the line uhlan regiments.

The other irregular force that existed was the "opolochenie," or militia. This had been raised in previous years, but never stood to arms very long. In 1806–1807 a total of thirty-two battalions of skirmishers and an unknown number of mobile battalions were raised. However, a week later two-thirds of them were disbanded. The only formation raised during this period that was not disbanded was the Imperial Militia Battalion which became part of the Guard.

The opolochenie raised in 1812 was a reaction to the French invasion, but plans had been laid for its formation as early as 1810. Even so, when raised, it was poorly organized and inadequately armed. Though a standard organization was issued, it was seldom attained. In addition, the men were armed with anything available, including muskets, though seldom, pikes, and hatchets.

The "druzhin" or cohorts (equivalent of a regiment) was the basic unit of the opolochenie. They were used as a source of replacements for the line units towards the end of the war. At Malo-Jaroslavets it was reported that pike-carrying opolochenie were used to fill out the third ranks of the companies. There are repeated references to the St. Petersburg opolochenie being absorbed into line units around the second battle of Polotsk. Other units, like the Count Saltiko Hussars of the Moscow contingent, did pass into the regular army.

Chapter V

Supply Considerations

In the seventeenth and eighteenth centuries the military had evolved a supply system based on the amassing of supplies in magazines and fortifications augmented by purchases from civilian contractors who followed in the wake of every army. These supply systems were rudimentary at best, and it was not possible for an army to sustain itself at any distance from its magazines. This restriction led to a system of military operations that were carefully planned, long in advance, and supported by the accumulation of military supplies for months prior to the actual inception of the campaign.

Once a war had begun, it was heavily influenced by supply considerations. There were no lightning maneuvers, troops marching hundreds of miles as was seen in the 1805 campaign. The wars of this period were like the jousting of turtles and seldom penetrated far into the country of either nation involved.

These wars were primarily wars of maneuver where one army attempted to establish itself in the enemy's territory in a strong position. It would then begin to ravage the enemy's territory until it forced the enemy to come to battle on as unfavorable terms as possible or was forced to move to fresh, unravaged country. These wars resulted in a continual squabbling over border provinces that exchanged hands every few years.

When the French Revolution erupted, the French military establishment found itself undergoing a major revolution itself. The logistical administration and its supply system rapidly decayed, proving incapable of providing the logistical support required by the newly raised French armies. As a result, the French armies were frequently on the verge of starvation. They lacked all logistical support, often going barefoot and in rags. By necessity they found themselves forced to fend for themselves, as their government had proven incapable of providing for them.

What began initially as the simple pillaging of the countryside by starving soldiers rapidly evolved into a systematic requisitioning and amassing of supplies in a given area. A relatively sophisticated system evolved, where individual companies would detach eight to ten men under the direction of a corporal or a sergeant on a periodic basis. These squads operated independent of the main body for periods of a week or a day, collecting supplies and material necessary for sustaining their parent company. They would then return and distribute this material amongst their fellows.

This organized "foraging" or "living off the land" should be distinguished from the actual marauding and pillaging committed by individuals and stragglers that followed the path of the advancing French armies like the tail of a comet. The latter case was often committed under threats of physical violence aimed at the long-suffering peasants. The former, however, was often controlled by treaties or other arrangements where the provision of such material was formally agreed to by the host nation. In this case the peasants were often paid in gold or paper that could theoretically be exchanged. There is, however, a period phrase, "Worthless as an assignat." Payment not in gold was in paper assignats, Revolutionary I.O.U.s which were absolutely without value. In the case of the French moving through conquered territory, there was seldom any remuneration. However, only rarely were provisions forcefully taken.

This system and the old system of supplying armies often stripped the countryside bare and caused serious problems for the local inhabitants, but it was nothing new to much of Europe. Though during the previous centuries armies had depended on magazines, starving armies had often moved through provinces, stripping them bare and wasting much of what they found. In contrast, the highly organized French system wasted little.

The French quickly became expert at estimating the ability of an area to support an army and developed skills in locating supplies in areas where other armies would have quickly starved if forced to live off the land. These skills had permitted the French to execute the massive maneuvers that gave them smashing victories in 1800, 1805, 1806, and

1809. It also led to the mystique that the French army could outmarch
every other army in Europe.

The ability to maneuver strategically had been seriously handicapped
for years by the necessity to provide a wagon train for supplies. These
wagon trains formed massive tails on every army, slowing them to a
snail's crawl. The French, lacking this military train and having the
ability to live off the land they were traversing, were able to march as
fast as their soldiers' legs could carry them, instead of at the pace of
the oxen pulling the wagons. The foraging bands would fan out across
the countryside behind the vanguard of the advancing army, collecting
provisions. Once that was done, they would close up to the main body
and distribute what they had gathered.

This often meant that the main bodies would reach their destination
sadly depleted by these detachments and other stragglers that fell behind.
It was not unusual, even in 1812, for a French army to stop to permit
the foraging parties to catch up with the main body. Despite this, the
French were capable of marches of up to fifty miles per day for short
periods and sustained marches of thirty or more miles a day for a week
or more.

Napoleon has often been accused of being overly optimistic about
the ability of his troops to provision themselves during the 1812 campaign.
He is accused of setting out on an ill-conceived operation that led to a
disastrous retreat and the destruction of the largest army seen to date.
However, an examination of the documents and facts refutes this. It is
highly unlikely that Napoleon was unaware of the Russian countryside.
He most certainly read the account of Charles XII's Russian campaign.
Even the Frenchman Guibert had described Russia as a "wasteland"
in his works. However, Napoleon most assuredly knew that it would
not be impossible for his troops to live off the land as they had in so
many previous campaigns.

In 1811 the French Depot de Guerre was ordered to carefully collect
all the information it could about Russia and to carefully examine all
the information it could find on the Russian campaign of Charles XII.
Their studies cannot have missed the Russian scorched earth tactic. This
realization is what probably prompted Napoleon to mass 1,000,000 rations in Stettin and Kustrin in April 1811. This was also the period
when Napoleon began a massive reorganization and expansion of his
military train.

By the end of 1811 the development of the French supply system in Poland had taken on a very offensive posture. His treaty with Prussia and the material provisions contained therein indicate a strong eastern orientation as early as February. If Napoleon had been defensively oriented, these supplies would have been deposited further away from the most probable areas of Russian advance. His supplies were positioned as far forward as the Vistula—not a defensive position.

In January 1812 it was ordered that Danzig be provisioned for war. By March sufficient supplies had been acquired there to support 400,000 men and 50,000 horses for 50 days. More supplies were stockpiled all along the Oder River. In addition, the French military train was raised to a total of twenty-six battalions.

Napoleon had begun in 1811 to expand his military train. He decided to concentrate on heavy wagons, despite warnings about the poor roads in Russia. In a letter dated 4 July 1811 he took the first steps. Prior to this period the supply wagons were drawn by four horses each and had a total capacity of one "miller" (one miller was approximately 1,000 French pounds, 489.6 kg, or 1,076 avoirdupoids) per horse drawing the wagon. In this letter Napoleon proposed adding two more horses to each wagon and increasing the load from four to six "millers" (4,304 avoirdupoids to 6,456 avoirdupoids). By this means he hoped to save one wagon in three, or thereby expand his existing cartage by one third. This had the one major drawback of increasing the load in each wagon and, as events were to show, this was a major problem vis-à-vis the Russian roads. During the first weeks of the invasion, as the French moved through Russian Lithuania, the skies poured rain on them, turning the roads into impassable morasses. Most of the wagons sank into the mud and were unable to move at any speed, let alone fast enough to feed the advancing French armies.

Somewhat in contrast to this, Napoleon also ordered the equipping of some train units "à la comtoise," that is, with light wagons, each drawn by a single horse. However, these wagons were also destined to be overloaded to the point where their "lightness" became a title only.

The provisioning of the army with artillery and munitions was undertaken on a massive scale. Magdeburg was the main distribution point and from there material was shipped down the Elbe into East Prussia. The munitions Napoleon gathered together for his 1812 campaign compare favorably with the efforts of the heavily industrialized nations during the First World War.

Napoleon knew that however well organized his supply system was, it would depend on horses, which are not the most rapid transport system. In addition, the horses also consume much of what they transport, seriously limiting the range of a horse-drawn supply system. Napoleon knew this and realized that it would make supplying an army of 200,000 men at the distance from the Niemen to Moscow a near impossibility. Evidence strongly suggests that Napoleon had recognized this when developing his campaign plans and did not intend that his supply system would be asked to stretch that far.

Indeed, it was Napoleon's plan to engage the Russian army quickly and destroy it near the Russian frontier. If pursuit became necessary, Napoleon intended to pursue the Russians only as far as Smolensk. When Napoleon reached Smolensk, his initial reaction was to establish himself there and build a supply base for the next jump forward in the spring. Other considerations appear to have caused Napoleon to vary from this plan and to advance towards Moscow.

By establishing his army in Smolensk, it is highly probable that Napoleon could have maintained his army with the supply system built there, if supplies had been supplemented by an organized foraging system of the surrounding countryside. This is substantiated by the actual situations of the wing army corps that did not advance so far into Russia and which were adequately supported by their supply arrangements. These armies, even that under Macdonald which operated on the extreme north, were in far better condition than the sad remnants of the main army falling back from Moscow. Their condition was so superior that the facts surrounding the conditions and the disaster that had befallen the main army were kept from them as long as possible. The truth was only revealed when the flanking forces finally merged with the main army between the Berezina and Smolensk.

Napoleon's army entered Russia with twenty-four days' worth of supplies; four on the backs of the men and a further twenty days' supplies in the wagons following the army. This would have been sufficient to support the limited operations that Napoleon had envisioned in his initial plan to bring the Russians to battle quickly and defeat them.

Though feeding the soldiers was reasonably well provided for, the provision of 250,000 horses with fodder was completely beyond the capabilities of every supply system in the world at that time. This single fact was probably more the cause of the destruction of the French cavalry than Murat's incessantly charging it around the countryside. That is not to say that Murat's actions did not make considerable contributions to the cavalry's destruction, as he often did not stop long enough to permit the proper care and maintenance of the horses. The reason for his actions is probably justifiably laid to his desire to bring the Russians to battle more than to the reckless stupidity he is often accused of by historians.

The Russian plans for the defense of their country also depended on logistical considerations. General Phull, a Prussian in service to Russia, had laid plans for the erection of a fortified position on the Drissa. He hoped to recreate a Torres Vedras situation and draw the French into an area that he felt was exceedingly poor, in order to stretch the French supply system to the breaking point. Once the French had been sufficiently weakened by the distance traveled, lack of supplies, and weather, he intended to sally forth and engage the French with a fresh army. The only problem with this plan was that when the French finally overran Drissa, Murat reported that the area around Drissa was not a desert, as the Russians had thought, but that it was relatively well provisioned and could easily support the French operations.

Once the French began their invasion, a number of supply problems quickly arose. First was the rains. Then came problems with the supply system's quality. It had been rapidly expanded, as had the rest of the army, and its ranks were filled with low-quality recruits and draftees. Their minimal training and professionalism was to tell; they simply couldn't cope with the situation.

The massive expansion of the rest of the army had its impact as well. The veteran troops were sadly diluted by the influx of recent recruits and the demands of the Spanish campaign. A similar expansion had occurred in 1809 when the French army was largely composed of new recruits. In both instances the recruits lacked the discipline and savoir faire to be able to sustain themselves in a foraging situation, but as the 1809 campaign was fought in Austria, the impact of this indiscipline on supplies was minimal compared to what it was to be in 1812.

As supplies became scarce in 1812, discipline broke down and the control over the troops diminished. They plundered indiscriminately instead of carefully requisitioning the supplies they found. Surprisingly, the officers refused to take part in these excesses and often suffered to a greater degree than the men they led.

This lack of discipline forced the inhabitants of the region to flee and hide those supplies that might have assisted the French army. If they had remained, a carefully established administration could have tapped the regional resources and provided more than sufficient supplies to support the French army.

This problem had yet another facet. A large part of the French army was composed of non-French, allied contingents that did not have the French skill at foraging. They lacked the skills necessary to find the supplies they required and had a bad tendency, when foraging, to think only of themselves. They tended to eat what they found when they found it and did not bring it back to their parent units. As a result, those men staying with the combat formations went hungry.

There was also an inequity of supply distribution. Each corps considered itself and its own supply problems only, not sharing its bounty with the next corps, which might be starving. The actual historical sequence was that the vanguard corps stripped the countryside and lived reasonably well, while those corps following it had slim pickings.

Despite this, once Lithuania and Belorussia were crossed, the countryside became richer and encouraged Napoleon's advance. Napoleon knew that the areas around Smolensk and Moscow were rich and could provide much of the needs of his army.

The internal supply problems of the Grande Armée were exacerbated by the systematic destruction of those available supplies by the Russian army as it retreated. This entailed the destruction of magazines and other stockpiles of provisions, such as those maintained by the peasants. However, as in the rest of Europe, when a nation attempted to destroy the supplies held by its peasantry, the peasants would hide it as actively as they did if threatened by the invaders. These peasants often considered their own governments to be as hostile to their well-being as the invaders were. Also, it should be remembered that Lithuania had been part of the Kingdom of Poland not too many years before. The sympathies of those people were actually pro-Napoleon, as he had recreated the crushed Polish kingdom in the shadow form of the Grand Duchy of Warsaw. This had revived their dreams of national identity and self-determination.

The Lithuanians actually raised and fielded five infantry regiments, one light infantry regiment, and four cavalry regiments to support Napoleon. This would suggest that there would have been a serious degree of regional support for Napoleon's efforts. Cooperation with his supply needs would have been a foregone conclusion, had he remained in Smolensk.

These attitudes should have mitigated much of the impact of the Russian army's effort to strip the Lithuanian countryside. Evidence suggests that it was only after the French left Lithuania that they faced "scorched earth." The Russian peasantry in the Russian provinces east of Smolensk had been stirred by the Orthodox priests with the idea that the French were heretics sent by Satan to destroy their religion. With this fear firmly implanted, the Russian peasants not only assisted the Russian army by withdrawing food, but engaged in guerrilla actions against the French foraging teams and stragglers.

Despite this cooperation, it is exceedingly unlikely that the peasants destroyed all the foodstuffs they held. A peasant who slaves in the fields and is barely able to feed himself was hardly likely to commit himself and his family to a winter of starvation simply because some Russian officer told him to do so. The peasants hid far more than they destroyed, in the hopes of it escaping the French. This meant that there was still a large volume of supplies for the French to utilize.

Then what was the primary cause of the starvation of the Grande Armée? There are two basic causes, both of which have been mentioned. The first was the undisciplined troops, which resulted in poor utilization of the supplies found. This discouraged any cooperation, or tacit nonintervention, by the peasants, whose supplies were to be requisitioned. The second cause was the change in plans that caused Napoleon to advance beyond the effective limitations of his supply system. The problems of heavy wagons and bad roads were more symptomatic than causal. The limited experience of the train personnel was apparent in their lack of care for their equipment and horses, but this too is a minor point. It contributed to, but did not cause, the collapse of the supply system.

When Napoleon began the disastrous retreat, the supply system had finally collapsed. The two factors mentioned had taken their toll. This indiscipline became rampant, and the corps of the weaker disciplinarians rapidly collapsed into hordes of stragglers that hovered around those few units that retained their discipline and organization. The full extent of the disaster that befell these men because of their indiscipline became tragically visible when they reached the Berezina. A thoughtless, mindless horde, thinking solely of its survival, pushed and shoved, struggling to survive one more minute and then sank into despair and resignation to its death.

The Russian Supply System

The Russian supply system was both different and not different from the French system. It was different in that the Russians never developed a system of foraging like that used by the French. It was similar in that the Russians depended on a system of magazines. The Russian system in the beginning of the campaign was based on a series of major magazines positioned in Vilna, Swezinia, Koltiniani, Grodno, Slonim, Slutz, Pinsk, Mosir, Brest, Kowel, Luzk, Dubno, Saslawl, Staro-Kostantof, and Ostrog. There was a secondary line of magazines in Riga, Dinaburg, Drissa, Sebesch, Velisch, Bobruisk, Rogatschef, Jitomir, Kiev, Novgorod, Veliki-Luki, Kaluga, Trubtschewska, and Sossniza. These magazines were positioned along the major lines of supposed operations, those lines running from the Niemen to St. Petersburg, Moscow, and Kiev. The Russians had positioned more than 1,200,000 bushels of meal, 112,000 bushels of barley, and 1,600,000 bushels of oats in them.

Prior to 1812 the Russian army was maintained through this system of magazines. The basic concept of a magazine was a functional idea, but the Russian system failed because the magazines were too big and too widely spaced. These great distances between magazines proved an embarrassment when the Russian train system had to operate between them, and the loss of a magazine to the French was a major supply disaster. This system was incompatible with the Russian plan of a rapid withdrawal. In addition, the Russian commissariat was plagued with a lack of bakers to produce the bread for the armies.

Knowing this, the Russians attempted to provide a flexible magazine system which operated in a specific area, gathering in supplies from the peasants to support the army. However, there was never sufficient time to establish these magazines and the carts employed to transport the provisions had a bad habit of being captured by the advancing French. In addition, because of the personal danger to the wagoners, they reacted in ways that protected themselves, but that acted to the detriment of the army they were to feed. They tended to take the long, safe route, and if it took two weeks, well that was too bad.

There was a further failure that resulted from the lack of proper preparation on the upper Dvina, the upper Dnieper, in Smolensk, and along the roads to Moscow and St. Petersburg. The initial Russian plan was to withdraw only as far as the Dvina, but the unexpected changing of plans totally upset the Russian supply plans. They were, as a result, obliged to supply their armies on an ad hoc basis during the middle phases of the campaign.

During the French withdrawal, the Russians provided their armies with supplies drawn by requisitions from the outlying cities and farming regions along the side of the French line of advance that had not been ravaged by the French. This material was passed through the flexible magazines described earlier. The supplies so gathered were transported in any and all available transportation, civilian and military. This system was one that sprang up to meet the needs of the army rather than a formally organized and planned military system. It did succeed in feeding the Russian army. Its vehicles were adapted to use on the notoriously bad Russian roads, and it was not subject to the ravagings of the cossacks or pillaging by its own troops who had lost all discipline. This does not mean that it functioned perfectly. It did not. It had its failures and, though the lot of the Russian soldiers was better, they weren't immune from the pain and hardships of hunger. They also died by the thousands from cold and hunger.

Chapter VI

Preparations for the Invasion

As Napoleon began reorganizing his army for the campaign, he quickly encountered manpower problems. His first step was to bring the fourth and sixth battalions of his infantry regiments up to strength by stripping the regimental depots of men and sending them forward in July 1811. On 1 July the conscripts forming the Class of 1811 were called to active duty. During August they departed for their depots.

The Expansion for War Begins

In December a new decree ordered a levy from the Class of 1812 as well as 7,920 new drafts from the Classes of 1810 and 1811 in the seven departments of Holland, the Rhine Estuary, Breda, and the Scheldt Estuary. A major recruiting campaign began on 10 February 1812 in an effort to raise still more manpower.

The increased recruiting and conscription could solve the numerical aspect of the manpower problem, but problems arose with the quality of the noncommissioned officers necessary to supervise and train the new recruits. Indeed, there were insufficient men available to be raised to noncommissioned officer status. On 1 July 1811 it was reported that many of the newly promoted noncommissioned officers in several of the newly formed sixth battalions did not have the prerequisite two years of service for the Fontainbleau noncommissioned officer school. Napoleon insisted that these unqualified men be returned to the ranks and that only qualified individuals, those with two years of service and attendance at the Fontainbleau school, be appointed to the ranks of noncommissioned officers.

Napoleon justified this by stating that he felt that a noncommissioned officer must have practical experience in war in order to be able to attend to the special needs of soldiers in the field. Anyone lacking this experience could not possibly function properly. To underscore this point, Napoleon issued the Decree of 2 August 1811, which stated that no conscript could become a corporal or brigadier until he had two years of service. This decree also set very specific periods of time before a soldier could be promoted to any of the other noncommissioned ranks. To become a corporal fourier or brigadier fourier required two and a half years of service. To become a sergeant or quartermaster sergeant required four years of service, and to rise from sergeant-major, quarter-master sergeant, or adjudant to lieutenant required eight years of service.

There was a great deal of concern regarding the quality of the soldiers being used to form the sixth battalions. On 25 August Davout reported to Napoleon that he had taken conscripts from the sixth battalions and spread them amongst the first four field battalions in an effort to even out the distribution of new drafts into his regiments. Concurrent with this he withdrew veterans from the first four battalions and placed them into the new sixth battalions to provide those battalions with a solid cadre of veteran soldiers.

Davout spoke of his shortage of noncommissioned officers or men who could qualify to become noncommissioned officers. Principally he spoke of the requirement that they be able to read and write. As a stopgap measure, Davout informed Napoleon that he was promoting individuals to the ranks of noncommissioned officers if they seemed capable, but did not fully meet the requirements.

In addition to the newly raised sixth battalions, Napoleon was giving serious consideration to raising a seventh battalion in each regiment or increasing the number of men assigned to each battalion. It had become apparent that the recruiting campaign and the drafts were producing more men than had been anticipated. Napoleon sought an efficient use of these men and consulted Davout. Davout's opinion, in a letter dated 10 September 1811, was that a battalion of 960 men was too large to be managed properly. He supported the idea of a seventh battalion.

Davout went on to say that if Napoleon's decision was to raise a seventh battalion, he would require six to eight weeks to pull sufficient cadres from his corps for this project. He also felt that despite the earlier discussions of a shortage of qualified noncommissioned officers, he could find enough of them for the seventh battalions.

Though there was frantic activity in 1811, the actual military preparations for the 1812 campaign began shortly after the 1809 campaign. Napoleon had no idea that by 1812 he would be at war with Russia, his nominal ally. The ground work for the Grande Armée of 1812 was being laid in the demobilization of the Grande Armée of 1809.

Changes After the 1809 Campaign

The French armies began withdrawing from Austria after the Peace of Schönbrunn. Many units returned to their garrisons in France, while others took up positions in Germany. Major formations occupied Düsseldorf, Hanau, Fulda, the Hanseatic cities, Hanover, Magdeburg, Bayreuth, Salzburg, and Rastibon. These cities were all occupied by late February 1810, but the demobilization of the French armies was to continue.

On 15 May Napoleon ordered the disbanding of the Armée d'Allemagne. In its place Napoleon ordered Davout to organize a new army. Davout did this and repositioned some of these forces. He moved forces into Passau, Danzig, Stettin, Küstrin, and Glogau, while maintaining garrisons in the cities mentioned earlier.

During 1812 the Armée de Barbant, which consisted of the French forces occupying Holland as well as the Dutch army, was disbanded. It had consisted of two divisions of infantry, a National Guard division, a light cavalry division, and a Dutch infantry division. All told it had 38,791 French infantry, 4,392 French cavalry, 9,369 Dutch infantry, and 1,007 Dutch cavalry. It was dissolved in April. The National Guard was demobilized and some of the French troops returned to garrisons in France.

On 1 May 1810 the Corps d'Observation de la Hollande was organized to replace the Armée de Barbant. Pursuant to the treaty of 16 March 1810, it consisted of 12,000 Dutch troops and those French troops remaining in Holland. This corps lasted only until 9 July 1810, when Holland was formally incorporated into metropolitan France. The Dutch army ceased to exist, and the Decree of 18 August 1810 incorporated it into the French army.

On 19 September 1810 Napoleon directed Prince Eugène, viceroy of Italy, to reorganize the Armée d'Italie. It had 27,000 men and a guard of 3,000. After the 1809 campaign it had stood down and been renamed the "Corps d'Observation d'Italie." The corps consisted of three infantry divisions, two cavalry divisions, and the Italian Royal Guard.

On 4 October 1810 Napoleon set about reorganizing the Armée d'Allemagne. It was to have three infantry divisions, a light cavalry division, and a heavy cavalry division. It was to be equipped with 110 guns and a double provision of ammunition. Its engineering corps was to consist of six sapper companies, one miner company, and two pontoonier companies. It was also to have a gendarme force of 100 men. It was renamed the Corps d'Observation de l'Elbe. Prior to completion of the reorganization, the three infantry divisions were increased to four divisions. This growth continued, and by August 1811 a fifth division was organized.

A sixth division was raised from the various allied contingents under the command of General Grandjean and became the garrison of Danzig. The eighth and ninth divisions were also raised in August. The eighth was formed in Münster and the ninth was raised in Nijmegen.

The Corps d'Observation du Rhin was renamed the Corps d'Observation des Côtes de l'Océan, but it underwent no changes until 1 January 1811. At that time its first two divisions were formed and held in Boulogne, the third was raised in Utrecht, and the fourth in Emden.

The Corps d'Observation de l'Elbe, Corps d'Observation des Côtes de l'Océan, and the Corps d'Observation d'Italie constituted the standing French army in early 1811. These three corps were to form the nucleus of the Grande Armée of 1812.

On 17 April 1811 Napoleon ordered the formation of the 2nd, 3rd, and 4th Cuirassier Divisions. The regiments that were to form these divisions were moved into Germany in September and began organizing in October in Bonn, Erfurt, and Cologne. The cuirassier division with Davout's corps was designated as the 1st Cuirassier Division.

Napoleon began gathering his artillery together in the forward magazines at Metz, Wesel, la Fère, and Strasbourg, where it would be ready to move into Germany quickly. At the same time Napoleon ordered the organization of a major bridging train in Danzig. The task of this train was to throw two bridges over the Vistula when Napoleon decided it was time to advance.

Napoleon also ordered the formation of two siege trains. One was formed in Danzig and the other in Magdeburg. He also began a selective recall of troops fighting in Spain. Efforts to accumulate provisions in

Magdeburg, Stettin, Küstrin, and Glogau were accelerated, while Danzig was to become the principal depot, repair facility, and construction center of the French forces deployed in eastern Germany.

Napoleon's Allies Prepare for War

During early 1811 Napoleon began urging the Grand Duchy of Warsaw and the Kingdom of Westphalia to expedite the mobilization of their armies. He was greatly concerned about the possibility of a preemptive Russian attack and wanted both armies ready to defend their borders. He also pushed the various other princes in the Confederation of the Rhine to do the same. Similar urgings were sent to Davout, Eugene, and Ney.

On 9 August 1811 Napoleon signed a conscription decree for the Army of Cleve-Berg. The decree called up a total of 1,850 men. With the addition of further drafts to replace desertions from the ranks, the actual total called up came to 2,150 men. Six hundred of these men were used to rebuild the 1/1st Regiment in Düsseldorf, 1,200 were to form the 4th Regiment, and the remainder went to the cavalry regiment and train units.

Napoleon hoped to rebuild the Berg army with this draft until the 1st Regiment had one 600-man battalion and the 2nd, 3rd, and 4th Regiments had two full 600-man battalions each. The cavalry was to have a total of 1,000 men and the artillery, train, and engineers were to have 1,500 men. However, the 1811 draft proved insufficient and a further draft was called in 1812.

Pressures were applied to the other German states, reaching a peak in December 1811. In February 1812 the first German division was organized with the contingents of Berg, Baden, and Hesse-Darmstadt. This division was assigned to General Daendels and sent north, where it occupied Swedish Pommerania, Stettin, and Küstrin in early March 1812. In addition, the forces of Frankfurt and Würzburg were joined to form the nucleus of the "division princiére" and stationed in Hamburg.

The two Mecklenburg contingents were formed into a brigade and assigned to the Corps d'Observation de l'Elbe, now known as I Corps. However, the armies of Saxony, Bavaria, and Württemberg were not expected to be mobilized until March 1812.

During the month of February the strength and positions of the allied contingents of the Grande Armée were as follows:

The Württembergers under the command of the Prince of Württemberg totaled 10,000 infantry, 2,000 cavalry, 1,000 artillery, and 30 guns. With the exception of the 7th Regiment, which was assigned to garrison Danzig, the entire Württemberg army was awaiting orders at Heilbronn on 26 February. It was assigned to the III Corps under the command of Marshal Ney.

The Bavarian army consisted of 14,000 infantry, 3,174 cavalry, and 1,016 artillerists and train. Between 10 and 15 February they left their garrisons and moved to the Saxon border. They were assigned to the VI Corps under the command of General St. Cyr.

Saxony provided two mixed divisions, each with about 9,000 men. Additional Saxon forces were serving as garrisons in Danzig and Glogau. Saxony provided a total of 624 officers, 19,013 men, 6,160 horses, and 59 guns. However, Saxony did not mobilize its forces until later in 1812, choosing to keep their forces in garrisons in Dresden, Torgau, Buben, Lübeck, and Kottbus.

The Westphalian army consisted of 20,000 men, 4,416 horses, and 40 guns, not including the 1st and 8th Infantry Regiments stationed in Danzig, the Chevauléger Regiment serving in Spain, and an infantry battalion also serving in Spain. The main Westphalian army was scattered through Westphalia in garrisons in Kassel, Halberstadt, Ascherlebe, Hildesheim, Brunswick, Mühlhausen, Nordhausen, and other cities.

The Westphalian corps was initially organized into three groups: a mixed brigade forming the advanced guard, a division of ten infantry battalions and a reserve formed of an infantry brigade, a cuirassier brigade, and the park. Napoleon found this arrangement awkward and in February directed Jérôme to reorganize this force into two infantry divisions and a cavalry brigade. The Westphalian corps assembled between 10 and 15 March near Halle and Dessau with orders to cross the Elbe if called. Though Jérôme was in command, all military considerations were left to Général de division Vandamme.

The Polish forces were fully organized and standing to arms in March. Napoleon made no further dispositions of their forces, but ordered the raising of a fourth battalion for every infantry regiment. He also directed that the cavalry regiments be raised from 850 to 1,050 men.

During January 1812 the Corps d'Observation de l'Elbe was divided into the I and II Corps. The I Corps had five divisions and the II Corps had three. Oudinot, who commanded the II Corps, moved his forces to Münster and Osnabrück.

The Corps d'Observation des Côtes de l'Océan was reorganized into the 7th, 10th, 11th, and 12th Divisions on 15 February. They then assembled in Mainz under the command of Marshal Ney as the II Corps. The Corps d'Observation d'Italie became the IV Corps and its divisions were numbered as the 13th, 14th, and 15th Divisions. On 15 February these divisions occupied Botzen, Tremot, Verona, and Bresica.

The cavalry reserve was divided into three corps, each having a light cavalry division and two divisions of either cuirassiers or dragoons. A remount depot was established in Hanover under the command of General Broucier. He was charged with securing sufficient horses from German sources to fully mount all three cavalry corps.

General Daendels' 26th Division was organized by Napoleon on 22 January 1812. It consisted of forces from Frankfurt, Würzburg, Mecklenburg-Schwerin, Mecklenburg-Strelitz, and the 4th, 5th, and 6th Rhinbund Regiments.

As the invasion drew closer, Napoleon began to look to the requirements of the first days of the campaign. He paid particular attention to the bridging requirements of the Niemen. To cross it he needed a bridging train capable of crossing a 600-foot-wide river. To solve this he had three bridging trains organized in Danzig. The first two had 100 pontoons each, while the third had none. It was equipped solely with cordage and other necessary equipment. The other pontoonier companies were in Danzig, and five fully equipped companies were with the advanced guard. Napoleon also ordered the outfitting of two battalions of "matelots" (sailors) to assist in the crossing. These men were to man the boats that were to transport the first assault waves of infantry across the Niemen.

Napoleon also organized his grand park. It was to have an additional 50 percent over the normal provision for the army's artillery and a 25 percent overprovision of infantry ammunition. However, this formation was not loaded until the invasion was imminent.

The French park had eight artillery train companies attached to it. Six were French, one was Guard, and one was Italian. A total of 2,016 wagons were attached to those units. In addition, there were four newly raised battalions "à la comtoise" with 2,424 wagons, and four ox-drawn battalions with a further 1,224 wagons.

Each regular wagon was capable of carrying an average of 30 metric hundredweights, the "comtoise" wagons would carry 12 metric hundredweights, and the ox wagons would carry 20 hundred-weights. This meant that the train could carry between 110,000 and 120,000 metric hundred-weight of supplies.

The effect of the call-up of the Class of 1812 on 24 December was substantial. By the end of January, half of the conscription was complete and approximately 120,000 draftees were called. Of that number, 112,249 were already in the depots being trained. The remaining 7,751 were retained in a reserve to be trained later.

The Situation Deteriorates

The political situation continued to deteriorate and on 15 March Napoleon knew that he had no option but the military one. He directed the I Corps to move on the Oder River, taking up positions on Küstrin, Stettin, Bomberg, and in the area between Ancalm and Stettin. Oudinot's II Corps was to advance on the Elbe River, positioning itself between Magdeburg, Brunswick, Helmstadt, Wesel, and Münster. The II Corps moved to Erfurt, Weimar, and Leipzig.

At the end of March the I Corps was on the Vistula River and encamped on its banks by 15 April. On 21 March II Corps crossed the Elbe River and moved on Brandenburg and Magdeburg. The II Corps was in Leipzig, and the IV Corps was in Dresden and Glogau. The V Corps occupied Prague and Moldin on the 29th and the VI Corps arrived on the Oder River on 30 March. The Saxons began to organize in March and arrived in Kalisch on 14 April. From there they moved towards the Vistula River.

The Westphalians of the IX Corps crossed the Elbe River on 24 March and moved to Spremberg, arriving in early April. From there they moved to Glogau and Kalisch. The Württemberg army joined Ney in Heilbronn.

The Prussian contingent organized in Königsberg, Berlin, and Breslau. On 25 March they moved to Breslau while the French Imperial Guard left France and began deploying in Germany. The first elements of the Guard reached Magdeburg on 29 March. The Vistula Legion arrived in Sedan, and four regiments of Young Guard were recalled from Spain.

Preparations Behind for Home Defense

Considering how much attention Napoleon gave to the needs and organization of his main army, one might imagine that he neglected other aspects of the French military situation. Perhaps any other commander would have, but Napoleon had an administrative genius that no other military leader of his age could hope to match.

Mindful of the British landings in the Scheldt estuary in 1809 while he was occupied in Austria, Napoleon had real concerns that this might happen again. He gave special attention, as a result, to his coast defenses. While the army's field artillery forces and the navy's shipboard gunners were highly professional, the coast artillery had become the dumping ground of the poor performer. These men continued to demonstrate their lack of skill by the low level of training in their new positions.

The coastal defense system was gravely inadequate. In 1811 the coast defense budget amounted to about 3,500,000 francs. Napoleon was ready to double this if he felt it was necessary to provide an adequate defense. "Nothing has been gained from having bad troops manning these defenses," he said, "and it is a ridiculous economy to charge militia captains with the defense of a coast that might be threatened by highly competent enemy regulars."

To remedy this potentially threatening situation, Napoleon deployed four field artillery regiments along the coast to reinforce the coastal units. A major reorganization of the staff and administration occurred. Money, equipment, administration, and training poured into the coast defenses.

Plans Are Developed

With his coasts attended to and relatively secure, Napoleon turned eastward once again. He feared a preemptive attack by the Russians and took steps to counter it by the careful disposition of his forces. He also developed his offensive plans. In a letter to General Lariboisiere, dated 14 March 1812, Napoleon outlined his plans for opening the campaign with a siege of Dinaburg and Riga. He requested all the information available to him on those two cities.

Napoleon also asked him to determine how many boats would be necessary to transport the siege train from Magdeburg. Napoleon stated that he wished to embark this train by 1 April and move it down the Vistula River to Bomberg, where he hoped to have it positioned by 1 May. He stated that he wanted this material in Vilna and ready for siege operations by 1 June. He also directed General Lariboisiere to maintain the target of these operations secret from everyone, including the commanding officer of the engineers.

Napoleon similarly directed that the Danzig siege train should travel via boat to Memel and on to Tilsit. He stated that he anticipated these two sieges to last only fifteen days: five days for investment, opening of trenches, construction of batteries, and the commencement; followed by ten days of sapping. These plans for sieges, however, do not reinforce the idea that Napoleon was considering the short campaign his twenty-four days' worth of supplies might otherwise have indicated.

On 25 March 1812, Napoleon wrote a series of instructions in case of a Russian attack before his preparations were complete. Jérôme and his Westphalians were to make no move unless the Russians attacked the Grand Duchy of Warsaw. If this occurred Jérôme was to take command of the V, VII, and IX Corps. He was to be provided with orders for Poniatowski and Reynier that put them under his command. Jérôme was to command the right wing of the French army while Davout took the left wing and began offensive operations against the invading Russians.

Russian Activity

The issuance of orders to Jérôme and Davout and some juggling of positions by the French completed Napoleon's dispositions. The evidence clearly indicates that at this point Napoleon was committed to war with Russia.

This is supported by Napoleon's overactive interest in the Russian military preparations and movements. As early as 6 January 1810, Napoleon received reports of major Russian troop redeployments from Finland into Lithuania and south. Since Russia was engaged in a war with the Turks at the time, it was thought that these troops were moving to join the Army of the Danube.

As time passed, Napoleon's intelligence community increased its efforts and the frequency of its reports. A report dated 30 September 1810 informed Napoleon that major magazines were being formed in Iourburg, Dinaburg, Riga, Drouia, Mohilev, Vitebsk, and Orsha.

In May 1811 Napoleon learned that the divisions of Wittgenstein, Lavrov, Konovnitzin, and Baggovout were located in northern Lithuania. There were also three divisions in central Lithuania, the 7th under Generallieutenant Kapsevitch, the 9th under Generallieutenant Suvarov, and the 22nd under Generallieutenant Lewis. The 9th and 22nd Divisions were advancing from Podolia through Volhynia and onto Pinsk.

These seven divisions all had the standard six-regiment organization.

Napoleon knew that the Russian battalions had an average strength of 700 men, which gave these divisions an average strength of 7,800 men. In addition, a single dragoon regiment of approximately 600 men and a cossack "pulk" were attached to each division, giving each of these divisions an average of 8,900 men. There were two further divisions in Podolia at this time, the Siberian Division under Generallieutenant Arakcheyev and the 18th Division under Generallieutenant Tchervatov. These divisions were weak and it was known that the total strength of both divisions did not exceed 11,100 men.

Napoleon's espionage system informed him that the Russians had organized three reserve cavalry divisions. The first two were commanded by Generallieutenants Korff and Pahlen. They were posted on the Polish border. Korff's division had a total strength of 9,250 men and consisted of four hussar regiments, four dragoon regiments, and five cossack pulks. Pahlen's division had 6,750 men in four cuirassier regiments, four dragoon regiments, and four uhlan regiments.

Napoleon knew that the infantry divisions were later reinforced by the activation of the third battalion. Once raised to full strength, the third battalions were to be sent to work on various fortifications. Napoleon's information was incomplete in that he only knew the names and numbers of these battalions, but he never learned of their true strength, which was very very low. He only saw battalions.

French intelligence located another cavalry division with forty squadrons under the command of the Grand Duke Constantine near Nizyn and another cavalry force under Generalmajor Tchlapitz in the districts of Ostang, Zaslavl, and Zwrachel.

In May General Docturov was recalled to St. Petersburg and his command was turned over to Kapsevitch. In addition, several other senior officers were recalled to St. Petersburg for consultations.

News arrived in Paris that magazines were being raised in Dubno, Zaslavl, and Korets. The provinces of Volhynia, Podolia, and Kiev had each been directed to provide 13,106,200 liters of wheat, 1,654,600 liters of flour, and 19,273,000 liters of oats to support the army.

Reports surfaced again that 30,000 men had been moved from the Swedish frontier with Finland and that a major magazine was being organized in Bobruisk. This magazine was to hold 14,780,000 liters of wheat and 24,580,000 liters of oats. Another immense magazine was being formed in Samogitia.

Fortifications Prepared for the Assault

In Kiev, fortifications were being erected by 3,000 men under the direction of an English colonel named Margrini. On 10 May 1811 it was reported that Dinaburg was being fortified by a Saxon officer named Hackel. Thirty-two battalions of recruits were being used to raise these fortifications, and they were expected to be reinforced during the year. The city was to be defended by 600 guns and surrounded by a trench thirty-six feet deep. It was to have three ranks of galleries and a glacis that was 360 feet long. The ground had been cleared for 9,000 feet around the fortification and a strong bridgehead established on the left bank of the Dvina River. It is little surprise that Napoleon was organizing a massive siege train to deal with this fortress.

There were also reports of a steady stream of forces being drawn away from the Russian Army of Turkey, and about 50,000 men appear to have been drawn away by April. The French did not consider this to be a significant withdrawal even when the Russians made the detachment of three divisions official. These last three divisions were destined for Slonim, Niesweiz, and Koltiniany.

In mid-May Napoleon learned that the Russian army was undergoing a major reorganization and that four army corps of about 30,000 men each were being formed. The new 1st Corps was stationed around Slonim, the 2nd Corps was in Vilna and Iourburg, the 3rd Corps in Koltiniany, and the 4th Corps in Riga. These corps had a total of 90,000 infantry and 30,000 cavalry, not counting cossacks. It was thought that they had a total of 250 guns.

General Engelhardt's division was reported to have moved on Orgeyev on 19 May 1811. He and his division had remained in Iassy until mid-April. On 23 May Napoleon learned that the 1st, 2nd, 3rd, and 4th Divisions were occupying Courland, Samogitia, and the northern parts of Lithuania. He also learned that the 7th, 9th, and 22nd divisions were in central Lithuania and Ploesie. The nine infantry divisions in Lithuania each had a dragoon regiment and a cossack pulk assigned to them.

The Siberian Division, commanded by Generallieutenant Arakcheyev, was in Podolia and still understrength. The 1st Grenadier Division and a reserve division were stationed on the Dvina River to act as a general reserve.

Word came that the third battalions of the infantry regiments were being used exclusively to construct fortifications and had not been organized into field divisions. More significantly, Napoleon learned that the

Russians had raised a number of new jager regiments, the 51st being among them.

Generals Pahlen and Korff commanded two of the three cavalry divisions in Lithuania, while the commander of the third division had not yet been named. Their forces were kept on the border to watch for any sign of the French advance. To support them, four cossack pulks that were stationed near Pinsk moved forward to join them.

Between 15 May and 1 June it was learned that Wittgenstein's division had moved from between Riga and St. Petersburg and was now heading towards Mitau. The divisions of Lavrov, Baggovout, and Konovnitzin were still in central and southern Lithuania. Kapsevitch's division was in Volhynia, but was moving towards Lithuania while Suvarov's division had moved from Wallachia through Russian Galacia and into southern Lithuania.

Arakcheyev's and Tchervatov's weaker divisions remained in Podolia. Napoleon learned that each of them had about 5,500 infantry, a dragoon regiment, and a cossack pulk.

The latest count of the Russian front line forces in Lithuania totaled 74,000 infantry, two cavalry divisions with 18,500 men, and a reserve division of 6,750 men.

In June Napoleon learned that Engelhardt's division was detached from Wallachia and had begun moving north into Lithuania. Another report dated 10 June stated that 10,550 men of Docturov's corps were being concentrated near Lutsk and Jitomir. It was also destined for Lithuania. Napoleon also learned that the nine Russian divisions in Lithuania had assumed positions extending in a line from Rosienne to Vladimir and Kamieniec-Podolski.

On 23 June Napoleon learned that there were 30,000 infantry near Riga. The report said that the city was fortified with a double wall and sixty heavy-caliber guns. Riga's magazine was known to have a 104.5-million-liter capacity.

On 21 June the Russians were beginning to fortify Stary-Konstantinov. By 17 June the Russian forces in Moldavia facing the Turks had been reduced to five divisions, and in early July General Lewis moved his division into Bobruisk, where he began to fortify and provision the city.

By August there were 100,000 men in Lithuania and a further 50,000 near Pinsk. Converged grenadier battalions were formed from the depots of the 4th, 5th, 14th, and 17th Divisions, but the French intelligence reports indicated that these battalions did not exceed 600 men each.

In August General Essen's corps was formed with the infantry divisions of Generals Lavrov and Konovnitzin. They were joined by Pahlen's cavalry division. In addition, a reserve was formed by the third battalions of the infantry regiments. It was, however, reported that the men in those third battalions were of very low quality and suited only to dig fortifications.

The Russians Expand Their Army

The fifth or depot squadrons were stripped out of the cavalry regiments and returned to their depots. Once in the depots these squadrons were organized into the 9th, 10th, and 12th Cavalry Divisions.

Napoleon was aware that the reserve battalions of the 4th and 14th Divisions had been organized into the 30th Division and that those of the 5th and 7th Divisions had become the 31st Division. He also knew that the 32nd, 33rd, 34th, 35th, and 37th Infantry Divisions and the 9th, 10th, and 12th Cavalry Divisions had been formed, but he was never to learn of their true organization and strength.

The strength of the new Russian divisions varied tremendously. The 32nd Division, commanded by Generalmajor Hamen, was so weak that it was reorganized into two converged infantry regiments. The reserve battalions of the 11th and 36th Jagers had about 240 men each. The average strength of the depot battalions of the 1st Grenadier Division was 314 men. The depot squadrons of the 1st Cuirassier Division, forming part of the 9th Cavalry Division, averaged about 126 men each. This force was organized into a converged cavalry regiment.

Russia was pulling together every soldier it could, and Napoleon knew it. The Russians were faced by the hostile Turks to the south and a growing threat from Napoleon in the west.

By the beginning of August, the Russian army covered the length of the Prussian and Polish borders and extended into Galacia. The Russian right consisted of the 4th Division in Vilna under Baggovout and the 17th Division in Dinaburg under Alexeiev. They were supported by Korff's cavalry division on the Niemen River.

The Russian center was commanded by Generallieutenant Essen in Slonim. He commanded the 3rd and 11th Divisions supported by Pahlen's cavalry. The Russian left was commanded by General Docturov and consisted of Kapsevitch's 7th Division and the 25th (Siberian) Division. It was supported by a reserve formed by the 1st Grenadier Division on the Dvina. The reserve for the left wing was the 24th Division posted in Kiev.

By August the French assumed that the reorganization of the Russian army to the standardized six-regiment division was complete. Their sources indicated that the average battalion had no more than 650 men, and when the regiments were joined by the third battalions, the regiments would have no more than 1,600 men. They reevaluated the Russian divisions as having 10,000 men with the addition of the third battalions.

Russian War Plans

Russia was also making plans for the coming war. It was decided that if Prussia declared for France, the Russians under Wittgenstein would move against Prussia and Danzig in an effort to knock them out of their alliance with France. In case of war with Sweden, which was allied with France, the Russian Guard was to join the 20,000-man corps on the Aaland Islands and along the Finnish frontier.

In case of war with Austria, General Kutusov was to refrain from any offensive action against the Austrians and assume a defensive position along the Danube. The 9th Division, commanded by Lewis, and the 18th Division were to observe the Austrian movements. In addition, four cuirassier regiments, one dragoon regiment, and two uhlan regiments were to be formed into a supporting cavalry corps.

In late August Generallieutenant Tuchkov and his three divisions were in Wallachia. General Docturov, with four divisions, joined Tuchkov in operations against the Turks. A force of 13,000 recruits was also moving south to join them, as was part of Tchlapitz's cavalry division.

It was in September that four cossack pulks were assigned to every cavalry division to provide it with an irregular scouting force. A single pulk was assigned to every infantry division.

On 14 August 1811 the Russian army was positioned as follows: The 1st Corps (Wittgenstein) was in Samogitia and Courland; the 2nd Corps (Baggovout) was in Vilna, Mohilev, and Plock; the 3rd Corps (Essen) was in Grodno and Minsk; and the 4th Corps (Docturov) was in Vinnitsa and Kiev. The 1st Grenadier Division, the reserve, was in Vilna and on the Dvina; the 24th Division was near Kijov and Bialoceskiev; a cuirassier division was near Duman and another was near Riga, Revel, and Pilten. The total Russian forces in the Polish provinces was 112,900 men: 87,000 infantry, 16,900 cavalry, and 12,000 cossacks.

This figure includes the third infantry battalions, which were not normally included in such figures. Without them the infantry strength was 55,000 men.

On 22 September it was reported that Kapsevitch's and Docturov's forces were moving north. In November it was found that the 9th and 17th Divisions had left the Dniester and moved into Moldavia. Some cadres of regiments destroyed in fighting the Turks were withdrawn to Podolie and the Polish Ukraine. From there they went to Kiev to be rebuilt with men drawn from the recruiting depots formed in 1810.

It was reported that the 7th, 18th, 24th, and 25th Divisions were ordered to detach some battalions into Moldavia to support Kutusov's operations against the Turks. For the most part, however, these were regimental reserve battalions. Those regiments that did not have their reserve battalions were obliged to send one of their field battalions. This movement of veteran forces north continued, and on 12 November a major transfer of veteran troops out of Moldavia was reported, despite the continuing war with the Turks. They were being replaced to a greater and greater extent with new recruits.

In January the French noted that the Russians had stopped withdrawing troops out of Moldavia because of the unsatisfactory state of the war with the Turks. However, just before the French invasion, the Russians negotiated and signed a treaty with the Turks, freeing their southern forces.

Between January and June 1812, when the invasion began, there were relatively few changes in the disposition of the Russian army. The forces north of the Pripet Marsh were formally organized into the 1st Army and 2nd Army of the West. Those forces south of the Pripet were still organizing and were to become the 3rd Army of the West. The 3rd Army was not to be completed until the invasion began.

Chapter VII

The Battle Is Joined

Geography and the Plans

The geography of Russia has always played a major role in its military history. This vastness is filled with every imaginable type of terrain and is sharply divided in the west by the Pripet River along an east-west line. Though the Pripet River is not a major river, it is surrounded by the largest marsh in Europe. It is an impenetrable and militarily impassable area of swamp, forest, and lakes pierced by very few roads.

Ancient Lithuania lies north of the Pripet. It is heavily wooded and liberally sprinkled with swamps and lakes, with little open terrain suitable for the deployment of a major army. Lithuania further complicates military operations with a series of rivers running north and south. Among these formidable barriers to an invading army are the Niemen, Vilia, Berezina, and Dvina Rivers, all of which must be crossed before an invader arrives before Moscow.

Any terrain in Russia was complicated, not eased, by the Russian road system. The roads through Lithuania were little more than dirt tracks. After a rain these tracks quickly turned to a sea of mud that sucked the boots off men's feet and strangled wagons in their grasp. If dry, the thousands of feet and hooves that were to pass over them quickly raised clouds of choking dust.

There were three main roads leading east from western Europe. The first passed through Brest-Litovsk and led on to Kiev. From there it moved to Smolensk and Moscow, passing around the Pripet Marsh from the south. The second road to Moscow ran through Grodno and Minsk, along the northern flank of the Pripet where it joined the main route east at Vitebsk. The third road ran from Kovno directly to Smolensk, the religious capital of Russia, and then on to Moscow.

In deciding which route to use for his lines of communication, Napoleon realized that the southern route through Brest-Litovsk would expose his communications to the mercies of the Austrians. Though he had recently married an Austrian princess, Austria had been his staunchest enemy for years. It was too great a risk to take. The central route had much the same problems.

The northernmost route, through Kovno, was the superior choice. It passed from the Grand Duchy of Warsaw, Napoleon's staunchest ally, through the heart of Lithuania, which could be counted on to receive the French as liberators.

Espionage had informed Napoleon that the main Russian forces were concentrated north of the Pripet. Barclay de Tolly commanded a total of six infantry corps and three cavalry corps over a front of 250 miles. His forces stretched from Slonim in southern Lithuania to Shavli in Courland. Bagration, with two other corps and a sizable cavalry contingent, was concentrating around Lutsk, 200 miles south of Slonim, to the south of the Pripet. Napoleon felt that the Russians had three military options. Their first option was to fall back and refuse to allow the French their decisive battle. In this instance, Napoleon felt he could outmarch them, pierce their center, and destroy the two fragments separately and in detail. Their second option was to abandon Vilna and fall back to a position between Grodno and Slonim. Here Napoleon planned to trap them against the Pripet and smash them.

The third option, and the most likely in Napoleon's opinion, was that the Russians would slowly give ground while Bagration moved up from south of the Pripet, took Warsaw, and cut Napoleon's communications. To counter this, Napoleon tasked Jérôme and Schwarzenberg to tie Bagration down while he advanced and seized Vilna. Prince Eugène was to advance along the main army's flank and prevent any unexpected blows from striking it. After about twelve days, Jérôme was to withdraw slowly up the Nraew River, drawing the Russians after him. When he contacted Eugène and Davout he was to stop, and the trap would slam shut as Napoleon concentrated 400,000 men against Bagration. He had every reason to expect another Ulm.

All of Napoleon's plans were aimed at bringing the Russians to battle and winning a total victory within twenty days of the beginning of the campaign. This is substantiated by the Grande Armée's being provisioned with twenty-four days' supplies as it crossed the Niemen. Once the Russian armies were destroyed, the czar would be at his mercy.

Despite the brilliance of this plan, it had not made allowances for the distances and roads. In his previous campaigns Napoleon had been able to communicate easily with his subordinate commanders. The roads were good and the distances relatively small. Thus he had been able to bring his forces into a decisive concentration at the critical point time after time, smashing his outnumbered and outmaneuvered enemies. To accomplish this Napoleon had dominated his subordinate commanders and directed their every move. This overcontrol had resulted in the stifling of initiative and confidence in many of these men. In consequence, when his corps commanders were forced to operate in Russia without this spoon-fed direction, they had to operate on their own skills and initiative. Unfortunately the results were often marred with fatal errors and misjudgments of Napoleon's desires.

The Camp at Drissa

The initial Russian defensive plan, designed by the Prussian general Phull, was based on the concept of an entrenched camp that would support the Russians while the French starved at its gates. Once the French were sufficiently weakened, the Russians would strike them and drive them back to Germany.

The position chosen for this camp was near Drissa, on the Dvina. Phull had induced the czar to dispatch Colonel Wolzogen, also a former Prussian officer, with instructions to select a site for this fortified camp. The position chosen had the sole advantage of being in a "U"-shaped bend in the Dvina with a gap of about three miles at its mouth. The camp extended beyond this gap in a slight curve that was supported on either end by the banks of the river. On the right bank of the Dvina, above and below the camp, there were several minor streams, of which the Drissa was the largest. These streams provided strong positions for any army wishing to assume a defensive posture.

The slightly curved front of the camp was fortified with a triple ring of works, closed and opened, planned by Phull himself. Communications eastward from the camp were secured by seven bridges. On the other side of the Dvina there were no fortifications, despite the fact that the river was shallow enough to be forded. As a result, the tactical strength of the position was not great and it could readily be turned.

Strategically, the location was even worse. It lay between the roads leading from Vilna to Moscow and St. Petersburg, but dominated neither of them. The shortest road to Moscow passed by Vitebsk, twenty-four miles from Drissa. The road to St. Petersburg passed four miles from Drissa.

Barclay de Tolly, Bennigsen, and Arenfeld disagreed with Phull's plan and attempted to persuade the czar to drop it. Their effort began with the proposal to accept battle at Vilna. At this point Wolzogen attempted to arrange an interview with Barclay in an effort to provide communications between him and Phull. He induced Barclay to request the services of an officer for the establishment of a small bureau to handle these communications. The choice fell upon Clausewitz, who rose to fame of his own accord in later years.

Clausewitz's first task was to evaluate the condition of the Drissa camp. When he arrived, he met considerable resistance from the suspicious commander, who considered Clausewitz a spy. This was neither unusual nor surprising. There was a great deal of resentment for all non-Russians in the czar's service.

According to Clausewitz the outer circle of fortifications

comprised a line of embrasures for musketry; some 50 or 60 paces back was a line of works alternately open and closed. The former were intended for batteries, the latter for single battalions that were to protect the batteries. Some 500 or 600 paces behind this enceinte was considered a reserve position; in the center, and in the third line, there was a still greater entrenched work, serving as a redoubt to cover a retreat.

Although this system of fortifications was evidently too artificial, the number of works was too great, and the whole deficient in a particular view, yet the defense of it with a considerable mass of men, and with the known valor of the Russians, promised serious resistance. One may even maintain with confidence that the French, if they had chosen to frontally attack this camp, would have consumed their force without gaining their objective.

The profile of the works was good, the ground however was sandy; and as no external devices for strengthening had as yet been resorted to, palisades, felled trees, wolves teeth, and etc., there was much to be desired on this side. (Clausewitz, *The Campaign of 1812 in Russia*. John Murray, London, 1943. P. 22)

When Clausewitz inspected the Drissa camp, he discovered that none of the required seven bridges had, as yet, been built, and that the camp commandant was incapable of the task.

Phull's idea was to garrison the camp with 50,000 men, and with another 70,000 advance against the French, who he assumed would have crossed the Dvina to attack the camp in the rear. If the French failed to leave sufficient force on the western bank, he hoped he would be able to break out of the camp, overpower and overwhelm those French left to guard the lines of communication, and cut off the main French army. The tactical advantage of the camp was "inside lines of communication."

To support such a plan, the location of the camp should have provided more favorable terrain for the battle. But the left bank was covered with woods and swamps that would not permit easy observation of the French. In addition, to support this maneuver, a fortified bridgehead on the right bank, behind the camp, was an absolute necessity. The probable result of adherence to this plan by the Russians would have been the loss of whatever unit was assigned to serve as a garrison of the camp.

On 28 June, when Clausewitz returned to the imperial headquarters, now at Svieciany, he presented his report on the Drissa camp to the czar. Phull was there, and Clausewitz's criticisms were hammerlike blows to his pride. Clausewitz's words caused the czar to reconsider the plan. When he conferred with his other officers, he found them even more outspoken than Clausewitz.

Scorched Earth

At this point the idea of using the great distances of Russia to defeat Napoleon arose. It originated in Berlin and was transmitted via Scharnhorst to Count Lieven, who spoke of its wisdom to the czar. The concept was that no battle should be permitted until the gates of Smolensk were under attack. Clausewitz informed Phull of this idea, but Phull was so entranced with his own plan that he failed to grasp the wisdom of what eventually became the Russian strategic plan. By the time the campaign had begun, Phull's plan had fallen into disrepute, but it was not entirely abandoned.

At the outbreak of the war, the forces of Bagration and Barclay de Tolly were dangerously separated and the fortifications at Dinaburg and Borisov were barely begun. Almost by default, the plan for drawing the French into the vastness of the Russian steppe was adopted. Barclay embraced this tactic and would pursue it as long as necessary. However, this commitment was to have serious detrimental effects on his command. No one, even Barclay, envisioned the distances that the retreat would entail. There was continuous pressure for him to turn and fight the French.

Initial Maneuvers

By 18 March 1812 the principal French forces were massed between Danzig and Warsaw as well as along the banks of the Vistula. On 23 June 1812 a closed carriage drawn by six horses suddenly appeared in the middle of the bivouac of the 6th Polish Uhlan Regiment. The troopers were even more startled when it stopped and Napoleon, himself, climbed out.

Spotting a major, Napoleon approached him, asking to see the regiment's commander. Major Suchorzewski, not mentioning that his colonel was still asleep, stated that he was temporarily in command and was awaiting Napoleon's orders. Napoleon asked the route to the Niemen River and the location of the most advanced Polish outposts. The next request was the most surprising. Napoleon requested Polish uniforms for himself and his staff. There was a standing French order that no French uniforms were to be seen on the Russo-Polish border. Napoleon did not wish to warn the Russians of the pending invasion. Napoleon and his staff quickly exchanged their uniforms with some very surprised Polish officers and headed for the border.

Two horses were provided. Napoleon and Berthier mounted them, moving towards the Niemen with Lieutenant Zrelski, whose company had the picket duty that day. As they approached the village of Alexota, near the jumping off points on the Niemen, Napoleon carefully examined the terrain.

As they returned from their reconnaissance, a hare sprang between the legs of Napoleon's mount, startling it. Napoleon was thrown to the ground, but quickly remounted. All those who witnessed it knew it was a bad omen. Marshal Berthier confided to Caulaincourt later, "We should do better not to cross the Niemen. This fall is a bad sign." (*With Napoleon in Russia, Memoirs of General de Caulaincourt . . .* N.Y., William Morrow & Co. 1935, P. 46)

At 10:00 P.M. General Morand passed three companies of the 13th Légère across the Niemen in small boats so they could serve as a screen to protect General Elbe's engineers as they raised the pontoon bridges. At the sight of this crossing, a group of Polish uhlans, probably belonging to the 6th Uhlans, spurred their mounts forward into the river, hoping to seize the honor of being the first to be on Russian soil. Unfortunately, the current proved too swift and they were quickly swept downstream, engulfed by the river. As the men slipped beneath its waters they were clearly heard to cry, "Vive l'Empereur!"

Meanwhile elements of the 13th Légère landed and began spreading across the far bank. They quickly encountered a company of Russian hussars. A Russian officer advanced and challenged the French skirmishers. They responded to this challenge with musketry.

Had Russians been on the bank when dawn broke, they would have seen three pontoon bridges across the Niemen and Morand's division deployed on the Russian bank. They were promptly followed by Murat and the greater part of the reserve cavalry. On 24 and 25 June the rest of the Grande Armée made an unopposed crossing and began to fan out across the Russian countryside.

Oudinot and II Corps turned north after crossing the Niemen and crossed the Vilia. Ney and III Corps had originally been scheduled to cross the Niemen at Prenn, but Napoleon began to feel uneasy about the lack of Russian contact. Napoleon felt that Ney was too isolated and directed him to redirect his forces to the main crossing site. On late 24 June, Kovno was occupied without opposition.

Napoleon had expected that Murat and the 1st and 2nd Reserve Cavalry Corps would have established contact with Barclay de Tolly by this time, but the continuing reconnaissance had revealed no indication of their presence. The French crossings had taken Barclay by surprise. He had expected the crossing to be on 25 June and had directed General of Cavalry Platov to concentrate near Grodno and attack the right flank of the Grande Armée. Barclay had intended to strike the French as they neared Vilna, and if no resistance was encountered, he planned to advance to Svencoiny to offer battle. Bagration was to support Platov's attack and conform to Barclay's movements. If forced to retreat, he was to move to Borisov.

The Grande Armée's advance a day earlier than anticipated forced Barclay to withdraw and concentrate around Sventisiani. Docturov, who apparently did not receive the orders to concentrate at Sventisiani, remained immobile. Napoleon had not expected Barclay's withdrawal, but he was even more surprised by Bagration's failure to advance on Warsaw. Bagration was also withdrawing north to join Barclay. This caused Napoleon to believe that the Russians had divined his main line of attack through Kovno and would not play into his hands.

Meanwhile Barclay moved towards Drissa, unaware that Bagration was attempting to join him. His movements delayed this union. The gap between these two armies attracted Napoleon and he hoped to trap Bagration by thrusting Eugène's corps into it. Jérôme's Westphalians were to change over from a defensive posture and advance so as to maintain the pressure on the 2nd Army of the West.

Unfortunately for the French, this opportunity slipped by. Eugène's forces were two days behind schedule. This delay prevented Napoleon from pushing forward until his flank was secure. Eugène had been delayed at the Niemen with the tangle of his supply train. It also became evident that Jérôme was not advancing quickly enough to maintain good contact with Bagration. Schwarzenberg and Reynier had conformed to the Russians' movements and moved towards the Bug River and Lublin. It was becoming quickly obvious that the lack of mobility was hindering Napoleon's strategic plans already.

Despite this, Napoleon continued to advance, sending Murat, Davout, and the Guard towards Vilna. Ney was to cover the left flank and Eugène was urged to advance more quickly. On the other side, Bagration, seeking to impress Alexander, was demanding authorization from him to advance into Poland.

Jérôme's forces continued to push forward. His column was led by Latour-Maubourg, who was followed by Poniatowski's V Corps and Jérôme's own VII Corps. On 7 June the French cavalry advance guard encountered Platov's rear guard. Platov had orders to hold Mir against the French advance.

Skirmish at Mir

On 8 June the French occupied the village of Korelitchi. Platov's forces (Illowaiski #5, #10, #11, #12, Syssoief #3, Karpov #2, Grekov #8, and Kharitonov Don Cossack Regiments, as well as two Don horse batteries) were deployed, for the most part, in the Iablonovchtchina woods, south of Mir.

Platov posted the Syssoief #3 Cossack Regiment on the southern edge of Mir such that one sotnia was on the road to Piasotchna, one to the left of the road, and one on the right of the road. On 9 June the 2nd Brigade of the 4th Light Cavalry Division (the 3rd, 15th, and 16th Polish Uhlans) advanced from Korelitchi on Mir with the 3rd Uhlans leading the way. The 3rd advanced in a column of three squadrons.

When the 3rd Uhlans reached Piasotchna, they threw back Platov's advanced post and traversed the village at a gallop until they encountered the Syssoief #3 Cossack Regiment on the far side of the village. The 3rd Uhlans reformed, but were quickly engaged by the bulk of Platov's cossacks and nearly annihilated. The few survivors escaped only with the greatest difficulty as the two flanking squadrons of the Syssoief #3 Cossacks had struck their flanks and rear.

General Turno brought up the remainder of the 2nd Brigade, but was only able to temporarily hold Platov. He was thrown back with 356 dead and wounded. Turno was then reinforced by the arrival of Dziewanowski's 28th Light Cavalry Brigade (2nd, 7th, and 11th Uhlans). At the same time, Platov was reinforced by the arrival of Generalmajor Vasiltchikov with the Akhtyrsk Hussars, the Kiev and New Russia Dragoons, the Lithuania Uhlans, and the 5th Jager Regiment. However, as they arrived, night fell and the battle broke off.

On 10 June Platov drew up his rear guard (Akhtyrsk Hussars, Kiev and New Russia Dragoons, Illowaiski #5, #10, #11, and #12, and two horse batteries) along the road to Mir and placed the rest of the cossacks in an attempt to ambush the Polish cavalry as it resumed the advance. Kouneinikov's brigade (five sotnias of the Ataman Don Cossack Regiment, Grekov #18, Simpheropol Tartar Regiment, and Kharitonov Don Cossack Regiment) found itself almost to Slobtzi when it was recalled to Simakovo.

While the 7th Uhlans followed the retiring Russian rear guard, the 3rd, 15th, and 16th Uhlans remained on the edge of Simakovo. The 2nd and 11th Uhlans stood on the northern edge of the village. Platov ordered his rear guard to turn on the 7th Uhlans, throwing them back on Simakovo and continuing to attack the 3rd, 15th, and 16th Uhlans. The 7th Uhlans were in echelon by the right, supported by one squadron of the 3rd Uhlans to their west and one squadron of the 16th to the east. Two squadrons of the 3rd stood in reserve.

Behind these elements came the 4th Division, Kaminski's division of the V Corps. When this cavalry battle began, Kaminski was near Tyrskiewicz, a half mile from Mir. The 4th Division received orders to hold there, and the cavalry battle raged for a total of six hours.

About 2,100 men of Kouneinikov's cossack brigade arrived and charged into the melee, throwing back the French left wing. At the same moment, Platov charged Turno's brigade again, disordered it, and threw it back. Platov's forces then advanced into Mir, where they encountered Tyskiewicz's brigade (the 4th Polish Chasseur à Cheval Regiment) and the divisional horse artillery. Platov decided to withdraw, leaving 600 dead and wounded Poles in his wake. The Russian losses were considerably less. So ended the skirmish at Mir.

The Advance Resumes

At dawn of 28 June the French reached Vilna and encountered their first Russian rear guard. General Bruyere's light cavalry attacked them, but after a couple of cannon shots, the Russians abandoned their positions and burned the city's magazines. Davout's infantry and Murat's cavalry entered the city that morning.

The day before, Jérôme had entered Grodno, opposed only by a few of Platov's cossacks. Reynier's Saxons seized Bialystok, while Schwarzenberg's Austrians concentrated at Syedletz. Oudinot pushed Wittgenstein's rear guard out of Vilkomir on the 28th of June and Macdonald advanced slowly, opposed only by a screen of cossacks.

Barclay ordered Platov to join him by way of Smorgony to destroy the magazine there. Bagration was to cover the southern flank of the 1st Army of the West, protect the Minsk-Borisov road, and maintain contact with Tormassov's 3rd Army of the West. Alexander, fearing that Napoleon would cut Barclay off from Drissa, ordered Bagration to move via Vilekya to join Barclay. The possibility of their junction forced Napoleon to act quickly. When Bagration's 2nd Army was reported east of Ochmiana, Napoleon readjusted his plans and directed Murat to pursue Barclay towards Sventisiani. For this purpose Murat was assigned five cavalry divisions and a new, ad hoc corps formed from Friant's and Gudin's divisions, which were detached from Davout's I Corps. This infantry formation was placed under the command of Count Lobau. On the left, Macdonald's forces were still advancing in front of Ney's forces. Two more of Davout's divisions, Dessaix and Compans, were to remain in Vilna and protect the massing French supply convoys. On the right, Jérôme was to move on Ochmiana in an effort to continue applying pressure on the Russians.

These maneuvers resulted in a pause in the French advance, which allowed Barclay to break contact with them. On 29 June Napoleon ordered a series of fruitful reconnaissances in his effort to reestablish contact with Barclay. These forces stumbled onto Docturov's corps, which had still not received orders to move. Napoleon thought Docturov was part of Bagration's army. Docturov realized his position was in peril and began moving without orders.

The weather had been hot up to this point in the campaign, but the weather broke with a day long deluge, flooding the roads and turning them into seas of mud. The French supply trains and all wheeled traffic bogged down quickly. The French troops broke into an undisciplined, aggressive foraging that alienated the Lithuanians. The number of horse losses rose alarmingly and many of the new recruits, less hardened to the life in the field, sickened and died. The artillery could barely move, and the rapid advance slowed to a crawl with the wheeled traffic falling farther and farther behind the vanguards.

Despite the heavy rains, on the 29th Davout's light cavalry, commanded by Bordesoulle, was advancing rapidly down the road from Lida to Wilkowszki. Pajol, with another force of light cavalry, advanced on Minsk. Davout had been given command of three columns. His goal was to trap Bagration, but the heavily wooded terrain quickly made this task impossible. Davout's losses from the advance were heavy and his report caused Napoleon to send reinforcements consisting of the 1st Chevauléger-lanciers de la Garde under the command of General Colbert and Claparede's division, drawn from the army reserves, on 4 July.

The French right column, commanded by Grouchy, consisted of Dessaix's division and two other brigades. Davout commanded the center column consisting of Compans, Pajol, Valance's cuirassiers, and the Guard lancers. The left-hand column was commanded by Nansouty and consisted of four heavy cavalry brigades and Morand's infantry division.

Davout's effort to trap Bagration went astray almost immediately. Eugène did not advance on Vilna as ordered, but spent the whole of 2 July in Piloni, fearing that a large Russian force was about to fall on his left flank. After a sharp tongue-lashing from Napoleon, he set out again and arrived in Vilna on the 4th. However, Napoleon also ordered the forces of Murat, Ney, and Oudinot to pause and allow their artillery to catch up. The mud had delayed it too long, and the lack of artillery was becoming dangerous.

Bagration had slipped the net. The slow advance of Jérôme had not been enough to hold him, and he easily broke contact. Not only had Jérôme dallied, but it took him forty-eight hours to inform Napoleon that the Russians had abandoned Ochmiana and that Bagration was moving off towards Slonim and Minsk with his seven divisions. Napoleon instructed Berthier to inform Jérôme "that it would be impossible to maneuver in worse fashion," and concluded, "he has robbed me of the fruit of my maneuvers and of the best opportunity ever presented in war—all on account of his singular failure to appreciate the first notions of warfare."* This was too much for Jérôme's ego, and about a week later, after a clash with Davout, he quit the Grande Armée, turning his corps over to his chief of staff and returning to Westphalia.

In the meantime, Barclay concentrated his army around Drissa and quickly became disenchanted with the position. On 1 July Bagration marched on Nikolajef and hoped to cross the Niemen there on 4 July. He knew that Davout was in Woloschin and turned towards Mir, in order to march to Minsk. As he moved into Schwerschin his vanguard made contact with Davout's advanced guard. He took a detachment from Docturov's corps commanded by General Doroschov and moved to Njeswich, seeking to contact Barclay's army. He remained there three days to allow his baggage and artillery to catch up.

Tormassov was still in Volhynia, organizing the 3rd Army of the West. When Barclay learned that Davout had cut his lines of communication, he decided to move on Minsk, along the southern bank of the Dvina. He ordered Platov to cover his flank by holding Volozhin until 8 July.

Murat's forces continued to push eastward, continually defeating Barclay's cavalry rear guards, and on 5 July, Jérôme finally began to advance once again. Jérôme wanted Davout to continue towards Minsk and to continue to draw Bagration southward so that the French might reach Vitebsk before him. Murat and Ney would continue to cautiously push Barclay while Napoleon gathered up Eugène, St. Cyr, and the Guard to form a strike force that would swing up from the south, advance through Vitebsk, and move into the gap between Bagration and Barclay to strike Barclay's isolated army. At this time Napoleon gave Davout the secret authority to take command of Jérôme's Westphalians, should the two armies come together, but ordered Davout to keep this authority secret. He had not informed his brother, Jérôme, of this decision.

Napoleon had calculated that the Russians could not possibly reach

---

* (David Chandler, *Campaigns of Napoleon*, N.Y. Macmillan, 1966. p. 776)

Minsk before 11 July and directed Davout to advance as quickly as possible. In the meantime, Alexander had determined to make the planned stand at Drissa. He rebuked Bagration for not moving through Minsk, fearing that Davout might bypass the Russian armies and march directly on Smolensk.

Barclay and the other generals began to loudly object to General Phull's plans and the Drissa encampment. After much argument it was decided that the Russians would withdraw to Vitebsk, beginning on 14 July, and take up a strong position in the hope that Bagration would join them. Bagration received the czar's letter on 11 July and sent a hot retort that he was holding the main French army by himself, stating that Barclay should attack, since obviously only minor forces were in front of him. Two days later he wrote that it was his plan to first defeat Jérôme and then Davout. He inferred that Russia was being betrayed by Barclay, who was of Scottish ancestry, and that all non-Russians were suspect. With that pronouncement he continued his retreat.

On 8 July, Davout's columns limped into Minsk, only to discover that Bagration had doubled back several days earlier and moved to Bobruisk when he learned of Davout's advance. Realizing that danger awaited them, the Russians had pursued a more southerly line of retreat than anticipated. After a nine-day march, Bagration reached Jesvizh and rested for seventy-two hours. If all had gone according to Napoleon's plans, Jérôme would have been there on the 7th to greet Bagration, but he was nowhere near. The result of Napoleon's first maneuver against Bagration had ended in a dismal failure. The muddy roads, the exhaustion of his men, Jérôme's infuriating failure to obey orders, and Napoleon's lack of energy—his age was beginning to tell—had contributed to its lack of success.

On 9 July, Napoleon issued orders for his renewed offensive. He ordered Macdonald to move on Jacobstadt along the Dvina. Davout was to move on Borisov and Orsha in an effort to keep Barclay and Bagration separated. Jérôme, supported by Schwarzenberg, was to continue his pursuit of Bagration.

Davout planned to move from Minsk to Mohilev and Borisov once his corps was concentrated. As Jérôme renewed his feeble advance, news came from Schwarzenberg that Tormassov had completed the organization of the 3rd Army of the West and was moving to join Bagration.

On 11 July, Napoleon ordered Davout to seize Borisov and move from there to Kokhanovo, where he would be able to move on Mohilev,

Orsha, or Vitebsk, as required. Reynier and his Saxons were to remain in Slonim and operate independently against Tormassov, while Schwarzenberg passed behind him towards Nesvizh and on to the Dvina River.

Jérôme Quits

On 12 July, when it became apparent that the Russians planned to make their stand at Drissa, Napoleon began the planned concentration on its southern flank. Davout's cavalry occupied Borisov and made contact with Jérôme. The next day, Davout saw an opportunity to destroy Bagration before turning north and informed Jérôme of the authority Napoleon had given him to take command of the Westphalians. In a fit of infantile rage, Jérôme halted the forward movement of his corps, turned the command over to his chief of staff, General Marchand, and deliberately did not tell him Napoleon's plans or orders. On the 15th, when Davout learned of Jérôme's childish resignation, he tried to make him change his mind, but failed. Since Davout was too weak to attack Bagration alone, he moved on Mohilev instead, to bar the shortest road northward to Vitebsk.

When Jérôme departed, he left Marchand totally in the dark about Napoleon's instructions. Marchand was forced to sift through all the orders before he was able to direct Poniatowski and Latour-Maubourg to advance on Bobruisk in an attempt to cut Bagration's line of retreat. This resulted in great confusion among the divisional commanders, and Poniatowski turned to Davout for instructions. Davout could give none.

Skirmish at Romanov

Platov had been charged with holding the French at Romanov until the 15th. He occupied the village with the 5th Jagers and placed his two 6-gun cossack horse batteries behind the Vousva River, to the northeast of Romanov. The bulk of his forces were on the right bank of the river. His right wing was commanded by Generalmajor Illowaiski with two regiments, and his left was commanded by Generalmajor Kouneinikov with three regiments. Platov established a reserve consisting of the Ataman Cossack Regiment behind the center. The Akhtyrsk Hussars, Kiev Dragoons, and Lithuania Uhlans were positioned in the village.

On the morning of 15 July the 1st Polish Chasseur à Cheval Regiment, the lead element of Latour-Maubourg's corps, encountered Platov's advanced guard. The cossacks withdrew, pulling the Poles into an ambush. The remaining cossacks attacked in their famous "lava" formation, where the sotnias were widely separated and the individual cossacks had a great deal of independence to maneuver. The 2nd squadron of the 1st Chasseurs broke into a skirmish formation as the remaining three squadrons formed in echelons by the left behind them. Latour-Maubourg ordered the Poles to attack. Their commander sent the 3rd and 4th squadrons forward. Illowaiski and Kouneinikov led their forces in a flank attack as the Karpov cossacks' attack struck the Poles frontally. The Poles lost 279 of the 700 engaged, and the battle ended with the arrival of the rest of the French corps. Platov recrossed the Vousva River, burning the bridge behind him. The battle was then taken up by the cossack horse batteries on the far bank. This dissolved into an artillery battle as Platov resumed his withdrawal.

Davout Takes Command

Davout received Jérôme's refusal to reassume command on 19 July and began issuing orders directly to the VII Corps divisional commanders. He directed Poniatowski to march on Slutsk via Igumen and Mohilev. Latour-Maubourg was to advance on Bobruisk in an attempt to locate Bagration, and Tharreau was to move on Borisov via Minsk.

Napoleon learned of Jérôme's departure on the 19th or 20th. He was furious with Davout, whom he accused of prematurely seizing command of the right wing. He directed Poniatowski to assume command and continue the pursuit of Bagration, while extending his left to maintain contact with Davout. He went on to order Reynier to remain in Slonim and Schwarzenberg to advance on Minsk. Davout was ordered to Mohilev, but no orders were issued to Tharreau, probably due to an oversight.

On 20 July, as the orders were being written, Davout was throwing the 2,000-man garrison out of Mohilev, and by 5:00 he had occupied the city, capturing its massive magazine intact.

As a result of some misinformation, Napoleon believed there were Russian forces maneuvering on his rear and Minsk. To cover this eventuality he detached some cavalry to his rear. While Napoleon was reacting to this imaginary threat, Davout was facing an impending attack by Bagration's forces, which had been reinforced by Ignatiev's reserve division. Davout was facing twice his number. Davout had only the 6,000 cavalry of Pajol's and Bordesoulle's light brigades and the cuirassiers of General Valence and the 22,000 infantry forming Compans', Dessaix's, and Claparede's divisions.

Battle of Saltanovka

On 21 July, Davout ordered the 3rd Chasseurs à Cheval from Bordes-soulle's brigade to make a reconnaissance towards Dashkovka, about four leagues from Mohilev. These chasseurs soon encountered Bagration's advanced guard. When they reached the heights above Bouritniki, their colonel and his advanced squadron found themselves surrounded by 3,000 cossacks. They were quickly taken prisoner, while the remaining three squadrons were thrown back. The survivors took shelter behind the French 85th Line Regiment, which was also advancing in reconnaissance under the personal direction of Davout. It quickly turned back the cossacks with a few shots from their accompanying artillery.

The pending encounter was to occur on a field surrounded by forests and deeply scored by a ravine with a small stream running along its bottom. The terrain around Saltanovka was constrictive and would not permit the Russians to profit from their numerical superiority.

Knowing of the impending storm, Davout spent the evening of the 22nd preparing his position. He had the bridge on the Staroi-Bickov road barricaded. On the right, his sappers broke down the bridge and dam by the Fatova mill. They also cut loopholes in all the neighboring buildings. On his right wing, in the village of Fatova, Davout placed five battalions of the 108th Line and one battalion of the 85th Line. To the left, near Saltanovka, he placed three battalions of the 85th Line and an independent company of voltigeurs. Behind the right wing, between Fatova and Seletz, he positioned four battalions of the 61st Line as a reserve. He established a general reserve consisting of one battalion of the 85th and 61st Line Regiments, Valence's cuirassier division, Chastel's 3rd Light Cavalry Division, and the 3rd Chasseur à Cheval Regiment near Seletz.

At 7:00 A.M. on the morning of the 23rd, the Russian general Raevsky advanced with orders to take Saltanovka with the 6th and 42nd Jagers in the lead. Bagration had given him five regiments of the 12th Division, five more from the 26th commanded by Paskevitch, twenty squadrons, three cossack regiments, and seventy-two guns. General Raevsky, with the 12th Division, was to attack the French frontally, while Paskevitch and the 26th Division were to attack Fatova after turning the French right.

At 7:30 A.M. the advancing Russians pushed the French advanced posts back. The 26th Division advanced, with a battalion of the Orel and another of the Nivegorod Infantry Regiments leading the way. Behind them advanced twelve guns, the Poltava Infantry Regiment, six more guns, the Ladoga Infantry Regiment, the second battalion of the Nivegorod Infantry Regiment, and finally the rest of the cavalry.

At the same time the skirmishers from Prince Charles of Mecklenburg's and Voronzov's divisions as well as those of the 18th Division attacked Atovka. This force encountered the battalion of the 85th Line in the woods near Fatova, pushing them back. At the same time Bagration posted a battery of twelve guns on the plateau dominating Atovka. A battalion of the 108th Line with a few guns advanced to the 85th, and the two battalions took up a position to the south of Fatova, on a low ridge, formed in columns and covered by a thick screen of skirmishers. Bagration then began deploying the heads of his column for the pending assault. Davout sent two battalions of the 61st Line to support the 85th and 108th.

The leading Russian battalions of Orel and Nivegorod, supported by twelve guns, attacked and carried the village. However, as they cleared it on the far side, they were struck by the four battalions of the 108th concealed in the wheat fields behind the village. At the same time the Poltava Infantry Regiment threw back the battalion of the 108th posted to the west of Fatova.

In its turn, the Poltava Infantry was pushed back by two battalions of the 61st led by General Guyardet. The Russians established a six-gun half-battery on their side of the stream, and its fire prevented the 61st from pursuing the retreating Poltava Infantry Regiment. Paskevitch positioned the Ladoga Infantry Regiment to the west of Fatova, and to its right, in the woods, he posted a chain of skirmishers. Though this shored up the Russian left, the two French battalions pushed back the two battalions of the Orel and Nivegorod Infantry that had crossed the stream. Paskevitch advanced the Poltava Infantry and four masked guns to stop the French advance and prevent their turning the Russian right wing.

The battalions of the 85th and 108th Line pushed back the Poltava Infantry and attacked the Russian guns, which showered them with cannister. Colonel Achard, with a battalion of the 108th and one from the 85th, advanced with great energy, crossed the stream near Atovka, and succeeded in capturing the Russian position. However, he was wounded at the critical moment, and the Russian counterattack pushed his forces back.

At the same time that Achard was advancing, Bagration formed the Smolensk Infantry Regiment into an attack column to act in concert with Paskevitch, when he resumed the offensive. The 6th and 42nd Jagers covered the head of the Smolensk Infantry as they advanced. Raevsky, flanked with his two sons, stood at the head of the Smolensk Infantry. Unfortunately, he did not hear the cannon shots that signaled Paskevitch's advance over the noise of the battle and started his advance too late. The Smolensk Regiment advanced into a terrible artillery fire directed by Chef d'escadron Polinier, which inflicted heavy casualties on it. The advance stopped, and as Raevsky learned of the advance of fresh French forces, he called off the attack and began to withdraw from the battlefield.

Davout assumed that Bagration's main effort was on the right, but by noon the reconnaissance he had directed towards this flank had encountered nothing. He then ordered the 111th Line, Chastel's light cavalry, and Valence's cuirassiers to advance in support of General de division Dessaix in a renewed attack on the Russian center at Saltanovka.

The successful battalions of the 61st and 85th Line crossed the stream and attacked the Russian left. Dessaix crossed between Fatova mill and the Saltanovka bridge, moving forward and attacking the Russian rear, throwing their center into disorder. Bagration, already disquieted by the French success on his left, ordered a general retreat.

General Compans, at the head of the 61st and 111th Line, charged the Russians again, pursuing them until nightfall. They were near Nowielski when the pursuit stopped.

The battle continued until nightfall. The French had outfought twice their number, killing 2,548 Russians and taking 200 prisoners, while losing 4,134 dead and wounded.

The Advance

The Battle of Saltanovka ended as General Raevsky withdrew from the field. He moved his corps towards Smolensk and arrived there on 4 August, two days after Bagration. Meanwhile, Grouchy had advanced through Kokhanovo on the 17th and established contact with Eugène on the 18th. On the 19th, Grouchy surprised Orsha, seizing the immense magazines there. The garrison fled before they could fire the supplies. Grouchy continued to force his passage over the Dnieper, and within three days his forces had passed through Babinovitshi and were reconnoitering the roads to Smolensk and Vitebsk.

Jérôme's VII Corps had been passed to General Vandamme, but later General Tharreau assumed command and marched on Minsk and Orsza to join the Grande Armée. Poniatowski and the V Corps continued to follow Bagration, but only as far as Romanova, where the great forests began. From there he moved on Igumen and Mohilev, where he arrived six days later. Latour-Maubourg pursued Bagration as far as Blusk, arriving on the 24th. However, he was unable to move on the fortress of Bobruisk, so he crossed the Berezina at Berezino and moved on Mohilev, arriving on 5 August.

Chapter VIII _____

The Northern and Southern Operations

To the south, Reynier, commanding the VII Corps, composed entirely of Saxons, and Schwarzenberg, commanding the Austrian Hilfkorps, were operating against Tormassov's 3rd Army of the West. Reynier moved against Tormassov, who was threatening to move against Lubin, but he had only 10,600 men to face Tormassov's numerically superior forces. Napoleon, under the mistaken impression that Tormassov had only about 10,000 men, assumed that Reynier could hold him at bay and intended to recall Schwarzenberg to the Grande Armée. He recommended that Reynier invade Volhynia so as to better defend Muchavetz and Precipiez. Reynier advanced and on 25 July found himself at Chomsk. From there he detached Klengel's brigade to Kobrin and other small detachments to Brest-Litovsk and Pinsk.

The Battle of Kobrin

In mid-July Tormassov received orders to advance. He moved on the French rear along a line that extended from Pinsk to Brest-Litovsk, but his main forces moved on Kobrin. Kobrin was a small country village at the junction of the Dvina-Pruszany and Brest-Pinsk roads, standing on the banks of the Murawiec River. There were only a few houses on the right bank of the river, connected to the village by a wooden bridge over which the road to Pruszany ran. The only stone building had been converted by the Saxons into a strongpoint. It was a small cloistered church on the left bank. Below the church, on the other side of the street, was a tumbled-down redoubt left over from the days of Charles XII of Sweden's invasion of Russia. It was completely surrounded by wooden buildings.

The terrain around the village was open, but beyond the village streets stretched a swampy lowland crossed only by the two main roads and narrow paths. The Murawiec River was only six to eight paces wide as it passed through the village and was quite shallow.

Klengel deployed his troops as follows: On each of the three main roads entering the city he positioned two or three companies of infantry with a pair of guns. In the market, in front of the church, he posted a battalion of the König Infantry Regiment as a reserve. On the right bank of the Murawiec there were two companies, two guns, and a squadron of the Prinz Clemens Uhlan Regiment under the command of Matthai. The approach to the city was barricaded, a single house being occupied. Major von Becka's squadron of the Prinz Clemens Uhlans stood a half-hour from the city on the road to Brest and that of Major Piesport stood on the road to Polska.

Klengel had 2,433 men under his command: the König and Niese-meuschel Infantry Regiment with 1,019 infantry and the regimental artillery with 2 officers and 123 men. There was sufficient ammunition on hand, but insufficient rations. Fifty of the brigade's train wagons loaded with rations had not reached the main body, even after a night march. Delayed by a broken bridge, the ox-drawn wagons had been forced to seek another route to Kobrin. The train was captured by cossacks.

On the morning of 27 July, thanks to a reconnaissance report from Major von Becka, Klengel learned that the road to Brest was swarming with "kalmucks and bashkirs." Von Piesport's squadron was also attacked, and both squadrons were driven back to Kobrin. The third squadron, posted on the right bank of the Murawiec, commanded by Matthai, pulled back to Kobrin as more Russian squadrons crossed the river to face them.

The main body of Tormassov's forces approached along the road from Antopol. The attacking Russians came from Zalesie. Major Bevillaqua, with two companies of the König Infantry Regiment and two 4pdr guns, faced them alone. Opposing him were twelve Russian squadrons and a battery of twelve guns. Bevillaqua had no choice but to withdraw into Kobrin.

The village was completely surrounded by Russian cavalry. The Russian artillery battered the city, and around 10:00 A.M. their dragoons attempted to break into it. Though the Saxon positions were still holding, Klengel ordered Colonel Zechwitz to break out in the direction of Pruszany with the Prinz Clemens Uhlans. They broke out and eventually rejoined Reynier's main force.

Around 11:00 A.M. the Russian assault columns approached the city along all three main roads. Colonel Gophardt, with a portion of the König Regiment, moved down the road towards Brest in an attempt to stop the Russians. Major Bevillaqua held the Antopol road with his two companies of the König Regiment. Major von Schlieben, with six companies of the Niesemeuschel Regiment, held the southern portion of the city and a furious house-to-house battle began.

An hour later, Major von Schlieben fell back to the market place. The König Regiment took up positions in the church, on the bridge, and in the redoubt. An hour later the Niesemeuschel Regiment also moved into the redoubt.

The Saxon infantry was running out of ammunition and the guns were down to fifty rounds when the columns began their assault on the redoubt. They struck "like a whirlwind" and General Klengel capitulated. Generals Markoff and Oldekopf accepted his surrender. In this action the Russians captured 62 officers, 1,992 men, 4 guns, and 4 flags. There were 13 officers and 260 Saxon officers hors de combat, while the Russians lost about 600 men.

Reynier had been marching to Klengel's aid, but he encountered the Russian advanced guard near Antopol and was forced to retire. Schwarzenberg, knowing of Tormassov's strength, had not moved to join the main army as Napoleon directed, but had remained at Slonim. With the fall of Kobrin he moved to Reynier's assistance, obtaining Napoleon's approval for his actions after the fact.

Northern Operations

On the northern flank of the main army, Marshal Macdonald was advancing against Riga while Marshal Oudinot operated between him and the main army. The Russians had detached Wittgenstein's 1st Corps to operate against Oudinot and maintain communications with General Essen, the garrison commander of Riga. On 18 July the principal battle formation of the Russian 1st Corps was in Balin with twenty-two battalions, eight squadrons and seventy-two guns, totaling 13,065 men. The second line of battle, under General Sazonov, had eight battalions and totaled 4,559 men. He was posted near Pridouisk to cover the reconnaissance forces of Prince Repnin and General Kulnieff. Prince Repnin had a detachment of two battalions, eight squadrons, and a position battery. This force had 1,607 men.

General Kulnieff, who commanded another reconnaissance force of four battalions, eight squadrons, and two guns, totaling 3,731 men, moved out at the break of dawn, sending his cossacks across the Dvina, forcing back the French pickets. His cossacks continued on to Onikschti, where they encountered eight squadrons of the 11th Chasseur à Cheval Regiment and the 10th Polish Hussar Regiment, detached from the 2nd Light Cavalry Division. The French cavalry advanced against the cossacks, attempting to push them back. However, the Russian advanced guard crossed the bridge at Drouia and began to deploy before the village. The cossacks continued to hold the French cavalry until Lieutenant Colonel Ridiger arrived with four squadrons of the Grodno Hussar Regiment. The Russian hussars immediately attacked the French and pushed them back to a ravine by Litichki. Here the French reformed their cavalry and formed them into four columns. Ridiger, seeing the remaining four squadrons of his regiment closing in, moved on the French flanks and threw them in great disorder to the village of Jaga. The French reformed their cavalry there.

While the French reformed, part of the chasseurs dismounted and formed a skirmish line. The Russian hussars charged again while the cossacks attacked the French in the flank. The French fell back with the Russians in pursuit until they reached Tschernevo.

The remainder of Kulnieff's forces remained in place to cover the movement of his cavalry against a potential advance of the French main body, which was camped near Drissa. Kulnieff learned that a considerable French force was advancing along the right bank of the Drouia and that more French infantry was between Trouia and Tschernevo. Having completed the reconnaissance and located the French forces, Kulnieff determined that they were making no offensive move in this area. He recalled his cavalry and recrossed the Dvina, leaving only the cossacks on the far bank.

This small clash cost the Russians twelve dead and sixty-three wounded, while the French losses were considerably higher. The main battle line of the Russian 1st Corps and the corps reserve moved to Pokahevzi to replace Baggovout's corps. Baggovout was forced to move because of the movements of the French on the Russian left. The reconnaissance assured Wittgenstein of the safety of this move.

Oudinot and the French II Corps had been surrounding the city of Dinaburg during this period. He received orders on 19 July to rejoin the main army. He evacuated his positions around the city and moved out.

In the face of the French, Wittgenstein made an attempt to cover the territory between Novgorod and the Dvina River. A chain of observation posts was established between Drissa and Dinaburg and north to Jacobstadt. Another bridge was erected by the Russians in Dinaburg, and Colonel Count Sievers erected a small fieldwork to defend the bridgehead. The bridge at Dinaburg was evacuated because of its isolation, and its guns were moved to Pskof. Six of those guns, however, were assigned to the garrison of Dinaburg.

On 21 July Colonel Baron Diebitsch made another reconnaissance across the Dvina with a large cossack force, three battalions and six squadrons. The force was unable to advance far and was forced to return after a long detour. On the same day, Generalmajor Hamen was sent to Dinaburg to assume command of its garrison, relieving Prince Jachwill, who returned to Wittgenstein's staff.

On 23 July the movement of the main Russian armies drew it away from Wittgenstein and caused a large gap to appear between them. To plug the gap and secure his communications, Wittgenstein sent General Balk with two battalions of converged grenadiers from the 5th Division, six guns from Horse Battery #3, and a detachment of the Riga Dragoon Regiment to Leschkova. Barclay gave Wittgenstein orders that if he were separated from the main army he was to move on Vitebsk and take the offensive at the first opportune moment. He was to act in support of Riga and prevent any successful siege of that city.

On 24 July Balk was reinforced by a battalion of the 36th Jagers, two more reserve battalions of grenadiers, two converged grenadier battalions from the 14th Division, a squadron of Guard Hussar Regiment, and six guns from Position Battery #28.

By 26 July Macdonald had advanced his X Corps into Courland and secured the Dinaburg bridgehead. His movements had, however, opened up a gap between himself and Oudinot, providing the Russians with an opportunity to cross the Dvina near Drouia and move on the French lines of communication.

The Russians began this maneuver on 26 July. Their reserve remained until a detachment from Kastschkovski arrived. General Balk was left in Wolinizi with two battalions of converged grenadiers from the 5th Division, three squadrons of the Riga Dragoons, and six guns from

Horse Battery #3. This small force was to screen the main body as it moved along the left bank of the Dvina and to scout any movements by Oudinot.

On 27 July General Kulnieff crossed the Drissa with the cavalry of General Balk and advanced to reconnoiter the proposed advance. Infantry detachments were placed in Siabki and Tobolki, later to be reinforced by General Helfreich's forces.

At 4:00 P.M. the French advanced against this force, and a skirmish began around Philipova, not far from Kliastitzy, between the Russian advanced guard, consisting of Grodno Hussars, a squadron of the Guard Hussars, and the Platov #4 Cossack Regiment, and the leading French elements, consisting of the 7th and 20th French Chasseur à Cheval Regiments and the 6th Polish Uhlan Regiment. A heavy cavalry battle ensued and only stopped with nightfall. Though relatively inconclusive, the Poles lost 167 men.

Wittgenstein learned from prisoners taken in this engagement that two divisions of Oudinot's corps were in Bieloe and the third division, that of General Merle, had passed the night near Lozovka. This information and other information concerning Macdonald's movements caused Wittgenstein to believe that his chance to strike Oudinot was at hand.

The Battle of Kliastitzy or Jakobovo

The next day Wittgenstein began moving his forces towards Kliastitzy, where he intended to give battle. At the same time Oudinot's forces redeployed. Wittgenstein's advanced guard consisted of the Grodno Hussars, Platov #4 Cossacks, 25th and 26th Jagers, and Horse Battery #1. This force had a total of 3,730 men and 12 guns.

The French had occupied Jakobovo with the 56th Line, 25th Légère, and 24th Chasseurs à Cheval. The 23rd Chasseurs à Cheval were posted on the road to Sebej. Verdier had moved his division towards Sebej, and General Merle had remained at Drissa to protect the baggage and artillery park.

When Wittgenstein learned of the French positions, he ordered the 23rd and 24th Jagers and Position Battery #14 to advance in support of Kulnieff's advanced guard. He ordered Kulnieff to attack without awaiting further reinforcements. Wittgenstein wished to seize the right bank of the Nitschtscha, a small river flowing behind Jakobovo, before the French could reinforce their garrison in Jakobovo. The remainder of his first line of battle was moving forward as fast as possible.

General Legrand's advanced posts were chased out of the woods before Olkhovka at 5:00 P.M. by Kulnieff's forces as he moved onto the plateau overlooking Jakobovo. Horse Battery #1 unlimbered near the road to Kliastitzy. The 25th Jagers took up position on its right, and the 26th were posted on its left. The Grodno Hussars took a reserve position behind the battery.

The remainder of Legrand's division, alerted by their pickets, moved across the Nitschtscha and formed near Jakobovo. Legrand, seeing the small force opposing him, attacked the Russian right with four battalions of the 36th Line, supported by four more battalions of the 26th Légère and four of the 19th Line. The intensive fire from the Russian battery broke up this attack and allowed the 25th Jagers to maintain their position until Wittgenstein arrived with the 23rd and 24th Jagers and Position Battery #14. This force placed itself to the right of the Russian line. The Grodno Hussars and the two new jager regiments moved to support the 25th Jagers. Position Battery #14 unlimbered next to Horse Battery #1 and began to pound the French.

The Russian right, now heavily reinforced, moved over to the attack, and the French were driven back to Jakobovo. The 23rd and 24th Jagers, under General Berg, moved on the woods to the left of Jakobovo. They were repulsed by the 36th Line. General Kulnieff detached the 25th to support Berg, but Maison's French brigade repulsed all three regiments and drove them back on Kastschkovski's division, which had just arrived on the field. A skirmish battle developed in front of the village while the French set it afire. The battle continued inconclusively in this position until nightfall.

Verdier's division passed over the Nitschtscha and took up a reserve position behind Legrand's center. Doumerc's cuirassiers were posted further to the rear. The Russians made preparations as well. Kulnieff's four regiments were supported by the converged grenadiers of the 5th and 14th Divisions and by the infantry and cavalry reserve of General Sazonov. Their right was supported by fourteen guns and their left by six.

The attack started again in the morning. Legrand struck at the Russian center. The fire of the two Russian batteries was heavy, and it disordered their ranks. However, the French continued advancing, forcing the Russian batteries to limber up and withdraw.

The Russian skirmishers, supported by the Kalouga and Sievesk Infantry Regiments drawn from the first line of battle, counterattacked and drove back the French, recapturing their original position. The French withdrew to Jakobovo, leaving part of their infantry in the village of Jakobovo.

During the night Wittgenstein moved up his reserve with the intention of attacking with all of his forces before dawn. He left only Repnin's forces in Katerinovo.

During the morning of 1 September, the Russian advanced guard and the first line of battle was placed before Jakobovo in the following order: the 24th, 25th, 23rd Jagers, Position Battery #5, two pieces from Battery #9, Sievesk, Kalouga, 26th Jagers, Light Battery #27, Perm, and Mohilev.

The Grodno Hussars and Batteries #1, #14, and the remainder of #9 were placed in the second line of battle. This force had arrived in Olkhovka at dawn and became the general reserve. All the Russian infantry was formed in battalion attack columns.

The French had maintained nearly the same positions they had held at the end of the previous day. The French left was secured on the woods. Verdier's division was held in reserve. The 5th Light Cavalry Brigade of Castex was spread along the French line, and Doumerc's cuirassier division was held in reserve by Kliastitzy. Merle's division was near Sivochino on the Drissa, and the 6th Light Cavalry Brigade was near Wolinzi.

At about 3:00 A.M. Colonel Frolov of the 23rd Jagers, posted before Jakobovo, noted that it was lightly held and advanced his regiment into the village. He was promptly chased out by the 26th Légère. A skirmish battle developed on the Russian right, and the fighting soon spread along the entire front of both armies. Marshal Oudinot had placed his artillery on the heights by Jakobovo and began to fire while his columns struck the Russian center.

This initial attack was stopped by the fire of Position Battery #5 and Light Battery #27. Oudinot reinforced his attack and sent it forward again. As this renewed attack began on the center, the French also struck at the Russian left. This second attack, with its greater mass of troops, was also stopped by the concentrated Russian artillery fire. As they recoiled, Wittgenstein launched a counterattack with General Berg's troops.

Generalmajor Kastschkovski lead the Sievesk and Kalouga Infantry and part of the Grodno Hussars against the French center. Generalmajor Prince of Siberia attacked the French right with the Perm and Mohilev

Infantry. The 23rd, 24th, and 25th Jagers advanced against the woods occupied by the French left wing. The Russian second line advanced to support this attack.

The Prince coordinated his attack with Kastschkovski's attack by spreading the 26th Jagers between them. The 26th Jagers moved in echelons behind Perm and Mohilev.

The Russian columns were animated and attacked vigorously with bayonets. The Russian attack on the center stalled initially, but as Sievesk and Kalouga moved in, the tide swung against the French. The entire French line fell back to the sandy hills along the Nitschtscha River. Oudinot had stationed Verdier's division there. Coupled with concentrated French artillery fire, Verdier's division stabilized the situation momentarily.

The Russians resumed their advance, and Oudinot reacted by withdrawing his artillery across the river while attacking with his center to cover their withdrawal. The French attack was stopped by the fire of Light Battery #27 and Position Battery #5, which had advanced with the Russian infantry. General Berg quickly counterattacked, taking the French positions and pushing the French back across the Nitschtscha.

The French withdrawal was orderly, and they quickly took up defensive positions on the far bank of the Nitschtscha, near Kliastitzy. They defended the single bridge with their artillery and filled the buildings of the village with skirmishers.

On their side of the river, the Russians spread jagers along the bank and continued the skirmish fire. To turn the French left, Wittgenstein sent his cavalry towards Gvozdy. General Balk detached the Riga Dragoons there and continued farther along the river with the Grodno Hussars and the Iambourg Dragoons to find a ford. Count Sievers set about raising a bridge with the two pontoonier companies near Gvozdy when it was learned that the ford was impassable. This bridging effort was covered by a battery of twelve guns.

When Oudinot learned of the Russian flanking maneuver, he began to withdraw, defending his center and left while attempting to fire the bridge at Kliastitzy. Wittgenstein responded immediately and directed the depot battalion of the Pavlov Grenadiers to rush the bridge. The grenadiers pushed across it and established themselves on the far bank. They were supported by the Russian skirmishers along the bank, two guns of Light Battery #27, and the Perm and Mohilev Infantry Regiments, who followed them over the bridge. They quickly began establishing themselves in the buildings of Kliastitzy despite the fire of the defending French horse artillery.

The successful seizure of the bridge forced the French to accelerate their withdrawal, and they abandoned some of their baggage. The remainder of the Russian infantry and artillery crossed the bridge while their cavalry crossed at the ford.

The bulk of the Russian 1st Corps paused to catch its breath and reorganize while Kulnieff led the pursuit of the beaten French with the Grodno Hussars, the Iambourg Dragoons, part of the Riga Dragoons, four guns from Horse Battery #1, the 1st Battalion of Converged Grenadiers of the 14th Division, and Wittgenstein's cossacks. They were supported by the Russian skirmishers who also advanced. Kulnieff's forces captured more baggage about four miles from Kliastitzy. They advanced down the road to Polotsk and captured 900 prisoners.

The Russian reserve had only entered the battlefield as the Pavlov Grenadiers had rushed the bridge at Kliastitzy. Being fresh they continued to advance in support of Kulnieff's pursuing forces and reached the Drissa River by nightfall.

Marshal Oudinot crossed the Drissa at Sivochino and joined Merle's division, occupying a position ten miles behind the village of Borachtchina. Prince Repnin was ordered to join the advanced guard by the diagonal road from Katerinovo to Sokolichtchi, but he found the road impractical and moved along the road to Kliastitzy.

Kulnieff was ordered to remain on the left bank of the Drissa until the next day and not to engage in any serious action with the French before the Russian main body joined him. However, the main body didn't begin to move until 8:00 A.M. the next day. He had been reinforced by the dispatching of the Perm and Sievesk Infantry Regiments and was joined by four regiments of General Sazonov's 14th Division, the four jager regiments, and a battalion of converged grenadiers from the 5th Division. His advanced guard consisted of 15,000 men and twenty-four guns.

The Death of Kulnieff

Kulnieff recommenced his pursuit as well. His light troops were stopped near the village of Moskolinki, and he advanced the Iambourg Dragoons and Horse Battery #1 to push back what he believed to be only a small French rear guard stalling for time. He hoped to seize the defile to Bieloe.

The French remained passive near Oboirazina, their three divisions in deep columns that were mutually supported by each other behind a ridge that hid them from Kulnieff's view. With them were Doumerc's cuirassiers and the 5th Light Cavalry Brigade. The 6th Light Cavalry Brigade was dispatched to watch the fords over the Drissa.

The advancing Russians were suddenly taken under fire by a concealed battery of French 12pdrs. They brought up six guns of Light Battery #27 to counter the French fire and supported the six guns with the Toula Infantry. The reserve of General Sazonov followed, as did the rest of the 5th Division. The Russian advanced guard continued to push slowly into the defile.

Oudinot permitted this gradual advance to continue before he opened up with the rest of his artillery, which was positioned around the Russians like spectators in an amphitheater. The heavy barrage was followed by the rapid advance of Legrand's and Verdier's divisions. The French pushed vigorously and the entire Russian advanced guard crumpled and fell back on the Drissa in great disorder. They lost three guns from Horse Battery #1, six from Light Battery #27, 1,000 dead, and 1,500 wounded.

The Russians were unable to maintain a foothold on the far bank, and Oudinot, wishing to profit from his success, continued to advance with all of his forces, Verdier leading the way. He did not wish to allow the Russian advanced guard the opportunity to reorganize itself.

General Kulnieff was trying to rally the Grodno Hussars when he was struck in the legs by a cannon shot, which killed him. His troops continued their rapid withdrawal with greater haste.

Count Wittgenstein's reserve was advancing to support Kulnieff, but it stopped to reorganize his shattered command by the village of Golovchitsa, not far from his starting position that morning. He extended his line from the farm of Stary Dvor to the bank of the Nitschtscha. The right wing of the first line, under General Berg, consisted of Perm, Mohilev, and the 25th and 23rd Jagers. The left wing, under Kastschkovski, consisted of Kalouga, Sievesk, and the 24th and 26th Jagers. The second line contained nine battalions and eight squadrons of reserve cavalry. An additional two squadrons, however, were detached from the reserve to watch the Russian left wing, which was uncovered.

General Prince Jachwill and General Helfreich were sent forward to take command of the shattered advanced guard. They pulled it back together and positioned it behind the general reserve, where it formed a third and fourth line. Horse Battery #1 was detached from it and placed on the right wing, and a squadron of the Riga Dragoons was posted to the left of Golovezitsy.

Verdier's division, leading the attack, advanced without waiting for the rest of Oudinot's corps to catch up with them. The 26th Légère led the attack.

The French skirmishers occupied the buildings of Stary Dvor, on the Russian right, but they were quickly dislodged by a battalion of the Perm Infantry. The 24th Jagers and part of the skirmishers of the Sievesk Infantry Regiment pushed back a tentative probe on their extreme left. The French main body organized itself on the heights during this time.

After a few minutes of artillery preparation, the infantry of Verdier's division moved forward against the Russian right and center. The defensive fire of Position Battery #14, Light Battery #27, and the surviving nine guns of Horse Battery #1 threw the advancing French columns into disorder.

The Russian first line counterattacked. General Berg led Perm, Mohilev, and the 24th and 26th Jagers against the French right. General Kastschkovski struck the French right flank with Kalouga, Sievesk, and the 24th and 25th Jagers supported by four squadrons. The Russian second line advanced against the French center, which was not uncovered by the first line's movements. The vigor and shock of the flank attack by Kastschkovski's forces pushed the French back. The French withdrew, occupying the woods on their right. These woods were turned by the Sievesk Infantry, and the 24th and 26th on the right, while the depot battalion of the Count Arakcheyev Grenadier Regiment, drawn from the second line, assaulted the woods frontally.

Two squadrons of the Guard and Riga Dragoons charged a dense French column which had not withdrawn fast enough and cut it off. Those French that were not killed were forced to surrender. Wittgenstein was wounded while leading this attack, but he had the wound bandaged in the field and continued to direct the Russian pursuit. The Russians pursued the French, who withdrew slowly in a skillfully managed withdrawal.

The Russian pursuit continued as far as Sokolichtchi. The French took up a position before the farm of Sokolichtchi, behind a ravine crossing the road. There was a single bridge over the road, and the French burnt it as they crossed it. The French supported one wing on the woods and the other on the Nitschtscha River. The Russians took that position with a quick frontal assault led by three battalions of the Sievesk and Mohilev Infantry Regiments. This assault was supported by Batteries #5 and #14. While the 24th Jagers moved against the French left, the 25th Jagers fired on it frontally, while two guns, which had crossed the river at a ford, fired into the French flank.

The French resumed their withdrawal and took another position on the plateau between Sokolichtchi and Sivochino, where they formed some cuirassier squadrons as a rear guard. Colonel Albrecht received orders to attack them with the depot squadrons of the Guard Uhlans and Dragoons. Before they could execute this charge, the French withdrew. Their exit was hurried by fire from Horse Battery #3.

The pursuit was resumed by Horse Battery #3, the Kalouga Infantry Regiment, and some jagers who moved into the defile. Oudinot's flanks were once again exposed, and he resumed his withdrawal, crossing the Drissa at Sivochino and burning the bridge behind him. Position Battery #5 unlimbered on the right bank and harassed the retiring French, while Russian jagers crossed the Drissa at a ford and stopped near Borarchtchina. The main battle line and the reserve were placed in echelons between Sokolichtchi and Sivochino.

Between 30 July and 1 August the Russians lost 3,000 men hors de combat and 1,300 prisoners. The French lost about 4,000.

On the following day the French withdrew towards Polotsk and the Russians moved on Bieloe. Wittgenstein took great care to watch the movements of Marshal Macdonald, but determined not to cross the Drissa with the bulk of his forces. He placed an advanced guard along the roads to Polotsk, Wolinizi, and Nevel, while his main body took up positions near Sokolichtchi. Wittgenstein reorganized his corps on 2 August.

Maneuvers on Polotsk

By 3 August the French had crossed the Dvina and taken up positions around Polotsk. Macdonald's movements had forced Prince Radziwill to destroy the works around Dinaburg and to withdraw the infantry and three cavalry regiments that had formed its garrison. Macdonald constructed a bridgehead near Kreutzburg and organized the X Corps behind Kalkoumen.

On 8 August, Wittgenstein ordered several bridges to be raised over the Dvina so he could counter any French move as well as to take advantage of any error on Macdonald's part that might open up his lines of communications to an attack. However, a French advanced guard moved into Drouia and captured much Russian equipment and their bridging train. The Russians had abandoned it during their march on Kliastitzy.

Colonel Albrecht was sent with two squadrons and a company of jagers to recapture this equipment. This force crossed the Dvina at a ford, chased out the small French force, and recaptured their bridging train.

On 9 August, the main body of the Russian 1st Corps was in Rasizi with its reserves in Babi. The same day the Russian advanced guard crossed the Dvina and occupied Drouia in force. Wittgenstein was still watching Oudinot and was concerned because he had learned that St. Cyr's VI Corps had joined him. Fearing that Oudinot might resume the offensive, he responded by placing his corps along the road to Kokhanovitsi and against Oudinot's flank. He feared that Oudinot would move along the road to Sebej, which would open up Wittgenstein's lines of communication to the French.

On 10 August the French advanced along the road to Volinza and Osevia. General Helfreich and Colonel Rudiger retreated to Kokhanovitsi, which they found occupied by the French. The arrival of Helfreich and Rudiger coincided with the arrival of General Auvray, chief of staff of the Russian 1st Corps, and his column. The French were attacked immediately by the forces of Helfreich and Kastschkovski. The French were pushed back to the heights along the right bank of the Svolna River. The Russian main body and reserve took up positions before Kokhanovitsi. General Hamen was ordered to close up with them.

The Battle of Svolna

During the morning of 11 August, General Auvray believed that the French movements were offensive in nature and braced his forces for their attack. When no attack occurred he grew to believe that he was facing only a small detachment which was awaiting reinforcements from either the II or the VI Corps. He ordered a reconnaissance in force. The two combined advanced guards, with the Iambourg Dragoons, pushed back the French outposts on the Svolna plain.

Once they occupied the plain, the Russians observed a major French force, Oudinot's II Corps, on the far bank of the river. The right bank was occupied by a strong French cavalry force and the villages of Pogarichtchi, Svolna, and Ostroy-Konez were heavily garrisoned with French infantry. The French line was fixed on its right in Pogarichtchi and on its left in Svolna. General Auvray determined to clear the French outposts from his bank of the river and sent the Grodno Hussars and Platov #4 Cossacks to do the job. Behind them came the rest of the Russian forces.

The two Russian cavalry units pushed the French cavalry on the plain back to the river, but the fire of supporting French artillery stopped their advance. The Russian infantry of the advanced guard and the 5th Division advanced in battalion columns onto the rising ground before Pogarichtchi. Auvray covered his flanks with his cavalry and two squadrons of the converged Guard Cavalry Regiment, which were posted on his right flank. The French withdrew before the larger Russian force.

The Grodno Hussars, Iambourg Dragoons, and two squadrons of the converged cuirassier regiment, which formed the Russian left wing, moved into Pogarichtchi. From there they advanced into the village of Kaprovitzki. The four infantry regiments of the 5th Division (Sievesk, Perm, Kalouga, and Mohilev) and Position Batteries #5 and #28 formed the Russian center. The six squadrons of the Grodno Hussars formed behind the Russian center, and the Russian right was formed with the 23rd and 25th Jagers, Light Battery #26, and two squadrons of converged cuirassiers. The remainder of the Russian forces formed their second line, which was posted behind Mamonovchtchina, and their reserve, which was at Paluikovchtchina.

As the Grodno Hussars advanced, the three Russian batteries fired to support their advance. The French withdrew from Svolna and Ostroy-Konez because their artillery on the far bank could not support them.

Several columns were detached from the French main body and moved towards Ostroy-Konez to reinforce its withdrawing defenders and recapture it. Ostroy-Konez was important to the French, as it was the strongpoint closest to the bridge. Auvray sent General Kastschkovski and Colonel Diebitsch, his quartermaster-chief, with the Tenguinsk and Estonia Infantry Regiments, supported by Position Battery #14, to push them out. Kastschkovski deployed the Iambourg Dragoons, placing artillery and infantry behind them, to form his left wing. He sent this force forward.

When they reached short cannon range of the French, the Iambourg Dragoons swung clear, opening the field of fire for Position Battery #14. This artillery fire disordered the French attack out of Ostroy-Konez, and the Russians counterattacked with bayonets, taking the village. The Russian skirmishers from the Perm and Estonia Infantry Regiments pursued as far as the river-bank, where they formed on the bank and continued to fire on the French.

Kastschkovski received orders to detach two squadrons, a battalion from the Estonia and Tenguinsk Infantry Regiments, and six guns of Position Battery #14 and send them to the Svolna farm. The French were putting up a stiff resistance before the farm because Oudinot had been able to move fresh troops across the bridge and reinforce his troops. Diebitsch, sent by Kastschkovski with troops detached from the left, positioned himself near a small copse of woods between Svolna and Ostroy-Konez. The four Russian guns with him began to fire on the French troops that were supporting the French by the bridge. He sent two battalions of the Perm and Mohilev Infantry Regiments under Colonel Lialin to attack the French flank. A musketeer company and the elite company of the Perm Regiment advanced under the command of Major Forbiev, driving back the French. The end of the retiring French column was cut off by Colonel Lialin and taken prisoner. The Russian artillery on the right wing closed up to the river bank and turned its fire on the French nearest the river, forcing them to elongate their position.

Skirmishers detached from Perm, Mohilev, and 3/Estonia moved forward to profit from the French retreat, passing over the bridge without orders. Some squadrons of Doumerc's cuirassiers, placed nearest the river, fell on them, driving them back in great disorder. The Russian jagers fled over the bridge with the cuirassiers in hot pursuit until the Grodno Hussars struck them in the flank and drove them back. The remainder of Doumerc's cuirassiers counterattacked, but withdrew as soon as the Russian artillery began to play on them.

Several French columns then moved towards Ostroy-Konez, and Kastschkovski directed the fire of Position Battery #14 on them while he advanced the Navajinsk Infantry Regiment to support the threatened Russians in Ostroy-Konez. This was sufficient to cause the French to withdraw.

The intensity of the Russian artillery fire made it difficult to expand the position of the advanced guard, so it withdrew and rejoined the main body on the left bank of the Svolna. This position, dominating the entire plain, could only be reached by the two bridges over the Svolna. Since the French positions were too strong for the Russians to force, Auvray stopped the Russian advance at the river's edge.

Skirmishers from Perm and Estonia, supported by a company from Kalouga and another from Navajinsk, established themselves on the left bank. Those of Perm and Estonia were before Ostroy-Konez. Here they covered the raising of a bridge to permit the Russians to resume the offensive, should the opportunity arise.

The battle of Svolna was inconclusive. Oudinot, with about 10,000 men, had clashed with about 9,000 men under the command of Auvray and had come out the worst for it. The French had lost 1,200 hors de combat and 300 prisoners, while the Russians lost only 800 hors de combat.

French Retreat on Polotsk

The next day the Russians remained in their positions near Svolna while the French withdrew to Volinzi. Their retreat was followed by a cossack patrol, and General Balk was sent to Tobolki to cover the Russian right.

During the night of 13 August, Wittgenstein was reinforced by nine of the ten battalions forming the garrison of Dinaburg. This force was the 32nd Division, which was formed of depot battalions. The line depot battalions were so weak that they were reorganized into the 1st and 2nd Converged Infantry Regiments. The depot battalions of the 11th, 18th, and 36th Jagers were converged into the Converged Jager Regiment. Though numbering only around 3,000 men, normally an insignificant number, these units assumed a more important role: the French thought they were facing full-strength units instead of the terribly understrength depot battalions actually before them.

On 14 August, Wittgenstein once again decided to move against Polotsk, and he reorganized his forces. Colonel Vlastov was detached with four squadrons of the Grodno Hussars, the 24th Jagers, two converged grenadier battalions from the 5th Division, and 200 cossacks. He moved on Kliastitzy and Sivochino to harass the French right.

Wittgenstein found himself obliged to contend with Oudinot operating an offensive based on interior lines of communication. He also had Macdonald to the north to contend with. Colonel Vlastov's forces were directed to move on Bieloe in order to menace the French right and communications. The French withdrew in the face of this move and moved on Polotsk. The Russians occupied Volinzi as a result.

The French continued to retreat on Polotsk, and on 16 August they surrendered Ropno to Helfreich. The Bavarian detachment in Bieloe withdrew along the road to Nevel, towards Polotsk, and joined Oudinot there.

It was on 17 August that Wittgenstein learned that the French II

and VI Corps had joined forces, but he still felt he should move forward
to observe the French. Despite unfavorable numbers, Wittgenstein was
determined to attack the French at Polotsk.

First Battle of Polotsk

General Helfreich's advanced guard, supported by the first line of
battle, moved to the defile at Ropno with the 25th and 26th Jagers and
the Perm and Mohilev Infantry under the command of the Prince of
Siberia. They encountered a French advanced guard, pushing it back.
A battalion of Perm took a road parallel to the main road to Pressemenitza.
By 5:00 A.M. Helfreich and the Prince of Siberia had cleared the French
out of the woods before Polotsk and established communications with
Vlastov. Vlastov had occupied the woods before the tavern of Borovka
with the 23rd and 24th Jagers.

On 18 August the Russian forces under Wittgenstein consisted of
the 1st Corps, the 32nd Reserve Division or Dinaburg garrison, and a
detachment of infantry commanded by Prince Repnin. This force totaled
about 20,000 men. On 30 August the French II Corps and Doumerc's
cuirassier division commanded by Oudinot had about 24,000. He had
been joined by the two Bavarian Divisions of VI Corps. This force had
suffered heavily during the beginning of the campaign, though entirely
from causes other than combat. Its original strength of 26,000 had been
reduced to about 20,000 men. This gave Oudinot a total of 44,000,
not including artillery and train personnel.

Oudinot had reason to suspect an attack and positioned his forces
around Polotsk to receive it. Polotsk is on the Dvina River. In front of
the city, to the northwest, is a plain encircled by heavy forest. The
Pelota River runs from the northwest of the city to the west of the city
where it joins the Dvina, intersecting this plain for about a mile and a
half.

The Pressemenitza farm stands near the forest, in the center of the
plain. The Spass convent stood on the right bank of the Pelota, about a
half mile from the Pressemenitza farm. The Bavarians had converted
the convent into a strongpoint and occupied it in great strength. Their
front line was held by the 20th Division under General Wrede, while
the 19th Division, under General Deroy, remained as a reserve behind
Spass.

Oudinot positioned Legrand's division, reinforced by a regiment
from Verdier's division and some light cavalry, in front of Polotsk, a

total of 7,000 men. On his left, extending to the Spass convent, were
the Bavarians, some 11,000 men. All of the Bavarian artillery, except
twelve guns, had been organized into a single battery. This battery dominated the center of the field. The remaining twelve guns were a reserve
under General Dulauloy and were posted near the river to cover any
potential retreat.

All of II Corps' artillery had been posted on the left bank of the
Dvina, with the exception of a few guns left with Legrand. The rest of
the II Corps, Doumerc's cuirassiers, Castex's light cavalry, and the 8th
and 9th Divisions, remained on the left bank as well.

Wittgenstein moved his forces forward during the night of the 16th,
and on the 17th he began his attack. His initial movement was to advance
General Helfreich's forces and the brigade of the Prince of Siberia towards
the Spass convent. The Bavarian massed battery took them under heavy
fire and drove them back into the woods. This initial Russian attack on
Spass consisted of the 23rd, 25th, and 26th Jager Regiments and six
guns on the Russian right. The center consisted of three infantry regiments
and thirty guns. The left consisted of the Perm and Mohilev Infantry
Regiments in the first line and twenty-four guns in the first line. The
second line consisted of nine battalions and all the Russian cavalry.
Vlastov's five battalions remained on the left flank of this attack.

General Berg advanced the remaining forces of the Russian first
line of battle and formed them in columns before the Pelota. The battle
was to be well developed by the time Wittgenstein arrived on the field.

Wittgenstein stopped his right wing's advance. He directed his left
wing to push no further than the convent and to act in support of Vlastov's
forces. He then placed his cavalry and second line of battle behind the
first. Count Sievers was detached with the I Corps pioneer company
and two battalions to build a bridge over the Dvina three miles below
Polotsk to distract the French threatening their flank.

The Russians were deployed and their first line was positioned as
follows: The right wing bordered on the main road to Drissa and started
with the 23rd, 25th, and 26th Jagers, six guns from Position Battery
#28, Kalouga, Sievesk, and converged infantry regiments. The center
consisted of Horse Battery #1, Position Battery #5, and Light Battery
#9. This artillery extended to the Pressemenitza farm, where it joined
the Russian left. The left consisted of the Perm and Mohilev Infantry,
six guns of Position Battery #28, Light Battery #26, and Vlastov's

detachment, which was secured on the road to Nevel. The artillery was positioned in front of the infantry, and the Russian reserves were in Ropno, some distance from the battlefield.

The two battalions of converged grenadiers of the 5th Division, the 24th Jagers, and one battalion of Perm and Mohilev Infantry Regiments began the attack on Spass. General Hamen supported the attack with one battalion of the Estonia, Toula, and Navajinsk Infantry Regiments and a battalion of the 18th Jagers, who positioned themselves to the right of Vlastov's detachment. The goal of this attack was to seize the convent and separate the Bavarians from the French. The Russians succeeded in seizing the closest buildings of the convent, but the Bavarians, supported by their own artillery and that on the left bank, quickly threw them back. As the battle began developing, Legrand's 8th Division crossed over the Dvina from the left bank and took up positions on the ramparts of the city. The 9th Division of General de division Merle remained on the far bank in reserve.

Prince Jachwill directed the fire of Light Battery #26 and Horse Battery #3, which had only six guns, to cover the retreat of the Russian left and to stop the pursuing Bavarians. The fire disordered the Bavarians and they were quickly counterattacked by the converged grenadiers, 1/Perm, 3/Mohilev, and the 24th Jagers. Their advance was supported on the right by 3/Perm and 1/Mohilev under the command of Colonel Diebitsch. The Bavarians fought bravely, but they were forced back to the buildings of the convent on the French side of the Pelota. Here they reestablished themselves and were reinforced by fresh troops. Two companies of grenadiers and a battalion of the 24th Jagers detached and moved towards the Pelota to strike a Bavarian column, which had crossed the river at a ford, and drove them back.

The crossfire of Batteries #1 and #28 raked Oudinot's troops as they advanced to make an assault against the Russian center. Oudinot's forces advanced twice, but they were repulsed each time. Oudinot was wounded during these assaults and was forced to turn command of his corps over to General St. Cyr.

The battle continued around the Spass convent. It dissolved into a skirmish fight, something in which the converged grenadiers of the 5th Division had a particular skill. They had participated in the 1808 campaign in Finland where they had engaged in many such battles against the Swedes.

As the Bavarians massed strong columns against the convent, Wittgenstein advanced part of the second line, sending Kalouga, Sievesk, and the converged infantry, under General Berg, to reinforce his center.

General Berg did not wish to advance directly, exposing his flank to the French artillery fire, so he moved around Nevel. His advance coincided with the French assault on Colonel Vlastov's front and flank. Vlastov was aided in his defense by the detachment of Position Battery #5, which was also detached from the center.

General Berg reinforced Colonel Vlastov with all of his skirmishers while he formed his three regiments in attack columns behind them. He was supported on his right by the Prince of Siberia with the Perm and Mohilev Infantry Regiments. He advanced his right flank. The Bavarians counterattacked, but fell back in disorder on the Spass convent. As General Wrede's troops withdrew, they set fire to the convent. The 1st Brigade, 20th Division, under General Vincenti, remained in the village near the convent until General Vincenti was badly wounded. When it withdrew, it obliged the withdrawal of the Bavarian battery posted next to the convent.

Wrede received reinforcements and attempted to reestablish his initial positions. His columns crossed the Pelota and were greeted by fire from Batteries #3, #5, #9, and #26. He was thrown back time and again with heavy casualties. During one advance his skirmishers actually advanced as far as Battery #3, only to be chased away by two squadrons of the Grodno Hussar Regiment.

General Berg established his troops near Spass as the skirmishers of Legrand's division of French moved on the Russian center again. General Hamen detached six guns from Position Battery #27, a battalion of the Toula Infantry Regiment, and the depot battalion of the 18th Jager Regiment from the second line and moved them forward. They drove back Legrand's skirmishers, but attracted the attention of the bulk of Legrand's division. The two Russian battalions were unable to stand up to the unequal battle and withdrew to the main line. Their withdrawal cleared the field of fire for Batteries #1 and #27 to fire on Legrand's troops. The skirmishers covering the Russian center were supported by two battalions drawn from the second line, one each from the Estonia and Navajinsk Infantry Regiments.

The Russian artillery fire forced Legrand's skirmishers back, exposing the French columns to their fire. The French began to withdraw and were pursued into the suburbs of Polotsk. General Hamen continued to push Legrand with success and was reinforced by a second battalion of the Toula Infantry Regiment. He was able to seize the scrubby terrain before Polotsk, but night fell, ending the battle.

The Russian right had remained inactive after repulsing the earlier French attacks. It was supported by the battalions placed on the left bank of the Dvina River. Colonel Sievers, charged with the construction of a bridge over the Dvina, was disturbed by the presence and fire from French troops on the far bank. The two battalions with him formed a line along the edge of the river and drove the French back, out of musket range, with a rolling fire. The French were unable to further hinder the construction of the bridge after that.

That evening Wittgenstein wished to extend his lines and was obliged to establish his headquarters in the Pressemenitza farm, the only remaining habitable buildings in the area. During the night of 17–18 August the Russians were reorganized and redeployed. They were now, from right to left, 23rd, 25th, and 26th Jager Regiments, Toula, Estonia, the depot of the 18th Jager Regiment, a battalion of the Navajinsk Infantry Regiment, Perm, Mohilev, Sievesk, and Kalouga Infantry Regiments, the converged infantry, the 24th Jager Regiment, and the converged grenadiers of the 5th Division.

The artillery was positioned, right to left, six guns from Position Battery #28, Horse Battery #1, six guns from Position Battery #27, six guns from Position Battery #5, Light Battery #9, six guns from Position Battery #28, Light Battery #26, six guns from Horse Battery #3, and six guns from Position Battery #5. The cavalry, the remainder of the infantry, and the artillery were posted in the second line behind the main line.

The right wing was in the same position it had occupied the day before the battle, but the left wing was supported on its right by Pressemenitza and on the left by the Pelota. Its advanced positions were strung along the Pelota River near the Spass convent. The Russian losses after the first day of battle totaled approximately 2,500 dead and wounded, though they claimed to have inflicted 4,000 casualties and taken 1,000 prisoners.

The Russian 1st Corps reserve had left Ropno during the night and advanced along the road to Nevel, where it took up positions to support the Russian left. Colonel Sievers received orders to raise another bridge on the Pelota River near Lozovka. The topography of the left bank was more favorable to an attack than that of the right, but Wittgenstein hoped to cross the bulk of his forces over Sievers' new bridge and strike the French in the rear if they were to cross the Dvina in force.

During the morning of the next day, St. Cyr encouraged these hopes and directed his baggage, under escort of Valentin's infantry and his cavalry, to file behind the Dvina in view of the Russians. At the same time he entered into negotiations with the Russians for the removal of the wounded.

St. Cyr redeployed his forces for the coming battle. A Bavarian thirty-one-gun battery was formed from the 1st, 5th, and 6th Bavarian 6pdr Foot Batteries, and the 2nd and 3rd Bavarian Light Batteries. It was established on the rise near the Spass convent, where the Bavarian batteries of Gotthard and Gravenreuth had been posted the day before. Merle's division was posted as a reserve, with Candras' brigade (1st and 2nd Swiss Regiments), to the north of the city to the east of the Pelota, and Coutard's brigade (123rd Line and 3rd Swiss) was posted in the city and on its walls.

At 3:30 A.M. Verdier's division, now commanded by General Valentin, passed over the Dvina, followed by Merle's division. Legrand's division used the valley of the Pelota to cover its movement and supported its right on the village of Spass. They were followed by all of the II Corps artillery (under General Aubry, who had replaced General Dulauloy), Doumerc's cuirassiers, and Corbineau's light cavalry. Doumerc followed and positioned his cuirassiers on Merle's right, behind the bulk of the army.

Legrand redeployed his division behind the Spass convent. Valentin was positioned some distance behind him, while Merle formed the French army's left, resting on the Dvina.

At 4:30 A.M. St. Cyr had the 6th Bavarian Artillery Battery give the signal for the attack. The Bavarian 20th Division was designated to attack the Gromeower forest, and Deroy's 19th Division was to attack Spass. This force was masked from the Russians' view by the Pelota's valley and the convent.

At 5:00 A.M. the French began a concentric attack under a heavy artillery cross fire from Bavarian and II Corps batteries. This fire was directed primarily against Pressemenitza and quickly threw General Berg's 5th Division and Vlastov's detachment into disorder. The fire on Position Battery #27 and Light Battery #9 shattered many of their guns and killed or wounded most of the batteries' horses.

The five guns of Light Battery #27, positioned by Colonel Diebitsch, had not been observed by the Bavarians. It took one of the Bavarian batteries in the flank and forced it to withdraw, lessening the fire on the Russians. Despite this, all thirty-one guns fired fifty rounds each, consuming most, if not all, of their artillery. This was of little matter at that point, for as the battle developed they were masked by their own infantry and had no opportunity to engage the enemy in any significant manner until later.

The Russian infantry was attacked by the Bavarians under Wrede and Deroy on their left. Legrand's 6th Division, supported by Doumerc's cuirassiers, struck them in their center, near the convent. Verdier advanced on Legrand's left. He left a single brigade to watch the Russian right. Merle was to the left of Polotsk.

On the left a Bavarian battalion under Laroche, with a single gun, moved on Hamernia, leading the 1st and 3rd Brigades. It encountered a Russian grenadier company covering the construction of a bridge, and five miles further it encountered a squadron of the Grodno Hussars. Both of these Russian units were quickly chased off.

The attack by the Bavarian 20th Division on Spass was led by the 2nd Brigade, with the 3rd Regiment leading the 7th Regiment. They broke into files and extended along the ravine formed by a tributary of the Pelota. This movement was not observed by the Russians.

The progress of the attack of the Bavarian 19th Division depended on the success of the 20th Division's attack. The 20th Division advanced in the following order: Raglovich's 2nd Brigade—3rd Jäger Battalion, 10th Line and 4th Line; the 3rd Brigade—8th Line and 4th Jägers; 1st Brigade—9th Regiment and 1st Line. The 4th Light Battery of Captain Gravenreuth followed only after the infantry had advanced out of the city.

Three companies of the 3rd Bavarian Jägers occupied the convent which the infantry left, and the entire battalion moved in a column by peloton with General Raglovich at its head. As the jägers arrived at the village of Spass, its skirmishers deployed to cover the deployment of the brigade. They were immediately followed by the 10th Regiment, which posted itself on their left. This movement was supported by the Bavarian 4th Light Battery posted to the left of Spass.

The Bavarian 4th Battery had chosen an advantageous position where it could engage a Russian battery placed before Pressemenitza. The Russian battery was posted where it could fire into the rear of Raglovich's advancing brigade.

Legrand's division advanced slowly to permit the Russians time to deploy their entire forces against the Bavarians. However, he advanced too slowly and allowed the Russians to be struck by the head of Deroy's column before he was in position. Deroy was only able to deploy slowly. Because of this and Wrede's position, the Russians concentrated their efforts on Becker's brigade until Raglovich's brigade arrived, punishing it severely.

The Russian artillery fire switched from its counterbattery effort and turned its fire on Raglovich. It stopped the first impulse of the main attacks. The 4th Bavarian Light Battery was taken under heavy fire and forced to withdraw to its original position. Vlastov, three squadrons of the Grodno Hussars, and the 5th Division moved forward into a furious melee. However, the numerical strength of the French and their heavy artillery fire forced the Russian 5th Division back, behind Presse-menitza. The 10th Regiment and the rest of the Bavarian right wing recoiled. At that moment the 4th Bavarian Line advanced. General Deroy had concealed it in a small depression. The Russian column received a heavy fusillade from them for a half hour. Recovering the initiative, the entire division of Deroy formed in line and advanced.

Raglovich's brigade recoiled, leaving Becker's brigade in a dire situation. His left flank was now exposed. The Russians tried to turn the right of the 2nd Brigade of the 19th Division. The Russians pushed into the gap, against the exposed flank of the 2nd Brigade of the 20th Division.

The Russians penetrated the gap between the two brigades and were engaged by the 2/7th Bavarian Line and cut it off from the rest of the brigade. A lively battle ensued and the Bavarians were forced to withdraw.

Becker's and Raglovich's brigades reformed and placed themselves in line. A part of the 4th Light Battery was posted with Raglovich's brigade and prepared to attack.

The 3rd Brigade of the 19th Division was followed by the 2nd in the following order: 8th Line and 4th Jägers formed the line between the 2nd Brigade and Legrand. The 8th Regiment had problems deploying and the 4th Jägers immediately responded, covering its movement.

The forces of Colonel Vlastov and the two battalions of converged grenadiers of the 14th Division, which were sent to support him, were placed before the woods on the road to Nevel.

At 5:00 P.M. three battalions under Siebein passed over the bridge on the Pelota: 1/ and 2/9th Regiment and the 1/1st Regiment. The 2/1st Regiment and the 1st Jägers remained provisionally in this position as a reserve. Two heavy French columns, four times as strong as the Bavarians, advanced alongside of the Bavarians, leading the way. The

French commenced a heavy cannonade on the Russian left flank, which was responded to by Position Battery #27 and Light Battery #9, posted before the farm. The French fire shot them to pieces, scattering their men and equipment.

The Bavarian division deployed to the left under heavy Russian artillery fire. It struck a country manor house occupied by the Russians, who were attacked by three French battalions. The French attack failed and was thrown back on the 9th Bavarian Line. The 9th advanced at the pas de charge against the Russians. They attacked the building with great courage and the Russians were driven back.

The three battalions under Siebein moved across the bridge and assumed positions in the city. The 2/1st Regiment was ordered forward to rejoin the 1st Battalion, and the part of the 4th Light Battery that had remained behind also crossed to rejoin that portion that had been engaged against the Russians all morning.

The 1/1st Bavarian Line and Gravenreuth's Battery (4th Light) were ordered to fall on the Russian left flank. The infantry arrived in time to protect the battery from a cavalry attack. The 2/1st Line arrived shortly thereafter and both formed square. After the cavalry charge was repulsed, one battalion moved to the left to recapture a battery of four French 12pdrs. Cossacks had taken it and killed or captured the crews. The rapid Bavarian advance retook the battery and freed many of the prisoners.

The Bavarian attack recommenced, but Deroy was quickly mortally wounded. Wrede was himself wounded, and the Bavarian attack stopped. To compound the situation, Legrand's attack on Pressemenitza was checked. St. Cyr moved to the center and ordered Siebein to support Legrand's resumption of the offensive. Wrede took command of the entire Bavarian corps and, judging that the time for the offensive was right, placed himself at the head of Deroy's division. His presence reassured the division, and the battle resumed.

Vlastov menaced the Bavarian left flank and forced them to withdraw. Vlastov then placed himself on the road to Nevel, forming a line along its right. The Russian left continued to battle in this position until the battle ended.

In the center, General Hamen profited from the fire of the six guns of Light Battery #27 and reformed his shattered forces. As he fought the advancing regiments of Legrand's division, other French forces turned the Pressemenitza position, which was weakly defended by a single battalion of the Sievesk Infantry Regiment. The French threw this battalion back and advanced on the Russian batteries near the Pressemenitza farm. The French advanced into a shower of cannister three times, eventually overrunning Battery #9 and part of Battery #28. The gunners defended themselves, but were forced to withdraw, abandoning seven guns to the French. General Hamen held his position and counterattacked in an effort to recover the captured guns.

Seeing that the Russian center had developed a gap between it and the 5th Division, General Hamen gathered the Toula and Estonia Infantry Regiments with a battalion from the Navajinsk Infantry, Tenguinsk Infantry, and 11th Jagers. These seven battalions formed themselves and began a counterattack as the French columns moved past the farm. The 8th Division was taken in the flank. The most advanced French unit, the 26th Line Regiment, recoiled in front of the attack of two squadrons of the Guard Cuirassiers under the command of Colonel Protassov. The 6th Division under Maison fell back in disorder. With the exception of one single regiment whose senior officers were hors de combat and whose troops were quite inexperienced, the withdrawal was not significant.

Legrand's division was struck again by two battalions of the Navajinsk and Tenguinsk Infantry Regiments. General Hamen's counterattack stabilized the Russian center and took up a strong defensive position. He fought back several less vigorous attacks by Legrand's division, the last attack being stopped by a notable effort by Colonel Harpe and a battalion of the Navajinsk Infantry Regiment.

The Russian 5th Division and reserve profited from this stabilization to begin their withdrawal towards Ropno, which Wittgenstein had designated as the rallying point for his battered army.

On the right flank, several columns of Valentin's division had advanced against the Russian right at the beginning of the battle, but the cross fire from Battery #1 and the six guns of Battery #26 had forced the French back to their original positions. One French column crossed the Pelota at a ford and moved against the rear of the Russian left flank, cutting off one of the Russian escape routes. The depot battalion of the Pavlov Grenadier Regiment pushed it back and then proceeded to fight its way through the French lines, making good its escape.

At the moment the principal French attacks began to slacken, the French reestablished the thirty-one-gun battery with the II Corps artillery and directed it against the Russian center. It supported the advance of several infantry columns and a large cavalry force that moved against the Russians. General Balk advanced his cavalry to meet that of General Corbineau, a detachment of the 24th Chasseurs à Cheval, which defended the II Corps battery. He struck the French cavalry frontally with the converged cuirassier regiment (depot squadrons of the Emperor and Empress Cuirassier Regiments), while a squadron of the Grodno Hussars under Major Semeka struck them in the flank.

The French cavalry fell back, directly over the battery. The Russian cuirassiers pursued them vigorously and so closely that the French gunners were unable to fire on them for fear of striking their own cavalry. The Russians continued their pursuit hot on the heels of the fleeing French cavalry, overrunning the battery and sabering many gunners. However, they were unable to maintain possession of the captured battery because the teams had been taken away by the fleeing French.

The 1st and 2nd Swiss Regiments formed square and stood like rocks, bayonets lowered, menacing friend and enemy alike, causing the Russian cavalry to swerve away.

The Russians continued forward, overrunning St. Cyr and his staff. St. Cyr was forced to throw himself into a ditch to escape them. The Russians continued towards Polotsk, entering into the middle of the French army, which surrounded them on all sides. The 9th Bavarian Line continued to advance, but Siebein formed the 1st Bavarian Line Regiment into a square on the left flank by the cuirassiers. It was supported by the 4th Light Bavarian Battery. The 1st Bavarian Line broke its square and advanced, recapturing the 12pdr battery that had been overrun by the Russians.

One hundred men of the 3rd Swiss Regiment had been placed in a cemetery surrounded by walls. It formed a veritable fortress. Their fire raked the charging Russians and stopped their advance.

A prompt and skillful attack by Berkheim's 4th Cuirassier Regiment and the 3rd Swiss Infantry Regiment led by Colonel de Lorencez struck the Russian right flank and drove them back in disorder. The Russians then withdrew to their lines.

The French stopped their attacks as the Russians accelerated their withdrawal. The Russian advanced guard of General Helfreich was the last to leave the battlefield, following the main body closely. It was night and fatigue ended the battle, neither side having decisively beaten the other.

The pursuit by the French was limited to Candras' Swiss brigade. The four battalions from Candras' brigade moved down the road to

Bieloe without much enthusiasm for the pursuit. They were fatigued from a long day of battle.

The Russians had left a company of grenadiers to cover the bridge they'd raised two miles below Polotsk, and a squadron of Grodno Hussars guarded a ford two miles further down the road. The French pursuit caught up with the Pavlov Grenadiers. Their cavalry teased the battalion in an effort to break it, but it held fast. Shortly afterward, four French battalions and a column of cuirassiers passed the first bridge, driving the defenders back and seizing the ford as well. The Pavlov Grenadiers were cut off, but they continued to withdraw, taking 100 French prisoners with them.

On the Russian extreme right, the 23rd Jagers and three squadrons of the Grodno Hussars covered the road to Dissna. The infantry brigade of General Amey and the light cavalry of General Castex attacked them. The French drove them back until they were taken under fire by Horse Battery #1. A timely charge by the Grodno Hussars stopped what remained of the pursuit.

The French retained Merle's division as a reserve. It was on the right of the army. Doumerc's cuirassiers were totally available as well, to support the attack of the four divisions. The Russian Converged Guard Cavalry Regiment attacked and drove back Corbineau, only to be driven back and suffer heavy casualties at the hands of Berkheim's 4th Cuirassiers, who put the Russians in flight.

The Russians assumed a new position between Ropno and Pressemenitza that night. On the 22nd they resumed their withdrawal, moving on Sivochina and Tokolitchie Tchitar on the right bank of the Drissa.

The French pursuit had been weak, not intended to punish, but merely to gather in some more fruits of the battle. The first battle of Polotsk was over. Though St. Cyr's 77 battalions, 36 squadrons, and 150 guns had defeated Wittgenstein's 45 battalions, 27 squadrons, and 98 guns, it was an inconclusive battle. The French lost about 2,000 dead and wounded, as well as about 500 prisoners. The Russians lost about 3,000, including 1,200 prisoners and 14 guns. It had been a heavy battle for the Bavarian artillery, which had fired 153 12pdr shot, 10 12pdr cannister, 1,374 6pdr shot, 132 6pdr cannister, 534 howitzer shells, and 30 howitzer cannister rounds.

The pursuit began on the 22nd in earnest. Around 4:00 P.M., General Wrede arrived before the new Russian positions. He encountered Vlastov's detachment near Belaia. The Russian infantry fire disordered the Bavarian main attack. Only the Bavarian attack on the Russian left continued its advance.

The Bavarian flanking maneuver advanced to the Belaia farm and threatened to turn their flank. However, Colonel Silin and two squadrons of the Grodno Hussars charged and threw them back. Colonel Roth and the 26th Jagers chased those who had succeeded in occupying the farm out of their positions as well. Vlastov pushed back the Bavarian left and center. The Bavarian right still maneuvered to turn the Russian flank. Its attack was stopped by Colonel Rudiger at the head of a squadron of the Grodno Hussars and the Platov #4 Cossacks. The failing light favored the Bavarians and allowed them to withdraw, leaving 153 prisoners and 500 dead and wounded. The Russians claim to have lost only ninety-four men.

Having established himself, Wittgenstein began to erect field fortifications to protect his position near Sivochina, and he fortified Sebije as well. He established his magazine, artillery park, and depots in Sebije. The French under General St. Cyr did the same, beginning construction of a massive series of earthworks around Polotsk.

Southern Operations

South of the main army, Schwarzenberg maneuvered against the Russian 3rd Army of the West. Napoleon directed that Schwarzenberg detach a small force of 4,000 men to operate behind his force and the main army under Napoleon. Schwarzenberg was not happy about having to detach more of his cavalry in face of an enemy he knew was decidedly his superior in that arm. He had disobeyed Napoleon's earlier order to close with the main French army and moved to support Reynier after the disaster at Kobrin. However, this time he did not disobey.

He detached Mohr's forces, which consisted of two battalions of the de Ligne Infantry Regiment, the Hesse-Homberg Hussar Regiment, a detachment of 200 horse, a company of jägers, two companies of the Beaulieu Infantry Regiment that had been detached earlier to Kleist, and an eight-gun 3pdr battery. Mohr was to maintain contact with both Schwarzenberg and Napoleon, who was on the Dnieper at this time. In addition, he was to march on Pinsk and determine the strength of the Russian forces in Volhynie before Schwarzenberg and Reynier invaded the region.

Tormassov maneuvered his 3rd Army of the West in the face of the Austro-Saxon forces. He detached General Knorring with the Tartar Uhlan Regiment and a force of cossacks to advance into Poland and disconcert the French rear.

His advance did that and even more. His advance on Warsaw stirred the city into a state of panic. Efforts were made to raise a national guard and use them to engage Knorring. Eventually, General Loison, the commander of Koenigsberg, was obliged to advance to Rastenberg with a force of 10,000 infantry. Warsaw was calmed, and Knorring rejoined Tormassov.

The advancing Austro-Saxon forces were beginning to threaten Tormassov's magazines in Prujany, so he adjusted his maneuvers to increase the level of pressure against the Austrians in an effort to slow their advance. Schwarzenberg and Reynier were confused about the strength of Tormassov's army. They knew that he had at least three infantry divisions, two cavalry divisions and a third force of new levees. Knowing the approximate size of the Russian forces, Schwarzenberg was surprised when Reynier said that he no longer required the support of the Austrian Hilfkorps. Schwarzenberg began to draw away, but was not moving quickly. He preferred to linger until he had firm information on the Russian strength and their positions. He sent out numerous reconnaissance forces to probe ahead of his advancing columns. For the most part, the Russian forces withdrew before him, drawing back on Prujany.

The Battle of Gorodetschna or Prujany

General Frelich encountered a small Russian cavalry force consisting of a few squadrons of the Vladimir Dragoon Regiment, the Loubny Hussar Regiment, and some cossacks near Tychin and Gorecz. They were quickly driven back, and Frelich located a large Russian camp containing infantry, cavalry, and artillery before him. He sent four squadrons of the Kaiser Hussar Regiment between Tychin and Gorecz, a squadron of the Blankenstein Hussar Regiment towards Prodosie, and held two more squadrons in reserve near the Bluden farm. A short skirmish developed and Captain Schage of the Kaiser Hussar Regiment charged with a half-squadron, driving back 200 Russian cavalry.

The Russians renewed their withdrawal, with the Austrians in pursuit, until they encountered a large Russian force at Seghnevitschi. This force consisted of General Tschlapitz' two light cavalry regiments, three infantry battalions, and twenty-four guns. Two miles behind him was Tormassov. Kamenski was posted nearby in the village of Janov.

The Russians advanced their light cavalry and some infantry against

Frelich's flank. Frelich sent two dispatches to Schwarzenberg that morning, and Schwarzenberg sent Siegenthal's division forward to support Frelich. Two battalions of the Catulinski Infantry Regiment were moved into Gorecz.

At 2:00 P.M. Schwarzenberg gave the order to attack Seghnevitschi. Frelich's brigade was to attack its right with Frimont's division advancing behind him. The principal attack would be by Mayer's brigade and consist of two battalions of the Catulinski and a battalion of the Czartorski Infantry Regiments. Mayer was to move on the left, detouring the swamps, in an effort to approach the village unobserved.

The battle was a disappointment, as the Russians withdrew after offering very little resistance. However, during their withdrawal the Austrian artillery extracted some casualties. The Austrians lost only two officers and six men dead, sixteen wounded, two prisoners, twenty horses killed, and twelve horses wounded.

As the Austro-Saxon forces resumed their advance, Tormassov took up a position halfway between Prujany and Kobrin in an effort to stop Reynier. Schwarzenberg and Reynier were anxious to avenge Kobrin and advanced on him rapidly. There were 13,000 Saxons and 25,000 Austrians facing Tormassov's 18,000 Russians.

Schwarzenberg directed Trautenberg to move from Oniceviczi against Prujany on the road from Malets. As he crossed the heights of Pavloviczi he heard a strong cannonade coming from the direction of Prujany. This was the Saxons moving on Vele Selo and engaging the Russians they'd encountered there. Trautenberg reacted by detaching two squadrons of the Kienmayer Hussar Regiment and two guns to establish contact with Reynier while the rest of the Austrian column hurried its advance towards the battle.

As the Austrians crossed the last ridge separating them from Prujany, they sent the Austrian 5th Jäger Battalion into the forest along the road. They were supported by the St. George Grenz, who deployed into the forest to the left. Both swept the forest clear of Russians.

The Kienmayer Hussar Regiment advanced in column towards Prujany and crossed the swamp to the left of the village with three squadrons to menace the flank and rear of the Russians. The rest of the regiment pushed directly into Prujany, supported by the fire of Lieutenant Schmidt's wurst battery. The Russians were forced to retire and destroyed the bridges behind them. Captain Grazer of the Austrian staff directed the rapid repair of the bridges. Once they were repaired, the pursuit resumed, until the hussars encountered formed Russian infantry.

At 4:00 P.M. Trautenberg ordered his division to attack the defile at Kozebrod. The brigade of Colonel von Suden led the attack with Pflacher's brigade in support. The rest of the division followed. Von Suden formed two small columns with his brigade. A company of the 5th Jägers led one column formed with two companies of the St. George Grenz on the right of the road. The third division of the St. George Grenz advanced on the road with Lieutenant Venzl's 6pdr foot battery. Eight companies of the Beaulieu Infantry Regiment were positioned to act as an immediate reserve. A second reserve was formed with two battalions of the Duka Infantry Regiment. One was to the right and the other to the left of the first reserve.

The fire began at 5:00 P.M. when the Austrian artillery began to provide covering fire for the advance of the 5th Jäger Battalion and the St. George Grenz Regiment against a hedgerow by Kozebrod. They captured two Russian guns posted by the hedgerow and drove back the Russian infantry. The terrain was difficult and made pursuit slow. The Russian artillery was able to position itself advantageously on the Horodezka heights, where it could shower shot upon the advancing Austrian infantry.

Major Franquen directed three companies of the Beaulieu Infantry Regiment to counter a Russian attack on the Austrian flank. When his forces came under cannister fire, Trautenberg sent two, then three, more companies of the Beaulieu Infantry Regiment under the command of Major Troaf to support Franquen.

As these troops were drawn from his reserve, Trautenberg sent the 1/Duka Infantry Regiment forward to take their place. Colonel Bakoney was sent with a company of his regiment to support the jägers in their attack on the Kozebrod hedge. He then ordered forward the last three companies of 1/Duka Infantry Regiment.

These last three companies advanced to the right side of a causeway that crossed the swamp, despite heavy cannister fire from the Russian batteries covering it. Lieutenant Pausner led his company forward. He drove the Russians out of a farm at bayonet point and seized it for himself.

The Russians placed three guns and a battalion of infantry in the Drohovice farm in an effort to threaten the Austrian flank anew and nullify the effects of their attacks. Captain Hofmeister of the 5th Austrian Jägers quickly led his company into the farm, supported by a platoon of the Duka Infantry Regiment, and drove the Russians out. It was only with the greatest effort that the Russians saved their guns.

At 8:00 P.M. the Austrians forced the defile at Kozebrod and began to repair the broken bridge with their pioneers. The Russians had taken up new positions behind the stream, facing them at the fork in the road that led to Gorodetschna and Kaments.

With the Austrian objectives achieved, the Austrian advanced posts were left to Colonel von Suden. A half-squadron of the O'Reilly Chevauléger Regiment watched the road to Gorodetschna and Kaments, a company of the Warasdiner St. George Grenz was posted at the fork in the road, a company of jägers was posted on the causeway by the hedge, another half-squadron of the O'Reilly Chevauléger and two companies of the Beaulieu Infantry Regiment were posted on the right of the road to Cherechev in a farm.

In support of these forces, a battalion of the Beaulieu Infantry Regiment was posted on the right wing, two squadrons of the O'Reilly Chevauxleger were posted in the center, two battalions of the Duka Infantry were in the rear, and on the left wing, near the causeway, were two companies of the 5th Jäger Battalion and five companies of the St. George Grenzer Regiment. The day's battle had cost the Austrians nineteen dead, ninety-nine wounded, and thirty-four missing.

After his withdrawal, Tormassov had taken up a strong position and was awaiting his 13,000-man reserve. He was positioned such that his front and right flank were covered by a swamp that extended about three miles along the river whose waters formed it. There was a thick wood, nearly one and a half miles long, that continued to bend around to within two miles of the Kobrin road. This road was important to the Russians, as it formed their only line of retreat. However, it was dangerous to them because it passed through a bottleneck formed by the woods. The Russian position resembled a half moon and was approachable by three dry passes: the road from Kobrin to Prujany, the road from Poddoubny which was not passable by artillery, and the road from Kobrin to Cherechev.

Tormassov believed that the road from Kobrin to Prujany was the only likely line of assault and positioned his forces accordingly. He had positioned his forces such that his first line consisted of the Vladimir and Tambov Infantry Regiments. Behind them, forming a second line, stood the Dnieper and Kostroma Infantry Regiments. The 28th Jagers covered their wings, and the Starodoub and Taganrog Dragoon Regiments were posted on their left to observe the plain. Two twelve-gun batteries were placed to cover the river crossing and the swamp to the left.

Realizing the strength of this position, Reynier and Schwarzenberg maneuvered to avoid what they knew could only be a bloody frontal assault. General Reynier suggested that they should maneuver to strike the Russian left flank and rear. Schwarzenberg agreed that it was the only reasonable approach to their problem and detached von Zechmeister's brigade to support the Saxon attack. Schwarzenberg later decided this wasn't enough and detached von Lilienberg's brigade as well, bringing the total to two chevauxléger and two hussar regiments sent to support the Austrians.

The Saxons advanced, led by a battalion of the 1st Light Infantry, the Prinz Anton Infantry Regiment, two light batteries, the Saxon Polenz Chevauxléger, the Prinz Clemens Uhlans, and the Saxon Hussars. Behind them came von Zechmeister's brigade of the Hohenzollern and O'Reilly Chevauxlégers, General Le Coq's Saxon division, and Sahr's brigade. Siegenthal's Austrian division moved on the road to Poddoubny.

The 2/2nd Saxon Light Infantry seized the crossing on the road to Tevele by a coup de main. Kamenski attacked and drove the light infantry back while he established a battery of twenty-four guns to hold the Austrians in check on the road to Poddoubny.

Reynier personally directed the successful main attack along a dry passage. His advanced guard was primarily the Saxon light cavalry under the command of Baglez. The advanced guard passed over the marsh and stream. It entered and deployed from the woods onto the plain behind the Russian left. They were followed by the rest of the Saxons and Austrians under Reynier, who remained concealed in the forest until 11:00 A.M., when Zechmeister moved his brigade out and formed it into two lines. His move was supported by the Saxon artillery along the edge of the heights on which the forest stood. Zechmeister positioned his brigade such that there was sufficient space for the infantry to exit from the woods and safely deploy. The 2/1st Saxon Light Infantry occupied the forest along the edge of the swamp. The 1/1st Saxon Light Infantry moved along the edge of the forest, and the Prinz Anton Regiment posted itself on the heights, to cover the passage of the rest of the infantry. A zug (platoon) of the 1st company, Saxon 1st Light Infantry, and the skirmishers of the Prinz Anton Regiment moved to the left, where they joined the 2/1st Light Infantry.

The second Saxon Division remained in reserve in the forest while Lilienberg's brigade moved to the left of the 1st Saxon Division. The Saxons gradually spread along the ridge. Sahr's brigade, all that remained of the second division, assumed the critical position anchoring the Saxon left on the swamp where they had crossed. The Austrian general Bianchi assumed command of Lilienberg's brigade after Lilienberg was wounded and moved it to a position on Sahr's right. The center was held by Le Coq's 21st Saxon Division, and Zechmeister, who commanded Gablenz's Saxon light cavalry as well as his own brigade, held the extreme right of the Saxon army. Zechmeister was directed to move to the east and cut the single line of escape of the Russians: the road from Kobrin to Gorodetschna.

Frimont positioned his forces across the river, facing Tormassov's position. He was in command of Trautenberg's division, Liechtenstein's brigade, two divisions of the Reisch Dragoons, two divisions of the Kienmayer Hussars, two Austrian wurst batteries, a 6pdr position battery, and a 12pdr position battery. Liechtenstein's brigade was formed in two lines. A division of the Reisch Dragoon Regiment was placed on the slope of the hill to the right of Liechtenstein. On their left were two battalions of the Duka Infantry Regiment and a twenty-gun battery on the heights.

The Saxon maneuver surprised Tormassov, who had not suspected that the ground in the swamp would support such a move. His line facing the Austrians across the river consisted of the Vladimir and Tambov Infantry Regiments in the front line and the Dnieper and Kostroma Infantry Regiments in the second rank. A battalion of the 28th Jagers was posted on either flank. The Starodoub and Taganrog Dragoon Regiments were posted at right angles to the infantry with the Position Batteries #9 and #18 deployed before them.

Tormassov saw and reacted to the Saxon move to his flank and rear. He stripped his right, leaving only the Riajsk Infantry Regiment, six guns of Position Battery #15, and the Tver Dragoon Regiment to watch the road to Gorodetschna. He positioned the Vladimir Infantry Regiment to watch the crossing at Poddoubny and moved the rest of his army to face the Saxons. Dnieper, Kostroma, and Tambov Infantry Regiments formed a line with the 28th Jagers on their left wing linking them to the Vladimir Infantry Regiment. On their right were the twenty-four 6pdr guns of Light Batteries #12 and #34. The Starodoub and Taganrog Dragoon Regiments formed behind them in echelon to the left.

Tormassov ordered Generallieutenant Markoff's corps—Nacheburg, Koslov, and Vitebsk Infantry Regiments, 10th Jagers, four squadrons of the Tartar Uhlan Regiment, six 12pdr guns of Position Battery #15—to turn about and face the Saxons. Under heavy Saxon artillery fire, Markoff moved his forces to the ridge of hills that ran between the village of Poddoubny and the village of Zavnice so that they faced the Saxons. To his right Kamenski extended his forces—Dnieper, Kostroma, Tambov Infantry Regiments, and 22nd Jagers—to the river.

To the south of Markoff, General Lambert deployed his forces—the Kourin Infantry Regiment, 14th Jagers, Alexandria Hussar Regiment, and six guns. Markoff formed his forces into two lines with the Tartar Uhlan Regiment forming the link with Lambert. The cossacks and kalmucks were posted further to Lambert's left as was the Pavlovgrad Hussar Regiment.

While the Russians and Saxons raced to extend their flanks towards Zavnice, a heavy battle began at the critical junction of Sahr's brigade and the Austrians on the far side of the river. For an hour the Austrians and Saxons were subjected to heavy Russian artillery fire. The Alvinzi Infantry Regiment lost ninety men to this fire. Sahr's forces were repeatedly charged by the Russian dragoons, but the support of the Austrian artillery on the far bank forced them back. The 2nd Light Infantry formed a line with the von Speigel and von Anger Grenadier battalions in square on either flank. Part of the 2nd Light Infantry was formed in skirmish order before them.

The 6th company of the 2nd Light Infantry was charged by the dragoons and formed klumpen (small knots of men sometimes known as "hasty squares") and bravely fought off the Russian dragoons with the support of the 2nd company. The 2nd Light Infantry lost 7 officers and 260 men during these attacks.

The Russian cavalry near Zavnice continually charged the Saxons, especially Le Coq's 21st Division, on whose right was all the Saxon cavalry. The first major Russian cavalry attack consisted principally of ten squadrons of cossacks and two dragoon regiments. They struck Zechmeister's brigade. Zechmeister faced them frontally with the Polenz Chevauléger Regiment and a few squadrons of the hussars, while he sent the Hohenzollern Chevauxléger Regiment into their flank, taking 150 prisoners.

Reynier ordered the Austrian chevauxlégers and Polenz Chevauxlégers to move against the Cherechev-Kobrin road and gain the Russian left flank. This maneuver was countered by the Pavlograd and Alexandria Hussar Regiments, who drove them back.

During the evening, as the battle slackened, Sahr's brigade renewed its attack on the Russian right, supported by the Alvinzi Infantry Regiment, the skirmishers of Le Coq's 21st Division, and 1/Collerado Mansfield Regiment. This Austrian battalion was positioned on the far side of the river. It crossed through the swamp and pushed forward against the Russian flank with bayonets, driving back the Russian infantry. Its advance was stopped by the threat of attack by the Russian cavalry. It was forced back to the edge of the swamp where it was supported by 2/Collerado Mansfield Regiment, which had also crossed the river. The Hiller Infantry Regiment moved up too, but did not cross the swamp. It had support from the Austrian artillery on the far bank.

Because of the threatening cavalry, the Alvinzi Infantry Regiment, also advancing to support the 1/Collerado Mansfield Regiment, formed bataillonmasse and continued to advance. General Frelich moved to support them with the Blankenstein and Kaiser Hussar Regiments. Further support came from the half-battery of Lieutenant Aust, which fired on the Russian left flank. Despite the ardor of the Russian attack, they were driven back after failing to dislodge the Austrians. Night began to fall, and the battle died out.

Before Gorodetschna, at about 5:00 P.M., General Frimont, who commanded the force watching the original Russian positions across the river from Gorodetschna, resolved to attack the Russians before him. To do this he established a 6pdr battery which directed its fire on them. He had noticed the slow drawing off of forces facing him across the river. When they did not respond to his artillery fire he advanced a Grenz infantry battalion, a battalion of the Beaulieu Infantry, and three divisions of cavalry into Gorodetschna, to support the 6pdr battery.

This alarmed the Russians, who responded by placing four battalions and eight guns by the Gorodetschna post office, three divisions of cavalry and eight more guns on the right, and, near the swamp, a further three divisions of cavalry. Behind them Frimont saw masses of infantry on the sandy hills and decided that the position was too strong to attack. About the time he withdrew, night was falling and the battle died down.

Tormassov was reinforced by the 13,000 men he had been expecting, but he had not engaged more than eighteen battalions and forty-eight squadrons of his total force of thirty-nine battalions and sixty-six squadrons. He decided that his position was too dangerous to continue to hold. Once night fell, he began to withdraw. He had lost about 4,000 men hors de combat and 500 prisoners. The Austrians had lost 2,000 men hors de combat and the Saxons lost 3 officers and 166 men dead, 16 officers and 644 men wounded, and 1 officer and 5 men missing. In addition the Saxons lost five guns, three of them from the von Roth horse battery, which were destroyed in the artillery duels during the day.

Russian Withdrawal

On 13 August Reynier advanced to renew his effort on the Russian left only to find their rear guard under General Count Lambert. The Russians fell back behind Mouk Navelsa and the allies occupied Kobrin without resistance.

On 15 August the Austro-Saxons attacked the Russian rear guard without serious effect near Novo Selki and again the next day at Divin. By the 17th the Russians reached Samary without opposition.

Tormassov reached Ratno on the 17th with detachments of Prince Khowanshoi's and Generalmajor Tschlapitz' forces. On the same day he learned of Admiral Tchichagov's approach after the conclusion of peace with Turkey. He determined to retrace his steps and moved back to establish his army on the Styr River. Schwarzenberg also heard of Admiral Tchichagov's approach and stopped his pursuit at the Styr.

The effect of this action, though technically a Russian failure, was to draw Schwarzenberg away from the main army and its ordered junction with Davout. It also prevented many of the Polish troops in the Grand Duchy of Warsaw from being sent to the rear areas of the main French army to support its operations. Instead they were tied to garrison duties in the Grand Duchy of Warsaw.

Northern Operations

To the extreme north of Oudinot and St. Cyr, Marshal Macdonald marched on Riga with his X Corps. When Barclay evacuated the Russian camp at Drissa, Wittgenstein was left in Pokemtsy with about 25,000 men, exclusive of the Riga garrison. He was charged with defending Riga and Pskof. While Wittgenstein maneuvered with his forces against Oudinot, Macdonald moved on Riga. Macdonald left Rossieny on 4 July and occupied the cities of Mitau, Bransk, and Jacobstadt with his Prussian forces.

The governor of Riga, General Essen, had long been preparing his city for siege. He had torn down the suburbs of the city to give the fortress a clear field of fire as well as to prevent the French from approaching the fortress unseen. In addition, every possible reinforcement had been added to the garrison. To strengthen his position, Essen dispatched General Lewis with several infantry battalions, a large artillery force, an uhlan regiment, some cossacks, and a large force of dragoons to occupy Eckau and the neighborhood of Bouske.

The Prussians of General Grawart were positioned between Mitau and Riga. Macdonald had his headquarters in Jacobstadt, and the Russian forces moving on Eckau threatened to cut the communications between Grawart and Macdonald. To prevent this possibility, Grawart moved to attack them with five battalions before they could accumulate sufficient forces to actually cut his communications. Grawart hoped to push the Russians back to Riga.

The Battle of Eckau

On the morning of 18 July, several small detachments of Prussian hussars were observed by the Russians as they reconnoitered the Russian positions. The Russian uhlan regiment posted there drove them off and captured a few prisoners. The appearance of the Prussian forces alarmed the Russians, and they leapt to arms. They prepared to receive the pending Prussian attack. One Prussian column moved from the vicinity of Ranken and, covered by the forces of General Kleist (three battalions and six squadrons), moved on to the left. Kleist seemed determined to take possession of the ground occupied by the Russians. A second Prussian column positioned itself on the main road leading to Eckau and moved towards the Prussian right and center.

The Prussian advance did not shake the Russians, who coolly awaited its arrival. As the Prussians closed, their left column was swept with heavy artillery fire from a strong battery on the heights that covered the Russian right flank. At the same moment the Prussian cavalry moved forward to charge the Russian uhlans, who were stationed near the entrance of a narrow defile. They moved to prevent the Russians from striking the Prussian infantry.

The cannonade caused heavy casualties on the advancing Prussian infantry. Kleist thought it necessary to respond to this by falling on the Russian left, but his initial assault failed. Kleist rallied his forces and sent them back repeatedly.

General Lewis found his right heavily pressed by the Prussians, who had just reinforced their attack. He was obliged to withdraw towards Riga and assume a new defensive position. The losses from this battle were not particularly high. The Russians lost about 600 men hors de combat, and the Prussians lost about the same number of men.

Northern Stalemate

After this clash, the forces of both sides settled down for nearly a month without any action. The French forces near Schlock received reinforcements and reports that the siege train of heavy artillery from Danzig for the siege operations against Riga had reached Marshal Macdonald. Essen learned that another French corps was advancing from Germany to assist Macdonald in his siege of Riga. Essen felt that if this force should arrive before the Prussians were defeated, he would be obliged to fight with terribly disadvantageous numbers. He resolved to lessen this by attempting to drive the Prussians back to Mittau and the opposite bank of the Aa River.

The Prussians were strongly placed. Their right was a short distance from the village of Eckau and ran across the main road near Draken, which was also occupied by the Prussians. The Prussians had further strengthened their position by digging earthworks that were well posted with artillery. The Prussian center was flanked on the left by the Mouss, a branch of the Aa. There was a large force placed between these positions and the Babite Lake.

General Essen decided that the Prussian right was the most vulnerable point in the Prussian line and directed his efforts against it. He ordered a brigade under General Viliamov to make a false attack on the Prussian center in an effort to draw off their reserves. Meanwhile he directed six British gunboats, ten Russian gunboats, and three bombards filled with troops from Dinamunde, under Admiral von Möller, to descend on Schlock. They were to land on the Prussian flank and rear.

Battle of Dahlenkirchen

On 22 August the Russians launched their attack. A furious assault began. The Russians landed their troops and sent Viliamov's brigade forward against their center. The Prussian left was swept from their entrenchments at bayonet point. The Russians lost control in the excitement of dislodging the Prussians and pursued them headlong towards the Prussian rear only to find a large body of Prussian cavalry awaiting them. The Prussian cavalry charged them before they were able to reform, and the Russians suffered severe casualties. Despite the heavy losses and the impact of the charge, the Russians succeeded in holding the Prussian earthworks.

While the Russians held off the Prussian cavalry, the Prussian infantry rallied. On the Prussian right, which had held, an eight-gun horse battery moved forward at General Grawart's order and unlimbered to pour heavy fire into the Russians. Despite this, the Prussian position was not strong enough, and they were forced to withdraw. The withdrawal of the Prussian right was followed shortly by the now unsupported Prussian center. The center had never been seriously engaged by Viliamov, and its withdrawal was not difficult.

At the moment of his success General Essen learned that only six of the gunboats under Razvozov had been able to move past Schlock and make the landing. This failure to pass Schlock prevented Essen's designs on the Prussian right. Though he did not destroy the Prussians, Essen had dislodged them from their positions and inflicted a serious loss on them. The Prussians withdrew to Mittau.

The Prussians had had about 1,500 men and a single battery under Oberst von Horn, while the Russians had attacked with twelve battalions and six squadrons, about 6,000 men total. The Russians inflicted about 800 casualties and suffered about 600 casualties.

The most unusual aspect of this battle was the combined army and naval operations. Though there was no official treaty ending hostilities between the Russians and English, there had been several instances of similar cooperation between Russian and British forces since 20 July. Admiral von Möller reported to General Essen that "there were six English vessels, under the command of Captain Stuart, detached up the River Aa, while ten of our (Russian) gunboats landed a thousand troops to attack the enemy, who occupied the town of Schlock and its environs."

Stalemate Resumes

After 23 August General Essen's forces became stationary, not engaging in any enterprise of note. His positions did not change significantly from those they assumed after their victory at Schlock. There was uninterrupted communication between Essen and Wittgenstein during this period.

Essen was informed that considerable portions of the division facing him had fallen back from Mittau, leaving only a very small garrison in the city. He lost no time in making preparations to seize the city, which he knew to be an intermediate depot for the Prussians. In addition, their artillery park and engineering park were in Ruenthal and Borsmunde, situated near the Aa River, about a mile apart and three short days' march from Riga.

Though the engineering park was of little value, the siege train contained the 130 guns necessary for the assault on Riga. The season was too advanced to undertake the siege, so the forces had been held back rather than be exposed to unnecessary risk. The train had come under Macdonald's command on 9 July and moved from Koenigsberg on the 12th. It had moved forward only slowly, passing Tilsit on 30 July and finally reaching Ruenthal on 30 August.

On 26 September Steingell and his Finnish corps joined General Lewis and advanced on Eckau with about 16,000 men. Eckau was only lightly held. Yorck was informed of Steingell's move and positioned Kleist before Mittau. He ordered Hunerbein to join him and to assume a position near Eckau with the bulk of his forces.

On the following day, before Hunerbein arrived, Yorck decided to fix his left so as to cover the park and establish himself behind the Aa on the heights of Ruenthal. He was unable to cover both the park and Mittau, so he ordered Kleist to join him as quickly as possible.

Steingell occupied Bausk with a small detachment (two infantry regiments) and took up a position opposite Yorck on the Aa. His force consisted of the Nizov Infantry Regiment and a battery of twelve guns. These positions remained unchanged until Kleist joined Yorck.

That junction occurred on 29 September, and Hunerbein was only a few miles from Bausk. Yorck decided to assume the offensive and had a bridge constructed over the Aa at Mesoten. Yorck began to move his infantry across at 1:00 P.M. His cavalry and artillery moved across at a ford a short distance away. Yorck's advanced guard quickly pushed back the Russian advanced parties, but stopped when they encountered Steingell's main body, which advanced against them. Steingell crossed below Mesoten, by Zemal, and moved on Grafenthal. Kleist was posted there and pushed the Russians back to the Aa.

While this was going on, General Essen moved on Mittau down the river in his gunboats and, with the support of 3,000 men sent by Steingell, seized Mittau on the 29th with little opposition. Here he captured 50 effective soldiers, 150 invalids, four brass guns, and a vast collection of provisions, including furs that had been requisitioned from Courland. These furs were a significant capture in this area, which was inclined to very harsh winters.

On 30 September Yorck learned that Hunerbein had retaken Bausk. He continued his offensive movements and attacked the Russians on both banks of the Aa. The Russians on the left bank of the Aa retired on Mittau and those on the right fell back to Olai. Yorck did not pursue them into the cities, but on 1 October, Steingell and Essen resumed their withdrawal and moved into Riga. This latest series of engagements had cost the Russians about 1,500 dead and wounded and about 2,500 prisoners. The Prussians lost about 900 dead and wounded and 350 prisoners.

Macdonald had left a feeble detachment in Dinaburg and moved the bulk of his forces on 30 September to join Yorck. By the time he arrived, the situation had once again returned to a state of lethargic inactivity.

Steingell decided that he did not wish to be closed into Riga and moved south to join Wittgenstein near Drissa on 10 October.

Macdonald established his headquarters near Stalgen, on the left bank of the Aa, between Bausk and Mittau. Immediately after his arrival he pulled Grandjean's division back to Illuks, a day's march from Dinaburg. He retained Hunerbein's brigade, with eight battalions, in its last position. Yorck remained near the Baltic and Eckau with a Polish brigade, a Prussian brigade, and six squadrons of Prussian cavalry. His right extended to Frederickstadt, and his reserves were in Mittau, Stalgen, and Anenburg. Jacobstadt also received a small garrison.

The Russians occupied Olai, Baldon, and Niegut. Macdonald decided not to surrender his advantages to the Riga garrison. The countryside had been heavily foraged and he could not afford to move his forces about the countryside to forage further. As a result he chose to hold his positions strongly.

During the month of October Macdonald ordered the siege train returned to Germany, but his forces remained in their siege positions around Riga for the entire month.

Chapter IX

Failure at Smolensk

On 16 July Murat reported Russian movements that appeared to be the attack for which Napoleon was longing. Napoleon responded by recalling the Guard and VI Corps, which he had sent to Bloubokie in the hopes of striking any Russian advance out of Drissa, to his south.

On the 19th, when the hoped-for Russian attack did not materialize and Murat reported that the Russians were evacuating Drissa and destroying the material that they could not take with them, Napoleon reacted swiftly. He thought that the Russians would move on Polotsk and effect a junction with Bagration. Instead, he discovered they were moving on Vitebsk. Napoleon responded by redirecting his troops to move from Kamen to Biechenkovski on the 21st. They arrived there on the 24th. Davout's battle at Saltanovka, near Mohilev, had denied Bagration the use of that road and redirected his movement. On the 24th, near Biechenkovski, a number of Russian stragglers were captured. These men informed Napoleon that Barclay was definitely in Vitebsk, on the left bank of the Dvina.

The Battle of Ostrovno

On 25 July Murat proceeded towards Ostrovno with his cavalry. At approximately 6:00 A.M., about three miles from Ostrovno, the French 8th Hussar Regiment encountered two squadrons of the Russian Guard Hussar Regiment and eight 6pdr guns of Horse Battery #7. This was Ostermann's advanced guard. The Russian cavalry, supported by the

artillery, drove the 8th Hussar Regiment back on the rest of Pire's 4th
Light Cavalry Brigade. The 8th Hussars joined the 16th Chasseur à
Cheval Regiment. They counterattacked, capturing the eight guns and
150 prisoners.

Ostermann fell back to await the arrival of the Russian infantry
that was following him and directed the Soum Hussar Regiment to attack
Pire. They quickly found themselves facing Murat's advanced guard,
the I Reserve Cavalry Corps under General Nansouty. General St. Germain
and two battalions of infantry advanced against the Russians, while all
of the corps horse artillery was formed into a single battery to play on
the Russians. When they arrived, Ostermann deployed Tchoglokov's
11th Division on both sides of the main road, and Bakhmetieff's 23rd
Division formed itself in battalion columns as a second line behind him.
Murat estimated the total force to be seven or eight battalions.

Murat advanced St. Germain's division, which was formed by brigades and supported by Bruyère's division. A heavy cannonade developed
and the Ingremannland Dragoon Regiment moved to take the French in
the right flank.

The French countered this by moving the 15th Light Brigade to
face them. This brigade consisted of two Polish uhlan regiments and
the combined Prussian Hussar Regiment. The brigade charged and drove
the Russians back, taking 200 prisoners. At the same time Ornano's
12th and 13th Light Brigades charged along the main road, only to be
thrown back by the Russian infantry's defensive fire.

Murat sent two battalions of the 8th Légère Regiment into the woods
on his left to support the 1st Cuirassier Brigade. The Russians responded
by sending three battalions to attack them. The Russian advance was
stopped by the 9th Polish Uhlans and the Prussian Combined Hussar
Regiment.

Ostermann attempted to force the French to retreat by threatening
their right, but the battalion he sent was struck by the 9th Polish Uhlan
Regiment supported by two squadrons of the Prussian Hussars and a
brigade of cuirassiers. A further 200 prisoners were captured, and the
Russians withdrew.

At the same time, two other Russian battalions moved against the
French right and were attacked by the 6th and 8th Polish Uhlans of the
15th Light Brigade, leaving 200 Russian dead and 150 wounded behind
them.

Murat's continued attacks forced Ostermann's infantry back into the woods. Murat soon realized that it was fruitless to attempt to attack them and backed off his cavalry. He had possession of the ground where the initial attack on the 8th Hussar Regiment had occurred. He positioned Bruyère's 1st Light Division and St. Germain's 1st Cuirassier Division where they could hold that position and watch the Russians.

As the French rallied and prepared their next attack they were reinforced by the arrival of Delzon's 13th Infantry Division, from Eugène's IV Corps. This division took position on the heights in time to stop an advance by the Russians. Two battalions of the 8th Légère Regiment stopped repeated attacks by the Russians.

Faced with this overpowering force, Ostermann had no alternative but to withdraw. This he did in good order, and the engagement broke off. He withdrew to favorable positions before Ostrovno.

As a serious battle seemed to be developing, the divisions of Morand, Friant, and Gudin, part of I Corps, III Corps, Sebastiani's division (then posted on the right bank of the Dvina), the 2nd and 4th Cuirassier Divisions from the II Reserve Cavalry Corps, as well as General Montbrun with the three regiments of Bavarian cavalry received orders from Napoleon to congregate on the scene.

Ostermann's new position was well chosen and commanded the ground in front of it. It overlooked all the roads that approached Ostrovno. The city stood astride the main road and was flanked by the Dvina River on the right, a ravine on its front, and a thick woods on the left. Ostermann was positioned so that he had communication with the magazines that supplied him as well as with Vitebsk, the regional capital. Ostermann intended to defend this city.

That evening Murat was joined by the remainder of Eugène's IV Corps. Ostermann was also reinforced by the 3rd Cavalry Corps and by Konovnitzin's 3rd Division. At 10:00 A.M. Murat sent Delzon's division forward against Konovnitzin's division, which was in a strong position behind the ravine. Konovnitzin's left wing was fixed in a forest that bordered the left of the battlefield.

Murat sent a strong reconnaissance against them, consisting of the French advanced guard and two battalions of the 8th Légère Regiment. The Russian infantry fire drove back the French cavalry, but the Russian advance was stopped by the French infantry supporting them.

Delzon sent the 84th Line Regiment in column by divisions under General Huard against the Russian right, while the 92nd Line and the 1st Provisional Croatian Infantry Regiment were directed to enter the heavy woods on the Russian left. The French artillery of Danthouard formed on their center, while the 106th Line Infantry Regiment and Nansouty's cavalry and artillery remained as a general reserve behind the ravine. The difficulties in pushing the Russians out of the woods slowed Huard's advance. He attempted twice to push Konovnitzin's division back, but the Russian reserve deployed to counter his thrust.

The Russians struck back. The 8th Légère and 84th Line Regiments vainly tried to hold them back. Their line gradually diminished, littering the ground in front of their position with their dead and the plain behind them with their retiring wounded. The stream of wounded was joined by others who abandoned their ranks. This trickle of deserters grew into a stream and eventually developed into a rout. The French artillery, perceiving itself abandoned, also began to retire, resulting in a general rout.

Reportedly, Murat saw this and darted forward, placing himself in front of the 8th Polish Uhlan Regiment. He excited them with his words and actions, though they were already enraged by the sight of the advancing Russians. Murat then ordered them forward. He had, apparently, only wished to stimulate them and send them against the Russians. He had no intention of throwing himself with them into the midst of a melee, from which he could neither see nor command, but the Poles were already crouched and condensed behind him. The charging cavalry covered the width of the field completely and pushed Murat before them. He could neither detach himself from them nor stop. He had no recourse but to charge in front of the regiment, where he had stationed himself to harangue them. Now, trapped, he submitted himself with some grace to what was, at best, an uncomfortable position.

At the same time, General Danthouard ran to his artillery men while General Girardin ran to his reserve, two battalions of the 106th Line Regiment. These generals rallied their forces and directed them against the Russian position. The 84th Line and Croatians, supported by the two battalions of the 106th, struck the Russians, reestablished their original positions, and captured two guns. This movement was seconded by General Roussel leading the 92nd Line Regiment in column from the forest.

On the Russian left, General Pire led the 4th Light Cavalry Brigade around the Russian flank. The Russians continued to hold the thick forest which broke the battlefield in two. The 92nd Line Infantry, intimidated by the heavy fire issuing from the forest, froze in its position, unable to advance or withdraw. Generals Belliard and Roussel moved to them and led them forward. They advanced into and seized the forest.

This success turned the strong Russian column that had advanced against the French right. Murat, perceiving this and having survived his charge with the Polish uhlans, drew his sword and exclaimed, "Let the bravest follow me!" The Russians saw the danger in their exposed situation and began to withdraw. They quickly plunged into the forest and intervening ravines which slowed Murat's cavalry sufficiently to permit their escape.

After their furious battle and their previous experience with Russians in the woods, Eugène and Murat were hesitant to commit themselves once again to a battle in the forests. Napoleon arrived at this time and took over tactical command of the battle. He quickly gave orders, and the woods that had stopped Eugène and Murat were swept end to end. That evening the residents of Vitebsk could see the French light troops emerging from the forests around the city.

The retreating Russians were reinforced by Tuchkov's remaining division, the grenadier division under Strogonoff which arrived at Dobrieka at about 5:00 P.M.

The battle had been exhausting and the movement through the woods had badly disordered the French. As night fell they stopped to reorganize and prepare for the night. Opposite the French lines, the skies were lit with the multitude of bivouac fires that marked the Russian positions. They had lost 2,500 men hors de combat during the battle, while the French lost 3,000 and about 300 prisoners.

On the dawn of 27 July, Napoleon appeared at the French advanced posts. In the growing light he saw the Russian army encamped on the elevated plain that commanded the approach to Vitebsk. The Lucizza River formed a deep channel that divided the French and Russian positions. Pahlen's 3rd Cavalry Corps, eight battalions of infantry, and two pulks of cossacks had replaced Ostermann and Konovnitzin in front of Vitebsk. The infantry was centered on the main road, while the cavalry was stationed on the right in a double line supported by the Dvina.

The Russian position was not squarely opposite the French position, but to their left. This was because they had changed their facing to conform to the course of the river.

General Pire's brigade was directed to the right to reconnoiter the terrain. To defend the passage of the French, a twelve-gun battery was established to the left of the road on a ridge overlooking the plain.

The French forces crossed a narrow bridge over a ravine and were obliged to deploy by a change of front to the left, with their right wing foremost, in order to preserve the support of the river on that side. General Broussier's division led the advance formed in square because of the threatening Russian cavalry. Delzon's division followed behind to form the second line. On the banks of this ravine, near the bridge and to the left of the main road, was a small hillock which had already attracted Napoleon's notice. From this vantage point Napoleon could observe both armies, yet not be in the middle of the battle.

The 14th Division, part of Eugène's IV Corps, under General Broussier, sent forward the 200 Parisian voltigeurs forming the three companies of voltigeurs of the 9th Line and the 18th Légère Regiment commanded by General de brigade Sivary. They pushed forward on the left, passing in front of the entire Russian cavalry force. They pushed the Russians out of a small village and took up a position where their flank was secured on the Dvina. The 16th Chasseur à Cheval Regiment followed them with a battery of horse artillery. The Russians coolly allowed the French to advance and permitted them to prepare to attack.

As the 16th Chasseurs prepared themselves and reorganized after traversing the broken terrain, they were attacked by the cossacks opposite them. They stood fast and unsuccessfully attempted to break the Russians' charge with carbine fire. They held their fire until the Russians were thirty paces from them and then fired a volley. Despite the effect of the French fire, the Russians closed with them and drove them back in disorder.

In their haste to escape, the 16th Chasseurs became trapped in the ravine. Murat reacted by drawing his saber and leading the sixty officers of his suite into the melee. During the course of this melee, one officer barely deflected a blow aimed by a cossack at Murat. The remains of the 16th Chasseurs rallied behind the 53rd Line Regiment, part of General Broussier's division, which had hastily formed squares in echelon. The fire of the 53rd drove the Russian cossacks back, saving the French artillery that was about to fall into the Russians' hands. The Russian cavalry charged the squares repeatedly, but were eventually driven back.

The charge of the Russian cossacks carried them to the foot of Napoleon's observation post on the hill. Some of the Chasseurs à Cheval de la Garde, posted to protect Napoleon, drove off a few aggressive cossacks with a few well-aimed shots. The Russian cossacks withdrew and passed directly over the voltigeurs of the 18th Légère Regiment. These men had escaped attention during the cavalry battle, but now became the center of attention. All eyes were locked on them as they disappeared in the midst of the cossacks. Only the voltigeurs knew that they were not lost. Their captains had fought their way across the ground, heavily cut by ravines and thickets bordering the Dvina. There the voltigeurs reunited, urged on by their officers and the danger that stalked them. In this emergency each looked to his neighbor for support, knowing that if one failed, all would be lost. They skillfully turned the ground to their benefit. The Russians became entangled in the brush and other obstructions as the voltigeurs calmly shot them down. As each fell, his body and that of his horse further encumbered the ground, making the Russian approach increasingly difficult. They soon lost heart and withdrew, to the delight of the French army.

Meanwhile, the rest of IV Corps and Murat's cavalry, followed by the three divisions of I Corps under the command of Count Lobau, attacked the main road and the woods on the right of the Russian line. Delzon's division was ordered to march parallel along the heights and to its right, to move rapidly on the Lucizza River and turn the enemy's rear in an effort to bar their escape towards Vitebsk. In this effort he was supported by a brigade of light cavalry and a cuirassier division. Once in place, their advance begun, Broussier's division attacked a small village defended by four battalions and ten guns. The village was taken and the defending Russians driven back.

This retreat was the signal for the Russian cavalry to begin withdrawing. The Russian vanguard retreated suddenly behind the ravine of the Lucizza River to avoid being pinned against it by the French advance. The result was that the entire Russian army was collected on the far bank of the Lucizza River and presented a united body of twenty-two battalions and sixty-four squadrons, about 20,000 men, to the attacking French.

The determined Russians had assumed a strong position in front of Vitebsk, the regional capital. The probability of a determined defense was high as a result. Napoleon assumed that they would feel their position was strong enough and their duty clear enough to warrant a serious defense. At 11:00 A.M. Napoleon ordered the French attack to cease in order to permit them to reorganize and prepare for the decisive battle expected on the next day. Napoleon spent the rest of the day studying the battlefield and awaiting the arrival of further reinforcements.

Generallieutenant Konovnitzin believed Bagration to be near Orsha and had resolved to fight until he was joined by Bagration. When he had learned that Bagration had retreated via Novoi-Bickov towards Smolensk, he quickly changed his mind, and on the morning of 28 July, the French awoke to find that the Russians had disappeared. The maneuver of Vitebsk ended in failure for the French when the Russians effected their second escape from Napoleon's traps. They left 2,700 dead and wounded and 1,100 prisoners behind them, but Barclay's forces had not been brought to battle.

The Advance Resumes

The French resumed their advance on the 29th. As they arrived in Sourai, Eugène was informed that a Russian convoy was passing nearby. He sent Colonel Banco, commander of the 2nd Italian Chasseur à Cheval Regiment, with 200 men to pursue this convoy. After marching twenty miles, Banco arrived at Veliz at the same moment the convoy departed from the far side of the village. Banco's forces charged as soon as they were within range, charging five times, but being repulsed by a force of infantry and cavalry that was their superior. Despite their initial failures, the Italians eventually prevailed. They took 500 prisoners and the abandoned Russian baggage. The Italian casualties were light in view of the fury of their attacks.

The French probed the roads tentatively, but for eight days Napoleon remained camped before Vitebsk to reorganize his army and allow the stragglers to catch up. During this reorganization, Junot assumed command of the Westphalian VIII corps, formally replacing Jérôme.

Before this second halt, Junot, Eugène, and Davout rejoined the main body with their forces. Davout rejoined on the 21st near Dubrovna, and Eugène joined it on the 24th near Briszikova. The VIII Corps joined on 4 August near Orsha.

Poniatowski and the Polish V Corps remained in Mohilev until 8 August, when he detached Latour-Maubourg with the IV Cavalry Corps and Dombrowski's division to move against General Hertel in Bobruisk. Latour-Maubourg eventually returned to the main body, but Dombrowski remained behind to cover Minsk.

The French had suffered considerably from their marches, the weather, and the occasional combat. Their numbers had also been reduced by the detachments of troops to form garrisons in the various strategic cities that the French had taken as they advanced. The size superiority Napoleon had enjoyed over Barclay was considerably diminished, and by 3 August his main army consisted of 185,000 men.

Of the original 375,000 men in the main army, 90,000 had been detached under St. Cyr, Oudinot, Latour-Maubourg, and Reynier. This should have left about 285,000 in the central army, but there was a deficit of 100,000 men which was a clear loss. The 185,000 remaining men were distributed between Murat and Ney, who were in Rudnia, Count Lobau's three divisions in Babinovicki, the Guard in Vitebsk, Eugène in Surasch and Welisch, and Davout and Junot on the left bank of the Dnieper.

Bagration arrived in Smolensk on 4 August. He immediately began to poison the political waters with lies about Barclay's true loyalties. Barclay was also being pressured by Alexander to assume the offensive and decided on 6 August to attack Napoleon. Though resolved to attack, Barclay was ignorant of the positions of Napoleon's forces. He intended to have the combined Russian armies advance on Rudnia, turn Eugène's flank and destroy his corps, then engage the rest of the French as they came to Eugène's aid.

Napoleon had expected some offensive Russian action and had moved Macdonald across the Dvina to assist Oudinot. He then ordered Oudinot and St. Cyr to remain on the offensive, to keep Wittgenstein from coming to Barclay's assistance. Napoleon then evolved what is known as the Maneuver of Smolensk, designed to place the Grande Armée in the rear of the Russian army, cut them off from Moscow, and force them into a decisive battle.

The final plans were not set when Barclay began his advance on Rudnia and Poryeche on the 7th. On 8 August Platov's cossack screen contacted the II Cavalry Corps. General Sebastiani had 3,000 cavalry, including Beurman's 14th Light Cavalry Brigade from III Corps, the 24th Légère Regiment, and the Württemberg horse artillery. He was engaged by the Russians near Inkovo and received a severe handling from Platov's forces, losing about 300 men hors de combat and a further 300 prisoners. During the night of 7–8 August, Barclay was misinformed that Eugène had two corps at Poryeche. He immediately suspected a trap and faced half of his army north, directing Bagration to move to Vidra. Platov had continued east, not having received orders since his battle at Inkovo. At long last, however, Barclay realized this, and Platov was recalled to cooperate with him in his proposed attack on Eugène.

Bagration feared that Davout might maneuver against the Russian left and became more insolent and openly insubordinate. He announced that his troops were sick and starving, then marched to Smolensk despite Barclay's orders. Barclay permitted this without too much argument and arranged his positions to account for Bagration's departure.

On 11 August Barclay remained stationary as his cavalry ineffectually engaged Murat's outposts. On the 12th he learned that Poryeche had been evacuated and ordered Platov to determine the direction of the French movements. Barclay then realized that 15 August was Napoleon's birthday and feared that it might be celebrated by a major French attack. He responded by retreating his army down the Vitebsk-Smolensk road. He ordered Bagration to send his light troops to Katan and mass the rest of his army behind Barclay's left.

Fearing a Russian attack, Napoleon's reaction to Inkovo was to stop his preparations for the move on Smolensk. Instead he chose to concentrate his army near Lyosno, around the III Corps, in preparation for battle. By the 10th, Barclay's irresolute actions convinced Napoleon that Barclay was not going to attack. He immediately stopped his concentration and reverted to his original plan of a move on Smolensk.

Napoleon ordered Davout to cross the Dnieper River at Rosasna, Junot to go to Romanovo, and Murat, Ney, and Eugène to move south, screened by Sebastiani's cavalry. Napoleon moved on instinct, not knowing Barclay's precise position. He intended to form a "bataillon carré" with his army and launch it across the Dnieper on a fifteen-mile front, through Orsha and Rosasna, as secretly as possible. There were to be two columns. The Rosasna column under Napoleon's personal command was to consist of Murat's cavalry, the Guard, III Corps, and IV Corps. The second Orsha column, under Davout, was to consist of I, V, and VIII Corps. As a diversion, Latour-Maubourg's cavalry was to attack further down the Dnieper. Once this massive formation crossed the Dnieper it was to advance along the left bank of the Dnieper, eastwards towards the Smolensk-Moscow road, which it was to cut. From there it would drive the remains of the Russian forces to the north.

In support of these carefully planned operations, Napoleon built up his communications by fortifying Vitebsk and garrisoning it with 3,800 men: the Flanker-Chasseurs, 1/1st Vistula Regiment, and a Hessian battalion. This garrison eventually grew to 7,000 men as various "bataillons de marche" arrived. Napoleon intended to redirect his operations once

Barclay realized his maneuver. Napoleon's communications would pass through Orsha and on to Vilna by way of Birisov and Minsk.

Napoleon began his concentrations for his maneuver. With a deep cavalry screen, his movements remained unknown to Barclay. During the night of 13–14 August, General Elbe erected four pontoon bridges over the Dnieper near Rosasna, and the French began to pour over them. By daylight 175,000 men had crossed and were advancing on Smolensk. The screen was formed by the cavalry of Grouchy, Nansouty, and Montbrun.

The Battle of Krasnoe

By 2:30 P.M. the leading elements of the French had reached Krasnoe, where they encountered the first Russian troops. Barclay had stationed Generalmajor Neverovski's 27th Division, some 7,200 infantry, three cossack pulks, the Polish Uhlan Regiment, and the Kharkov Dragoon Regiment, totaling 1,500 cavalry. In addition, Neverovski had a position battery commanded by Colonel Apouchkin. Barclay's decision to post him on the main road to Smolensk proved to be a very wise decision.

The ground was unequal, but bare and very suitable for cavalry. Murat took possession of the ground, but the bridges to Krasnoe were broken. The French cavalry was forced to move to the left and cross at a bad ford some distance from the main forces. Once the cavalry was across the river they found Neverovski ready to receive them. Realizing the potential for a smashing victory, the French cavalry launched a quick attack. Though they acted hastily and lost time, they immediately dispersed the Russian cavalry.

Neverovski had detached the 49th Jagers and two guns into Krasnoe and the 50th Jagers and the cossacks at full speed to Korythnia, halfway to Smolensk, where they were to take up position and check any further French advance should they be forced to retreat. Facing Neverovski's nine battalions, the Kharkov Dragoons, and ten guns was all of Murat's cavalry and Ney's infantry.

The initial French advance was not certain. Grouchy led with Chastel's light cavalry and Delahoussaye's dragoons on the left. The light cavalry of I and II Corps, with the 24th Légère Regiment, were personally led by Marshal Ney and formed the center. Montbrun's two cuirassier divisions were on the right with Nansouty's corps behind him.

The 24th Légère attacked, supported by the entire 10th Division, and carried Krasnoe at about 3:00 P.M., chasing out the 49th Jagers and capturing the two guns posted there. The 9th Polish Uhlan Regiment pursued them over the bridge. They advanced against the Russians in good order. When the Kharkov Dragoons appeared about to charge, the Poles faced them, supported by Bordessoulle's brigade. The Kharkov Dragoons were chased back. Neverovski sent them to the rear, forming his infantry into two dense columns, and began to withdraw.

The French cavalry rapidly moved over the bridge. As soon as Murat had some squadrons across the Lossmina ravine, he threw them against the Russian rear guard, disordering it and capturing five or six more guns. Neverovski rallied his broken troops and, apparently doubting their steadiness, ordered his young recruits into one large square with some 130 yards on a face and six ranks deep. This massive square of 5,000 men continued withdrawing towards Smolensk.

As the French cavalry regiments crossed the ravine, they charged individually into the Russian square. These uncoordinated attacks were quite haphazard. Murat seemed to exercise little general control, acting more like a regimental commander than a corps commander. He rode about furiously, directing isolated charges rather than regrouping his entire command for a single, consolidated assault. In one attack the 4th Chasseurs and the 6th Polish Uhlans charged one after the other, each being repulsed in its turn.

Most of the French artillery remained behind the Lossmina, but a Württemberg battery did come into the action, showering them with cannister. Ney's infantry was unable to move up and attack the Russians, because Murat's clumsy handling of the cavalry blocked their advance.

The Russian fire was at best erratic, but the steadiness of the troops was exceptional. Though the Württemberg artillery did manage to take the square under fire, six guns were inadequate to break it.

During the advance Neverovski had one very critical moment. His column was marching through a field of ripe rye to the left of the main road. His forces suddenly encountered a stout palisade. The retreating square stopped, and being so pressed by the French, had insufficient time to make a gap in it. At this moment a Württemberg cavalry regiment penetrated into the square, only to be thrown back out.

The failure of the Württembergers gave the Russians time to clear the fence and continue their withdrawal. Neverovski moved towards a defile where Grouchy had been directed in anticipation of this move.

Murat, however, was deceived by a false report and diverted the bulk of Grouchy's cavalry towards Elnia, leaving him only about 600 horses. Grouchy directed the 8th Chasseur à Cheval Regiment, part of the 11th Light Brigade, to seize the defile, but they were too weak to hold it against Neverovski. The 6th Hussar Regiment charged the column's left, but were wholly unsuccessful. Neverovski retreated like a lion, leaving 1,500 dead and wounded, 800 prisoners, and seven lost guns behind him. The French lost 500 men.

Neverovski broke away from the French and retreated into Smolensk, where he slammed the gate shut behind him. The French lost their chance to seize Smolensk undefended. In response to Neverovski's pleas for assistance, Bagration sent the 7th Corps under General Raevsky to cover his retreat into Smolensk. Raevsky requested a cuirassier division and more explicit instructions, but after receiving neither, he marched to the southern bank of the Dnieper, near Smolensk, arriving in the early hours of the 15th.

Move into Smolensk

Barclay learned of the French offensive of Neverovski, and both he and Bagration began to retrace their steps to Smolensk. Napoleon, in contrast, ordered a surprising twenty-four-hour halt in the French advance.

Barclay's initial reaction to Napoleon's movement was that it was a retreat. He prepared to advance back to Vitebsk. He suggested to Bagration that he should move south of the Dnieper River. Bagration protested, pointing out that Smolensk, Neverovski, and Raevsky were in great danger. Bagration counterproposed a crossing to the southern bank of the Dnieper at Katan and was given authorization to do so. His actual movements were limited to sending a few cavalry squadrons to make that maneuver.

Barclay did not wish to take decisive action and limited his movements until Platov had scouted further to the west. Barclay placed the 7th Corps of General of Infantry Docturov at Bagration's disposal, while he warned the governor of Smolensk to evacuate his archives.

Nansouty and Grouchy, under Murat's direction, halted three miles short of the gates of Smolensk without discovering the presence of Raevsky's eight regiments and six batteries in Smolensk. Murat hoped for a battle and was keeping his cavalry concentrated rather than allowing them to spread out and scout the countryside for the Russians. Murat neglected to scout the southern bank of the Dnieper as a result. Montbrun received some reports of a Russian bridge near Katan. This was passed to Napoleon, who responded by sending the Guard Lancers to examine the area. Junot had lost his way, taking the wrong road, and wandered about aimlessly. Eugène and Pajol moved north along the Dnieper and made no contact with the Russians.

The Russians had become convinced that the French would approach Smolensk from the northern bank of the Dnieper and had positioned the greater part of their forces to meet a threat from that direction. The French had, however, arrived before Smolensk via the southern bank. The Russians discovered that they had been turned and hastily repositioned their forces. Czar Alexander had left his army shortly before this and had turned command of the combined armies over to Barclay with orders to defend Smolensk.

The Battle of Smolensk

After leaving Loubna, Ney moved on Smolensk and arrived before its suburbs to find a few sections of dragoons and numerous cossack pulks deployed before him. Raevsky's forces had risen to 15,000 troops and 72 guns. Raevsky knew that Barclay and Bagration were quickly closing on Smolensk and that his job was to keep the French out until they arrived. He deployed his twenty-three battalions to the west and south of the city. The 26th Division of Paskevitch was placed in the Krasnoe suburb of the city and in the ditch before the Royal Citadel. Behind the curtain, between two bastions, he positioned the Vilna Infantry Regiment, and in the cemetery to the left he placed the Odessa and Tarnopol Infantry Regiments as well as three regiments of Neverovski's 27th Division. In the Mstislavl suburb he posted eight battalions of the 12th Division. An additional brigade was posted in the Roslavl suburb as a reserve. Raevsky went on to position eighteen guns in the citadel and the remainder of his guns behind the earthen ramparts of the city's defenses. During the night he was reinforced by the arrival of the Lithuanian Uhlan Regiment and the New Russia Dragoons, which gave him twelve more squadrons.

At about 1:30 P.M. the Russian cavalry was driven back into the suburbs. The first assault on the city was made by the Württembergers on the Krasnoe suburb. Raevsky's forces were so thin that a strong attack would have broken through them. In strengthening his troops in the Krasnoe suburb, he had to shift his other forces to meet the Württemberg assault, but they too were threatened by the French. He had only two regiments in reserve when he learned that the French had penetrated the city on his left. He directed his reserve to counter this breakthrough, only to learn after they'd departed that the report was false.

Ney saw that the Royal Citadel was being denuded of troops and sent a battalion of the 46th Line Regiment to dash forward in the hope of seizing it by a coup de main. They scaled the earthen rampart and penetrated into the interior, where they engaged the garrison in a desperate battle. Raevsky and his reserve responded, driving the French back over the rampart as a second battalion of the French 46th Line arrived. The panic of the first battalion infected the second and both withdrew quickly, leaving the citadel to the Russians.

The city of Smolensk straddled both sides of the Dnieper. On the southern bank stood the Old City, which was surrounded by a massive, but decayed, wall. This wall was some 6,000 paces long, 10 feet wide and 25 feet tall. It was broken by thirty-six massive bastions that were armed with small batteries. The wall was covered by a deep ditch, a covered way, and a glacis. On the north bank, opposite the Old City, lay the St. Petersburg suburb. It was connected to the Old City by a single bridge, but the Dnieper was not very deep where it passed through the city.

The French spent the remainder of 16 August in a reconnaissance of the countryside around Smolensk. Ney stayed on the left and moved towards the Dnieper. Davout assumed a central position, and Poniatowski moved to the far right. Murat and the cavalry remained in reserve with the Guard and Eugène's IV Corps. The Westphalians of the VIII Corps were expected shortly, but Junot was still lost and leading them about the countryside.

During the night of 16–17 August, the Russian 7th Corps was relieved and reinforced by the arrival of the 6th Corps of Docturov, 7th and 24th Divisions, and by the 3rd Division of Konovnitzin. Generalmajor Neverovski's 27th Division and the 6th Jagers of the 12th Division remained in the city. This brought the total Russians in Smolensk to 20,000 men and 180 guns. They were facing 183,000 French and allies equipped with 300 guns.

At 8:00 A.M. on 17 August the Russians sortied from the Old City and engaged the French in the suburbs. Raevsky's troops had departed during the night, but had returned almost immediately to rejoin Bagration's forces that morning. They assisted Docturov's and Konovnitzin's forces, which were engaged in battle with the French. On the far side of the Dnieper, Barclay's lines remained immobile on the heights of the St. Petersburg suburbs.

A total of 12,000 Russians were posted in the front lines. On the right was Konovnitzin's 24th Division. One of his brigades was posted in the city, and the other two were in the esplanade between the Malakhov gate and the suburb. The 6th Jager Regiment was positioned to the left of the gate. Generalmajor Neverovski had his 27th Division in the Ratchevka suburb, and the Guard Jager Regiment was positioned in the city, between the city wall and the Dnieper River.

Napoleon had gone to sleep the night before with the hope of a major battle in the morning. Smolensk was a major religious and provincial capital. Napoleon was sure that the Russians would make a stand before it.

At about 4:00 A.M., on the French left flank, the Württemberg outposts (three companies of the 2nd Württemberg Regiment) before the Stasnaia suburb discommoded the Russians so much that they attacked them. Koch's brigade sent three companies of the 6th Württemberg Regiment at 4:30 and the 1/2nd Württemberg Line to support them at about 6:00 A.M. Knowing of the battle, Napoleon had directed that three battalions be sent to the left from the center at about 5:00 A.M. The two battalions of the 6th Regiment and Coronnette's battalion were selected.

This movement was supported by Stockmayer's brigade, which placed the 2nd Jäger Battalion to the right of the 2nd Württemberg Line Regiment. The remaining two battalions of the brigade were posted behind the line in column to provide support if needed. However, the fighting was inconclusive.

General of Infantry Docturov had his forces on the left bank of the Dnieper, the 3rd, 7th, and 24th Divisions, the Smolensk Infantry Regiment, the 6th Jager Regiment, and part of the 4th Cavalry Corps. He was engaged in a lively battle with the French at 8:00 A.M. He occupied the suburbs with the 7th and 24th Divisions, supported by cavalry. The latter, placed on the left bank, was later joined by the Guard Jager regiment. Docturov had placed 120 guns on the defenses to support his forces. Some of the guns were placed in the towers on the city walls.

In the center, about 8:00 A.M., the 4/ and 6/21st Line and 1/127th Line relieved the advanced posts of the 12th Line Regiment. The skirmishing between the Russians and the French was so violent that General Leclerc was obliged to engage part of his brigade.

General Belliard, tired of the uncertainty of the pending battle, led a small cavalry force off to the Dnieper and explored it for fords and Russians. He encountered and drove off a small band of cossacks above the town and discovered that the Russians were not redeploying for a major battle. He immediately informed Napoleon of this.

His hopes for a major battle dashed, Napoleon sought to send part of his army around the Russians to cut their lines of communication and force a battle. Unfortunately the cavalry he sent out to find a ford across the Dnieper went six miles and only succeeded in drowning a few horses.

The initial phase of the battle lasted until about 10:00 A.M., when the French began to slacken their artillery fire. It was fought entirely in the suburbs. The Russians were to maintain their positions in the suburbs until 4:00 P.M.

Ney was to attack the citadel to the west of the city, now defended by Lichatcheff. Lichatcheff was also directed to defend the Krasnoe suburb.

At about 1:00 P.M. Ney gave the order for the Württembergers to take the Stasnaia suburb. Hugel's brigade advanced to the left of the main road with Stockmayer's brigade on the right. At 3:00 P.M. it was supported by the 6th Württemberg Line Regiment. Hugel's brigade took heavy fire from the Russian batteries on the far side of the Dnieper and two Württemberg batteries, the 2nd Horse Battery and the 1st 12pdr Battery, were directed to return their fire.

To assure liaison with the 2nd Brigade and the artillery, Hugel deployed the 2/1st Württemberg Line Regiment as a skirmish screen. The rest of the brigade followed in open columns. In this formation, and under artillery fire, the brigade entered the suburb. The battle to take the suburb was violent. The front line, formed as skirmishers, was pushed back six times. Successively, the brigade was reinforced by the 2/1st Württemberg Line Regiment, three companies of the 2nd Württemberg Line Regiment, and one company of the 6th Württemberg Line Regiment. At the same time Stockmayer's brigade pushed into the suburb with the 2/1st Württemberg Line Regiment. Covered by Württemberg artillery posted just inside the range of the Russian skirmishers, the infantry pushed into and took the cemetery. The battle was such that the Württembergers twice expended their ammunition.

Stockmayer's brigade was moving to threaten the flanks of the Russian columns in the suburb. The 1/2nd Württemberg Line Regiment relieved Coronette's battalion and Stockmayer pushed forward with this battalion and two companies of the 2nd Württemberg Jäger Regiment. The rest of the brigade was in column behind them.

Disquieted by this and by Hugel's advance, the Russians sent a strong column against them. Stockmayer threw the 1/2nd Jäger and two companies of the 2nd Jägers into their flank, while the 1/2nd Württemberg Line Regiment formed a liaison between them and the main line.

At 1:00 P.M. Morand's division massed on the road to Krasnoe behind a mill, with the 13th Légère Regiment in the lead. It was supported by the 30th Line Regiment, which was posted to its right. Gudin's division marched on his left under the direct command of Count Lobau. Gerard's 3rd Brigade had relieved the advanced posts of the 2nd Brigade earlier in the morning with the 4/ and 6/21st Line and 1/127th Line. When forming for the attack, the division formed as follows: the 12th Line Regiment formed in line with the 6/21st deployed in skirmishers in front of it. To the right, the 4/21st was also deployed in skirmishers and posted on the heights. On the left, the 1/127th Line was in column behind the 2/127th, which was in line and supported by its two pieces of regimental artillery. The 2/127th was supporting the left of the 12th. The other battalions of the 21st Line and 7th Légère were in echelons by battalion. Those of the 21st were in columns by division.

The formation advanced unchanged until it entered the leading buildings of the suburb. However, it was not wide enough to cover the entire front of the Russians, who could outflank it on the left if they so chose. The 127th Line was moved to prevent that, and two battalions of the 21st moved to fill the gap between the 127th and the rest of the division. The entire movement was supported by the division's light artillery. Dessaix's division took up a position on the road to Roslovl while Compans replaced it as the reserve. The suburb was defended by Kapsevitch.

About 1:00 P.M., the light cavalry of General Bruyere's 1st Light Cavalry Division chased a Russian battery off the plateau that overlooked the Smolensk bridges. They seized the position, and a French sixteen-gun battery was positioned there. The French gunners then began to shower shot on the Russians posted on the north bank of the Dnieper. In response the Russians erected a twenty-four-gun battery, and a devastating artillery duel began.

Poniatowski's Poles attacked the Nicolskoi suburb on the East, the

French right. His goal was the suburb and the Malakov gate. The 20th Light Cavalry Brigade, supported by a battery of light artillery, chased the cossacks out of the suburb. The Polish artillery, supported by the French, engaged in a heavy artillery duel in an effort to silence the Russian batteries firing on the advancing 16th and 18th (Polish) Divisions. A Polish battery, posted between the two advancing divisions, tried to drive back the Russian skirmishers, which formed a line along the edge of the suburb. Three companies of voltigeurs were detached and sent into a ravine in which the Russians were concealed. They were supported by two additional companies. This action was supported by heavy artillery fire.

Prince Poniatowski directed two battalions of converged voltigeurs and a battalion of the 8th Polish Line Regiment against the suburb of Malakov. The 12th and two battalions of the 13th Polish Line Regiments moved on the Malakov Gate, the 15th Polish Line Regiment moved on the Saint Nikolas Gate, and the 2nd Polish Line Regiment moved on the suburb on the banks of the Dnieper. As the Poles passed over the ravine and advanced into the suburbs, they were taken in the flank by Russian artillery on the far bank. Their progress into the suburb was not good.

In an effort to disrupt the Russian communications, Poniatowski raised a battery of sixteen guns and directed its fire on the bridges. However, this battery was too exposed and suffered heavily from Russian artillery fire.

Despite Russian reports that the Polish artillery was silenced, it was not. The Poles divided their artillery into three groups. The first was assigned to fire counterbattery on the right bank of the river. Four 3pdrs were placed such that they could engage a Russian battery. The second group was placed on the left, where it supported the attack on St. Nikolas. The rest of the Polish artillery fired on the bridges over the Dnieper.

Platov's and Karpov's cossacks were at Katan, which worried Napoleon. Ney sent Mortier's cavalry brigade, six battalions of Württemberg infantry, and six guns of the Imperial Guard Artillery to protect against a possible flank attack. A sharp action resulted, which cost the French 11 officers and 200 men hors de combat.

Napoleon found his forces being held back by the walls of Smolensk. Though old and decayed, they held the French out of the city. Napoleon drew the Guard artillery and thirty-six 12pdrs together into a single battery under General Sorbier. The goal of this battery was to batter a hole in the walls. However, the 6pdr and 12pdr guns were too light to beat a hole in the walls. Seeing the futility of their fire, the Guard artillery redirected their fire into the covered way and promptly cleared it of Russian infantry.

A second French battery was established above the city, with howitzers stripped from various companies. It began to rain shells into the Russian positions.

At 5:00 P.M. Junot finally appeared at the heights above Smolensk. The French offensive was gaining ground. Morand and Gudin had penetrated through the suburbs and up to the city walls. Friant's division had overrun the Roslavl suburb and pushed the Russians back with severe losses. This had caused Barclay to send Prince Württemberg forward. Württemberg pushed his four battalions through the Nikolas and Malakov gates to engage the French. Lobau and Poniatowski engaged him and drove him back.

Only Ney's attack was not succeeding. He had met with stiff resistance and made little headway until the others succeeded. All of the French columns left trails of dead and wounded behind them as they pushed into the city. All that separated the Russians and French now was the city walls. Napoleon was rapidly growing tired of this pointless battle. He felt it to be as desperate as Ney's sending the 46th Line against the Royal Citadel earlier.

At 5:00 P.M. the Poles attacked the Malakov Gate very heavily. At the same time they struck the Ralschenka suburb. The Polish attacks steadily drove the Russians back, and they moved on the bridge. Barclay directed the fire of a powerful battery against the Ratchevka suburb, but the news that Docturov sent to him about his difficulty in holding his position forced him to do more. In response Barclay sent General Prince Württemberg to assist him. Württemberg lead four regiments to the Malakov gate, and General Rossi took the Tobolsk and Volhynie Infantry Regiments forward to relieve the Guard Jager Regiment. Puchnizki's brigade was sent to support Lichatcheff's division, and the 4th Jager Regiment advanced to the Malakov Gate.

These orders were followed with great zeal, and the Polish brigade of General Grabowski was thrown back, Grabowski being killed in the assault. The Russian assault recaptured Ratchevka, but it was ordered to evacuate the suburb and take up a position in the covered way so as to defend the eastern part of the city in conjunction with the 6th Jager Regiment and the Guard Jager Regiment.

The 4th Jagers pushed out of the Malakov Gate in an effort to take back the buildings there. They took possession of the covered road. The 34th Jagers were posted behind them as a reserve. A lively firefight developed between the skirmishers of both sides. The V Corps was pushed by Rossi's brigade, and Puchnizki became heavily involved with the III Corps. This was important to Barclay's plans, for if he wished to sortie his armies from Smolensk to engage the French, he would have to have control not only of these important gates, but also of the suburbs immediately outside them.

The battle for Smolensk was very bloody. It was remarked that during the advance one battalion lost a whole rank of one of its platoons to a single ball, which struck down twenty-one men when it hit.

Those French forces not in the battle were held in reserve upon the heights above the city. Their positions gave them an amphitheater view of the battle below them. They watched in silence as their comrades advanced through the shower of shot and fire. They were so moved that they responded by clapping their hands to express their approval. The noise of this applause was so great that it could be heard by the attacking columns.

On reaching the walls of the Old City, the attackers were screened from the Russian musketry. The artillery fire continued and became more brisk. Napoleon grew fatigued of the assault and decided to call it off. Lobau, however, convinced him to continue the attack.

General Konovnitzin was charged with the evacuation of the city. Württemberg placed himself at the head of the 4th Jagers to lead the withdrawal. As the 4th Jagers reached the bridge over the Dnieper, the French artillery that had been firing on the north bank of the Dnieper took them under fire. The jagers moved to the right and into the covered way. Once in this position they were attacked by the French and a firefight developed. Their timely occupation of the covered way prevented the French from entering the city. The 34th Jagers dropped off a battalion to act as a reserve for the 4th Jagers and passed over the bridge. The French stopped their attacks and no longer pressed the Russians at the Malakov Gate.

At this time Württemberg was informed of Rossi's success against the Poles. General Konovnitzin dispatched General Puchnizki's brigade to the right side of the citadel, where Ney's Württembergers had begun a heavy assault. The 6th Jager Regiment fell back from their bridge when Prince Württemberg arrived. The battle was already decided. The

French greeted Prince Württemberg's arrival with a heavy cannonade, which caused heavy casualties in the 1st Brigade of the 4th Division.

Night fell, and Napoleon returned to his tent. Lobau could no longer maintain his position in the ditch surrounding the city. Howitzer shells were fired into the city to cover his retreat. Thick black smoke began to rise from several points in the city. This smoke was soon lit by long spires of flame rising from the city. Numerous smaller fires gradually swelled and merged until the entire city was engulfed in flames.

Count Lobau was dismayed by so great a disaster, which he believed to be the result of the howitzer fire he had ordered. The combat ceased and the dark of the night was lit by the light of the burning city. Almost as soon as darkness fell the Russians began to withdraw. The corps of General of Infantry Docturov and the 3rd Division took up positions in the St. Petersburg suburb, and the jagers of Prince Chakoffski's brigade, the 3rd Division (20th and 21st Jager Regiments), occupied the city. General Korff and the 30th Jagers had been given the task of holding the ramparts and were ordered to fire the city when they withdrew. Korff's last act was to order the 30th Jagers to destroy the bridge over the Dnieper after the last Russian forces had crossed it.

At 2:00 A.M. Ney discovered that the walls in front of his corps were unoccupied, and he entered the city. Shortly after, the French passed through the Malakov Gate. Though the bridge was broken, the river was only four feet deep. At 9:00 A.M. 600 Württembergers and Portuguese waded across the Dnieper to attack the 30th Jagers. The attack was successful, and the Russians surrendered their positions to them. Hugel's Württemberg brigade quickly followed the lead elements across the river, and Ney brought his artillery up to the river's edge to support his bridgehead. Barclay was only able to mask this penetration with his rear guard, under General Korff, who now commanded several jager regiments and three uhlan and hussar regiments.

During the day, the jagers of the 3rd and 17th Divisions were placed along the bank of the Dnieper, where they engaged the French for most of the day with their skirmish fire. The jagers of the 4th Division were held in reserve on the heights behind the St. Petersburg suburb, and the rest of the 4th Division moved to join the 17th Division on the extreme right of the Russian army. They were exposed to heavy artillery fire along the length of the river for the entire day's battle. Generals Skalon and Balla were killed during the battle for Smolensk.

The Russian losses were, according to Barclay, about 4,000 men.

Bogdanovich speaks of 6,000 men hors de combat. Prince Eugène of Württemberg's division lost 1,300 men alone, so the 6,000 figure is probably more accurate. Furthermore, it is reported that Docturov's corps had only 6,000 men capable of further combat.

Though Napoleon gives his losses at 700 killed and 3,100 to 3,200 wounded, the losses to the divisions of I Corps present at Smolensk and commanded by Count Lobau were about 6,000. Gudin's division alone lost 60 officers and 1,658 men. The Poles lost 18 officers and 500 men dead and 47 officers and 765 men wounded. The Württembergers lost 80 dead and 559 wounded. The 25th Division had had 4,007 men under arms on 3 August, but after Smolensk it had only 2,827 men. Gudin's division lost 155 officers and 3,860 men dead and wounded.

The French lost General Grabowski killed and Generals Dalton, Grandeau, and Zayonschlek wounded.

The French began their occupation of the city and started extinguishing the fires. August 18th was spent in reorganizing and repairing the bridge over the Dnieper. On the Russian side, the final breakdown in relations between Bagration and Barclay occurred. Bagration set out, without Barclay's orders to do so, for Solovievo. He left only four cossack pulks to cover the vital crossroads at Lubino. It was late when Barclay began to follow Bagration, and Napoleon's inactivity once again cost him the chance of separating the two armies and defeating them in detail.

Chapter X

The March on Moscow

The Pursuit

At 4:00 A.M. the French pursuit of the fleeing Russian armies began as Ney advanced his corps across the Dnieper. His first job was to cover the crossing of the rest of the Grande Armée. His second job was to determine the direction taken by the Russians. Meanwhile Murat crossed the Dnieper at a weir near the Stragan Brook and moved down the road to Moscow.

Ney's troops climbed to the heights behind the St. Petersburg suburb in the flickering light of the burning buildings. His troops proceeded slowly, with a thousand detours to avoid the flames. The Russian rear guard managed to block his advance at every corner; they had barricaded all of the major intersections.

When Ney's troops finally broke out of the suburbs, they encountered only the few cossacks left behind by Bagration to cover the vital crossroads. These crossroads were the main roads to Moscow and St. Petersburg. Ney pondered the direction the Russians had taken. He had neither prisoners nor civilians to tell him, and the ground bore signs in both directions.

During the previous night Barclay learned that only Karpov's cossacks covered the Loubino crossroads and dispatched Generalmajor Tuchkov with the Elisabethgrad Hussars, the Revel Infantry Regiment, the 20th and 21st Jager Regiments, and a horse battery to occupy the crossroads.

Ney remained uncertain where to go until about 2:00 P.M., when word came that Murat had encountered Russian troops on the road to Moscow. Ney, having orders to pursue the Russians, set out after them and would have quickly overhauled them, but for the numerous ravines and streams that crossed the road, providing strong positions for the Russian rear guard to delay Ney's advance.

Barclay had not, however, taken the Moscow road. He had taken the St. Petersburg road because it swung away from the Dnieper more abruptly and exposed his men to less chance of discovery by the French. This road made a long swing, longer than the Moscow road, which it rejoined further away.

Barclay pushed his forces down this road, committing his long train and artillery to a narrow pass through the dense forests. This heavy column traversed what was not the shortest route between him and his goal. Every horse and wagon that became stuck down with heavy mud or that overturned stopped the column and let the pursuing French close in. Time was wasted, and every second counted as the sound of Ney's guns moved down the Moscow road and eventually overtook them. Ney's actions slowed Barclay's withdrawal, and Nansouty, under Murat, moved rapidly down the road to Moscow in support of Ney.

Barclay's forces advanced with the first column under General Tuchkov I to the right. Tuchkov I's forces consisted of the 2nd, 3rd, and 4th Infantry Corps as well as the 1st Cavalry Corps. A second column, under General of Infantry Docturov, consisted of the 5th and 6th Infantry Corps, the 2nd and 3rd Cavalry Corps, the 1st Cuirassier Division, and the army's entire artillery reserve. The Russian rear guard was commanded by Adjutant General Korff and consisted of the 7th Jager Regiment, three cossack pulks, and a horse battery. Korff commanded a total of fourteen battalions of jagers from the 2nd and 4th Infantry Corps, the Polish Uhlans, and the Soum and Mariuopol Hussar Regiments.

In support of the retreating army, Pavlov had dispersed his cossacks in a chain of vedettes that stretched from Smolensk to Poretchie. They acted as the first line of defense against the advancing French. However, their job was more to warn of the French approach and to stop French scouting parties than to engage in serious battle.

Barclay ordered Tuchkov III to lead a detachment formed with three cossack pulks, the Elisabethgrad Hussar Regiment, the 20th and 21st Jager Regiments, the Revel Infantry Regiment, and a horse battery to the vital crossroads at Loubino and, if possible, to advance along the route to Smolensk and support General Karpov, who was leading the cossacks forming the rear guard of the 2nd Army of the West. Tuchkov III departed at 8:00 P.M.

Bagration had detached a small force under Generallieutenant Prince Gortchakov and posted it at Chein-Ostrog, four miles from Smolensk, where it remained until Barclay's forces arrived. It was with these troops that Tuchkov III established communications.

The Russian retreat continued doggedly, and as Barclay's troops reached Gorbunovo, Ney and Nansouty's forces caught up with and engaged the head of the Russian column. The French hastened their advance and began to deploy to engage the Russians.

The French appearance stopped Tuchkov III's movements to join Bagration and forced him to deploy along the main road in reaction to the French assault. The 20th Jagers were on the right of the main road and the 21st Jagers were on the left. Both occupied thickets, and between them the Russian rear guard deployed. The artillery company positioned itself on the road with the Revel Infantry Regiment, and the Elisabethgrad Hussars acted as a reserve. The three cossack regiments were detached to the left, towards the Dnieper, to watch for a French advance from that quarter.

The 1st Cuirassier Division and the 3rd and 4th Infantry Corps had passed Loubino and were moving on Bredikhino. Tuchkov I, having succeeded in carrying out his orders and occupying the crossroads, sent the Leib Grenadier and the Count Arakcheyev Grenadier Regiments with six guns to reinforce the advanced guard of Tuchkov III.

The 2nd Infantry Corps under Generallieutenant Baggovout was unable to follow the 3rd and 4th Infantry Corps. They were engaged by the French near Gorbunovo.

The Battle of Loubino or Valoutina-Gora

Barclay watched the French movement along the heights behind Gorbunovo and realized that it was important for him to hold that position if he was to pass the rest of his army to safety. He stopped the Tobolsk Infantry Regiment and four guns. He directed Württemberg to take and hold Gorbunovo with them. He called back the Bieloserk and Wilmanstrand Infantry Regiments, as well as a squadron of the Isoum Hussar Regiment, and sent them to join Württemberg. Barclay then ordered Korff to hasten his march and pass part of his troops to Tschottkino, to the right, and to form a second line behind Württemberg's forces.

Korff positioned himself between Tyczinina and Loubino. He placed his eight battalions on the plateau that overhung the main road. On his right he placed eight horse guns. Behind this artillery was the Leib Grenadier Regiment, as well as the Jeletz and Ekaterinburg Infantry Regiments. To their right, in a small woods, the Revel Infantry Regiment was posted and to their left were the 20th and 21st Jager Regiments. Behind the jagers was a battalion of converged grenadiers and a battalion of the Revel Infantry Regiment. The rest of the infantry was posted further to the left on the heights. The Bourtirki and Rilsk Infantry Regiment were in a village.

Count Orlov-Denisov was on the extreme left, towards Martino. His forces consisted of the Elisabethgrad, Soum, and Mariuopol Hussar Regiments, two squadrons of the Isoum Hussar Regiment, and four horse guns. Karpov's cossacks were posted before the Russian left wing, near Goumninczino and Martino. The Russian advanced guard totaled about 5,000 men and was positioned behind the Stragan River, in support of Württemberg's forces.

Württemberg's forces were posted as follows: a battalion of the Tobolsk Infantry Regiment, under Major Baron Wolf, occupied the wooded heights above Gorbunovo. A battalion of the Wilmanstrand Infantry Regiment was placed in the brush along the small stream that ran between Gorbunovo and the road to Moscow. This stream was dry at the time and represented only a minor obstacle to the French. Württemberg burned the bridge over it and placed the other battalion of the Wilmanstrand Infantry Regiment with two guns to hold what remained of the bridge.

The advancing forces of Ney's corps stopped and placed a battery to face the two Russian pieces across the stream. Several battalions from this column, including Razout's division and the Portuguese Legion among them, moved to the left against Gorbunovo and towards the heights where Major Wolf was positioned. The Tobolsk Infantry Regiment and a battalion of the Bieloserk Infantry Regiment formed a column that attacked the French left. The French were pushed back, but returned to engage the Russians in a firefight. The battalion of Major Wolf had taken position in an old fortification on the height. It protected his troops from much of the effect of the French fire, and he held off the French attacks from noon until about 2:00 P.M.

Ney formed his forces as follows, from left to right: Ledru's 10th Division, Marchand's 25th Division, Razout's 11th Division. Their force covered approximately a league. Razout's division concentrated its efforts on a village which covered the Russian left.

Despite all the time that had elapsed during this initial phase of the battle, the Russian train had still not passed the crossroads. The jam was such that Württemberg suggested erecting a second bridge over the Stragan stream. A squadron of hussars was dismounted, at Lowenstern's direction, and set to tearing down houses to provide materials for the pioneers, under Baron Salza, raising this new bridge. The second bridge was eventually raised and greatly alleviated the jam at the stream.

The grind of the heavy traffic tore up the crude Russian road, making it impassable in many places. The holes were filled with corduroy and fascines to permit the artillery and other wheeled traffic to pass. The gunners and drivers, encouraged by Count Kutaisov, dragged their guns and wagons forward with superhuman effort. Not a single gun or wagon was abandoned.

The French efforts increased, and eventually Württemberg was forced to order Wolf's lone battalion to withdraw. Before he could pull back, the French launched a renewed attack on Gorbunovo. They captured the two guns guarding the burnt bridge. The Bieloserk Infantry Regiment charged forward and recaptured the guns. Wolf took advantage of this distraction to move his battalion into and retake Gorbunovo. However, he was caught by the Württemberg chevauxlégers and sabered.

At 3:00 P.M. a battalion of converged grenadiers from the 3rd Division was sent forward by General Tuchkov and took up position behind the Stragan.

The rearguard was forced to recoil behind the Stragan River, but at 4:00 P.M. Barclay led forward a 12pdr battery, a battalion of Volhynie Infantry Regiment, and two hussar regiments: Elisabethgrad and Isoum. He returned the Bieloserk and Wilmanstrand Infantry Regiments to the 2nd Infantry Corps. The 3rd and 4th Infantry Corps had reached Loubino, but Baggovout and Korff were too far to the rear to intervene quickly. The Russian baggage was jamming the crossroads, making their intervention even more difficult. Barclay deployed his forces and ordered Yermolov to bring forward the 3rd and 4th Infantry Corps. He had a total of sixteen battalions organized behind the Stragan. The 4th Infantry Corps gradually took up position as the Jeletz, Rilsk, and Ekaterinburg Infantry Regiments fell into position. The 3rd Infantry Corps had moved out along the main road a half hour before the 4th Corps.

After the highway crossed the Stragan, it passed across the southern end of a low, wooded plateau that extended to the north for two miles. South of the road was a dry marsh that extended to the Dnieper. On the numerous low hills that rose out of this marsh were several hamlets and copses. One of these villages which dominated the road was occupied by the Russians.

Konovnitzin's 3rd Division and Tchoglokov's 11th Division arrived, bringing a total of seven new regiments and a horse battery with them. Tchoglokov's forces moved forward to support the hussars of Count Orlov-Denisov while Konovnitzin's infantry moved to the center of the field. A battalion of converged grenadiers from the 3rd Division joined the battalion of the Count Arakcheyev Grenadier Regiment, which was placed on a hill to the left, behind a woods near Boubleievo. Boubleievo was occupied by the Rilsk Infantry Regiment, and Karpov and his cossacks were now near Goumniczino and Martino.

The left of the Russian position was covered by a swampy valley formed by the Samili stream and a large swamp to its left. This stream cut the Russian position. It was impossible for the Russians to pull behind the Samili without uncovering the road to Gorbunovo, which was on the left bank of the Samili. Besides uncovering the critical road, such a move would also expose the flanks of Baggovout and Korff. Similarly, if the heights to the left were abandoned, the French could threaten the Russian line of retreat.

The Russians were posted across this terrain as follows: the 1st Artillery Brigade was on the heights to the north of the main road such that they swept it with their fire. To their right and rear were the Guard Grenadier Regiments, Jeletz and Ekaterinburg Infantry Regiments held in column. On the extreme right the Revel Infantry Regiment held the woods near Greitschichki, with a battalion of the Count Arakcheyev Grenadier Regiment in support. To the left of the road the 2nd, 20th, and 22nd Jager Regiments, under the command of Generalmajor Chakowski, defended a swamp. Posted behind them was a battalion of converged grenadiers from the 3rd Division and a battalion of the Count Arakcheyev Grenadier Regiment.

Learning of a pending attack and its specific targets from two Württemberg deserters, Orlov-Denisov hastily moved the 1st Cavalry Corps from Bredikhino and placed it behind the swamp. To the south of the swamp, Tuchkov established himself with the Soum, Elisabethgrad, and Mariuopol Hussars and two squadrons of the Isoum Hussar Regiments, a total of twenty-six squadrons, and four horse guns. These squadrons were formed in four lines at the interval of a squadron within a half musket shot of the thick bush to their front. The horse artillery was posted on a small knoll to their right. Five cossack pulks and two squadrons of the Isoum Hussar Regiment were posted on their left wing.

Once Orlov-Denisov had these dispositions prepared, he called on Barclay to send him some more horse artillery and a brigade of infantry to cover his right.

Around 5:00 P.M. the French III Corps arrived. Ney's first attack consisted of Ledru and Razout's divisions. The Württemberg artillery engaged the Russian center. The initial French frontal attacks failed. The 3rd Division advanced on the right of the III Corps. The 7th Légère Regiment crossed the first stream supported by two battalions of the 21st Line Regiment. It succeeded in seizing a foothold, but could not take the plateau. A little later the 12th Line Regiment joined it. The French then attempted a flanking move through the swamp to take the Russian battery there. The 20th and 21st Jager Regiments stopped them, while the converged grenadiers of the 3rd Division and the Count Arak-cheyev Grenadier Regiment counterattacked, driving the French back.

At the same time, Ney stopped his corps behind the heights of Tebenkova. French cavalry moved across the stream in front of the Wilmanstrand Infantry Regiment and attacked the Russian skirmishers. Württemberg had only a single squadron of the Isoum Hussar Regiment to counter this. The Russian hussars attacked successfully, probably because the French cavalry was disordered as a result of the thick brush in which they were operating. The French withdrew.

General of Infantry Docturov was pleased by the hussars' and Strogo-noff's attacks. However, his pleasure was short-lived. A French battery opened fire from across the Dnieper and began to inflict casualties on his forces as heavy columns of French infantry advanced against his center. The advancing forces were General Gudin's 3rd Division, I Corps. Generals Ledru and Marchand moved their divisions in support.

The 3rd Division advanced in columns by peloton. The 7th Légère Regiment led the column, followed by the 12th, 21st, and 127th Line Regiments. General Gudin personally led the 7th Légère Regiment across the stream and was struck by a cannon shot that broke both legs, killing him. Command passed to General Gerard. When the French saw that Gudin, a favorite, had fallen, they charged furiously and drove the Russian infantry from its positions to the south of the road. This threatened to break Barclay's thin position. He countered by sending Konovnitzin's four infantry regiments forward. He reinforced the left with the Ekaterino-slav Grenadier Regiment and sent the Pernau and Polotsk Infantry Regiments and a company of horse artillery to the right to support the cavalry on that wing. The 1st Cavalry Corps was ordered to deploy on the heights in front of Doukhovskoie, to the right of the Kexholm Infantry

Regiment, all that remained of the 4th Corps reserve near Loukanovo. The Pavlov, Tauride, and St. Petersburg Grenadier Regiments were organized into the last reserve and posted near Loubino with three artillery companies.

The attack of the French 3rd Division was paralleled with an attack by Razout's 11th Division, III Corps. He pushed back the Rilsk Infantry and began pushing the 20th and 21st Jager Regiments. This French thrust was countered and stopped by an attack by a battalion of converged grenadiers from the 3rd Division and a battalion of the Rilsk Infantry.

In addition to Razout and Gudin's attack, the French cavalry attacked the cossacks and Soumy Hussar Regiment, driving them back. Orlov-Denisov counterattacked with the Elisabethgrad and Mariuopol Hussar Regiments, striking the French in the flank and driving them back. Yermolov advanced the 3rd and 4th Infantry Corps to assist Tuchkov I and the 1st Cuirassier Division while they crossed Loubino and took up new positions behind and to the left of the Kixholm Infantry Regiment.

The French 3rd and 11th Divisions renewed their attacks, with the 10th and 25th Divisions in reserve. They attacked the Russian center, but Konovnitzin's fresh infantry, the Mourmonsk, Tchernigov, and Korporsk Infantry Regiments, counterattacked with bayonets and drove them back. Davout renewed the attack again, only to be repulsed with heavy casualties.

The Russian 2nd Infantry Corps arrived at 7:00 P.M. with the rear guard of Baron Korff. The 17th Division, which was at the head of this column, moved to the right wing, and the 4th Division was placed in reserve behind it. Their rear guard was positioned near Kochaevo. This completed the flank movement of the Russian army.

In the center and on the French left, Marshal Ney sent the Württemberg light brigade forward in skirmish order with two line brigades in support. The other brigades of the III Corps took the same formation, and a general assault began. Three times this formation attacked the Russians until night had long since fallen.

On the main route General Gerard reinforced his line with three battalions of the 21st and 127th Line Regiments and resumed the attack, but night also forced him to stop his attacks.

At about 9:00 P.M. night fell and the French 3rd Division crossed the ravine once again to attack the Russian right wing. It was thrown back by Tuchkov III, commanding the Ekaterinoslav Grenadier Regiment. Tuchkov was wounded and taken prisoner.

Further to the right, Junot's Westphalian corps had been resolutely advancing through the day. From Stubna the high road turned left and ascended some heights to avoid the swamps and tributaries of the Dnieper. There was a shorter side road that ran straight across these obstacles and rejoined the main road behind the plateau of Valoutina. While Ney was pursuing the Russians down the main road, Junot crossed the Dnieper at Prudichevo and took this side road. An aggressive attack on Junot's part would have assured a decisive victory for Ney, as the Russians were heavily engaged to their front by Ney. Junot's attack would have struck their rear, and they would have been lost. As they rushed to escape the pincer movement they would have had to pass through several narrow defiles, and the resulting confusion would have resulted in their complete destruction.

Murat, judging Junot had had sufficient time to arrive in his assigned position, grew concerned when he did not hear Junot's attack. On seeing the firmness of the Russians before him, Murat realized that Junot had not attacked. He plunged into the woods at the head of a small escort until he arrived at Junot's headquarters. Murat's wrath descended upon the hapless Junot, who only whined that he had no orders to attack, that his Westphalian cavalry was shy, its efforts feigned, and that it could not be brought to charge the Russians.

Murat finally bullied Junot into acting and sent two light infantry battalions, the Guard Chevauxléger Regiment, both hussar regiments, the Guard Grenadier Battalion, the Jäger-Karabinier Battalion, and the Guard Jäger Battalion forward. This attack was supported by the fire of two batteries. This force moved out of the woods on the east of Bableveja. The voltigeur companies of the 1st and 2nd Jäger Battalions were detached and formed a skirmish line behind which the remainder of the Westphalians advanced. They advanced against a birch woods that was filled with Russian skirmishers. Behind this copse stood the main Russian army on an open plain.

While the voltigeurs engaged the Russian skirmishers, they were struck in the flank by a column of cossacks, the Elisabethgrad Hussar Regiment, and two squadrons of the Isoum Hussar Regiment moving up from the Russian left wing. The voltigeurs of the 2nd Jäger Battalion fell back to the right and escaped the attack, but those of the 1st Jäger Battalion were not so lucky. Captain Bucher formed his company into square and engaged the Russians with peloton fire. The cossacks engaged this tiny band and tried to crush it.

Hammerstein, the commander of the Westphalian cavalry, formed his cavalry into echelons and struck the superior force of Russian cavalry. His attack was not very successful. The Guard Chevauxléger Regiment lost one dead and seven wounded officers, thirty-six dead and ninety-three wounded men, and five prisoners.

The voltigeurs remained besieged until the Guard Jäger Battalion and the Jäger-Karabinier Battalion arrived. They advanced with the voltigeur companies of the 1st, 2nd, and 6th Westphalian Line Regiments. Two batteries of Westphalian artillery covered their advance. The Russians were driven back.

It was not only on the left that the Russians had narrowly escaped. General Morand had led his 1st Division, I Corps, around the right flank of the Russians. If he continued his advance he would fall on the Russian rear much as Junot should have done. His appearance would have had the same impact as an aggressive attack by Junot should have had. However, Napoleon was unaware of the terrain and had ordered him recalled to the point where he and Count Lobau had started that morning. What could have been a double envelopment failed totally.

The next day, when the battle was reviewed, Napoleon realized that Junot had failed him and ordered him replaced by General Rapp. However, Rapp refused to supplant his old friend. His manner and words calmed Napoleon, whose anger always subsided after it had vented itself in words.

The French had fielded 50,000 men, of whom about 37,000 were seriously engaged. The Russians gradually fielded about 30,000 men. Losses on both sides were heavy. Gerard's 3rd Division, formerly Gudin's division, had lost 2,297 hors de combat. Ney is believed to have lost about 4,000. Junot's casualties are estimated to have been about 700. The total French losses were probably about 8,500. The Russians are estimated to have lost about 5,500 men.

The Advance on Smolensk Resumes

This action marked the end of the Smolensk maneuver and was Napoleon's second strategic failure. It had been thwarted by Barclay's dispatching of the 7th Corps to Smolensk. This action alone had kept Ney and Murat from seizing the city undefended.

The decayed defenses of Smolensk had proven stronger than suspected, and Raevsky was able to hold the French off long enough to permit the main Russian army to arrive. The French had foolishly wasted August 15th by not advancing, and they had surrendered much of the surprise that might have been theirs. More than one opportunity was lost. Napoleon would have been better served if he had bypassed Smolensk and cut the Moscow road, but he further slowed his advance by engaging in an assault on a fortified position. Napoleon had hoped that Russian pride and religious fervor would force them into a full-scale battle, as urged by Barclay's generals, but the results were disappointing to both.

While the French army regrouped and licked its wounds from the action at Valoutina-Loubino, Barclay moved his troops as quickly as he could. His column was entangled in the crossroads and did not extricate itself until near midnight. Junot's failure was providential for the Russians. On the 20th the Russian column continued its retreat on Slobeneva, where it joined Docturov's column. The French had not engaged Docturov during his retreat from Smolensk.

The Russian Withdrawal Resumes

For two days the Russian army moved across the Dnieper, except for Platov. Platov remained behind, on the right bank, with a rearguard formed of the Soum, Mariuopol, and Elisabethgrad Hussar Regiments, the Polish Uhlan Regiment, and the cossacks of the 1st Army of the West. Supporting him on the left bank was General Rosen with six jager regiments and some horse artillery.

The same day, Bagration reached Dogoromunde and established communications with Moscow. Platov was under attack by the French advanced guard, but crossed his forces over the Dnieper under the support of General Rosen.

With the fall of Smolensk, Napoleon had a decision to make. He was faced with several alternatives. He was miles from his bases in Poland and eastern Prussia. His strength had been steadily drained by exhausting marches, battles, and detached garrisons, and he had still not brought the Russians to account in a decisive battle. His initial plan of a decisive battle within the first twenty days had long vanished. At first Napoleon allowed supply considerations to govern his moves, and, according to Caulaincourt, he intended to clear the position around Smolensk of Russian troops, dig his forces in, and prepare to winter his army at Smolensk. During the winter he could bring up supplies and reinforcements, reorganize Poland with the newly conquered Lithuanian provinces, and make preparations for a renewed offensive in the spring. However, the idea of a two-year campaign was alien to Napoleon. In all of his previous campaigns Napoleon had been able to come to grips with his enemy and force the decisive battle within a single season. The lack of a decisive battle weighed heavily on his mind.

By unifying Poland he would have a very strong Polish army allied to his cause in the spring. He also knew that it was another 280 miles to Moscow from his position in Smolensk. To cover that distance would take most of the remaining season, and there was no certainty that the Russians would offer battle if he did advance. He did know that the Russians would ravage the countryside as they withdrew, further compounding his supply problems. Napoleon's supply system was already stretched to the limit and could not hope to handle such great distances. There were powerful reasons to remain in Smolensk.

In contrast, there were powerful political and military reasons to resume the advance. Napoleon's initial reasons for entering the war with Russia were economic. Napoleon still had the Continental System in his mind, and his war with Russia had increased the trickle of British goods into Russia to a flood of both goods and military aid. Napoleon had to stop it as quickly as possible. A long delay, six months or more, would allow the Russians to redeploy their Finnish and Danube armies, recently released because of treaties with Sweden and Turkey. A six-month delay would allow the raising and training of new troops to fill out the various reserve divisions and replace their campaign losses. Though Napoleon could raise a large Polish army, the combination of Russian manpower and British armaments more than offset that advantage.

Napoleon feared that a reinforced Russian army would be tempted to attack his overextended army if he were to surrender the offensive to them. Napoleon's lieutenants had shown themselves to be, for the most part, incapable of acting independently, and this had compounded his fears.

The recreation of ancient Poland also had its problems. It would not endear him to either Prussia or Austria, his nominal allies, because they had participated in the last partitioning of Poland and feared the retribution of a reestablished Poland.

By 4:00 P.M. on August 20th Napoleon had weighed all the alternatives and ordered Murat and Davout to advance. Latour-Maubourg was directed to fall in on the French army's right flank and pass through Roslavl. Dombrowski was sent back to cover Mohilev and Minsk, while Pino,

Pajol, and Guyon were ordered to clear out the last vestiges of the Russian army around Smolensk before they, too, joined the advance. There was a reorganization and shifting eastward of reserves and garrison troops. Victor was given command of the French rear areas, and Macdonald was given authorization to take Riga.

The Grande Armée resumed its advance in three columns. The central column consisted of the Guard, Murat's cavalry, and the I and III Corps. Eugène was to command the left column and Poniatowski commanded the right. Napoleon's main army consisted of 124,000 infantry, 32,000 cavalry, and 587 guns.

The weather was dry as the French advanced. Wells and streams dried up or were spoiled by the retreating Russians, compounding the French army's problems. The countryside was stripped by the Russians, but Eugène and Poniatowski, advancing down the flanks, found sufficient supplies and intact villages to support them. Murat advanced down the main road, but by keeping his cavalry concentrated, he compounded their supply and forage problems. The French cavalry suffered cruelly from their privations. Murat and Davout soon had a serious disagreement, as Davout wished to conserve what remained of the army's strength, while Murat was always charging off every time a cossack showed his face. Murat's flamboyant actions continually whittled away at the cavalry's strength. Napoleon, however, took Murat's side in this argument, crossly accusing Davout of being "overcautious."

Morale and discipline began to suffer, and the troops began to forage with greater desperation. They began to encounter hostile peasants who, combined with the cossacks, began to take a heavy toll of the French forage parties. Despite these problems, couriers arrived daily from Paris, convoys followed the army and were seldom molested, supplies accumulated in the advanced supply depots, Napoleon's military governments were establishing their control and organizing their resources, and the Lithuanian army was beginning to take shape.

The Lithuanian Army Is Raised

This last organization lasted only a few short months, with few units surviving into the 1813 campaign. It was organized as an extension of the army of the Grand Duchy of Warsaw. The Poles had seventeen consecutively numbered infantry regiments and sixteen consecutively numbered cavalry regiments. The Lithuanians were to raise five infantry and four cavalry regiments which were numbered in sequence with those of the Grand Duchy. In addition, the Lithuanians raised the only light infantry to exist in the army of the Grand Duchy of Warsaw.

The establishing and organizing of these units was directed by Governor Hogendorp. The infantry was under the direction of General Niezetowski and the cavalry under General Wawrecki. The colonels for the Lithuanian regiments were selected from the great landed families of Lithuania who had previous military experience.

There were limits on the monies provided by Napoleon for the formation of these regiments. He provided only 400,000 francs when 4 million were needed. As a result, each noble enrolled was expected to contribute towards the organization of his regiment. The actual field commander of the regiment was to be a major, while the colonel was the honorary commander. These units were organized identically to their Polish counterparts.

The officers were selected from among the most distinguished Polish officers available. Most of them were veterans of the old legions of Italy and the 1807 campaign. Napoleon allowed other officers to be drawn from the Vistula Legion as well as from the army of the Grand Duchy of Warsaw.

The Order of the Day, dated 13 July 1812 and originated in Vilna, nominated the officers for the regiments, directing the raising of the Lithuanian regiments. In addition to the regular troops it directed the organization of the Lithuanian national guard and the Lithuanian gendarmerie. The function of these units was to maintain internal order and security. They were more of a police force than a military formation.

These units were filled by a conscription which began in August. However, the lack of money, officers, supplies, equipment, and horses, coupled with the incessant raids of cossacks, slowed their organization.

The organization of the Lithuanian army was relatively complete by the time Napoleon began the withdrawal from Moscow. They were ordered to concentrate, and on 20 December three of them arrived in Augustovo. From there they were sent to Warsaw. The 19th Regiment, under Hogendorp, attempted to reach Vilna, but encountered the Russians and was severely handled. Only a fragment succeeded in reaching the XI Corps in Königsberg, from whence they passed to Warsaw. The 22nd Regiment was engaged at Minsk and almost entirely captured. Only its officers escaped to Warsaw.

The cavalry was more fortunate. The 17th and 20th Regiments joined the XI Corps and were able to withdraw with it. They were untrained, but still committed to action. The survivors later reached Eugène's Corps d'Observation, where they were placed under the command of Gerard.

Evidence suggests that the 18th and 19th Regiments, the light infantry, and the gendarmes à cheval were at Berezina during the crossings.

The 3rd Chevauléger-lanciers de la Garde were ambushed and destroyed near Slonim in October, only a few survivors making it back to the French lines, where they were incorporated into the 1er Chevauléger-lanciers de la Garde. The Lithuanian Tartars never exceeded a squadron and were also absorbed into the 1er Chevauléger-lanciers de la Garde.

However, before all of this transpired, the campaign had much to undergo. As the French pursued the Russians after Smolensk, both suffered. The morale of the Russians fell, desertion and illness increased. The Russian generals protested that Barclay was mismanaging the retreat and began to accuse him of not being a true Russian because of his Scottish ancestry.

Russian Plans

The czar was pressured into abandoning Barclay's fabian tactics and on 24 July, while in Moscow, he made a public plea to every Russian capable of bearing arms, for assistance. His request for assistance was answered by all of Russia. Moscow alone offered 80,000 militia. He stirred up the Russian will to resist with a religious fervor. The Russian Orthodox Church joined in his efforts by stirring up the peasantry into a holy crusade, and the icon of the Black Virgin of Smolensk was given to the army for its protection.

In response to pressure by Bagration, Barclay offered to give battle with the French near Usvyatye. However, Bagration objected and the plan was dropped. On 27 August the Russians continued their retreat. The French advanced guard drove the Russians towards Viazma. The army, thirsty from the march, the heat, and the dust, was in want of water. The troops disputed the possession of a few muddy pools and fought near the springs which were soon rendered turbid and exhausted.

The French advance continued, and they encountered the Russians in positions on the Ozma, near the village of Rouibki, with an 8,000-man cavalry rear guard. Murat moved to turn their left and sent the 4th Chevauléger-lancier Regiment forward to attack them. The Russians turned and retreated on Viazma.

On 28 August the French found themselves on the banks of the Viazma River. During the night the Russians had destroyed all of the bridges over the Viazma, plundered the town, and set it afire. Murat and Davout advanced quickly in an effort to extinguish the flames. The Viazma was found to be fordable near the ruined bridges, and the French infantry crossed over, attacking the incendiaries. The flames were quickly extinguished.

A few chosen men were sent forward to the advanced guard with orders to watch the Russians closely and to ascertain if they indeed were the incendiaries. The reports of these men eradicated all doubt on that issue. It was indeed the Russians who had begun a scorched-earth policy. Despite the fires and pillaging, supplies were still found in the city.

Beyond the Viazma, behind a ravine in an advantageous position, the Russians had once again appeared and shown themselves ready for battle. The cavalry on both sides immediately engaged in battle, and as infantry became necessary, Murat placed himself at the head of one of Davout's divisions. He sought to send it forward against the Russians.

Davout hastened up, calling his men to halt, loudly censuring the maneuver and reproaching Murat for it. Davout forced his generals to obey him. Murat appealed to his dignity, his rank, and to the situation, but in vain. Murat finally set out to complain to the Emperor.

Napoleon was infuriated by Davout's actions and placed the division in question, Compen's 5th Division, under Murat's control. However, the battle was over at that time. Murat was so incensed over the issue that he was ready to snatch up his sword and attack Davout. Belliard stopped him and persuaded him not to commit such a mistake.

After the Viazma incident the Russians were reinforced by 15,000 regular troops and 10,000 opolochenie, Russian militia.

Kutusov Takes Command

When Barclay reached Tsarevo Zaimische, he intended to make a stand against the French, but he discovered that the czar had replaced him with Kutusov. Kutusov's appointment had been forced on the czar by the frightened Russian aristocracy. He was sixty-seven years old and so corpulent that he was unable to mount a horse. Despite his greedy, lazy nature, he was popular with the troops. He was a Russian with a Russian-sounding name in contrast to Barclay's foreign extraction and name. It was felt that Kutusov's "true Tartar character" would save the Russian national honor.

Kutusov was dispatched from St. Petersburg, and as he traveled through the villages between there and the Russian army, his carriage was constantly swamped by the peasants who crowded around him to receive his blessing and to show him their children. On 26 August he encountered the British military liaison officer, General Wilson, who was to become one of his harshest critics. On 27 August Kutusov arrived in Gzatsk, on the Smolensk-Moscow road, and watched the passage of the demoralized Russian army.

With his arrival, there appeared a rumor in the army that a huge eagle had been seen flying over his head, circling slowly above him as he reviewed the troops. This was interpreted as a strong omen and raised the confidence of the army.

Kutusov set about seeking a position for the battle he intended to have with the French. His first plans were for a battle near Gzatsk, and the Russian army began to concentrate there on 31 August. In a letter of that date, Kutusov ordered Tormassov and Admiral Tchichagov to renew their offensive against Napoleon's southern flank and announced his intention to offer battle at Mozhaizk.

The French occupied Gzatsk on 1 September, and the Russians resumed their withdrawal covered by a rear guard under General Konovnitzin. Napoleon once again chose to halt his advance, giving his stragglers two days to catch up. The rest of his army was allowed to rest.

On 2 September, Napoleon ordered the complete mustering of his army, and the returns showed about 128,000 men, with an additional 6,000 able to return to the ranks in five days. On 4 September the French once again began their advance, but their progress was marked by constant skirmishes. None of these skirmishes developed into a serious action, and the Russians vanished as soon as Eugène's flanking column began to threaten an envelopment of the Russian rear guard. At about 2:00 P.M. on 5 September, Murat led the French advanced guard onto the plains around Borodino.

Chapter XI

Kutusov Turns to Fight

Geography of a Battlefield

Before him, Murat saw a rolling, open plain speckled with occasional clumps of pine and birch. Along the north of the plain ran the new road from Smolensk to Moscow. To the south of the field ran the old Smolensk road. These two roads united at Mozhaizk, behind the plain. From there a single road continued through the forest. The Kolocha stream ran along the north of the plain, swinging north to eventually join the Moscow River. It and its tributaries had deeply scored the ground and were marked with steep banks that would prove to be serious military obstacles.

Though they were invisible to Murat, the plain had been fortified with a number of entrenchments by the tiny Russian engineering establishment. Twenty-six guns were positioned behind the Kolocha in what was to be known as the "Great" or "Raevsky Redoubt." Two further batteries with a total of twelve guns (nine in the forward battery and three in the rear battery) were placed "en echelon" near Gorki.

To the south, near the right flank, were a number of small streams running approximately north-south. They were the Voinak, Semenovka, Kamenka, and the Stonets, all of which flowed into the Kolocha. Kutusov chose to make his stand on the east bank so he could take advantage of a low ridge, which gave his gunners the fullest advantage of their fire, and of the gullies of these streams, which would provide some handicap to the attacking French.

The Raevsky Redoubt was constructed in the shape of a "V" with two short epaulments (shoulders) at the tops of the "V." The work was originally open at the back, but a wooden palisade was raised to close it off. Modest Bogdanovich made some unusual comments regarding the strength of this work and states that

> it was desired to construct a strong work in the fashion of a bastion, with half-tenailles at the sides. However, both the means and the time were lacking for this, so that this position, contrary to the claims of foreign histories, was only weakly fortified. The guns placed in this redoubt were unable to sweep the surrounding terrain properly. The entrenchment of earth was on the downslope, and in consequence of this, had a counterscarp noticeably lower than its scarp, while the entrenchment itself was not very deep to begin with. The construction of the entrenchment had only begun on 6 September (Gregorian Calendar), and therefore only on the evening before (the first day of the battle). This was because the personnel of the Moscow Government's militia, to whom the work had been assigned, had not been provided with pickaxes and shovels, and did not have the slightest concept of how to manufacture gabions or fascines.
>
> At daybreak on the 7th, the embrasures for only nine guns had been completed, and the redoubt was still not generally ready. The digging was generally extraordinarily difficult, on account of the rounded stones with which the heights of the Borodino battlefield were covered. For this reason, the cross section of the work could not be given the requisite bulk, and because of the shortage of fascines, the slopes could not be faced. There was nothing to speak of in the way of palisades or other hindrances to the approach. (M. Bogdanovitch, *Geschichte des Feldjagers im Jahre 1812.*)

The Russian Positions

Despite his demotion, Barclay still commanded the 1st Army of the West and was charged with holding the Russian right flank. He placed a mobile reserve on the right flank consisting of Platov's cossack and the 1st Cavalry Corps. Kutusov had positioned Baggovout and his 2nd Infantry Corps with the 4th Infantry Corps of Ostermann-Tolstoy behind the Kolocha in an unassailable position. Docturov's 6th Infantry

Corps stretched from these forces to the Raevsky Redoubt. The redoubt was manned by Paskevitch and men of his 26th Division, part of the 7th Infantry Corps.

Korff and Kreutz, commanders of the 2nd and 3rd Cavalry Corps, were positioned behind the redoubt to support it. In the village of Borodino, some distance in front of the redoubt, the Guard Jager Regiment was posted in a most vulnerable and isolated position. These dispositions clearly indicated that Kutusov anticipated the main French advance along the new Smolensk road.

To the south Kutusov's position was not so impregnable. There was an open stretch of 2,500 yards devoid of any terrain protection other than the banks of the Semenovka stream. The village of Semenovskaya dominated this position, but it was a military liability because of its totally wooden construction. As a result it was totally dismantled and burned to provide a clear field of fire.

On the left of this position were three more field fortifications. These three "V" flèches were "en échelon" and known as the "Bagration fléches." About a mile in front of these flèches was the Shevardino Redoubt, another "V," which was erected to warn of any French advance in that direction.

Kutusov positioned General Raevsky's corps, one division of which occupied the redoubt, south towards the village of Semenovskaya. He had the 4th Cavalry Corps positioned to support Raevsky. Still further south was Voronzov's 2nd Converged Grenadier Division, which occupied the Bagration flèches. Neverovski's 27th Division was behind the flèches. All of this infantry, part of the 8th Infantry Corps of Generallieutenant Borosdin, were formed in battalion columns.

A general Russian reserve was formed with the 1st and 2nd Cuirassier Divisions. The Guard Infantry and Tuchkov's 3rd Infantry Corps and twenty-six batteries, 300 guns total, were part of this reserve.

Kutusov's tactical dispositions reflected his inability to grasp the possibility of a French advance from the south. As a result, initially, he made little effort to defend his southern flank. When he did react to the appearance of the French, he only sent 8,000 men from Tuchkov's 3rd Corps, 1,500 cossacks, and 7,000 opolochenie. This force took up positions around the Utitza mound. No fortifications were raised, even though this mound offered a strong position that would have been invulnerable if fortified. His only action was to place Tuchkov's forces in the woods so they could spring an ambush on the French should they advance rashly. He hoped that once the French had committed their last reserves against Bagration's flank, these forces could swing out and strike their flank and rear.

To the north of this ambush, Kutusov strung out the 11th, 20th, 21st, and 41st Jager Regiments in an extended skirmish line that spread over a mile of open terrain. They formed the link between the ambush and Bagration's southern flank.

General Bennigsen passed through this area on the 6th and was buried with complaints about these dispositions by the commanding officers of these jager regiments. He overrode Kutusov's orders and directed Tuchkov to abandon the ambush and take up a position on the open plain to calm the jagers' fears.

Kutusov was not informed of this change and it was presumed that the changes in the positions had been made by Tuchkov, who died on the 7th. When Bennigsen's actions were discovered, he incurred Kutusov's wrath.

Kutusov's star had fallen after the disastrous battle of Austerlitz in 1805. In the time since his retirement, many tactical and operational changes had occurred in the Russian army. Kutusov was totally unfamiliar with them and made little effort to rectify this lack of knowledge. This lack of familiarity was probably the source of his irrational distribution of commands. Docturov commanded the center, which consisted of the 6th Infantry Corps and the 3rd Cavalry Corps. Prince Constantine commanded the Reserves. The right was commanded by Miloradovitch and consisted of the 2nd and 4th Infantry Corps as well as the 2nd and 3rd Cavalry Corps. Prince Gorchakov commanded the left, which was formed with practically the entire 2nd Army of the West.

Kutusov's positioning of forces was not unusual for the Russians, but were in striking contrast to those used by Wellington. Kutusov had placed his troops in dense columns on the forward slopes of the position, in full view of the French and their artillery. Wellington's practice was to place as much of his forces as possible on the reverse slopes, where they were hidden from view and fire.

The French were well aware of the disadvantages of this type of position, and Davout's instructions to his artillery were very explicit when he stated that these vulnerable columns were to be their principal target. The Russian plan and the French doctrine doomed thousands of Russians to die. The Preobragenski and Semenovski Guard Infantry Regiments, who did not fire a shot in anger, were to suffer 273 casualties from the French artillery.

Kutusov's dispositions dismayed his generals. Clausewitz said,

> The best side of the position, however, the right wing, could be of no avail to redeem the defects of the left. The whole position too strongly indicated the left to the French as the object of operation, to admit of their forces being attracted to the right. It was, therefore, a useless squandering of troops to occupy this portion. It would have been far better to have let the right wing lean on the Kolocha itself in the neighborhood of Gorki, and merely to have observed the remaining ground as far as the Moskva, or have pretended to occupy it. (Clausewitz, *Campaign of 1812 in Russia*, p. 150)

General Toll, the quartermaster general of the 1st Army of the West as well as quartermaster general of the entire Russian army under Kutusov, and Clausewitz both favored the deep formation that Kutusov had adopted. They considered such a position "to afford the best means in a defense of resuming the offensive, and of depriving the assailant of the advantage of the last disposition, and thus of surprise." Some things would never change in Russian military thought, and this was one of them.

Clausewitz indicates that it was most probably General Toll's influence that had resulted in the deep Russian formation. Clausewitz, though favoring deep formations, did not concur with Toll "as to the application of his principle in this instance." Clausewitz felt that the Russians were too compact and that the reserves were positioned much too close to the front line. He said that

> the depth of the ground, was too much neglected. The cavalry stood from 300 to 400 paces behind the infantry, and from these to the great reserve was scarcely 1,000 paces. The consequence was that both the cavalry and the reserve suffered heavily from the enemy's fire without being engaged. If we recollect what masses of artillery were used in this battle by the Russians, that the Russian artillery, on account of the quantity of small ammunition carts it uses, takes up more room than any other, we may imagine how the space was filled and crammed up. The author retains to this moment the effect produced on his mind by the spectacle with which position presented in this particular. (Clausewitz, *Campaign in Russia in 1812*, p. 155)

As the Russians stood awaiting the French offensive, Napoleon concentrated his efforts on bringing up his straggling columns. Seeing the strength on the Kolocha, he concentrated his army against the Russian left. Early on the afternoon of 5 September he rode forward to personally review the Russian position and the Shevardino Redoubt. Though of little military significance, it prevented Napoleon from making a close inspection of the Russian position and hindered the deployment of the French army with its twelve guns.

After studying the Russian positions, Napoleon turned and rode back to his generals to make plans for the initial French attacks. He directed Poniatowski to move his V Corps to the south in an effort to flank the Russian left. He then directed Compans' 5th Division to assault the Shevardino Redoubt commanded by Generallieutenant Gorchakov II.

Gorchakov had spread the 5th, 49th, and 50th Jager Regiments before the redoubt in a skirmish line extending from Alexinka to Fomkina along the Doronino ravine and in the brush extending towards Ielnia. The 27th Division was positioned behind the redoubt in dense columns, covered by the 12pdr guns in the redoubt. To the left and behind the infantry was the 2nd Cuirassier division, consisting of the Military Order, Little Russia, Gluchov, and Novgorod Cuirassier Regiments. It was posted in regimental columns. With it were eight horse guns, two squadrons of the Akhtyrsk Hussar Regiment, the New Russia, and the Kiev Dragoon Regiments detached from the 4th Cavalry Corps. To the right of the infantry were the Karkov and Tchernigov Dragoon Regiments, also from the 4th Cavalry Corps, and four horse guns. Generalmajor Karpov and six cossack regiments were posted on the Old Smolensk Road to observe the movements of Poniatowski.

The Battle of Shevardino

After throwing bridges over the stream that separated the two armies, Compans' 5th Division rolled forward, supported by the 1st and 2nd Reserve Cavalry Corps under Nansouty and Montbrun. The Russian skirmish screen fired on the advancing French and quickly withdrew.

The French advanced in dense columns preceded by a cloud of skirmishers and passed through Fomkino and Doronino, pushing back all Russian resistance. Compans established a strong battery near Valoueava. This battery was on a low ridge. It fired in support of the French, limbered up, and advanced with the column, unlimbering to fire on the Russians time and again until it was within cannister range of the Russians. The gunners were supported by six or seven companies of voltigeurs that took up positions on a small mound near the gunners' final position.

Compans' battery fired on the redoubt for nearly two hours and then moved against the village of Doronino and the adjacent woods. At the same time Poniatowski advanced against Ielnia, driving out the 5th Jager Regiment. The Kiev Dragoon Regiment charged, driving back the French skirmishers that had recklessly exposed themselves. A portion of the Akhtyrka Hussar Regiment, under Rittmeister Alexandrovich, charged a column which marched against the Russian guns the hussars were to protect. The French were driven back.

While the Russian skirmishers were retreating on the Russian right, the Novgorod Dragoon Regiment passed between the brush and the south side of the Doronino, disordering two French columns as well as throwing back a French cavalry probe. However, they too were obliged to withdraw as Poniatowski's Poles began to advance down the Old Smolensk Road and threatened their flank.

Generalmajor Lowenstern misread the situation and returned to Bagration with a glowing report of the valiant defense of the redoubt. On his return he found the artillery and some of the defending infantry streaming back towards the main Russian lines. He reacted by sending forward another battery and committing a brigade of the 27th Division. These forces advanced and supported the redoubt with point-blank musketry aimed at the advancing French.

Six companies of voltigeurs, supported by one battalion of the 61st Line Regiment, had occupied a mound 250 feet from the redoubt in support of Compans' battery. Compans sent the 57th and 61st Line Regiments, under General Duppelin, to attack the left wing of Neverovski's 27th Division. The right wing of the French 5th Division, the 111th and 25th Line Regiments, were to turn the Russian right. Simultaneously Morand and Friant moved on the village of Shevardino. A violent fusillade began at a range of sixty feet and stopped the French advance. Compans brought up four guns behind the cover of the 57th Line Regiment to break the stalemate. They began to fire cannister into the dense green lines of Russians. The artillery fire shook the Russians, and they crumbled under a bayonet assault by the 57th and 61st Line Regiments. These two regiments swept into the redoubt and found that the skirmish fire had killed every living thing in it. Morand quickly followed this success up by occupying the redoubt with his division.

Though it had begun as a small argument over maneuvering room, the battle around Shevardino was rapidly escalating into a general battle between the two armies' wings. Prince Gorchakov dispatched the 2nd Grenadier Division to relieve the battered 27th Division. The 2nd Grenadier Division and the rest of the 8th Corps were sent to take the redoubt, and they captured it after a bloody assault. The sole intention of Gorchakov was to hold the redoubt long enough to let night fall and end the battle.

The French columns began to close in on the 2nd Grenadier Division from the left. Colonel Tolbouzin, commanding the Little Russia and Gluchov Cuirassier Regiments, charged the French columns, driving them back. They continued their charge into the French lines, where they took a battery on the heights near Doronino, dragging off three pieces. At the same time the Karkov and Tchernigov Dragoon Regiments dispatched two squadrons each in a charge on the 111th Line Regiment. In response the 111th formed square, but lost its two regimental guns in the battle. It was heavily pressed and only saved by the timely arrival of the Joseph Napoleon Regiment, a regiment of pressed Spanish soldiers from Friant's 2nd Division.

The fall of darkness did not end the battle. Poniatowski was turning the redoubt's southern flank. Generalmajor Karpov observed this calmly. The redoubt was half destroyed by the violence of the initial assaults. Around 11:00 P.M. Bagration received the order to withdraw his forces. The rear guard was made up of the 2nd Cuirassier Division and a battalion of the Odessa Infantry Regiment.

As they withdrew, Murat's cavalry came forward once again. Neverovski, in an effort to halt the French advance, ordered the Odessa Infantry Regiment to raise their voices and beat their drums as loudly as possible in an effort to exaggerate their numbers. The cuirassiers advanced to meet the French. The engagement was fought in total darkness, and in the confusion the Russians completed their withdrawal. The French brought 35,000 men to play against 18,000 Russians. Both sides seem to have lost about 8,000 men in the engagement.

As the battle died down, both armies settled into their bivouacs. Russian fires lit the horizon to the east, but the French army sat sullen in the darkness. They had been unable to procure firewood or the other scarce comforts of field bivouacs.

Preparations for the Next Day's Battle

The night was marked with serious arguments in the Russian staff. General Yermolov contended that Shevardino was a superfluous position as a result of the Bagration flèches, and that it stood out of artillery range and consequently there was no point in defending and maintaining it. He was very outspoken in his opinion, stating that holding the position had allowed the French to strike an inferior, isolated portion of their army with little risk to themselves. Barclay agreed and urged that the redoubt be evacuated before a general assault was launched against it. Bagration's defense of this position was heated, probably because he had personally selected its site and his ego was involved. The result had been the sacrifice of 8,000 Russians. The decision to withdraw did come, but late in the evening.

There was also an argument concerning the weakly defended Old Smolensk Road, which was open to the classical Napoleonic flanking maneuver. Bennigsen and Kutusov were firm in their contention that the opolochenie was sufficient to hold this flank, and that Tuchkov's entire 3rd Infantry Corps was in a position to support them should they become too heavily involved with the French.

At dawn Napoleon began another review of the Russian positions, paying particular attention to their weak left and center. He advanced as far as the Russian outposts to insure that he had seen everything as clearly as possible. Poniatowski told him that he had not encountered heavy resistance, but Napoleon hesitated in deciding whether or not to attempt a grand tactical maneuver against the Russian left flank.

In the afternoon he again moved out to inspect the Russians, wishing to ascertain if there was any gap between the Bagration flèches and the right of the Russian 3rd Infantry Corps. As he stood on the heights opposite Borodino, Davout rode up and proposed taking the I and V Corps in a flanking maneuver around the Russian left flank. His proposal would bring him into the Russian flank and rear in the same manner as Junot should have done at Valoutino. The result would almost certainly have been the destruction of the Russians.

Such a maneuver was normally what Napoleon would have ordered, but in this instance he stated, "No! The movement is altogether too great! It would lead me away from my objective and make me lose too much time."[*] Many things no doubt passed through his mind. Foremost was the possibility that the Russians might once again refuse battle and disappear as they had at Smolensk. Or perhaps he feared that the Russians might go over to the offensive and strike him while a major portion of his army was maneuvering and unable to support him. He decided to

[*] (C. Duffy Borodino, *Napoleon Against Russia, 1812,* p. 84)

commit the French to a bloody frontal assault. It is probable that he felt that he could have afforded the losses in men and material if he could have extracted an equal loss from the Russians and destroyed their only standing army. Having done so, he could have then brought up those forces he had left behind and have still had a substantial field force.

Above all Napoleon wanted a smashing victory which would force the Russians into political collapse. Another unsuccessful maneuver would merely waste time and leave him miles from his bases, far from the security of winter quarters in Smolensk and having obtained nothing for his gamble. No, he had committed too much and could not afford to let the Russians escape him again. He had no real choice but to pin them in place and pound them into submission.

As Napoleon returned to camp, Murat reported that the Russians appeared to be withdrawing. Napoleon moved back to the front quickly to see what was happening. What he saw was troops moving onto the field, not away from it.

The French Battle Plans

Napoleon's plans for the battle evolved during the remainder of the day. He decided to send Poniatowski's V Corps on a limited flanking maneuver along the Old Smolensk Road. He determined to make his main thrust against the Russian center, along a sector of about one and a half miles. Here he planned to mass 85,000 men of the three divisions of I Corps and the I, II, and IV Reserve Cavalry Corps. He formed his forces into a deep columnar formation. Behind the I Corps he placed Ney's III Corps, Junot's Westphalians, the Guard Cavalry, the Young Guard, and finally the Old Guard. The Old Guard was designated as the last reserve. The assault formation was one-and-a-half miles long.

Napoleon posted Eugène north of the Kolocha with the IV Corps, Gerard's division of I Corps, and the III Reserve Cavalry Corps of General Grouchy. His task was to take the village of Borodino and the Raevsky Redoubt.

The Russian Positions

The Russians spent 6 September finishing off their entrenchments and positioning their forces. The 1st Army of the West was organized under the command of General of Infantry Miloradovitch. On its extreme right was the flank detachment of Colonel Vlasov III. His forces consisted of the Vlasov III Don Cossack Pulk and five sotnias of the Ataman Cossack Regiment.

Next came the Maslovo detachment of Generalmajor Passek who commanded the 4th, 30th, and 48th Jager Regiments. This force was positioned in the brush near Maslovo and the nearby woods. The Borodino detachment consisted of the Guard Jager Regiment, a section of the Guard Marine Equipage Battalion, and fourteen supporting guns.

In Gorki, Lieutenant Colonel Dieterichs III commanded the 11th and 36th Jager Regiments. They were positioned at the west entrance of Gorki and on both sides of the road.

The 2nd Infantry Corps, commanded by Generallieutenant Baggovout, was positioned as follows: the 4th Division, Tobolsk, Volhynie, and Krementchug Infantry Regiments, 4th and 34th Jagers, and the Minsk Infantry Regiment. The 17th Division was positioned next and arranged left to right as follows: Riazan, Bieloserk, and Brest Infantry Regiments, 30th and 48th Jager Regiments, and Wilmanstrand Infantry Regiments. This force was supported by two battalions of Moscow opolochenie and seventy-two guns.

The 4th Infantry Corps, under Generallieutenant Ostermann-Tolstoy, was deployed as follows: 11th Division—Kixholm, Pernov, and Polotsk Infantry Regiments, 1st and 33rd Jager Regiments, and the Jeletz Infantry Regiment; 23rd Division—Rilsk, Ekaterinburg, and one battalion of the Seleguinsk Infantry Regiments and the 18th Jager Regiment. The corps was supported by forty-eight guns.

The 1st Cavalry Corps had the Niejine Dragoon Regiment and Polish Uhlan Regiment in the first rank, with the Guard Dragoon Regiment, Guard Hussar Regiment, Guard Uhlan Regiment, Guard Cossack Regiment, and twelve horse guns in the second rank. The 2nd Cavalry Corps had the Pskof and Moscow Dragoon Regiments in the front rank and the Elisabethgrad and Isoum Hussar Regiments in the second rank. The Kargopol and Ingremanland Dragoon Regiments had been detached, but ten horse guns remained with the 2nd Cavalry Corps.

General of Cavalry Platov was positioned with an independent force of cossacks consisting of the Don Cossacks of Ilowaiski #5, Grekov #18, Kharitonov #17, Jirov, five sotnias of the Ataman Regiment, Simpheropol Tartar Regiment, and twelve horse guns.

The center of the Russian position was commanded by General of Infantry Docturov. The first detachment from the center was under Colonel Voutich I and consisted of the 19th and 40th Jager Regiments. They were posted in the ravine to the right of the Raevsky Redoubt. The second detachment was under Generalmajor Alexapol. He commanded the 1st Jager Regiment, which was spread between the Raevsky Redoubt and Borodino. In the woods bordering the Kolocha, the 6th and 20th Jager Regiments were posted in a skirmish screen that reached to the Kamenka stream.

Docturov had deployed his 6th Infantry Corps with the 7th Division on his right. It was deployed, left to right, as follows: Moscow, Pskof, and Sofia Infantry Regiments, 36th Jager Regiment, and the Libau Infantry Regiment. To their left was the 24th Division under Generalmajor Lichatcheff. They were, left to right, Oufa, Chirvan, and Bourtirki Infantry Regiments, 19th and 40th Jager Regiments, and the Tomsk Infantry Regiment.

Generalmajor Kreutz and his 3rd Cavalry Corps were posted in the center as well. The Kourland Dragoon Regiment and three squadrons of the Orenburg Dragoon Regiment were in the first line. The Soum and Marioupol Hussar Regiments were in the second line. The Siberian, Irkhoutsk, and one squadron of the Orenburg Dragoon Regiment and ten guns were detached to the road to the left as a rear guard.

The Russian main reserve consisted of the 5th Infantry Corps. The Guard Division was arranged with the Preobragenski, Semenovski, and Ismailov Guard Regiments in the first line. The Lithuanian and Finland Jager Guard Regiments were in the second line.

In addition to the Guard, the reserve contained the 1st Converged Grenadier Regiment which had three battalions drawn from the 4th and three battalions from the 17th Divisions, the 1st Cuirassier Division, and the main artillery reserve, 306 guns.

The left wing was commanded by General of Infantry Prince Bagration. The first detachment was under Colonel Goguel and consisted of the 5th, 41st, and 42nd Jager Regiments. This force was spread in a skirmish screen from west of the Kamenka to the detachment of General Alexapol. The second detachment, under Generalmajor Prince Chakoffski, consisted of the 49th and 50th Jager Regiments, Tauride Grenadier Regiment, and the 21st Jager Regiment. This detachment was positioned from the leftmost flèche to the village of Utitza, where it occupied all the woods and brush in between.

The 7th Corps was posted with the 26th Division consisting of the Ladoga, Poltava, and Nivegorod Infantry Regiment, the 5th and 42nd Jager Regiments, and the Orel Infantry Regiment. To their left was the 12th Division with the Smolensk, Narva, and New Ingremannland Infantry Regiments, 6th and 41st Jager Regiments, and the Alexopol Infantry

Regiment. This corps had two batteries, twenty-four guns, support-ing it.

The 8th Infantry Corps was to the left of the 7th Infantry Corps. It was commanded by Generallieutenant Borozdin. The 2nd Grenadier Divi-sion was posted slightly behind and to the left of the 12th Division. It consisted of the Kiev, Astrakhan, Moscow, Siberia, Little Russia, and Fangoria Grenadier Regiments.

Behind the flèches was the 27th Division, consisting of the Vilna, Simbrisk, and Odessa Infantry Regiments, the 49th and 50th Jager Regi-ments, and the Tarnopol Infantry Regiment. This corps was supported by two batteries, twenty-four guns. It should be noted that portions of the 2nd Grenadier Division were occupying the three flèches.

The 4th Cavalry Corps was behind the 12th Division. It consisted of the Karkov, Tchernigov, Kiev Dragoon, and New Russia Dragoon Regiments. Behind them was the Akhtyrsk Hussar Regiment, the Lithua-nian Uhlan Regiment, and a horse battery of twelve guns.

The reserve of the right wing consisted of the 2nd Converged Grena-dier Division and the 2nd Cuirassier Division. The 2nd Cuirassier Division was posted behind the 2nd Grenadier Division. It consisted of the Military Order, Ekaterinoslav, Gluchov, Novgorod, and Little Russia Cuirassier Regiments formed in two lines and a single horse battery.

A small detachment of eight cossack pulks was placed on the right flank of the 27th Division. This force was under the command of General-major Karpov and was in a picket screen that extended south towards Utitza.

The 3rd Infantry Corps was posted around Utitza. In the plain behind the village was Konovnitzin's 3rd Division. It consisted of the Mour-monsk, Revel, and Tchernigov Infantry Regiments, the 20th and 21st Jager Regiments, and the Seleguinsk Infantry Regiment. Behind them stood the 1st Grenadier Division consisting of the Leib, Count Arak-cheyev, Pavlov, Ekaterinoslav, Tauride, and St. Petersburg Grenadier Regiments. The 1st, 2nd, and 3rd Opolochenie Divisions, under the command of Generallieutenant Markov, and the Smolensk Opolochenie, commanded by Generallieutenant Lebedev, were posted behind the 1st Grenadier Division.

The Russians had divided their position by army corps. Each corps was supported by a small complement of artillery, while the bulk of the army's artillery was held in the general reserve. Two divisions occu-pied each sector. Initially all of the jagers were deployed as skirmishers before their respective divisions. Only the 33rd and 34th Jagers remained formed. The cavalry was formed in regimental lines, in two lines and behind the infantry, as a general rule.

In preparation for the coming battle, Kutusov toured the army, encouraging it. He was preceded by the Black Virgin of Smolensk icon. Kutusov read a proclamation to his soldiers saying, "Soldiers, fulfill your duties. Think of the sacrifices of your cities to the flames—of your children who implore you for protection. Think of your emperor, your lord, who regards you as the source of all his strength; and tomorrow, before the sun sets, you will have traced your faith and allegiance to your sovereign and country, in the blood of the aggressor and of his hosts." Kutusov's passage through the ranks was preceded and followed by the incantations and prayers of the Russian Orthodox priests who sprinkled holy water, swung their censers, and blessed the troops and their colors. The Russian army was whipped up to a religious fervor with exhortations to drive the satanic invaders from the sacred soil of mother Russia.

As at Austerlitz, Kutusov issued only limited, last-minute orders. He left much of the execution of the pending battle to the local commanders. He did insist that they retain their reserves intact as long as possible, that they prevent the "troops from banging off with their muskets for no purpose, and to get the gunners to economize as far as possible their ammunition." He fell back on the old Russian preference for the bayonet and stated that it would be the "fundamental tactic" of the day.

The commander of the 1st Army of the West's artillery, General Koutaissof, was an innovator and wished to stop a rather unfortunate habit of the Russian artillery. When threatened, the artillery would limber up and withdraw, fearing the loss of a gun more than being concerned for the infantry it left in the lurch. Koutaissof told his subordinates that they were

> to remind the companies from me that they are not to make off before the enemy are actually sitting on the guns. Tell the commanders and all the officers that they must stand their ground until the enemy are within the closest possible cannister range, which is the only way that you will insure that we do not cede a yard of your position. The artillery must be prepared to sacrifice itself. Let the anger of your guns roar out! A battery which is captured

after this will have inflicted casualties on the enemy which will more than compensate for the loss of the guns.

Although in this battle the Russian gunners obeyed these instructions, their habit of saving the guns at the expense of the infantry continued into the twentieth century and World War I.

French Battle Instructions

During the afternoon of 6 September, Napoleon received a courier from Paris who brought a new painting of his son, the king of Rome. He also brought news of Marmont's disastrous defeat at Salamanca at the hands of Wellington.

After that news, Napoleon set about preparing and dispatching his orders to the various corps. He ordered that the break of dawn should be marked by the fire of two new batteries organized during the night by Davout's corps against the flèches opposite them. Napoleon was still unaware that there was a third flèche in this group.

At the moment General Pernety, commander of the I Corps artillery, with thirty guns from Compans' divisional artillery and all of the howitzers from Dessaix's and Friant's divisions shall commence to fire and crush with their shells the enemy battery, which shall have by this means, against it twenty four of the Guard's pieces, thirty from Compans' division and eight from the divisions of Dessaix and Friant; a total of sixty two guns.

General Foucher, commander of the artillery of III Corps, shall advance with all the howitzers of the III and VII Corps, which number sixteen, around the battery which forms the redoubt on the left. This will make forty guns against this battery.

General Sorbier shall be ready for the first command to detach himself with all the Guard howitzers and advance on one or the other redoubt.

During this cannonade Prince Poniatowski shall advance from the village towards the forest and turn the position of the enemy. General Compans shall skirt the forest to carry the first redoubt.

The cannonade on the right shall commence at the same moment as the cannonade on the right. A strong skirmish shall be started by Morand's division and by the divisions of the Viceroy (Eugène) as soon as they see the attack on the right begin. The Viceroy shall seize the village (Borodino), cross via the three bridges to the heights, as Generals Morand and Gerard advance under the Viceroy's orders to seize the (Raevsky) redoubt and form the line of the army.

All shall be done with order and method and having care to retain always a large quantity of reserves.

In addition to his orders to his generals, Napoleon had circulated to the lowest levels of his army his own proclamation, saying, "Soldiers, here is the battle that you have so desired. It will give us abundance, good winter quarters, and a prompt return to the fatherland. Conduct yourselves as at Austerlitz, Friedland, Vitebsk, Smolensk, and posterity will remember with pride your conduct on this day; that it shall be said of you: He was in the great battle under the walls of Moscow."

Generally 6 September was spent by both sides in the preparation of orders and less strenuous activities. Lieutenant Bogdanov, of the Russian engineers, was the one officer who was truly busy. He was charged with strengthening the Raevsky Redoubt. He spent the day digging a number of wolfpits about one hundred yards in front of the battery and extending the epaulments to a length of twenty-five yards. Taking timber from dismantled houses, he built a double palisade around the rear of the battery. The first stood upright and was about eight feet tall. The second was angled outwards and was about six feet in length. He left gaps on either end to permit troops and artillery limbers to enter or exit the redoubt.

After he inspected the work, General Raevsky said, "Now gentlemen, we may rest in security. When daylight comes Napoleon will espy what seems to be a single open battery, but his army will come up against a virtual fortress. The approaches are swept by more than 200 guns (he is counting those of the nearby field batteries), the ditch is deep and the glacis is solid."

When night fell, no one in either camp slept soundly. The air was as full of tension as were the soldiers who looked forward to what might be the last day of their lives. The night echoed with the sounds of rumbling wheels as the armies made last-minute adjustments. The horizons were lit by a countless multitude of camp fires.

Napoleon slept less than all others. Still fearing that the Russians might decamp on him, he rose repeatedly to reassure himself that the

Russians were still there. He rose at 3:00 A.M., spoke to his aides for a while, and finally joined Berthier and worked until 5:00 A.M. At dawn he rode out to the Shevardino Redoubt and remarked to his staff, "It is a trifle cold, but the sun is bright. It is the sun of Austerlitz!"

Chapter XII

The Turning Point—The Battle of Borodino

The Battle Begins

The first cannon shots broke the stillness of the dawn, and the Russians began their reply. It was quickly discovered that the three batteries, a total of 102 guns, that Napoleon had ordered formed on September 6th were out of range of their targets. The guns had to be prolonged forward 1,600 paces until they were within range.

The firing spread to the I and III Corps. The air was torn by the shriek of round shot. Death and destruction had begun to rain on both armies, with shots indiscriminately smashing all that they encountered.

Eugène's forces advanced into the village of Borodino, as directed, and engaged the Russian Guard Jager Regiment with the 106th Line Regiment. Barclay had recognized the dangerous position of the Guard Jagers and sent Lowenstern to recall them. As Lowenstern arrived, so did the French, at "an unbelievable speed." Delzon's 13th Division had caught the Guard Jagers, commanded by Colonel Bistrom, and one French brigade hurried them across the Kolocha. Another brigade sent forward skirmishers who fired on the fleeing Russians as they crossed the bridge. The crowding was so thick and the fire so heavy that the regiment lost half of its strength before it had completely crossed the bridge.

So rapid was the advance of the 106th Line Regiment and the retreat of the Russian Guard Jagers, that the French were able to cross the intact bridge and advance on Gorki. However, the French began to lose their organizational integrity, and, as they grew fatigued, they were struck frontally by the regrouped Guard Jagers and in the flank by the 1st, 19th, and 40th Jager Regiments. The 106th Line was thrown back across the Kolocha, where it reformed behind the 92nd Line Regiment. The Russians quickly reoccupied the lost ground on their side of the Kolocha, while the Russian Guard Equipage Battalion destroyed the bridge.

Delzon's division occupied the village as the Bavarian cavalry deployed behind the village to the east. Eugène prepared to renew his assault across the river by organizing a twenty-eight-gun battery near Borodino. This battery was positioned so that it could bring the Raevsky and Gorki earthworks under fire. Since the village was untenable, the Russians quickly lost interest in Borodino, and the French deployed around it. Ornano moved to Bezzoubovo, and the divisions of Gerard and Broussier, the Italian Guard, and Grouchy's III Reserve Cavalry Corps supported Morand's division as he prepared to recross the Kolocha.

Barclay began a tour of his army, and as he passed through the Russian Imperial Guard he was showered with shot. Lowenstern recalled that the young grenadiers preserved a truly military bearing and calmly welcomed Barclay's appearance. The shots were already working to devastating effect in their ranks, but the men stood stoically and silently, with their muskets by their sides, and they coolly closed up their ranks whenever a missile claimed its victim. The effect was shaking to all, but hardest on the officers. General Lavrov was so shaken by the carnage that he suffered a nervous breakdown.

The Battle for the Bagration Flèches

As Napoleon heard the battle around Borodino develop, and when he judged that Poniatowski had had enough time to reach his jumping-off positions, he directed that Davout's I Corps begin its attack of the Bagration flèches. The flèches had been under fire of the 102 guns of Sorbier, Pernety, and Foucher since 7:00 A.M., but most of their fire had been directed on the Raevsky Redoubt and the village of Borodino. Thirty-eight guns had taken an enfilade position against the lines of the 2nd Army of the West, while the others had enfiladed the 1st Army of the West. In the middle of this cannonade, General Compans' 5th Division advanced with the support of thirty guns. He moved on the flèches, to the right of Sorbier's battery, and crossed the woods. Teste's 25th and 57th Line Regiments cleared them of Russian skirmishers while the entire division pushed along the southern edge of the woods. Friant and the 2nd Division remained behind as a reserve. To the south, Poniatowski had also become engaged in battle.

Compans' men marched into the fury of the Russian 11th and 32nd Light Companies. The Russian fire took such a heavy toll of the advancing infantry that the columns thinned perceptively as they advanced. Not only was the cannister fire from the flèches taking a toll, but Russian skirmishers stationed between the flèches and Utitza, under Prince Chakoffski, kept the French under heavy fire.

A stray shot from a Russian skirmisher struck General Compans and put him out of the battle. Shortly after Marshal Davout's horse was killed beneath him, throwing him to the ground and stunning him. With the temporary loss of these two, General Dessaix took command of the assault, and Compans' two-pronged assault fell to the side. The 57th Line Regiment advanced into and seized the westernmost flèche. However, the fire from the Russian skirmishers and a counterattack by the 2nd Converged Grenadier Division and a few battalions of the 27th Division threw them out.

General Voronzov's forces reestablished themselves in the flèche while General Sievers advanced with the Akhtyrsk Hussar Regiment, Lithuanian Uhlan Regiment, and the New Russia Dragoon Regiment. General Sievers pursued the recoiling French back to their main lines and captured twelve guns. However, in its turn, the Russian cavalry was attacked by the 2nd and 4th Württemberg Chevauxlégers and thrown back. The French recaptured their guns.

The 5th Division was scattered in the ditches and folds of the ground before the flèches. General Rapp came forward to assume command of the division from Dessaix. This permitted him to concentrate his attention on his 4th Division, which had replaced the 5th in the front line.

Ledru's 10th Division moved forward at 9:00 A.M. as the third assault against the flèches, with three regiments in battalion columns. He was supported by Junot's VIII Corps, which was positioned to the left of Shevardino, and the IV Reserve Cavalry Corps. Davout's renewed advance was supported by the I Reserve Cavalry Corps.

Bagration saw the assault coming and brought up the rest of Neverovski's 27th Division to support the 2nd Converged Grenadier Division. The French did not observe this and were still unaware of the existence of the third flèche, behind the flèche designated as Ledru's target. As Ledru advanced on his target flèche, Junot was chasing the Russian jagers from the woods to the south of the flèches.

Bagration ordered Raevsky to shift part of his 7th Infantry Corps towards the flèches, and the 2nd Grenadier Division of Prince Carl of Mecklenburg was to move to the left of Semenovskaya. The 2nd Cuirassier Division was to position itself to the left of the grenadiers. Bagration then ordered the 3rd Infantry Corps of General Tuchkov I to detach the 3rd Division towards the flèches. He also demanded and received from the reserve the Guard infantry regiments Ismailov, Lithuanian, and Finland, the Emperor and Empress Cuirassiers, eight battalions of the converged grenadiers, the two Guard Position Batteries—Emperor and Arakcheyev, and the 1st Guard Horse Battery. Though reinforcements were on the way, it would take one-and-a-half hours before all of them would arrive.

This was sufficient time to allow the French to fully develop their attack. The 24th Légère and the 57th Line Regiments struck the leading flèche from the south simultaneously as Ledru struck the flèche from the north. It was at this time that the French realized that there was a third flèche. The French attack finally drove the 2nd Converged Grenadier Division out of the flèche.

By this time Bagration had sent the 27th Division, four battalions of the 12th Division, the 2nd Grenadier Division, the 2nd Cuirassier Division, the Akhtyrsk Hussar Regiment, the Lithuanian Uhlan Regiment, the New Russia Dragoon Regiment, and five horse guns into the cauldron brewing around the flèches.

The French had been reinforced by the light cavalry brigades of Beurmann and Bruyère. The Württemberg cavalry, under Beurmann, was sent to stop a Russian infantry force moving to retake the flèches, but was struck by Duka's Gluchov, Novgorod, and Little Russia Cuirassier Regiments. The Württembergers were thrown back, and Duka's cavalry struck the head of Dessaix's 4th Division. Six guns were lost to the Russians momentarily.

Duka's cuirassiers were quickly countercharged by 100 volunteers of the 6th Polish Uhlan Regiment under Major Sucharzewski. They were stopped and brought under the concentrated fire of the French artillery.

General Rapp was in the front lines directing his forces when he was struck twice by spent musketballs, a third ball grazed his arm, and a fourth shot struck him in the hip and threw him from his horse. Dessaix once again assumed the command of both divisions, only to be shot in the arm by a musketball.

Ledru's division succeeded in its fourth attack, at about 10:00 A.M., and took possession of the flèche once again. During the course of the capture of the flèche, Russian generals Neverovski and Gorchakov II were wounded. The French had barely reoccupied the flèche as Konovnitzin's 3rd Division, supported by the Soum and Marioupol Hussar Regiments, and the Kourland and Orenburg Dragoon Regiments counterattacked and drove them out.

Upon seeing the Russians retake the flèche, Murat seized control of the Württemberg König Jägers and the 72nd Line Regiment. He led them forward, retaking the southernmost flèche once again. The Russian cuirassiers charged Murat's force, surrounding him and his jägers in the flèche with a sea of hostile cavalry. The remainder of the Württemberg division advanced to save their fellows.

Napoleon was informed of the capture of the flèches and decided that Junot's VIII Corps was no longer required to support Davout's attack. He directed Junot to move between Davout and Poniatowski. When Napoleon learned of the checking of Ney's forces, he sent him Friant's 2nd Division. A total of 26,000 French were massed before the flèches occupied by only 18,000 Russians.

Heavy batteries on both sides pounded the other's infantry. Bagration was struck by a cannister ball that eventually killed him. Both his chief of staff, St. Priest, and Konovnitzin were wounded.

Though the French retook the flèches again at 11:00 A.M., they were thrown out by Generallieutenant Borosdin's 8th Infantry Corps, supported by the Kiev, Moscow, Astrakhan, and Siberia Grenadier Regiments of the 2nd Grenadier Division.

By 11:30 A.M. it was clear that the French had finally seized permanent control of the flèches. Konovnitzin withdrew his troops behind the ravine of the Semenovskaya, while General of Infantry Docturov took command of the 2nd Army of the West. The French had committed about 45,000 men and 400 guns to the battle over the flèches. The Russians had faced them with about 300 guns. The battle had lasted five hours before the French found themselves in indisputable control of the flèches.

The Assault on the Raevsky Redoubt

To the north of the battlefield, Eugène, after capturing the village of Borodino, directed Delzon to hold it with his division and brought Morand, Gérard, and Broussier across a pontoon bridge he had raised over the Kolocha above the village. He made preparations for his assault on the Raevsky Redoubt. Eugène's slow preparations and advance caused the Russians to think that his actions were purely diversionary, so they had begun shifting their forces along the northern flank towards the south to reinforce the battle around the flèches.

Raevsky's 7th Infantry Corps had been assigned to defend the redoubt and the surrounding terrain. He had formed a massive skirmish line with the 5th, 6th, and 41st Jager Regiments from the 7th Infantry Corps, the 19th and 40th Jagers from the 6th Infantry Corps, and the 18th Jager Regiment from the 4th Infantry Corps. This force was posted in the ravine of the Semenovskaya stream. Four battalions of the 12th Division were posted to the left of the redoubt. They were supported by six field batteries.

A powerful artillery barrage prepared the way for Eugène's assault. This fire was directed primarily on the 3rd Cavalry Corps, posted to the left and rear of the redoubt. Horse Battery #9 was destroyed by this fire, but its position was quickly filled by another battery. The Alexandria Hussar Regiment and three dragoon regiments standing near the redoubt were severely mauled by this fire.

Shortly before 10:00 A.M., Raevsky easily threw back a French reconnaissance in force led by Broussier. When Bagration was wounded, Raevsky took command in his place and began to move to Semenovskaya. Raevsky decided that it was too dangerous for him to leave his troops, who were threatened with attack. He sent Konovnitzin to handle things as best he could. Shortly afterwards, he found French grenadiers pouring through the embrasures of his redoubt.

It was 11:00 A.M. when the lead elements of Morand's 1st Division advanced in the "ordre mixte." Five battalions of the 30th Line Regiment and two battalions of the 2nd Baden Infantry Regiment, Bonamy's brigade, advanced directly on the redoubt. Great holes were ripped in their ranks by the cannister belching from the redoubt's 12pdr cannons. Bonamy led them forward at the "pas de charge." They passed over the redoubt's wall, and the Russian gunners fought for their lives with their rammers. A bloody hand-to-hand battle ensued, and the French 30th Line Regiment swept through and beyond the redoubt, chasing the surviving gunners before them. Only a single battalion of the 13th Légère Regiment was unengaged and able to exploit the gap in the Russian lines. The other battalions were too heavily engaged to move through the gap.

Barclay, having sent Lowenstern to investigate the commotion around the redoubt, learned of its loss and moved to the 6th Infantry Corps. He sent the two battalions of the Tomsk Infantry Regiment forward to turn the right of the redoubt.

General Yermolov, chief of staff of the 1st Army of the West, was also passing this vicinity of the redoubt. He noted the 18th, 19th, and 40th Jager Regiments were fleeing in complete disorder. They were incapable of interfering with the French reorganization and consolidation of the recently captured redoubt. Yermolov took command of the 3/Oufa Infantry Regiment and directed it up the hill, towards the redoubt. Behind them he reorganized the jagers and directed them to follow it. He also directed Colonel Nikitin to take three horse batteries and support their advance.

At the same time Generalmajor Kreutz, with part of the 3rd Cavalry Corps, consisting of the Siberian, Orenburg, and Irkhoutsk Dragoon Regiments and a horse battery, moved against the Italians. The Italians were advancing on the French left, and this attack stopped their advance.

The commanders of the Russian 12th and 26th Divisions rallied their troops and were moving to crush the French 30th Line Regiment. They pierced the center of the 30th Line Regiment with the support of Colonel Nikitin's three horse batteries, now posted to the left of the redoubt. The French holding the redoubt fled before the massive Russian assault. Those that remained put up a desperate fight that lasted no more than ten minutes. General Yermolov took a handful of crosses of the Order of St. George and threw them at the redoubt to encourage the jagers, but they were out to avenge their insult and this was unnecessary. Those that remained of the French 30th Line Regiment were pushed out at bayonet point and suffered heavily. Only 268 men of the 30th Line Regiment remained to reform behind the French lines, despite support from the carabiniers.

General Bonamy had been wounded fifteen times and was abandoned by his retreating troops in the redoubt. He was about to receive his sixteenth wound from a poised bayonet when he cried out that he was Murat, king of Naples. The grenadier who was about to bayonet him seized him by the collar and led him off to Kutusov. Kutusov's only action when he saw the bloody Bonamy was to see that his wounds were quickly tended to, and Bonamy passed into captivity.

In the engagement around the redoubt, the Russians suffered the loss of General Koutaissof, chief of artillery to the 1st Army of the West. He had forgotten his true duties and had led a party of Russian infantry along the right of the redoubt. His death removed the only guidance and supervision that the Russian artillery reserve had. Once he died, movement from the artillery reserve to the battle stopped.

As the French fell back from the redoubt, their artillery stopped firing, so as to not hit them. Silence fell for the Russians as well, for they were unable to fully re-man and serve the guns in the redoubt they had just recaptured. The French quickly reorganized and began to bring another powerful attack column against the 7th Infantry Corps and the redoubt. Another bloody battle swept over the redoubt.

Prince Eugène of Württemberg was leading the 17th Division of the 2nd Infantry Corps south towards the battle around the flèches and halted it behind the redoubt at 10:00 A.M., when the French attacked him. He was resting his troops when he found himself attacked by the French III Reserve Cavalry Corps. The three cuirassier and four dragoon regiments moved forward with their light cavalry brigade screening their advance. This mass of cavalry swarmed around the Russian infantry, forcing it to form square quickly.

Grouchy's III Reserve Cavalry Corps inflicted heavy losses on the 17th Division. Kreutz's Russian 3rd Cavalry Corps advanced to assist Prince Eugène, but his forces were insufficient to stop the carnage. Yermolov was twice forced to turn the guns in the redoubt around to fire on French cavalry in his rear. Despite the threat to their rear, Yermolov's forces stood fast.

Around 11:00 A.M. the battle slackened, and the French artillery took up the pace. Prince Eugène of Württemberg was dehorsed by a cannon shot and, as he remounted, a howitzer shell killed the second horse. He finally mounted a draft horse from an artillery unit and led the second brigade (Krementchug and Minsk Infantry Regiments) towards the area behind the Bagration flèches, where he had been directed.

Yermolov was struck in the neck by a cannister shot and passed command of the redoubt to Generalmajor Lichatcheff, commander of the 24th Division.

The French Strike the Russian Center

As the actions around the Bagration flèches and Raevsky Redoubt raged, Napoleon chose to direct elements of the I and III Corps, the I and IV Reserve Cavalry Corps, and a large force of French artillery to strike the Russian center. This force was directed against the Russian

line around the village of Semenovskaya, which was defended by eight
battalions of the 2nd Converged Grenadier Division. This force, commanded by Generalmajor Voronzov, was immediately in front of the
village. They were supported by the Russian Guard regiments Ismailov,
Lithuanian, and Finland, posted to the south of Voronzov, and the 1st
Cuirassier Division, posted behind him. The converged grenadiers, cuirassiers, and the guard infantry had been sent forward from the reserve to
fill this position. Somewhat to their rear was the 3rd Division, which,
though primarily concerned with the flèches, could assist the center if
problems arose. They acted as a second line to the forces around Semenovskaya.

The French attack on the center was led by Friant's 2nd Division.
He was flanked by the heavy cavalry of the I and IV Reserve Cavalry
Corps. This force advanced directly on the rubble that had been Semenovskaya. The assault was heralded by a tremendous artillery barrage that
furthered the destruction of the already ravaged village.

The Russian artillery replied and directed much of its fire on the
French cavalry. About 10:00 A.M. the French assault began, and the
cavalry quickly began their advance. Latour-Maubourg's forces advanced
in half-squadrons, his forces divided into two columns. As he crossed
the Semenovskaya stream, his right-hand column was the 7th Cuirassier
Division, commanded by Lorge. The right column contained the Saxon
cuirassier regiments—Garde du Corps and Zastrow (eight squadrons);
the Polish 14th Cuirassier Regiment (two squadrons); and the 1st and
2nd Westphalian Cuirassier Regiments (eight squadrons). The left column
was formed by the 4th Light Cavalry Division: 3rd, 11th, and 16th
Polish Uhlan Regiments (twelve squadrons).

As the leading two-and-a-half squadrons of the Saxon Garde du
Corps crossed the stream, they encountered a Russian battery supported
by the 2nd Grenadier Division formed in squares. General Thieleman
formed the remaining squadrons in echelon to the left and charged the
Russians. One square was broken and the others forced back. In their
pursuit of the withdrawing Russian infantry, they encountered the dragoons of General Sievers' 4th Cavalry Corps. The dragoons were supported by the fire of the 2nd Guard Light Artillery Battery. This was
insufficient to halt the Saxons, and they pressed beyond the village and
found themselves facing the Ismailov and Lithuanian Guard Infantry
Regiments formed in six battalion squares.

The French cavalry assault was furious, but the Ismailov Guard withstood them. In one of three historically recorded instances, the Ismailov Guard actually executed a bayonet charge against the attacking cavalry. They did so with the support of the 1st Guard Light Battery and the two Guard Position Batteries.

At the same time, General Borosdin II, with his 1st Cuirassier Division (Emperor, Empress, and Astrakhan Cuirassier Regiments) struck the Saxons frontally, and the Akhtyrsk Hussar Regiment struck them in the flank. The Saxons suffered heavy casualties from the ensuing cavalry battle because they had left their cuirasses in Saxony. They were driven back behind a crest to the right of Semenovskaya.

The Polish uhlans of the 28th Light Brigade, who had advanced to the left of the Saxons, had become involved in battles around the Raevsky Redoubt and captured eight guns. The toll was heavy and the 11th Uhlan Regiment lost nearly all of its officers and most of its men hors de combat.

A lull developed as the cavalry withdrew and Friant brought the 15th Légère and 48th Line Regiments into the ruins of Semenovskaya. The cavalry engagement renewed itself as the blown Russian cavalry was struck by the Westphalian cuirassiers. The Russian cavalry was pushed off the battlefield.

As the two cavalry battles raged on the sides of Semenovskaya, the 2nd Converged Grenadier Division reformed and established a weak line in front of the village. General Docturov slowly fed the Moscow and Astrakhan Grenadier Regiments into the village to provide support for the converged grenadiers.

The Russian resistance in Semenovskaya was impressive. Friant's officers were so discouraged by the Russian resistance that one colonel ordered his regiment to withdraw. After an exchange with Murat, which embarrassed the colonel, he turned to his men and said, "Soldiers, about face! Let's go and get killed!"

Friant's renewed attack crushed what resistance remained in the grenadiers, and the 15th Légère and 48th Line Regiments swept over the ruins of Semenovskaya. The breach in the Russian lines had finally been formed, and it lay directly in the path of the French reserve.

This was the classical time for the Napoleonic coup de grace, but it did not occur. Murat and Ney had been conducting the battle uninterrupted by Napoleon's direction. They sent a courier to Napoleon requesting the release of the reserves, specifically the Young Guard. Napoleon slowly considered the situation and initially consented. He quickly recanted, however. General Lobau and the Young Guard, disappointed by this, slowly edged forward on the pretext of correcting the alignment of their ranks. Napoleon saw this and immediately brought it to a halt.

From this gap the Lithuanian and Finland Guard withdrew in perfect order, while the rest of the 2nd Army of the West, which had defended the flèches, withdrew in great disorder into the woods behind Semenovskaya. With his line pierced, Barclay turned the 4th Infantry Corps south in order to seal the threat to his army from that flank. At the same time Platov began his maneuver to the north of Eugène on the French bank of the Kolocha.

General Belliard arrived at noon with a second request for the release of the Young Guard. His request was denied when Napoleon said, "Before I commit my reserves I must be able to see more clearly on my chessboard." No doubt he was thinking of the miles between his army and France as well as the pending winter. Ney was not pleased, but Murat received the news with more grace.

Napoleon's failure to release the Young Guard had given Docturov and Konovnitzin time to reform what remained of the 2nd Army of the West. At the same time Barclay maneuvered the 4th Infantry Corps. These movements obliged Napoleon to release General Sorbier and the sixty pieces of Guard artillery, which he had held in reserve. General Sorbier quickly deployed them in support of General Friant. The Guard artillery, eager to join the battle, galloped forward.

Once in position, the artillery began an enfilading fire on Ostermann-Tolstoy's infantry, which had moved into the gap behind Semenovskaya. Despite the heavy and accurate French artillery fire, the Russians marched as if machines, filling the gaps that were ripped in their ranks by the artillery fire as if they were on parade. They continued to close until the French took them under fire with cannister, which blew away entire pelotons with a single blast. As the Russians reached their assigned position, they halted and remained there. They were swept with heavy artillery fire for five hours without stirring. The only movement was as new troops stepped forward to fill the ranks emptied by artillery fire. After the battle, their positions could still be seen, clearly marked by the dead, whose bodies were still arranged in formation.

Activity on the Northern End of the Battlefield

Platov's maneuver to the north, mentioned earlier, had begun when the cossacks discovered an unknown ford. Hoping to exploit this, Platov sent word to Kutusov and suggested sending the cavalry reserve across the ford to threaten the French left. This reserve was then located on the northern side of the Russian army and had not yet been committed to the battle. As word of the discovery arrived, so did word of the fall of the Raevsky Redoubt. Despite this, Colonel Toll suggested to Kutusov that the entire cavalry reserve of the Russian right should be sent on this maneuver, and Kutusov agreed.

This order released 8,000 Russian cavalry that had sat idle while the rest of the Russian army was heavily engaged to their south. The forces of Generallieutenant Ouvarov's 1st Cavalry Corps (the Russian Guard cavalry) consisted of twenty-eight squadrons of cavalry and a single Guard Horse Battery with twelve guns. This force was joined by 5,000 cossacks and two Don Cossack Horse Batteries, and the entire force moved across the Kolocha near Maloe about 11:00 A.M. The first French forces they encountered were the 84th Line Infantry Regiment and the Bavarian and Italian light cavalry of General Ornano.

The Russians formed the Elisabethgrad Hussar Regiment and the Guard Cossacks into their first rank. Behind them formed the Guard Dragoon, Uhlan, and Hussar Regiments, the Niejine Dragoon Regiment, and the 2nd Guard Horse Battery. The Guard Hussar Regiment attacked the 84th Line Regiment, which was in square. They attacked three times without artillery preparation or success. Eventually, the Russian artillery unlimbered and forced the 84th Line Regiment to withdraw behind the river and abandon its two regimental guns. The remainder of the Russian cavalry drove back the Bavarian and Italian cavalry.

Platov had crossed the Kolocha with nine cossack pulks in an attempt to maneuver on the French rear, but the regular cavalry operating with them was stopped by Delzon's division and the reformed Italian and Bavarian cavalry. The French moved cavalry north to support that flank. General Grouchy's III Reserve Cavalry Corps was the first to move north. The 11th Light Brigade, formed by the 6th Hussar and 8th Chasseur à Cheval Regiments, engaged the Russians with deadly effect. Napoleon, reacting to the Russian advance, detached part of the troops attached to the Guard to act as a reserve for that flank. The Vistula Legion, an elite formation of Poles, advanced and established themselves in Eugène's rear, relieving his fears of Platov's cossacks striking him from behind.

The cavalry reinforcements pushed the Russians back to the Kolocha, and they lost the French guns they had captured. Though there was much recrimination on the Russian side and accusations of lethargic efforts by Platov's cossacks, the Russians did not realize the actual impact of their maneuver. If they had realized its impact, they would not have been so quick to pass the blame. This diversion had paralyzed the French left and center from about noon to 2:00 P.M. The word that the much-feared cossacks were in the French rear had spread terror as far south as Shevardino. The Imperial Guard made ready to receive cavalry in their rear. Though Napoleon had earlier made the decision not to commit his Guard, this incident reinforced his desire not to commit them.

The Russian maneuver had diverted a total of sixteen regiments north to support this flank. Grouchy had retained only four regiments of his cavalry south of the Kolocha. Eugène had moved north to supervise the conduct of the operations on the northern flank personally. Napoleon also shifted his position north and remained there until about 3:00 P.M.

On the Russian side, Kutusov made little personal effort in directing the conduct of the battle. Barclay and Bagration were left to make the tactical efforts unaided. Barclay was astonished when Kutusov sent the Guard Infantry to support the 2nd Army of the West, though it was heavily engaged in the defense of Semenovskaya.

The stopping of the infantry assaults on the Raevsky Redoubt and the successful advance against Semenovskaya had opened a gap in the French lines. The only force available to fill this gap was the IV Reserve Cavalry Corps. As a result, for the best part of three hours, these magnificent and expensive horsemen were used to fill the gap. They were then subjected to the undivided attention of the Russian artillery in and around the redoubt. The 1st Brigade of the 7th Cuirassier Division, under General Thieleman, was badly mauled and lost about half its strength. The Westphalians of the 2nd Brigade, under General Lepel, were singled out for special attention and suffered even more cruelly as they stood in the open.

The II Reserve Cavalry Corps was positioned under this fire as well. The bright copper cuirasses of the Carabinier Regiments also attracted the attention of the Russian gunners. General Montbrun, commander of the II Reserve Cavalry Corps, was struck while maneuvering Pajol's division under some cover. He was taken from the field and died of his wounds at about 5:00 P.M. Napoleon sent General August de Caulaincourt, brother to the Grand Equerry, to take command of the II Reserve Cavalry Corps upon Montbrun's death.

More Attempts to Take the Raevsky Redoubt

While the French cavalry was being battered, the French were massing 170 guns. This "grande batterie" directed its fire on the redoubt and the eight Russian reserve horse batteries that were positioned near it. The breastwork forming the redoubt was battered, and the earth forming it was blown back into the trench, filling it in. Casualties were heavy, and the horse battery of Colonel Nikitin lost 93 of 235 men and 113 horses in a single hour.

At 2:00 P.M. Napoleon ordered Eugène to resume his attacks. The divisions of Broussiere, Gerard, and Morand advanced, supported on the left by part of Chastel's 3rd Light Cavalry Division. This force was to strike the right and front of the redoubt, while Wathier's 2nd Cuirassier Division and Lorge's 7th Cuirassier Division attacked the left of the redoubt.

Barclay had positioned the 4th Infantry Corps to the left of the Raevsky Redoubt, his left wing refused. He placed the 7th Infantry Corps and the Preobragenski and Semenovski Guard Infantry Regiments behind the 4th Corps as a second line. He then began forming a third line with the 2nd and 3rd Cavalry Corps. They were reinforced by the Chevalier Guard and Horse Guard Regiments. The 2nd Cavalry Corps had not arrived by the time the French assault began. In addition, a large portion of the 3rd Cavalry Corps had been detached to the left wing.

The desire of the French, Saxon, Polish, and Westphalian horsemen to come to grips with the gunners who had had them under fire for so long caused them to move quickly. Once they were ordered forward, they quickly outstripped their supporting infantry. The flashes of fire from the redoubt's guns tore more holes in their ranks, but they pressed on.

General Wathier's 2nd Cuirassier Division arrived at the redoubt first, and as they were about to enter its rear they were greeted by a heavy volley from the infantry stationed there. General Caulaincourt, at the head of the 5th Cuirassier Regiment, was struck and killed. Wathier's division was repulsed, and the IV Reserve Cavalry Corps moved in to fill the gap. Lorge's 7th Cuirassier Division, composed of the Saxons, Poles, and Westphalians, and Rozniecki's light cavalry formed in two lines to their left, and the corps horse artillery advanced. They were met by the fire of the 33rd Jager Regiment, as well as that of the Perm and Kixholm Infantry Regiments at sixty paces. This fire brought them to a halt, but General Thielemann continued to push forward with the Saxon Garde du Corps.

The Garde du Corps drew out to the left and advanced directly on the redoubt's breastwork, unmasking the Zastrow Cuirassier Regiment. The Garde du Corps and the nearest squadrons of the Zastrow Cuirassier Regiment poured up and over the breastwork, while the other squadrons forced their way through the rear and embrasures of the breastwork. As the Saxons passed over the top of the breastwork they were greeted by the uplifted bayonets of a compact mass of troops that occupied the redoubt. They were supported by the fire from the Russian infantry posted around the redoubt. The dead tumbled into the redoubt, but they were quickly followed by their enraged fellows. A bloody melee ensued in which all sense of military discipline and organization disappeared.

The French infantry had advanced close on the heels of the cavalry, occupying the redoubt with the 9th Line Regiment and consolidating their gains. Despite the fury of the battle around the redoubt, the Russians succeeded in withdrawing six of the guns from the redoubt. Two others were abandoned in the northern entrance, and the third was thrown into the ditch. A further ten were found dismounted in the redoubt. The capture of this redoubt by heavy cavalry was an act unparalleled in military history.

Once the redoubt was secured, Eugène began to mass all available cavalry behind it, including the II and IV Reserve Cavalry Corps. Grouchy's III Reserve Cavalry Corps was released when the Russian threat to the northern flank had passed. At that time Grouchy's cavalry joined the others behind the redoubt. Once these three cavalry corps had completely reorganized, they advanced beyond the redoubt to face the Russians again.

Barclay took personal command of the forces in the Gorki ravine and directed the 24th Division to retake the redoubt. However, before the counterattack could begin, the 14th Polish Cuirassiers descended into the ravine in a column of threes, stopped the counterattack, and drove the Russians back.

The French cavalry fell back all along their front after the attacks against the Russian 4th and 6th Infantry Corps proved unsuccessful. The Russian infantry was formed in battalion squares and successfully resisted their repeated attacks. Latour-Maubourg, supported by Defrance's 4th Cuirassier Division, charged one of the batteries and some of the infantry of the 6th Infantry Corps. The gunners stood encouraged by the artillery commander of the 6th Infantry Corps, while Generalmajor

Korff arrived with the 2nd Cavalry Corps, and Generalmajor Kreutz arrived with the 3rd Cavalry Corps.

Generals Defrance, Chastel, and Houssaye and part of the French V Corps charged the Russian 7th Division. The Chevalier Guard and the Horse Guard were posted on a ridge before the village of Kniazkovo, behind the 7th Division. When the French carabiniers broke through the 7th Division, crushing the 19th Jager Regiment's squares and sabering the gunners of the 2nd Guard Horse Artillery Battery, these two Guard cavalry regiments charged. They recaptured the battery and turned to engage the IV Reserve Cavalry Corps.

The Chevalier Guard was formed by squadrons, in two lines with gaps between the two squadrons in the first line sufficient to permit the squadrons of the second line to pass through. The Horse Guard was posted in line to their left. Facing them were the Saxon Garde du Corps, followed by the Zastrow Cuirassier Regiment and the Polish 14th Cuirassier Regiment. The Horse Guard moved against the flank of the advancing Saxons and were countered by the 14th Cuirassiers. The Poles, having already been heavily engaged and having suffered many losses, were insufficient to hold them back. The Poles and Saxons were forced back.

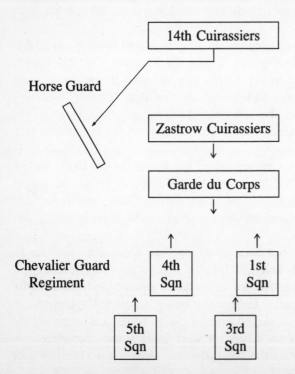

At the same time the 2nd Cavalry Corps arrived, and the Isoum Hussar Regiment and the Polish Uhlan Regiment attacked Wathier's and Defrance's forces. The Russians were not able to halt the French advance and were themselves thrown back by the 1st Cuirassier Regiment and a half-squadron of chevauléger-lanciers.

The Pskof Dragoon Regiment, Commanded by Colonel Sass, attacked the right of the redoubt and threw back part of Houssaye's dragoons. Grouchy quickly reacted by throwing several regiments at them, driving them back. The Russian dragoons withdrew under the protective fire of the 2nd Guard Horse Artillery, who had advanced to support them. In response, a French twelve-gun battery began to fire on the Russian artillery, killing Captain Ral, the Russian battery commander.

The Russian 3rd Cavalry Corps arrived on the field and dispatched five of its six regiments into what quickly developed into a two-hour melee. The cavalry of both armies intermingled; dust rose obscuring all vision. Small groups of cavalry pulled into and out of the battle to rally, reorganize, and charge back into the fray. All control of the battle passed from the hands of the generals and into the tiny knots of soldiers.

By 5:00 P.M. the cavalry began to abate and the Russian generals began to fear that Napoleon would finally unleash his still fresh Imperial Guard to decide the battle. This was not, however, Napoleon's intention. He said, "I will not have my Guard destroyed. When you are eight hundred leagues from France you do not wreck your last reserve."[*] Napoleon was already thinking of the long march home.

Activity to the South of the Battlefield

To the south of the battlefield, Poniatowski's Poles had advanced to their positions early in the morning. About the same moment that the 57th Line Regiment was making its first advance against the flèches, Poniatowski's forces became heavily involved around Utitza.

The first shots began about 8:00 A.M. when Poniatowski encountered Generallieutenant Strogonoff's 1st Grenadier Division about one mile south of the flèches. The Russians had been weakened by the detachment of the 3rd Division, which had been sent to help around the flèches. The Leib and Count Arakcheyev Grenadier Regiments of Geltoukhin's brigade were positioned to the right of the mound. Behind them, forming

[*] (Duffy, C. *Borodino* . . . N.Y. 1973. p 131)

a reserve, was the Pavlov Grenadier Regiment. On the mound itself were four 12pdr cannons. To the left of the mound were the Ekaterinoslav and St. Petersburg Grenadier Regiments, and a twelve-gun battery was posted between them. The Tauride Grenadier Regiment was detached to the right, where it reinforced the six jager regiments of Prince Neverovski and Prince Chakoffski. These jagers were in the brush and formed the link between the Russians around the flèches and the Utitza mound. Behind Tuchkov and on either side of the mound were 4,000 Moscow opolochenie armed with pikes and thirty-six cannon.

At 10:30 A.M. Poniatowski renewed his advance. He moved twenty-two guns (another source says forty) forward and directed their fire on the Russians around the Utitza mound. Things were rapidly becoming dangerous for the Russians. Word was sent to Kutusov, and he ordered Baggovout to dispatch the 17th Division, and later the 4th Division, south to assist Tuchkov. Eventually, the entire 2nd Infantry Corps was shifted south, and only the six jager regiments remained in their original positions.

The 2nd Infantry Corps had not been engaged before this time, but it was now marching into one of the hottest battles on the field. Baggovout detached two regiments from the 17th Division to cover his flank as he moved south. He also left part of the 12pdrs of Position Battery #17 to support the badly outgunned artillery of the 4th Infantry Corps. At the request of Tuchkov, he detached a force to move ahead of the main body of his forces. The Bieloserk and Wilmanstrand Infantry Regiments as well as the remainder of Position Battery #17, under the command of Colonel Gluckhof, set out ahead of the main force to reinforce Tuchkov as quickly as possible.

Position Battery #17 was immediately directed to the Utitza mound, where it established itself the moment Poniatowski's twenty-two-gun battery opened fire. A combination of an uneven artillery duel and the rapid advance of the Poles forced Position Battery #17 to limber up and withdraw. The Polish advance was met by the Bieloserk Infantry Regiment, who held a position on the mound. A bloody fight began.

At noon the 2nd and 3rd Infantry Corps moved forward, advancing as far as the village of Utitza. During this advance Tuchkov was killed while leading the Pavlov Grenadier Regiment forward, and Baggovout assumed command of the southern flank.

Poniatowski's artillery engaged in a three-hour duel with the Russians, in an effort to prepare the way for the pending infantry assault. He planned a two-column attack against the mound. Once the attack was launched, two Polish columns advanced around the northern flank of the mound until they encountered the 2nd Infantry Corps: the Minsk, Riazan, Wilmanstrand, and Brest Infantry regiments, and 500 pike-armed opolochenie.

The Polish left column was a diversion, and it succeeded in that function very well. Poniatowski's main force advanced to the southern foot of the mound. Baggovout counterattacked with Karpov's cossacks, the 1st Grenadier Division, and the 17th Infantry Division. This force only barely succeeded in stopping the Polish advance. This stabilized the battle for the Russians momentarily. However, the situation to the north left Baggovout's position very exposed. He was obliged to fall back along the Old Smolensk Road, abandoning his positions to Poniatowski.

Poniatowski sent his divisions forward against the mound. The 13th Polish Hussar Regiment, supported by three other cavalry regiments of the V Corps, moved forward to strike Baggovout's left flank. Karpov's cossacks counterattacked and brought this attack to a halt. Prince Eugène of Württemberg took command of a rear guard consisting of four guns and the Krementchug Infantry Regiment. The Krementchug Infantry Regiment had barely 300 men and was soon joined by the Minsk Infantry Regiment which had only about 200 men. Supported by the four guns and eventually by the Brest and Riazan Infantry Regiments who came up behind them, this tiny force of 500 Russian infantry advanced against the Poles.

Condition of the French and Russian Forces

The Minsk Infantry Regiment was smothered with musketry and attacked by the 12th Polish Uhlan Regiment. The Russian regiment fell back, its numbers reduced to less than 350. This was the last Russian formation to withdraw from its original position. With the withdrawal of this last force, the Russians began to concede that the battle was lost. Barclay sent Wolzogen to Kutusov to inform him of the serious situation on the battlefield. Barclay asked Wolzogen to insure that he got any orders in writing, fearing that Kutusov might give orders that he might later deny having issued, causing Barclay to take the blame for any failure that might result.

Wolzogen reported that he

duly embarked on my report concerning the position and the state of the Russian army, and I explained that apart from the right wing, which was on and to the left of the Smolensk Road, we had lost all our important positions and that every regiment was in a state of extreme exhaustion and disarray. I was still speaking when Kutusov cut me short with a cry: 'You must have been getting drunk with some flea-bitten sutler woman to give me a report like that! We have victoriously repulsed the French attacks along the whole length of our front, and tomorrow I shall place myself at the head of the army and drive the enemy without more ado from the soil of Russia!' With this he looked around challengingly at the members of his suite, who nodded enthusiastic approval.

Kutusov, who had spent the entire battle busily engaging in drinking champagne and eating sweetmeats, had no idea of the actual course of the battle. This response enraged Wolzogen, who then carried Kutusov's instructions to Barclay.

Kutusov conferred with Colonel Toll and then dictated an order telling Barclay to move the army about 1,000 paces to the rear and assume a new position aligned with the Gorki Hill on the right and the Utitza woods on the left. He felt that the French had suffered as much as the Russians and intended to continue the action. He hoped to restore the army's organization and replenish their ammunition during the night in order to renew the battle in the morning. He felt that to withdraw then would result in the loss of all the Russian artillery. He sent a similar set of orders to Docturov, the acting commander of the 2nd Army of the West.

Barclay was dismayed by the orders he received and knew that his troops were incapable of continuing the action the next day. They had undergone twelve hours without food or water, under continual heavy exertion. There was very little hope of feeding the army during the night either.

The Russian army was obliged to fall back to the position occupied by its reserve artillery. The 6th Infantry Corps touched the battery near Gorki and extended south towards Semenovskaya. The 4th Infantry Corps touched the 6th Infantry Corps on the north and extended south until it encountered the Guard infantry regiments of Finland and Semenovski.

These two Guard infantry regiments capped the salient formed by the 2nd Army of the West. The 2nd Infantry Corps fell back from that position to the Old Smolensk Road and was joined by the 3rd Infantry Corps. Both corps were now commanded by Baggovout. The Russian cavalry withdrew to the newly formed second line. The 5th Corps, Preo-bragenski, and Semenovski Guard Infantry Regiments, as well as part of the Guard and Lithuanian Jager Infantry Regiment were held in reserve. Behind the right wing, following the course of the lower Kolocha, were the 4th, 30th, 34th, and 48th Jager Regiments. The jagers had not taken part in the battle and were fresh. The total reserves of the Russian army consisted of 5,000 men, while the French still retained 20,000 fresh Imperial Guardsmen.

At this point Kutusov reported that a massive artillery duel had occurred, causing immense damage on the advancing French, who were finally forced to withdraw. Kutusov had completely fabricated this and, believing he had won a great victory, sent a report to this effect to the czar. The courier was a light infantryman who had not been engaged in the battle. Therefore he only knew what he was told. There was much rejoicing in Moscow, and Kutusov was promoted to the rank of field marshal. Kutusov sent Colonel Toll and another aide to investigate the state of his army. They discovered that the artillery had shot off most of its ammunition and that the gun carriages and other equipment were in a terrible state. They discovered that the infantry was in an even worse condition. Colonel Toll encountered one unit and asked what regiment it was. The response was that "they are the 2nd Division!" The 7th Infantry Corps could barely muster 700 men, and both armies had no more than 50,000 fatigued and starving troops.

At 10:30 P.M. these conditions were reported to Kutusov, who then decided to retreat the following morning. His explanation to the czar was that he could more easily consolidate his forces by withdrawing them to the heights of Mozhaizk.

The French had also suffered severely during the battle, and they too withdrew from the battlefield to settle for the evening around fires made from broken carriages and musket stocks. Eventually the French sank into an exhausted slumber. The Russians sent some cossacks out on a reconnaissance and reported that the French had withdrawn behind the Kolocha. Shortly after, the cossacks swarmed over the battlefield. At daybreak, Barclay, seeing the French had abandoned the Raevsky Redoubt, sent General Miloradovitch and several battalions, accompanied by an artillery battery, to reoccupy the shattered redoubt.

By dawn the Russian baggage and artillery had moved some distance down the road to Mozhaizk. Kutusov discovered that the wagons he had ordered for the transport of the army's wounded had not been arranged, but he was still able to carry off many of the army's wounded in the mass of carts that followed his army. Slowly the ponderous column of retreating Russians drew away from the battlefield, and the French showed no inclination to pursue them.

The French spent the day after the battle counting the bodies and tending the wounded. Napoleon was in a state of extreme depression. Though he had finally gotten his battle, it had been a bloody meatgrinder, rather than the subtle strokes of a master. The Russians had survived to fight another day. Though bloodied, they were still capable of considerable resistance. They were in the middle of their own country, able to replenish and reinforce their army far more easily than the French, who were at the end of a very long, tenuous supply line. The battlefield yielded few trophies, only a handful of prisoners and some broken guns. The manner in which the Russians had stood, like machines, allowing themselves to be mown down by the massed French artillery amazed Napoleon, and he feared the prospect of meeting such an army again.

Murat began a tardy cavalry pursuit the afternoon of 8 September, but it was stopped by the Russian cavalry rear guard near Mozhaizk.

Various sources put the Russian losses at Borodino at between 38,500 and 44,000, but the official records show 43,924 dead, wounded, and missing. Among the Russian losses were twenty-three generals.

The true extent of the punishment absorbed by the Russian army is best illustrated by more graphic descriptions of individual formations. The 2nd Army of the West had been reduced from 20,000 to 14,000 men. Many battalions had fewer than 200 men remaining around the colors. The six grenadier battalions which had defended the Bagration flèches were reduced to a total of about 300 men. The Empress Cuirassier Regiment had entered the battle with 400 men and now had only 95.

The French losses were around 30,000, including fourteen generaux de division, thirty-three generaux de brigade, thirty-two staff officers, eighty-six aides-de-camp, and thirty-seven regimental colonels. Both armies were totally exhausted, both physically and mentally. This was accentuated by the indecisive nature of the battle. It is interesting to note that in salvaging what was left on the battlefield, the French collected 20,000 artillery balls with which to restock their supplies.

The Pursuit Resumes

The distance from Borodino to Moscow is only fifteen miles. The Russian army passed through Moscow on 14 September. Its rear guard, under General Miloradovitch, consisted of 10,000 infantry and about as many cavalry. It included the Guard Cavalry Corps under Generallieutenant Ouvarov. This was one of the few Russian forces that was not heavily engaged during the battle at Borodino.

It was this force that Murat had encountered near Mozhaizk. It was evening and, after some hours of skirmishing and cannonade, the Russians retired behind their positions, and both sides settled down for the evening. Both were still heavily infected by fatigue from the battle at Borodino.

On 10 September Miloradovitch found his rear guard only one mile from the main army when the French again made contact with him. It was an hour before sunset, and the French advanced with infantry, cavalry, and artillery. He was forced to give battle. His infantry occupied a low ridge and defended it vigorously. Though the French attacks were relatively serious, they lacked real motivation. This particular engagement continued until 11:00 P.M. Miloradovitch remained close behind the battlefield.

As the Russians retreated from Borodino they received every possible provision from the Russian people, whose support had risen to the demand. Only the Russian rear guard suffered, because the horses were seldom given the opportunity to be unsaddled and receive proper care.

According to Clausewitz, the original forces that had been under Barclay and Bagration, after the detachment of Wittgenstein and not including cossacks, had totaled 110,000 men. Approximately 30,000 reinforcements had joined them since the campaign began, but now the Russian main army consisted of no more than 70,000 men. This indicates a loss of 70,000 men to battle, disease, fatigue, and the other hazards of a military campaign.

As Napoleon followed the retreating Russians, he found himself facing supply difficulties. Normally he would have expected to gather supplies from the civilian population and military magazines. In contrast to the beginning of the campaign, the Russian people now made great efforts to deny the French any and all supplies. Magazines were burned, and in the process the entire village often burned. In order to escape the impact of the burning villages, permit his forces to maneuver more rapidly and spread their impact on what supplies existed, as well as to reassume his strategic maneuvering formation, the battalion carré, Napoleon marched his army in three columns: one central and two flanking. This reduced the number of men attempting to forage in any given terrain, and the flanking columns often found themselves in unravaged territory, well capable of meeting their needs. The infantry fared better than the cavalry. The horses suffered because most of the suitable forage had been removed or destroyed, and the cavalry had to fan out over a much greater distance to obtain the necessary forage.

The weather also conspired against both sides. It remained hot and dry. Wells and streams dried up, forcing the troops to scatter in search of water.

On 13 September Kutusov halted just west of Moscow and called a council of war. He probably hoped that this council would relieve him of his promise to defend Moscow, but to his surprise it voted to give battle once again. Barclay spoke out and contended that such an enterprise would result in both the destruction of the army and the capture of Moscow. He recommended that the army move north to defend against a possible move against St. Petersburg, but Colonel Toll urged they withdraw towards Kalouga and the rich territory around it. It would be capable of supporting and reanimating the Russian army as well as allow- ing a possible link with Admiral Tchichagov's army as he moved up from the south. This plan was accepted. However, Poniatowski's corps was moving to cut them off from Kalouga, so Kutusov was forced to move south towards Kolomna.

On 14 September the Russian army passed through Moscow. The rear guard followed it on the 15th. General Miloradovitch was entrusted to conclude an agreement with Murat that would allow a delay of several hours between the Russian evacuation of Moscow and its occupation by the French.

General Miloradovitch advanced a party under a flag of truce to the French pickets and requested an audience. After a few hours it was announced to him that General Sebastiani would see him. This did not please Miloradovitch, though he agreed to see him. After a long conference and repeated assurances from Sebastiani that the French would prevent disorder in the city, the conference ended.

General Sebastiani had promised that the leading elements of his advanced guard would not enter the city until two hours after the Russians had vacated it. However, Miloradovitch was surprised to see two light cavalry regiments deploy before Moscow prior to this. He once again sent out a flag of truce, but Murat refused to meet with him. General Miloradovitch met with Sebastiani again, and he protested this breach of faith and of the agreement. While this conference went on, a continual stream of carriages and civilians flowed out of the city.

Clausewitz accompanied Miloradovitch in this interview and was surprised to discover that the uhlan regiment deployed before him was the Brandenburg Uhlan Regiment, from his native Prussia. It was part of the 15th Light Cavalry Brigade assigned to Nansouty's I Reserve Cavalry Corps.

Chapter XIII

The Hollow Victory

The French Enter Moscow

Eventually the interview between Generals Miloradovitch and Sebastiani broke off, and the Russians finished their evacuation. The French cavalry advanced into the city and were surprised to find it totally evacuated. Gradually the entire French army entered into the city and found their bivouacs. When Napoleon arrived he expected to be greeted by a delegation of boyars that would beg him to spare their city. He was disappointed. His expression of disappointment resulted in a frantic search of the city for anyone that was a resident of the city. This resulted in the corralling of a few members of the lowest classes, who were wheeled before Napoleon. This did not please him at all. This began the first breakdown of Napoleon's plans for an occupation of Moscow. He had no local administration to assist him in organizing the city's resources to support his army.

Fires had been observed as the French moved into the city; even Clausewitz remarks that he saw them. However, during the night of 15–16 September, a major conflagration broke out. The French discipline suffered seriously as a result of this fire and efforts to put it out. Once the fires were extinguished, large sections of the city were found to have been destroyed. It was clear that the city had been deliberately torched. French soldiers, who had been enjoined from looting, now ran amuck in an orgy of pillage. A great waste of materials occurred until the 19th, when order was finally restored, and a systematic organization of supplies and material began under the administration of the French.

As the French settled down in Moscow, the Russians continued to move west, leaving a screen of cossacks behind them, across the Kolomna road, and the regular cavalry was sent on towards Mozhaizk on a series of raids. Murat's cavalry had almost lost contact with the Russians and reported that the Russian forces were disintegrating. However, once the French cavalry reached Bronnitzo, it became apparent that the Russians had out-maneuvered them, not disintegrated. Reports of raiding cavalry in Mozhaizk were brought to Napoleon's attention. He dispatched Bessieres to reconnoiter towards Polotsk with a strong force to try to find Kutusov.

Bessieres found Kutusov's tracks and began a vigorous pursuit. Kutusov refused to accept battle, being still seriously concerned about his army and busy reorganizing it. He continued to retreat, leaving a rear guard near Trautino. Kutusov moved south of the Nara River to commence a serious refitting of his army. Replacements and supplies were plentiful, allowing a rapid filling out of his force. Though his infantry was weakened and very undertrained, the Russian cavalry was still a powerful force. It was also during this period that it was decided to send the cossacks to operate against Napoleon's lines of communication.

Napoleon kept his army in Moscow until October, when he began to become concerned about the coming winter. He made up his mind to withdraw slightly into friendly country and establish himself at Velizh. Here he could operate with Victor and Oudinot supporting him from a new position in Velikyi Luki. To supplement this, Napoleon opened negotiations with the Russians and sent Lauriston to Kutusov with the hopes of arranging an armistice as well as to present peace proposals.

The Russian Offensive Begins

The Russians had decided to start a counter-offensive. St. Cyr was selected as Wittgenstein's target. Wittgenstein was to drive him north, away from the main French forces; Essen and Steingell would attack Macdonald and then move on St. Cyr, where they would combine with Wittgenstein to destroy him in turn. From there they would move on Vilna. Admiral Tchichagov was to engage Schwarzenberg and Reynier, driving them westward, and then link up with Wittgenstein. Together Tchichagov and Wittgenstein would place themselves along a line behind the Berezina River and cut Napoleon's most likely line of retreat.

The Russians started to put this plan into operation on 29 September, when Essen and Steingell began to move out of Riga. However, Yorck quickly drove them back into their old positions. On the 22nd Tchichagov began crossing the Styr River, and Schwarzenberg and Reynier began a slow retreat to a line from Warsaw to Bialystok, gathering in their garrisons and reinforcements. Tchichagov attempted to cross the Bug River several times, but failed. Finally, on 29 October, he detached Sacken to face the Austro-Saxon forces while his main force moved on Minsk. Once this move became apparent, Schwarzenberg and Reynier moved in pursuit, with Sacken following.

The growing attacks by cossacks on his lines of communications forced Napoleon to take steps to preserve them. On 6 September Napoleon had ordered Marshal Victor to advance into Lithuania, where he formed a central reserve for the Grande Armée between Vitebsk and Smolensk. Napoleon had given him the discretion to operate on Vilna or Minsk if either was threatened. He also misinformed Victor that Tchichagov's force totaled no more than 40,000. Victor's forces had arrived in Smolensk on 24 September. The 4th, 7th, and 9th Polish Line Regiments were detached to form the garrison of the city.

With this force around Smolensk, Napoleon decided to withdraw on Smolensk and pass the winter there before beginning his 1813 campaign against the Russians. However, before he could begin his withdrawal the Russians began to assume the offensive and struck near Vinkovo.

The Battle of Vinkovo

Murat's forces were stationed between the Chernischnia's junction with the Nara River and the village of Teterinka, a distance of three miles, and Spass-Koupolia, four miles to the south. Vinkovo, south of Chernischnia, was occupied by Claparede's Poles and supported by the III Reserve Cavalry Corps and a division of the I Reserve Cavalry Corps. To the left of Vinkovo lay Dufour's division and the remainder of the I Reserve Cavalry Corps. Poniatowski's V Corps was stationed with Sebastiani's 2nd Light Cavalry Division to his extreme left. Latour-Maubourg's IV Reserve Cavalry Corps was watching the Narva River on the right rear. This entire force, commanded by Murat, totaled about 25,000 men. The 9000–10,000 cavalry in this force was miserably horsed, and the horses of the 180 guns assigned to it were in even worse state.

The Russians, under the command of Bennigsen, advanced in five columns. The first three were directly under his control. The first of those was commanded by General Adjutant Orlov-Denisov and consisted of ten cossack regiments, the 20th Jager Regiment, and twenty horse guns. He was to turn the French left and occupy the road near Voronovo. It was followed by the reserve of Generalmajor Müller-Zakomelski, who commanded the Guard Light Cavalry Division, Niejine Dragoon, and six horse guns. The second column was under Generallieutenant Baggovout. It consisted of the 2nd and 3rd Infantry Corps and sixty guns. Baggovout was to attack the French left flank and move obliquely to the right in support of the first column.

The third column was commanded by Ostermann-Tolstoy and consisted of the 4th Infantry Corps and twelve guns. Ostermann was to assure the liaison between the two leading columns and the two that followed.

The second force consisted of the fourth and fifth columns. The fourth was commanded by Generallieutenant Docturov and consisted of the 6th Infantry Corps and twenty-four guns. The fifth column was under Generallieutenant Raevsky and consisted of the 7th and 8th Infantry Corps and forty-six guns. Docturov and Raevsky were to cross the Nara near Trautino and move on Vinkovo to fix the French. This would facilitate the Russian encirclement of their left wing.

A general reserve followed the second force and consisted of the 1st and 2nd Cuirassier Divisions and the artillery reserve. All five columns were led by an advanced guard under the command of Generallieutenant Miloradovitch. This advanced guard consisted of the 2nd and 4th Cavalry Corps, four cossack regiments, a few jager battalions, and a few horse batteries. It was to remain in place until the battle began and then advance with the fourth and fifth columns.

The battle was to begin at 6:00 A.M. upon a signal from the Russian right wing. The first column was at Stremilovo, the second at Khorsosino, and the third on the road from Spass-Kouplia. The fourth column, fifth column, and advanced guard were between Dedni and Gliadovo.

It was at 7:00 A.M. that the brigade of jagers leading the second column moved out of the forest and made contact with the French. With the appearance of the first column in the French rear, General Sebastiani's division fell into disorder, and its confusion spread to the other troops around it. The entire French left hastily fell back behind the Chernischnia. The third column was held back while the second column leisurely pursued the French to the river. The Russian 3rd Infantry

Corps was directed more to the left, on the Teterinka. The first column was unable to hinder the French withdrawal behind Spass-Kouplia. The 4th Cavalry Corps of Generallieutenant Vasil'chikov saw the French disorder, crossed the Chernischnia, and attacked them.

Vasil'chikov sent the 3rd Jager Regiment and a grenadier regiment against a forest occupied by French infantry. They took the woods and pushed the French back to Spass-Kouplia. Vasil'chikov pursued them vigorously, as did Orlov-Denisov and Müller-Zakomelski, supported by the 2nd and 4th Infantry Corps. The 3rd Infantry Corps crossed the Dimitrovka to protect the Russian right wing, but the 6th, 7th, and 8th Infantry Corps stopped along the Chernischnia. The Russian pursuit stopped at Spass-Kouplia when the Russians received erroneous reports of French reinforcements. Murat quickly reorganized his troops at Voronovo, and the Russians withdrew to Trautino, leaving a rear guard in Vinkovo that consisted of Miloradovitch's advanced guard and the 2nd and 4th Infantry Corps. The Russians lost about 500 killed, including General Baggovout, while the French lost about 2,000 dead, including Generals Lery and Fischer. In addition, they lost about 1,500 prisoners, one standard, thirty-eight guns, and much baggage.

The French Retreat Begins

The news of this battle brought Napoleon from his lethargy and forced him into action. He suspected that Kutusov had received reinforcements of 10,000 cavalry from Wallachia and believed that he had not a moment to lose if he was to escape from Moscow with his army. He also wished to avenge Murat's humiliation and to demonstrate that it was not the cause of his sudden retreat.

On 19 October the Grande Armée began to file out of Moscow, taking with it 95,000 men, 500 cannon, and as many as 40,000 wagons piled high with the loot of Moscow. Among all the unofficial loot, a number of objects were taken at the express order of Napoleon. Among those articles were a fragment of wood believed to be from the true cross, the preserved hand of Saint Andrew, a number of golden and bejeweled church objects, an icon of St. Virege, numerous jewels and other valuable objects, 147 standards and flags, and six suits of armor.

In addition to the loot, Napoleon took with him a greatly diminished Grande Armée. On 18 October it consisted of:

Corps	Infantry	Cavalry	Guns*	Caissons & Forges
Imperial Guard	17,871	4,609	112	275
I Corps	27,449	1,500	144	633
III Corps	8,597	901	71	186
IV Corps	23,963	1,661	92	450
V Corps	4,844	868	49	239
VIII Corps	1,916	775	54	130
Dismounted Cavalry	4,000	—	—	—
I, II, III, & IV Cavalry Corps	—	5,000	67	157
Total	89,640	15,314	569	2,070

* Includes both field and regimental guns.

The First Russian Offensive Moves

Kutusov's camp at Trautino was chosen to block the Tula and Kalouga roads. It was located in one of the richest provinces of Russia and had the advantage of being between Napoleon and the Tula arms factory and the Braunsk gun foundry. They had to be held if the Russians were to rearm their army. In addition to keeping these important resources for the Russians, it denied Napoleon the supplies his army desperately needed. Napoleon's only alternative to this southern route was to recross the countryside that had already been ravaged by his advancing armies.

While Kutusov remained in his camp, he continually received everything he required: new weapons, supplies, and new recruits. His army was swelled with the arrival of opolochenie. This force was quickly absorbed into the depleted Russian army's ranks. Despite their lack of training, the opolochenie were incorporated into the infantry companies, where they were used to form the third ranks. Many of the opolochenie were armed only with pikes, there not being sufficient muskets to arm them properly.

Napoleon's first move was to advance on Trautino and come to Murat's assistance. On his departure he left Mortier behind in Moscow with specific orders to blow up the Kremlin and retire on Vereya. In coordination with this, Murat dispatched Poniatowski to secure the area around Vereya. Eugène led the army's advance south, supported by

Ney. Ney was to advance to the Motsha River and serve as a screen. After that he was to become an advanced guard for the advancing French. Junot was to move down the Borodino road and support the French right.

As the French retreat began, there was little movement in the Russian camp. The main French force was moving over a single bridge on the Lutza River, near the small village of Malo-Jaroslavets. After crossing the river, the road immediately went up a very steep bank, past a small church, and into the village. The march had been hampered by rains that had turned the roads into mud. The poor condition of the underfed draft horses pulling the carts, which were overladen with loot and sank into the mud, further slowed the column's movement.

The Russians had made no effort to pursue their gains at Vinkovo. And again they failed to interfere with Napoleon's advance towards Malo-Jaroslavets. On 22 September Docturov's 6th Infantry Corps moved out of Trautino to shadow Napoleon's retreat. When Docturov realized the importance of the defile at Malo-Jaroslavets, he ceased to act only as a shadow and rapidly outmarched the overburdened French columns, moving to seize the defile.

Kutusov was aware of the French movement and had only to move ten miles to seize the defile himself. Docturov left Aristovo at 7:00 P.M. and advanced through a countryside that lacked any direct road to Malo-Jaroslavets. Winding his way across the flat meadowlands heavily cut by ravines and small streams greatly slowed the progress of his artillery. Despite these problems Docturov reached Malo-Jaroslavets at 3:00 A.M.

The Russians were ignorant of the locale and were forced to deploy along the roads leading into the village because of the poor light. Special efforts were made to secure the road to Spasski, for it was felt to be the most probable line of advance for the French that day.

The Battle of Malo-Jaroslavets

On 23 October Eugène's advanced elements reached Malo-Jaroslavets and, finding no Russians there, bivouacked for the evening. The nature of the position had caused Delzon to encamp most of his division on the northern bank and not across the stream, in the village.

Malo-Jaroslavets was built on the summit of a high bank that rises immediately above the Lutza River. A single bridge spans the ravine through which the Lutza flows, connecting the village with the northern bank of the Lutza. The ground on both flanks of the village rises up steeply from the river and is heavily wooded. The ground to the left was heavily cut by ravines and fissures that made maneuvering artillery over it very difficult. The entire town was made of wood and was located near the summit of a hill. In the center of the village there was a large open-market square. At the edge of the river's bank was a church surrounded by a cemetery and a few other buildings that commanded the approaches to the bridge.

At 4:00 A.M. Docturov sent forward four regiments of jagers to rush the town. This sudden rush caught the sleeping French by surprise and quickly pushed them out of the village. The only portion they were able to hold was the church and the few buildings between the village and the bridge. Here they stopped the Russians. Docturov personally led forward a horse battery and positioned it so that it could fire on the French attempting to cross the bridge and support their fellows in the churchyard. It took only three volleys of cannister to stop Delzon's advance and force it back.

For an hour, Delzon's 13th Division had stood relatively inactive under heavy artillery fire. Eugène, drawn by the sound of the Russian guns, had quickly evaluated the situation and realized that it was vital that the bridgehead be retained and expanded. The Russian fire was quickly making Delzon's position untenable, and Eugène chose to order him forward.

The Russians had seized the entire village and established themselves strongly in it. However, the survivors of the French garrison still held the churchyard.

Delzon's forces crossed the bridge and rushed forward with bayonets fixed. He believed that his forces were pushing the Russians back and sent word to that effect to Eugène. However, his troops began to waver under heavy Russian pressure. Delzon advanced to urge them forward and was struck in the forehead by a musketball, dying instantly. His brother threw himself upon him and would have carried him away, but was struck himself and died.

Guilleminot succeeded Delzon, and his first action was to push one hundred grenadiers into the church. They immediately loopholed it, turning it into a small fortress. Five times the Russians were to push past the church pursuing the French, and five times they were swept by fire from the French in the church. This cross fire proved too much for the Russians each time and invariably forced them to retire.

Guilleminot continued to press forward, and, though reinforced by General Broussier's 14th Division, he still could not advance beyond the central market square. At 10:00 A.M. Ney and Davout's corps arrived, and it became more evident that the French were intent on crossing in strength.

In response to the French reinforcements, Docturov sent a string of staff officers to Kutusov to inform him of the progress of the battle. He hoped to pressure Kutusov into expediting the sending of reinforcements.

At length, the entire 14th Division pushed up the road, onto the village, and engaged with the Russians. Its third push up the road had been successful, and the French were beginning to push through the village and into the plain. However, each time they exposed themselves on the plain, they came under heavy Russian artillery fire.

At this critical moment the Russian 7th Infantry Corps under General-lieutenant Raevsky arrived and moved into position. Its fire shook the French infantry and drove them back into the village. Raevsky's grenadiers were ordered to take the town. They advanced boldly, sweeping the French before them. Their advance carried them through the village. Again the Russians captured everything except the critical church position, which once again swept them with heavy fire.

The obstacles of the ground had increased the confusion in the French ranks. The French descended the road precipitously, abandoning their hold on the village. During the course of the French withdrawal, the Russian artillery showered the village with shot and shell, which set the village on fire. The Russian recruits pursued the French furiously through the flaming streets. A frantic hand-to-hand battle began between small scattered groups. In the fury of the battle, individuals struggling together tumbled down the slope and into the flames.

Eugène still had the 15th Division under General Pino held back and intact on the far bank of the river. It advanced a single brigade into the village's left and another into its right. This division was composed of Italians who had not previously engaged in battle, and they were eager to prove their prowess. They moved forward, shouting enthusiastically, ignorant of or ignoring the danger awaiting them.

The shock of the Italian advance was more than the Russians could endure, and they were forced back. The village was reconquered for the fourth time, and the eager Italians of the 15th Division overrode the wisdom of their officers. Once again Eugène's forces pushed out of the village and onto the plain. They immediately drew the concentrated fire of the Russian artillery posted on the plain awaiting them. The Italians quickly recoiled back into the village.

The Russians, emboldened by the continual stream of reinforcements they were receiving and the failure of the last attack, moved forward once again. They moved their right forward, in hope of trapping the Italians before they could cross the bridge. Eugène had nothing left but his last reserve. This was the Italian Guard, and it was committed to the battle. He rallied the shaken remains of the 13th, 14th, and 15th Divisions for their fifth assault on the village. They advanced and swept into the village again.

Colonel Peraldi and the Italian Conscripts of the Guard charged with their bayonets lowered, throwing the Russians defending the bridge back. The smoke and fire of the burning village so intoxicated them that they continued their charge through the village and emerged on the plain above the village. They then impetuously charged the Russian batteries on the plain. They came under heavy fire and found but limited shelter in a ravine in the plain. They too recoiled into the village.

The fires in the wooden village had become so intense that the French and Italians were able to hold only the outskirts of the village. Those few remaining Russians in the village were pounded by the artillery that the French had brought into the village to sweep the interior of it clean of resistance. The battle began to die down, and the last Russian jagers surrendered their positions to the French at 11:00 P.M.

Both armies had committed about 24,000 troops to the battle. The French losses are estimated to be about 6,000, while those of the Russians were about 8,000.

Docturov retired on Kutusov's main body, taking his artillery with him and abandoning the entrenchments his troops had raised on the plain above Malo-Jaroslavets. Napoleon did little to interfere with their withdrawal other than to establish his artillery on the northern bank and fire on the withdrawing columns. Napoleon felt that Kutusov might counterattack again with very short notice. He was unwilling to commit a large force across the Lutza, where it might be attacked with overwhelming force and pinned against the steep banks of the river, where it would be destroyed.

During 24 October the French remained idle, and on the 25th Napoleon advanced with two squadrons of the Chasseurs à Cheval de la Garde Imperiale as an escort. He wanted to personally view the situation and make his plans for the next events of the campaign. Suddenly a formation of cossacks appeared from a nearby woods and charged straight for him.

A swarming melee evolved and one cossack got to within twenty yards of Napoleon. Napoleon's staff officers joined into the melee in an effort to defend their emperor. Other guard units nearby advanced to join in the fray. One staff officer lost his sword in the battle and seized a lance from a cossack. Because of his nonuniform cloak and his weapon he was mistaken as a cossack by a Grenadier à Cheval de la Garde Imperiale, who ran him through with his saber. Despite the seriousness of his wound, this officer survived to return to France. The skirmish ended as the cossacks found themselves badly outnumbered and fled.

The proximity of the cossacks to the main French army and the shock of their attack combined with the bloody nature of the battle the previous day led Napoleon to reconsider his plans. Perhaps it was the fear of attempting a crossing and becoming heavily engaged, but whatever it was, Napoleon changed his plans and decided to return along his original line of advance from the Niemen.

Napoleon was unaware that Kutusov had entirely abandoned his position above Malo-Jaroslavets and even the slightest reconnaissance by the French would have advanced without opposition. His decision threw away all of the fruits of the previous day's victory and condemned his army to its eventual destruction.

Chapter XIV

The Russian Northern Offensive

Wittgenstein Begins His Offensive

To the north, Russian General Steingell marched south to join Wittgenstein as planned. On 23 September he departed Riga and moved by forced marches. Count Wittgenstein prepared to act with Steingell. He was joined by the promised reinforcements, but they were not as numerous as he had hoped for. Steingell advanced in two columns. The right column, which passed through Sebej, was composed of two battalions of the Navajinsk Infantry Regiment, two squadrons of the Polish Uhlans, and six cohorts of the St. Petersburg Opolochenie, a total of 5,322 men, of whom 3,775 were opolochenie. The second column moved on the left, through Veliki-Louki, and consisted of four squadrons of the Mitau Dragoon Regiment, the depot battalion of the Polotsk Infantry Regiment, two battalions of the 1st Marine Regiment, two light artillery companies, and six cohorts of the St. Petersburg Opolochenie. The second column had a total of 9,025 men, of whom 6,581 were militia. The Novgorod opolochenie had not organized as quickly as that of St. Petersburg and didn't arrive until later.

To cross the Dvina, Wittgenstein had to make several preparations. His force lacked a pontoon company, so he was obliged to begin assembling the required material and carts at Sivochino. Count Sievers detached his engineering colonel with the two converged infantry regiments, the pioneers, and four horse guns to prepare the material necessary for the passage near Dissna.

Generalmajor Beguiczev, commander of the reinforcement column that came through Veliki-Louki, was ordered to detach Generalmajor Alexseiev with the 1st Marine Regiment, the Mitau Dragoon Regiment, a cohort of opolochenie, and six guns. This detachment was to move on Gorodok and Kosiany. From there it was to move to Goriany, where it was to search for a suitable ford. General Alexseiev was to defend the projected bridgehead as it was constructed, as well as to cover the march of General Beguiczev.

Beguiczev moved to Nevel on 28 September. On the 29th he was in Krasnopolie, where he was met by Generalmajor Diebitsch's detachment (seven battalions, four squadrons of dragoons, and one hundred cossacks). Lieutenant Colonel Bedriagua was sent to Pridrovik with his converged hussars to act as an advanced guard for Steingell.

On 28 September the Sebej column joined Wittgenstein. The six opolochenie cohorts were disbanded and incorporated into the infantry regiments of the 14th Division and the two jager regiments of the 15th Division as replacements. Some cohorts were used as a third or reserve battalion for other regiments. These forces were ordered to be held in the second line. Any attack by the opolochenie cohorts was to be a bayonet attack and was always to be supported by the two battalions of regular infantry to which they were attached. All of their movement was to be done in column, and they were always to be screened by skirmishers drawn from the regular battalions.

On 2 October General Beguiczev remained in Krasnopolie. His advanced guard, under General Diebitsch, had been reinforced with six guns and sent to Lipova. Count Steingell continued his movement south.

Wittgenstein, hearing of Steingell's approach, began to make preparations for the coming operations. He divided his force into three columns. The left-hand column was commanded by Beguiczev and consisted of an infantry battalion, eight opolochenie cohorts, and a battery of twelve guns. It totaled 6,273 men. The advanced guard of the left column was commanded by General Diebitsch and consisted of seven battalions, four squadrons, six guns, and one hundred cossacks. It totaled 2,792 men. This force followed the road from Nevel to Polotsk. The central column was commanded by Wittgenstein in person. It moved from Sivochino to Jourevicz. His advanced guard, under General Balk, consisted of five battalions, four squadrons, a cossack regiment, and six guns. It had a total of 3,222 men. The main battle force was commanded by General Berg and consisted of eight squadrons, eight battalions, and thirty guns. In addition, the central column had a reserve, commanded by General Kakhoffski, which consisted of four squadrons, five battalions, and twenty guns. It had a total of 3,630 men.

The left and center columns were united in Jourevicz and formed the principal corps that was destined to move along the left bank of the Dvina. The right-hand column was commanded by General Prince Jachwill and was assigned to move directly on Polotsk via the road from Sebej. It was to contain and distract the French. His advanced guard was commanded by General Vlastov and consisted of four squadrons, four battalions, two cohorts of opolochenie, a cossack regiment, and six guns. It had a total of 4,062 men.

Jachwill's main body was commanded by General Sazonov. It consisted of three squadrons, ten battalions, four cohorts of opolochenie, and sixty-four guns. It had a total of 7,351 men.

On 16 October the left-hand column reached Dretounn, while its advanced guard was in Miczoulitchi. Balk's forces were in Jartzi, and Wittgenstein and his reserve stopped in Arteikovczi. Prince Jachwill had his main forces in Sivochino, and his advanced guard was in Beloie.

Steingell crossed the Dvina at Drouia and advanced to Milacheva. General Alexeiev encountered a French detachment near Kosiany. It consisted of about 2,000 infantry and 1,500 cavalry. Alexeiev attacked them and pursued them ten miles down the road to Polotsk.

The Russian advance continued, and on 17 October General Balk's forces encountered 4,000 French at Jourevicz. He was unsuccessful in his initial attempts to push them out. When General Diebitsch arrived with further Russian forces, the French withdrew across the Polota. In their haste they failed to destroy the bridge. The two advanced guards combined under the command of General Balk and pursued the French about three miles.

That evening the Russians moved into Jourevicz, where Wittgenstein established his headquarters, and there was a reorganization of the Russian forces. Seven cohorts of militia were absorbed into the four infantry regiments belonging to the 5th Division and the three grenadier depot battalions assigned to the 1st Infantry Corps. Three converged grenadier battalions were drawn from the advanced guard, as well as the twelve guns assigned to General Beguiczev's force, and were incorporated into the reserve. The reserve was then given to Beguiczev. The advanced guard was stripped of three more battalions and three squadrons, which were replaced by a cohort of opolochenie. This new advanced guard was placed under Colonel Stolypin and sent to Losovka to maintain communications with General Jachwill.

While Steingell and Wittgenstein maneuvered on St. Cyr's forces, seeking to destroy him, St. Cyr remained stationary. He had held his positions in Polotsk since 18 August. His forces had erected an entrenched camp before the walls of Polotsk. The French were strongly positioned in the city. The French camp was well provisioned and shows what Napoleon could have done had he chosen to spend the winter in Smolensk. Its barracks were built by their occupants and were more spacious than the houses belonging to the Russian peasants. They were properly entrenched and well protected from assault.

For two months the Russians and French around Polotsk had engaged in a war of small skirmishes. The French had attempted to extend themselves over the countryside and secure provisions, but the Russians had actively stripped it bare and filled it with ambushes. This type of warfare favored the Russians, since the French were ignorant of the local language, customs, and countryside.

The result was hunger and disease, which had seriously sapped the strength of St. Cyr's forces and reduced them to about half of their original strength. At the same time the constant stream of reinforcements and replacements had doubled Wittgenstein's forces. In addition, the Bavarians had a shortage of fodder which restricted their ability to reconnoiter the area around Polotsk and give warning of the advancing Russians.

St. Cyr learned of the advance of Steingell and Wittgenstein as they drove back his outposts. He sent a pressing letter to Macdonald asking him to engage Steingell as he crossed Macdonald's front, but Macdonald did not feel himself authorized to execute such a maneuver without orders. He also mistrusted Yorck, who he suspected of having intentions of allowing the Russians to capture the French siege train. Macdonald believed his first priority and concern was this siege train, so he would not move. He also refused St. Cyr's request for 15,000 reinforcements.

This permitted the Russians to become bolder in their actions. Wittgenstein seized all the defiles through the woods surrounding Polotsk on the Russian bank of the Dvina. He threatened the French with battle, which he didn't believe they would accept.

The French in Polotsk

St. Cyr had not sufficiently entrenched himself to oppose such a large force, and insufficient works had been built to cover what forces he still had. The left of the French position rested on the Dvina and was defended by batteries placed on the left bank of the river. This battery was the strongest point in the French position. The French left was relatively weak and was separated from the main forces by the Polota River, which flowed into the Dvina to the north of the city.

St. Cyr had placed Corbineau's light cavalry brigade and three battalions of Bavarians on the left bank of the Dvina, near Bononia. They were to observe and contain Steingell. The right wing of the French line was held by Verdier's 8th Division, now under Maison. On his extreme right were two squadrons of cuirassiers, one squadron of lancers, and one squadron of chasseurs à cheval. Legrand's 6th Division was supported on the right by Maison and on the left by the Polota. Merle's 9th Division and the Bavarian divisions occupied the entrenched suburbs on the right of the Polota. There was an additional detachment of Bavarian infantry posted near Strouria to observe any Russian attack on the left.

Second Battle of Polotsk

On 18 October Wittgenstein sent his advanced guard, under General-lieutenant Jachwill, to threaten the French forces around Spass from the left, while he maneuvered to threaten them from the right. General Balk pushed the French from Gromy and advanced through the woods. The 26th Jager Regiment and two squadrons of the Grodno Hussar Regiment, accompanied by twelve guns, advanced along the road to Polotsk that crossed the Polota River. The 25th Jager Regiment and the depot battalion of the Kixholm Regiment with four guns moved past Lake Volovi. Another two squadrons of the Grodno Hussar Regiment and a cossack regiment advanced along a small road on the extreme left.

The French in Polotsk were positioned as follows: The 6th Division of Legrand was on the left bank behind the Polota. Its right wing was posted on Redoubt #7. The 8th Division, under General Maison, was to the left of the 6th Division and faced east. The 9th Division, with General Merle, was further to the left, along the right bank of the Polota. In the redoubts were four Bavarian batteries. About 600 Bavarians formed the garrison of the Struwnia Bridge, one hour's march upstream from Polotsk. The Bavarian regiment of Ströhl, formed of two weak battalions, formed the flank on the southernmost end of the French lines.

Candras' brigade, 9th Division, was posted with the 1st Swiss Regiment in the first line. Dulliker's battalion of converged voltigeurs was in an advanced post facing Ropna. The second line was formed with a converged grenadier battalion.

The 2nd Swiss Regiment stood to the left of the 1st. Füssli's battalion was posted in the front line and Von der Weide's battalion was in the second line. The Croatians were posted further to the left.

The 4th Swiss Regiment was posted on the ramparts of Polotsk and on the bridges over the Polota. The 3rd Swiss Regiment arrived after 3 P.M. and joined the 4th Swiss in its positions.

Wittgenstein's first advance was rather rash, and the two squadrons that St. Cyr had retained charged Wittgenstein's vanguard and overthrew them, taking its artillery and capturing Wittgenstein himself. However, a quick counterattack by the Grodno Hussar Regiment and the Converged Cuirassier Regiment forced the French back. This, coupled with the failure of the French to realize who they had captured, caused them to leave their prize behind.

The Russians then rushed from the woods and exhibited their entire force. The French advanced to attack the Russian right and center. Wittgenstein advanced the 26th Jager Regiment and reinforced them with the Sievesk Infantry Regiment. He then reinforced the 25th Jager Regiment with the Perm and Mohilev Infantry Regiments.

One of the first Russian volleys wounded St. Cyr, but he remained in the midst of his troops, even though he had to be carried about. Wittgenstein was determined to seize the French positions. The Russians advanced three 12-gun batteries to the edge of the forest. They began a lively cannonade. On the Russian left the Kalouga Regiment and the converged guard cavalry advanced along the road from Vitebsk.

The French shifted one squadron from the 20th Chasseur à Cheval Regiment and one from the 8th Chevauléger-lancier Regiment to face them. The French cavalry charged the interval between the Russian left and center. They captured Light Battery #7 and then split in an effort to widen the gap between the Russian left and center.

In the center General Diebitsch stopped this threat with the Mohilev Infantry Regiment, and the 6th Cohort of the St. Petersburg Opolochenie turned to face the French cavalry. On the left Wittgenstein countercharged with the converged guards and some squadrons of the Grodno Hussars, recapturing the battery and driving the French back. The French cavalry fell back until it was covered by two squadrons of the 14th Cuirassiers positioned on the right of Maison's division.

The French renewed their attack. Wittgenstein ordered General Beguiczev to move the converged cuirassiers and three battalions of grenadiers behind the center of their line to reinforce it. The two guard depot battalions moved behind the 25th Jager Regiment, and a grenadier depot battalion moved to support the right. Two battalions of infantry and a cohort of opolochenie were left as a reserve behind the center.

The battle continued with skirmishers, mostly opolochenie, advancing to the edge of the French trenches. Wittgenstein ordered Diebitsch to support the militia with some troops from the center, while his right drove the French back to their trenches. A French counterattack pushed the Russian skirmishers back, but the Perm Infantry Regiment and a grenadier depot battalion counterattacked.

The French fell back to their trenches again. Legrand's division supported its left wing on the redoubt known as "des Tuleries." Maison's division stood behind the Wolowoi Lake and was supported by Redoubt #9.

The French were pushed too hard and surrendered the redoubt "des Tuleries." This redoubt had been defended by the Valaison battalion 11th Légère Regiment and the 2nd and 37th Line Regiments. Colonel Ridiguer led the 25th Jager Regiment and two Guard depot battalions, supported by two squadrons of the Grodno Hussar Regiment, against Legrand's left. Legrand was thrown back to the lake.

General Beguiczev followed Ridiguer with his converged grenadiers. General Berg, who was detached from the left with the Kalouga Infantry Regiment and the converged guard cavalry, moved back to the center, establishing his artillery so it could continue shelling the French.

The French attempted to push the Russians back by maneuvering two squadrons of the 14th Cuirassier Regiment, two squadrons of the 20th Chasseur à Cheval Regiments, and two squadrons of the 8th Chevau-léger-lancier Regiment. The Riga Dragoon Regiment, the converged guard cavalry, and the converged cuirassiers counterattacked the French cavalry and threw them back. The French reformed under their artillery, but the Russians turned their right flank and forced them back into Polotsk.

During this cavalry action the French infantry fell back to their trenches. The intense artillery they directed at the "des Tuleries" redoubt forced the Russians to evacuate the redoubt, and the French reoccupied it.

Wittgenstein decided not to press his attack on the trenches. Diebitsch took command of the advanced guard when Balk was wounded and reestablished the skirmish screen before the Russian lines. Night fell and the French remained in control of their trenches, but they were filled with the dead of both armies.

On the right, the victory appeared to belong to the French, but on the left, the victory was in some doubt. At 4:30 P.M. Jachwill's attack had begun. He sent Vlastov forward with four battalions, eight squadrons, and six guns. His attack was supported by Sazonov, who led three squadrons, ten battalions, eight cohorts of opolochenie, and sixty-four guns. Jachwill's attack had a total of 17,500 men, while Merle's 9th Division had barely 4,000.

Merle had been ordered to avoid any serious combat and began to redeploy his forces behind Redoubts #4 and #5, occupied by the Bavarians, and Trench #16 with his first echelon. The Russians increased their pace and closed on Candras' brigade, the 1st and 2nd Swiss Regiments. The voltigeur battalion of the 1st Regiment left the front line, recrossed the barracks, and took up position in its original position.

The Russian artillery directed its fire on the ramparts of Polotsk, while the 1st and 2nd Swiss Regiments formed to face the pending attack. The 1st Swiss Regiment formed in column of attack and was supported by the 2nd Swiss Regiment. The Russian attack was strong. The 1st Swiss Regiment met them with fire by peloton, marched forward, and fired again and again. The 1st and 2nd Swiss Regiments then advanced with bayonets and became embroiled in a violent melee with the Russian columns. The Swiss repelled Vlastov's infantry and cavalry attacks, forcing him back on Sazonov's forces.

This setback did not deter Jachwill, who quickly renewed his attacks. Merle, who saw two Russian divisions forming to advance against the two weak Swiss regiments, responded by once again attempting to withdraw, but he was too hotly engaged to do so. He was supported by fire from Redoubts #4 and #5.

Jachwill sent his cavalry forward to strike these weak regiments. However, they were met with cold steel and resolve. The Swiss held their fire until the Russians were seventy paces from them. Each volley cut great holes in their ranks. The Chevalier Guard withdrew, but Dulliker was killed and his battalion passed to Zingg's command. Colonel Castella had two horses killed beneath him and was wounded himself. The eagle of the 2nd Swiss Regiment fell, but was grabbed by Captain Müller before it could be carried away. The 1st Swiss Regiment lost thirty-three of its fifty officers hors de combat in this action.

General Amey's brigade, consisting of the 3rd and 4th Swiss Regiment and the Croatians, saw their comrades' danger. They were posted on the ramparts of the city. The 3rd Swiss, posted in a bastion, moved behind Redoubt #3. The 4th Swiss was behind the Polota, near the 5th Battery. Covered by the cannister fire from these two batteries, they charged forward in an effort to throw this Russian attack back. The fire from the Bavarian batteries and those in Redoubts #3 and #4 tore great holes in the Russian ranks. They caused a momentary pause in the Russian advance, and Merle resumed his withdrawal.

While Merle retired at the "pas ordinaire," the Russian light troops moved to turn his flanks and take his rear. The Russians moved into the ravine of the Polota. Merle quickened his pace and arrived just in time to defend the trenches. The Russian incursion was stopped by concentrated musketry from the lines along the ravine, the fire of two cannons positioned in Entrenchment #3, known as the "Croat Entrenchment," and artillery from Redoubt #4 that had been pulled from the ravine and formed into a battery to sweep the ravine. The fire from the guns drawn from Redoubt #4 formed a cross fire with the Bavarian guns in Redoubt #11, on the left bank of the Dvina.

The Russian losses were, as a result of this concentration of artillery fire, quite heavy. They withdrew, reformed, and renewed their attack. Candras' Swiss struck their right flank while Amey's Swiss and Croatians struck their left, driving them back. Favored by the falling dusk, the Russians withdrew to the edge of the woods.

Prince Jachwill supported his right on the Dvina and detached Vlastov towards Pressemenitza to make contact with Wittgenstein's advanced guard, now commanded by Diebitsch. Wittgenstein withdrew the bulk of his forces towards Gromy, where he established his headquarters.

The night passed quietly. St. Cyr sent out cavalry on a reconnaissance that brought him the erroneous news that the Russians had not passed over the Dvina either above or below Polotsk. However, Steingell and 13,000 Russians had crossed the river at Drissa and were now moving on the left bank with the objective of taking St. Cyr in the rear. This would shut St. Cyr into Polotsk and seal his fate.

The morning of the 19th found Wittgenstein's troops under arms and preparing to renew the attack. But no advance occurred. St. Cyr realized that it was not his feeble fortifications holding back Wittgenstein and realized that some maneuver must be underway. He knew it must be an attempt to seal him into Polotsk, so he sent out his cavalry again.

At 10:00 A.M. an aide-de-camp came in at a full gallop to announce that Steingell was marching up the Lithuanian side of the Dvina with 5,000 infantry, 12 squadrons, and 12 guns. Steingell had defeated Corbineau's cavalry, blocking his way, and was moving south. News of this victory elated Wittgenstein and convinced St. Cyr of the danger of his position.

St. Cyr immediately dispatched the 7th Cuirassier Regiment, a Swiss regiment, and a Bavarian brigade under the command of Wrede to assist Amey's beaten forces. Every moment the noise of Steingell's artillery moved closer and closer to Polotsk. The French batteries on the left bank were turned around to face this new threat. All this was observed by Wittgenstein, but his forces remained immobile. Before Wittgenstein moved, he felt he had to see, not only hear, Steingell's guns.

St. Cyr's generals urged him to retreat, but he steadfastly refused. He believed that 50,000 Russians were waiting to pounce on him the moment he began to withdraw.

General Wrede advanced with three columns against two jager regiments under Tourczaninov, part of Steingell's forces. On Wrede's right was a column under General Baron von Strath, the left was General Amey's brigade, and the center was led by Wrede himself. At 4:30 P.M. the center column struck the Russian advanced guard, surprising it, dispersing it, and taking 1,800 prisoners. Steingell was stunned. Though only a half-hour from Polotsk, he stopped his advance and withdrew towards Bononia. A thick fog fell over the town and battlefield about 6:00 P.M. and lasted until dusk.

St. Cyr waited for dusk to fall and immediately began his withdrawal. Slowly the French and Bavarians began to file across the river. When Legrand's division began to cross, they were covered by Maison. From habit or a desire to deny the Russians their cantonments, the French torched their positions. Shortly the entire French lines were in flames.

The fire disclosed the French withdrawal to the Russians, who immediately opened fire with their artillery. The Russian infantry rushed forward, but the withdrawing French forced them to fight for every foot of ground. The French crossed the bridge, effecting their withdrawal in good order. The French rearguard action was fought by the Swiss regiments commanded by Castella and Requetti, the Croatians, and the 123rd Line Regiment. The Russians were unable to occupy the city until 3:00 A.M.

A total of 27,000 French and Bavarians had engaged 32,000 Russians. The French lost about 7,000 dead and wounded, leaving 2,000 prisoners behind them. The Russians lost about 10,000 dead and wounded, while leaving about 2,000 prisoners in French hands.

St. Cyr and Oudinot Retreat

Wittgenstein was unable to cross the Dvina and pursue St. Cyr because the bridges were destroyed. Steingell was falling back in disorder on Dissna. St. Cyr withdrew without opposition. He decided to detach Wrede with what remained of the Bavarian VI Corps. Wrede was to move to Glubokoye and cover the road to Vilna. This would permit the II Corps to move unmolested on Lepel, where it could then protect Wrede as he withdrew in a leapfrog fashion.

On the morning of the 20th, General Wrede moved against the Finnish forces of Steingell. Wrede advanced his forces in three columns. The left column was commanded by Amey and consisted of the 2nd Swiss, 124th Line, a detachment from the 11th Légère, a half-battery of French horse artillery, and three squadrons of Corbineau's light cavalry. The center column was commanded by Wrede and contained the 19th and 37th Line Regiments, Corbineau's light cavalry (less three squadrons), the 7th Cuirassier Regiments, nine 6pdr guns, and six 12pdr guns. The right column consisted of the cadres of the Bavarian brigade of Baron von Strohl, thirty chevauxlégers, and three 6pdr guns.

The right-hand column was ordered to move along the Dvina to the mouth of the Ouchatsch, while the central column attempted to throw the Russians out of the Polotsk-Bononia defile and back towards Ouchatsch. General Amey was to move on Roudnia, but he learned that Wrede was heavily engaged and maneuvered along the left bank of the Ouchatsch to fall on the Russian right flank.

This force started its march at 3:00 A.M., but contrary to expectations, the Russians attacked at 4:00 A.M. Wrede had given the order not to fire, but to march at the "pas de charge" in column in a bayonet attack on the enemy. The Russians were thrown back in disorder on Ouchatsch, losing as prisoners a colonel, a major, a large number of other officers, and 1,800 men. The shattered remains of the Russian advanced guard were pursued by a few pelotons of the 7th and 20th Chasseur à Cheval Regiments.

Between the Bononia chapel and the defile, the Russians massed all of their cavalry and some artillery in a faint-hearted attempt to stop Wrede's advance. However, as Wrede's artillery opened fire, the Russians departed quickly, crossing to the far side of the Ouchatsch. Wrede deployed his central column and advanced on the chapel.

The Russians on the far bank were in an extremely strong position. They had placed twelve guns and about 8,000 infantry and cavalry to receive Wrede's attack. Wrede, however, positioned his artillery on a knoll overlooking the Russians and began an artillery duel.

After a half-hour the Russian artillery fell silent and began to withdraw. It was time for General Amey's maneuver, but he was late. Wrede decided not to wait for his arrival and planned to force a passage over the Ouchatsch. He moved quickly, his columns crossing a ford. The Russians hastily abandoned their positions and much material on the battlefield. Wrede pursued them as far as Benkovitz, but stopped. He feared becoming too widely separated from General Amey. He preferred to await his arrival and the chance to reorganize his forces.

That evening St. Cyr was ordered to return with the French troops and resume command of his Bavarian forces. Once with the Bavarians, he was to move with them, Corbineau's brigade, and the 7th Cuirassier Regiment on Roudnia and take up a defensive position.

Victor Arrives

Victor was sent word of St. Cyr's danger and advanced to support him. Victor's forces joined St. Cyr on 28 October. Both corps were reorganized into a single formation. St. Cyr was forced to relinquish command to Victor because of a very painful wound received during the battle of Polotsk. Marshal Victor reorganized the two corps as follows:

Right Wing
General Daendels

6th Division: General Legrand (II Corps)
26th Division: General Daendels (IX Corps)

Center
General Merle

9th Division: General Merle (II Corps)
12th Division: General Partoneaux (IX Corps)

Left Wing
General Girard

8th Division: General Maison (II Corps)
28th Division: General Girard (IX Corps)

Corps Cavalry
General Doumerc

3rd Cuirassier Division: General Doumerc
5th Light Cavalry Brigade: Castex
6th Light Cavalry Brigade: Corbineau
25th Light Cavalry Brigade: Fournier
26th Light Cavalry Brigade: Delatre

On the 29th this formation moved on Beszenkoviczi, and the Baden Lingg Jäger Battalion was detached and sent to Buterova, on the Ula River. The baggage was sent to Babinoviczi. In Buterova a battalion from Legrand's division acted as a garrison, and a Bergish battalion was left behind to cover Vitebsk. This battalion was pushed out a few days later, and the city was retaken by the Russians.

Wittgenstein's forces left the Polotsk area and began to move on Ula in an attempt to push Victor back. On the evening of the 30th his forces contacted Victor. The next day the French 26th Division moved on Buterova, where it joined Legrand's 6th Division. Both divisions moved to Czaszniki. In an attempt to break contact with the Russians, they engaged in a night march over a freezing, narrow, bad road. Victor wished to show only this portion of his forces to the Russians and to conceal the junction of the II and IX Corps from them.

The merging of the II and IX Corps was to occur during the night of 31 October–1 November, but by the morning of 31 October only the 26th Division had actually made contact with the II Corps. At daybreak on the 31st, the Russians confronted this weak force. It was located near Czaszniki, and the Russians immediately brought it under a heavy cannonade. Legrand initially defended Czaszniki, but shortly abandoned the village, recrossed the river, and moved to support himself with the other divisions of the II Corps.

Victor wished to permit the Russians to move onto the plain so he could better judge their strength. This wish was quickly granted as Wittgenstein's forces passed over the Oula and occupied Czaszniki, attacking the II Corps. The II Corps was formed in line. Around 11:00 A.M. the 26th Division organized itself in echelon behind the II Corps. The Baden brigade positioned itself behind Merle's Division, consisting of the three Swiss and one Croatian regiments.

The Baden Infantry moved forward in a battle column so they could better defend their assigned positions. General Daendels detached five companies of the Hessian Leibregiment and sent them with a Bergish battalion and four Bergish guns across the Ula with orders to support that flank. In the course of the battle, the Russian converged Guard cavalry charged them repeatedly.

The Battle of Smoliantsy

A skirmish battle developed, and the voltigeur company of the 2/Leibregiment of the Hessian brigade engaged the Russians until its ammunition was expended. It was relieved by a company drawn from the 3rd Baden Line Regiment. This company was engaged by Russian artillery and suffered heavy casualties. More men were detached from the 3rd Baden Line Regiment to support their heavily pressed fellows. They advanced at a run. The entire battle dissolved into a wasteful skirmish between the light infantry and artillery of both sides. As night fell, the battle died away, and the French received orders to withdraw about an hour-and-a-half behind their position. They took up new positions in the woods located there.

Around midnight the Hessian detachment of Colonel von Franken and the Lingg Jägers that had been sent across the Ula to support the French flank returned. The clash on the 31st had cost both sides about 400 dead and wounded, but the French left some 800 prisoners behind.

The order to retreat was given, and the two French corps withdrew in good order on the Smoliantsy palace, where they made an effort to recross the river. However, the Russians quickly stopped this effort. The two corps continued to move towards Senno. Wittgenstein made no further attempt to interfere with the French withdrawal. He established the Russian bridgehead at Smoliany with his advanced guard, while his forces positioned themselves to move to their best advantage as the situation developed. He chose, as things evolved, to wait for the arrival of Admiral Tchichagov's forces.

That evening the two French corps completed their merger and took up positions that they were to hold until 3 November. On 4 November they began to move on Torbinka, and on 5 November they moved to Czereia. That day the French encountered cossacks which Oberst von Cancrin, of the Baden Hussar Regiment, allowed to cross over a bridge near the Krasnogura castle before he attacked. Once they were in the narrow defile, he struck and captured nearly all of them.

The Withdrawal Continues

The French advance resumed with Legrand's division, four Baden horse guns, and the 25th Light Cavalry Brigade acting as the advanced guard. They moved from Czereia towards Lukonil, and on the 8th they were again attacked by the Russians. The Baden Hussars and the Baden

Horse Artillery, under Captain Zensburg, drove them back. The advanced guard was quickly supported by the Berg Brigade, under General Damas, which stationed itself near Stroczeviczi. Eventually the Russians were driven back.

On the same day Marshal Oudinot was sufficiently recovered from his wound to resume command of the II Corps. The two corps separated, and the II Corps drew off to the right.

Colonel LaRoche advanced with the 25th Light Cavalry Brigade and assumed the duties of the advanced guard for the IX Corps on the 12th. He quickly encountered Russian cavalry and artillery near Truchanovicz. He did not have his own artillery to support him, but despite its lack he held his position with great tenacity. However, during this engagement Oberst von Cancrin, commander of the Baden Hussar Regiment, was killed by a Russian licorne shell.

The remainder of the French corps advanced, its flank being masked from Russian fire by the detached voltigeur companies from Hochberg's Baden regiments. The detached companies rejoined their parent regiments once the engagement ended.

After a fatiguing march, the rear guard was gathered in at Mielskoviczi. It rejoined the corps at about 1:00 A.M. where the main body was bivouacked. On the 13th Marshal Victor moved back towards Czaszniki in order to strike Wittgenstein and throw him back across the Dvina. Victor hoped that he could force Wittgenstein back and away from Napoleon's line of retreat on the Berezina. To this end Partoneaux's division and the IX Corps cavalry advanced to engage the Russian advanced positions. That evening Daendels' division moved into Zeulaszi.

The Russians advanced a weak skirmish line the next morning, and it was turned away by the voltigeur company of the Lingg Jäger Battalion and a company of the 2nd Berg Infantry Regiment. The 26th Division was heavily engaged by Russian artillery, but night fell and brought the battle to an end.

On the morning of 15 November the IX Corps rose to arms early, expecting a renewed battle. There was no assault for two hours. Both armies contented themselves with an artillery duel. Instead of the order to attack, the French corps suddenly received the order to withdraw. The new French offensive was given up because of the receipt of orders from the Imperial headquarters in Smolensk. They had been brought by Colonel Chateau, one of Victor's aides-de-camp. He also brought news of the main army's retreat from Moscow.

On the 16th the IX Corps passed Putski on the road to Senno. On the 17th it reached Ulianovicz, and on the 20th it moved on Czereia. The great loss of staff officers in the IX Corps had resulted in a reorganization of the Baden brigade. It was organized into the equivalent of two regiments, one commanded by General Lingg and the other by Colonel Bruckner.

On the 22nd the retreat began in earnest with the rear guard being formed with two cavalry regiments, three line infantry battalions, the Lingg Jäger Battalion, and two horse guns under General Delaitre. On the 23rd the other light cavalry brigade was detached to form the rear guard. On the 23rd Daendels and Girard arrived in Doknitza, and Partoneaux arrived in Batrun.

On the 24th Victor assembled the IX Corps in Batrun and departed there about noon. Hochberg and the Baden brigade was ordered to support the rear guard under Delaitre with two battalions, should it be necessary. As the march began, Delaitre sent word that he was heavily engaged by the Russians. Hochberg sent one of the provisional Baden regiments back to support him. The engagement did not last long, and the rear guard assumed a position 600 to 800 paces behind the village.

As the battle began anew, the Russians brought forward more men and guns. A battalion of the provisional Baden regiment deployed in skirmish order to support the right wing of the rear guard. The other battalion was held in reserve behind the left wing. The remaining battalion was in echelon behind the right wing, and two Bergish battalions were held in reserve further back.

The position was further reinforced by the arrival of the 25th Light Cavalry Brigade, composed of the Baden Hussar Regiment and the Hessian Chevauxléger Regiment. Fournier decided to assemble all four of the corps cavalry regiments into a single formation and turned command of the battle over to Hochberg. Fournier then withdrew the cavalry from the forested terrain where the battle was being fought.

For the first time in his career, Hochberg found himself in command of eleven battalions and commanding a major battle. He had earlier sent the Baden Horse Artillery back, out of the battle. He still had four French horse guns which he deployed advantageously. They began to shell Batrun in an effort to delay the Russian advance. However, the French howitzer was dismounted after its third shot, and Hochberg was forced to withdraw the remaining guns. The Russians established a battery of twelve 12pdrs that began to heavily engage Hochberg's forces. This was followed by an energetic assault by the Russians on Hochberg's right wing. The Russians were seeking to seize the defiles through which Hochberg had to retreat. He sent a single battalion to defend these defiles and insure his control of them, while the disordered troops reorganized themselves and began moving through the defile. During their withdrawal, the Baden, Hessian, and French troops suddenly came under unexpected Russian musket fire. A battalion of the Hessian Leibregiment, placed near the rear, observed the Russian maneuver and advanced at a run to counter the threat to the defile.

Once the Leibregiment secured the defiles, the IX Corps' rear guard began to pass through it. The losses from this engagement amounted to twenty-six dead and sixty-three wounded from the Baden contingent, with similar losses from the other contingents engaged in the battle.

Napoleon's orders to Victor directed that he be in Borisov on 26 November. He was to form the rear guard for the main army on its march to Minsk. Victor reached the main road at Bobr at 2:00 P.M. that afternoon. Hochberg's brigade formed the advanced guard and Partoneaux's division formed the rear guard.

Chapter XV _____

The Russian Southern Offensive

Tchichagov Advances in the South

At the same time St. Cyr was under attack around Polotsk, there were significant developments on the southern flank of Napoleon's army. General Dombrowski abandoned Minsk, and General Lambert occupied it on 16 November, finding 5,000 sick and two million rations in an immense magazine that also contained a great quantity of gun powder and cannon barrels. He captured a total of forty days' supplies for 100,000, some 30,000 pairs of shoes, clothing, and other equipment in equal proportions.

The Russian and Austrian positions along the Styr had remained static since mid-September. The only actions were patrols like the one that occurred on 23 September. This resulted in two officers and eight soldiers captured and seven dead. The influence of the numerically superior Russian cavalry was beginning to make itself felt. Because of the cavalry problem, a strong mobile column was organized under the command of General von Zechmeister. This column contained the O'Reilly Chevauxlégers, 62 Saxon Hussars under Major von Czettritz, 42 Chevauxlégers from the Saxon von Polenz Regiment, and 3,000 Polish cavalry. Initially this column moved away from the Styr in the direction of Polonka and Radomysl, but the far side of the river was strongly held by the Russians. To avoid the Russians, Zechmeister's column built a bridge and crossed where the Russians were not in strength. The greater part of the Russian Army of Moldavia was moving towards Dubno and Lutsk in order to reinforce the 3rd Army of the West. It had just recently been freed from duty in Wallachia as a result of a peace treaty signed with Turkey.

On 19 September the Russian generals brought von Zechmeister's reconnaissance to a halt and sent the greater portion of their cavalry on a reconnaissance towards Lutsk. Von Zechmeister was ordered to watch the Russians. He wrote Reynier on 20 September,

> This morning I set out from Polonka, with orders to move on Nieseviec. An hour from there I was informed that the Russians were there and that a picket of thirty Polish horse had been ambushed. I detached Major von Czettritz with 100 horse from my left flank with the order to maneuver so as to cut the Russians off from Radomysl to prevent Russian reinforcements from reaching the position. As I descended from the woods I found a Russian detachment of 250 horsemen formed before Nieseviec, which I struck and dispersed, fleeing in disorder towards Radomysl. Major von Czettritz moved into Radomysl with 300 horsemen. (G. Fabry, *Campagne de Russie*, Paris)

On 21 September von Zechmeister's column was struck by a stronger Russian force. It was encamped when 600 cossacks, 300 hussars, and 300 dragoons swept down on it. The Russians captured three Saxon officers and forty Saxon troopers, ninety-two from the O'Reilly Chevaux-léger Regiment, and twenty Poles. In the meantime, the Russian 5th Division, part of the Army of Moldavia and under the command of Admiral Tchichagov, moved down the Styr River, where it joined the corps of Tormassov. The Saxon corps was then struck by this force and driven across the Bug near Lumbovl on 28 September. The Saxon losses, however, were small. On 3 October the Saxon and Austrian forces reunited near Brest and moved on Muraviec.

Schwarzenberg believed that the position he held at the beginning of October extending from Brest to Vilna could be held once he was joined by the French main army. The Saxons stood on the left wing. The Austro-Saxon forces remained in these positions until 10 October. When the Russian 3rd Army of the West was joined by Tchichagov's forces, it moved forward in an attempt to drive the Austro-Saxon forces away from any possible junction with Napoleon and the main army.

Near the village of Baila, the Saxon VII Corps and part of the

Austrian forces encountered cossack outposts and drove them back on Zalesie, where they joined the Schusselburg Infantry Regiment. Admiral Tchichagov advanced on Baila as quickly as he could with General Essen's III Corps. This consisted of thirteen battalions, ten squadrons, two cossack regiments, and twenty guns. He dispatched Generalmajor Goulatyov to Pechatz with twelve battalions, two dragoon regiments, an uhlan regiment, two cossack regiments, and three batteries.

Essen's corps was led by the 1st Battalion of Converged Grenadiers and a squadron of the Smolensk Dragoon Regiment. This force crossed the Tzna River near Voskrinitza. They struck and drove back the two squadrons of the Saxon Hussar Regiment and Prinz Clemens Uhlan Regiment that they encountered.

The road from Voskrinitza to Baila went through a thick forest which was occupied by two other squadrons of the Saxon Hussar Regiment. However, rather than engage the Russians, once threatened, the Saxons withdrew across the river. The second Saxon division was posted on the far bank with eighteen guns, and the first was concealed in the woods before the village of Kozouli. Essen sent the 37th Jager Regiment and 1st Converged Grenadier Battalion forward to attack the Saxon right wing near Seletz. The 2nd Converged Grenadier Battalion and the Jitomir Dragoon Regiment advanced against the Saxon left near Kozouli.

When they found they were being attacked by such feeble forces, the Saxons went over to the offensive. The Saxon skirmishers attacked a Russian battery and captured one gun. Three other guns were taken, but lost when the Jitomir Dragoon Regiment counterattacked. Essen found himself facing more than he cared to face. He learned of the massive Saxon advance and speedily withdrew before the Saxons.

Both the Austrian and Saxon corps fell back on Drohiczyn, in order to cover Vilna and Warsaw, as Essen withdrew on Brest. The Austro-Saxon forces took up a position on the Bug River and remained there until 28 October. The Saxons bivouacked on the left bank near Skrezeszev. For the first time since they left their homeland, the Saxons received reinforcements of 1,700 fresh Saxon troops. On 25 October the Saxons had a total of 12,283 men. There were also 2,621 sick and wounded in hospitals and 2,655 known prisoners.

Tchichagov had his corps between Brest and Kaminiec-Litovsk. He had united his forces in hopes of executing a drive that would drive Schwarzenberg and Reynier back to Warsaw. However, despite this plan, Tchichagov received orders calling him back. The czar had ordered the 3rd Army of the West to divide into two equal forces. One was to be commanded by General von Sacken and to assume the duties observing the Austro-Saxon forces. The other force was to move towards the Berezina in the hopes of blocking Napoleon's escape.

Schwarzenberg responded to this weakening of the Russian forces by once again advancing on Slonim. The Saxons were to advance over the Rudnia River while the Austrians occupied Slonim. For the third time the Saxons crossed over the Bug. When they reached their new positions the temperature was falling, and there was a great shortage of supplies, wood, and straw. The lack of wood and straw was especially harsh on the men and horses since they were obliged to camp in the open. The next morning they began a long march eastward.

After three weeks of marching, the Saxons finally contacted the Russians near Visocky. On 1 November a squadron from von Frolich's brigade was struck by the Loubny Hussar Regiment, the Vladimir Dragoon Regiment, and a cossack regiment. The Austrian cavalry was driven back. The Leichtenstein Hussar Regiment and two squadrons of the Prinz Clemens Uhlan Regiment, under Major von Seydlitz, counterattacked, driving the Russians back.

Though harassed and swarmed by the Russians, the Saxons continued advancing and arrived in Lapinika on 12 November. The Austrians arrived in Slonim with little interference, but the Saxon VII Corps found itself assailed on all sides. The Saxons learned from prisoners that their principal opponent was the Russian 7th Infantry Corps, and that its goal was to keep them separated from the Austrians. Despite the efforts of the 7th Infantry Corps, the Saxons advanced towards their rendezvous in Volkovysk with the 32nd Division, commanded by Duruette, part of Augereau's XI Corps.

Reynier arrived in Volkovysk and established his headquarters there. He covered his position with Le Coq's 21st Division. Duruette's 32nd Division, also there, was composed of young, relatively untrained soldiers. Five of its regiments were penal regiments formed entirely of pardoned deserters. The remaining regiment was from the German state Würzburg. The entire division was short of every type of material, and the only truly reliable troops were the Wurzburgers.

The Battle of Volkovysk

At about 3:00 A.M. on the night of 15 November, three Russian battalions and about 100 cavalry rushed the city. The Russians had advanced on Volkovysk since 10:00 A.M. the previous day. The Saxons were unaware of their advance until late that afternoon. Sacken's forces, totaling 16,000 infantry, 6,000 cavalry, and 5,000 cossacks, greatly outnumbered Reynier and Duruette's 15,000 infantry and 1,000 cavalry. The Russian assault awoke the French with the noise of its musketry. They had closed on the French unnoticed and entered Volkovysk to find it occupied by a few soldiers assigned to guard the corps headquarters and the Saxon baggage.

A battalion of the 39th Jager Regiment moved directly against Reynier's headquarters and quickly became involved in a desperate struggle with the 1/1st Saxon Light Infantry Regiment. The Saxon light infantry was supported by the von Anger and von Spiegel Grenadier Battalions. They were quickly joined by the 2/Prinz Friedrich August Regiment and part of Duruette's division. Reynier was surprised by two Russian companies commanded by a Russian officer named Magers and only barely escaped through a window, his clothes in his hand.

The confusion in the ensuing battle was indescribable. A furious house-to-house struggle raged through the streets. The Saxons were unable to push the Russians out of the city and actually lost ground. The 1/1st Light Infantry lost four officers and eighty-one men, while the 2/Prinz Frederich August Regiment lost its standard.

Le Coq dispatched an adjutant to Schwarzenberg to inform him of the battle and to obtain help. Though assistance was to arrive, it was unable to reach the Saxons before 16 November. During this time the Russians were able to maneuver the greatest portion of their forces against the Saxons until the last of the Saxons were driven from the city and forced to assume positions north of the city.

The 21st Division was positioned between Volkovysk and the road between Bialystok and Mosty. To their left and below them stood the 22nd Division. Duruette's forces were behind them formed in two echelons. The cavalry was held north of the Ortes River. The Saxon position was such that their artillery made any Russian assault unlikely to succeed.

Despite the strength of the Saxon position, the Russians began their assault at 8:00 A.M. on 15 November. It began with a heavy assault by the numerous Russian cavalry against the Saxon left flank. General von Gablenz and his Saxon cavalry brigade had taken a position on the left during the night. This force moved to counter the Russian attack. His attack was lead by the Saxon Hussar Regiment, and it became entangled in a wild melee. The Saxon colonel was struck from his horse by a cossack and wounded seven times in the fight. His hussars recoiled, reformed, and charged again with the support of the Polenz Chevauxléger Regiment and the Prinz Clemens Uhlan Regiment. They drove back the Russian cossacks to the right bank of the Volkovysk River. The fire of von Roth's Saxon Horse Battery inflicted heavy casualties in the cossack forces as they withdrew over the bridge to return to their lines. In the late afternoon the Russians moved forward once again to strike the Saxon left flank, but they were thrown back by the bayonets of the 2/1st Light Infantry Regiment and a company of the Prinz Anton Infantry Regiment.

On 16 November the Saxons attempted to assault the city, but the effort proved fruitless. As the assault fell back, the air was filled with three distinct salvos, the signals that the Austrians were fast approaching. With that reassuring signal, the Saxon artillery began a heavy barrage on the city, and twelve companies of the 32nd Division surged forward in an assault.

Sacken's forces were strongly positioned, but he lost his nerve. The Russians had heard the signal too and quickly abandoned their positions. They began maneuvering on Sqislocz. Schwarzenberg's lead elements began appearing on the battlefield. Schwarzenberg had with him the two infantry divisions of Trautenberg and Bianchi and the cavalry of Frolich and Wrede. The remainder of the Austrian Hilfkorps had remained in Slonim to watch Admiral Tchichagov's forces.

New Russian Maneuvers

On 24 November Sacken moved to Brest-Litovsk and Kobrin, but he continued to move eastward towards Lubolm and Kovel. Reynier followed him, occupying Brest-Litovsk, and Schwarzenberg reoccupied Kobrin. This was, however, as far as they were to advance, because Schwarzenberg had received orders to fall back on Warsaw. Reynier formed the rear guard, and on 1 November their withdrawal began.

Sacken's maneuvers had cost him 7,000 men and several guns, but he had seriously impacted Napoleon's plans and hurt the outcome of the campaign. He had diverted Schwarzenberg from his pursuit of Admiral Tchichagov, though if Schwarzenberg was to resume the pursuit by 14 November, he still could have caught him.

On the night of 20 November the 3rd Ukrainian Cossacks were surprised by the Austrians, and three squadrons were captured at Pruhany. At the same time 8,000 Poles under General Kossenki were turned back in their attempt to penetrate Volhynia via Oustilony by General Moussin Pouchkin as he advanced on Vladimir.

The French at Borisov

The French governor of Minsk had retreated on Borisov, where he gathered together a small garrison of 3,000 men. Dombrowski, who heard of the capture of Minsk while in Semlo, moved to Berezino, seeking a safe route to Borisov. His force had shrunk to 5,000 men. A Lithuanian regiment commanded by General Kossenki and a Württemberg battalion were detached and lost at Koidanov. Another regiment had been detached on the Bobruisk road to act as a rear guard. The column had a total of twenty guns with it.

Hagendorp, the former governor of Minsk, had established himself in Borisov and occupied a weak bridgehead with a single battalion of the 95th Line Regiment. He was blissfully ignorant of the danger that threatened him, and instead of urging Victor to advance quickly to support him, he persuaded Victor and Pampeluna that there was no danger of attack.

Tchichagov Closes In

Admiral Tchichagov sent Lambert to Jouknovo on 19 November while Tschlapitz covered his left, and Colonel Loukoffkin was detached with a cossack regiment to watch the road to Igumen. The cossacks encountered six Russian infantry battalions, four squadrons, and another cossack regiment detached by General Ertel moving from Oozyr to reinforce Tchichagov. Ertel had been ordered to join Tchichagov with his entire force, but chose to send only part of it. Tchichagov was so enraged by this disobedience that Ertel was relieved and command passed to Tuchkov.

Colonel Loukoffkin's detachment of cossacks contacted Dombrowski's rear guard near Igumen and pursued it. On 20 November Lambert reached Jodin and pushed on towards Ouperecoiczi. His move was supported by Lambert, also in Jodin, and Tschlapitz in Zembin.

Dombrowski moved as quickly as he could towards the French bridgehead at Borisov by advancing along the Berezina. He arrived there at midnight on 20 November. He was not met by any knowledgeable individual, and, as a result, he was forced to encamp his forces as best he could in the dark. He set his right on the works on the road to Zembin. His left had nothing to secure itself against and hung in the open.

The Battle of Borisov

The works around the bridgehead were far from finished. Many of them were little more than tracings on the ground where bridgeheads were to be built. At dawn on 21 November, Lambert appeared before

Dombrowski's positions. The 14th Jager Regiment attacked Dombrowski's right, the 38th Jager Regiment hit his left, and the 7th Jager Regiment were to hit his center. The two flanks were to be taken before the 7th Jagers hit the center.

The Russian 11th and 12th Horse Batteries advanced, one on each flank, while Lambert's other two infantry regiments and the advanced guard's cavalry formed a reserve on the road to Jodin.

The battalion of the French 95th Line Regiment, stationed near the bridgehead, was surprised and driven back across the bridge. The 14th Jager Regiment seized the redoubt on the right, but the 38th Jagers were unable to hold their ground against the Württemberg battalion advancing from Borisov.

The Russian General Engelhardt, who advanced at the head of his 7th Jager Regiment, turned his regiment to support the 38th Jager Regiment, but was killed. Despite the loss of its general, the regiment continued its movement and recaptured the redoubt on the left.

Dombrowski was alerted to the action and realized the danger to his forces if the Russians seized the bridgehead. He moved to join the Württemberg battalion in the central works that covered the bridge.

By noon Dombrowski had established his brigade so that it straddled the main road to Minsk. He proceeded to move his baggage and artillery park over the bridge. He established six guns in a battery on the far side of the river to cover his retreat.

Lambert positioned his artillery so that it might sweep the bridge as Dombrowski's Poles retreated over it. An artillery duel began, and a heavy cannonade lasted until 5:00 P.M. Lambert was wounded while rallying the 7th Jager Regiment, which had fallen back from its unsuccessful attack on the central works. Colonel Krussovski succeeded Lambert. Krussovski drew up his forces under the cover of a twelve-gun battery placed to the left of the redoubt. His forces then advanced and carried the whole line of entrenchments, the village, and the bridge.

Dombrowski led his troops across the bridge and attempted to rally them for the defense of a mill on the Orsha road. However, the Russians had too much momentum for him to stop them, and he was pushed back towards Lochnitza. Dombrowski left 1,500 dead, 2,500 wounded, two standards, and eight guns on the battlefield. The Russians suffered about 2,000 casualties out of the 3,500 engaged.

Langeron heard the cannonade and was marching to the sounds of the guns. However, he was unable to join the advanced guard until nightfall and did not participate in the battle. Admiral Tchichagov followed close behind and established his headquarters in Borisov that night.

Tchichagov Moves on the Berezina

During the same day as the battle at Borisov, Colonel Loukoffkin and his cossacks had overtaken the single regiment forming Dombrowski's rear guard near Oucha. They drove it over the Berezina River at Usza and took two to three hundred prisoners.

On 22 November Voinov's corps and the reserve under Savaneieff passed over the Berezina and took up a position astride the road to Bobr. Tschlapitz withdrew from Zembin and advanced to the new Russian headquarters at Borisov.

General Pampeluna and his brigade, detached from the 6th Division, part of Oudinot's II Corps, had been posted in Vesselovo and received the first news of the fall of Borisov. The news was duly passed on to Oudinot, who responded by moving his corps to Nemonitza, where he met Dombrowski's shattered forces. On 23 November Admiral Tchichagov directed Generalmajor Pahlen, who had replaced Lambert as the commander of the advanced guard, to advance with his forces down the road to Bobr. As he reached the heights of Nemonitza, he was shocked to find that he had encountered Oudinot's advanced guard marching on Borisov under the command of Dombrowski.

A quick action resulted, and Pahlen found himself unable to deploy. Pahlen found himself quickly bundled up and hustled in great disorder down the road. He fled back over the bridge at Borisov with a loss of 1,500 prisoners, the headquarters baggage, and the advanced guard baggage. Castex's brigade, the 23rd and 24th Chasseur à Cheval Regiments, pursued him. Dombrowski was leading 2,500 infantry, 1,100 cavalry, and 12 guns. The results were not a surprise when one considers that the Russians had only 2,800 infantry.

Oudinot's seizure of Borisov and the bridge had trapped three Russian jager regiments and 3,000 cavalry on the east bank of the Berezina. They escaped his wrath only because a peasant showed them a ford near Brill.

Tchichagov had been dining in Borisov as Oudinot's II Corps arrived. He escaped, but lost all his correspondence and baggage. He did succeed in cutting the bridge and establishing batteries along the river to prevent Oudinot from repairing it.

On 29 November Napoleon ordered Schwarzenberg to move against Admiral Tchichagov, but too great a distance separated them, and there was little point in the pursuit. Schwarzenberg had carried their pursuit of Sacken too far for him to be able to intervene.

Napoleon and the Main Army

The actions by the II, VI, and IX Corps to the north and that of the VII and Austrian Hilfkorps to the south were little more than a sideshow for the withdrawal of the main army from the battlefield at Malo-Jaroslavets.

Napoleon spent the day after the battle of Malo-Jaroslavets in deep contemplation. He pondered the options open to him. Murat, as usual, urged a resumption of the attack across the Lutza River. Davout urged a withdrawal through Medyn and Elnya. However, the other marshals consulted urged a quick withdrawal through Mozhaizk. Napoleon accepted the decision of the majority, and even though he later learned that Kutusov was in full retreat himself, he continued the French withdrawal through Mozhaizk.

The French army began to retrace its steps of the last five months along the roads from Borodino to Smolensk. As it crawled along the poor roads, it was burdened by heavy wagons overloaded with loot and hundreds of sick and wounded that were accumulated in the various hospitals along the way rather than left to the mercies of the cossacks. The Grande Armée filed past the battlefield at Borodino which was still littered with the putrefying corpses of the dead and broken implements of war. It proved a haunting spectacle for all that passed. As the army passed over this thoroughly ravaged land, it was unable to provision itself. Discipline began to break down as the soldiers began to forage more savagely than they had in the past.

Soldiers were competing for an ever-diminishing supply of food. Officers became bored with the pace of the war. The senior officers left every decision to Napoleon, and the younger officers lacked the experience and knowledge to sustain themselves and their troops. Regiments began to dissolve into disorder, and swarms of stragglers dogged the flanks and rear of the army in ever-growing numbers. Davout's I Corps was the rear guard. It was swamped with stragglers and the mass of lagging baggage and artillery. This mass was more than even the many-talented Davout could handle, and he received much unjust criticism from Napoleon. He was accused of delaying the retreat by his inability to manage this horde. The situation for Davout's forces was even worse than for the rest. This was because he had to pass over terrain that had been ravaged during the advance to Moscow and again by the rest of the army as it preceded him across it in retreat. The countryside had been picked clean of everything, including forage. The horses were weakened by the lack of forage and died by the thousands. This further slowed the advance of Davout's charges. Eugène advanced just ahead of Davout. He advanced as slowly as possible, to spare the wear and tear on his corps.

Kutusov had lost contact with the French during his retreat from Malo-Jaroslavets. He lost further time by looking for the French down the road to Medyn, but on 27 October he learned of their line of retreat and set off in pursuit. He began to position himself such that he always remained a threat to Napoleon's withdrawal but remained relatively secure from attack himself. Napoleon's forces were preceded by Ozharovski, who raided ahead of Napoleon in an attempt to destroy all of the supplies possible, while Miloradovitch's and Platov's cossacks hounded his flanks and rear.

Napoleon had reason to fear such an effort from Kutusov, and, suspecting that he might be cut off from his base in Smolensk, he marched ahead of the main body with his guard, reaching Viazma on 31 October. When he arrived in Viazma, his army was stretched over sixty miles of road, and he did nothing to close it up other than to scold Davout for not moving fast enough.

In Viazma Napoleon found dispatches from Paris, Warsaw, St. Cyr, and Victor. These documents confirmed his fears of a Russian offensive. He learned of Schwarzenberg's and Reynier's movement northward and of Wittgenstein's pursuit of Victor. He urged Victor to turn on Wittgenstein and push him back across the Dvina. Napoleon recalled d'Hillers and ordered him to join the main line of withdrawal. He ordered Ney to take a position in Viazma until Davout could pass through it. Ney was then to assume the position of rear guard.

On 31 October Platov's cossacks made contact with the rear of the French army and began to dog its heels. They continued their harassing pursuit. On 3 November Miloradovitch and his two divisions appeared before Viazma, attempting to interpose themselves between Eugène and Davout and cut off the French rear guard.

As the Russians arrived, Eugène's scouts and baggage were only a mile from the city. Nothing was visible to indicate the presence of the Russians to Eugène. The French were badly drawn out along the road, and Eugène stopped the lead elements to allow the straggling column to catch up. Shortly after the halt, Chef d'escadron Labedoyere arrived in Viazma with word of the Russian presence.

The Battle of Viazma

General Nagel's brigade of the 13th Division formed Eugène's rear guard. He was attacked in the left flank about two miles from Viazma by several squadrons of Russian cavalry. This cavalry moved into the gap separating the I and IV Corps. Eugène saw the danger and began to redeploy his forces to the right of the road near Foederovskoe. He placed his Polish forces a bit forward of the rest of his forces. The divisions of I Corps closed up quickly to support those of the IV Corps.

The Russian cavalry was supported by an infantry division of 12,000 men. Eugène's forces were able to check their advance, except on the right, near Viazma, where the Italians were dislodged. The Russians held the Italian position until a regiment from Ney's III Corps moved out of Viazma to attack them.

At the same time Compans' 5th Division, part of I Corps, joined the rear guard. They cleared the way to Viazma and engaged the Russians while the rest of I Corps passed along the left side of the road. Compans remained to support Eugène's rear guard.

When Davout completed this maneuver, he assumed a position on the right of Eugène's forces, linking them to Viazma. Eugène allowed the 13th Division, the old rear guard, to pass behind the 14th Division. The 14th Division assumed the duties of the rear guard, and Compans' division preceded it.

The 15th Division followed the 13th Division and remained with the Italian Royal Guard near Viazma, where they formed a reserve. When this maneuver was complete, the Russian infantry once again advanced, and a violent action began. The Russians had a massive artillery superiority and had been encouraged by the confusion generated by the French maneuvers. They took it for a rout and maneuvered their artillery at a gallop to take advantage of that confusion.

The Russian artillery moved obliquely to the flank of the French lines, which it began to cut down. The French guns in Viazma were ordered to return and provide support for the infantry. However, they could only maneuver with difficulty. Davout's forces advanced and forced the Russians to withdraw their artillery, lest it all be overrun. Three guns were captured. The audacity of this action astonished both the Russians and the French.

Miloradovitch realized that the French were escaping him and sent the British military observer General Wilson to Kutusov to request assistance. Wilson found Kutusov within earshot of the battle, unconcernedly resting his army and himself. Wilson became furious and called him a traitor, declaring that he would dispatch one of his escorts to St. Petersburg to denounce his actions to the czar.

This had no effect whatsoever on Kutusov. He seemed to be of the opinion that the Russian winter alone would bring about Napoleon's demise. He felt that nature had not sufficiently weakened the French for him to fully commit himself to a battle with them, to quote Wilson. However, it is more likely that Kutusov realized that the French before Miloradovitch were the battle-hardened core of the French army. It was the best of the French army, and his army was newly flushed out with new conscripts and would be no match for the French. It is reasonable to consider that an ill-advised attack at this point would have been an open invitation to disaster, throwing away all the Russian gains to date.

Kutusov, no doubt, did feel that it was wiser to permit the winter to work on the French a little longer before he committed himself. Wilson's perspective was seriously tainted by a great hatred of the French and a strong desire to see them punished at any opportunity. In this case, Kutusov's military judgment was far superior to his.

Miloradovitch, left to his own devices, tried to break the French lines. However, the French were still strong enough to resist him and prevented his penetrating their lines. Despite their strength, the men of the I and IV Corps were weakening. They became worried as they heard another action beginning to their rear. They imagined that the rest of the Russian army was approaching Viazma via the Yuknov road, the passage Ney was defending.

It was only a small Russian advanced guard, but it alarmed Eugène by threatening to cut off his escape route. The action was broken off as soon as all the French baggage had made its escape. The French retrograde movement encouraged the Russians, who renewed their efforts. Only the efforts of the 25th, 57th, and 85th Regiments, part of I Corps, along a ravine, prevented the Russians from breaking the I Corps, turning its right flank, and destroying it.

Eugène was not heavily engaged and was able to move more rapidly through Viazma. The Russians pursued him closely and penetrated into the city limits. The Russians then blocked Davout's passage as he attempted to pass through the city. He was being pursued by 20,000

Russians and under the fire of eighty cannons. Morand's 1st Division entered first and was unaware of the Russian presence. They struck him and drove him back. Morand rallied his division, restored the situation, and fought his way through the city.

It was Compans' 5th Division that finally put an end to the battle. He marched his division towards the city. When Miloradovitch's forces came too close, he turned suddenly and, like an annoyed lion on a pack of jackals that ventured too close, gave them something to consider. He then returned to his retreat, marching off the field of battle without further molestation.

A combination of night, the river, the town, and Marshal Ney's rear guard separated the Russians from the retreating French. When the danger ceased, the French settled down for the night and began reorganizing. Four thousand were either dead or missing, and many others were separated from their units. The French had once again shown their military prowess, but there were great gaps in their ranks. Each regiment scarcely had the strength of a battalion, and battalions were the strength of a peloton. Soldiers were no longer in their accustomed positions with their comrades and officers.

A sad reorganization took place in the light of the burning city of Viazma. The night was continually disturbed by the noise of Ney's rearguard artillery. Everytime the artillery fire broke out anew, the weary French seized their arms, fearing they were under attack again.

The Retreat Resumes

The next day winter arrived, and snow began to fall. The temperature fell, turning the roads into sheets of ice. The snow prevented the horses from grazing, and the icy roads prevented the starving beasts from maintaining their footing. Because the horses were in such poor condition, the French found themselves forced to begin abandoning more and more of their artillery, equipment, and baggage. Morale fell further, and discipline began to erode seriously.

The retreat continued, and losses grew more rapidly than ever. There were nearly 30,000 stragglers following the column, and very little mounted cavalry remained. The few wagons and carts that still remained with the army were filled with the wounded. However, discipline had fallen so badly that when one of the wounded would fall from the cart in which he had been riding, no one would stop to pick him up. The shortage of food was so acute that if a horse slipped on the ice he would be butchered by hungry soldiers before he could rise to his feet.

The army was quickly falling into a state of survival of the fittest and every man for himself. The organized, disciplined units began to shrink as the weaker fell away and forgot that their organization was their best chance for survival.

On 6 November Napoleon received more dispatches from Paris and learned of the abortive coup attempted by General Malet. Malet had attempted to seize power on 22 October and reestablish a republican government. He had asserted that Napoleon had perished in Russia and induced several colonels of the Paris garrison to bring out their men. With their assistance he attempted to seize control, but his bluff was called, and he was shot. Though it was obviously the work of a madman, no one had rallied to the king of Rome. Some of the officials had actually carried out Malet's orders. Napoleon began to wonder how strong his support in Paris actually was. His strength was weakening, and he knew it.

The retreat continued, and once in Dorogobuzh, Napoleon ordered Eugène to take the side road through Dukhovschina. The Italians were continually surrounded by swarms of cossacks, who picked off stragglers and harassed the column's flanks. As the Italians advanced, the Russians sent a force ahead of them to occupy Dukhovschina. When the IV Corps reached the Vop River they found it only lightly frozen, not enough to bear the weight of a crossing army. The Italian Guards waded across the river, breaking the ice with their chests. The rest of the army followed, but many wagons and guns became stuck in the mud of the river bottom and had to be abandoned.

The IV Corps bivouacked about three miles from the Vop until the morning of the 10th. Their line of march was littered with abandoned caissons, guns, elegant coaches, and booty taken from Moscow. It took little effort on Eugène's part to get his corps moving, as the riverbank was swarming with cossacks who plied their bloody trade with a passion on every straggler they caught.

The Italians bivouacked in the fields. They had little cavalry and artillery remaining with them. Only fourteen guns remained with the 14th Division. The advance was led by the Italian Royal Guard and the entire force continued its march on Dokhovschina. As they approached the village, several cossack regiments sortied from the village and maneuvered across the plain in an effort to surround the Italians. The Italian Guard formed itself into square, while those Italian dragoons and Bavarian chevauxlégers that were still mounted advanced by squadrons to drive the cossacks away. The road was cleared, and the IV Corps resumed its advance, with the lead elements supported by the 13th Division.

Dokhovschina had not been on the initial line of advance of the French army as it penetrated into Russia in July and August. As a result, it was well supplied and the buildings were intact. It proved a welcome windfall to the starving and cold troops. Eugène was so pleased with his situation that he detached an aide-de-camp with the 15th Division to move on Smolensk and inform Napoleon of his intention to rest his forces in Dokhovschina on 11 November. On 12 November the IV Corps resumed its march, and, as it departed, Dokhovschina was burned.

Upon arriving at the heights above Smolensk, Eugène placed himself at the head of the Italian Guard. The cold was so intense that thirty-two grenadiers froze to death in formation. General Broussier was forced by the Russians to evacuate his forces from an entrenched village but was able to break through their lines and joined Eugène.

Eugène wished to move the remains of his baggage into Smolensk and ordered the second brigade of the 14th Division to dislodge a Russian battery that was sweeping a bridge with its fire. General Heyligers moved forward with two guns and about fifty infantry. He assumed a position on the heights that turned the Russian battery's position and forced them to withdraw. The IV Corps renewed its advance and entered Smolensk.

Napoleon and his guard arrived in Smolensk on 9 November. Here he learned of the capture of a brigade under d'Hillers and of Wittgenstein's capture of Vitebsk on 7 November. Napoleon had sent Count Baraguay d'Hillers along the road to Elnya to stop the advance of the Russian forces under Count Orloff. The French had advanced with fresh troops organized into "bataillons de marche." They took positions around the villages of Yazvino, Liakhovo, and Dolghmoste. D'Hillers had entrenched his troops in position, hoping to hold off 5,000 Russian cavalry and 3,000 infantry, but his first brigade was forced to capitulate. He found himself about three miles to the rear, and, fearing the rest would be enveloped, he withdrew the remains of his forces to Smolensk. He was convinced that his small force could not stop such a superior Russian force.

Napoleon reorganized his remaining cavalry under Latour-Maubourg and gave specific instructions for the distribution of rations to his army. However, these instructions were not carried out. The masses of stragglers were refused food, being told that it would only be issued to organized formations after the presentation of proper requisitions. The crowds were so enraged that they broke into the magazines, looting and wasting much of the material so carefully stored there. Despite the looting and waste, Napoleon was still able to replace all the ammunition expended by his army to date and to add five new, fully equipped batteries to his army.

Of the 100,000 men leaving Moscow, only about 41,500 remained at their colors. The Guard alone accounted for 14,000 of these and a further 5,000 dismounted cavalry still retained their discipline. Eugène's IV Corps had 5,000 effectives and Davout's I Corps had 10,000. The V and VIII Corps (Poles and Westphalians) were merged and totaled only about 1,500. Ney's once-powerful III Corps had about 3,000. As a result, Napoleon had great hopes for the relatively fresh troops of II and IX Corps.

Napoleon left Smolensk in the company of his Guard. He was followed by Davout on the 16th and Ney on the 17th. On the morning of the 14th, when the Guard departed, its march was firm. The gloom and silence of the column was interrupted only by the squeak of the multitude of wheels in the column. On the first day the column advanced only fifteen miles, but the Guard artillery required twenty-two hours to cover that distance.

The following units in the column arrived in Korythinia with Junot's Westphalian corps, totaling 900, in the lead. Only fifteen miles separated Korythinia from Krasnoe and the road was flanked by the Dnieper River. A second road ran parallel to the main road, running from Elnya to Ktadnor. Kutusov used that road to move his 90,000 men. He quickly outstripped the French and sent forward several columns to intercept the French.

The Battle of Krasnoe

The forces of Ostermann arrived at Korythinia at the same time as the French vanguard entered the village. A second column, under Milora-dovitch, with 20,000 men had taken positions nine miles in advance of the French. They posted themselves to intercept the French near Nerlino and Mikoulina, behind a ravine skirting the main road. Here they lay in ambush awaiting the French advance.

The third Russian column reached Krasnoe, taking it by surprise, but Sebastiani, the local commander, drove them out. The fourth Russian column moved between Krasnoe and Liady, farther down the road, and captured the many stragglers they found there.

The French passed the night in Korythinia and the next morning moved down the road again. They were led by a horde of stragglers, all eager to reach Krasnoe. As they came within five miles of the city, they were suddenly confronted by a row of cossacks positioned on the heights to the left of the road. The cossacks were quickly driven off by a volley, and the march began anew.

A Russian battery began to fire on the advancing column, and thirty Russian squadrons advanced to threaten the Westphalians. The stunned Westphalians froze, making no effort to deploy. An unknown officer called out to them and assumed command. The soldiers ignored normal military convention. They began responding to the orders of this strange general. It was, in fact, General Exelmans of the Grenadiers à Cheval de la Garde. He moved forward, and the Russians were content to remain in their position and shell his new command.

Exelmans was supported by the Vistula Legion under General Claparede and the Guard who followed him. The force crossed the bridge and advanced into Krasnoe. As the Old Guard passed across the gorge under the Russian artillery fire, it formed its ranks tightly about Napoleon, and its band struck up the popular military march, "Where can we be happier than in the bosom of our family." Napoleon ordered them to stop, insisting that they play, "Let us watch over the Empire."

The Russian fire was becoming troublesome, and Napoleon ordered it silenced. The gorge was becoming congested. The Guard artillery was dragged by hand up to a plateau that overlooked the road. General Devaux's Young Guard Artillery had not lost a gun since they departed Moscow, due to the foresight of Colonel Villeneuve. Villeneuve had ordered every wagon and cart loaded with plenty of oats. As a result, his horses were still fit and able to draw their guns and equipment.

After two more hours the French advanced guard, commanded by General Sebastiani, entered Krasnoe. His Guard grenadiers drove out Ozhrovski's cavalry, part of the Russian third column.

While Napoleon's forces cleared the gorge, Eugène struggled in Smolensk to gather up and reorganize his corps. It had joined in the pillage and looting of the Smolensk magazines. He had great difficulty pulling them away from their plunder and only succeeded in rallying 8,000 men by 15 December. The next morning he departed, abandoning those who would not follow.

The advanced guard, 1,500 men of the 14th Division, were approached by a Russian officer under a flag of truce. He approached Eugène, stating that Eugène's tiny band was surrounded by 20,000 Russians under the command of General Miloradovitch. He went on and stated that Napoleon and his forces had been captured and that Eugène had no choice but to surrender.

Before Eugène could respond, General Guyon moved forward and shouted in a loud voice, "Return immediately to whence you came and tell him who sent you that if he has 20,000 we have 40,000!" Shortly after the emissary withdrew, the hills to the left began to belch smoke and flames as the Russian batteries located there opened fire. Eugène's tiny formation organized itself quickly and advanced, bayonets bristling.

Eugène ordered the two guns remaining to him to open fire, and he brought the 13th Division forward. General Ornano led them forward, and as he did, a near miss knocked him from his horse. He was thought to be dead, but he was only stunned and arose quickly. Colonel Delfanti was sent forward with a battalion to rally the units shaken by Ornano's fall. He was also struck down and had to be carried from the field. As he was carried off, he was wounded by a second cannonball that also carried away the head of General Villeblanche.

Delfanti's 200 men moved to support a square formed by the 35th Line Regiment under General Heyligers. However, deprived of their commander, they were poorly placed. The Russian cavalry quickly struck them, massacring them and seizing the guns which had been abandoned due to a lack of ammunition. The 35th Line Regiment was disorganized by the attack as well, and General Heyligers was taken prisoner.

The Russian artillery inflicted heavy casualties on the Italians, but they continued to advance. Eugène had just finished a reorganization of the 14th Division when the Russians moved to envelop it. Eugène ordered the remainder of his corps to profit by this. They filed along the right, behind the Italian Guard. As they made their escape in the dark, they advanced as silently as possible, hoping to escape detection. Suddenly a challenge in Russian broke the silence, and everyone froze. The Polish Colonel Kliski quickly ran over to the sentinel and rebuked him in his own language, saying, "Be silent fellow! Don't you see that we belong to the corps of Ouvarov, and that we are going on a secret expedition!" The simple Russian soldier, outwitted by his own language, held his tongue. This ruse allowed all but the 15th Division under General Triarie, which was acting as the rear guard, to escape. Triarie was to effect his escape later.

That same night the Russian campfires burned to the south and south-west of the Lossmina River, but Kutusov did not attack the French in

Krasnoe. The prestige of Napoleon and his Guard were still sufficient to prevent an attack, even though Kutusov had 90,000 men to Napoleon's 50,000.

At 9:00 P.M. Napoleon ordered Roguet to take the 2nd Guard Division and attack Ozhrovski's camp. This camp was two miles from Krasnoe and stretched for a distance of five miles. Roguet formed his four battalions of fusiliers into three columns and moved them on Buyanovo on the right, Maleievo in the center, and Chirkova on the left. They advanced in complete silence, their watches synchronized for a simultaneous attack. Roguet led the middle column personally.

At midnight, in a cold that was so intense that the Russians were comatose around their fires, the Fusilier Chasseurs and Fusilier Grenadiers fell on them with bayonets. The Russians were driven into the darkness in great disorder after taking heavy casualties. The French lost about 300 men in this attack, but the Russian losses were far greater.

This attack caused Kutusov to become more cautious in his maneuvers, and he halted his enveloping maneuver. He ordered Tormassov's corps to cut across the road between Krasnoe and Liady. He ordered a halt to operations for the evening, but the cossacks continued to loot the wagons stuck in the mire of the Lossmina that the French had abandoned earlier in the day.

Napoleon was faced with a decision. He could either continue his advance or remain in Krasnoe until Eugène, Davout, and Ney arrived. He decided to remain. General Durosnel was sent back towards Smolensk with a battalion of the Chasseurs à Pied de la Garde under General Boyere, two squadrons of the 1st Chevauléger-lanciers de la Garde, and two guns under Chlapowski to open the road for Eugène.

Durosnel moved forward along the left of the road to Katova, chasing the cossacks before him. He was quickly confronted by some regular Russian cavalry on his right. Durosnel ignored them, sending a few Polish lancers forward to inform Eugène of his advance. As he closed the Russian line, he directed the fire of his guns on it, but was promptly charged by the Russian cavalry supported by their own horse artillery. His men advanced steadily in square, firing at their antagonists. However, the Russians received a steady stream of reinforcements, and Durosnel was forced to retreat. This retreat was made in good order, but Napoleon, worried for his "children," had seconded this with an order carried by Latour-Maubourg to return.

Though Durosnel's effort was not an obvious success, it did draw enough of the Russians away from Eugène's front to permit Eugène to be able to close with Napoleon. Napoleon was doubly pleased: he had saved both his chasseurs and Eugène.

The Russian 6th Infantry Corps moved past Sorokino under the cover of their advanced guard and formed a line of battalion columns facing the main road. The 5th and 8th Infantry Corps did the same, forming a second and third line. Three regiments of the 1st Cuirassier Division deployed to the left of this infantry, and the entire force was directed to move behind the French advanced guard and maneuver on the French rear.

Prince Galitzin, with the 3rd Infantry Corps and the 2nd Cuirassier Division, was ordered to Ouvarova to attack the French frontally. He joined Miloradovitch, who commanded the 2nd and 7th Infantry Corps and 1st and 2nd Cavalry Corps, near Larionovo, in an effort to cut Davout off from Napoleon. If Davout succeeded in escaping them, Miloradovitch was to turn and pursue his rear guard, supporting Galitzin's attack. In addition, the detachment of Count Ojarovski was to operate to the left of the main column.

On 17 December Napoleon surveyed his situation. He had the columns of Miloradovitch, Strogonoff, and Galitzin on his right with 80,000 men and 100 guns, as well as a swarm of cossacks. They were moving on Liady and Orsha. It became obvious that if their maneuver succeeded, Napoleon would be cut off from Poana and separated from Ney and Davout.

Napoleon's forces still contained about 14,000 Guard, a few squadrons of Guard cavalry, about 400 horse under Latour-Maubourg, and a few guns that still had horses to pull them. He also had Eugène's greatly diminished IV Corps.

Napoleon posted Mortier with 5,000 Young Guard to the east and southeast of Krasnoe, along the Lossmina gorge. They were to hold that position for a day and blunt the advance of the Russians' attack. With the exception of a single battalion of chasseurs on Mortier's left, the Old Guard remained with Napoleon.

Roguet and his fusiliers were posted in front and to the left of Katova, facing it. Claparede, escorting the baggage and the Imperial treasury, was stationed west of Krasnoe to cover Eugène's retreat on Liady. Tindal, with a battalion of the 3rd Guard Grenadier Regiment, the army's wounded, and a force of dismounted cavalry barricaded the two and prepared to defend it. Drouot stripped the last horses from the guns and had the gunners burn their caissons, throwing their ammunition into a small lake.

Mortier made his dispositions along the heights above the Lossmina. In front of and along the bank occupied by the Old Guard, Mortier placed Prince Emil of Hesse's brigade of 600 men. This formation formed his left. In the center he placed Lanabeze's brigade, which consisted of the 1st Voltigeur and 1st Tirailleur Regiments. On the right, by Voskresnie, he placed a battalion of the 3rd Guard Grenadiers. He reorganized his infantry companies in two ranks so that the frontage of the battalions was more nearly normal. The remainder of Delaborde's 1st Division, with a squadron of the 2nd Guard Lancer Regiment and a squadron of the Portuguese Chasseur à Cheval Regiment under the Marquis de Loule, occupied the French second line.

The Russians opened the action by shelling the Hessians with thirty guns. Shortly later there were 100 guns in action all along the Russian front. The French attacked Ouvarova, which was occupied by the Tchernigov Infantry Regiment. The Russians were hard pressed, and Galitzin sent the Seleguinsk Infantry Regiment to support them. On the right, Voskreseniye was furiously contested and changed hands several times. Captain Aurnaud's company of the 1st Voltigeur Regiment was sent forward to block a Russian column that threatened to outflank the French position. His company withstood several charges until he was wounded.

The French advances stopped, and the Russian artillery fire from the heights on the right of the Lossmina, coupled with the advance of the 2nd Cuirassier Division, forced them back. The cuirassiers crossed the Lossmina below the village, but Galitzin was too weak to follow up his success.

At 4:00 P.M. the light began to fade and the battle ended. Ahead and on the left, Davout's guns could be heard mingled with the musketry of Roguet's troops as they both engaged Miloradovitch. To the south, east, and west, the entire horizon was ablaze with campfires. Claparede reported Bennigsen had cut the road to Liady, and only the road north to the Dnieper remained open.

Miloradovitch had positioned his superior forces to engage Davout as he attempted to join Napoleon. The French formed their forces into square and advanced under heavy fire that rained on them from the heights. As the artillery fire tore holes in the French formations, Russian cavalry would sweep forward in an attempt to breach them. However, the French steadfastly repulsed their attacks. The desperate situation was stabilized when General Morand's 1st Division, I Corps, arrived and stopped the Russian assaults.

The last escape route for the French to the Dnieper was suddenly closed as the Russians set up a horse battery on it and began to shell the Guard. Delaborde's guns were manhandled into position, but their response was feeble. The Duke of Teviso was ordered to hold out until nightfall. The 1st Tirailleur Regiment fell back on Krasnoe at the express orders of the marshal. The 1st Voltigeur Regiment continued to fight in their original positions.

The Novgorod and Little Russia Cuirassier Regiments took possession of the field. As the 1st Voltigeur Regiment and 3rd Dutch Grenadier Regiment abandoned their position, the Russians instantly positioned their artillery there, shelling the retreating French.

The new position of the Guard was quickly becoming untenable. A regiment was sent forward to drive off the Russian artillery. It recoiled from the heavy fire, and a second regiment advanced in its place. As this regiment reached the foot of the battery, it was driven back by the Novgorod and Little Russia Cuirassiers. It formed square and greeted the attacking cavalry with heavy musketry, driving them back. The Russian cavalry struck a third time, supported by two guns that poured cannister into the Guard Infantry. The square was broken and the soldiers massacred as the Mourmansk and Revel Infantry Regiments finished them off with bayonets.

The situation was rapidly becoming desperate, and Napoleon was obliged to quit the field before he could assure the safety of Ney. He ordered Mortier and Davout to make every effort to save Ney while he and the Guard moved on Liady.

Roguet's fusiliers and flankers relieved the Old Guard and were shelled furiously as they attempted to hold the Russians away from the road. Despite the fire it was hoped that the III Corps would pass. The Russians were charged by the Guard Flankers, but they repelled the attack. The Guard Fusiliers charged and stabilized the situation.

Under the cover of night the Russian cuirassiers attacked the plateau and Roguet's forces posted on it. The French guns were dragged away by hand because the horses were dead. Finally Mortier ordered Roguet to retire from the field.

Krasnoe was on fire as the Russian cuirassiers entered it. They sabered everything they encountered. A battalion of the 3rd Dutch Grenadiers stationed in the city made one last stand and then withdrew, being the last to retire behind the Young Guard and Roguet's division. General Tindal's infantry was so reduced in strength that the companies had an average of twenty men apiece. Roguet's division had suffered about 760 casualties.

The Old Guard and its comrades advanced westward. They moved with great difficulty over steep and icy roads. They lowered their wagons and guns down the hills on ropes because the horses couldn't safely traverse the slopes. Despite these measures, many guns and wagons were lost. Those who were mounted ran a very serious risk of being crushed if their horses slipped. Many men were crushed. A column of Davout's forces was caught and destroyed during the retreat by the Military Order and Ekaterinoslav Cuirassier Regiments under the command of Generalmajor Kretov as it moved towards Androssvanda.

On 17 November Napoleon directed Eugène to lead the advance on Orsha and the bridges over the Dnieper. Napoleon and the Old Guard followed, closely pursued by the rest of the Guard. In Krasnoe, the Russians took two standards, 45 guns, 6,229 prisoners, and a large quantity of baggage, including Davout's marshal's baton.

Orsha proved a great windfall for the ragged army that poured into it. Its commander and administration were both competent and capable. They had a well-stocked magazine system and systematically provided all that was so sorely needed by the Grande Armée. As much as possible the stragglers were fully equipped and returned to their proper formations.

Napoleon consolidated his forces and ordered the burning of all excess and unnecessary wagons and coaches. His enthusiasm for lightening his baggage train went too far: besides burning his own personal baggage, he also had his only remaining pontoon train burned.

Despite the serious objections of General Elbe of the Guard Engineers, the train was consigned to the flames. Elbe, however, feared the worst and managed to save two field forges and eight wagons loaded with coal and tools. He also had each of his sappers carry a tool, spikes, and clamps.

Ney's Finest Hour

Ney's III Corps had even greater problems than the rest of the army. It was the rear guard and was forced to pass over the same road as the main army, but by the time it arrived the Russians had already had time to prepare to receive it. He reached Krasnoe on 18 November and was greeted by a demand to surrender from an aide de camp of General Miloradovitch. His response was, "A Marshal never surrenders. There is no parlaying under an enemy's fire. You are my prisoner!" And with that he promptly took the emissary prisoner. After this his attempts to break through the Russian lines at Krasnoe proved fruitless.

The Russians prepared for Ney's approach. The 5th, 6th, and 8th Infantry Corps were placed near Debroie, facing Liady. Miloradovitch and Galitzin awaited Ney in strong positions by Krasnoe. General Depreradovitch, with the Chevalier Guards, the Horse Guards, and the Astrakhan Cuirassier Regiment, was sent to Winnyie-Louki to prevent Ney's crossing to the right of the main road.

The pursuit of Napoleon was abandoned to Count Ojarovski, General Borosdin, and the advanced guard of General Rosen, which was reinforced by six battalions of the 6th Infantry Corps and a regiment of Borosdin's cossacks. The pursuit was under the overall command of General Yermolov.

On 18 November, near 3:00 P.M., the cossacks announced Ney's approach. Miloradovitch arranged the 7th Infantry Corps in two lines. The 26th Division formed the first line and the 12th Division formed the second line. Both were supported on the right by the Lossmina. Behind them was the 3rd Infantry Corps with the 1st Grenadier Division in the front line and the 3rd Division in the second line. This force extended from the main road to the extreme left. Behind these two corps the 2nd Infantry Corps was held in reserve. Their entire front was covered by the Lossmina. The 2nd Cuirassier Division supported the 3rd Infantry Corps, and the 1st Cavalry Corps supported the 7th Infantry Corps. The 2nd Cavalry Corps stood near Ouvarova to cover the small plain between Loguinova and the Lossmina as well as the right flank of the 7th Infantry Corps.

A dense haze concealed Ney until his lead elements were 250 paces from forty Russian guns. Despite the heavy cannister fire that erupted once they were observed, the French crossed the Lossmina and passed into the guns. General Paskevitch, commander of the 26th Division, sent the Orel Infantry Regiment and the 5th and 42nd Jager Regiments, supported by the Guard Uhlan Regiment, forward to drive them back. The French recoiled and lost an eagle to the Russians.

Other French columns crossed the Lossmina to the right of the main road and were driven back by the Pavlov Grenadier Regiment. The battle raged for four or five hours, during which the French were raked by the fire of twenty-four guns on the right of the main road. Ney realized that he was hopelessly outnumbered and that he could never pass through Krasnoe. He withdrew towards the village of Dniakova.

That night he drew his men around Dniakova, north of the road, and had them build numerous fires to give the semblance of preparing for the night's bivouac. Once night had fallen and the Russians had settled down, Ney led his weary men through the darkness towards Syrokorense, on the Dnieper. When day broke on the 19th Ney was well on his way. The Russians discovered the ruse and sent Platov and his cossacks bounding off like a pack of hounds to locate the escaped prey.

The cossacks quickly closed on Ney and began trying to stop his advance. Ney formed his troops into square and, taking a musket in his own hands, led them onwards. By midnight III Corps had reached Guisnoe on the Dnieper. During the night his forces crossed over the ice. The ice was too thin to permit the passage of wagons so Ney was obliged to abandon all his train and artillery. Ney was still forty-five miles from Napoleon and Orsha. He covered that gap, and on 21 November he arrived outside Orsha, despite the continual harassment of the cossacks that had followed him across the Dnieper.

Ney sent a Polish officer to Orsha for help. Eugène responded by sending out rested forces to open the way for Ney's troops. Ney's arrival in Orsha raised the morale of the entire army. It proved an inspiration to everyone. However, Napoleon also received news of Oudinot's failure to hold the Borisov bridge.

Chapter XVI

The Nightmare at the Berezina

Advance on the Berezina

Napoleon was doubtful that the Borisov bridge could be secured and was informed of a ford, near Veselovo, about ten miles upstream from Borisov. Napoleon ordered Oudinot to recapture the bridgehead at Borisov or to locate another crossing some place between Berezino, twenty-five miles to the south of Borisov, and Veselovo. Oudinot was to build two bridges if he found a ford and fortify the bridgeheads to protect them.

Oudinot advanced his forces and captured the eastern bank of the Berezina at Borisov, but he was unable to secure the far bank because of the presence of Admiral Tchichagov. The destruction of the bridge forced him to seek the reported fords.

Oudinot learned of two fords. The first was at Studianka and was reported to him by General Corbineau, whose 6th Light Cavalry Brigade had been assigned to II Corps. The other ford was near Borisov. However, after Oudinot's Polish scouts reported it to him, the Russians also found it and sealed it off. Oudinot decided to move on Studianka.

On 20 November Napoleon ordered Victor to move to Borisov and form the rear guard of the army there on 26 November. In response, Victor moved south to Bobr and uncovered Oudinot's rear. If Wittgenstein had been alert he might have struck Oudinot in the rear and seized the last crossing available to Napoleon. He was unaware of the opportunity and pursued Victor instead.

Napoleon realized this error and on 23 November ordered Victor to return to the north and assume a position in Kholopenichi. Here he could cover Oudinot's rear. However, Victor had already advanced too far south, and, because of pressure from Wittgenstein, he was unable to execute this order.

Between 20 and 22 November Kutusov continued moving on Kopys. His headquarters were in Lannxi. His army took up positions near it. Miloradovitch and the advanced guard, formed with the 2nd and 7th Infantry Corps and the 2nd Cavalry Corps, were near Goriany. The Russians spent 22 November reorganizing and resting their army. The 3rd and 27th Divisions were organized into the newly reorganized 8th Corps, and the 1st and 2nd Grenadier Divisions became the newly reorganized 3rd Corps. Only General Platov continued to push forward against the French.

As Corbineau arrived at the Studianka crossing, he found that it was held by a strong Russian force on the western bank. In addition, he discovered that the warmer weather had melted much of the ice and snow, flooding the river. It was now five feet deep and flowing swiftly with great chunks of ice. The swamps had also begun to melt and would quickly become impassable for wheeled traffic.

Oudinot's other reconnaissance units reported fords at Ucholodi and Bolshoi-Starkov. However, they too were garrisoned by the Russians. When Oudinot learned of these garrisons, he canceled his order to march on Studianka.

Though Tchichagov and Wittgenstein had established contact with the French, Tchichagov was worried about Schwarzenberg's approach. He began to shift forces south to face this threat. Oudinot observed this, but suspected it was a feint. Napoleon had no knowledge of the approach of Schwarzenberg and had decided to withdraw through Vilna. He ordered Elbe, his pontooniers, and all available engineering and naval units to proceed to Oudinot. Napoleon ordered Dombrowski's and Alorna's detachments to join V Corps. He also ordered half the wagons of these two corps burnt so that the horses could be freed to draw the remaining artillery.

Napoleon intended that the bridges he planned to build would be used continuously. As soon as they were complete, Oudinot would cross and establish his forces on the western bank to defend the bridgehead. Once Oudinot was established near Bolshoi-Starkov, Ney was to follow and assume a position to his left. Both were to face the Russians to the south. The Imperial Guard was to cross after Ney and take a position to the north, near Brille, where it would form the general reserve. Eugène was to come next, then Davout, and finally Victor. Victor was to hold the eastern bank as a rear guard until the remains of the Grande Armée had crossed. The last act would be when General Elbé burned the bridges. At this point the Grande Armée had the following forces:

Corps	Commander	Infantry	Cavalry
Old Guard	Lefebvre	4,500	
Young Guard	Mortier	2,200	
Guard Cavalry	Bessières		2,000
I Corps	Davout	1,500	
II Corps with Dombrowski & Minsk Garrison	Oudinot	9,300	1,800
IV Corps	Eugène	1,600	
III & V Corps, Vistula Legion & Mohilev Garrison	Ney	5,400	400
V & VIII Corps	Junot	1,500	
IX Corps	Victor	11,000	1,200
IV Reserve Cavalry Corps	Lautor-Maubourg		50
	Total	36,700	5,450

During the night of 23–24 November, the weather grew cold enough to refreeze the marshes. Early in the morning Napoleon ordered Oudinot to cross the Studianka and sent Mortier's Young Guard south to Borisov.

On 25 November Generals Elbé and Chasseloup, the army's engineers, arrived at Borisov. They detached a small unit of engineers to give credence to the feinted crossing attempts being made by Oudinot. At 6:00 P.M. Oudinot's main forces silently abandoned their positions at Borisov and slipped north to Studianka where they began to establish themselves. The village of Studianka was quickly demolished and its lumber used to build the two bridges.

The first unit across the ford was Corbineau's brigade. His 400 men attacked the cossacks and their two guns on the far bank. A French battery of forty-four guns was drawn up on the eastern bank, and after brief cannonade, the combined action of Corbineau and the artillery drove the Russians away.

The Bridges Are Built

Corbineau's brigade was followed by Elbé's engineers, who threw themselves into the freezing water and began their labors. The night of

25–26 November was spent building a 100-yard bridge that linked the two banks. The first bridge was completed in the afternoon of 26 November. Oudinot and Dombrowski, with 11,000 men, immediately crossed, accompanied by Doumerc's cuirassiers and a few horse guns. The second, and larger, bridge was completed about 3:00 P.M., and the remainder of Oudinot's artillery and the Imperial Guard crossed.

Despite the efforts of Elbé and his engineers, the weight of the crossing army repeatedly broke down the bridges. As a result, they needed unceasing attention. The engineers were broken into teams that rotated the duties of maintaining the bridges during the crossing.

Oudinot's infantry caught Tschlapitz deploying for a counterattack and drove him back on Bolshoi-Starkov. Oudinot sent his cavalry westward to Zembik, where it secured a series of vital bridges, through the swamps, that Tschlapitz had neglected to burn.

While Ney, reinforced by Claparede, crossed the Berezina, Junot and Victor took up positions around Borisov. Davout assumed a position near Loshnitsa. Tchichagov spent 26 November in Usha, reconnoitering across the Berezina River in an attempt to discover Napoleon's plan, but learned nothing other than that he had been deceived. Wittgenstein was slowly dragging his army along the roads to Kostritsa. Vlastov led Wittgenstein's advanced guard, consisting of four cossack regiments, seven battalions, two cohorts of opolochenie, and six guns. The road was so bad that Wittgenstein was forced to leave twelve artillery companies in Kopya in order to double up the teams on the other companies. The 1st Cavalry Corps (the Russian Guard Cavalry) was left on the Dnieper to refit and reequip. Kutusov, with the rest of the army, now reduced to the 3rd, 4th, 5th, 6th, and 8th Infantry Corps, 4th Cavalry Corps, and two cuirassier divisions, moved down the main road to Borisov. Miloradovitch dispatched a new advanced guard under General Vassilczikov, composed of a jager regiment, one cossack regiment, and the 4th Cavalry Corps.

On 27 November the bulk of the French army crossed over the bridges, and by the end of the day only the IX Corps and a horde of stragglers remained on the eastern bank.

The Battles of the Berezina Crossing

Tchichagov, realizing his error, moved rapidly northward, but was distracted by the mob of stragglers at Borisov. He stopped to oppose their passage. Not being certain of the French maneuvers, he detached his advanced guard northward to observe the northern fords.

Wittgenstein had reached Kostritsa on the night of 26 November and learned of the French bridges at Studianka. He departed from the better road to Veselovo and pushed across the poorer country paths to Stari-Borisov in the hope of intercepting Victor. Instead of Victor's entire force, he encountered Partoneaux's 12th Division, which had become lost on the backroads to the east of the Berezina River. Partoneaux and his staff had ridden forward and were captured before they could return to the cover of their troops. The main body did not know of the capture of their commander, but found themselves surrounded by the entire Russian 1st Infantry Corps. They held their ground until morning, but were forced to surrender. The Russians captured 4,000 fresh and well-disciplined infantry, 500 cavalry consisting of the Saxon Prince Johann Chevauxléger Regiment and the Berg Chevauxléger-lancier Regiment, and four guns. Only 160 men escaped the disaster to tell the story to Napoleon.

When he learned of this, Napoleon ordered Hochberg's brigade to recross the Berezina to rejoin the rest of the IX Corps. It was only with the greatest difficulty that the brigade was able to return to the other side, forcing its way through the stream of stragglers that flooded across the bridges. That stream of humanity was so heavy that the Baden artillery was unable to cross and was left on the western bank.

Tchichagov seized the east bank of the Berezina at Borisov and repaired the bridges on 28 November. He went on to establish communications with Wittgenstein, who was then in Stari-Borisov. The two Russian generals made plans for a morning attack. Tchichagov's cavalry was to move to seize the vital bridges at Zembik that were then in French hands. Yermolov joined Tchichagov, and Platov moved up in support. However, despite the excellence of their service up to this time, the cossacks failed miserably during the crossing operations.

Tchichagov advanced at dawn to find Ney had pushed Langeron and Tschlapitz back to Bolshoi-Starkov. Tchichagov counterattacked very poorly near Veselovo with 9,000 infantry and 1,500 cavalry.

Oudinot held the right and center, while Ney held the left. Oudinot had posted the 123rd (Dutch) Line Regiment and the four Swiss regiments in the front line. The Croatians were around the Zavniki redoubt. The extent of the French front was about a mile and a quarter. The ground was broken by open woods and only partially cultivated.

Seven Russian jager regiments (7th, 12th, 14th, 22nd, 27th, 28th, and 32nd), under the command of General Sabaniev, occupied the woods between Siakhov and Brill, supported by the Pavlograd Hussar Regiment. The hussars had been broken into independent squadrons and were spread behind the infantry in small meadows. A lively skirmish began, and Oudinot was wounded again. Ney assumed command. About 10:00 A.M. Ney counterattacked with the Vistula Legion, the 3rd Cuirassier Division, the four Swiss regiments, the 123rd Line Regiment, and the Croatians. The force of three to four thousand men struck the Russian left, in the middle of the woods, nearly a mile from the road. There were two small meadows, open patches of only a few hundred square yards each, in which the Russian 18th Division of Prince Tchervatov was posted. It was formed in deep columns and did not expect attack because of the heavy forest cover.

General Doumerc and his 3rd Cuirassier Division struck the 18th Division. The 4th, 7th, and 14th Cuirassier Regiments, totaling 400 men, struck them suddenly and successfully. They had passed through the brush and woods, quickly reformed, and fallen on the Russian columns. They sabered more than 600 men, by Russian reports, and took 2,000 prisoners as well as a few guns.

A flank attack by General Berthezène's brigade of the 1st Division of the Young Guard struck the Russian right where the brigade formed of the 12th and 22nd Jager Regiments was posted. General Gangeblov had been obliged to turn his command over to General Rudzevisch. Rudzevisch had deployed this force along the river. The attack of the Young Guard nearly destroyed them, reducing them from 4,000 men to 700 battered survivors in a matter of minutes.

The French cavalry continued their assault, taking advantage of their impetus, and bore down on the eight regiments of the 9th and 18th Divisions that General Savaneieff was bringing up to support Tschlapitz. Savaneieff had scattered much of his force into a skirmish screen that was very vulnerable to destruction at the hands of the formed French infantry. Opportunity had placed Tschlapitz at the head of two squadrons of the Pavlograd Hussar Regiment. He led them forward in a brilliantly executed charge that halted the French long enough for Savaneieff to rally and reform his infantry. The French II Corps advanced and established itself in the woods before Starkov and engaged Savaneieff's forces. Ney and Poniatowski responded by moving up their forces to support Oudinot's II Corps. Despite Russian reinforcements and counterattacks, the French successfully held their wooded positions until night fell and the battle ended.

On the east bank of the Berezina, Marshal Victor had established his corps on both sides of the village of Studianka. To the right of the village, towards Borisov, stretched a small, unobstructed plain. This plain was bordered on the east by a woods and stretched to the banks of the Berezina. The plain was split by the road that ran from Borisov to the site of the newly erected bridges. Though there were no major obstacles on the plain, it was cut by a valley that had a small stream in its bottom. The banks of this stream were steep. On the southern side of the valley was a ridge that overlooked the village of Studianka. Behind the southern ridge was a thick woods that obscured the view of the approaching roads.

It was on the plateau of Studianka that Victor placed his troops. Hochberg's Baden brigade, a battalion of the French 55th Line Regiment under Chef de bataillon Joyeaux, and four French 12pdrs formed the allied right. Its flank was secured on the Berezina and its left on Studianka. The center was held by the Berg brigade, and the allied left was held by Girard's 28th Division. The Poles (4th, 7th, and 9th Regiments) stood forward, supported by Kleingel's Saxon brigade (von Low and von Rechten Infantry Regiments), which were held in reserve.

Girard's left flank was unable to secure itself against the woods to the east of the plain and hung in the open as a result. The gap between the flank and the woods was filled by what little cavalry remained to the corps. This was the 350 cavalry of the Baden Hussar Regiment and the Hessian Chevauxléger Regiment under General Fournier. Behind the left, on a low ridge, was a reserve of fourteen French guns. Spread ahead of the main battle line was a thin skirmish line that acted as an advanced picket. On the far bank, Napoleon placed a battery of artillery from his reserve to support the Baden brigade with flanking fire.

In the beginning of the battle, the Russians quickly engaged the allied right. Vlastov, followed by Berg's corps, had taken position on the heights along the edge of the forest that overlooked the allied positions. As Vlastov established himself before the allied position, he sent Colonel Herngross to attack the French left with the converged hussars and the Rodinov #2 Don Cossack Regiment. The cossacks' attack was turned back by Fournier, who was in his turn driven back by the converged hussars. While this cavalry battle was going on, Vlastov established a twelve-gun battery to fire on the Baden brigade on the allied right.

This battery began to shell the bridges. The Russians also began a skirmish fire all along the entire length of the line. Timed with this was a major Russian assault against the Baden brigade. This assault attempted to push between the infantry and the Berezina in order to open a passage to the bridges. A hard-fought battle began, and the French battalion and the Lingg Jägers were pushed back after they had exhausted their ammunition. General Lingg was wounded, but ordered the 2/3rd Baden Infantry Regiment forward to fill the gap. As it approached the Russians it advanced with lowered bayonets, driving the Russians back into the woods. The Baden infantry attacked without any artillery support, yet despite this, it was successful.

While this was occurring, the Russians continued their heavy can-nonade on the allied left. The Russian line extended itself towards the allied right and began redeploying their artillery to threaten the most exposed portion of the allied line. In response to this threat, Victor ordered General Damas to attack the Russian artillery on the heights with the Berg brigade.

The Berg brigade advanced in two columns, each with the approximate strength of a battalion, from the plateau, with the support of the Baden Hussar Regiment and the Guard battery on the far bank of the Berezina. As they reached the bottom of the valley, they paused and took shelter behind the bank of the small stream. This offered some cover from the plunging artillery fire. As they resumed their advance, the Russian skir-mish line gave way. The Russians quickly reestablished their skirmishers several hundred paces behind their original line. The skirmishers stood before a defile through the woods. The 24th Jager Regiment stood in column in this defile. They engaged the assaulting Berg infantry with musketry.

Twice the Berg infantry attacked them and failed with great losses. They were faced by the Russian General Berg who commanded thirty-six guns, the Sievsk Infantry Regiment, the 1st Marine Regiment, and the 10th Cohort of St. Petersburg opolochenie. As this force was reinforced by the Perm Infantry Regiment, it went over to the attack.

As the first Bergish column fell back, the second column advanced in its turn. It had been deployed for such a contingency, but it too failed in its attack. Both columns fell back in disorder. Both columns fell back to their original positions near Studianka.

During this attack the Baden brigade underwent another heavy barrage of artillery and musketry fire on its extreme flank. Hochberg rotated his infantry battalions into the line, relieving each as it expended its ammunition. The Russian cannon fire was, by this time, reaching the masses of unformed stragglers that swarmed about the two brigades. The fire raised them to a panic, and they stampeded the bridges in terror. Others attempted to swim the freezing Berezina.

The withdrawal of the Berg brigade forced the Poles to fill in the gap. They did not recognize the Baden infantry and almost fired on it. As the fire of the Russian Horse Battery #23 intensified, the 34th Jager Regiment as well as the Nisov and Vorohenz Infantry Regiments advanced. They engaged the 7th and 9th Polish Infantry Regiments in a lively fusillade. The Hessian Chevauxlégers and Baden Hussars moved forward to attack. They totaled no more than 350 men. Fournier, their commander, was quickly wounded, and the command passed to Colonel de LaRoche. These brave men threw themselves against the flank of the advancing Russian column and, after a short fight, broke it. They captured 500 men of the 34th Jager Regiment and drove the other two regiments back.

Two squadrons of the Russian converged cuirassiers and the Pavlov Grenadier Depot Battalion advanced to counterattack LaRoche's forces with the supporting fire of Position Battery #11. The Hessian and Baden cavalry charged them. LaRoche, already wounded by a bayonet thrust in the first attack, was wounded a second time and taken prisoner. After that he was hit by another musket ball and received a saber cut to his shako. Wachtmeister Springer rushed to his commander's aide and freed him. The two German cavalry regiments were forced back. Once reformed and rallied it was found that there remained only 50 men. Though a costly attack, it had reestablished the center of the French lines. The Russian general Fock brought up his reserves and moved against the French left. The Saxons and 4th Polish Infantry Regiment fought off this last Russian attack.

As the IX Corps moved back, the Russians advanced their skirmishers against its right flank. The 2/2nd Baden Infantry Regiment was detached to hold them off. When it had expended its ammunition, the 1/1st Baden Infantry, under Captain Poln, advanced to fill its place.

The battle died down after this, and the Russians contented themselves with renewing their artillery and skirmish fire on the French lines. In the lull after the active attacks, the main French forces continued their retreat across the bridge. The press was so great, however, that it was still impossible to bring over the Baden artillery. The effort was eventually abandoned.

Losses were heavy on both sides. The Baden brigade lost 28 dead and wounded officers and 1,100 dead and wounded men. The Baden brigade had a total of 900 men remaining to arms. The Berg brigade was reduced to 60 men, and the Poles had 250 men.

At midnight the weakened forces from the IX Corps began withdrawing across the bridges. The grenadier company of the 1st Baden Infantry Regiment, commanded by Captain von Zech, formed their rear guard. Behind them, on the eastern bank of the Berezina, they left a mass of despondent and resigned stragglers. They were concerned with huddling around their meager fires and scavenging amongst the multitude of broken wagons and abandoned equipment that littered the bank. Escaping the Russians was not in their minds.

The French losses in the crossing operations were heavy. On 29 November the Old Guard had only 2,000 men and the Young Guard was reduced to 800. Hunger and cold had taken a heavy toll on the Russians as well.

The Retreat Resumes Again

On the 29th the French retreat began with the Guard leading the way. They moved from Zembik to Vilna. Had the Russians been able to seize these roads earlier, they would have totally destroyed the French. Fortunately for the French, these vital bridges were intact, and the security of Poland lay before them.

Napoleon Leaves the Grande Armée

At 10:00 P.M. that evening Napoleon quit the Grande Armée with an escort of 200 guardsmen. The 150 Guard horses that were still fit for duty were sent to Oshmiany, and a squadron of Guard Lancers formed relays between Smorgoni and Oshmiany. Murat was given command of the remains of the Grande Armée and ordered to bring it back to Poland.

At 9:00 A.M. on 29 November the Russian cossacks moved against the stragglers on the banks of the Berezina. Tchichagov did not stir to pursue the French. Ney once again assumed the rearguard duties and covered the French rear with the remains of the II, III, and V Corps. As they passed over the bridges through the marshes, General Elbé burned the major bridges between Brili and Zembik, blocking the Russian pursuit for twenty-four hours. Lanskoi's forces, consisting of twenty squadrons and a cossack regiment, moved to the vicinity of Pleshenitsy, sixteen miles from Zembik. He was stopped and held back by Oudinot and a collection of officers and batmen until Junot's Westphalians appeared and drove them off.

Wittgenstein was unable to cross the Berezina until Tchichagov provided the pontoons necessary to bridge it. The pursuit by the Russian armies finally got under way in a serious manner when Tschlapitz's light forces, composed of eight jagers, twenty-four squadrons of cavalry, eight cossack regiments, and three horse batteries, moved across the river. He quickly encountered the burnt-out bridges, which stopped his advance. Once it resumed, he stopped again when he encountered Platov's corps, which had been wandering about aimlessly, attempting to contact the French. Tschlapitz didn't contact Ney's rear guard until 2 December. Coming out the worse for that encounter, Tschlapitz assumed a respectful distance from Ney and contented himself with shadowing the retreat. The French still commanded respect.

On 2 December the main French army consisted of:

Advanced Guard:	I Corps & IV Corps	400 men
Main Body:	IX Corps	2000
	Guard	2800
Rear Guard:	Vistula Legion	200
	Dombrowski's Division	800
	IV Corps	300
	II Corps	500

The weather began to deteriorate again, and the temperature dropped below zero. Both armies suffered cruelly from the ravages of the climate, lack of food, and typhus. Organization and discipline disintegrated as never before, and the cossacks took advantage of this, looting and killing with abandon.

On 9 December the French reached Vilna. Napoleon had sent word that it was to prepare to receive and provision the army, but the administration learned of the disaster and fled in terror of the cossacks. The city was filled with supplies that were looted and wasted by the undisciplined soldiers. The bountiful supplies so allured the stragglers that it was only with the greatest effort that Lefebvre and Ney were able to rally enough of them to chase off the cossacks. It was at this time that Berthier remembered that Schwarzenberg and Macdonald had not been given orders. Berthier took it upon himself to order Macdonald to withdraw through Tilsit and Schwarzenberg to withdraw to Bialystok. A new rear guard was formed from the remains of the VI Corps under Wrede and the 31st Division of Loison.

The French left Vilna on 10 December, and the cossacks instantly entered the city. As Ney retreated over the river he set fire to the remaining supplies. Murat reached Roumcziki on 11 December, and the army halted again. He advanced to Kowno with an escort, where he contacted the garrison of 1,500 German levies and forty-two guns. Twenty-five of the guns were well horsed. He also found large magazines and a well-stocked treasury with 2.5 million francs. As strong as this position might have been, the Niemen was frozen, and the position could not be held. Murat continued to retreat with the Guard on 13 December. He placed a nine-gun battery on a hill overlooking the approaches to Kowno to hold the way for Ney.

Ney made his entrance into Kowno with 1,000 combatants and found the city full of dead and drunk men. The magazines had been looted and little remained. Platov and his cossacks arrived around 2:00 P.M. and began to fire on the bridge. An error resulted in the spiking of the guns on the heights and the recruits manning them fled. Ney and Gerard moved to the threatened gate and stabilized the situation. General Marchand led a sortie that drove the cossacks back and recaptured the heights.

At 9:30 A.M. the next morning Ney abandoned the city and fired the bridges over the Niemen. He moved through the Polviski forest to elude his Russian pursuers, but he was obliged to abandon the last guns belonging to Loison's 31st Division because of the roughness of the terrain.

On 14 December the main body of the Grande Armée had recrossed the Niemen. The army that had once mustered thousands now amounted to 400 infantry and 600 cavalry. Of the over 800 guns that they had taken into Russia, with the exception of some Polish guns, only nine remained.

The withdrawal continued, and on 19 December Murat and the lead elements arrived in Koenigsberg. Murat ordered that the stragglers be collected from the Prussian countryside. The V Corps was directed to Warsaw, the VI Corps to Plock, the I and VIII Corps to Thorn, the II and III Corps to Marienwerder, the Guard to Insterburg, and the reinforcements were drawn together to form the new 30th Division under Heudelet. Heudelet commanded the largest body of organized French in Germany. It consisted of 12,000 men and twenty guns.

The main Russian forces under Tchichagov entered Vilna on 10 December around noon. Efforts were made to round up the French stragglers and to restore order.

Wittgenstein had arrived in Kamen on 4 December and reached Sviranki on the 10th. From there he moved on Koidany to intercept Macdonald.

Marshal Kutusov arrived in Vilna on 13 December. From there he dispatched the 4th, 6th, and 8th Corps with the cavalry of General Vasil'chikov on Vologin. Ojarovski arrived in Vologin on 7 December and watched Schwarzenberg, who was in Slomin. Tuchkov replaced Ertel's division, which consisted of fifteen battalions, fourteen squadrons, two cossack regiments, and two artillery companies. Ertel's division was sent to join Ojarovski.

Kutusov joined Miloradovitch's advanced guard and accompanied them. General Wilson reported that 90,000 Russians perished in the march from Berezina to Vilna. Of a force of 10,000 recruits sent to Vilna to reinforce the Russian army, only 1,500 arrived, and the greater part of them were taken directly into the hospitals because of illness and frostbite.

Macdonald's Withdrawal

Months earlier, while the main army was occupying Moscow, Macdonald had pushed his corps forward towards Riga. The greater portion of his forces were formed of the Prussian Hilfkorps commanded by General Grawert. However, on 13 August Grawert was replaced by General Yorck. The campaign had been very stagnant until General Essen, commander of the Russian garrison in Riga, began his own campaign to break the relationship between Macdonald and Yorck.

Essen urged Yorck to turn on Macdonald, arrest him, and throw him into the fortress of Riga. Yorck did not bother to reply. He had already made known his attitude towards this idea in his comments at the execution of Tiedemann, when he said, "It is a good thing that he is dead; now we shall have more peace. In the last days of his life he also made himself contemptible, not only by often inciting our troops to desertion—in vain, fortunately,—but shamefully proposing to Major Crammon on the 6th (of August) at Schlock that he and his battalion should capitulate." When Paulucci succeeded Essen as governor, he attempted to persuade Yorck and failed as well.

With the withdrawal of the Grande Armée from Moscow and the disasters that had befallen it, coupled with the shaky relationship between Yorck and Macdonald, things began to change. With the Grande Armée moving back towards the Niemen, the Russians feared that Macdonald might move southward to support him. Wittgenstein was, as a result, ordered north to head off any such movement by Macdonald. Macdonald, in fact, never received such orders. Indeed, he received no orders to withdraw until Murat was in Vilna and Berthier took it upon himself to give orders. Even then, the orders did not reach him in Mitau until 18 December. The messenger, a Prussian, was so frightened of falling into Russians hands that he made a detour via Tilsit.

In the meantime, Macdonald became more and more uneasy about Yorck's loyalty. On 19 December he began to move south in four columns, three of which were formed from Prussian troops and commanded by Yorck, Massenbach, and Kleist. The roads were bad and snow lay thickly upon the ground. Yorck gradually became separated from Macdonald's lead column by a distance of about six miles.

At the same time the Russian 1st Infantry Corps, under Wittgenstein, advanced north to intercept him. Wittgenstein had rested his exhausted troops in Niemzim on 16 December and resumed his march on the 17th. Fearing to make contact with the French before he was ready to give battle, he sent forward two advanced reconnaissance units in addition to the usual advanced guard.

One of these reconnaissance forces was commanded by the Prussian General Diebitsch. Clausewitz was his chief of staff, and his force was formed principally of cossacks. On 20 December Diebitsch was in Koltiniani. The Russians had no idea of Macdonald's whereabouts. They had thought that he would be moving towards Memel in order to use the Kurische Haff, a narrow strip of land between the lake at the Niemen estuary and the sea. General Diebitsch had advanced with that concept in mind, but he discovered that Macdonald had already passed them by. He turned about and marched on Verni. From there he hoped he could intercept Macdonald the next day near Koltiniani.

After an early start, Diebitsch's corps reached the town of Verni at about 10:00 A.M. and learned that Macdonald had already passed through it ahead of them. Diebitsch also learned that he had interposed himself between the French column and what Diebitsch thought was their rear guard under the command of General Kleist. Kleist commanded four infantry battalions, two cavalry squadrons, and an artillery battery. The Russians faced them with about 1,400 men.

Though outnumbered, Diebitsch decided to attempt a deception and asked Clausewitz to go forward to try to arrange a truce with Kleist. Diebitsch hoped to convince Kleist that he, and not the Russians, were in an inferior position.

The Prussian Defection

When negotiations began, Kleist inadvertently stated that he was unable to enter into such negotiations, but that his commander, General Yorck, was behind him, and that he could speak with Diebitsch. The Russians were shocked to learn that they were in the middle of the entire corps. Yorck and Kleist had about 10,000 men behind them, Macdonald had 4,000 men at Koltiniani, and Grandjean was in Tauroggen, four miles south of Koltiniani, with 6,000 more troops. Diebitsch was in a most precarious position.

Growing anxious about Yorck and the Russians, Macdonald slowed his southern advance. He sent scouts to try to contact the Prussians, but the cossacks intercepted them all. Both Yorck and Macdonald were kept ignorant of each other's actions. Kleist informed Yorck of his contact during a meeting early in the evening of Christmas day. Yorck agreed to talk to Diebitsch, and they met in the Prussian camp that night.

Diebitsch told Yorck the size of his small force and continued to tell him that, though he couldn't stop Yorck, if the Prussians resumed their advance, Diebitsch could cut their baggage and artillery off and destroy it. He went on to outline to Yorck the disaster that had befallen Napoleon's Grande Armée. He also told Yorck that the czar had ordered that the Prussians were not to be treated in the same fashion as the French. Diebitsch offered up any military advantages he might have if the Prussians would commit themselves to be neutral.

Yorck refused to commit himself, but hinted that he might come to an agreement if he could preserve the honor of his corps. However, this was something that he could not justify at the moment. The two generals agreed to a temporary armistice for the night. In the morning Yorck made a reconnaissance and marched towards Lavkove, as if attempting to turn the Russian flank. Diebitsch moved to Schelel and remained in front of the Prussian forces.

As they continued their contacts over the next few days only a light screen of cossacks separated Yorck from Macdonald. Eventually a courier from Macdonald pierced this screen. He removed all doubt. If Yorck's troops did not arrive the issue of Prussian loyalty would be settled. Yorck had been holding up this moment of decision in the hope that Wittgenstein would arrive in force and resolve the issue. With this hope, Yorck signed the Convention of Tauroggen, which neutralized the Prussian corps in the struggle between Russia and France. Among the terms of this convention was the stipulation that the Prussian corps would not operate against the Russians for two months.

This convention had tremendous implications for the military, diplomatic, and internal political situation of Prussia. It was the first step towards the "Befreiungskrieg" or "War of Liberation" that was to rage across the face of Germany and France in 1813 and 1814. In addition to these long-range implications, it had the short-term effect of stripping Napoleon of 14,000 fresh troops that could have assisted Napoleon in his attempts to hold East Prussia and Silesia. That would have held the Russians away from his assembly areas while he reorganized his army and would have slowed the eventual Austrian defection.

The news of Yorck's defection reached Murat and caused him to lose his nerve. He abdicated his command to Eugène and fled to Naples. The remaining troops were moved into strong positions, and Eugène attempted to restore order. A crisis brewed over Eugène's assumption of command, as he was not initially inclined to accept command. However, Berthier persuaded him that no other marshal could command the obedience of the others and persuaded him to accept the task.

Schwarzenberg and Reynier had taken up winter quarters near Bialystok, but Schwarzenberg decided to retire into Galacia, an Austrian province, to be nearer his source of supply and his commanders. This retreat forced Reynier and his Saxons to withdraw to Glogau after a bloody clash with the Russians near Plock.

Macdonald's remaining forces withdrew into Danzig and joined Heudelet's division there. Eugène's main army totaled about 10,000 men of all nationalities formed into ad hoc provisional regiments.

Wittgenstein crossed the Vistula on 13 January with 30,000 men, but was forced to detach a major portion of his force to watch Danzig, where there were 20,000 French still capable of combat. Wittgenstein stopped his advance to await the arrival of Tchichagov and Kutusov. Admiral Tchichagov was advancing on Thorn with 20,000 men, and Kutusov with another 30,000 men was advancing into Pommerania.

Eugène Takes Command

Eugène initially organized his forces into four weak divisions and reorganized the 2,000 mounted cavalry that remained to him. Beyond these forces he had the 31st Division of XI Corps and Grenier's Italian division of 10,000 men. Grenier's Division had been called up from Italy and was divided into two smaller divisions. It was organized with the 31st Division to form the new XI Corps under the command of St. Cyr.

The main Russian forces stopped their advance and began to concentrate and reorganize. However, Wittgenstein detached three strong columns of cossacks, about 1,500 men, each armed with a few horse guns, and sent them forward under the commands of Tettenborn, Benkendorf, and Czernitchev. Their goal was to raid the countryside.

Eugène's advanced forces were eventually driven back to Frankfurt-am-Oder, and Wittgenstein's cossacks pushed nearly as far as Berlin. At this time Eugène had 30,000 men in Frankfurt, Reynier had 9,000 in Glogau, Augereau had 6,500 in Berlin, and Lauriston was in Magdeburg with two divisions of V Corps and awaiting the arrival of two more divisions. General Morand had 2,000 Saxons in Swedish Pommerania and the garrisons of Stettin, Küstrin, and Glogau, which provided another 17,000 men. Poniatowski had 8,500 men in Galacia, but they were neutralized by Schwarzenberg when he signed his own armistice with the Russians.

The Russian forces were not very strong at the beginning of 1813. Wittgenstein had 19,000 men available on 18 February, 150 miles from the Oder in Pommerania. Kutusov had 40,000 men, and Sacken had 20,000 watching Schwarzenberg in Galacia. Though Prussia had not yet defected, Yorck was close behind Wittgenstein, and other forces under Blucher and Bulow were rapidly organizing in Breslau and Colburg. As long as the bulk of Prussian territory was occupied by the French it was unlikely these forces would defect. However, this did not last long. Eugène's position was relatively secure. Eugène, however, fell under the influences of Augereau, who feared the possibility of a revolt in Berlin, in the French rear. Augereau persuaded Eugène to withdraw behind the Oder, and this encouraged the anti-French Prussians. Frederick Wilhelm signed the Treaty of Kalisch on 28 February 1813, which allied Prussia with Russia against Napoleon. This treaty remained secret until 27 March. The announcement of this treaty brought 30,000 fresh and well-armed Prussians into the Russian camp under the commands of Yorck and Bulow.

The Russians were emboldened by this and by the continuous French retreats. They pushed forward again, and Eugène responded by withdrawing behind the Elbe.

These maneuvers, though they occurred in early 1813, were the last maneuvers of the 1812 campaign. They rapidly developed into a new campaign as the French halted their withdrawals and reformed their armies. Once this was done, the French armies advanced, as was their tradition. They pushed their enemies before them, beginning one of the hardest-fought campaigns of Napoleon's career.

Chapter XVII _____

Aftermath—The French Phoenix

With the return of the remains of the French armies to Germany and Poland, a lull in the campaign occurred. When hostilities finally resumed, the 1813 campaign in Germany began. However, before the 1813 campaign began, there was a series of developments that can be considered to belong to the 1812 campaign.

Of the 680,500 men that Napoleon had organized for his invasion of Russia, barely 93,000 remained. The main army had suffered the harshest casualties and had dwindled from 450,000 to 25,000 men. The flanking and rearguard forces under Schwarzenberg, Reynier, Macdonald, and Augereau had returned with a total of 68,000 men, but many of these men had not ventured very far into Russia, and those of Schwarzenberg, Reynier, and Macdonald had not been as heavily engaged as the main army.

Records suggest that 370,000 French and allied soldiers died either from battle or other causes, while 200,000 were taken prisoner by the Russians. Of those taken prisoner, nearly half died in captivity.

Napoleon had taken 176,850 horses with him into Russia, and barely any of them survived the campaign. The Russians reported burning the corpses of 123,382 horses as they cleaned up their countryside of the debris of war. So heavy were the horse losses that one of Napoleon's most serious handicaps in the 1813 campaign was his inability to reconstitute his once-powerful cavalry.

Of the 1,800 cannon taken into Russia, the Russians reported capturing 929 of them, and only 250 were brought out. The remainder were lost or thrown into swamps and lakes so that they might not be captured. Though the loss of cannons was serious, the loss of horses was more devastating to Napoleon. France's arsenals and industrial facilities would soon replace the lost weaponry.

Of the 66,345 men that had belonged to Davout's corps in June 1812, there remained only 2,281. The 50,000-man Imperial Guard had been reduced to 500 men under arms and a further 800 sick, of whom 200 would never return to arms. Similar casualties were suffered by the II, III, and IV Corps.

The French army of 1813 would be rebuilt around these few survivors, Augereau's XI Corps, the two Italian divisions, and the garrisons of various German cities.

The one hopeful spot in all this despair was that most of those who had survived the campaign were officers and noncommissioned officers. These men would be indispensable if Napoleon was to reconstitute his army. They would form the cadres of experience around which the new levies would be formed.

The French were not the only ones to suffer and incur heavy losses during this campaign. The Russians suffered 150,000 dead from all causes and probably suffered a further 300,000 more crippled and maimed from wounds and frostbite. Despite these heavy losses, they had not been shaken. They had driven the invaders from the soil of sacred mother Russia, and they had inflicted the first truly major defeat on Napoleon and his vaunted armies.

Napoleon had left the army for many reasons. He was greatly concerned about his political security, and his return quieted many of these dangers. He also returned so that he might begin the gigantic task of reorganizing his army.

While still in Russia, during September, Napoleon had already begun taking steps towards this end. The Draft Class of 1812 had been nearly exhausted, and Napoleon obtained the Senatus Consultum calling for 120,000 drafts from the Class of 1813. This number was eventually raised to 137,000. This additional 17,000 was to fill out the National Guard. By the time Napoleon arrived in Paris, the greater portion of these draftees had already been received by their depots and had begun their training.

The most immediate reinforcements were the eighty-eight cohorts of the National Guard. Napoleon had had them raised in March of 1812 as a precaution. They were a force to protect France should a threat arise while Napoleon had a majority of the French army in Russia and Spain.

Initially 100 cohorts of National Guard were to have been raised, but it was reduced to 88. These cohorts were not to render service outside of metropolitan France and were raised by the various military divisions of France. Each cohort was to have a strength of 1,080 men, but this strength was seldom reached. The average strength was 850 men. The total National Guard totaled 78,000.

Initially these cohorts were pressured to volunteer for foreign service. Napoleon was unwilling to wait for volunteers and bodily transferred them to the regular army by the Senatus Consultum of 11 January 1813. Each cohort was organized into a regiment with four battalions. The artillery companies attached to each cohort were reduced to one per regiment, and the remainder were used to form three artillery regiments.

The Senatus Consultum of 11 January 1812 had authorized the drafting of an additional 100,000 men from the Classes of 1809–1812. In February, Napoleon took the surprising step of having 150,000 conscripts drawn from the Class of 1814.

In addition to this, Napoleon coerced the various departments and larger cities to offer an additional 15,000 to 20,000 armed, mounted, and equipped men. The Municipal Guard of Paris, totaling 1,050 men in two battalions, was sent to Erfurt to form the nucleus of another new regiment. The municipal guards of the other large cities were combined to form the 37th Légère Regiment.

The navy was not immune from Napoleon's scavenging either. There were twelve regiments of marine artillery in the various French ports. This force was divided into twenty-four battalions with a total of 16,000 men. These weak battalions were reinforced by the addition of 2,000 levies from the Classes of 1809–1812 and a further 2,000 from the Class of 1814.

On 3 April 1813 another Senatus Consultum authorized the drafting of a further 80,000 men from the Classes of 1807–1812 that belonged to the first "ban" or draft class of the National Guard. It drew a further 90,000 from the Class of 1814 and authorized the raising of 10,000 Gardes d'honneur. Though they were purportedly volunteers and had flashy uniforms, the Gardes d'honneur were little more than hostages to insure the loyalty of the French middle class.

These efforts should have theoretically provided Napoleon with a new army of 656,000 men. However, there were problems associated with the forces he had attempted to call up. The men drawn from the municipal guards were generally older, retired soldiers. The sailors were untrained in land maneuvers and warfare. The new recruits were totally untrained and needed time to be brought up to any proficiency. The National Guard were poorly officered, but the men forming the cohorts were well trained, sound, and capable soldiers. The marine artillery was also quite capable and was to prove a worthwhile addition to the Grande Armée.

Napoleon ordered the remains of the army in Germany to be redeployed and used as cadres or garrisons. Initially only the fourth battalions were sent to France, while the others remained in Germany. However, Napoleon later decided to send the third battalions as well. Each regiment was reorganized with 100-man companies led by three officers. These companies were organized into provisional battalions which were used as garrisons in the various cities. In this manner III Corps provided a single battalion of 600 men that became the garrison of Spandau.

The cadres of the third and fourth battalions were supplemented by cadets from the various military academies, and many of their older sergeants and corporals were promoted into the officer ranks to fill the numerous vacancies.

Napoleon decided that the thirty-six regiments that belonged to the first four corps of the Grande Armée would be rebuilt to a four-battalion strength. Napoleon set about sweeping up the various depot battalions that were in France. There were 100 field battalions in France from other regiments serving outside France that were also available. Napoleon filled these battalions out to full strength with new levies from the Class of 1813 and organized them into provisional regiments. Napoleon also transferred two old regiments, a total of nine battalions, from Italy to Germany.

With these forces Napoleon began organizing the Corps d'Observation de l'Elbe. It was to have three divisions and a total of forty-eight battalions. On 15 February it began organizing near Magdeburg. By 15 March it was complete and consisted of units that had been National Guard cohorts.

The First Corps d'Observation du Rhin was formed under Marshal Ney around Mainz in March. It was to have four divisions totaling sixty battalions.

The Second Corps d'Observation du Rhin formed under General Marmont. It was to have fifty battalions. It was to begin by forming three divisions around Mainz between late March and early April. A fourth division was not completed until late May.

The Corps d'Observation d'Italie was formed with four divisions and fifty-four battalions. The new I Corps was to be raised with four divisions and sixty-four battalions. The new II Corps was to have four divisions and forty-eight battalions. Druette's division and the two divisions of Saxons became the new VII Corps, and the Guard was reconstituted around the survivors of the Russian campaign and new drafts of veterans drawn from Spain.

On 6 January Napoleon had begun reorganizing his Guard. He started by forming two "bis" battalions of Guard Chasseurs and Grenadiers. He drew 3,000 veterans with eight-and-a-half years of service from 250 battalions serving in Spain and ordered that the five battalions serving with the navy provide six veterans per company. He drew 2,000 other veterans from the rest of the army, and with these 5,000 veterans he reformed his Guard.

He also formed two auxiliary fusilier battalions on 6 January, and on 10 January he ordered the forming of the 3–6th "bis" Voltigeurs. On 17 January he ordered the raising of the 3–6th "bis" Tirailleurs and began stripping the Pupilles de la Garde for his other Guard units.

Napoleon found reorganizing his cavalry more difficult. There were only a few Italian Gardes d'Honneur, a few Berg Lancers, and about 100 Italian Guard Dragoons with Eugène. To supplement them, Napoleon sent all available cadres to Paris and the depots in Fulda and Gotha. General Walther took 1,000 dismounted officers and men to Fulda, where he formed four squadrons with horses donated by the Rhinish princes.

About 9,000 or 10,000 dismounted cavalry had survived Russia. Napoleon supplemented them by drawing 3,000 officers and noncommissioned officers from the gendarmerie and further increased the numbers with drafts.

For political reasons, the troops provided from the territory around Paris were incorporated into the Guard Grenadiers à Cheval, Chasseurs à Cheval, Dragoons, and 2nd Lancer Regiment. They were, however, made into the newly formed Young Guard squadrons.

Napoleon intended to reconstitute and increase the Guard Cavalry beyond its 1812 strength and to reorganize fifty-two cavalry regiments in two line cavalry corps. The corps were to consist of three heavy and four light divisions. The newly reconstituted cavalry regiments were formed around cadres drawn from Spain. This ambitious plan was handicapped from the outset. The main horse-breeding areas were in eastern Prussia and central Germany. The military developments quickly pulled those two areas out of Napoleon's grasp, and he was forced to rely on the limited resources of western Europe.

The Guard Chasseurs à Cheval were raised to a strength of 2,411 officers and men, including five Young Guard squadrons. The Mamelukes were reformed and their ranks filled out with Frenchmen. The 2nd Guard Lancers had their Young Guard squadrons organized from the cavalry of the Paris Municipal Guard.

The Guard 1st Lancers were reorganized in Friedberg with a total of 1,500 men. The necessary horses were donated by the Rhinish princes, and 600 horses were bought in Hanover.

The Guard artillery began reforming with the organization of two horse and four foot batteries for the Old Guard. The Old Guard artillery was later raised to six horse and six foot batteries. There was a Young Guard artillery force raised, and it eventually consisted of fourteen foot and fourteen horse companies. The pontooniers were reconstituted from the line pontoonier units.

In February Napoleon directed that the Guard Infantry should consist of two grenadier à pied regiments, two chasseur à pied regiments, the fusilier-chasseur and fusilier-grenadier regiments, the flanker-chasseur and flanker-grenadier regiments, seven voltigeur and seven tirailleur regiments, and four bataillons of pupilles.

The four regiments of grenadiers and chasseurs were filled out with reinforcements drawn from France. The ''bis'' battalions of Guard raised in January were abolished in February and redesignated as the 1st Battalion of the newly forming regiments. Initially only the first battalion of the regiments was filled out, and once complete, the second battalions were filled out. The 2nd Grenadiers and 2nd Chasseurs were formed in Fulda and assigned to the Middle Guard. Only their officers and NCOs were designated as Old Guard. The 3rd Grenadier à Pied Regiment, the Dutch Grenadiers that had fought so bravely at Krasnoe, were disbanded, and the survivors were incorporated into the 1st Grenadier Regiment. The two battalions of the pupilles were transformed into the 7th Voltigeur Regiment, and the National Guard Regiment was transformed into the 7th Tirailleur Regiment.

As drafts of veterans arrived from Spain, Napoleon found he had 6,000 additional men and chose to form them into the 8th Voltigeur and 8th Tirailleur Regiments. As levies continued to flow into the depots, Napoleon raised further voltigeur and tirailleur regiments until there were thirteen regiments of each.

The lack of horses affected his artillery as well. This was further complicated when Napoleon directed an increase in the normal complement of regimental artillery. He knew that his green conscripts needed the morale boost that these guns gave.

By 20 April 1813 Napoleon had a field army totaling 210,000, of whom 35,000 were allied forces. Of the 175,000 French, 75,000 were conscripts from the Class of 1813. The 1814 levies had not yet arrived, and there were problems developing in arming them. There were proposals for arming them with foreign equipment, but the problems would be quickly surmounted. Napoleon had rebuilt his army into a functional military force and was able to take to the field sooner than his enemies.

Though it was filled with conscripts, the core of the new French army was built on solid, well-trained cadres able to provide direction to their new comrades. The newly formed regiments fought in the 1813 campaign with the same skill and brilliance that their predecessors had shown in Napoleon's earlier campaigns. Napoleon's administrative genius had once again demonstrated itself, and from the remains of a shattered army, like a phoenix, there arose a powerful new force ready to take up the challenge.

Romanov

Poles

1. 1st Squadron 1st Polish Chasseurs
2. 2nd Squadron (in skirmish line)
3. 3rd Squadron
4. 4th Squadron

Russians

A. Kouteinikov Cossacks
B. Karpof Cossacks
C. Ataman Cossacks
D. Ilowaiski Cossacks
E. 5th Jagers
F. Akhtyrski Cossacks
G. Kiev Dragoons
H. Lithuanian Uhlans

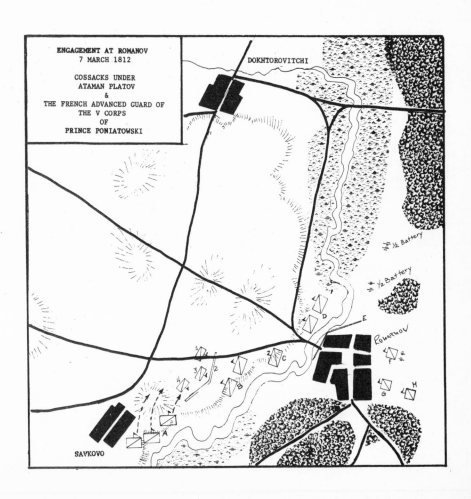

ENGAGEMENT AT ROMANOV
7 MARCH 1812

COSSACKS UNDER
ATAMAN PLATOV
&
THE FRENCH ADVANCED GUARD OF
THE V CORPS
OF
PRINCE PONIATOWSKI

Polotsk

1. 23rd Jaggers
2. 25th Jagers
3. 26th Jagers
4. Kalouga Infantry
5. Sewsk Infantry
6. Converged Infantry
7. Perm Infantry
8. Mohilew Infantry
9. Vlastof's Detachment
10. ½ Position Battery #28
11. Horse Battery #1
12. Position Battery #5
13. Light Battery #9
14. ½ Position Battery #28
15. Light Battery #26
16. Russian Reserve Infantry
17. Russian Cavalry

A. Wrede's Division
B. Deracy's Division
C. Legrand's Division
D. Verdier's Division
E. Doumerc's Cavalry Division
F. Brigade Corbineau
G. Brigade Castex

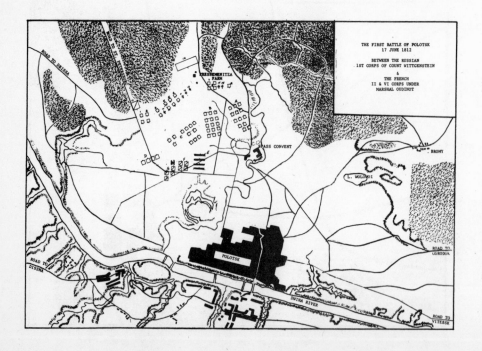

Mir

French
2. 2nd Polish Uhlans
3. 3rd Polish Uhlans
7. 7th Polish Uhlans
11. 11th Polish Uhlans
15. 15th Polish Uhlans
16. 16th Polish Uhlans

Russians
A. Perekopski Tartars
B. Syssoief #3 Cossacks
C. Ilowaiski Cossacks
D. Ilowaiski Cossacks
E. 5 Sotnias of Ataman Cossacks
G. Ilowaiski Cossacks
H. Grekov #8 Cossacks
I. Kharitonov #7 Cossacks
J. Simferopolski Tartars
K. Kiev Dragoons
L. Akhtyra Hussars

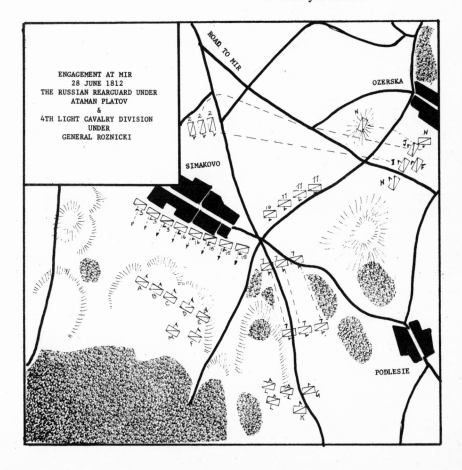

ENGAGEMENT AT MIR
28 JUNE 1812
THE RUSSIAN REARGUARD UNDER
ATAMAN PLATOV
&
4TH LIGHT CAVALRY DIVISION
UNDER
GENERAL ROZNICKI

Saltanovka

Russians
- C. 12th Division marching to the attack
- D. 26th Division
- E. Cavalry
- F. Cossacks
- H. 12th Division in battle
- J. 26th Division

- K. Cavalry
- L. Cossacks

French
- A. Infantry before the battle
- B. Cavalry before the battle
- C. Infantry in the battle

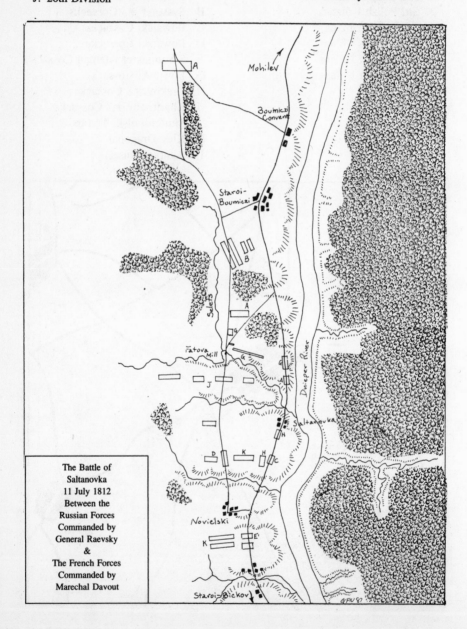

The Battle of
Saltanovka
11 July 1812
Between the
Russian Forces
Commanded by
General Raevsky
&
The French Forces
Commanded by
Marechal Davout

Ostrowono

Russians
- A. Soum Hussars
- B. Ingermanland Dragoons
- 11. 11th Division
- 23. 23rd Division

French
- 1. 4th Corps
- 2. 1st Reserve Cavalry Corps
  - a. 1st Cuirassier Division St. Germain
  - b. 1st Light Division Bruyeres
  - c. 5th Cuirassier Division 6th Paluhla Brigade

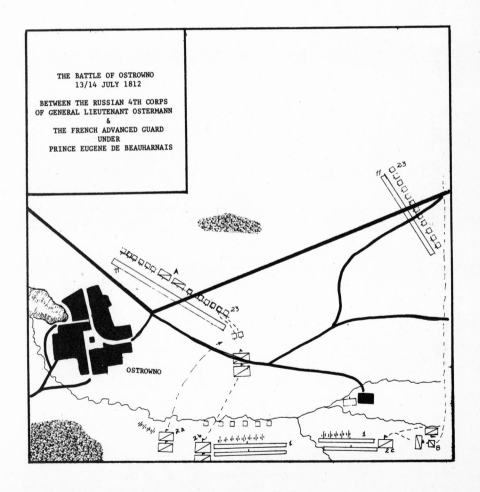

THE BATTLE OF OSTROWNO
13/14 JULY 1812

BETWEEN THE RUSSIAN 4TH CORPS
OF GENERAL LIEUTENANT OSTERMANN
&
THE FRENCH ADVANCED GUARD
UNDER
PRINCE EUGENE DE BEAUHARNAIS

OSTROWNO

Jakobovo

The Battle of Jakobovo
19 July 1812
Between the French II Corps
Commanded by
Marechal Oudinot
&
The Russian 1st Corps
Commanded by
General Count Wittgenstein

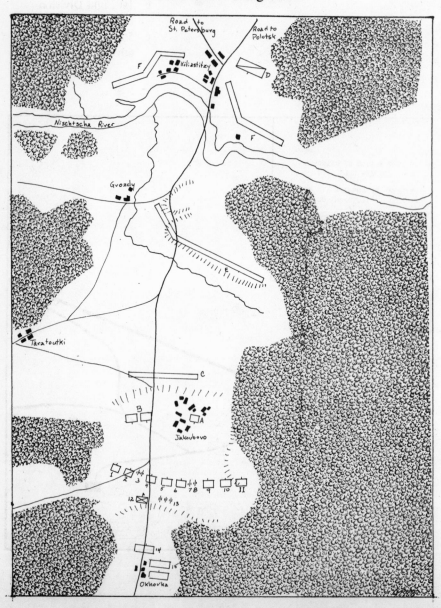

Russians
 1. Mohilev Infantry Regiment
 2. Perm Infantry Regiment
 3. Light Battery #27
 4. 26th Jager Regiment
 5. Kalouga Infantry Regiment
 6. Sevesk Infantry Regiment
 7. 2 Guns of Light Battery #9
 8. Position Battery #5
 9. 23rd Jager Regiment
10. 25th Jager Regiment
11. 24th Jager Regiment
12. Grodno Hussar Regiment
13. Horse Battery #1, Light Battery #14, 10 guns of Light Battery #9
14. 1st Corps Cavalry
15. 2nd Russian Line of Battle

French:
A. 26th Legere Regiment
B. 19th & 56th Line Regiment
C. 8th Division (Verdier) & 5th Light Cavalry Brigade (Castex)
D. 3rd Cuirassier Division (Doumerc)
E. 2nd French Position
F. 3rd French Position

Loubino

&

**The Russian Army
Commanded by
Marshal Barclay de Tolly**

**The Battle of Valoutina—Gora or Loubino
7 August 1812
Between the French Grande Armee
Commanded by
Emperor Napoleon I**

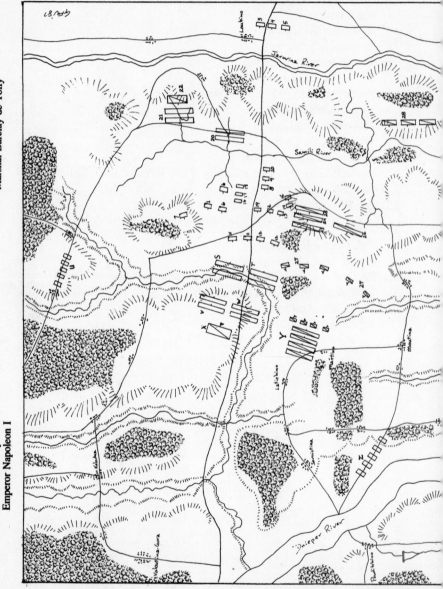

Russians:

1. Leib Grenadier Regiment
2. Count Arakcheyev Grenadier Regiment
3. Pavlov Grenadier Regiment
4. Tauride Grenadier Regiment
5. St. Petersburg Grenadier Regiment
6. Ekaterinoslav Grenadier Regiment
7. Mourmon Infantry Regiment
8. Revel Infantry Regiment
9. Czernigov Infantry Regiment
10. Koporie Infantry Regiment
11. 20th Jager Regiment
12. 21st Jager Regiment
13. Kexholm Infantry Regiment
14. Pernau Infantry Regiment
15. Polotsk Infantry Regiment
16. Jelets Infantry Regiment
17. Rylsk Infantry Regiment
18. Ekaterinburg Infantry Regiment
19. Converged Grenadier Battalion assigned to 3rd Division
20. 4th Division
21. 17th Division
22. Korff's Rearguard
23. –26. Elisabethgrad, Mariapol, Soumy & Isoum Hussar Regiment
27. Cossacks
28. 1st Reserve Corps

French:

U. 1st Division (Morand)
V. 10th Division (Ledru)
W. 25th Division (Marchand)
X. 9th & 10th Light Cavalry Brigades (Wollwrath)
Y. Murat's Reserve Cavalry
Z. VIII Corps (Junot)
S. 3rd Division (Gudin)
T. 11th Division (Razout)

Smolensk

The Battle of Smolensk
7 August 1812
Between the French Grande Armee
Commanded by
Emperor Napoleon I

&

The Russian Army
Commanded by
Marshal Barclay de Tolly

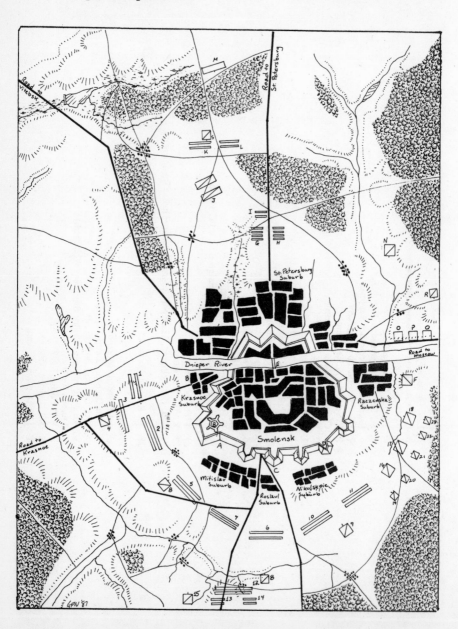

French
1. 10th Division (Ledru)
2. 25th Division (Marchand)
3. 11th Division (Razout)
4. III Corps Cavalry (Wollwrath)
5. 3rd Division (Gudin)
6. 1st Division (Morand)
7. 2nd Division (Friant)
8. I Corps Cavalry (Pajol)
9. V Corps Cavalry (Kaminski)
10. 16th Division (Zayonchek)
11. 18th Division (Kamienicki)
12. Young Guard (Mortier)
13. Old Guard (Lefebvre)
14. Vistula Legion (Claparede)
15. Guard Cavalry (Bessieres)
16. 3rd Light Cavalry Division (Lahoussaye)
17. 2nd Light Cavalry Division (Sebastiani)
18. 1st Light Cavalry Division (Bruyere)
19. 6th Heavy Cavalry Division (La Haussay)
20. 2nd Cuirassier Division (Wathier)
21. 4th Cuirassier Division (Defrance)
22. 1st Cuirassier Division (St. Germain)
23. 5th Cuirassier Division (Valence)

Russians
A. 7th Division (Kapsevitch) in Mitislavl Suburb
B. 24th Division (Lichatcheff) in Krasnoe Suburb and Citadel
C. 3rd Division (Konovnitzin) in Roslavl Suburb
D. 6th Jager Regiment in Nikolskoe Bastion
E. Guard Jagers in reserve at bridge
F. Dragoon Brigade
G. 2nd Corps (Baggovout)
H. 4th Corps (Schouwalov)
I. 1st Grenadier Division (Strogonoff)
J. 1st Cavalry Corps (Ouvarov)
K. Guard Division (Yermolov)
L. Converged Grenadiers
M. Guard Cavalry
N. 2nd Cavalry Division (Korff)
O. 7th Corps (Raevsky)
P. 8th Corps (Borosdin)
Q. 4th Cavalry Division (Sievers)
R. 3rd Cavalry Division (Pahlen)
S. Cossacks (Platov)

Gorodetchna

The Battle of Gorodetchna
12 August 1812
Between the Austro-Saxon Forces
Commanded by
Feld-Marschal Schwarzenberg

&

The Russian 3rd Army of the West
Commanded by
General Tormassov

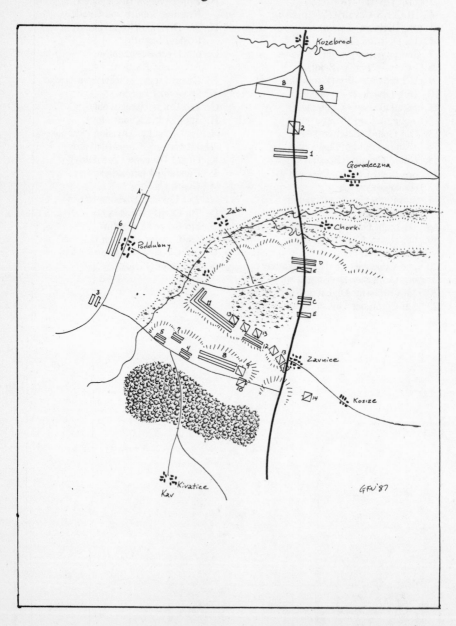

Austro-Saxon Forces
(Large Scale)
A. Saxon Positions 11 August
B. Austrian Positions 11 August

1. Trautenberg's Division 12 August
2. Frimont's Division 12 August
3. Hesse-Homberg's Division 12 August
4. Lilienberg's Brigade 12 August
5. Funcke's Brigade 12 August
6. Siegenthal's Division 12 August
7. Sahr's Brigade 12 August
8. LeCoq's Division 12 August
9. Fröhlich's Division 12 August
10. Saxon Advanced Guard 12 August

Russians
C. 19th Division 11 August
D. 9th Division 11 August
E. Corps Cavalry 11 August
11. 18th Division 12 August
12. 9th Division 12 August
13. Corps Cavalry 12 August
14. Pavlograd Hussar Regiment 12 August

Gorodetchna

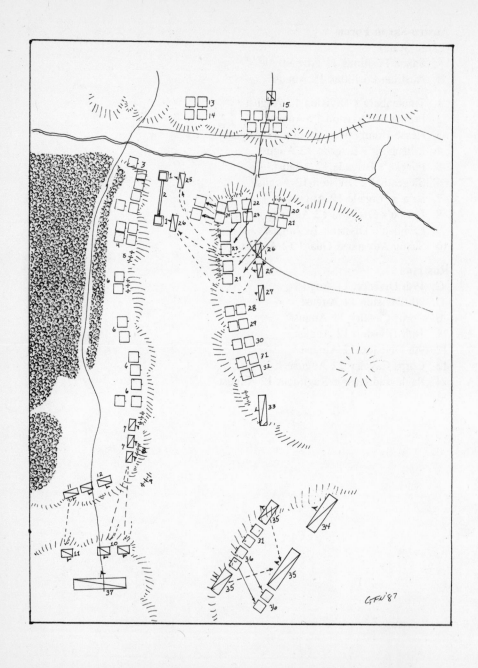

Austro-Saxon Forces

(Detailed)

1. Saxon Grenadier Battalions von Anger & von Spiegel
2. Saxon 2nd Light Infantry Regiment
3. Funcke Brigade
4. Lilienberg Brigade
5. Sonntag Battery
6. Saxon 21st Division (LeCoq)
7. Austrian Frölich Brigade
8. Saxon von Branst Battery
9. Saxon 1st and 2nd Horse Batteries
10. Austrian Hohenzollern & O'Reilly Chevauxlegers
11. Saxon Polenz Chevauxlegers
12. Saxon Prinz Clemens Uhlans & Saxon Hussars
13. Austrian Hiller Infantry Regiment
14. Austrian Colloredo Infantry Regiment
15. Austrian Siegenthal Division

Russians:

20. Vladimir Infantry Regiment
21. Dnieper Infantry Regiment
22. Tambov Infantry Regiment
23. Kostroma Infantry Regiment
24. 28th Jager Regiment
25. Starodoub Dragoon Regiment
26. Tanganrok Dragoon Regiment
27. Tver Dragoon Regiment
28. Koslov Infantry Regiment
29. Nacheburg Infantry Regiment
30. Vitebsk Infantry Regiment
31. Kour Infantry Regiment
32. 10th Jager Regiment
33. Tartar Uhlan Regiment
34. Kalmucks & Cossacks
35. Alexandria Hussar Regiment
36. 14th Jager Regiment
37. Pavlovgrad Hussar Regiment

Borodino

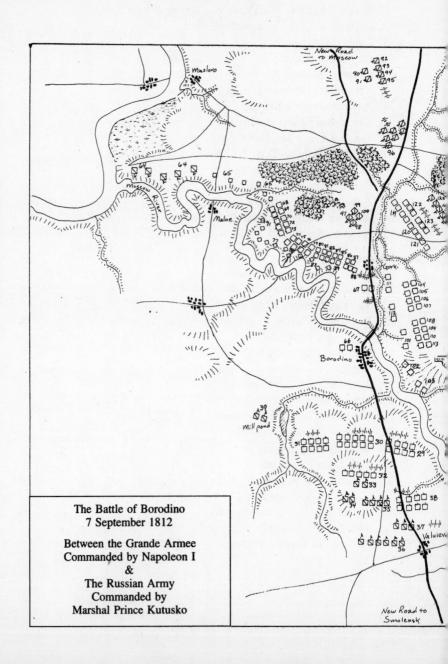

The Battle of Borodino
7 September 1812

Between the Grande Armee
Commanded by Napoleon I
&
The Russian Army
Commanded by
Marshal Prince Kutusko

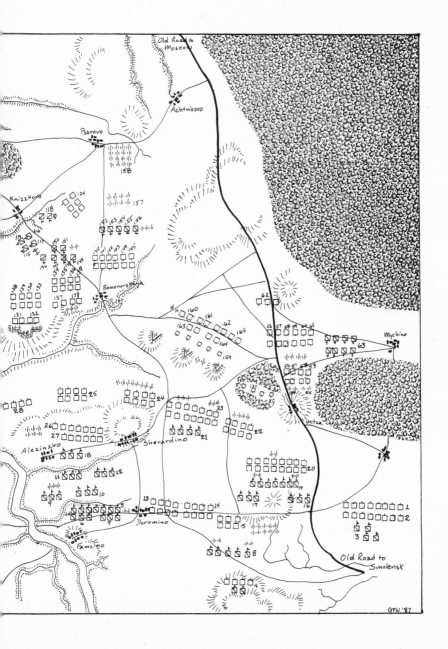

Battle of Borodino

French

V Corps: Prince Poniatowski
1   16th Division   —General Zagunczk
2   18th Division   —General Kniazieqicz
3   V Corps Cavalry   —General Kaminski

Guard:
4   Headquarters Guard
8   Guard Cavalry   —General Walthier
13 2nd Guard
    Division   —General Roguet
14 Old Guard
    Division   —General Curial
15 Vistula Legion   —General Claparede

I Corps: Marechal Davout
20 2nd Division   —General Friant
21 I Corps Cavalry   —General Girardin
22 4th Division   —General Dessaix
23 5th Division   —General Compans
29 1st Division   —General Morand
38 3rd Division   —General Girard

III Corps: Marechal Ney
24 10th Division   —General Ledru
25 11th Division   —General Razout
28 25th Division   —General Scheler
11 9th Light
    Brigade   —General Mouriez
12 11th Light
    Brigade   —General Beurman

IV Corps: Prince Eugene
30 13th Division   —General Delzons
31 14th Division   —General Broussier
32 Italian Guard   —General Lecchi
33 Italian Guard
    Cavalry   —General Triaire
34 1st Light Brigade—General Villata
35 V Corps Cavalry   —General Preysing
39 12th Light
    Brigade   —General Guyon

VIII Corps: General Junot
26 23rd Division   —General Tharreau
27 24th Division   —General Ochs
18 24th Light
    Brigade   —General Wolff

I Reserve Cavalry Corps: General Nansouty
16 5th Cuirassier
    Division   —General Valence
17 1st Cuirassier
    Division   —General St. Germain
19 1st Light
    Cavalry Division —General Bruyere

II Reserve Cavalry Corps: General Montbrun
5   2nd Light
    Cavalry Division —General Pajol

6   2nd Cuirassier
    Division   —General Wathier
7   4th Cuirassier
    Division   —General Defrance

III Reserve Cavalry Corps: General Grouchy
36 3rd Light
    Cavalry Division —General Chastel
37 6th Heavy
    Cavalry Division —General Haussey

IV Reserve Cavalry Corps: General Latour-Maubourg
9   4th Light
    Cavalry Division —General Rozniecki
10 7th Cuirassier
    Division   —General Lorge

Russians

3rd Corps: Generallieutenant Tutchkoff
3rd Division: General Konowitzin
50 Mormon Infantry Regiment
51 Revel Infantry Regiment
52 Czernigof Infantry Regiment
53 Kopor Infantry Regiment
54 21st Jagers in skirmish order
55 20th Jagers in skirmish order
1st Division: Generallieutenant Strogonoff
56 Leib Grenadier Regiment
57 Arakcheev Grenadier Regiment
58 Pavlov Grenadier Regiment
59 Ekaterinoslav Grenadier Regiment
61 St. Petersburg Grenadier Regiment
62 1st, 2nd & 3rd Opolochenie Divisions
63 Karpov's Cossacks
64 Don & Ataman Cossacks
65 4th, 30th, & 48th Jagers in skirmish order
66 Guard Jagers & Guard Marine Equippage Battalion
67 11th Jager Regiment

    2nd Corps: Generallieutenant Baggovout
    4th Division: Generallieutenant Prince Eugene of
    Wurttemberg
68 Tobolsk Infantry Regiment
69 Volhynie Infantry Regiment
70 Krementsoug Infantry Regiment
71 4th Jagers in skirmish order
72 34th Jagers in column
73 Minsk Infantry Regiment
17th Division: General Olsoufieff
74 Riazan Infantry Regiment
75 Belozersk Infantry Regiment
76 Brest Infantry Regiment
77 30th Jagers in skirmish order
78 48th Jagers in skirmish order
79 Willmanstrand Infantry Regiment

4th Corps: Generallieutenant Ostermann-Tolstoi
23rd Division: General Bakhemtieff
86 Rylsk Infantry Regiment
87 Jekaterinburg Infantry Regiment

88 Seinguinsk Infantry Regiment
89 18th Jagers in skirmish order

11th Division: General Tchoglokof
80 Polotsk Infantry Regiment
81 Pernau Infantry Regiment
82 Kexholm Infantry Regiment
83 1st Jagers in skirmish order
84 33rd Jagers in column

1st Cavalry Corps: Generallieutenant Ouvarov
90 Negin Dragoon Regiment
91 Polish Uhlan Regiment
92 Guard Dragoon Regiment
93 Guard Hussar Regiment
94 Guard Uhlan Regiment
95 Guard Cossack Regiment
96 Platov's Cossack Corps—7 Cossack Pulks

2nd Cavalry Corps: Generalmajor Korff
97 Pskov Dragoon Regiment
98 Moscow Dragoon Regiment
99 Elisabethgrad Hussar Regiment
100 Isoum Hussar Dragoon Regiment
101 19th & 40th Jagers in skirmish order
102 1st Jagers in skirmish order
103 6th & 20th Jagers in skirmish order

6th Corps: General of Infantry Docturov
7th Division: Generallieutenant Kaptsevitch
104 Moscow Infantry Regiment
105 Pskov Infantry Regiment
106 36th Jagers in skirmish order
107 Libau Infantry Regiment
24th Division: Generalmajor Lichatcheff
108 Oufa Infantry Regiment
109 Chirvan Infantry Regiment
110 Boutirki Infantry Regiment
111 19th Jagers in skirmish order
112 40th Jagers in skirmish order
113 Tomsk Infantry Regiment

3rd Cavalry Corps: Generalmajor Kreutz
114 Kourland Dragoon Regiment
115 Orenburg Dragoon Regiment (3 sqns)
116 Soumy Hussar Regiment
117 Marioupol Hussar Regiment
118 Irkutsk, Siberian & 1 sqn of Orenburg Dragoon
    Regiments

5th Corps: Grand Duke Constantin
Guard Infantry Division: Generallieutenant Lavrov
119 Preobragenski Guard Infantry Regiment
120 Semenovski Guard Infantry Regiment
121 Ismailov Guard Infantry Regiment
122 Finland Guard Jager Regiment
123 Lithuanian Guard Infantry Regiment
124 1st Converged Grenadier Division
    (6 bns)

1st Cuirassier Division:
125 Chevalier Guards, Horse Guards, Emperor
    Cuirassiers, Empress Cuirassiers and Astrakhan
    Cuirassiers
126 11th, 26th, and 41st Jagers in skirmish order
127 20th & 21st Jagers & Tauride Grenadiers in
    skirmish order

7th Corps: Generallieutenant Raevsky
26th Division: Generalmajor Paskevitch
128 Ladoga Infantry Regiment
129 Poltava Infantry Regiment
130 Nijegorod Infantry Regiment
131 5th Jagers in skirmish order
132 42nd Jagers in skirmish order
133 Orel Infantry Regiment
12th Division: Generalmajor Vasil'chikov
134 Narva Infantry Regiment
135 Smolensk Infantry Regiment
136 New Ingremanland Infantry Regiment
137 6th Jagers in skirmish order
138 41st Jagers in skirmish order
139 Alexopol Infantry Regiment

8th Corps: Generallieutenant Borosdin
2nd Grenadier Division: Generalmajor Prince Charles
of Mecklenbourg
140 Kiev Grenadier Regiment
141 Astrakhan Grenadier Regiment
141 Moscow Grenadier Regiment
143 Siberian Grenadier Regiment
144 Little Russia Grenadier Regiment
145 Fangoria Grenadier Regiment

4th Cavalry Division:
146 Kharkov Dragoon Regiment
147 Tchernigov Dragoon Regiment
148 Kiev Dragoon Regiment
149 Novgorod Dragoon Regiment
150 Akhtyrsk Hussar Regiment
151 Lithuanian Uhlan Regiment

2nd Cuirassier Division: Generalmajor Knorring
152 Military Order Cuirassier Regiment
153 Ekaterinoslav Cuirassier Regiment
154 Gluckov Cuirassier Regiment
155 Little Russia Cuirassier Regiment
156 Novgorod Cuirassier Regiment

Others:
157 Horse Artillery Reserve
158 Artillery Reserves
159 2nd Converged Grenadier Division
27th Division: Generalmajor Neverovski
160 Vilna Infantry Regiment
161 Simbrisk Infantry Regiment
162 Odessa Infantry Regiment
163 49th Jagers in skirmish order
164 50th Jagers in skirmish order
165 Tarnopol Infantry Regiment

Trautino

The Battle of Czernicznia or Trautino
6 October 1812
Between the Russian Army Commanded by
Marshall Prince Kutusov
&
The French Advanced Guard
Commanded by
Murat, King of Naples

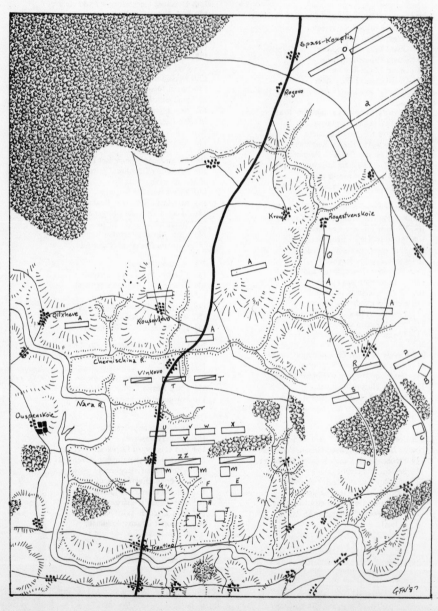

French

A. French advanced guard on the morning of the 6th
O. French forces during the battle

Russians

B. 1st Column, evening of 5th
C. 2nd Column, evening of 5th
D. 3rd Column, evening of 5th
E. 6th Corps, evening of 5th
F. 7th Corps, evening of 5th
G. 8th Corps, evening of 5th
H. 5th Corps, evening of 5th
J. 1st Cuirassier Division, evening of 5th
K. 2nd Cuirassier Division, evening of 5th
L. 3rd Jager Regiment
M. 2nd & 4th Cavalry Corps, evening of 5th
P. 2nd Column of 2nd Corps that divided and moved to positions Q and R during the Battle.
S. 4th Corps during the battle
T. 2nd & 4th Cavalry Corps during the battle
U. 3 Jager Regiments of advanced guard during the battle
V. 8th Corps during the battle
W. 7th Corps during the battle
X. 6th Corps during the battle
Z. 1st Cuirassier Division during the battle
ZZ. 2nd Cuirassier Division during the battle
a. Detachment of Count Orlov-Denisov

Polotsk

THE SECOND BATTLE OF POLOTSK
18 OCTOBER 1812

BETWEEN THE RUSSIAN
1ST CORPS OF COUNT WITTGENSTEIN

&

THE FRENCH
II & VI CORPS UNDER
MARSHAL ST. CYR

ROAD TO ST. PETERS...

ROAD TO DEISSA

KRESNENITZA FARM

CORPASS CONVENT

L. HOLOWOI

BROMY

ROAD TO GORODOK

ROAD TO VITEBSK

DWINA RIVER

POLOTSK

ROAD TO DISSNA

Russians

Advanced Guard of General Balk

1. 26th Jagers
   2 Squadrons of Grodno Hussars
   12 guns
2. 25th Jagers
   Kexholm Infantry Depot Bn.
   4 Guns
3. 2 Squadrons of Grodno Hussars
   Radinof Cossacks

Main Body

4. Perm Infantry Regiment
   Mohilew Infantry Regiment
5. Sewsk Infantry Regiment
6. Kalouga Infantry
   Converged Guard Cavalry
7. 2nd Column of General Major
   Debitsch
8. Detachment of Colonel Stolypin
9. Corps of Prince Jachwill

French

A. 8th Division (Maison)
B. 6th Division (Legrand)
C. 9th Division (Merle)
D. Bavarian 19th–20th Divisions
E. French evening positions

The Battle of Malo-Jaroslavetz
24 October 1812

Russians (Marshal Prince Kutusov)
A. 8th Corps
B. 3rd Division
C. 7th Corps
D. 2nd Corps
E. 4th Corps
F. 1st Grenadier Division
G. 6th Corps
H. 5th Corps
J. 2nd Cavalry Corps
K. 4th Cavalry Corps
L. Cuirassier Corps
M. 1st Cavalry Corps

N. General Dorokhof's detachment
O. Cossacks

French (Emperor Napoleon I)
P. 13th Division (Delzon)
Q. 14th Division (Broussier)
R. Division Pino
S. Italian Guard (Lecchi)
T. 12th and 13th Light Cavalry
    Brigade (d'Ornano)
V. 5th Division (Compans)
W. 3rd Division (Gerard)

Smoliantsy

Russian

A 1st Line and part of 2nd of Corps
  Steingel

B Regiment of 2nd Line Corps
  Steingel

C Corps of Berg

D Fock's Reserve

E Advanced Guard of Prince
  Jachwille

French

F Rout of French Corps arriving from
  Senno

G Point of initial French attacks

H Movement of French towards
  Smoliantsy

J French infantry during battle

K French cavalry during battle

L French cavalry advancing after
  battle

M Position of French corps after battle

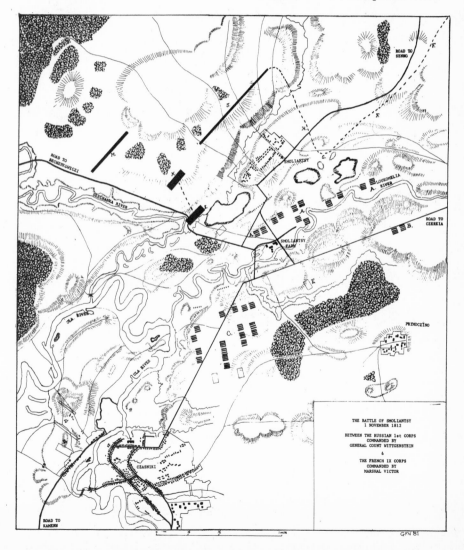

THE BATTLE OF SMOLIANTSY
1 NOVEMBER 1812

BETWEEN THE RUSSIAN 1st CORPS
COMMANDED BY
GENERAL COUNT WITTGENSTEIN
&
THE FRENCH IX CORPS
COMMANDED BY
MARSHAL VICTOR

Krasnoe

The Battle of Krasnoe
5 November 1812
Between the Russian Army
Commanded by
Marschal Prince Kutusov

&

The French Grande Armée
Commanded by
Emperor Napoleon I

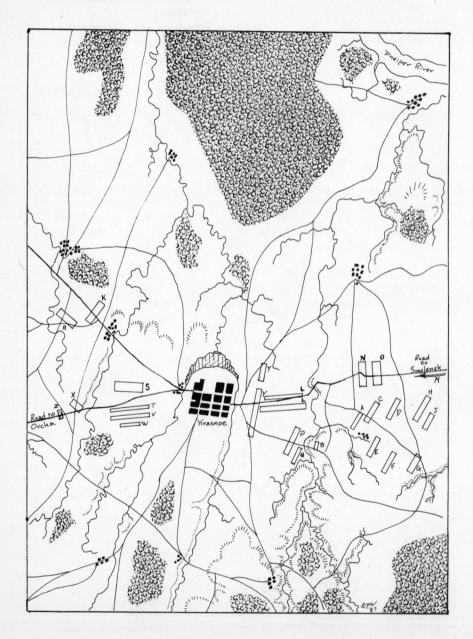

Russians

A. 3rd Corps (morning of the 5th)
B. Czernigov Regiment
C. 2nd Cuirassier Division & 8th Corps
E. 6th Corps
F. 5th Corps
G. 1st Cuirassier Corps
H. 2nd & 7th Corps
J. 1st & 2nd Cavalry Corps
K. Detachment of Count Ojarovshoi
N. 2nd & 7th Corps (evening of 5th)
O. 1st & 2nd Cavalry Corps
P. 3rd Corps
Q. Detachment of Count Ojarovshoi
S. Advanced Guard of General Rosen
T. 6th Corps
V. 8th Corps
W. 5th Corps
X. 1st Cuirassier Division

French

L. French Army (morning of 5th)
M. Davout's Corps marching on Krasnoe
Y. French Rear Guard
Z. French Army retreating on Orcha

Berezina

THE BATTLES OF THE BEREZINA:
STUDIANKA AND STAHKOV

16 NOVEMBER 1812

BETWEEN THE FRENCH ARMY
COMMANDED BY
EMPEROR NAPOLEON I

&

THE RUSSIAN ARMIES
COMMANDED BY
ADMIRAL TCHICHAGOF
AND
COUNT WITTGENSTEIN

Studianka

French

1. Battalion of 55th French Line
2. 4 French 12pdr guns
3. Hochberg's Baden Brigade and Damas Bergish Brigade
4. 28th French Division
5. Baden Hussars and Berg Chevaulegers
6. French Army the evening of the 5th

Russians

A. 1st Corps Cavalry
B. 1st Corps and Berg's Advanced Guard
C. 2nd Line of Berg's Corps remaining in position due to misunderstood orders

Stahkov

French

7. French Old Guard
8. I and IV Corps (Davout & Eugene)
9. II Corps (Oudinot)

10. III Corps (Ney), Vistula Legion (Claparde), & 3rd Cuirassier Division (Doumerc)
11. V Corps (Poniatowski)
12. 1st Division Young Guard (Delaborde)

Russians

G. 7th, 14th, 27th, 28th, & 32nd Jagers
H. Pavlovgrad Hussars
I. 12th & 22nd Jagers
J. Platof's Cossacks
K. Yermolof's Detachment
L. Admiral Tchichagof's Army of the Danube (Main body)
M. Steingel's Corps disarming Partoneaux's 12th Division

Night of the 15th

Z. Admiral Tchichagof's Army of the Danube
Y. General Platof's Cossacks
X. Detachment of Yermolof
W. 1st Corps of Count Wittgenstein
V. Detachment of General Tschaplitz

Appendix I

Treaties and Political Documents

The Treaties of Tilsit

Peace treaty between His Majesty, the Emperor of the French, King of Italy and His Majesty, the Emperor of all the Russias.

HIS MAJESTY, the Emperor of the French, King of Italy, Protector of the Confederation of the Rhine River, and His Majesty, the Emperor of all the Russias, both being animated by an equal desire to put an end to the calamity of war, have to this effect named as their Plenipotentiaries, that is to say: His Majesty, the Emperor of the French, King of Italy, Protector of the Confederation of the Rhine River, Charles Maurice Talleyrand, Prince of Benevente, his Great Chamberlain and Minister of Foreign Affairs, grand-cordon of the Légion d'Honneur, Chevalier grand-croix of the Orders of the Black and Red Eagle of Prussia and St. Hubert.

And His Majesty, the Emperor of all the Russias, Prince Alexandre Kourakin, his actual Private Advisor, Member of the Cabinet, Senator and Chancellor of all the Orders of the Emperor, actual Chamberlain, Ambassador Extraordinary and Plenipotentiary Minister at the Court of the Emperor of Austria for His Majesty, the Emperor of all the Russias, Chevalier of the Russian Orders of St. Andre, St. Alexandre, St. Anne first class, St. Volodimir first class, the Black and Red Eagle of Prussia, St. Hubert, Daneborg, the perfect union of Danemark, Bailli grand-croix of the sovereign order of St. John of Jersuleam; Prince Dimitri Labanoff de Rostoff, Lieutenant-general of the Armies of His Majesty, the Emperor of the Russias, Chevalier of the Orders of St. Anne, the Military Orders of St. George and the Orders of Volodimir, third class.

Who, after having exchanged their full and respective powers have agreed upon the following articles:

Art 1. Complete and perfect peace and amity shall take place between His Majesty, the Emperor of the French, King of Italy, and His Majesty, the Emperor of all the Russias, beginning on the day of the exchange of ratifications of the present treaty.

Art 2. All hostilities shall cease immediately, on land and sea wherever war is being waged, when news of the signing of the present Treaty is officially announced. High ranking members of the contracting Parties shall see that special couriers are dispatched in haste without undue delay to their respective generals in the field of battle and all command posts.

Art 3. All battleships or other ships belonging to a contracting Party or any of its respective subjects captured before the signing of the present Treaty, shall be restituted or in the case of sale, the sale price of said ships shall be restituted in full.

Art 4. His Majesty, the Emperor Napoleon, out of regard for His Majesty, the Emperor of all the Russias, and wishing to give proof of his sincere desire to unite the two nations in lasting friendship and trusting bonds, agrees to restitute to His Majesty, the King of Prussia—ally of His Majesty, the Emperor of all the Russias, all the conquered countries, cities and territories named as follows, that is to say: The section of the Duchy of Magdeburg situated to the right of the Elbe River, Priegnitz, the Uckermark River, the Middle and the New Mark of Brandenburg, with the exception of the Cotbuser Kreise, or Cotbuser Circle in Lower Lusace, which shall belong to His Majesty the King of Saxony: the Duchy of Pomerania; high, low and new Silesia with the county of Glatz; the section of the Netze River district, situated north of the causeway from Driesen to Schneidemuhl to the Vistula River via Waldau, following the borders of the Bomberg Kreis, the navigation right on the Vistula River, reciprocally and free of all tolls; the Pomerelie River, the Island of Nogat and the Vistula River, to the west of Old Prussia and the north of the Kulm Kreise, the Ermeland River and finally the Kingdom of Prussia as it was the 1st of January 1772, with the strongholds of Spandau, Stettin, Kustrin, Glogau, Breslau, Schweidnitz, Neisse, Brieg, Kosel, and Glatz, and generally all the strongholds, citadels, castles, and forts of the above mentioned countries in the State where said strongholds, citadels, castles, and forts are to be found now, and also the town and citadel of Graudenz.

Art 5. The provinces which were part of the Kingdom of Poland as of the first of January 1772, and which have passed on since then at various periods to Prussia shall, with the exception of the countries named in the preceding article and those specified in Article 9 of this Treaty, be possessed in full sovereignty by His Majesty, the King of Saxony. These possessions shall be given the name of Grand Duchy of Warsaw and be governed by constitutions which shall assure the people privileges and liberties in conformance to their neighbors tranquillity and welfare.

Art 6. The city of Danzig surrounded with a two kilometer radius shall be given its independence under the protection of His Majesty, the King of Prussia and His Majesty, the King of Saxony and shall be governed by the laws which were in effect at the time she ceased to govern herself.

Art 7. In order to communicate between the Kingdom of Saxony and the Duchy of Warsaw, the King of Saxony shall have free use of military roads crossing the possessions of His Majesty, the King of Prussia. The particular road, number of troops permitted to travel it, and bivouac areas shall be determined at a special meeting to take place between their Majesties under the mediation of France.

Art 8. Neither His Majesty, the King of Prussia, nor His Majesty, the King of Saxony, or the city of Danzig shall have authority to establish tolls and taxes of any kind or prohibit the navigation of the Vistula River.

Art 9. In order to establish natural borders between Russia and the Duchy of Warsaw the following territory surrounding the actual Russian frontiers shall be united for perpetuity to the Russian Empire: from the Bug River to the mouth of the Lossosna River; a border line starting at the mouth of the Thalweg-Bobra River, the Thalweg-Narew River to Stratz, from the Lisa River to its source, near the village of Mien, from the tributary of the Nurzek, taking its source from the same village from the Nurzek River to its mouth above the Nurr, and finally from Thalweg of the Bug River ascending from it to the actual Russian frontiers.

Art 10. No individual, of whatever class or station in life domiciled or owning properties in territories specified in the preceding article shall be affected in anyway by the exchange be it in his rights, rank and status or his properties, pensions and revenues or any other benefits coming to him; nor shall he be pursued in anyway, be it politically or militarily for any part he played in the present hostilities being terminated by this Treaty. Said specifications shall apply to individuals domiciled in the Old Kingdom of Poland which shall be restituted to His Majesty, the King of Prussia and be known as the Duchy of Warsaw.

Art 11. His Majesty, the Emperor of all the Russias and His Majesty, the King of Saxony undertake all obligations of the former owners be they public charges or religious, military or divine benefits, creditors or pensioners; each being responsible according to the territory acquired under Articles 5 and 9 of the present Treaty, without restriction exception, or any kind of reservation thereof.

Art 12. Their Serene Highnesses, the Dukes of Saxe-Coburg, Oldenburg, and Mecklenburg-Schwerin shall be reinstated in the full possession of their Serene States, but the ports of the Duchies of Oldenburg and Mecklenburg shall continue to be occupied by French garrisons until the ratifications of the future definite peace Treaty between France and England.

Art 13. His Majesty, the Emperor Napoleon, accepts the offer of mediation from His Majesty, the Emperor of all the Russias, to negotiate and conclude a definitive peace treaty between France and England providing this mediation offer is acceptable to England, one month after the exchange of the ratification of the present Treaty.

Art 14. For His part, His Majesty, the Emperor of all the Russias, wishing to prove how much he desires to establish the most enduring and amicable relations between the two Empires, recognizes in full His Majesty, the King of Naples, Joseph Napoleon, and His Majesty, the King of Holland, Louis Napoleon.

Art 15. His Majesty, the Emperor of all the Russias, in like manner recognizes the Confederation of the Rhine River, the actual State possessed by each sovereign which partake in it, the titles given to some among them, either by the Acts of Confederation or by Treaties of subsequent accession. Said Majesty promises to recognize, upon notification given him by His Majesty, the Emperor Napoleon, the Sovereigns who shall in the near future become members of the Confederation on a par in rank which shall be given to them by the Charter admitting them to the Confederation.

Art 16. His Majesty, the Emperor of all the Russias, cedes in full propriety and sovereignty to His Majesty, the King of Holland, the manor of Jever in East Friesland.

Art 17. The present Treaty of Peace and Friendship is declared in effect for their Majesties, the King of Naples and the King of Holland, and all confederate Sovereigns of the Rhine River, allies of His Majesty the Emperor Napoleon.

Art 18. His Majesty, the Emperor of all the Russias also recognizes his Highness, Prince Jerome Napoleon, as King of Westphalia.

Art 19. The Kingdom of Westphalia shall be composed of possessions ceded by His Majesty, the King of Prussia, to the left of the Elbe River and other States now in the possession of His Majesty, the Emperor Napoleon.

Art 20. His Majesty, the Emperor of all the Russias, promises to recognize the disposal of territories drawn in Article 19 and arranged by His Majesty, the Emperor Napoleon, with proper notification to His Majesty, the Emperor of all the Russias.

Art 21. All hostilities shall cease immediately on land and sea between the armies of His Majesty, the Emperor of all the Russias, and those of His Highness in all other places where official news of the signing of the present Treaty has arrived.

The high contracting Parties shall send special messengers without delay in order that their respective generals and commanders receive this news as soon as possible.

Art 22. The Russian troops shall withdraw from the Provinces of Wallachia and Moldavia; however, these provinces may not be occupied by His Highness' troops until the ratification of the future definitive Treaty between Russia and the Ottoman Porte have been exchanged.

Art 23. His Majesty, the Emperor of all the Russias, accepts the mediation of His Majesty, the Emperor of the French, King of Italy, for the purpose of negotiating and concluding a peace that shall be advantageous and honorable for both Empires. Their respective Plenipotentiaries shall meet in the place to be determined by the two parties concerned, in order to open and pursue the negotiations.

Art 24. The time stipulated in which the contracting Parties shall withdraw their troops from the places they must evacuate according to the above stipulations, as well as the execution of the various clauses included in the present Treaty shall be determined by special agreement.

Art 25. His Majesty, the Emperor of the French, King of Italy, and His Majesty, the Emperor of all the Russias, guarantee one another the integrity of their possessions and those of the Powers included in the peace treaty as they are or shall be in consequence of the above-mentioned stipulations.

Art 26. Prisoners of war taken by each contracting Party, or included in the present Treaty, shall be mutually exchanged in a body.

Art 27. Commerce between the French Empire, the Kingdom of Italy, the Kingdoms of Naples and Holland, and the Confederated States, on the one hand, and the Russian Empire, on the other, shall be restored on the same footing as before the war.

Art 28. Protocol between the two Courts, The Tuileries and St. Petersburg, with regard to Ambassadors, Ministers and Envoys, who shall be accredited, shall be established on principles of absolute and complete reciprocity.

Art 29. This present Treaty shall be ratified by the Emperor of France and by His Majesty, the Emperor of all the Russias. The exchange of ratifications shall take place in this City within four days of the signing of this Treaty. Done at Tilsit, the 7th of July (25 June), 1807.

Signatures
Charles Maurice Talleyrand
Prince of Benevente.
Prince Alexandre Kourakin
Prince Dimitri Labanoff de Rostoff

Peace Treaty Between His Majesty, the Emperor of the French, King of Italy, and His Majesty, the Emperor of all the Russias, signed at Tilsit, the 9th of July, 1807.

His Majesty, the Emperor of the French, the King of Italy, Protector of the Confederation of the Rhine, and His Majesty, the King of Prussia, equally desirous to put an end to the war hostilities, have nominated as their Plenipotentiaries, that is to say:

His Majesty, the Emperor of the French, Protector of the Confederation of the Rhine, Charles Maurice Talleyrand, Prince of Benevente, High Chamberlain and Minister of Foreign Affairs, grand cordon of the Légion d'Honneur, Chevalier of the Prussian Orders of the Black and Red Eagle and the Order of St. Hubert.

And His Majesty, the King of Prussia, Field Marshal von Kalkreuth, Chevalier of the Prussian Orders of the Black and Red Eagle; Count von Glotz; Private Advisor and Envoy Extraordinary and Plenipotentiary Minister to His Majesty, the Emperor of all the Russias, Chevalier of the Russian Order of the Red Eagle.

Who, after having exchanged their full respective powers, have agreed upon the following articles:

Art 1. Peace and friendship shall be established between His Majesty, the Emperor of the French, King of Italy, and His Majesty, the King of Prussia, as of the day of exchange of ramifications of the present Treaty take place.

Art 2. The section of the Duchy of Magdeburg, situated to the right of the Elbe River, Priegnitz, the Uckermark River, the Middle and the New Mark of Brandenburg, with the exception of the Cotbuser Kreise, or Cotbuser Circle in Lower Lusace, which shall belong to His Majesty, the King of Saxony; the Duchy of Pomerania; high, low and new Silesia with the county of Glatz; the section of the Netze River district, situated north of the causeway from Driesen to Schneidemuhl to the Vistula River via Waldau, following the borders of the Bomberg Kreis, the navigation right on the Vistula River, reciprocally and free of all tolls; the Pomerelie River, the Island of Nogat and the Vistula River, to the west of Old Prussia and the north of the Kulm Kreise, the Ermeland River and finally the Kingdom of Prussia as it was the 1st of January 1772, with the strongholds of Spandau, Stettin, Kustrin, Glogau, Breslau, Schweidnitz, Neisse, Brieg, Kosel, and Glatz, and forts of the above mentioned countries in the State where said strongholds, citadels, castles and forts are to be found now. The city and citadel of Grandenz, including the villages of Neudorf, Porschkou, Swierkorzy, will also be restituted to His Majesty, the King of Prussia.

Art 3. His Majesty, the King of Prussia, recognizes his Majesty, the King of Naples, Joseph Napoleon, and His Majesty, the King of Holland, Louis Napoleon.

Art 4. His Majesty, the King of Prussia, in like manner recognizes the Confederation of the Rhine River, the actual State possessed by each sovereign which partake in it, the titles given to some among them, either by the Acts of Confederation or by Treaties of subsequent accession. Said Majesty promises to recognize, upon notification given him by His Majesty, the Emperor Napoleon, the Sovereigns who shall in the near future become members of the Confederation on a par in rank which shall be given to them by the Charter admitting them to the Confederation.

Art 5. The present Treaty of Peace and Friendship is declared in effect for their Majesties, the King of Naples and the King of Holland, and all confederate Sovereigns of the Rhine River, allies of His Majesty, the Emperor Napoleon.

Art 6. His Majesty, the King of Prussia, also recognizes His Highness, Prince Jerome Napoleon, as King of Westphalia.

Art 7. His Majesty, the King of Prussia, cedes in full propriety and convereignity to the Kings, Princes or Grand Dukes who shall be designated by His Majesty, the Emperor of France, King of Italy, all the Duchies, Marquisettes, Principalities, Counties, Seigniories, and generally all territories or part thereof, as well as the domains and properties, which His said Majesty, the King of Prussia, possessed officially or otherwise, between the Rhine River and the Elbe River at the beginning of the present war.

Art 8. His Majesty, the King of Prussia, shall be composed of possessions ceded by His Majesty, the King of Prussia, to the left of the Elbe River and other States now in the possession of His Majesty, the Emperor Napoleon.

Art 9. His Majesty, the King of Prussia, shall recognize the arrangements made by His Majesty, the Emperor Napoleon, as stated in the two preceding articles, in the same manner as if these were effected and incorporated in the present Treaty.

Art 10. His Majesty, the King of Prussia, renounces for himself, his inheritors and successors, all actual or eventual rights which he might have or might claim,

1.) on all territories, without exception, situated between the Rhine River and the Elbe River other than those designated in Article 7.

2.) on those possessions belonging to His Majesty, the King of Saxony and the House of Anhalt, which are situated on the right bank of the Elbe River. Likewise, all actual or eventual rights and claims of States situated between the Elbe River and the Rhine River on territories in the possession of His Majesty, the King of Prussia, as they shall be recognized in the present Treaty, are and shall be obliterated for perpetuity.

Art 11. All pacts, agreements, treaties of alliance, manifest or secret, which might have been concluded between Prussia and any of the countries situated to the left of the Elbe River, and which would not have been broken during the present war, shall become obsolete and shall be considered null and void.

Art 12. His Majesty, the King of Prussia, cedes in all perpetuity and sovereignty the Cotbuser Kreis or Cotbus Circle in Lower Lusace to His Majesty, the King of Saxony.

Art 13. His Majesty, the King of Prussia, renounces for perpetuity possession of all provinces which belonged to the Kingdom of Poland and after the 1st of January 1772 passed at various periods under Prussian rule, with the exception of Ermeland and the countries situated west of Old Prussia, east of Pomerania, north of the Kulm Kreise, following a line going from the Vistula River at Schneidermuhl through Waldau following the confines of the Bromberg and the causeway going from Schneidermuhl to Dreisen, which shall with the city of and the citadel of Gradenz and the villages of Neudorf, Parkschken, and Swierkorzy, continue to be possessed in all propriety and sovereignty by His Majesty, the King of Prussia.

Art 14. His Majesty, the King of Prussia, also renounces for all perpetuity possession of the City of Danzig.

Art 15. The provinces renounced by His Majesty, the King of Prussia, in Article 13 will be, with the exception of the territories listed in Article 18, given in all propriety and sovereignty to His Majesty, the King of Saxony. These territories shall be given the name of the Duchy of Warsaw and be governed by constitutions safeguarding the liberty and privileges of the people in these territories and in no way disturbing the peace and tranquillity of their neighbor States.

Art 16. In order to communicate between the Kingdom of Saxony and the Duchy of Warsaw, the King of Saxony shall have free use of military roads crossing the possessions of His Majesty, the King of Prussia. The particular road, number of troops permitted to travel it, and bivouac areas shall be determined at a special meeting to take place between their Majesties under the mediation of France.

Art 17. From Dreisen to the Vistula River and Reciprocally, there shall be no tolls imposed for the navigation of the Netze River and the Bromberg Canal, which will be free and open in every respect.

Art 18. In order to establish natural borders between Russia and the Duchy of Warsaw, the following territories surrounding the actual Russian frontiers shall be united for perpetuity to the Russian Empire: from the Bug River to the mouth of the Lossosna River; a border line starting at the mouth of the Thalweg-Bobra River, the Thalweg-Narew River to Stratz, from the Lisa River to its source, near the village of Mien, from the tributary of the Nurzek, taking its source from the same village from the Nurzek River to its mouth above the Nurr, and finally from Thalweg of the Bug River ascending from it to the actual Russian frontiers.

Art 19. The city of Danzig surrounded with a two kilometer radius shall be given its independence under the protection of His Majesty, the King of Prussia and His Majesty, the King of Saxony, and shall be governed by the laws which were in effect at the time she ceased to govern herself.

Art 20. Neither His Majesty, the King of Prussia, nor His Majesty, the King of Saxony, nor the city of Danzig shall have the authority to establish tolls and taxes of any kind or prohibit navigation of the Vistula River.

Art 21. The city, port and territory of Danzig shall be closed for the duration of the present naval war to all English commerce and navigation.

Art 22. No individual, of whatever class or station in life domiciled or owning properties in territories specified in the preceding article shall be affected in any way by the exchange be it in his rights, rank and status or his properties, pensions and revenues or any other benefits coming to him; nor shall he be pursued in any way, be it politically or militarily for any part he played in the present hostilities being terminated by this Treaty. Said specifications shall apply to individuals domiciled in the Old Kingdom of Poland which shall be restituted to His Majesty, the King of Prussia and be known as the Duchy of Warsaw.

Art 23. In a like manner, no individual born, living in or owning property in countries belonging to Prussia prior to the 1st of January 1772, and which is now to be restituted to His Majesty, the King of Prussia, under the terms of Article 2, as stipulated in this Treaty, and moreover, no individuals, that is to say, no civilians or members of the police force of Berlin who have taken arms to safeguard peace, shall be punished or pursued personally; nor shall their property, income or revenues, pensions, rank or stature be effected in any way whatsoever, for any kind of activity in which they might have participated during the present war.

Art 24. Debts, obligations and promises, which His Majesty, the King of

Prussia, might have previously assumed or contracted, prior to the present war, on territories, properties, or revenues which His said Majesty cedes or renounces under the present Treaty shall revert to the new possessors who shall undertake these obligations without reserves, exceptions, or restrictions.

Art 25. Stocks and capital funds belonging either to private citizens or public, religious, civil or military establishments, in countries ceded or renounced by His Majesty, the King of Prussia, under the present Treaty, and which might have been placed either in the Berlin Bank, the Maritime Society, or any other such establishment in the Kingdom of His Majesty, the King of Prussia, shall not be confiscated or seized. However, owners of said capital funds shall be free to dispose of them or continue to benefit from them as they wish and also collect interest issued as stipulated in past or present contracts. These terms shall be reciprocal for stocks and capital funds of private citizens or any public establishment which the Prussian Monarchy might have placed in countries which His Majesty, the King of Prussia, now cedes or renounces in the present Treaty.

Art 26. Archives holding ownership titles, documents and papers concerned in any way with countries, territories, properties and personal domains which His Majesty, the King of Prussia, cedes or renounces as a result of the present treaty, shall be delivered by His said Majesty within three months of the exchange of the ratifications, that is to say, to Emissaries of His Majesty the Emperor Napoleon, for countries ceded on the left bank of the Elbe, and to the Emissaries of His Majesty, the Emperor of all the Russias and His Majesty, the King of Saxony, and the city of Danzig for countries that Their Said Majesties and the city of Danzig shall possess as a result of the present Treaty. All maps, layouts of citadels, castles and fortresses situated in the countries in question shall also be remitted in the same manner.

Art 27. Until the day of the exchange of ratifications of the future Peace Treaty between France and England, all countries under the jurisdiction of His Majesty, the King of Prussia, shall, without exception, be closed to the English for navigation or commerce. No traffic shall be allowed from Prussian ports to the British Isles, and no ships coming from England or her colonies shall be allowed to dock in said Prussian ports.

Art 28. An immediate agreement shall be made in order to regulate the time period and methods by which all territories shall be restituted to His Majesty, the King of Prussia. In addition, all details pertaining to the civil and military administration of these countries shall also be discussed in this agreement.

Art 29. All prisoners of war shall be exchanged en masse as soon as possible.

Art 30. The present Treaty shall be ratified by His Majesty, the Emperor of the French, King of Italy, and by His Majesty, the King of Prussia; the ratification shall be exchanged at Koenigsberg no later than six days following the signing of the Treaty, or sooner, if possible.

Done and signed at Tilsit the 9th of July, 1807.

Signed:
(L.S.) CH. Maurice Talleyrand
Prince of Benevente
(L.S.) Marshal, Graf von
Kalkreuth
(L.S.) August, Count of Glotz

Agreement concluded between Major General Prince de Neuchatel, on the one hand and Field Marshal von Kalkreuth, on the other, as Plenipotentiaries of Their Sovereigns, with regard to Article 18 of the Treaty, concluded at Tilsit between their Majesties, the Emperor Napoleon and the King of Prussia signed at Koenigsberg the 12th of July 1807.

Art 1. Commissioners, from the respective countries, shall be named without delay. These shall post stakes at the frontiers of the Duchy of Warsaw, of the Old Prussian territory of Danzig, and at the frontiers which separate the Kingdoms of Prussia and Westphalia.

Art 2. The city of Tilsit shall be restituted the 21st of July; Koenigsberg, the 25th of July, and the countries up to the Parssarge River, where the Army's former encampment was, the 1st of August. Old Prussia shall be evacuated to the Vistula River, the 20th of August, and on the 5th of September, the rest of Old Prussia shall be evacuated to the Oder River. The borders of the Danzig territory shall be computed in a circumference of two kilometers, and affixed with stakes marked with emblems of France, the territory of Danzig, Saxony and Prussia. By the 1st of October, all of Prussia shall be evacuated to the Elbe River. On the same day, Silesia shall also be evacuated in order that the entire evacuation of the Kingdom of Prussia shall be terminated in two and one half months. The section of the province of Magdeburg, situated on the right bank of the Elbe River, and the provinces of Prenzlau and Passewalk shall be evacuated on the 1st of November; however, sentries shall surround Berlin so that no troops whatsoever may enter that city.

The Plenipotentiaries shall determine the exact date for the evacuation of Stettin, and 6,000 Frenchmen shall remain in that city until the evacuation takes place. The districts of Spandau, Kustrin, and in general, most of the districts of Silesia shall be restituted to His Majesty, the King of Prussia, on the 1st of October.

Art 3. Artillery, all war equipment, and in general, all that is to be found in the districts of Pillau, Colberg and Grandenz shall remain in their actual state, and the same shall hold forth in the districts of Glatz and Kosal if the French have not taken possession of these above-mentioned districts.

Art 4. The aforesaid arrangements shall be executed within the time period allotted, in countries where taxes imposed therein have been paid. Taxes and fines shall be deemed paid when sufficient and proper guarantees have been given, and if these have been properly acknowledged by the Senior Quartermaster General of the Army. All fines not publicly recognized before the exchange of ratifications shall be considered null and void.

Art 5. All the Kingdom's revenues shall be paid into the King's treasury, as of the day ratifications are exchanged and made payable to the account of His Majesty, so that contributions which ought to have been paid, and those payments were rendered from the 1st of November, 1806, to the date of the exchange of ratifications are paid in full.

Art 6. Commissioners shall be named respectively so that amicable agreements on all legal points shall be drawn up: said Commissioners shall travel to Berlin the 25th of July in order to accelerate the evacuation.

Art 7. French troops and prisoners of war shall be nourished in the said country until the evacuation takes place. Whatever provisions are found in the army warehouses shall be used for this purpose.

Art 8. If the hospitals have not yet been evacuated when troops retire, the sick from France shall be taken care of by the King's Personal Representatives, who shall see that they receive proper care under medical officers.

Art 9. The Present agreement shall be effected in full. Done in good faith and signed with our seal in Koenigsberg, the 12th of July, 1807.

Signed:
Marechal Alexander Berthier
Field Marshal, Graf von Kalkreuth

The Berlin Decree
21 November 1806

Considering:

1. That England makes no recognition of the law of nations which is universally followed by all civilized peoples;
2. That she counts every individual belonging to an enemy state as himself an enemy, and consequently makes prisoners of war not only the crews of vessels armed for war, but also the crews of trading-ships and merchant vessels, and even the commercial agents and traders who travel for business purposes;
3. That she extends to the ships and merchandise of traders and to the property of individuals the right of conquest which can only apply to the property of the enemy state;
4. That she extends to unfortified towns and ports of trade, to harbors and the mouths of river, the right of blockade which, according to season and the usage of all civilized peoples, is only applicable to fortified places;

   That she even declares to be in a state of blockade places which all her combined forces would be incapable of blockading, entire coasts and a whole empire;
5. That this monstrous abuse of the right of blockade has no other object but to impede communications between peoples and raise the commerce and industry of England upon the ruins of the industry and commerce of the Continent;
6. That such being the evident aim of England, whoever trades in English merchandise upon the continent is by this fact furthering her designs and making himself her accomplice;
7. That this conduct of England—conduct in all ways worthy of the earliest ages of barbarism—has procured the advantage of this power to the detriment of all others;
8. That it is the natural right to oppose an enemy with the arms which he himself makes use of, and to combat in the manner in which he combats when he repudiates all those ideas of justice and those liberal sentiments which are the effect of civilization upon human society:

   We have resolved to apply to England the methods which she has sanctioned in her maritime code.

   The dispositions of the present decree shall always be considered as a fundamental principle of the empire, until England has recognized that the laws of war are one and the same on land and sea; that hostilities cannot be extended either to private property of any kind whatever, or to the persons of individuals who are unconnected with the profession of arms; and that the right of blockade must be restricted to fortified places genuinely invested by forces of adequate strength;

We have in consideration decreed and do decree the following:

Art 1. The British Isles are declared to be in a state of blockade.

Art 2. All commerce or correspondence with the British Isles is forbidden. In consequence, letters or packets addressed either to England or to an Englishman, or written in the English language, will not be allowed to pass through the post and will be seized.

Art 3. All individuals, subjects of England, of whatever state or condition they may be, who are in the countries occupied by our troops or by those of our allies, shall be made prisoners of war.

Art 4. Any commercial establishment, any merchandise, any property of any kind whatever belonging to an English subject, shall be declared a lawful prize.

Art 5. Trading in English merchandise is forbidden; and all merchandise belonging to England or coming from its factories or its colonies is declared to be a lawful prize.

Art 6. A portion of the receipts from the confiscation of merchandise and the properties declared as lawful prizes by the preceding articles shall be employed to compensate those merchants who have suffered losses by the seizure of merchant vessels by English privateers.

Art 7. No ship coming directly from England or the English colonies, or having been there since the publication of the present decree, will be received into any port.

Art 8. All vesels, which, by means of false declaration, that contravene the spirit of this decree, shall be seized; and the vessel and its cargo shall be confiscated as if it were English property.

Art 9. Our Prize Tribunal in Paris is charged with the final judgment of all contestations which should occur in our Empire or in the countries occupied by our French armies, relative to the execution of the present decree. Our Prize Tribunal in Milan shall be charged with the final judgment of such contestations which should occur in the Kingdom of Italy.

Art 10. The communication of this decree shall be given, by Our Foreign Minister, to the Kings of Spain, Naples, Holland and Etruria, and to Our other allies, whose subjects are victims, as are Ours, of the injustice and barbarity of the English maritime legislation.

Art 11. Our Foreign Minister, Ministers of War, the Navy, of Finance, the Police, and Our General Postal Directors, are charged, as each is concerned with the execution of this decree.

Napoleon

British Orders in Council
7 January 1807

Order in Council prohibiting Trade to be carried on between Port and Port of Countries under the domination or usurped control of France.

At the Court at the Queen's Palace, the 7th of January 1807; Present, the King's most excellent Majesty in council. —Whereas, the French government has issued certain Orders, which, in violation of the usages of war, purport to prohibit the Commerce of all Neutral Nations with his majesty's dominions, and also to prevent such nations from trading with any other country, in any articles, the growth, produce, or manufacture of his majesty's dominions; and whereas the said government has also taken upon itself to declare all his majesty's dominions to be in a state of a blockade, at a time when the fleets of France and her allies are themselves confined within their own ports by the superior valour and discipline of the British navy; and whereas such attempts on the part of the enemy would give his majesty an unquestionable right of retaliation, and would warrant his majesty in enforcing the same prohibition of all commerce with France, which that power vainly hopes to effect against the commerce of his majesty's subjects; a prohibition which the superiority of his majesty's naval forces might enable him to support, by actually investing the ports and coasts of the enemy with numerous squadrons and cruisers, so as to make the entrance or approach thereto manifestly dangerous; and whereas his majesty, though unwilling to follow the example of his enemies, by proceeding to an extremity so distressing to all nations not engaged in the war, and carrying on their accustomed trade, yet feels himself bound by a due regard to the just defense of the rights and interests of his people, not to suffer such measures to be taken by the enemy, without taking some steps on his part to restrain this violence, and to retort upon them the evils of their own injustice; his majesty is therefore pleased, by and with the advice of his privy council, to order, and it is hereby ordered, That no vessel shall be permitted to trade from one port to another, both which ports shall belong to or be in the possession of France or her allies, or shall be so far under their control, as that British vessels may not freely trade thereat; and the commanders of his majesty's ships of war and privateers shall be, and are hereby instructed to warn every neutral vessel coming from any such port, and destined to another such port, to discontinue her voyage, and not to proceed to any such port; and any vessel after being so warned, or any vessel coming from any such port, after a reasonable time shall have been afforded for receiving information of this his majesty's Order, which shall be found proceeding to another such port, shall be captured and brought in, and, together with her cargo, shall be condemned as a lawful prize; and his majesty's principal secretaries of state, the lords commissioners of the admiralty, and the judges of the high court of admiralty, and courts of vice admiralty, are to take the necessary measures herein as to them shall respectively appertain.

Principal Order: Blockade Ordinance
Order in Council; declaring the Dominions of his Majesty's Enemies, and of Countries under their Control, in a state of Blockade, under the Exceptions specified in said Order.

At the Court at the Queen's Palace, the 11th of November 1807; Present, The King's most excellent Majesty in council. —Whereas, certain Orders establishing an unprecedented system of warfare against this kingdom, and aimed especially at the destruction of its commerce and resources, were some time since issued by the government of France, by which the British Islands were declared to be in a state of blockade, thereby subjecting to capture and condemnation all vessels, with their cargoes which should continue to trade with his majesty's dominions. —And whereas by the same Orders, "all trading in English merchandise is prohibited; and every article of merchandise belonging to England, or coming from her colonies, or of her manufacture, is declared lawful prize;" —And whereas the nations in alliance with France, and under her control, were required to give, and have given, and do give, effect to such Orders; — And whereas his majesty's Order of 7 January last, has not answered the desired purpose, either of compelling the enemy to recall those Orders, or of inducing neutral nations to interpose, with effect, to obtain their revocation; but, on the contrary, the same have been recently enforced with increased rigour; —And whereas his majesty, under these circumstances, finds himself compelled to take further measures for asserting and vindicating his just rights, and for supporting that maritime power which the exertions and valor of his people have, under the blessing of Providence, enabled him to establish and maintain; and the maintenance of which is not more essential to the safety and prosperity of such states as still retain their independence, and to the general intercourse and happiness of mankind: —His majesty is therefore pleased, by and with the advice of his privy council, to order, and it is hereby ordered, That all the ports and places of France and her allies, or of any other country at war with his majesty, and all other ports, or places in Europe, from which, although not at war with his majesty, the British flag is excluded, and all ports or places in the colonies belonging to the commanders of ships of war and privateers, and to the judge of the high court of the admiralty, and the judges of the courts of vice-admiralty, directing that the ships and goods belonging to the Inhabitants of Hamburg, Bremen, and other places and countries in the north of Germany, which vessels and goods shall be employed in a trade to or from the ports of the united kingdom, shall until further order be suffered to pass free and unmolested, notwithstanding that the said countries are or may be in the possession or under the control of France and her allies; and that all such ships and goods so trading, which may have been already detained, shall be forthwith liberated, and restored; . . .

Additional Instructions to the Commanders of Ships of War and Privateers, to the Judge of the High Court of Admiralty

Our will and pleasure is, that the ships and goods belonging to the inhabitants of Hamburg, Bremen, and other places and countries in the north of Germany, which vessels and goods shall have been employed in a trade to or from the ports of our united kingdom, shall, until further order, be suffered to pass free and unmolested, notwithstanding that the said countries are or may be in the possession or under the control of France and her allies; and all such ships and goods so trading which may have been already detained shall be forthwith liberated and restored.

11 November 1807

Order in Council; containing certain Regulations under which the trade to and from the enemies Country shall be carried on:

At the Court at the Queen's Palace, the 11th of November 1807; Present, The King's most excellent Majesty in council. —Whereas, articles of the growth and manufacture of foreign countries cannot by law be imported into this country, except in British ships, or in ships belonging to the countries of which such articles are the growth and manufacture, without an Order in Council specially authorizing the same: —His majesty, taking into consideration the Order of this day's date, respecting the trade to be carried on to and from the ports of the enemy, and deeming it expedient that any vessel, belonging to any country in alliance or at amity with his majesty, may be permitted to import into this country articles of the produce or manufacture of countries at war with his majesty: —His majesty, by and with the advice of his privy council, is therefore pleased to order, and it is hereby ordered, That all goods, wares, or merchandises, specified and included in the schedule of an act, passed in the 43rd year of his present majesty's reign, entitled, "an act to repeal the duties of customs payable in Great Britain, and to grant other duties in lieu thereof," may be imported from any port or place belonging to any state not at amity with his majesty, in ships belonging to any state at amity with his majesty, subject to the payment of such duties, and liable to such drawbacks, as are now established by law upon the importation of the said goods, wares, or merchandise, in ships navigated according to law; and with respect to such of the said goods, wares, or merchandise, as are authorized to be warehoused under the provisions of an act, passed in the 43rd year of his present majesty's reign, entitled, "an act for permitting certain goods imported into Great Britain, to be secured in warehouses without payment of duty," subject to all the regulations of the said last-mentioned act; and with respect to all articles which are prohibited by law from being imported into this country, it is ordered, That the same shall be reported for exportation to any country in amity or alliance with his majesty. —And his majesty is further pleased, by and with the advice of his privy council, to order, and it is hereby ordered, That all vessels which shall arrive at any port of the united kingdom, or at the port of Gibraltar, or Malta, in consequence of having been warned pursuant to the aforesaid order, or in consequence of receiving information in any other manner of the said Order, subsequent to their having taken on board any part of their cargoes, whether previous or subsequent to their sailing, shall be permitted to report their cargoes for exportation, and shall be allowed to proceed upon their voyages to their original ports of destination (if not unlawful before the issuing of the order) or to any port at amity with his majesty, upon receiving a certificate from the collector or comptroller of the customs at the port at which they shall so enter (which certificate the said collectors and comptrollers of the customs are hereby authorized and required to give) setting forth, that such vessels came into such port in consequence of being so warned, or of receiving such information as aforesaid, and that they were permitted to sail from such port under the regulations which his majesty has been pleased to establish in respect to such vessels; but in case any vessel so arriving shall prefer to import her cargo, then such vessel shall be allowed to enter and import the same, upon such terms and conditions as the said cargo might have been imported upon, according to law, in case the said vessel had sailed after having received notice of the said Order, and in conformity thereto. —And it is further ordered, That all vessels which shall arrive at any port of the united kingdom, or at Gibraltar, or Malta, in conformity and obedience to said Order, shall be allowed, in respect to articles which may be on board the same, except sugar, coffee, wine, brandy, snuff and tobacco, to clear out to any port whatever, to be specified in such clearance; and, with respect to the last mentioned articles, to export the same to such ports and under such conditions and regulations only as his majesty, by any license to be granted for that purpose, may direct . . .

25 November 1807

Order in Council; establishing certain Regulations as to Vessels clearing out from this Kingdom, with reference to the Order of the 11th of November instant.

At the Court at the Queen's Palace, the 11th of November 1807; Present, The King's most excellent Majesty in council. —Whereas his majesty, by his Order in council, dated 11th of Nov. instant, respecting the trade to be carried on with his majesty's enemies, was pleased to exempt from the restrictions of said Order all vessels which shall have cleared out from any port or place in this kingdom under such regulations as his majesty may think fit to prescribe, and shall be proceeding direct to the ports specified in the respective clearances; his majesty, taking into consideration the expediency of making such regulations, is pleased, by and with the advice of his privy council, to order, and it is hereby ordered, That all vessels belonging to countries not at war with his majesty, shall be permitted to lade in any port of the united kingdom any goods, being the produce or manufacture of his majesty's dominions, or East India goods or price goods (all such goods having been lawfully imported) and to clear out with, and freely to convey the same to any port or place in any colony in the West Indies or America, belonging to his majesty's enemies, such port or place not being in a state of actual blockade, subject to the payment of such duties as may, at the time when any such vessel may be cleared out, be due by law on the exportation of any such goods, or in respect of the same being destined to ports of the colonies belonging to his majesty's enemies, and likewise to lade, clear out with, and convey as aforesaid, any articles of foreign produce or manufacture which shall have been lawfully imported into this kingdom, provided his majesty's license shall have been previously obtained for so conveying such foreign produce or manufactures; and it is further ordered, That any vessel, belonging as aforesaid, shall be permitted to lade in any port of the united kingdom any goods, not being naval or military stores, which shall be of the growth, produce or manufacture of this kingdom, or which shall have been lawfully imported, (save and except foreign sugar, coffee, wine, brandy, snuff and cotton) and to clear out with, and freely to convey the same to any port, to be specified in the clearance, not being in a state of actual blockade, although the same shall be under the restrictions of the said Order, and likewise to lade, clear out, and convey foreign sugar, coffee, wine, brandy, snuff and cotton, which shall have been lawfully imported, provided his majesty's license shall have been previously obtained for the exportation and conveyance thereof: and it is hereby further ordered, That no vessel shall be permitted to clear out from any port or place in this kingdom, to any port or place of any country subjected to the restrictions of the said Order, with any goods which shall have been laden, after notice of the said Order, on board the vessel which shall have imported the same into this kingdom, without having first duly entered and landed the same in some port or place in this kingdom; and that no vessel shall be permitted to clear out from any port or place in this kingdom to any port or place whatever, with any goods, the produce or manufacture of any country subjected to the restrictions of the said Order, which shall have been laden, after notice as aforesaid, on board the vessel importing the same, without having so duly entered and landed the same, or with any goods whatever which shall have been laden after such notice in the vessel importing the same, in any port or place subjected to the restrictions of said Order, without having so duly entered and landed the same in some port or place in this kingdom, except the cargo shall consist wholly of flour, meal, grain, or any article or articles the produce of the soil of some country which is not subjected to the restrictions of the said Order, except cotton, and which shall have been imported in an unmanufactured state direct from such country into this kingdom, in a vessel belonging to the country for which such goods have been brought, and in which the same were grown and produced; and it is further ordered, That any vessel belonging to any country not at war with his majesty, may clear out from Guernsey, Jersey or Man, to any port or place under the restrictions of the said Order, which shall be specified in the clearance, not being in a state of actual blockade, with such articles only, not being naval or military stores, as shall have been legally imported into such islands respectively, from any port or place in this kingdom direct; and with respect to all such articles as may have been imported into the said islands respectively, from any port or place under the restrictions of the said Order, it shall not be permitted to any vessel to clear out with the same from any of the said islands, except to some port or place in this kingdom.

The Milan Decree
24 December 1807

Napoleon, Emperor of the French, King of Italy, Protector of the Confederation of the Rhine:

In view of the Orders in Council of the British government, dated 11 November 1807, which subjugates the vessels of the neutral powers, friends and British allies alike, not only to visits by British privateers, but also to an obligatory port call and the imposition of an arbitrary tax on their cargo, which is regulated by English legislation;

Considering that, by these acts, the English government has denationalized the vessels of all European nations; that it is not within the power of any government to compromise the rights and independence of another, that all the sovereigns of Europe are jointly responsible for the sovereignty and independence of their colors, which if, by inexcusable weakness, which would be an ineffaceable blemish in the eyes of posterity, one permits to pass in principle and dedication by the use of such tyranny, the English in taking such action to legally establish, as they have profited by the tolerance of the governments to establish the infamous principle that the flag does not cover merchandise, and to give them the right to an extended, arbitrary and criminal blockade of the sovereignty of all states;

We have decreed and do decree the following:

Art 1. All vessels, of which ever nation, which suffer the visit of an English vessel or which submit to a port call in England, or shall pay any tax to the English government, is, by that act alone, declared denationalized, and lose the guarantee of their flag and are considered English property.

Art 2. Should such vessels, denationalized by the arbitrary measures of the British government, enter into our ports or those of our allies, should they fall into the power of our warships or our corsairs, they are declared as lawful prizes.

Art 3. The British Isles are declared in a state of blockade on sea and on land. All vessels, of whatever nation, whose cargo, coming from British ports or the ports of its allies or countries occupied by the English, or going to England, or going to English colonies or countries occupied by British troops, are declared lawful prize by this decree; it shall be captured by our warships or corsairs, and adjudged upon capture.

Art 4. These measures, which are but a just reciprocation for the barbaric system adopted by the British government, which likens its legislation to that of Algeria; ceases to have their effect for all nations which shall oblige the British government to respect their flags. These measures shall continue to be in effect until such time as this government returns to the principles of law which regulate the relations of civilized nations in the state of war. The dispositions of this shall be abrogated and nullified by the act of the British government returning to the principles of the rights of men, which also are those of justice and honor.

Art 5. All of the ministers are charged with the execution of this decree, which shall be published in the Legal Bulletin.

The Decree of 19 October 1810

Art 1. All merchandise of English manufacture and which is prohibited, presently existing in France, be they in warehouses or in the magazines of the customs, shall be publicly burned.

Art 2. In the future, all merchandise of English manufacture, confiscated by the customs or by seizures, shall be burned.

Art 3. All English merchandise found in Holland, the Grand Duchy of Berg, the Hanseatic cities, and generally near the Mein to the sea shall be seized and burned.

Art 4. All the English merchandise found in our Kingdom of Italy, no matter to whom it belongs, shall be seized and burned.

Art 5. All English merchandise found in the Illyrian provinces shall be seized and burned.

Art 6. All English merchandise found in the Kingdom of Naples shall be seized and burned.

Art 7. All English merchandise found in the Spanish provinces occupied by our troops shall be seized and burned.

Art 8. All English merchandise found in the cities and upon their occupation by our troops shall be seized and burned.

Napoleon

Treaty Concluded Between France and Prussia
8 September 1808

Art 1. The raising of the sums due from the Prussian states to the French army, as well as the special revenues due for late payment, is fixed at 140 million francs and, for payment of said sum, all claims of France on Prussia for war reparations, shall be canceled. This sum shall be paid, in the twenty days after the ratification of this present treaty, to the treasury of the Comptroller General of the Army, as follows:

Part in silver letters of credit, good and accepted payables, at the rate of six million francs per month, from the date of the exchange of the ratifications and the payment shall be guaranteed by the Prussian treasury.

Art 2. The Prussian revenues belong to the French administration from the date of the signing of the treaty, and after this day, to His Majesty, the King of Prussia.

Art 3. The claims His Majesty, the King of Prussia, has on particulars of the Duchy of Warsaw, according to the terms of the Treaty of Tilsit, are ceded without any reservation.

Art 4. All the dismembered provinces of the Prussian monarchy that that government wishes to reclaim, shall be the object of special arrangements.

Art 5. The States of His Majesty, the King of Prussia, shall be evacuated by the French within the interval of thirty to forty days after the exchange of ratifications, or sooner if possible.

Art 6. The places of Glogau, Stettin and Kustrin shall remain in the possession of the French until the complete discharge of letters of credit and deeds given in payment of the reparations enumerated in the first article. Glogau shall be returned when half of the payments are made and the other two shall be returned upon the complete payment of the debt.

Art 7. The French garrison which remains in Glogau shall consist of 2,500 infantry, 600 cavalry, and 200 artillerists, in total 3,300 men.

The garrison of Kustrin shall be 2,000 infantry, 600 cavalry and 200 artillerists, in total 2,800 men.

The garrison of Stettin shall be 3,000 infantry, 600 cavalry and 300 artillery, in total 3,900 men.

The total of these three garrisons: 10,000 men.

Art 8. The pay of these garrisons shall be paid by the treasury of the French administration; but the lodging, lodging compensation, food, forage, heating and light, shall be furnished by the Prussian administration, except for the troops of the general staff of each place, in conformance with the tariffs established by French regulations.

Art 9. There shall be in each of these places a siege provisioning of six months furnished by the French magazines of Prussian administration. In the first case, the administration, from the time of evacuation, shall fall to the French administration.

Art 10. From the evacuation of the aforementioned locations, the artillery, the munitions, and the guns belonging to the French army shall also be evacuated; the means of transport shall be furnished by the Prussian administration, which shall equally nourish the French troops until their departure from Prussian territory.

Art 11. During the time of the occupation of these places by the French army the administration of revenues and that of justice belongs to the King of Prussia, but the police shall be in the hands of the French commandant.

Art 12. No Prussian troops shall approach within one days march of any of these three places.

Art 13. There shall be a military road from:

Glogau to Kustrin
Kustrin to Stettin
Stettin to Stralsund
Glogau to Kalish
Glogau to Saxony
Stettin to Magdeburg
Stettin to Danzig

These roads shall serve for the movements of recruits, replacements, and in general for the needs of the French garrisons in the three reserved places.

Art 14. When the Treaty of Tilsit was signed, it was assumed by error that the city of Magdeburg lie entirely on the left bank of the Elbe. This river was then set as the territorial limit of Prussia, but the citadel of Magdeburg was on the right bank. His Majesty, the King of Prussia, consents to surrender the territory measuring 2,000 paces from the outworks of the citadel.

The stakes shall be placed by the French and Prussian commissioners in the five days following the exchange of this treaty.

Art 15. His Majesty, the Emperor and King, guarantees to His Majesty, the King of Prussia, the integrity of his territory on the condition that he remain a faithful ally of France.

Art 16. His Majesty, the King of Prussia, recognizes as King of Spain and the Indes, His Majesty, Joseph Napoleon, and as King of the Two Sicilies, His Majesty Joachim Murat.

Art 17. This treaty shall be ratified and the ratifications shall be exchanged within 30 days or sooner if possible.

Convention Between France and Prussia

His Majesty, the Emperor of the French, King of Italy, Protector of the Confederation of the Rhine, Mediator of the Swiss Confederation, and His Majesty, the King of Prussia, having fixed their attention on the declaration postponed during the month of April by the Russian ministers near the different courts and notably near that of Berlin, on the war preparations which they are pursuing and that of others and on the new commerce system of colonial merchandise established in Russia in opposition to the Treaty of Tilsit, find themselves authorized by such circumstances to provide for a change of dispositions on the part of the Petersburg Court and the possibility of a rupture more or less near, conserving always the hope that their apprehensions, some founded strongly, shall not be confirmed by events, but wishing only, should war come, that all shall be regulated and confirmed in advance between themselves for the execution of a treaty of alliance on this day, have resolved, conforming to Article III of the aforementioned treaty, do decree on this consideration by a contingent and special convention and have, to this end, named for their plenipotentaires the following:

His Majesty, the Emperor of France, King of Italy, etc., Hugues Bernard, Count of Maret, Duke of Bassano, etc.

And His Majesty, the King of Prussia, Frederick Wilhelm-Ludwig, Baron of Krusemark, etc.;

Whom, after having communicated their respective full powers, have agreed upon the following articles:

Art 1. In the case of war breaking out between France and Russia, His Majesty, the King of Prussia, shall make common cause with His Majesty, the Emperor and King.

Art 2. His Majesty, the King of Prussia, shall provide a contingent of 20,000 men comprised of 14,000 infantry, 4,000 cavalry and 2,000 artillerists with 60 cannons, having a double ration and the military equipage necessary to transport flour for ten to twenty days.

This contingent shall always be held complete at the aforementioned number present under arms.

Art 3. This contingent shall, as much as possible, be retained in the same army corps and employed by preference for the protection of Prussian provinces, but His Majesty, the King of Prussia, shall make no restrictions on the military dispositions of the army in which these troops are employed.

The troops who shall compose the aforementioned contingent shall be organized as follows: Those which find themselves in Silesia in Breslau, those near the Oder at Berlin, and those in the eastern provinces at Koenigsberg.

They shall be ready to begin operations at these diverse points on 15 March.

Art 4. Independent of the aforementioned corps, a corps of Prussian troops composed of 4,000 men shall form the garrison of Colberg and furnish, if necessary, detachments for the defense of the coasts. A Corps of 1,200 men shall garrison Potsdam. In the case His Majesty, the King of Prussia, judges to establish himself in the aforementioned residence, this garrison may be raised to 3,000. A corps of 10,000 men shall be furnished to garrison the fortresses in Silesia. A corps of 3,000 men shall form the garrison of Graudenz.

The commandants of Colberg and Graudenz shall regularly transmit the status of their position and garrison to the General Staff. They shall be obedient to the orders of the General Staff for the service of the army.

They shall receive in these locations, the officers which the General Staff judges suitable to establish there for the objectives of the service and the artillery squads which shall be sent there for the preparation of munitions, but no other troops shall be permitted entry.

There shall be no new work in this harmony with the French generals.

Art 5. His Majesty, Imperial and Royal, promises and engages himself to take part in such a war with all the forces at his disposal.

Art 6. The French troops and their allies may cross and occupy the Prussian provinces, with the exception of Upper Silesia, the country of Glatz, and the principalities of Breslau, Oels and Brieg. The French troops shall not enter this part of Silesia, nor in the counties which are not part of the lines of operations.

The city of Potsdam shall be exempt from the passage of troops and garrisoning by the French and their allies.

A company from the Potsdam garrison may be detached as a guard for the palace of Charlottemburg and another for the guard of the King's palace in Berlin.

No officer or employee may, under any pretext, enter or take up residence in the aforementioned palaces, without the permission of the government, which shall be established by His Majesty, the King of Prussia.

Art 7. The lines of operations shall be in the countryside between the Elbe and the Oder, between the Oder and the Vistula, and between the Vistula and the Memel or the Niemen. There shall be on these lines of operations no other Prussian troops other than the bourgeois militia, the gendarmerie, and those men strictly necessary for the maintenance of order.

Art 8. The French commandants who shall be established on the lines of operations shall not involve themselves directly, or indirectly, in the civil government or administration. They shall have in their sphere of authority all that concerns itself with requisitions, the supplying of material to the troops, service of the military hospitals, the police and the maintenance of order, and security of the rear of the armies concerned.

Art 9. The French administration or commandants may make, in case of need, requisitions on the local authorities or Prussian Commissariats for food and transport.

Payment will be made, in such a case, in three months by the Senior Commissariat Officer of the army. The individual receipts shall be combined into a general receipt and the cost shall be paid by a reduction of the Prussian contributions or at the end of the campaign.

Art 10. Should it become necessary to draw artillery, powder, shot, cartridges and other munitions from the Prussian fortresses, His Majesty, the King of Prussia, makes the promise to make them available to the French and their allies, with reduction in contributions or payment at the end of the campaign, all the aforementioned that His Majesty does not judge necessary for the defense of those places by his army.

Art 11. The Prussian army shall call no draft or military concentration during that time when the French army occupies its territory or that of the enemy, if it is not to the advantage of the alliance and harmony of the two powers.

Art 12. Those individuals who commit misdemeanor offenses shall be judged by the military commissions of the generals of the offended army. The defendant shall have a council for his defense from his own nation.

Art 13. In the case of a victorious outcome of the war with Russia, if, despite the vows and hopes of the contracting parties, His Majesty, the Emperor, shall engage himself to procure for His Majesty, the King of Prussia, an indemnity in territory to compensate the sacrifices and burdens taken by His Majesty for his support during the war.

Art 14. With regard to the positions at Glogau, Kustrin and Stettin, presently occupied by French troops, the expense for the garrisons and their approvisionment for siege, etc., shall date from the signing of this convention, for that of Glogau, and on the day when His Majesty, the King of Prussia, shall fill the contractual arrangements of the convention by a contribution, signed simultaneously with those present for Stettin and Kustrin, to the charge of His Majesty, the Emperor. A specific arrangement shall be made between the sovereigns on the duration of the occupation of these places by French troops.

Art 15. The present convention shall remain secret and shall in no case be made public or communicated to a foreign government by one or the other of the two contractual parties.

This shall be ratified and the ratifications exchanged in Berlin in a space of ten days or sooner if it can be done.

Signed: Duke of Bassano

Signed: Baron von Krusemark

Arrangements with Prussia Relative to the Execution of the Convention of 8 September and 5 December, 1808, and Concerning the Payment of the Contributions Due.

His Majesty, the Emperor of the French, King of Italy, Protector of the Confederation of the Rhine, Mediator of the Swiss Confederation, and His Majesty, the King of Prussia, wish to regulate, by a new arrangement, the execution of the convention of 8 September and 5 December, 1808, by the nomination of their plenipotentiaries as follows:

His Majesty, the Emperor of France, King of Italy, etc., Hugues Bernard, Count of Maret, Duke of Bassano, his minister of Exterior Relations.

And His Majesty, the King of Prussia, Henrich von Beguelin, Counselor of State of His Majesty, and his empowered proxy, etc.:

Whom, after having communicated their respective full powers, have agreed upon the following articles:

Art 1. During the time that the French troops are on the territory of the King of Prussia and during all the duration of the war with Russia, if Prussia comes to have place, the payment in silver of contributions remaining due by His Majesty shall be suspended; the interests being charged to His Majesty.

Art 2. His Majesty, the Emperor of the French, accepts, to the reckoning of said contributions and in lieu of money, the commodities and munitions which His Majesty, the King of Prussia, engages to furnish, upon concurrence of quantities to be determined later.

Art 3. His Majesty, the King of Prussia, engages himself:
1.) To pay by quarters, from month to month, beginning on the upcoming 1 March, in the French magazines:

200,000 quintel of rye
24,000 quintel of rice and dried vegetables

2,000,000 bottles of brandy
2,000,000 bottles of beer

2.) To pay by eights, from month to month, to be paid on 1 March, in the French magazines

400,000 quintel of wheat
650,000 quintel of hay
350,000 quintel of straw
6,000,000 bushels of oats

3.) To furnish by sixths, from month to month, at the beginning of 1 March:

44,000 cattle

Among this 44,000 cattle shall be 600 draft oxen, which shall be delivered to Danzig.

4.) To be furnished by quarters, month to month, at the beginning of 1 March, 15,000 horses:

6,000 for light cavalry
3,000 for heavy cavalry
6,000 for artillery or military equipage

5.) To be furnished by quarters, month by month:

600,000 pounds of powder
300,000 pounds of lead

6.) To be furnished for the transport of the army:

3,600 drawn wagons and provisions for the drivers, each carrying a weight of 1,500, composed in 120 brigades of 30 wagons each, and formed in three divisions formed at:

1st at Magdeburg on the Oder
2nd at the Oder on the Vistula
3rd at the Vistula on the Russian frontiers

7.) To establish hospitals for 20,000 sick and to furnish for said hospital, the buildings, furniture, linen, provisions, medications, medical attendants, and health officers, who shall serve concurrently with the French health officers.

Art 4. These substances shall be paid in the locations which have been designated by the managing general of the army: part shall be delivered on the Oder and the Vistula, including Modlin, and the other part at locations in eastern and western Prussia.

Art 5. These horses shall be delivered to the depots that shall be designated by the managing general of the army.

Art 6. The powder and lead shall be delivered to Modlin, Thorn, and Danzig, in proportions to be determined by the artillery commander.

Art 7. The hospitals shall be established in the places which shall be designated by the managing general of the army.

Art 8. The transport shall be delivered to the places designated by the managing general of the army.

Art 9. The assessment, as well as the price of the commodities, travel expenses, journeys of the hospitals and 3,600 wagons, shall be made voluntarily by both sides between the managing general and the commissioner of His Majesty, the King of Prussia.

Art 10. The acknowledgment of commodities which shall be paid shall be delivered in the measure of payment; the deductions shall be made every three months by the managing general of the army. The individual receipts shall be consolidated into a general receipt and establish the dates of payment. He shall make an accounting of the contributions and part of the interest which ceases to run.

Art 11. All the commodities and provisions which are found in Colberg and Graudenz which exceed the quantities for the provisionment of those places during one year: in Colberg for a garrison of 4,000 and in Graudenz for a garrison of 3,000 men, shall in eight days following the ratifications of this convention, be sent to the magazines of Kustrin, Stettin and Danzig, and received towards the totals required in Article 3.

Art 12. The surety acts furnished by the States of the Prussian Provinces for the security of payment of the contributions shall be sent to His Majesty, the King of Prussia, and exchanged against an obligation of the Prussian government, by whose raising shall be the same as said surety acts.

Art 13. As soon as the payments and delivery is made in execution of this convention and have been totally met, the general accounting of their quantity and value shall be stopped, as well as the definition in capital and interests of the contributions due by the King of Prussia as defined. There shall then be made new arrangements between the two contracting parties for the acquittal of the balance which results from said accountings, to the expense of one party or the other.

Art 14. This convention shall remain secret.

Art 15. This convention shall be ratified and the ratifications shall be exchanged in Berlin in the space of ten days or sooner if it may be accomplished.

Made and signed in Paris on 24 February 1812
Signed: Hugues Bernard
    Count of Maret
    Duke of Bassano
    French Minister of Exterior Relations

Signed: Henrich von Beguelin
    Counselor of State of His Majesty
    The King of Prussia

Convention Between France and Denmark
7 March 1812
Paris

His Majesty, the Emperor of the French, King of Italy, Protector of the Confederation of the Rhine, Mediator of the Swiss Confederation:

And His Majesty, the King of Denmark and Norway, etc.,

Wish by the alliance in which they unite, to come to an agreement on the measures to be taken for the common good, have named for the plenipotentiaries:

His Majesty, the Emperor of France, King of Italy, etc., Hugues Bernard, Count of Maret, Duke of Bassano, his minister of Exterior Relations.

And His Majesty, the King of Denmark and Norway, etc., Ernst-Frederick von Walterstorff, etc.;

Who, having communicated their respective full powers, have agreed upon the following articles:

Art 1. His Majesty, the Emperor and His Majesty, the King of Denmark, confirm and renew in its totality, in the most express and absolute manner, the clauses of the treaty concluded at Fontainbleau on 31 October, 1807, and notably the mutual guarantees expressed in Article 4 of said treaty.

Art 2. His Majesty, the King of Denmark, engages himself to maintain in the duchies of Holstein, Schleswig and in Jutland a force of 9,000 infantry, 1,000 cavalry and 50 cannon. These troops shall form a division of two brigades, each composed of 5,000 men and 25 guns.

One of these brigades shall be formed between Altona and the sea, near the Elbe, and be able to cross to the left bank within 24 hours. The other brigade shall be formed where it is able to join the first in as short a time as possible.

Art 3. His Majesty, the Emperor, shall maintain a division of similar force in the departments of the Bouches-de-Elbe (Mouth of the Elbe), Mecklenburg, and the Swedish Pomerania.

Art 4. The Danish division may be called upon to advance to the Weser, the Jade and the Ems, just to Delfzyl, Groningue, and Harlingen, or to any other enemy enterprise.

It can equally be called, for the same purpose, to Mecklenburg or Swedish Pomerania up to the mouth of the Oder, the isles of this river included.

It may also, in case of attack or insurrection in Holland, be required to move to the right coast of the Zuyderzee.

The Danish troops may in no case be outside the indicated territories, except with the orders of their sovereign.

Art 5. The status of this division shall be forwarded each month to the commanding general of the 32nd Military Division. This status shall contain the names of the generals and senior officers, the strengths of the different arms, the batteries of artillery with their strength present under arms and their emplacement.

Art 6. The position of Gluckstadt shall be armed and provisioned. The military edifices and gun boats of His Majesty shall not be used except in the case of the need of protection from the enemy. There shall exercise in these areas no police or other military jurisdiction, and they shall observe the military regulations of that post.

Art 7. The division of troops from His Majesty the Emperor and King, or that part of this division, which the commanding general for His Majesty, the King of Denmark, in Holstein judges sufficient, shall move in the duchies of Holstein and Schleswig and into Jutland as soon as they should be required to oppose a descent, an insurrection or any other enemy enterprise.

Art 8. If Norway or the Islands of Seeland are attacked and if the King of Denmark judges to retire his troops from Holstein he shall inform the Emperor and the commander in chief of the army. In this case he shall permit the entry of a French division or such part of said division to guard the country.

Art 9. Troops may be reciprocally requisitioned, in the case and for the reasons designated in the preceding articles, by the commanding general of His Majesty, the Emperor, or by the commander of the Danish forces in Holstein. They shall return to their respective cantonments should the case for which they were called cease to exist or should the requisitioning party no longer require their assistance.

Art 10. As soon as such troops should enter the country of the requisitioning country they shall be provided for by the requesting nation, but shall remain in the pay of their sovereign.

Art 11. To re-affirm as strongly as possible the bond that unifies these two states, there shall be concluded a commercial treaty on the basis most favorable to the mutual prosperity of the two nations.

Art 12. This present convention shall be held secret. It shall be ratified and the ratifications shall be exchanged at Copenhagen after a delay of twenty days or less if possible.

Duke of Bassano
Ernst-Frederick Walterstorff

Capitulation of 28 March 1812

Napoleon, by the grace of God and the constitution, Emperor of France, King of Italy, Protector of the Confederation of the Rhine, Mediator of the Swiss Confederation, having seen and examined the capitulation concluded, stopped, and signed in Berne on 28 March 1812 by Our Chamberlain, the Count August de Talleyrand, Officier of the Legion d'Honneur, Our envoy extraordinaire and minister plenipotentiary in Switzerland in full powers which we have conferred to this end, the gentleman Rodolphe de Watteville, general of the Confederation, former Landamman of the Swiss and envoy of the Canton of Berne; Jean Conrad d'Escher, Burgomeister of the Canton of Zurich; Joachim Pancrace Reutti, member of the Petit Council of the Canton of Saint-Gall; Nicholas Herr, Landamman of the Canton of Glaris, and August Pidou, member of the Petit Council of the Canton of Vaude, equally granted full powers, of which capitulation, follows:

Napoleon, Emperor of the French, King of Italy, Protector of the Confederation of the Rhine, Mediator of the Swiss Confederation, and the Helvetic Diet of the 19 Swiss Cantons, desires to establish on the most convenient bases, a draft and the organization of Swiss troops which France shall enter into her service in virtue of the military capitulation concluded on 27 September 1803 have named plenipotentiaries to this effect, as follows:

For H.M. Emperor of the French, King of Italy:

Monsieur le Count de Talleyrand, officer of the Legion d'Honneur, envoy extraordinaire and minister plenipotentiary of H.M. in Switzerland.

And for the Diet of the Swiss Confederation:

Monsieur Rodolphe de Watteville, General of the Confederation, former Landamman of the Swiss and envoy of the Canton of Berne; Jean Conrad d'Escher, Burgomeister of the Canton of Zurich; Joachim Pancrace Reutti, member of the Petit Council of the Canton of Saint-Gall; Nicholas Herr, Landamman of the Canton of Glaris; August Pidou, member of the Petit Council of the Canton of Vaude.

Who, having exchanged their full powers, have agreed upon the following articles:

Art 1. H.M. the Emperor of the French, King of Italy, shall retain and maintain in his service four regiments of Swiss troops, forming in total 12,000 men, less general staff.

Art 2. Each regiment shall be composed with a general staff, three field battalions, a demi-battalion for a depot, and a single artillery company.

Art 3. Each field battalion shall have six companies of 140 men each, organized such that there be one grenadier, one voltigeur and four fusilier companies. Each depot battalion shall have three companies of fusiliers with the same number of men.

Art 4. The organization of these regiments, battalions and companies shall be the same as that of the French troops.

Art 5. Conforming to the preceding article, the general staff of each regiment shall be organized in the following manner.

1 Colonel
1 Major
3 Chefs de bataillon
4 Adjutants-major
1 Quartier-maître
1 Paymaster
1 Adjudant-major, capitaine d'habillement
   (captain of uniforms)
1 Chaplain
1 Minister
1 Judge
1 Chirurgien major
3 Chirurgien aides-major
4 Chirurgien sous-aides
8 Adjudant sous-officiers (adjudant
   noncommissioned officers)
1 Music master
7 Musicians
1 Provost
1 Master Tailor
1 Master Armorer
1 Master Cobbler
<u>1</u> Master Gaitermaker
45 Total

Each company shall be organized as follows:

1 Capitaine
1 Lieutenant
1 Sous-lieutenant
1 Sergeant-major
4 Sergeants
1 Caporal-fourrier
8 Corporals
121 Fusiliers, grenadiers, or voltigeurs
<u>2</u> Drummers
140 Total

The artillery company attached to each regiment shall be organized as follows:

> 1 Lieutenant
> 1 Sous-lieutenant
> 3 Sergeants
> 3 Corporals
> 20 Gunners
> 2 Artisans
> <u>40</u> Train soldiers
> 70 Total

Art 6. The pay, the salaries, the funds of the four regiments shall be established and paid on the same footing as those of the French line infantry.

The military members of this corps of troops shall have the same rights as French military veterans to retirement pension providing they meet the requirements set by French law for time in service or have received wounds in the service of France; they shall participate in all the advantages accorded to the French troops.

Service pre-dating the Capitulation of 27 September, 1803, shall be counted towards retirement, if rendered in the service of pre-Revolutionary France or countries annexed into the territory of the Empire.

Art 7. The officers and non-commissioned officers, who find themselves without positions after the new organization of the four regiments shall be maintained in the service of France, retaining their salary until returned to active duty. They shall remain with their unit and continue service until they can be moved into a vacant billet commensurate with their pay grade or take their retirements which is their right.

Art 8. The men who are admitted into these regiments must be of Swiss origin, of the age 20 to 40, and a height of at least 1.678 meters (5'5") and having no infirmity: however, the men necessary to form the voltigeur companies may be shorter, but they must be no less than 1.556 meters (5'1") tall. These men shall contract to serve with fidelity during the four years of service to H.M. the Emperor Napoleon and his heirs.

Military leave will be granted four times a year, and as often as possible during the first month of each trimester, to the men whose enlistment shall expire in the following quarter.

Art 9. Replacements of men in these regiments shall be provided for in the following manner:

Dated from the signing of this capitulation, the Swiss government shall be obliged to furnish a fixed number of 2,000 men each year as replacement for those killed in service or those who retire for reasons of wounds, infirmity, war or long service contracts, or those, who by reason of the termination of their enlistment wish an absolute discharge.

In the case of war in Italy or Germany, they shall provide each year 1,000 additional men as an extraordinary war draft. Switzerland shall furnish each three months 250 men; the first draft to arrive three months after the notification of a state of war is communicated to Switzerland by the French government. This draft shall continue until the conclusion of peace.

The Swiss government shall engage to deliver to the replacement depots all the men it is required to furnish. The depots shall be placed near the Swiss frontiers.

The colonel general shall determine in which corps or which battalion these annual replacements shall be placed.

It is, therefore, no departure from these articles that the Swiss have contracted to furnish 3,160 men on 1 January 1812 and 500 men on 1 February and 1 March following, conforming to the determination of the Diet of 11 July 1811. These men who have not yet been sent shall be sent to the depots by the signing of this capitulation.

Art 10. The Swiss government, independently of the number of men it is to furnish each year for the maintenance of these four regiments in the service of France, shall be obliged to replace at its own expense all deserters, in the quantities which shall be indicated to them. They shall not be obligated to replace other than those who desert during the first two years of enlistment, upon entering to fill the engagement expressed in the following article.

Art 11. The Swiss government shall not engage to have any regiment in the service of any power other than France, to recall all Swiss who are serving abroad, and to employ, to cause them to decide to return to their country, all the means of persuasion and authority which are in their power.

Art 12. The recruitment shall be conducted by the Swiss Confederation. The officers, non-commissioned officers and soldiers of these regiments may be employed from time to time by the Cantonial governments, when those governments judge that this will be useful to the success of recruiting; the soldiers absent on six months furlough who are so employed shall be reported when so assigned.

Art 13. For discharge from the initial cost of recruitment and for the cost of passage of the 2,000 men which the Swiss government has engaged to furnish annually, and the additional 1,000 men they are obligated to provide in the case of war in Italy and Germany, as provided for in Article 9, there shall be placed at the disposition of the Swiss government the sum of 130 francs per man, which shall be taken from the fixed recruitment fund of 180 francs per man.

The Swiss shall receive in advance and every four months a third of the sum accorded by H.M. for the annual recruiting of Swiss troops.

The funds for the extraordinary draft shall be equally furnished in advance.

The 50 francs per man which form the balance of this fund shall be reserves held by France to be employed at the first placement of men and their outfitting with small equipment, according to the regulations established for French recruits.

There shall be nothing allocated for the engagement and the passage funds of men who for infirmities or other valid motives are refused after their arrivals at the depots or who do not appear because of desertion or other motive.

There shall be nothing allocated for the replacements of men who have deserted their flags and the Swiss government shall be required to provide from its own funds.

The recruits shall date, for their length of service, from the day of their enlistment, but they shall not include for pay purposes the day they arrived at the recruiting depot.

The re-enlistment funds shall continue to be administered by the regimental councils. These re-enlistments shall not count as part of the annual number of men which the Swiss have engaged to furnish according to Article 8 of this capitulation.

There shall be allocated to these councils, for each man who re-enlists a sum as follows:

100 francs for 2 years
200 francs for 4 years
300 francs for 6 years
400 francs for 8 years

Art 14. There shall be allotted each year two leaves of 6 months among the non-commissioned officers and soldiers of each company and one 6 month leave for the officers.

Art 15. A battalion composed of four companies of grenadiers taken by detachment from the different Swiss regiments, as well as the officers necessary from the general staff, shall be admitted as part of the Imperial Guard, once H.M. has determined the time and relative dispositions.

Art 16. The office of colonel general of the Swiss is to be retained. This superior officer shall command the Swiss troops in Paris and shall have supervision of the rest; he is named by H.M. the Emperor.

The colonel general shall receive the administrative regulations, service regulations, compatibility regulations and execute all the directives.

There shall be, in addition, two Swiss brigadier generals to oversee training, service, administration, and the discipline in the four regiments.

Art 17. The three field battalions of each regiment shall be commanded by the colonel. The depot battalion will be commanded by the major.

Art 18. The brigadier generals, the colonels, the chefs de bataillon and the majors shall be nominated by H.M. the Emperor. He shall arrange in his service those individuals, favoring Swiss officers, which he judges the most worthy by their time in service.

Art 19. The captains, lieutenants and sous-lieutenants of grenadier companies shall be chosen by H.M. the Emperor, on the recommendation of the colonel general, from amongst the officers of the same grade of the regiments from which they are part.

Art 20. Promotion to the grade of captain and lieutenant shall be made in the regiments when a vacancy exists by members of that regiment; promotions shall be given by seniority by H.M., on the recommendation of the colonel general: recommendations shall be presented to the colonel general by the captains of each company and those of whom are chosen from among the non-commissioned officers of the regiment of which they belong.

The other part shall be taken from the cantons which do not have a proportional number to those of the soldiers who they must furnish and they shall be presented to the colonel general by the Swiss government in the name of the cantonal governments.

Art 21. H.M. the Emperor shall name, equally, upon the recommendation of the colonel of each regiment the following, approved and presented by the colonel general: the adjutant-majors, the standard bearers, the chaplains, the ministers, the judges and the surgeons. The judge shall rank as a captain; the standard bearer as a non-commissioned officer.

Art 22. The adjutant non-commissioned officers, the drum major, the drum corporal and provost of each regiment shall be named by the colonel upon the recommendation by their chef de bataillon.

Art 23. The administrative council of each regiment and that of the grenadier battalion which becomes part of the Imperial Guard shall be composed according to the regulations established on the same subject in the French army.

Art 24. The Swiss troops in the employ of France shall only be employed in Europe or the islands which are part of it.

Art 25. They shall retain the liberty to exercise their religion and be judged by their own laws and those who breach discipline shall be tried only in Swiss military tribunals, no matter what the case.

Art 26. The Swiss troops shall be assimilated, with regard to rank and required service, in the same state and regulations that re-adopted for the French troops, except as stipulated in Article 24.

Art 27. There shall be admitted to the Ecole Polytechnique of France, twenty young men on the recommendation of the Swiss Landamman after they have taken the prerequisite examinations required by law.

Art 28. The Swiss officers shall be rendered all charges and military dignities that exist in France.

Art 29. The seniority of the Swiss regiments shall be after that of the French regiments. Their seniority among those foreign regiments in the service of France shall be based upon their date of organization.

Art 30. If unforeseen circumstances should render it necessary to disband the Swiss regiments in totality or in part before the expiration of this convention, or if at the end time, the French government refuses to renew it, the officers, non-commissioned officers, and soldiers who comprise these regiments shall receive a discharge commensurate to their years of service and rank held.

Art 31. In the case where Switzerland finds itself, as a result of war, in imminent peril, H.M. the Emperor engages himself to send to the assistance of Switzerland, upon formal request of the Helvetic Diet and within ten days after such request, part or all of these regiments as the circumstances demand.

In this case the appointments, the pay, the travel allowances and the transport shall be at the expense of the requesting power.

Art 32. The military capitulation of 1803 is abrogated by the present capitulation, which shall last for 25 years and the contracting powers may after this period continue the agreement or renounce it.

In trust of which, we, envoy extraordinaire and a minister plenipotentiary of H.M. the Emperor of the French, etc., and we, plenipotentiary commissioners of the Swiss Confederation, have signed the present capitulation. Ratifications shall be exchanged in Paris in the space of twenty days or sooner if possible.

Made in duplicate between us in Berne on 28 March, 1812.

The Convention Concluded Between France and Saxony
25 February 1812
Dresden

Art 1. The 5th, 10th and 11th Infantry Regiments of the Duchy of Warsaw, each having four battalions of six companies each, shall be brought, without delay to a strength of 140 men per company.

   To render these regiments available in their entirety, there shall be added to each regiment a twenty-fifth company or a depot company, which shall have 140 men and be raised in the shortest time.

Art 2. The other regiments of the Duchy of Warsaw (not including those presently in Spain) shall be augmented by such means that, other than the depot companies, the companies shall be raised from 140 to 160 men per company.

Art 3. All the companies, without exception, of each of the fifteen cavalry regiments of the Duchy shall also be raised from 100 horses, their actual complement, to 120 men and 120 horses.

Art 4. His Majesty, the Emperor and King, takes as his expense: 1.) the expense of the first act, the pay and the organization of these 20 men to augment the complement of 140 men per company, 2.) the expense of the purchase of the horses, the first clothing issue, equipment and harness, the pay and organization of the 20 augmenting men for the raising of the complement from 100 men and 100 horses per company.

Art 5. If the effective force of said companies should be found to be below the old complement, raised by the stipulations above to 160 men per infantry company and 120 men and 120 horses per cavalry company, His Majesty, the Emperor and King, does not intend to cover the expenses necessary to raise those men necessary to meet the old complement. He will, however, pay for the raising of the 141st infantryman and the 101st cavalry man per company.

Art 6. Immediately after the signing of this convention the orders shall be given by the government of the King for the raising of the men and the purchase of the necessary horses, as well as the equipment and clothing, equipment and harnesses.

Art 7. A French commissioner shall be sent to those places with the funds necessary to pay for the purchase of the horses and the expenses of clothing, equipment and harnesses.

   The present convention shall be ratified and the ratifications shall be exchanged in Paris in the period of one month, or sooner if possible.

Signed: Jean-Charles, Baron de Serra
Signed: Frederick-Chretieu-Louis von
Sneft Pilasch

The Treaty Between Austria and France
14 March 1812

Art 1. Austria shall not keep the assistance stipulated by Article 4 of this treaty obvious in any war that France shall undertake, or against England or south of the Pyrenees.

Art 2. If war should break out between France and Russia, Austria shall furnish said assistance stipulated in Articles 4 and 5 of this treaty. The regiments which will comprise this assistance shall march and canton themselves in such a manner so as to be able to move in at least fifteen days to Lemberg after 1 May.

    Said corps shall have a double provisionment of artillery munitions as well as the military equipage necessary to transport twenty days of provisions.

Art 3. On his side the Emperor of the French shall make all dispositions necessary to operate against Russia, in the same period, with all the forces disposable.

Art 4. The corps of troops furnished by his majesty, the Emperor of Austria, shall be formed in three divisions of infantry and one division of cavalry, commanded by an Austrian General, at the choice of the Emperor of Austria.

    This force shall act on the line which shall be prescribed by His Majesty, the Emperor of the French, and act under his immediate orders.

    This force shall never be divided and shall always act as a separate and distinct corps.

    This force shall be provided for, in the enemy country, in the same manner as a French army corps, with nothing changed with regard to the regimes and usages established by Austrian military regulations for the nourishment of the troops.

    The trophies and booty that shall be taken from the enemy shall belong to the Austrian forces.

Art 5. In the case where, as a result of the war between France and Russia, the Kingdom of Poland shall come to be reestablished, His Majesty, the Emperor of the French, gives special guarantees, as she presently guarantees to Austria, the possession of Galacia.

    If, in the aforementioned case, Austria should choose to cede, for the purpose of reunification to the Kingdom of Poland, a part of Galacia, in exchange for the provinces of Illyria, His Majesty the Emperor of France, engages himself to consent to the exchange. The part of Galacia to be ceded shall be determined on the basis of population, extent of territory, revenues, of the sort which the estimation of two objects of exchange shall not be regulated by the extent of territory only, but by their real value.

Art 6. In the case of a happy outcome of the war, His Majesty, the Emperor of the French, engages himself to procure for His Majesty, the Emperor of Austria, the indemnities and territories, not solely to compensate for the sacrifices and expenses of cooperation with His Majesty in the war, but which will form a monument to the intimate and durable union which exists between the two sovereigns.

Art 7. If, in hatred of the bonds and engagements contracted by Austria towards France, should be menaced by Russia, His Majesty, the Emperor of the French, shall regard this attack as an attack directed against himself and shall immediately commence hostilities.

Art 8. The Ottoman Empire shall be invited to enter into a treaty of alliance on this day.

Art 9. The articles of this treaty shall remain secret between the two powers.

Art 10. It shall have the same force as if it were inserted in the treaty of alliance, and it shall be ratified and those ratifications exchanged in the same manner and at the same time as said treaty of alliance.

Made and signed in Paris
14 March 1812

The Convention of Tauroggen

Art 1. The Prussian Corps shall occupy the interior of the Prussian territory along the line from the frontier near Memel and Nimmerstat to the route from Woinuta to Tilsit. From Tilsit, the route which passes by Schillapischkew and Melankew to Lobiau and includes the villages and cities it touches, shall determine the extent of the country the aforementioned Prussian corps may occupy.

The Prussian troops, it is understood, may come and go along those aforementioned routes, but they may not take their quarters in this area.

Art 2. The Prussians shall remain neutral in the area designated in Article 1 until the arrival of orders from His Majesty, the King of Prussia. In case of orders to rejoin the French, the Prussians shall not engage in combat with the Russians for the space of one month from this date.

Art 3. In case of His Majesty, the King of Prussia, or His Majesty, the Emperor of Russia, refusing to ratify this convention, the Prussian corps shall be free to carry itself where the orders of their king call them.

Art 4. The Russians will surrender to the Prussians all stragglers which they find along the main route to Mittau and equally all military equipment found there. With regard to the branch of supply and train of the aforementioned corps, all which composes it, shall cross without obstacles through the Russian lines to rejoin the Prussian Corps.

Art 5. In the event of orders from Lieutenant General Yorck reaching Lieutenant General Massenbach, the troops under his command shall be included in this convention.

Art 6. All the prisoners captured by the Russians commanded by Major General Diebitsch from those commanded by General Massenbach, shall be equally included in this convention.

Art 7. The Prussian corps shall conserve the right to concert all that is relative to its provisionment with the provincial regencies of Prussia. This case is not excepted when those provinces are occupied by Russian forces.

The aforementioned convention has been dispatched in duplicate and carries the signature and seal of the undersigned.

Made in the Poschernu Mill on 18–30 December 1812.

Signed: Von Yorck
Lieutenant General in service of Prussia

Von Diebitsch
Major General in service of Russia

Appendix II

Orders of Battle 1810–1811

French Garrisons in Germany
1 January 1811

City and commander	Garrison during 1810	Garrison during 1811
Danzig General Rapp	French Artillery (2 coys +)	Same as 1810 French (270 men)
	Saxon 2 Battalions & Artillery Det.	Allies (3,246)
	Polish 10th Infantry (1) 11th Infantry (2) Artillery Det. (2,803)	
Stettin General Liebert	French 33rd Line (1) 7th Foot Artillery (2 coys)	Same as 1810 (354)
	Saxon 1 Infantry Battalion Artillery Det.	Allies (1,369)
	Polish 10th Infantry (1) Artillery Det. (1,158)	
Kustrin General Fornier-d'Albe	French 1 Bataillon de march Artisan Det. (949)	French 1 Foot Artillery Coy. Artisan Det. (129)
	Polish 5th Infantry (2) (1,043)	Same as 1810 (1,302)
Glogau General Rheinwald (Replaced 6/22/10) General De Beaupre	French Foot Artillery Coy. Artisan Coy. (89)	Same as 1810 (132)
	Saxon	Same as 1810

City and commander	Garrison during 1810	Garrison during 1811
	3 Battalions—1 of recruits. (1,416)	plus 1 Polish Uhlan Sqn. (1,627)
Magdeburg General Michaut	French Foot Artillery Coy. Det. Regiment de Prusse (164)	French 2 Foot Artillery Coys. (154)
	Westphalian Artillery, sappers, gendarmes & veterans (397 men)	Same as 1810

French Garrisons in Germany
2 April 1811 to 31 January 1812

City and General	Garrison	Strength
Danzig	French 9th Foot Artillery (2 coys) Polish 10th Infantry Regiment (3) 11th Infantry Regiment (3) 9th Polish Uhlan Regiment (3) Artillery Company Saxon von Rechten Infantry Regiment (2) Artillery Company Bavarian 2 Infantry Battalions Württemberg 1 Infantry Battalion	13,557
	Permanent Garrison: 2nd Chasseur à Cheval Regiment 5th Foot Artillery (4 coys) Sappers, Miners, Pontooneers	1,817
Settin General Liebert	French 33rd Line Regiment (1 coy) 7th Foot Artillery (2 coys) Berg	2,808

City and General	Garrison	Strength
	2nd Infantry Regiment (2)	
	3rd Infantry Regiment (2)	
	Artillery Company	
	Train Company	
	Permanent Garrison:	6,585
	85th Line Regiment	
	108th Line Regiment	
	Det. 7th Hussar Regiment	
	Train & Artillery	
Kustrin	French	1,089
General Teste	7th Foot Artillery (1 coy)	
	Berg	
	1st Infantry Regiment (2)	
	Regiment des Princes (1)	
	Permanent Garrison:	2,444
	5th Polish Infantry Regiment (3)	
	7th Hussar Regiment (4)	
Glogau	French	2,861
General de Beaupre	7th Foot Artillery (1 coy)	
	Saxon	
	von Low Infantry Regiment (2)	
	Artillery Company	
	Wurzburg Infantry Regiment (1)	
	7th Polish Uhlan Regiment (1)	

Development of the 1st Corps
(Corps d'Observation d'Elbe)

	6/11	9/5/11	1/31/12
1st Division: General Morand	3 Bn	5 Bn	5 Bn
13th Légère Regiment	3	5	5
17th Line Regiment	3	5	5
30th Line Regiment	3	5	5
2nd Baden Line Regiment	0	0	2
2nd Division: General Friant			
15th Légère Regiment	3	4	5
33rd Line Regiment	3	5	5
48th Line Regiment	3	5	5
Joseph Napoleon Regiment	0	0	2

	6/11	9/5/11	1/31/12
3rd Division: General Gudin			
7th Légère Regiment	3	5	5
12th Line Regiment	3	5	5
21st Line Regiment	3	5	5
127th Line Regiment	0	0	2
4th Division: General Dessaix			
33rd Légère Regiment	3	4	5
85th Line Regiment	3	5	5
108th Line Regiment	3	5	5
Hesse-Darmstadt Regiment	0	0	2
5th Division: General Compans			
25th Line Regiment	0	4	5
57th Line Regiment	0	5	5
61st Line Regiment	0	5	5
111th Line Regiment	0	5	5
Light Cavalry:			
2nd Chasseur à Cheval Regiment	4 Sqn	4 Sqn	4 Sqn
9th Polish Uhlan Regiment	4	4	4
1st Chasseur à Cheval Regiment	4	4	4
3rd Chasseur à Cheval Regiment	4	4	4

Development of the French Army
1811–1812

Corps d'Observation du Rhin, 1 July 1811
1st Division
  Brigade
    24th Légère Regiment (4)
    4th Regiment (4)
  Brigade
    19th Regiment (4)
    123rd Regiment (4)
  Brigade
    1st Portuguese Regiment (2)
    4th Swiss Regiment (2)
2nd Division
  Brigade
    26th Légère Regiment (4)
    72nd Line Regiment (4)

Brigade
    46th Line Regiment (4)
    126th Regiment (4)
Brigade
    2nd Portuguese Regiment (2)
    Illyrian Regiment (20
3rd Division
Brigade
    18th Line Regiment (4)
    93rd Line Regiment (4)
Brigade
    56th Line Regiment (4)
    124th Line Regiment (4)
Brigade
    Joseph Napoleon Regiment (2)
    3rd Swiss Regiment (2)
4th Division
Brigade
    Tirailleurs du Po and Corsica (2)
    2nd Line Regiment (4)
Brigade
    37th Line Regiment (4)
    125th Regiment (4)
Brigade
    2nd Swiss Regiment (4)
    3rd Portuguese Regiment (2)

Corps d'Observation des Côtes de l'Ocean, 2 January 1812
(Formerly the Corps d'Observation du Rhin)
1st Division
    24th Légère Regiment (4)
    46th Regiment (4)
    72nd Regiment (4)
    126th Regiment (3)
    1st Portuguese Regiment (2)
2nd Division
    4th Line Regiment (4)
    18th Line Regiment (4)
    93rd Line Regiment
    2nd Portuguese Regiment (2)
    Illyrian Regiment (4)
3rd Division
    29th Légère Regiment (4)

44th Line Regiment (4)
Provisional Regiment of Bolougne (2)
125th Line Regiment (3)
129th Line Regiment (2)

Corps d'Observation d'Italie, 20 April 1811
1st Division: General Delzons
    8th Légère Regiment (2)
    1st Provisional Croatian Regiment (2)
    84th Line Regiment (3)
    92nd Line Regiment (3)
2nd Division: General Broussier
    9th Line Regiment (4)
    13th Line Regiment (4)
    29th Line Regiment (4)
    112th Line Regiment (4)
    52nd Line Regiment (4)
    53rd Line Regiment (4)
    35th Line Regiment (4)
    106th Line Regiment (4)
3rd Division: General Partoneaux
    1st Line Regiment (3)
    62nd Line Regiment (3)
    101st Line Regiment (3)
    Joseph Napoleon Regiment (2)
4th Division: General Fontanelli
    Italian Regiments (15 battalions)
Guard: General Pino
    6 Battalions
    2 Squadrons
Light Cavalry Division: General Grouchy
  1st Brigade
    6th Hussar Regiment
    8th Chasseur à Cheval Regiment
  2nd Brigade
    6th Chasseur à Cheval Regiment
    25th Chasseur à Cheval Regiment
  3rd Brigade
    4th Chasseur à Cheval Regiment
    9th Chasseur à Cheval Regiment
  Reserve:
    3 French Dragoon Regiments
    1 Italian Dragoon Regiment

Artillery:
    Regimental guns—40 guns
    Foot Artillery—60 guns
    Horse Artillery—40 guns
Military Equipage:
    9th Battalion

Corps d'Observation d'Italie, 1 July 1811
1st Division: General Delzons
    8th Légère Regiment (2)
    1st Provisional Croatian Regiment (2)
    84th Line Regiment (4)
    92nd Line Regiment (4)
2nd Division: General Broussier
    9th Line Regiment (3)
    13th Line Regiment (3)
    53rd Line Regiment (3)
    106th Line Regiment (4)
3rd Division:
    35th Line Regiment (3)
    Joseph Napoleon Regiment (2)
    29th Line Regiment (2)
    112th Line Regiment (2)
    Illyrian Regiment (2)

Corps d'Observation d'Italie, 2 January 1812
1st Division: General Delzons
    8th Légère Regiment (2)
    1st Provisional Croatian Regiment (2)
    84th Line Regiment (4)
    92nd Line Regiment (4)
2nd Division: General Broussier
    18th Légère Regiment (2)
    9th Line Regiment (4)
    35th Line Regiment (4)
    53rd Line Regiment (4)
    Joseph Napoleon Regiment (2)
3rd Division
    3rd Italian Légère Regiment (4)
    Dalmatian Regiment (3)
    2nd Italian Line Regiment (3)
    3rd Italian Line Regiment (4)
    5th Italian Line Regiment (2)

Light Cavalry Division: General Grouchy
  1st Brigade
    6th Hussar Regiment
    8th Chasseur à Cheval Regiment
  2nd Brigade
    6th Chasseur à Cheval Regiment
    25th Chasseur à Cheval Regiment
  3rd Brigade
    4th Chasseur à Cheval Regiment
    9th Chasseur à Cheval Regiment
  Reserve:
    7th Dragoon Regiment
    23rd Dragoon Regiment
    28th Dragoon Regiment
    30th Dragoon Regiment
Italian Guard

Artillery, Engineers, and Military Equipage

Organization of the
French Heavy Cavalry
1811

	17 April 1811	25 December 1811	15 February 1812
1st Division	2nd Cuirassiers 3rd Cuirassiers 9th Cuirassiers 12th Cuirassiers	2nd Cuirassiers 3rd Cuirassiers 9th Cuirassiers	Assigned to I Corps
2nd Division	5th Cuirassiers 8th Cuirassiers 10th Cuirassiers 11th Cuirassiers	5th Cuirassiers 8th Cuirassiers 10th Cuirassiers	Assigned to II Corps
3rd Division	4th Cuirassiers 6th Cuirassiers 7th Cuirassiers 11th Cuirassiers	4th Cuirassiers 6th Cuirassiers 7th Cuirassiers	Assigned to III Corps
4th Division	1st Carabiniers 2nd Carabiniers 1st Cuirassiers	1st Carabiniers 2nd Carabiniers 1st Cuirassiers	
5th Division	Not formed	6th Cuirassiers 11th Cuirassiers 12th Cuirassiers	

Organization of the French Light Cavalry
25 December 1811

1st Brigade:
  2nd Chasseur à Cheval Regiment
  9th Polish Uhlan Regiment
2nd Brigade:
  1st Chasseur à Cheval Regiment
  3rd Chasseur à Cheval Regiment
3rd Brigade:
  7th Hussar Regiment
  9th Chevauléger Regiment
4th Brigade:
  8th Hussar Regiment
  7th Chasseur à Cheval Regiment
5th Brigade:
  23rd Chasseur à Cheval Regiment
  24th Chasseur à Cheval Regiment
6th Brigade:
  7th Chasseur à Cheval Regiment
  20th Chasseur à Cheval Regiment
  8th Chevauléger Regiment
7th Brigade:
  11th Chasseur à Cheval Regiment
  12th Chasseur à Cheval Regiment
8th Brigade:
  5th Hussar Regiment
  9th Hussar Regiment
9th Brigade:
  11th Hussar Regiment
  6th Chevauléger Regiment
10th Brigade:
  6th Chasseur à Cheval Regiment
  25th Chasseur à Cheval Regiment
11th Brigade:
  6th Hussar Regiment
  8th Chasseur à Cheval Regiment
12th Brigade:
  9th Chasseur à Cheval Regiment
  10th Chasseur à Cheval Regiment
13th Brigade:
  2nd Italian Chasseur à Cheval Regiment
  3rd Italian Chasseur à Cheval Regiment

French Divisional Artillery Equipment
November 1811

Artillery Pieces

Division	12pdrs	Guns 6pdrs	3pdrs	Howitzers 6.33″	5.5″	Total
1st Division	—	10	—	—	4	14
2nd Division	—	10	—	—	4	14
3rd Division	—	10	—	—	4	14
4th Division	—	10	—	—	4	14
5th Division	—	10	—	—	4	14
Heavy Cavalry	—	8	—	—	4	12
Reserve	12	—	—	4	—	16
Grand Park	—	—	—	—	—	0

Space Carriages

Division	12pdrs	Guns 6pdrs	3pdrs	Howitzers 6.33″	5.5″
1st Division	—	1	1	—	—
2nd Division	—	1	1	—	—
3rd Division	—	1	1	—	—
4th Division	—	1	1	—	—
5th Division	—	1	1	—	—
Heavy Cavalry	—	2	—	—	1
Reserve	2	—	—	1	—
Grand Park	—	3	5	—	4

Caissons

Division	12pdrs	Guns 6pdrs	3pdrs	Howitzers 6.33″	5.5″
1st Division	—	15	—	—	8
2nd Division	—	15	—	—	8
3rd Division	—	15	—	—	8
4th Division	—	15	—	—	8
5th Division	—	15	—	—	8
Heavy Cavalry	—	24	—	—	16
Reserve	36	—	—	12	—
Grand Park	36	75	10	12	40

Division	Infantry caissons	Pyrotechnic caissons	Tool wagons	Munition wagons	Field forges
1st Division	15	—	—	4	2
2nd Division	15	—	—	4	2
3rd Division	15	—	—	4	2
4th Division	15	—	—	4	2
5th Division	20	—	—	4	2
Heavy Cavalry	—	—	—	4	2
Reserve	—	—	—	4	2
Grand Park	84	2	2	12	2

Munitions

Division	12pdrs	Ball 6pdrs	3pdrs	Howitzers 6.33″	Shell 5.5″
1st Division	—	1706	—	—	435
2nd Division	—	1899	—	—	576
3rd Division	—	1905	—	—	600
4th Division	—	1812	—	—	636
5th Division	—	1886	—	—	584
Heavy Cavalry	—	2936	—	—	1162
Reserve	2429	—	—	612	—
Grand Park	2134	8631	2220	576	2728

Division	12pdrs	6pdrs	Cannister 3pdrs	6.33″	5.5″
1st Division	—	351	—	—	30
2nd Division	—	405	—	—	23
3rd Division	—	391	—	—	24
4th Division	—	345	—	—	24
5th Division	—	400	—	—	24
Heavy Cavalry	—	620	—	—	63
Reserve	516	—	—	58	—
Grand Park	522	1876	300	45	—

Division	Infantry cartridges	Loose musket balls
1st Division	291,520	15,432
2nd Division	240,145	14,286
3rd Division	262,145	7,951
4th Division	274,060	24,000
5th Division	316,220	29,100
Heavy Cavalry	—	—
Reserve	—	—
Grand Park	1,497,880	116,946

French Regimental Artillery Material
November 1811

	3pdr guns	3pdr caissons	Infantry caissons	Field forges
1st Division				
13th Légère	4	6	5	1
17th Line	4	6	5	1
30th Line	4	6	5	1
2nd Division				
15th Légère	4	6	5	1
33rd Line	4	6	5	1
48th Line	4	6	5	1
3rd Division				
7th Légère	4	6	5	1
12th Line	4	6	5	1
21st Line	4	6	5	1
4th Division				
33rd Légère	4	6	5	1
85th Line	4	6	5	1
108th Line	4	6	5	1
5th Division				
25th Line	4	6	5	1
51st Line	4	6	5	1
61st Line	4	6	5	1
111th Line	4	6	5	1

	3pdr ball cartridges	3pdr cannister	Infantry cartridges	Ambulances	Wagons
1st Division					
13th Légère	1,263	199	84,720	1	6
17th Line	1,128	201	84,240	1	6
30th Line	1,243	218	87,120	1	6
2nd Division					
15th Légère	1,406	248	78,980	1	6
33rd Line	1,180	177	85,230	1	6
48th Line	1,265	206	81,120	1	6
3rd Division					
7th Légère	1,266	193	84,040	1	6
12th Line	1,140	183	81,870	1	6
21st Line	1,160	174	71,462	1	6
4th Division					
33rd Légère	1,496	232	64,146	1	6
85th Line	1,028	171	86,040	1	6
108th Line	930	235	77,555	1	6
5th Division					
25th Line	916	248	68,050	1	6
51st Line	970	264	77,610	1	6
61st Line	1,026	214	82,340	1	6
111th Line	1,087	238	68,625	1	6

Siege Provisions at Danzig

Siege provisions	Desired quantity	Quantity on hand 1 October 1813
Flour	5,000 metric cwt	0 metric cwt
Grain	20,000	21,885
Rye	8,100	3,465
Biscuit Rations	611,173 rations	611,173 rations
Rice	1,915 metric cwt	499 metric cwt
Dried Vegetables	1,475	813
Salt	1,278	1,273
Fresh Meat	7,237	0
Salted Beef	2,250	194
Salted Lard	1,800	0
Cheese	1,800	0
Edible Oil	108	0
Hay	79,689	7,437
Straw	22,850	11,798
Oatmeal	612,000 decaliters	254,368 decaliters
Wine	720,000 liters	67,921 liters
Brandy	230,400	132,616
Vinegar	100,800	21,160
Firewood	42,750 cubic meters	160 cubic meters
Candlesticks	576 metric cwt	446 metric cwt
Flammable Oil	54	2
Reserve magazine		
Wheat	50,000 metric cwt	0 metric cwt
Rye	50,000	0
Rice	2,000	0
Dried Vegetables	2,000	0

Contingents to be Provided by the Confederation of the Rhine

Name of the state	Total	Already provided & in Spain or Germany	Remainder to be furnished
Bavaria	30,000	2,278	27,727
Saxony	20,000	3,098	16,902
Westphalia	25,000	4,064	20,936
Würtemburg	12,000	1,200	10,800
Baden	8,000	4,060	3,940
Cleve-Berg	7,000	3,423	3,577
Hesse-Darmstadt	4,000	3,118	882
Wurzburg	2,000	768	1,232
Frankfurt	2,800	586	2,214
Nassau	3,781	3,259	522
Saxe-Weimar, Saxe-Gotha Saxe-Meiningen, Saxe-Hildburghausen & Saxe-Coburg-Saalfeld	2,800	—	2,800
Anhalt-Dessau, Anhalt-Bamburg, & Anhalt-Coethen	862	—	862
Anhalt-Detmold & Lippe-Schaumburg	840	—	840
Schwarzburg-Sonderhaus Schwarzburg-Rudolstadt	650	—	650
Reuss-Greitz, Reuss-Sohleiz, Reuss-Ebersdorf & Reuss-Lobenstein	459	—	459
Mecklenburg-Schwerin	1,900	—	1,900
Mecklenburg-Strelitz	400	—	400

Russian Provision Depots and Commissaries
August 1811

Provisions Service Section: St. Petersburg

Commissions for provision depots located in:

St. Petersburg	Krementchug
Orenburg	Kiev
Tobolsk	Hrothirbek
Moscow	Vitebsk
Jassy (Temporary for the Army	Riga
of Moldavia)	Abö

Commissaries:

Vyburg	Revel
Novgorod	Mohilev
Kazan	Omsk
Theodosie	Fort West-Kamenogorskaïa
Irkoutsk	Iakoutsk
Okhotsk	Nijine-Kamtchatsk
Astrakhan	Fortress of St. Dimitri
Rostovsky	

Principal provisions magazines:

Uleaborg	Vasa	Abö
Sveaborg	Revel	Vyborg
Riga	Dinaburg	Chavli
Vilna	Slonim	Helsingfors
Disna	Pinsk	Frederikshamm
Bobruisk	Mozyr	St. Petersburg
Kiev	Jitomir	Brest-Litovsk
Kovel	Doubno	Staro-Constantinov
Ostrog	Zaslavl	

Minor provisions magazines:

Hamlekarlebi	Newkarlebi	Christianstadt
Biörnborg	Raumö	Nystad
Aland Island	Hangö	Borgö
Salo Fortress	Poïo	Tvastehus
Kymmenegard	Nyslott	Wilmanstrand
Kexholm	Weissenberg	Novaïa-Ladoga
Kronstadt	Narva	Louga
Hapsal	Derpt	Pernau
Arensburg	Mitau	Toukoum
Libau	Baousk	Jakobstadt

Minor provision magazines (cont.):

Pskof	Porkhovq	Veliki-Louki
Velij	Souraj	Vitebsk
Polotsk	Breslavl	Chklov
Mohilev	Stary-Bykhov	Novaïa-Bielitsa
Mstislavl	Telchi	Jurburg
Kovno	Orany	Grodno
Rojanka	Lida	Velikaïa-Brestovitsa
Novgroudok	Proujany	Volkovisk
Vyssoko-Litovsk	Kobrin	Bielostok
Briansk	Bielsk	Sokolka
Droguitchin	Minsk	Borissov
Igoumen	Nesvij	Sloutsk
Vassilkov	Oboukhov	Bielaïa-Tserkov
Bogouslav	Oumane	Zvenigorodka
Iekaterinopol	Lipovetz	Makhnovka
Radomysl	Berditchev	Lioubar
Dombrovitsa	Kovel	Loutsk
Choumsk	Bielgorodka	Laboune
Proskourov	Medjiboj	Khmielnik
Litin	Vinnitsa	Novo-Constantinov
Nemirov	Bratslav	Kamenetz-Podolsky
Balta	Berchad	Olgopol
Ielisavetgrad	Doubrossary	Tirapol
Odessa	Ovidiopol	Otchakov
Kherson	Berislavl	Kinbourgh
Pereskop	Eupatoria	Simferopol
Sebastapol	Ienikale	Karassoubazar
Theodosie	Fangoria	Anapa

Additional handling sights along the Dniester at:

Mohilev	Ataki	Jvanetz
Khotin	Iampol	Soroki
Balta	Rachkov	

Recruit processing Depots:

Government	Depots	Government	Depots
Olonetz:	Kargopol, Olonetz	Iekaterinoslav	Iekaterinoslav
Novgorod:	Korostyn & Starodoub		Ivanovsk
Pskof:	Kholm & Toropetz		Dmitrovsk
Minsk:	Zaslavl & Ivenetz	Kazan	Tetiouchi
Jaroslavl:	Jaroslavl	Tobolsk	Tara

Recruit processing Depots (cont.):

Government	Depots	Government	Depots
Tchernigov:	Gloukhov	Kiev	Bielgorodka
	Novgorod-Sieversky	Smolensk	Kiev
Kherson:	Olviopol &	Moscow	Dmitrov
	Novomirgorod	Orel	Briansk
Slobodas-	Vladimir &	Vladimir	Rosslavl
Ukraine:	Akhtyrka	Orenburg	Oufa
Nijine-	Nijine-Novgorod		
Novgorod:			

Russian Hospitals
1811

City	Capacity	City	Capacity
St. Petersburg	2,550 sick	St. Petersburg	1,840**
Moscow	1,840	Riga	1,220
Slonim	1,220	Georgievsk	610
Oranienbaum	610	Grodno	610
Kamenetz-Podolsky	610	Vilna	610
Odessa	610	Vyborg	610
Kiev	610	Simperopol	610
Frederikshamm	610	Helsingfors	610
Tiflis	610	Azov	610
Revel	610	Kazan	300
Narva	300	Rotchensalm	300
Kuopio	300***	Doubno	300***
Orenburg	300	Kherson	300
Aland Island	300	Stavropol	150***
Minsk	600***	Derpat	150***
Iekaterinograd	150	Vladicavkaz	150
Smolensk	150	Pskov	150
Omsk	150	Bobrouisk	300
Dinaburg	300	Mohilev	300
Triaspol	— (1)	Glousk	300
Arkhangel	200***	Tavastehus	200***
Jassy	3,000(2)	Bender	200(2)
Khotin	150(2)	Kilia	110(2)
Fokchani	700(2)	Craiowa	700(2)

City	Capacity	City	Capacity
Polïechi	1,500(2)	Brailov	3,000(2)
Bucharest	1,000(2)	Special mobile Hospital	3,000(2)

Unless otherwise indicated, these hospitals are assigned to the army.

**   Artillery Hospital
*** Temporary Hospitals
(1) No count set
(2) Army of Moldavia

Assignments of Cossacks
1811

Don Cossacks

In Finland:
Kisselev II Cossack Regiment
Lotchilin Cossack Regiment
Isaeva #2 Cossack Regiment

Along the border from Polangen to the Dniester:
Selivanov Don Cossack Regiment
Popov Cossack Regiment
Platov #4 Don Cossack Regiment
1st Bug Cossack Regiment
2nd Bug Cossack Regiment
3rd Bug Cossack Regiment
Denissov #7 Don Cossack Regiment
Illowaiski #4 Don Cossack Regiment
Illowaiski #7 Don Cossack Regiment
Tcharnusubov #5 Cossack Regiment
Slioussarve #2 Cossack Regiment
Simpheropol Tartar Regiment
Perecop Cossack Regiment

Army of Moldavia:
Andreinov Cossack Regiment
Gardeieff Cossack Regiment
Souline #9 Cossack Regiment

Astakhov #7 Cossack Regiment
Illowaiski #2 Cossack Regiment
Illowaiski #5 Cossack Regiment

Denissov #6 Don Cossack Regiment
Ataman Cossack Regiment
Kutainikov #4 Cossack Regiment
Barbantchikov Cossack Regiment
Melnikov Cossack Regiment
Loukoffkin Cossack Regiment
Sisava Cossack Regiment
Melnikov #3 Cossack Regiment
Isaeva Cossack Regiment
Platov #5 Cossack Regiment
Tchikilev #1 Cossack Regiment
Melentriev #2 Cossack Regiment

In the Caucasus:
Colonial Regiment of Astrakhan
Colonial Regiment of Mozdok
Colonial Regiment of the Volga
Colonial Regiment of Khoper
Colonial Regiment of the Caucasus

Regiments in the Don:
Grekov #8 Cossack Regiment
Apaostolov Cossack Regiment
Pozdiëev Cossack Regiment
Moltchanov #2 Cossack Regiment
Ilyne #1 Cossack Regiment
Petrov #1 Cossack Regiment

Regiments in Georgia:
Denissov #9 Don Cossack Regiment
Ejov #1 Cossack Regiment
Danilov Cossack Regiment
Popov #16 Cossack Regiment

Cossacks in the State of Orenburg:
Orenburg Cossacks
Stavrapol Kalmuck Regiment
1st Teptar Cossack Regiment
2nd Teptar Cossack Regiment
Tcherevkov #2 Don Cossack Regiment

Illowaiski #10 Cossack Regiment
Illowaiski #11 Cossack Regiment
Illowaiski #12 Cossack Regiment
Grekov #8 Don Cossack Regiment
Vlassov #2 Don Cossack Regiment
Pantelev Cossack Regiment
Mikhailov Oral Cossack Regiment
Isaeva #4 Cossack Regiment
1st Orenburg Cossack Regiment
2nd Orenburg Cossack Regiment
Ivanov #2 Cossack Regiment

Voisko of Terek & Kizliar
Voisko Semeïnoïe
Voisko Grebenskoie
Colonial Regiment of Kouban
Mountain Detachment of Mozdok

Baladin Cossack Regiment
Arakantsev Cossack Regiment
Krasnov Cossack Regiment
Perrsianov #1 Cossack Regiment
Karchine #4 Cossack Regiment
Samolov #1 Cossack Regiment

Arguieiev #2 Cossack Regiment
Pozdieiev #8 Cossack Regiment
Bogatchev #1 Cossack Regiment
Cossack Voisko of the Orals

Russian Recruit Depots and the Levy of 1811

Assignment of Depots and Divisions:

Depot	Division	Depot	Division
Viazma	3rd	Zmiev	15th
Toropetz	4th	Olivopol	16th
Kholm	5th	Biely	17th
Kargopol	6th	Konotop	18th
Starodoub	7th	Taganrog	19th
Novomirgorod	8th	Azov	20th
Izioum	9th	Olonetz	21st
Ielisavetgrad	10th	Tchigurin	22nd
Akhtyrka	11th	Elnia	23rd
Roslavl	12th	Novgorod-Sieversky	24th
Ivanovka	13th	Podgoscz	25th
Staraia-Roussa	14th	Romny	26th

Distribution of Recruits of the Levy in the Processing Depots:

1st Line of Depots	Recruits	2nd Line of Depots	Recruits
Kargopol	1,004	Petrozavodsk	2,269
Olonetz	1,215	Novgorod	4,123
Podgodcz	4,029	Tver	4,571
Staraia-Roussa	4,264	Moscow	7,553
Kholm	4,033	Kalouga	6,668
Romny	4,242	Tula	3,694
Toropetz	4,213	Orel	3,526
Beily	4,005	Kursk	3,237
Viazma	4,004	Kharkov	4,469
Elnia	4,235	Iekaterinoslav	3,973
Roslavl	3,975		43,083
Starodoub	4,200		
Novgorod-Sieversky	4,205	General Total	130,635
Konotop	4,242		
Akhtyrka	4,200	To the Jeletz Regiment	535
Zmiev	3,975		
Izioum	4,103	By Regional Governors	
Ivanovka	3,929	Tobolsk	1,540
Taganrog	2,875	Tomsk	1,315
Azov	3,022	Irkoutsk	1,592
Tchiguirin	3,556	Astrakhan	151
Novomirgorod	3,576	Caucasus	228
Ielisavetgrad	3,001	GRAND TOTAL	136,066
Olviopol	3,449		
	87,552		

Shipments of Recruits to the Various Reserve Depots
of the 2nd and 3rd Line
Resulting from the Extraordinary Levys
of 1811

Governments	1st Levy	2nd Levy	3rd Levy	4th Levy	5th Levy	Depot
Archangle	176	352	528	704	881	Petroavodsk
Olonetz	193	387	581	774	968	
Vyborg	185	370	556	741	927	
Total	554	1,009	1,665	2,219	2,776	
Kurland	386	773	1,160	1,546	1,933	Novgorod
Lithuania	527	1,054	1,581	2,108	2,636	
Estonia	205	410	616	821	1,026	
St. Petersburg	365	731	1,097	1,462	1,828	
Novgorod	589	1,178	1,767	2,356	2,945x	
Total	2,072	4,146	6,221	8,293	10,367	
Pskof	608	1,216	1,826	2,433	3,041	Tver
Tver	953	1,906	2,859	3,813	4,766	
Jaroslav	743	1,487	2,231	2,974	3,717	
Total	2,304	4,609	6,915	9,220	11,524	
Vitebsk	702	1,404	2,107	2,809	3,512	Moscow
Moscow	902	1,805	2,708	3,611	4,514	
Vladimir	887	1,764	2,661	3,548	4,435	
Total	2,941	4,963	7,476	9,968	12,461	
Grodno	633	1,267	1,900	2,534	3,168	Kalouga
Vilna	1,006	2,012	3,018	4,025	5,031	
Smolensk	908	1,817	2,727	3,635	4,544	
Kalouga	743	1,487	2,231	2,975	3,718	
Total	3,290	6,586	9,876	13,169	16,461	
Minsk	815	1,630	2,445	3,260	4,075	Tula
Mohilev	758	1,517	2,276	3,035	3,794	
Tula	871	1,742	2,613	3,485	4,356	
Total	2,444	4,889	7,344	7,780	12,225	

Governments	1st Levy	2nd Levy	3rd Levy	4th Levy	5th Levy	Depot
Volhynie	1,039	2,078	3,117	4,156	5,195	Orel
Tchernigov	1,010	2,021	3,032	4,042	5,053	
Orel	960	1,921	2,881	3,842	4,082	
Total	3,009	6,020	9,030	12,040	15,050	
Poltava	1,294	2,588	3,882	5,176	6,470	Kursk
Kursk	1,437	2,287	3,431	4,575	5,718	
Total	2,437	4,875	7,314	9,751	12,188	
Kherson	262	524	786	1,048	1,311	Kharkov
Iekaterinoslav	466	933	1,401	1,868	2,334	
Tauride	73	147	221	195	368	
Kharkov	800	1,601	2,402	3,203	4,004	
Voroneje	982	1,964	2,946	3,929	4,911	
Total	2,583	5,169	7,756	10,343	12,928	
Podolie	1,402	2,085	4,128	4,171	5,123	Iekaterinoslav
Kiev	1,069	2,139	3,210	4,279	5,349	
Total	2,471	4,224	7,338	8,450	10,562	
Vologda	567	1,134	1,701	2,269	2,836	Vologda &
Kostroma	787	1,574	2,362	3,149	3,937	Jaroslav
Viatka	905	1,811	2,717	3,623	4,529	
Total	1,692	3,385	5,079	6,772	8,466	
Nijine-Novgorod	826	1,653	2,480	3,307	4,134	Vladimir
Perm	808	1,617	2,426	3,236	4,044	
Total	1,634	3,270	4,906	6,543	8,178	
Penza	688	2,011	2,427	3,237	3,443	Riazan
Kazan	810	977	1,496	3,469	4,053	
Total	1,498	2,998	4,598	6,097	7,496	
Samara	809	1,618	2,427	3,237	4,046	Tobolsk
Orenburg	498	1,734	2,601	3,469	4,336	
Total	1,307	2,615	3,923	5,229	6,539	

Governments	1st Levy	2nd Levy	3rd Levy	4th Levy	5th Levy	Depot
Tambov	993	1,986	2,980	3,973	4,967	Voronej
Riazan	867	1,734	2,601	3,469	4,336	
Total	1,860	3,720	5,581	7,442	9,303	
Voisko on Don	141	282	423	564	705	Tcherkask
Saratov	755	1,511	2,267	3,022	3,778	
Total	896	1,793	2,690	3,586	4,483	

The Source of Russian Levies in 1811 by Province

Government	Recruits	1st Line Depot	Division
Tver	2,213	Toropetz	4th
Jaroslav	2,000		
Pskof	2,433	Kholm	5th
Tver			
Archangle	704	Kargopol	6th
Olonetz	300		
Minsk	700	Starodoub	7th
Mohilev	2,500		
Tula	1,000		
Poltava	1,576	Novomirgorod	8th
Podolie	2,171		
Kiev	830		
Iekaterinoslav	900	Izioum	9th
Kharkov	3,203		
Grodno	1,000	Roslavl	11th
Kalouga	2,975		
Kursk	420	Akhtyrka	12th
Voronej	3,929	Ivanovka	13th
Lithiania	1,908	Staraia-Roussa	14th
Novgorod	2,305		
Poltava	3,600	Zmiev	15th
Kiev	3,446	Olviopol	16th

Government	Recruits	1st Line Depot	Division
Vitebsk	1,405	Viely	17th
Moscow	2,600		
Volhynie	400	Konotop	18th
Orel	3,842		
Kherson	1,048	Taganrog	19th
Iekaterinoslav	968		
Tauride	295		
Voisko on Don	564		
Staratov	3,022	Azov	20th
Olonetz	474	Olonetz	21st
Vyborg	741		
Volhynie	3,556	Tchiguirin	22nd
Vitebsk	1,404	Elnia	23rd
Smolensk	3,625		
Minsk	1,720	Novgorod-Sieversky	24th
Tula	2,435		
Kurland	1,546	Podgoscz	25th
Lithuania	200		
Estonia	821		
St. Petersburg	1,462		
Volhynie	200	Romny	26th
Tchernigov	4,042		

Government	Recruits	2nd Line Depot
Vologda	2,269	1st at Petrozavodsk
Kostroma	3,149	2nd at Novgorod
Jaroslav	974	
Viatka	3,623	3rd at Tver
Moscow	1,011	4th at Moscow
Nijine-Novgorod	3,307	
Perm	3,235	
Kazan	3,243	5th at Kalouga
Vilna	3,425	
Penza	2,854	6th at Tula
Minsk	840	
Grodno	1,534	7th at Orel

Government	Recruits	2nd Line Depot
Orenburg	2,992	
Simbrisk	3,237	8th at Kursk
Riazan	3,469	9th at Kharkov
Tambov	3,973	10th at Iekaterinoslav

Statistics of Illness and Casualties during the Reconstruction of the Fortress of Riga

Division & regiment	Time period	Reported ill at the beginning	Cured	Dead	Still in treatment
14th Division					
Toula (9 cos)	1 April	384	312	4	59
Navaguinsk (5 cos)	1 April	224	202	10	12
25th Jagers (9 cos)	2 May	309	231	15	63
		917	745	29	134
5th Division		81	19	—	62
Sievsk (9 cos)	28 June	105	17	2	56
Kalouga	3 July	186	36	2	118
Depot Battalions					
Perm	29 April	43	12	—	31
Sievsk	30 April	90	52	4	34
Mohilev	8 May	39	7	9	23
Kalouga	21 April	70	31	3	36
23rd Jagers	1 May	20	6	4	10
24th Jagers	2 May	36	11	2	23
		298	119	22	157
Overall Totals		1,401	939	53	409

Distribution of the Russian Engineering Staff
on Special Assignment
1811

Army of Moldavia
  1 Generalmajor
  3 Lieutenants
  6 Captains
  6 Lieutenants
  4 Under Lieutenants
  1 Ensign
Army Corps of Georgia
  1 Lieutenant Colonel
  3 Captains
  3 Lieutenants
Assigned to the Caucasus
  1 Captain
  3 Lieutenants
  2 Second Lieutenants
Assigned to Barclay de Tolly, Aide-de-camp to the Czar
  2 Captains
  2 Lieutenants
  2 Second Lieutenants
To the Ministry of the Navy
  1 Lieutenant
To General-Major Lavrov
  1 Captain
In Krioukov to erect the Commissariate Facilities
  1 Lieutenant Colonel
  1 Lieutenant
To General of Cavalry Prince Volkonsky
  1 Captain
To Kazan to Erect the Commissariate Facilities
  1 Lieutenant
Detached to General-Lieutenant Steingel
  1 Captain

Organization of the Russian Army
as Reported by General Rapp
to Marshal Davout
On 17 July 1811

1st Army Corps: General Wittgenstein (in Riga)
  5th Division: General Koslakovski (in Riga)
    4 Infantry Regiments
    2 Jager Regiments
    2 Position Batteries
    1 Battery with 6 guns
    1 Horse Battery
  14th Division: General Sazonov (between Riga & Revel)
    4 Infantry Regiments
    2 Jager Regiments
    2 Position Batteries
    1 Battery with 6 guns
    1 Horse Battery
  1st Cavalry Division: General Kokhovski (in Lithuania and on the frontier
      of Samogitie)
    2 Hussar Regiments
    2 Cossack Pulks
  1st Cuirassier Division: General Depreradovitch (in St. Petersburg)
    Emperor Cuirassier Regiment
    Empress Cuirassier Regiment
    4 Dragoon Regiments
2nd Army Corps: General Baggovout
  Infantry Division: General Count Strogovitz (in Vilna)
    5 Grenadier Regiments
    1 Horse Artillery Battery
    1 Park of 48 field pieces
  4th Division: general unknown (outside Vilna)
    4 Infantry Regiments
    2 Jager Regiments
    1 Position Battery with 12 guns
    1 Light Battery with 12 guns
    1 Horse Battery
  17th Division: General Alexeiev (Dunabourg)
    4 Infantry Regiments
    2 Jager Regiments
    1 Position Battery with 12 guns

1 Light Battery with 12 guns
1 Horse Battery
3rd Army Corps: General Essen (in Slonim)
  11th Division: General Lvrov (between Slonim & Jourovitsa)
    4 Infantry Regiments
    2 Jager Regiments
    1 Position Battery with 24 guns
    1 Horse Battery
    Park & Train
  3rd Division: General Konovnitzin
    2 Infantry Regiments
    2 Jager Regiments
    12 12pdr guns
    12 6pdr guns
    1 Light Battery
  3rd Light Cavalry Division: General Pahlen (in Novgorodek)
    2 Hussar Regiments
    4 Cossack Pulks
4th Army Corps: General Docturov (in Doubno)
  7th Division: (in Volhynie)
    4 Infantry Regiments
    3 Jager Regiments
    1 Position Battery with 12 guns
    1 Light Battery with 12 guns
    1 Light Battery
  24th Division:
    4 Infantry Regiments
    3 Jager Regiments
    1 Position Battery with 12 guns
    1 Light Battery with 12 guns
    1 Light Battery
  Cuirassier Division: General Koutouzov (In Volhynie)
    4 Cuirassier Regiments
    4 Dragoon Regiments
  4th Light Cavalry Division: General Tchlaitz (in Volhynie)
    2 Hussar Regiments
    4 Cossack Regiments
  25th Division:
    Not yet attached, but destined to join later

Organization of the Russian Army as Reported by General Rozniecki on 1 August 1811

Right Wing: General Baggovout
  4th Division—in Vilna
  17th Division—Dunabourg
  Cavalry Division of General Korff
    16 Squadrons of Dragoons
    16 Squadrons of Hussars
    2,000 Cossacks

Center: General Essen in Slonim
  3rd Division: General Konovnitzin (between Slonim & Novgorodek)
  11th Division: General Lavrov
  Cavalry Division: General Pahlen

Left Wing: General Docturov (in Loutsk)
  7th Division: General Kapsevitch (in Loutsk)
  25th Division: General Likhatchev (Old Siberian Division) (in Medjiboj & Letitschev)
  Cavalry Division of General Tchlapitz (in the provinces of Bratslav & Podsolie)

Reserves:

Right Wing Reserves:
Grenadier Division on the Dvina between Vitebsk & Polotsk

Center Reserves:
3rd Battalions of various regiments working on the fortifications of Bobrouisk

Left Wing Reserves:
  24th Division in Kiev in July. In August part of this division joined the 7th Division.

The right is flanked by the corps of General Wittgenstein, comprised of the 5th and 14th Divisions, stationed between Mitau and St. Petersburg, and a division of cavalry under the temporary command of General Kokhovski composed of 16 squadrons of hussars, 16 squadrons of dragoons and 8 squadrons of uhlans.

Stationed on the Dniester were the three infantry divisions of Souvarov, Lewis and the former division of Docturov, with the cavalry division of Knorring composed of 16 cuirassier squadrons and 8 uhlan squadrons. This totals 21,600 men and 2,500 cavalry.

On the Polish frontier were the 16 regiments of cossacks, each with no more than 500 horses. These cossacks belong to the divisions of Kokhovski, Korff, Pahlen and Tchlapitz. They were reinforced in August with two new regiments from the interior, becoming a total of 18 regiments.

Organization of the Russian Army as Reported by General Rozniecki on 14 September 1811

1st Corps: General Wittgenstein (in Riga)
  5th Division (in Samogitie & Courland)
  14th Division (in Samogitie & Courland)
  Cavalry Division of General Kokhovski (in Samogitie & Courland)

2nd Corps: General Baggovout (in Vilna)
  4th Division (In Vilna, Mohilev & Polotsk)
  17th Division (In Vilna, Mohilev & Polotsk)
  Cavalry Division of General Korff (In Vilna, Mohilev & Polotsk)

3rd Corps: General Essen in Slonim
  3rd Division (In Grodno & Minsk)
  11th Division (In Grodno & Minsk)
  Cavalry Division: General Pahlen (In Grodno & Minsk)

4th Corps: General Docturov (Replaced by Bagration in October)
  7th Division: General Kapsevitch
  25th Division: General Likhatchev (4 musketeer regiments only)
  Cavalry Division of General Tchlapitz
    (in Vinnitza and Kiev, but in December it moved between Brest and the Dniester)

Cossacks:
  24 Regiments en échelon on the frontier.

Reserves:
  Grenadier Division (4 regiments) (between Vilna & Dvina)
  24th Infantry Division (near Kiev)
  Cuirassier Division: General Knorring (4 cuirassier & 1 Uhlan regiments) (Near Ouman and in the Ukraine)
  Cuirassier Division: General Depreradovitch (8 cuirassier & 9 chasseur squadrons) (Near Revel & Riga)

Russian Magazines
Levels of Provisions at the Beginning of the Campaign

Cities	Divisions to be Provisioned	Days Provisions
Riga	8 Infantry Divisions	30 days
	4 Cavalry Divisions	30 days
Dinaburg	8 Infantry Divisions	30 days
	4 Cavalry Divisions	30 days

Cities	Divisions to be Provisioned	Days Provisions
Veliki-Luki	8 Infantry Divisions 4 Cavalry Divisions	60 days 60 days
Bobruisk	2 Infantry Divisions 1 Cavalry Division	30 days 30 days
Mohilev	2 Infantry Divisions 1 Cavalry Division	60 days 60 days
Kiev	9 Infantry Divisions 4 Cavalry Divisions	30 days 30 days
Sessinza	9 Infantry Divisions 4 Cavalry Divisions	60 days 60 days
Schavli	1 Infantry Division ½ Cavalry Division	30 days 30 days
Vilna	8 Infantry Divisions 4 Cavalry Divisions	30 days 30 days
Svenziani	8 Infantry Divisions 4 Cavalry Divisions	15 days 15 days
Grodno	2 Infantry Divisions 1 Cavalry Division	30 days 30 days
Brest	2 Infantry Divisions 1 Cavalry Division	30 days 30 days
Slonim	2 Infantry Divisions 1 Cavalry Division	30 days 30 days
Sluzk	2 Infantry Divisions 1 Cavalry Division	30 days 30 days
Pinsk	2 Infantry Divisions 1 Cavalry Division	30 days 30 days
Mosir	2 Infantry Divisions 1 Cavalry Division	30 days 30 days
Luzk	9 Infantry Divisions 4 Cavalry Divisions	60 days 60 days
Ostrog	9 Infantry Divisions 4 Cavalry Divisions	15 days 15 days
Jitomir	9 Infantry Divisions 4 Cavalry Divisions	15 days 15 days

Appendix III

Orders of Battle for the 1812 Campaign

Russian Army Organization
1 January 1812

Corps: Count Steingell (in Finland) (30,652)
  2 Dragoon Regiments
  6th Division
  21st Division
  25th Division
Guard Corps: Grand Duke Constantine (in Petersburg) (28,526)
  Guard Cavalry Division
  Guard Infantry Division
  2 Cuirassier Regiments
  2 Grenadier Regiments
  1 Infantry Regiment
Corps: Count Wittgenstein (in Lithuania & Kourland) (34,290)
  1st Cavalry Division
  5th Division
  14th Division
Corps: General Baggovout (in Vilna & Vitebsk) (47,520)
  1st Cuirassier Division
  2nd Cavalry Division
  1st Division (less two grenadier regiments)
  4th Division
  17th Division
Corps: General Essen (in Grodno, Minsk, & Mohilev) (41,045)
  3rd Cavalry Division
  23rd Division
  3rd Division
  11th Division (less 1 infantry regiment)
Army: Prince Bagration (in Volhynie & Podolie) (104,322)
  2nd Cuirassier Division
  4th Cavalry Division
  5th Cavalry Division
  2nd Division
  7th Division
  12th Division
  18th Division
  24th Division

Army: General Kutusov (on the Danube) (87,026)
  6th Cavalry Division
  7th Cavalry Division
  9th Division
  9th Division (less 8 battalions)
  10th Division
  15th Division
  16th Division
  22nd Division
Corps: Duke Richelieu (in Crimea) (19,501)
  8th Cavalry Division
  13th Division
  8 Battalions from the 9th Division
Corps: General Rtitchev (in Caucasus) (9,928)
  19th Division
  1 Dragoon Regiment
Corps: General Paulucci (in Georgia) (23,745)
  2 Dragoon Regiments
  20th Division
Garrison: in Moscow (10,641)
  27th Division
Other:
  In addition to the forces listed above, there were 2,417 instructional troops, 4,051 pioneers, 4,851 reserve artillerists, and 69,166 garrison and invalid (retired) troops on active duty. This gave a total of 517,682 active duty personnel

French Artillery and General Engineering Park
Posted in Depots and Lines of Communication
Early 1812

Danzig:
Commanding Officer—General de brigade Lepin
  6/5th Foot Artillery (2/108)
  9/5th Foot Artillery (2/106)
  19/5th Foot Artillery (2/119)
  10th Saxon Foot Artillery Company (3/88)
  16th Polish Foot Artillery Company (4/123)
  3rd Bavarian Foot Artillery Company (1/26)
  6th Artillery Artisan Company (3/101)
  1st Armorer Company (1/50)

Magdeburg:
Commanding Officer—Colonel Bardenet
  1/, 5/9th Foot Artillery Company (2/203)
  11th Artillery Artisan Company (2/36)
  3rd & 5th Armorer Companies (3/100)
Stettin:
Commanding Officer—Colonel Pont-Bodin
  12/7th Foot Artillery Company (3/105)
Custin:
Commanding Officer—Chef de bataillon Poulet
  14/7th Foot Artillery Company (2/105)
Glogau:
Commanding Officer—Chef de bataillon Perrault
  18/7th Foot Artillery (1/110)
  9th Saxon Foot Artillery Company (4/117)
Erfurth:
  2/1st Foot Artillery Company (2/118)
Straslund:
  17/8th Foot Artillery Company (2/112)
Spandau:
  8/1st Foot Artillery (3/109)
  6/, 13/3rd Foot Artillery (5/213)
  1/8th Foot Artillery (2/111)
  4/, 16/, 17/9th Foot Artillery (7/284)
Praga:
  18th Polish Foot Artillery Company (3/88)
Zamose:
  13th & 17th Polish Foot Artillery Company (8/199)
Modlin:
  9th & 15th Polish Foot Artillery Company (6/163)
Thorn:
  Polish Foot Artillery Company (5/121)
Marienburg:
  18/8th Foot Artillery Company (4/64)
Pillau:
  9/9th Foot Artillery (3/115)
General Engineering Park:
  1/, 3/, 5/, 6/1st Miner Battalion (10/382)
  1/, 5/2nd Miner Battalion (4/182)
  1/, 3/, 4/1st Sapper Battalion (4/441)
  det. & 2/3rd Sapper Battalion (1/358)
  1/, 2/, 3/, 4/Sappers de l'Isle d'Elbe (12/509)

General Engineering Park (cont.)
  Det. Engineering Artisan (1/75)
  Marine Battalion & Military Artisans of the Danube (16/794)
  4th Équipage de Flotille (28/811)
  17th Équipage de Flotille (31/803)
  5/, 6/Engineering Train Battalion (5/430)

Russian Armies at the Beginning of the 1812 Campaign

1ST ARMY OF THE WEST

Commanding General —Barclay de Tolly
Chief of Staff   —Lavarov (Paulucci, Tormolov)
Quartermaster General—General Muschkin (Colonel Toll)
Service Chief   —Colonel Kikin
Chief of Artillery   —General Koutaissof
Chief of Engineers   —General Trousson

1st Corps: Generallieutenant Wittgenstein
5th Division: Berg
  Brigade: Kozaczkoffski
    Sievesk Infantry Regiment (2)
    Kalouga Infantry Regiment (2)
  Brigade: Generalmajor Prince of Siberia
    Perm Infantry Regiment (2)
    Mohilev Infantry Regiment (2)
  Brigade: Colonel Frolov
    23rd Jager Regiment (2)
    24th Jager Regiment (2)
    Converged Grenadier Battalions of the 5th Division (2)
  Artillery Brigade:
    Position Battery #5 (8–12pdrs & 4 Licornes)
    Light Batteries #9 & #10 (8–6pdrs & 4 Licornes ea)
14th Division: Generalmajor Sazonov
  Brigade: Colonel Harpe
    Toula Infantry Regiment (2)
    Navajinsk Infantry Regiment (2)
  Brigade: Generalmajor Helfreich
    Tenguinsk Infantry Regiment (2)
    Estonia Infantry Regiment (2)

Brigade: Colonel Denissev
    25th Jager Regiment (2)
    26th Jager Regiment (2)
    Converged Grenadier Battalions of the 14th Division (2)
Artillery Brigade: Colonel Staden
    Position Battery #14 (8–12pdrs & 4 Licornes)
    Light Batteries #26 & #27 (8–6pdrs & 4 Licornes ea)
    Pioneer Company
1st Cavalry Division: Generalmajor Kakhoffski
    3rd Brigade: Generalmajor Balk
        Riga Dragoon Regiment (4)
        Iambourg Dragoon Regiment (4)
    Part of 5th Brigade: Koulnieff
        Grodno Hussar Regiment (8)
    Cossacks:
        Rodinov #2 Don Cossack Regiment
        Platov #4 Don Cossack Regiment
        Selivanov #2 Don Cossack Regiment
    Artillery:
        Position Battery #28 (8–12pdrs & 4 Licornes)
        Horse Batteries #1 & #2 (8–6pdrs & 4 Licornes ea)
        Pontooneer Companies #1 & #2
2nd Corps: Generallieutenant Baggovout
4th Division: Prince Eugène of Württemberg
    Brigade:
        Krementchug Infantry Regiment (2)
        Minsk Infantry Regiment (2)
    Brigade: Rossi
        Tobolsk Infantry Regiment (2)
        Volhynie Infantry Regiment (2)
    Brigade:
        4th Jager Regiment (2)
        34th Jager Regiment (2)
    Artillery:
        Position Battery #4 (8–12pdrs & 4 Licornes)
        Light Batteries #7 & #8 (8–6pdrs & 4 Licornes ea)
17th Division: Olsoufieff
    Brigade: Tehoubarov
        Riazan Infantry Regiment (2)
        Bieloserk Infantry Regiment (2)
    Brigade: Tuchkov III
        Wilmanstrand Infantry Regiment (2)
        Brest Infantry Regiment (2)

Brigade: Potemkin
   3rd Jager Regiment (2)
   48th Jager Regiment (2)
Artillery Brigade: Walewacz
   Position Battery #17 (8–12pdrs & 4 Licornes)
   Light Batteries #32 & #33 (8–6pdrs & 4 Licornes ea)
   Horse Battery #4 (8–6pdrs & 4 Licornes)
Part of 8th Brigade: Wsewologski
   Elisabethgrad Hussar Regiment (8)
3rd Corps: Generallieutenant Tuchkov I
3rd Division: Konovnitzin
  Brigade: Tuchkov III
   Mourmonsk Infantry Regiment (2)
   Revel Infantry Regiment (2)
  Brigade: Voeikov
   Tchernigov Infantry Regiment (2)
   Korporsk Infantry Regiment (2)
  Brigade: Prince Chakoffski
   20th Jager Regiment (2)
   21st Jager Regiment (2)
   Converged Grenadier Battalions (2)
  Artillery:
   Light Batteries #5 & #6 (8–6pdrs & 4 Licornes)
   Position Battery #3 (8–12pdrs & 4 Licornes)
1st Grenadier Division: Strogonoff
  Brigade: Tsvilenev
   Pavlov Grenadier Regiment (2)
   Ekaterinoslav Grenadier Regiment (2)
  Brigade: Geltoukhin
   Count Arakcheyev Grenadier Regiment (2)
   Leib Grenadier Regiment (2)
  Brigade: Pock I
   St. Petersburg Grenadier Regiment (2)
   Tauride Grenadier Regiment (2)
  Artillery Brigade:
   Position Battery #1 (8–12pdrs & 4 Licornes)
   Light Batteries #1 & #2 (8–6pdrs & 4 Licornes ea)
   Horse Battery #2 (8–6pdrs & 4 Licornes)
4th Corps: Generallieutenant Schouwalov
11th Division: Tchoglokov
  Brigade: Philissov
   Polotsk Infantry Regiment (2)
   Jeletz Infantry Regiment (2)

Brigade:
  Kexholm Infantry Regiment (2)
  Pernov Infantry Regiment (2)
Brigade: Bistrom
  1st Jager Regiment (2)
  33rd Jager Regiment (2)
Artillery Brigade: Cotliarev
  Position Battery #2 (8–12pdrs & 4 Licornes)
  Light Batteries #3 & #4 (8–6pdrs & 4 Licornes ea)
23rd Division: Bakhmetieff
  Brigade: Okoulov
    Rilsk Infantry Regiment (2)
    Ekaterinburg Infantry Regiment (2)
  Brigade: Alcksapol
    Seleguinsk Infantry Regiment (2)
    18th Jager Regiment (2)
  Artillery Brigade: Goulewicz
    Position Battery #23 (8–12pdrs & 4 Licornes)
    Light Batteries #43 & #44 (8–6pdrs & 4 Licornes ea)
  Brigade:
    Isoum Hussar Regiment (8)
5th Corps: Grand Duke Constantin
Guard Division: Yermolov
  Brigade: Baron Rosen
    Preobragenski Guard Infantry Regiment (3)
    Semenovski Guard Infantry Regiment (3)
  Brigade:
    Ismailov Guard Infantry Regiment (3)
    Lithuanian Guard Infantry Regiment (3)
  Brigade: Bistrom
    Guard Jager Infantry Regiment (3)
    Finland Guard Infantry Regiment (3)
  Artillery:
    Guard Position Battery (8–12pdrs & 4 Licornes)
    Count Arakcheyev Position Battery (8–12pdrs & 4 Licornes)
    1st & 2nd Guard Light Batteries (8–6pdrs & 4 Licornes)
    Guard Horse Battery (8–6pdrs & 4 Licornes)
1st Converged Grenadier Division:
  Brigade:
    Guard Marine Equipage Battalion (1)
  Brigade:
    Converged Grenadiers of the 1st Division (2)
    Converged Grenadiers of the 4th Division (2)

Brigade:
    Converged Grenadiers of the 17th Division (2)
    Converged Grenadiers of the 23rd Division (2)
Brigade:
    Pioneer Companies (3)
1st Cavalry Division: Depreradovitch
Brigade: Borosdin
    Emperor Cuirassier Regiment
    Empress Cuirassier Regiment
    Astrakhan Cuirassier Regiment
Brigade: Cheviez
    Chevalier Guard Regiment
    Horse Guard Regiment
6th Corps: General of Infantry Docturov
7th Division: Kapsevitch
Brigade:
    Moscow Infantry Regiment (2)
    Pakof Infantry Regiment (2)
Brigade:
    Libau Infantry Regiment (2)
    Sofia Infantry Regiment (2)
Brigade: Balla
    11th Jager Regiment
    36th Jager Regiment
Artillery Brigade: Dewell
    Position Battery #7 (8–12pdrs & 4 Licornes)
    Light Batteries #12 & #13 (8–6pdrs & 4 Licornes ea)
24th Division: Lichatcheff
Brigade: Tschoulski
    Oufa Infantry Regiment (2)
    Chirvan Infantry Regiment (2)
Brigade: Denissieff
    Tomsk Infantry Regiment (2)
    Bourtirki Infantry Regiment (2)
Brigade: Wouitch
    19th Jager Regiment (2)
    40th Jager Regiment (2)
Artillery Brigade: Jefremov
    Position Battery #24 (8–12pdrs & 4 Licornes)
    Light Batteries #45 & #46 (8–6pdrs & 4 Licornes ea)
Part of 11th Brigade:
    Soum Hussar Regiment (8)
    Horse Battery #7 (8–6pdrs & 4 Licornes)

Guard Cavalry Division
  1st Brigade:
    Guard Dragoon Regiment (4)
    Guard Uhlan Regiment (4)
    Guard Hussar Regiment (4)
  Brigade:
    Kourland Dragoon Regiment (4)
    Kasan Dragoon Regiment (4)
    Niejine Dragoon Regiment (4)
    Horse Battery #2 (8–6pdrs & 4 Licornes)
2nd Cavalry Division: Generalmajor Baron Korff
  6th Brigade: Davydov
    Pskof Dragoon Regiment (4)
    Moscow Dragoon Regiment (4)
  7th Brigade: Panczoulidzeff
    Kargopol Dragoon Regiment (4)
    Ingermannland Dragoon Regiment (4)
  8th Brigade:
    Polish Uhlan Regiment (8)
  Artillery:
    Horse Battery #6 (8–6pdrs & 4 Licornes)
    Position Batteries #28, #29, & #30 (8–12pdrs & 4 Licornes ea)
3rd Cavalry Division: Generalmajor Count Pahlen
  Brigade: Skalon
    Orenburg Dragoon Regiment (4)
    Siberia Dragoon Regiment (4)
  Brigade: Klebeck
    Irkhoutsk Dragoon Regiment (8)
    Mariuopol Hussar Regiment (8)
    Horse Battery #9 (8–6pdrs & 4 Licornes)
Cossacks: General of Cavalry Platov
  Ataman Don Cossack Regiment
  Denissov Don Cossack Regiment
  Illowaiski #4 Don Cossack Regiment
  Illowaiski #8 Don Cossack Regiment
  Kharitonov Don Cossack Regiment
  Vlassov Don Cossack Regiment
  1st Bug Cossack Regiment
  2nd Bug Cossack Regiment
  Denissov #6 Cossack Regiment
  Gardeieff #1 Cossack Regiment
  Simpheropol Tartar Regiment

Perecop Cossack Regiment
1st Bashkir Regiment
Kalmucks Regiment
Don Horse Battery

2ND ARMY OF THE WEST

Commanding General —Prince Bagration
Chief of Staff   —Generalmajor Count St. Preist
Quartermaster General—Generalmajor Vistitski II
Service General   —Colonel Marin
Chief of Artillery   —Generalmajor Lowenstern
Chief of Engineers   —Generalmajor Forster

7th Corps: Generallieutenant Raevsky
26th Division: Paskevitch
  Brigade: Liebart
    Ladoga Infantry Regiment (2)
    Poltava Infantry Regiment (2)
  Brigade:
    Orel Infantry Regiment (2)
    Nivegorod Infantry Regiment (2)
  Brigade: Gogel
    5th Jager Regiment (2)
    42nd Jager Regiment (2)
  Artillery Brigade: Schoulmann
    Position Battery #26 (8–12pdrs & 4 Licornes)
    Light Batteries #47 & #48 (8–6pdrs & 4 Licornes ea)
12th Division: Kolubakin
  Brigade: Ryleieff
    Smolensk Infantry Regiment (2)
    Narva Infantry Regiment (2)
  Brigade: Pantzerbieter
    New Ingremanland Infantry Regiment (2)
    Alexopol Infantry Regiment (2)
  Brigade: Palitzin
    6th Jager Regiment (2)
    41st Jager Regiment (2)
  Artillery Brigade: Sablin
    Position Battery #12 (8–12pdrs & 4 Licornes)
    Light Batteries #22 & #23 (8–6pdrs & 4 Licornes ea)

Part of 14th Cavalry Brigade: Wassilezikov
  Akhtyrsk Hussar Regiment (8)
  Horse Battery #8 (8–6pdrs & 4 Licornes)
8th Corps: Generallieutenant Borosdin
2nd Grenadier Division: Generalmajor Prince Charles of Mecklenburg
  Brigade: Chatilov
    Kiev Grenadier Regiment (2)
    Moscow Grenadier Regiment (2)
  Brigade: Buxhowden
    Astrakhan Grenadier Regiment (2)
    Fangoria Grenadier Regiment (2)
  Brigade: Hesse
    Siberia Grenadier Regiment (2)
    Little Russia Grenadier Regiment (2)
  Artillery Brigade: Bogoslavski
    Position Battery #11 (8–12pdrs & 4 Licornes)
    Light Artillery Batteries #20 & #21 (8–6pdrs & 4 Licornes ea)
2nd Converged Grenadier Division: Voronzov
  Brigade:
    Converged Grenadiers of the 7th Division (2)
    Converged Grenadiers of the 24th Division (2)
  Brigade:
    Converged Grenadiers of the 2nd Division (2)
    Converged Grenadiers of the 12th Division (2)
    Converged Grenadiers of the 26th Division (2)
2nd Cuirassier Division: Generalmajor Knorring
  2nd Brigade: Kretov
    Military Order Cuirassier Regiment
    Ekaterinoslav Cuirassier Regiment
  3rd Brigade: Duka
    Gluchov Cuirassier Regiment
    Novgorod Cuirassier Regiment
    Little Russia Cuirassier Regiment
  Artillery:
    Position Batteries #31 & #32 (8–12pdrs & 4 Licornes ea)
4th Cavalry Division: Generalmajor Sievers
  12th Brigade: Pantchaulidseff
    Karkov Dragoon Regiment
    Tchernigov Dragoon Regiment
  13th Brigade: Emmanuel
    Kiev Dragoon Regiment
    New Russia Dragoon Regiment

Brigade:
  Horse Battery #10 (8–6pdrs & 4 Licornes)
  Pontooneer Company #4
  Pioneer Companies (4)
Irregular Troops: Illowaiski
    Andreinov #2 Cossack Regiment
    3rd Bug Cossack Regiment
    Mussareff #2 Cossack Regiment
    Illowaiski #12 Cossack Regiment
    Karpov #2 Cossack Regiment
    Syssoief #3 Cossack Regiment
    Illowaiski #10 Cossack Regiment
    Illowaiski #5 Cossack Regiment
    Illowaiski #11 Cossack Regiment
    Don Cossack Horse Battery
27th Division: Generalmajor Neverovski
  Brigade: Kniajnin
    Vilna Infantry Regiment (2)
    Simbrisk Infantry Regiment (2)
  Brigade: Stavitski
    Odessa Infantry Regiment (2)
    Tarnopol Infantry Regiment (2)
  Brigade: Woiekov
    49th Jager Regiment (2)
    50th Jager Regiment (2)

3RD ARMY OF THE WEST

Commanding Officer —Generallieutenant Tormassov
Chief of Staff   —Generalmajor Inzoff
Quartermaster General—Generalmajor Renne
Chief of Artillery   —Generalmajor Sievers

Corps: General of Infantry Kamenski
18th Division: Prince Tchervatov
  Brigade: Bernardos
    Tambov Infantry Regiment (2)
    Vladamir Infantry Regiment (2)
  Brigade: Prince Khowanski
    Dnieper Infantry Regiment (2)
    Kostroma Infantry Regiment (2)

Brigade: Metcherinov
  28th Jager Regiment (2)
  32nd Jager Regiment (2)
Brigade:
  Converged Grenadiers of the 9th Division
  Converged Grenadiers of the 15th Division
  Converged Grenadiers of the 18th Division
Brigade:
  Pavlovgrad Hussar Regiment (8)
Artillery Brigade:
  Position Battery #18 (8–12pdrs & 4 Licornes)
  Light Batteries #34 & #35 (8–6pdrs & 4 Licornes ea)
  Horse Battery #11 (8–6pdrs & 4 Licornes)
Corps: Generallieutenant Markoff
15th Division: Nasimov
  Brigade: Oldecop
    Kourin Infantry Regiment (2)
    Kolyvan Infantry Regiment (2)
  Brigade: Stepanov
    Koslov Infantry Regiment (2)
    Vitebsk Infantry Regiment (2)
  Brigade: Prince Wiasemski
    13th Jager Regiment (2)
    14th Jager Regiment (2)
  Artillery Brigade:
    Position Battery #15 (8–12pdrs & 4 Licornes)
    Light Batteries #28 & #29 (8–6pdrs & 4 Licornes ea)
9th Division: Generalmajor Udom
  Brigade: Reichel
    Riajsk Infantry Regiment (2)
    Apcheron Infantry Regiment (2)
  Brigade: Seliverstov
    Iakout Infantry Regiment (2)
    Nacheburg Infantry Regiment (2)
  Brigade:
    10th Jager Regiment (2)
    38th Jager Regiment (2)
  Part of 17th Cavalry Brigade: Madetof
    Alexandria Hussar Regiment (8)
  Artillery Brigade:
    Position Battery #9 (8–12pdrs & 4 Licornes)

Light Batteries #16 & #17 (8–6pdrs & 4 Licornes ea)
Horse Battery #12 (8–6pdrs & 4 Licornes)
Corps: Generallieutenant Sacken
  Brigade: Sorokin
    Reserve Battalions of the 15th Division (6)
  Brigade:
    Reserve Battalions of the 18th Division (6)
11th Cavalry Division: Lasskin
  Brigade:
    Reserve Squadrons of the 4th Cavalry Division (4)
    Reserve Squadrons of the 5th Cavalry Division (8)
    Reserve Squadrons of the 2nd Cuirassier Division (4)
  Artillery:
    Position Battery #33 (8–12pdrs & 4 Licornes)
    Horse Battery #13 (8–6pdrs & 4 Licornes)
  Part of 26th Cavalry Brigade:
    Loubny Hussar Regiment (8)
Cavalry Corps: Generalmajor Lambert
5th Cavalry Division:
  15th Brigade: Berdiaief
    Tver Dragoon Regiment (4)
    Starodoub Dragoon Regiment (4)
  16th Brigade: Khroutchov
    Jitomir Dragoon Regiment (4)
    Arasmass Dragoon Regiment (4)
  Part of 17th Cavalry Brigade: Knorring
    Tartar Uhlan Regiment (8)
8th Division: Generalmajor Tschlapitz
  24th Brigade: Barkov
    Serpuchov Dragoon Regiment (4)
    Vladimir Dragoon Regiment (4)
    Taganrog Dragoon Regiment (4)
  Artillery Reserve:
    Position Battery #34 (8–12pdrs & 4 Licornes)
    Pontooneer Company #5
    Pioneer Company (1)
Irregular Corps:
    Platov #5 Don Cossack Regiment
    2nd Bashkir Regiment
    Barbantchikov #2 Cossack Regiment
    Vlassov #2 Don Cossack Regiment

1st Kalmuck Regiment
2nd Kalmuck Regiment
Theodosic Tartar Regiment
Eupatorie Tartar Regiment
Diatchkin Cossack Regiment
(Total of 30 squadrons)

The Army of the Danube

Commanding General—Admiral Tchichagov

8th Division: Essen II
  Brigade:
    Archangle Infantry Regiment (2)
    Schusselburg Infantry Regiment (2)
  Brigade:
    Old Ingremanland Infantry Regiment (2)
    Ukraine Infantry Regiment (2)
  Brigade:
    8th Jager Regiment (2)
    39th Jager Regiment (2)
  Artillery Brigade:
    Position Battery #8 (8–12pdrs & 4 Licornes)
    Light Batteries #14 & #15 (8–6pdrs & 4 Licornes ea)

10th Division: Lieven
  Brigade:
    Jaroslav Infantry Regiment (2)
    Kursk Infantry Regiment (2)
  Brigade:
    Crimea Infantry Regiment (2)
    Bieloserk Infantry Regiment (2)
  Brigade:
    9th Jager Regiment (2)
    39th Jager Regiment (2)
  Artillery Brigade:
    Position Batteries #10 & #30 (8–12pdrs & 4 Licornes ea)
    Light Batteries #18 & #50 (8–6pdrs & 4 Licornes ea)

13th Division: Langeron
  Brigade:
    Vieliki-Loutzk Infantry Regiment (2)
    Saratov Infantry Regiment (2)
  Brigade:

Galitz Infantry Regiment (2)
Pensa Infantry Regiment (2)
Brigade:
   12th Jager Regiment (2)
   22nd Jager Regiment (2)
Artillery Brigade:
   Position Battery #13 (8–12pdrs & 4 Licornes)
   Light Batteries #24 & #25 (8–6pdrs & 4 Licornes ea)
16th Division: Bulatoff
Brigade:
   Netchlot Infantry Regiment (2)
   Okhotski Infantry Regiment (2)
Brigade:
   Kamchatka Infantry Regiment (2)
   Mingrelia Infantry Regiment (2)
Brigade:
   27th Jager Regiment (2)
   43rd Jager Regiment (2)
Artillery Brigade:
   Position Battery #16 (8–12pdrs & 4 Licornes)
   Light Batteries #30 & #31 (8–6pdrs & 4 Licornes ea)
8th Cavalry Corps:
6th Cavalry Division
   18th Brigade:
      Saint Petersburg Dragoon Regiment (4)
      Lithuania Dragoon Regiment (4)
   19th Brigade:
      Sieversk Dragoon Regiment (4)
      Kinbourn Dragoon Regiment (4)
   20th Brigade:
      White Russia Hussar Regiment (8)
      Volhynie Uhlan Regiment (8)
7th Cavalry Division
   21st Brigade:
      Smolensk Dragoon Regiment (4)
      Pereiaslav Dragoon Regiment (4)
   22nd Brigade:
      Tiraspol Dragoon Regiment (4)
      Dorpat Dragoon Regiment (4)
   23rd Brigade:
      Olivopol Hussar Regiment (8)
      Tchougouiev Uhlan Regiment (8)

Attached:
  Grekov #7 Don Cossack Regiment
  Grekov #8 Don Cossack Regiment
  1st Orenburg Cossack Regiment
  2nd Orenburg Cossack Regiment
  Astakhov #7 Cossack Regiment
  Melnikov #5 Cossack Regiment
  3rd Orel Cossack Regiment
  4th Orel Cossack Regiment
  Melnikov #3 Cossack Regiment
  Loukoffkin Cossack Regiment
  Tourtchaininov Cossack Regiment

OTHER RUSSIAN FORCES

Caucasus:
19th Division: Rutcheff
  Brigade:
    Kazan Infantry Regiment (2)
    Bielov Infantry Regiment (2)
  Brigade:
    Sebastapol Infantry Regiment (2)
    Sousdal Infantry Regiment (2)
  Brigade:
    16th Jager Regiment (2)
    17th Jager Regiment (2)
  Artillery Brigade:
    Position Battery #19 (8–12pdrs & 4 Licornes)
    Light Batteries #36 & #37 (8–6pdrs & 4 Licornes ea)
20th Division: Paulucci
  Brigade:
    Troitsk Infantry Regiment (2)
    Kabardinsk Infantry Regiment (2)
  Brigade:
    Tiflis Infantry Regiment (2)
    Volgoda Infantry Regiment (2)
  Brigade:
    9th Jager Regiment (2)
    15th Jager Regiment (2)
  Artillery Brigade:
    Position Battery #20 (8–12pdrs & 4 Licornes)
    Light Batteries #38 & #39 (8–6pdrs & 4 Licornes ea)

25th Brigade:
  Narva Dragoon Regiment (4)
  Borisoglievsk Dragoon Regiment (4)

St. Petersburg:

25th Division: Baschutski (from Finland)
  Brigade:
    Vorohenz Infantry Regiment (2)
    1st Marine Infantry Regiment (2)
  Brigade:
    2nd Marine Infantry Regiment (2)
    3rd Marine Infantry Regiment (2)
  Artillery Brigade:
    Position Battery #14 (8–12pdrs & 4 Licornes)

Riga: Commanding Officer—Essen I

22nd Division: Lewis
  Brigade:
    Viborg Infantry Regiment (2)
    Viatka Infantry Regiment (2)
  Brigade:
    Staroskol Infantry Regiment (2)
    Olonetz Infantry Regiment (2)
  Brigade:
    29th Jager Regiment (2)
    45th Jager Regiment (2)
  Artillery Brigade:
    Position Battery #22 (8–12pdrs & 4 Licornes)
    Light Batteries #41 & #42 (8–6pdrs & 4 Licornes ea)

Finland: Commanding Officer—Steingell

6th Division: Rachmanoff
  Brigade:
    Azov Infantry Regiment (2)
    Ouglitz Infantry Regiment (2)
  Brigade:
    Nisov Infantry Regiment (2)
    Briansk Infantry Regiment (2)
  Brigade:
    3rd Jager Regiment (2)
  Artillery Brigade:
    Position Battery #21 (8–12pdrs & 4 Licornes)
    Light Battery #27 (8–6pdrs & 4 Licornes)

21st Division: Demidoff

Brigade:
  Neva Infantry Regiment (2)
  Petrovsk Infantry Regiment (2)
Brigade:
  Lithuania Infantry Regiment (2)
  Podolsk Infantry Regiment (2)
Brigade:
  2nd Jager Regiment (2)
  44th Jager Regiment (2)
Artillery Brigade:
  Position Battery #21 (8–12pdrs & 4 Licornes)
  Light Batteries #11 & #40 (8–6pdrs & 4 Licornes ea)
  Pioneer Company
27th Brigade:
  Finland Dragoon Regiment
  Mitau Dragoon Regiment
  Lotchilin Cossack Regiment

Composition of
Russian Reserve Divisions
1812

Reserve Division	Source of the Depot Battalions	Number of Battalions	Commander
30th	14th Division	6	
	4th Division	6	
31st	5th Division	6	
	17th Division	5	
32nd	1st Grenadier Division	6	Generalmajor Hamen
	23rd Division	4	
	11th Division	5	
33rd	3rd Division	3	Generalmajor Villiaminov
	7th Division	7	
34th	24th Division	6	
	26th Division	6	
35th	2nd Grenadier Division	6	Generalmajor Zapolskhoi
	18th Division	6	
36th	12th Division	6	Generalmajor Sorokin
	15th Division	6	
37th	27th Division	6	
	9th Division	6	

Reserve Battalions

39th	Podgochtch	6	Major Korpotov
	Staraia-Roussa	6	Major Frykine
40th	Kholm	6	Major Jerdieiev
	Torpetz	6	Major Netelhorst
41st	Viely	6	Major Glasenap
	Viazma	6	Major Matov
42nd	Elnia	6	Major Timtchenko-Roubane
	Rosslavl	6	Major Stchervob
	Starodoub	6	Major Kotchetoura
43rd	Novgorod-Sieversky	6	Major Joukov
	Konotop	6	Major Voinov
44th	Romny	6	Major Kraievsky
	Isioum	6	Major Svietchine II
45th	Zmiev	6	Major Khodakovsky
	Isioum	6	Major Svietchine II
46th	Tchiguirin	6	Major Inguistov
	Novomirgorod	6	Major Medviedev
47th	Elisabetgrad	6	Major Efimovitch
	Olivopol	6	Major Mamontov

Cavalry

9th	1st Cuirassier Division	4	Generalmajor Prince Repnin
	Guard Cavalry	3	
	1st Cavalry Division	8	
	2nd Cavalry Division	8	
10th	3rd Cavalry Division	8	
	4th Cavalry Division	6	
11th	5th Cavalry Division	8	Generalmajor Lasskin
	2nd Cuirassier Division	4	
12th	6th Cavalry Division	8	
	7th Cavalry Division	8	

Reserve Squadrons

13th	Podgochtch	4	Lt. Col. Lobko
	Staraia-Roussa	4	
	Kholm	4	Major Knabe
	Torpetz	4	
	Elnia	4	Major Dymtchevitch
	Rosslavl	4	

15th	Romny	4
	Akhtyrka	4
16th	Tchiguirin	4
	Novomirgorod	4
	Elisabetgrad	4
	Olviopol	4

Organization of Reserve Corps

I Reserve Corps: Muller
  9th Cavalry Division
  32nd Division
  33rd Division

II Reserve Corps: Ertel
  27th Division
  34th Division
  35th Division
  36th Division
  10th Cavalry Division
  11th Cavalry Division

Riga Garrison: Labanov
  30th Division
  31st Division

Moldavia:
  12th Cavalry Division

Royal Prussian Army Corps
13 May 1812

Advanced Guard: Generallieutenant von Massenbach (in Goldbach)

Right Wing: Colonel von Czarnowsky (in Tapiau)
  1st Combined Hussar Regiment (4)
  2nd Combined Hussar Regiment (2)
  East Prussian Jager Battalion (2 coys)
  Fusilier Battalion 1st Infantry Regiment
  Horse Battery #3

Left Wing: Oberstleutnant von Jurgass (in Labiau)
  2nd Combined Dragoon Regiment (2)
  East Prussian Jager Battalion (2 coys)

Fusilier Battalion 5th Infantry Regiment
Fusilier Battalion 3rd Infantry Regiment
Foot Battery #1
Corps of Battle: General of Infantry von Grawert (in Kongisberg)
   Right Wing: Oberst von Below
      2/1st, 1/3rd Infantry Regiment
      1/4th, 1/5th Infantry Regiment
   Left Wing: Oberstleutnant von Horn (in Caymen)
      2/2nd, 1/10th Infantry Regiment
      1/, 2/Leib Infantry Regiment
      Fus/Leib Infantry
      1/6th Infantry Regiment
      1st Combined Dragoon Regiment (4) (1/4th, 2/4th, 1/5th, 3/5th)
Artillery: Major von Schmidt (in Koenigsberg)
   2nd Prussian Foot Battery (6–6pdrs & 2 How)
   3rd Prussian Foot Battery (6–6pdrs & 2 How)
   4th Brandenburg Foot Battery (6–6pdrs & 2 How)
   Horse Battery #1
   Horse Battery #2
Pioneers: Major Markoff (in Koenigsberg)
   1st Pioneer Company
   2nd Pioneer Company
Train: Major von Herzberg (in Koenigsberg)
   Prussian Park Columns #1, #2, #3, & #4
   2 Bridging Trains

Russian I Corps
10 June 1812

Commanding General—Generallieutenant Count Wittgenstein
Chief of Staff   —Generalmajor d'Auvray
Artillery Commander —Generalmajor Jachwill
Quartermaster Chief   —(vacant) (later Baron Diebitsch)
Service Colonel   —Baron Diebitsch
Chief of Engineers   —Colonel Count Sievers

Advanced Guard: Generalmajor Koulnieff
     Rodinov #2 Don Cossack Regiment (465)
     Platov #4 Don Cossack Regiment (410)
     Grodno Hussar Regiment (4)(560)

Brigade: Colonel Denissiev
  23rd Jager Regiment (2)(1,269)
  24th Jager Regiment (2)(1,227)
Artillery: Colonel Pering
  Light Battery #9 (8–6pdrs & 4 Licornes)

Main Battle Line: Generalmajor Berg
  Brigade: Colonel Frolof
    26th Jager Regiment (2)(1,225)
    25th Jager Regiment (2)(1,309)
  Brigade: Generalmajor Prince of Siberia
    Perm Infantry Regiment (2)(1,267)
    Mohilev Infantry Regiment (2)(1,270)
  Brigade: Colonel Loukoff
    Sievesk Infantry Regiment (2)(1,136)
    Kalouga Infantry Regiment (2)(1,135)
  Brigade: Generalmajor Helfrich
    Tenguinsk Infantry Regiment (2)(1,254)
    Estonia Infantry Regiment (2)(1,279)
  Artillery:
    Position Battery #27 (8–12pdrs & 4 Licornes)(251)
    Position Battery #5 (8–12pdrs & 4 Licornes)(216)
Cavalry: Generalmajor Balk
  Brigade: Colonel de la Caste
    Riga Dragoon Regiment (4)(562)
    Grodno Hussar Regiment (4)(560)
  Artillery: Lt. Col. Suchosantes
    Horse Battery #1 (8–6pdrs & 4 Licornes)(220)
    Horse Battery #3 (8–6pdrs & 4 Licornes)(220)

Reserve
Infantry: Generalmajor Sazonov
  Brigade:
    Converged Grenadiers of 5th and 14th Divisions (4)(1,984)
  Brigade: Colonel Harpe
    Toula Infantry Regiment (2)(1,160)
    Navajinsk Infantry Regiment (2)(1,183)
  Artillery: Colonel Staden
    Light Battery #26 (8–6pdrs & 4 Licornes)(152)
    Light Battery #27 (8–6pdrs & 4 Licornes)(152)
    Position Battery #27 (8–12pdrs & 4 Licornes)(233)
    Pioneer Company (93)
    1st & 2nd Pontooneer Companies (308)

Cavalry: Colonel Falk
 Iambourg Dragoon Regiment (4)(569)

Detached Forces
 Kazan Dragoon Regiment (4)
 Polish Uhlan Regiment (8)
 Riga Dragoon Regiment (4)
 Selivanov Cossack Regiment

Russian I Corps
30 June 1812

Commanding General—Generallieutenant Count Wittgenstein
Chief of Staff   —Generalmajor d'Auvray
Artillery Commander —Generalmajor Jachwill
Quartermaster Chief —(vacant) (later Baron Diebitsch)
Service Colonel   —Baron Diebitsch
Chief of Engineers   —Colonel Count Sievers

Advanced Guard: Generalmajor Koulnieff
 Platov #4 Don Cossack Regiment (336)
 Grodno Hussar Regiment (4)(1,044)
 Brigade: Colonel Denissiev
 23rd Jager Regiment (2)(1,408)
 24th Jager Regiment (2)(1,268)
 Artillery: Colonel Pering
 Position Battery #28 (6 guns)(160)
 Light Battery #9 (8–6pdrs & 4 Licornes)(179)

Main Battle Line: Generalmajor Berg
 Brigade: Colonel Frolof
 25th Jager Regiment (2)(1,285)
 Brigade: Generalmajor Prince of Siberia
 Perm Infantry Regiment (2)(1,215)
 Mohilev Infantry Regiment (2)(1,235)
 Brigade: Kozaczkoffski
 Sievesk Infantry Regiment (2)(1,160)
 Kalouga Infantry Regiment (2)(1,165)
 Brigade:
 Reserve Battalion of 11th Jagers (1)(240)
 Reserve Battalion of 36th Jagers (1)(234)
 Artillery:
 Position Battery #27 (8–12pdrs & 4 Licornes)(213)

Position Battery #5 (8–12pdrs & 4 Licornes)(251)
Light Battery #27 (8–6pdrs & 4 Licornes)(141)
Brigade:
Converged Dragoon Depot Squadrons (4)(501)
    (Moscow, Pskof, Ingremanland, & Kargopol Dragoon Regiments)
2nd Line of Battle: Generallieutenant Kakhoffski
Riga Dragoon Regiment (4)(500)
Iambourg Dragoon Regiment (4)(409)
Horse Battery #1 (8–6pdrs & 4 Licornes)(213)
Reserve Grenadier Battalions
  Leib Grenadiers (1)(228)
  Tauride Grenadiers (1)(302)
  Ekaterinoslav Grenadiers (1)(363)
  Pavlov Grenadiers (1)(304)
  Arakcheyev Grenadiers (1)(267)
  St. Petersburg Grenadiers (1)(357)
  Converged Grenadiers of 5th and 14th Division (4)(1,016 & 972)
Reserve: Generalmajor Sazonov
Converged Cuirassier Depot Squadrons (4)(533)
Converged Guard Depot Squadrons (3)(404)
    (Hussars, Dragoons & Uhlans)
26th Jager Regiment (2)(1,243)
Brigade: Generalmajor Helfrich
Tenguinsk Infantry Regiment (2)(1,204)
Estonia Infantry Regiment (2)(1,1,231)
Brigade: Colonel Harpe
Toula Infantry Regiment (2)(1,1,156)
Navajinsk Infantry Regiment (2)(1,126)
Artillery:
Light Battery #26 (8–6pdrs & 4 Licornes)(160)
Position Battery #14 (8–12pdrs & 4 Licornes)(213)
Position Battery #28 (6 guns)(159)

1st Reserve Division
1 July 1812

Commanding Officer: General Loison
Brigade: Major de Tracy
  1st Demi-brigade de marche
    1st Battalion de marche
      3 companies of 5/7th Légère Regiment (10/428)
      3 companies of 5/33rd Légère Regiment (11/431)

2nd Battalion de marche
   3 companies of 5/13th Line Regiment (8/377)
   3 companies of 5/15th Line Regiment (7/425)
3rd Battalion de marche
   2 companies of 5/17th Line Regiment (5/332)
   2 companies of 5/25th Line Regiment (5/300)
   1 company of 5/12th Line Regiment (2/140)
2nd Demi-brigade de marche: Major Dambrujac
  1st Battalion de marche
   2 companies of 5/48th Line Regiment (3/326)
   2 companies of 5/108th Line Regiment (5/327)
   2 companies of 5/85th Line Regiment (7/332)
  2nd Battalion de marche
   2 companies of 5/30th Line Regiment (6/332)
   2 companies of 5/33rd Line Regiment (6/330)
   2 companies of 5/21st Line Regiment (5/321)
  3rd Battalion de marche
   2 companies of 5/57th Line Regiment (4/327)
   2 companies of 5/61st Line Regiment (6/329)
   2 companies of 5/111th Line Regiment (6/320)
3rd Demi-brigade de marche: Major Aberjoux
  1st Battalion de marche
   3 companies of 5/26th Légère Regiment (6/485)
   3 companies of 5/11th Légère Regiment (10/323)
  2nd Battalion de marche
   2 companies of 5/2nd Line Regiment (5/332)
   2 companies of 5/37th Line Regiment (3/328)
   2 companies of 5/37th Line Regiment (6/330)
   2 companies of 5/93rd Line Regiment (6/330)
  3rd Battalion de marche
   3 companies of 5/24th Légère Regiment (6/489)
4th Demi-brigade de marche
  1st Battalion de marche
   2 companies of 5/19th Line Regiment (6/266)
   2 companies of 5/46th Line Regiment (5/303
   2 companies of 5/18th Line Regiment (5/299)
  2nd Battalion de marche
   2 companies of 5/4th Line Regiment (4/296)
   2 companies of 5/72nd Line Regiment (8/273)
   2 companies of 5/56th Line Regiment (6/307)
6/19th Line Regiment (20/685)
6/37th Line Regiment (15/691)

6/56th Line Regiment (10/709)
6/93rd Line Regiment (16/882)
6/46th Line Regiment (13/793)

Danish Division
1 July 1812

Division: Generallieutenant Ewald
  Brigade: Generalmajor Wegener
    1/, 2/, 3/, 4/Oldenburg Infantry Regiment (4)(56/2,578)
    1/, 2/Schleswig & Holstein Light Infantry Regiment (2)(32/947)
    2/, 6/Hussar Regiment (2)(13/325)
    1/, 2/Jutland Dragoon Regiment (2)(98/287)
  Brigade: Generalmajor Dorrien
    Queen's Infantry Regiment (1)(23/1,138)
    1/Sionie Infantry Regiment (3)(21/938)
    3/Schleswig Infantry Regiment (1)(16/562)
    3/Holstein Infantry Regiment (1)(13/562)
    2/Schleswig Jager Regiment (1)(18/495)
    1/, 2/, 3/, 4/Holstein Cavalry Regiment (4)(23/583)
  Artillery: Major Muck
    Foot Artillery (4/325)
    Horse Artillery (9/460)
    40 guns & 10 howitzers

Russian I Corps
18 July 1812

Commanding General—Generallieutenant Count Wittgenstein
Chief of Staff   —Generalmajor d'Auvray
Artillery Commander —Generalmajor Jachwill
Quartermaster Chief —(vacant) (later Baron Diebitsch)
Service Colonel   —Baron Diebitsch
Chief of Engineers   —Colonel Count Sievers

Advanced Guard: Generalmajor Koulnieff
    Platov #4 Don Cossack Regiment (370)
    Grodno Hussar Regiment (8)(724)

Brigade: Colonel Denissiev
   25th Jager Regiment (2)(1,193)
   26th Jager Regiment (2)(1,168)
Artillery: Lt. Col. Suchosanets
   Horse Battery #1 (8–6pdrs & 4 Licornes)(216)
Main Battle Line: Generalmajor Berg
  Brigade: Generalmajor Prince of Siberia
   Perm Infantry Regiment (2)(1,215)
   Mohilev Infantry Regiment (2)(1,235)
  Artillery: Baikov
   Light Battery #27 (8–6pdrs & 4 Licornes)(140)
  Brigade: Colonel Loukoff
   Sievesk Infantry Regiment (2)(1,160)
   Kalouga Infantry Regiment (2)(1,065)
  Artillery: Lt. Col. Paring
   Light Battery #9 (8–6pdrs & 4 Licornes)(140)
  Brigade:
   24th Jager Regiment (2)(1,285)
   23rd Jager Regiment (2)(1,208)
  Artillery:
   Position Battery #5 (8–12pdrs & 4 Licornes)(213)
   Position Battery #14 (8–12pdrs & 4 Licornes)(234)
   Light Battery #27 (8–6pdrs & 4 Licornes)
   Pioneer Company (93)
2nd Line of Battle: Generallieutenant Kakhoffski
  Brigade:
   Converged Grenadier Battalions of 5th & 14th Divisions (4)(1,984)
  Brigade:
   Position Battery #27 (8–12pdrs & 4 Licornes)(140)
  Brigade:
   Reserve Grenadier Battalions (1,581)
     Leib Grenadiers (1)
     Tauride Grenadiers (1)
     Ekaterinoslav Grenadiers (1)
     Pavlov Grenadiers (1)
     Arakcheyev Grenadiers (1)
     St. Petersburg Grenadiers (1)
  Artillery: Captain Bistrom
   Horse Battery #3 (8–6pdrs & 4 Licornes)(224)
  Cavalry: Generalmajor Balk
   Riga Dragoon Regiment (4)(500)
   Iambourg Dragoon Regiment (4)(409)

Reserve: Generalmajor Sasonov
  Brigade: Colonel Harpe
    Toula Infantry Regiment (2)(1,081)
    Navajinsk Infantry Regiment (2)(1,051)
  Artillery:
    Light Battery #26 (4–6pdrs & 2 Licornes)(72)
  Brigade: Generalmajor Helfrich
    Tenguinsk Infantry Regiment (2)(1,129)
    Estonia Infantry Regiment (2)(1,153)
  Artillery:
    Light Battery #26 (4–6pdrs & 2 Licornes)(73)
Reserve Cavalry: Prince Repnin
    Converged Cuirassier Depot Squadrons (4)(500)
    Converged Guard Depot Squadrons (3)(370)
      (Hussars, Dragoons & Uhlans)
    Depot Squadron of Pskof Dragoon Regiment (1)(127)
    Converged Jager Regiment (Depot Bns) (374)
    Position Battery #26 (8–12pdrs & 4 Licornes)(236)

Army of Moldavia
19 July 1812

Commanding General —Admiral Tchichagov
Chief of Staff   —Generallieutenant Sabaneiev
Quartermaster General—Generalmajor Berg
Service General   —Generalmajor Tuchkov II

I Corps: Generallieutenant Langeron
13th Division: Generallieutenant Langeron
    Vieliki-Loutzk Infantry Regiment
    Galitz Infantry Regiment
      (5 Battalions)
    Saratov Infantry Regiment (2)
    29th Jager Regiment
    45th Jager Regiment
      (5 Battalions)
    Position Battery #22 (8–12pdrs & 4 Licornes)
    Light Batteries #41 & #42 (8–6pdrs & 4 Licornes ea)
    Grekov #7 Don Cossack Regiment
    Panteleieff #3 Cossack Regiment
    1st Orenburg Cossack Regiment

18th Brigade:
  Saint Petersburg Dragoon Regiment (4)
  Lithuania Dragoon Regiment (4)
  Horse Battery #14

2nd Corps: Generalmajor Essen II
8th Division: Generalmajor Essen II
  Archangle Infantry Regiment
  Schusselburg Infantry Regiment
    (5 battalions)
  Old Ingremanland Infantry Regiment (2)
  Ukraine Infantry Regiment (2)
  37th Jager Regiment (2)
  Horse Battery #15 (8–6pdrs & 4 Licornes)
  Light Batteries #14 & #15 (8–6pdrs & 4 Licornes ea)
  Position Battery #8 (8–12pdrs & 4 Licornes)
  Smolensk Dragoon Regiment (4)
  Sieversk Dragoon Regiment (4)
  Grekov #8 Don Cossack Regiment
  2nd Orenburg Cossack Regiment
  Astakhov #7 Cossack Regiment

3rd Corps: Generallieutenant Voinov
10th Division: Generalmajor Lieven
  Kursk Infantry Regiment (2)
  Crimea Infantry Regiment (2)
  Bieloserk Infantry Regiment (3)
  9th Jager Regiment (2)
  39th Jager Regiment (2)
  Position Batteries #10 & #30 (8–12pdrs & 4 Licornes ea)
  Light Batteries #18 & #50 (8–6pdrs & 4 Licornes ea)
  Kinbourn Dragoon Regiment (4)
  White Russia Hussar Regiment (8)
  3rd Orel Cossack Regiment
  4th Orel Cossack Regiment
  Melnikov #3 Cossack Regiment

4th Corps: Generalmajor Bulatoff
16th Division: Generalmajor Bulatoff
  Okhotski Infantry Regiment (2)
  Kamchatka Infantry Regiment (2)
  Mingrelia Infantry Regiment (2)
  Position Battery #16 & #39 (8–12pdrs & 4 Licornes ea)
  Light Battery #31 (8–6pdrs & 4 Licornes)

Horse Battery #17 (8–6pdrs & 4 Licornes)
Pereiaslav Dragoon Regiment (4)
Tiraspol Dragoon Regiment (4)
Dorpat Dragoon Regiment (4)
Tchougouiev Uhlan Regiment
Melnikov #5 Cossack Regiment

Reserve Corps: Generallieutenant Savanief
Jaroslav Infantry Regiment (3)
Olonetz Infantry Regiment (3)
7th Jager Regiment (3)
Olviopol Hussar Regiment (8)
Loukoffkin Cossack Regiment
Horse Battery #16 (8–6pdrs & 4 Licornes)

Detached for Service: General Linforst
Neutchlot Infantry Regiment (3)
27th Jager Regiment (3)
43rd Jager Regiment (3)
Tourtchaininov Cossack Regiment
Kirejov Cossack Regiment
Volhynie Uhlan Regiment (8)
Light Battery #30 (8–6pdrs & 4 Licornes)

Russian 3rd Army of the West
20 July 1812

Commanding Officer —Generallieutenant Tormassov
Chief of Staff   —Generalmajor Inzoff
Quartermaster General—Generalmajor Renne
Chief of Artillery   —Generalmajor Sievers

Detachment Adjudant General Count Lambert (Moving on Ratno)
Brigade:
10th Jager Regiment (2)
14th Jager Regiment (2)
Part of 17th Cavalry Brigade: Madetof
Alexandria Hussar Regiment (8)
15th Brigade: Berdiaief
Tver Dragoon Regiment (4)
Starodoub Dragoon Regiment (4)
Horse Battery #12 (6 guns)

Cossacks:
  3 Cossack Pulks

Detachment: Generalmajor Prince Tchervatov (Moving on Ratno)
  Part of 17th Cavalry Brigade: Knorring
    Tartar Uhlan Regiment (8)
    Eupatorie Tartar Regiment
    Vladamir Infantry Regiment (2)
    Dnieper Infantry Regiment (2)
    28th Jager Regiment (2)
    Horse Battery #11 (8–6pdrs & 4 Licornes)
    Light Battery #34 (8–6pdrs & 4 Licornes)

Advanced Guard: Generalmajor Tschaplitz
  Brigade:
    Pavlovgrad Hussar Regiment (8)
    Loubny Hussar Regiment (6)
  Brigade: Prince Wiasemski
    13th Jager Regiment (2)
    Horse Battery #12 (6 guns)
    Pioneer Company of Captain Kuzewitsch
    Barbantchikov #2 Cossack Regiment

Corps: Generallieutenant Markoff
Division:
  Brigade: Bernardos
    Tambov Infantry Regiment (2)
    Kostroma Infantry Regiment (2)
9th Division: Udom
  Brigade: Reichel
    Riajsk Infantry Regiment (2)
    Apcheron Infantry Regiment (2)
  Brigade: Seliverstov
    Iakout Infantry Regiment (2)
    Nacheburg Infantry Regiment (2)
  Artillery Brigade:
    Position Battery #2 (8–12pdrs & 4 Licornes ea)
    Light Batteries #16, #17, & #35 (8–6pdrs & 4 Licornes ea)
15th Division: Nasimov
  Brigade: Oldecop
    Kourin Infantry Regiment (2)
    Kolyvan Infantry Regiment (2)
  Brigade: Stepanov
    Koslov Infantry Regiment (2)
    Vitebsk Infantry Regiment (2)

Artillery Brigade:
   Position Battery #15 & #18 (8–12pdrs & 4 Licornes)
   Light Batteries #28 & #29 (8–6pdrs & 4 Licornes ea)
24th Cavalry Brigade:
   Taganrog Dragoon Regiment
   Vladimir Dragoon Regiment

Reserve: Generalmajor Chowanski
Brigade
   38th Jager Regiment (2)
Brigade:
   Converged Grenadiers (4)
Artillery:
   Light Battery #34 (8–6pdrs & 4 Licornes)
   Horse Battery #13 (8–6pdrs & 4 Licornes)

Detachment:
   Loubny Hussar Regiment (2)
   Serpuchov Dragoon Regiment (4)
   Converged Grenadier Battalions (2)
   23rd Jager Regiment (2)

Order of Battle for Kobrin
27 July 1812

RUSSIAN FORCES

On the North: (Road to Pruszana) Lt. Col. Matadov
   Alexandria Hussar Regiment (2)
   Cossacks (1 Sotnia)

Second Wave
   Alexandria Hussar Regiment (2)
   Starodoub Dragoon Regiment (2)
   Tartar Uhlan Regiment (1)

   These troops were, after the fall of Brest, moving from Brest to Kobrin.

On the West: (Road to Antopol)
   Pavlovgrad Hussar Regiment (8)
   13th Jager Regiment

On the South: (Road to Bulkovo and Brest)
   Starodoub Dragoon Regiment (2)
   Tver Dragoon Regiment (2)
   10th Jager Regiment
   14th Jager Regiment

SAXON FORCES

Brigade: Generalmajor Klengel
        König Infantry Regiment (2)
        Niesmeuschel Infantry Regiment (2)
Cavalry: Prinz Clemen Uhlan Regiment (3)
Artillery: 2 Regimental Batteries (4–4pdrs ea)

French Grande Armée
1 August 1812

Commander-in-Chief: Emperor Napoleon Bonaparte

Chief of Staff: Major General Berthier, Prince of Wagram and Neuchatel

Aides-de-camp to Bonaparte:

Baron Lejeune	Colonel of Engineers
Baron Flahaut	Colonel
Baron Pernet	Adjudant Commandant
Baron de Fesenzac	Chef d'escadron
D'Astorg	Chef d'escadron
Bongars	Chef d'escadron
Baron de Montesquiou	Capitaine
Baron Noailles	Capitaine
Baron Lecouteulx	Capitaine

Baggagemaster to the Chief of Staff: Capitaine Rieggert

General Staff of the Grande Armée

General de division	Count Sanson	Topography
	Caulaincourt	Commandant of General Staff
General de brigade	Count Bailly . . . . de Monthion	Chief of staff
. . . .	Baron Guillemont	Commander of lesser staff
. . . .	Baron Jomini	Staff historian
Commanding Adjudants .	Puthon, Simonin, Aubert, Michal, Prince de Hohenzollern, Falkowski, Pinthon de Fernig, Thery, Dupuy, Meynadier, Hulot, Lorinet	
Colonel	Gourry	
Chefs d'escadron or . . . . Chefs de bataillon	Galbois, Bedos, Stoffel, Fontenilles, Laczinski, Malezewski, Blakwel, Saint-Remy, Varmaesen, Allouis, Saint-Simon, Marquessac, Latte,	

	Dufouard, Dubourg, Gauthier, Pariset, Zadera, Laroche, Saint-Donat
Captains	Morot, Freval, Mathey, Deschamps, Blouin, Bonamy, Villemereuil, Ginnet, Bellanger, Meckenem, Prysie, Meresse, Deyragues, Guillot de la Poterie, Sainte-Croix, Levasseur, Theubet, Motte, Roucy, Garnier, Mirebeau, Descharmes, de Mondreville, Ledoux, de Courbon, de Soucy, de la Moussaye, Brunier, Delaplace

Geographical Engineers

Chef de bataillon	Boclet
Capitaines 1er Classe . . .	Delahaue, Bagetti (Sr.), Desnoyers
Capitaines 2e Classe . . .	Perripont, Regnault, Simondi, Chandellier
Lieutenants	Berlier, Aymard
Designers	Beuvelot, Bernard, Soinard, Guillard

Imperial Gendarmerie

General de brigade	Lauer	Commander
Chef d'escadron	Weber	Commander of the public force
Lieutenant	Coutant	Baggagemaster of General Staff

General Officers, Senior Officers, and others assigned to the General Staff:

General de division	Count Rapp
. . . .	Count Milhaud
. . . .	Count Baraguey d'Hillers
General de brigade	Lancantin, Heyligers, Franceschi, Bertrand, Barthiez de Saint-Hilaire, Lambert, Jalras, Corsin, Normand, Godard, Fabre, Evers, Margaron
Adjudants commandants	Amira, Thomasset
Chef de bataillon	Bosse

Other General Officers, Senior Officers and others assigned to the army:

		Posts during Campaign
General de division	Count Hogendorp	Governor of Lithuania in Vilna
. . . .	Baron Durutte	in Berlin
. . . .	Count Dutaillis	in Warsaw
. . . .	Count Charpentier	in Vitebsk
. . . .	Gomes Freyre	in Glouboke
. . . .	Marquis d'Alorna	in Mohilev
. . . .	Baillet-de-la-Tour	in Elbing
General de brigade	Castella	in Koenigsburg
. . . .	Corsin	in Pillau Fortress

....	Jomini	in Vilna
....	Plauzonne	in Plock
....	Ferrière	in Bialystok
....	Tarayre	in Kowno
....	Voyezinski	in Thorn
....	Wedel	in Wilkowski
....	Brun	in Grodno
....	Bronikowski	in Minsk
Adjudants commandants	Barrin	in Erfurt
....	Rippert	in Posen
....	Kossakowski	in Polotsk
Major	Cothias	in Gloubokoe

ADMINISTRATION OF THE IMPERIAL QUARTERS

Chief disbursing officer	Jonville		
Assistant inspector of reviews .	Vilain		
Health Service	Chardel	....	Physician
....	Saulnier	....	Surgeon major
....	Demarbaix	..	Surgeon major
....	Ruchet	.....	Pharmacist major

Administration

General Director	Count Dumas ...... General de division
Disbursing Agents	Chambon, Le Gorgne de Boigne, Trousset, Dumast, Robinet, Barthomeuf, Jacqueminot, Blin-Mutrel, Sartelon, Derville
War Commissioners ...	Lajard, Genet, Daudy, Renoud, Rolland, Dorigny, Alisse

INSPECTOR OF REVIEWS

Chief Inspector	Vienot Vaublanc
Assistant Inspector	Drolenvaux
Inspector of Cavalry Reviews	Lamer

Administrative Services

Health Service	Desgenettes ...	Chief Physician
......	Larrey	Chief Surgeon
......	Laubert	Chief Pharmacist
......	Bourdin	General Hospital Manager
......	Courtin	General Hospital Manager
Subsistances	Bagieu	Bread
......	Teubell	Bread
......	Valette	Meat
......	Aumont	Forage
......	Levrault	Printing

ARTILLERY STAFF

Commander of Artillery	Lariboisière ...	General de division
Chief of staff	Charbonnel	General de brigade
Assistant Chief of Staff	Marion	Colonel
Director of Grand Park	Neigre	Colonel

Bridging Train

Commander in Chief	Eblé	General de division
Chief of Staff	Chapelle	Colonel
Park Director	Zabern	Chef de bataillon
Commander of 1st Train	Peyerimhoff ...	Chef de bataillon
Commander of 2nd Train	Cahpuis	Chef de bataillon
Commander of 3rd Train	Larue	Chef de bataillon

SIEGE TRAIN

Danzig Siege Train

Train Commander	Darancey	General de brigade
Director	Gargant	Major
Assistant Director	Noël	Chef de bataillon

Magdebourg Siege Train

Train Commander	Traviel	General de division
Director	Cachardy	Major
Assistant Director	Paravicini	Chef de bataillon

GENERAL ENGINEERING STAFF

Commander of Engineers	Chasseloup	General de division
Chief of Staff	Liédot	Colonel

Engineering Park

Director	Montfort	Colonel
Assistant Director	Nempde	Chef de bataillon

Imperial Guard

Commander-in-Chief	Mortier	Maréchal d'Empire
Chief of Staff	unknown	

Headquarter Guard:
Neuchatel Battalion (1 + artillery co)(2–6pdrs)
Guides de la Chef (1 sqn)

Old Guard:

Commander-in-Chief	Lefebvre	Maréchal d'Empire

3rd Division: General de division Curial
   Brigade: General de brigade Boyer
    1st Chasseur à Pied (2 + artillery co)(34/1452)
    (2–3pdrs)*

* These companies are detachments from the 1st & 2nd companies of Cannonier
  Conscrits de la Garde

2nd Chasseur à Pied (2 + artillery co)(41/1,245)
(2–3pdrs)*
Brigade: Général de brigade Michel
1st Grenadier à Pied (2 + artillery co)(31/1,294)
(2–3pdrs)*
2nd Grenadier à Pied (2 + artillery co)(33/1,079)
(2–3pdrs)*
3rd Grenadier à Pied (2 + artillery co)(41/1,165)
(2–3pdrs)*
Artillery Reserve:
Brigade: Général de brigade Desvaux
1st Old Guard Horse Artillery (4/103)
(4–6pdrs & 2 How ea)
2nd Old Guard Horse Artillery (4/78)
(4–6pdrs & 2 How ea)
3rd Old Guard Horse Artillery (3/79)
(4–6pdrs & 2 How ea)
4th Old Guard Horse Artillery (4/82)
(4–6pdrs & 2 How ea)

Young Guard:
Commander-in-Chief . . . . . .   Mortier . . . .   Maréchal d'Empire
Chief of Staff . . . .   Meinadier . . . .

1st Division: General de division Delaborde
Brigade: General de brigade Berthezène
(brigade assigned later)
4th Voltigeur Regiment (2)
4th Tirailleur Regiment (2)
5th Voltigeur Regiment (2)(28/917)
Brigade: General de brigade Lanusse
6th Voltigeur Regiment (2)(25/621)
6th Tirailleur Regiment (2)(22/548)
5th Tirailleur Regiment (2)(28/1,011)
Artillery: General de brigade Nourry
4th Company Cannoniers Conscrits (3/81)(8–3pdrs)
5th Artillery Train Company (1/143)
2/5th Sapper Battalion (2/90)
2nd Division: General de division Roguet
Brigade: General de brigade Boyledieu
1st Tirailleur Regiment (2)(25/788)
1st Voltigeur Regiment (2)(22/928)

* These companies are detachments from the 1st & 2nd companies of Cannonier
Conscrits de la Garde

Brigade: General de brigade Lanbere
  Flanquers Regiment (2)(25/1,134)
  Fusilier Chasseur Regiment (2)(33/1,322)
  Fusilier Grenadier Regiment (2)(30/1,391)
Artillery: Colonel Villeneuve
  13/, 14/8th Foot Artillery (8/178)
  6/4th Train Battalion (1/97)
  2/7th Train Battalion (0/41)
  Sappers (5/102)
  Train des equipages (0/44)
  Administration (2/44)
Vistula Legion: General de division Claparède
  Brigade: General de brigade Cholpicki
    1st Vistula Regiment (2 + artillery co)
      (19/1,319)(2–3pdrs)
    2nd Vistula Regiment (2 + artillery co)
      (28/1,256)(2–3pdrs)
    (3rd Battalions joined their regiments later)
  Brigade: General de brigade
    3rd Vistula Regiment (2 + artillery co)
      (27/1,245)(2–3pdrs)
    4th Vistula Regiment (2 + artillery co)
      (2–3pdrs)
    (3rd Battalions joined their regiments later)
Attached to the Guard:
  Brigade:
    Portuguese Chasseur à Cheval Regiment (3)
    7th Chevauléger Regiment (4)
  Brigade:
    Velites of Turin (1)
    Velites of Florence (1)
    Italian Gardes d'Honneur (1 sqn)
    Spanish Pioneer Battalion
  Artillery: General de division Nourry
    3rd Conscrit Cannonier Company (4/77)(8–3pdrs)
    1st & 2nd Old Guard Foot Artillery (8/182)
      (6–12pdrs & 2 How ea)
    3rd & 4th Old Guard Foot Artillery (9/199)
      (6–6pdrs & 2 How)
    5th & 6th Old Guard Foot Artillery (6/217)
      (6–6pdrs & 2 How)
    Artillery Artisans (0/6)
    3/2nd Train Battalion (1/108)

1/,2/1st Train Battalion (2/125)
3/,4/1st Train Battalion (1/152)
Equipage Train (1/62)
3rd Division Artillery Artisans (2/62)
Other Artillery Artisans (2/89)
Guard Cavalry: Maréchal Bessières
Division: General de division Walther
  Brigade: General de brigade St. Sulpice
    Empress Dragoon Regiment (4)(65/1,015)
    Grenadier à Cheval Regiment (5)(70/1,096)
  Brigade: General de brigade Guyot
    Chasseur à Cheval Regiment (5)(70/1,107)
    Mameluke Squadron (8/67)
  Brigade: General de brigade Krasinski
    1st Chevauléger lancier de la Garde Regiment (Polish)
      (4)(69/887)
  Brigade: General de brigade Colbert
    2nd Chevauléger lancier de la Garde Regiment (Dutch)
      (4)(57/1,095)
    Gendarmerie d'Elite (2)(28/363)
Artillery: General de brigade Devaux
  1/, 2/1st Horse Artillery (5/124)
  2/, 3/7th Principal Train Battalion (2/146)
Artillery Reserve: General de division Sorbier
  2/,3/,4/Young Guard Horse Artillery (7/173)
    (4–6pdrs & 2 How ea)
  1/1st Guard Train Battalion (1/125)
  1/,5/Young Guard Horse Artillery (6/157)
    (6–6pdrs & 2 How ea)
  1/,2/Young Guard Foot Artillery (6–6pdrs & 2 How ea)
  2/,6/2nd Guard Train (7/214)
  6/2nd Guard Train Battalion (1/152)
  5/,6/1st Horse Artillery (5/134)
    (6–6pdrs & 2 How ea)
  3/,4/Young Guard Foot Artillery (6/195)
  3/,4/2nd Guard Train Battalion (2/267)
  5/,6/Young Guard Foot Artillery (7/214)
  1/,5/2nd Guard Train Battalion (2/226)
  15/,16/8th Foot Artillery (5/174)
  5/7th Principal Train Battalion (1/150)
Reserve Artillery Park:
  Det. Conscrit Cannoniers (1/42)(2–3pdrs)
  Det. Guard Artillery Artisans & Pontooniers (3/236)

3/,6/1st Guard Train Battalion (2/287)
Det. Conscrit Cannoniers (1/53)(2–3pdrs)
2/1st & 1/,2/,3/,6/2nd Guard Train (3/285)
Det. Conscrit Cannoniers (1/45)(2–3pdrs)
Det. 16th Artillery Artisans (2/41)
6/7th Principal Train Battalion (2/150)
1/,6/4th Principal Train Battalion (2/210)
3/1st Pontoonier Battalion (2/115)
2/,3/4th Principal Train Battalion (4/267)
1/,2/,3/,5/,6/13th Train (bis) Battalion (5/682)
10/8th Foot Artillery (3/93)
12/8th Foot Artillery (3/88)
14/8th Foot Artillery (4/91)
15/8th Foot Artillery (3/79)
16/8th Foot Artillery (3/78)
1/8th Horse Artillery (3/64)
   (4–6pdrs & 2 How ea)
2/1st Horse Artillery (3/65)
   (4–6pdrs & 2 How ea)
5/1st Horse Artillery (3/62)
   (4–6pdrs & 2 How ea)
6/8th Horse Artillery (3/65)
   (4–6pdrs & 2 How ea)
Det. 16th Artillery Artisans (0/9)
Engineer Park: General de brigade Kirgener
   6/5th Sapper Battalion (3/117)
   1st Cleve-Berg Sapper Company (3/118)
   Marine Artisan Battalion & 1st Battalion of l'Escaut
     (16/824)
   1/, 7/Guard Marine Battalion (8/221)
   Guard Equipage (3 companies)(8/516)
   1/,2/,3/,4/,5/,6/7th Equipage (15/705)
Equipage of the General Quarters:
   3/,4/,5/,6/2nd Equipage Battalion (8/445)
   1/,2/,3/,4/,5/,6/10th Equipage Battalion (15/772)
   1/,2/,3/6th Equipage Battalion (9/396)
   4/,5/,6/9th Equipage Battalion (4/390)
   1/,2/,3/,4/,5/,6/14th Equipage Battalion
   1/,2/,3/,4/,5/,6/15th Equipage Battalion (11/775)
   1/,2/,3/,4/,5/,6/16th Equipage Battalion
   1/,2/,3/,4/,5/,6/17th Equipage Battalion
   1/,2/,3/18th Equipage Battalion (9/380)

1/,2/,3/,4/,5/,6/20th Equipage Battalion (13/199)
1/,2/,3/,4/,5/,6/21st Equipage Battalion (12/491)
1/,2/,3/,4/,5/,6/22nd Equipage Battalion (13/470)
1/,2/,3/,4/,5/,6/23rd Equipage Battalion (12/467)
1st & 2nd Artisans of Military Equipage Companies (5/237)
1st Ambulance Company (3/107)
Artillery General Park
    10/1st Foot Artillery (3/98)
    21/2nd Foot Artillery (3/104)
    17/,22/5th Foot Artillery (5/216)
    8/9th Foot Artillery (2/90)
    15th & 18th Artillery Artisans Companies (2/140)
Bridging Train:
    1/,7/,9/1st Pontoonier Battalion (6/282)
    2/,3/,4/,5/,6/2nd Pontoonier Battalion (11/346)
    1/,2/,3/,4/,5/,6/8th Pontoonier Battalion (8/567)
    1/,2/,3/,4/,5/,6/9th Pontoonier Battalion (7/606)
Siege Trains:
  Danzig Siege Train: General de brigade Darancey
    4/5th Foot Artillery (3/124)
    6/,12/9th Foot Artillery (4/219)
    1/,10/,11/,14/,21/4th Foot Artillery (7/484)
    16 Mortars
    30 24pdrs
    60 12pdrs
    24 Howitzers
  Magdeburg Siege Train: General de division Taviel
    5/,16/5th Foot Artillery (3/216)
    15/,19/,21/,22/7th Foot Artillery (7/422)
    20 24pdrs
    40 12pdrs
    20 Howitzers
    20 Mortars
  Siege Equipage Train:
    4/,6/2nd Principal Train Battalion (2/262)
    3/3rd Principal Train Battalion (1/119)
    2/11th Principal Train Battalion (1/155)
    3/12th Principal Train Battalion (1/140)

I CORPS

Commander-in-Chief . . . . . .   Davout . . . .   Maréchal d'Empire
Chief of Staff . . . .   Baron Romeuf   . . . .   General de brigade

1st Division: General de division Morand
  1st Brigade: General de brigade d'Alton
    13th Légère Regiment (5 + artillery co) (102/3,406)
      (4–3pdrs)
  2nd Brigade: General de brigade Gratien
    17th Regiment (5 + artillery co) (96/3,498)
      (4–3pdrs)
  3rd Brigade: General de brigade Bonnamy
    30th Line Regiment (5 + artillery co) (93/3,715)
      (4–3pdrs)
    2nd Baden Line Regiment (2 + artillery co) (45/1,343)
      (2–3pdrs)
  Artillery: Chef de bataillon Raindre
    1/7th Foot Artillery (3/103) (6–6pdrs & 2 How)
    7/1st Horse Artillery (3/88) (4–6pdrs & 2 How)
    7th Artillery Artisan Company (0/4)
    1/, 2/1st Principal Train Battalion (1/156)
    6/3rd Sapper Battalion (3/98)
    1/12th Military Equipage Battalion (1/75)
2nd Division: General de division Friant
  1st Brigade: General de brigade Dufour
    15th Légère Regiment (5 + artillery co)(113/3,674)
      (4–3pdrs)
  2nd Brigade: General de brigade Vandedem
    33rd Line Regiment (5 + artillery co)(110/3,359)
      (4–3pdrs)
  3rd Brigade: General de brigade Grandeau
    48th Line Regiment (5 + artillery co)(98/3,270)
      (2–3pdrs)
    Joseph Napoleon Regiment (2 + artillery co)(47/1,678)
      (2–3pdrs)
  Artillery: Chef de bataillon Cabrie
    2/7th Foot Artillery (3/100)(6–6pdrs & 2 How)
    5/3rd Horse Artillery (3/79)(4–6pdrs & 2 How)
    Det. Artillery Artisan (0/4)
    4/, 6/1st Principal Train Battalion (1/154)
    5/5th Sapper Battalion (2/110)
    4/12th Military Equipage Battalion (2/120)

3rd Division: General de division Gudin
  1st Brigade: General de brigade Desailly
    7th Légère Regiment (5 + artillery co)(107/3,600)
      (4–3pdrs)
    12th Line Regiment (5 + artillery co)(115/3,760)
      (4–3pdrs)
  2nd Brigade: General de brigade Leclerc
    127th Line Regiment (2 + artillery co)(46/1,366)
      (2–3pdrs)
    21st Line Regiment (5 + artillery co)(113/3,629)
      (4–3pdrs)
    8th Rhinbund (Mecklenburg-Strelitz) Battalion (18/399)
  Artillery: Colonel Pelgrin
    3/7th Foot Artillery (3/104)(6–6pdrs & 2 How)
    4/3rd Horse Artillery (4/89)(4–6pdrs & 2 How)
    Det. Artillery Artisan (0/4)
    1/, 4/1st Principal Train Battalion (1/174)
    9/5th Sapper Battalion (3/117)
    1/, 3/12th Military Equipage Battalion (Det)(1/63)
4th Division: General de division Dessaix
  1st Brigade: General de brigade Barbanègre
    33rd Légère Regiment (4 + artillery co)(66/2,470)
      (4–3pdrs)
  2nd Brigade: General de brigade Frederichs
    85th Line Regiment (5 + artillery co)(109/3,930)
      (4–3pdrs)
  3rd Brigade: General de brigade Leguay
    108th Line Regiment (5 + artillery co)(103/3,647)
      (4–3pdrs)
  Artillery: Chef de bataillon Thevenot
    9/7th Foot Artillery (3/109)(6–6pdrs & 2 How)
    2/5th Horse Artillery (3/95)(4–6pdrs & 2 How)
    Det. Artillery Artisans (0/4)
    3/, 6/Principal Train Battalion (1/191)
    3/2nd Sapper Battalion (2/114)
    4/12th Military Equipage Battalion (2/83)
5th Division: General de division Compans
  1st Brigade: General de brigade Duppelin
    25th Line Regiment (5 + artillery co)(68/2,004)
      (4–3pdrs)
  2nd Brigade: General de brigade Teste
    57th Line Regiment (5 + artillery co)(97/3,575)
      (4–3pdrs)

3rd Brigade: General de brigade Guyardet
 61st Line Regiment (5 + artillery co)(101/3,570)
  (4–3pdrs)
 111th Line Regiment (5 + artillery co)(85/3,762)
Artillery: Chef de bataillon Klie
 2/6th Foot Artillery (3/92)(6–6pdrs & 2 How)
 16/7th Horse Artillery (2/105)(4–6pdrs & 2 How)
 Det. Artillery Artisans (0/4)
 2/, 4/9th Principal Train Battalion (2/156)
 5/3rd Sapper Battalion (2/117)
 3/, 5/12th Military Equipage Battalion (3/89)
Corps Cavalry: General de division Pajol
 1st Light Cavalry Brigade: General de brigade Pajol
  2nd Chasseur à Cheval Regiment (4)(40/816)
  9th Polish Lancer Regiment (4)(32/645)
 2nd Light Cavalry Brigade: General de brigade Bordessoulle
  1st Chasseur à Cheval Regiment (4)(35/824)
  3rd Chasseur à Cheval Regiment (4)(34/828)
Artillery Reserve:
 3/, 17/1st Foot Artillery (5/226)(6–12pdrs & 2 How)
 6/7th Foot Artillery (3/99)(6–6pdrs & 2 How)
 11/, 14/9th Foot Artillery (6/192)(6–6pdrs & 2 How ea)
 7th Artillery Artisan Company (3/32)
 1/, 5/, 6/1st Principal Train Battalion (2/223)
 5/1st Pontoonier Battalion (2/90)
 1/, 5/, 6/1st Principal Train Battalion (2/76)
 6/3rd Principal Train Battalion (0/30)
 1/, 2/, 3/, 4/, 5/9th Principal Train Battalion (6/431)
Engineering Park:
 8/5th Sapper Battalion (2/100)
 1st Engineering Train Company (3/115)
 1/, 3/, 4/, 5/, 6/12th Military Equipage Battalion (6/200)
 3rd Ambulance Company (2/106)
 Gendarmes à Cheval (6/92)

II CORPS

Commander-in-Chief . . . . . .   Oudinot . . . .   Maréchal de France
Chief of Staff . . . .   De Lorencez . . . . . .   General de brigade

6th Division: General de division Legrand
  1st Brigade: General de brigade Albert
    26th Légère Regiment (4 + artillery co)(81/2,931)
    (2–3pdrs)
  2nd Brigade: General de brigade Maison
    19th Line Regiment (4 + artillery co)(85/2,791)
    (2–3pdrs)
  3rd Brigade: General de brigade Moreau
    56th Line Regiment (4 + artillery co)(82/2,678)
    (2–3pdrs)
  4th Brigade: General de brigade Pamplona
    128th Line Regiment (2 + artillery co)(34/1,318)
    (2–3pdrs)
    3rd Portuguese Regiment (2 + artillery co)(37/1,264)
  Artillery: Chef de bataillon Bogaert
    11/5th Foot Artillery (3/100)(6–6pdrs & 2 How)
    6/3rd Horse Artillery (3/92)(4–6pdrs & 2 How)
    Det. 17th Artillery Artisan Company (0/4)
    3/3rd Train (bis) Battalion (1/126)
    4/3rd Sapper Battalion (2/96)
    Gendarmerie (1/10)
8th Division: General de division Verdier (Maison)
  1st Brigade: General de brigade Vivés (Albert)
    11th Légère Regiment (4 + artillery co)(82/3,118)
    (4–3pdrs)
    2nd Line Regiment (5 + artillery co)(104/3,127)
    (4–3pdrs)
  2nd Brigade: General de brigade Pouget
    37th Line Regiment (4 + artillery co)(79/2,540)
    (4–3pdrs)
    124th Line Regiment (3 + artillery co)(6/1,447)
    (2–3pdrs)
  Artillery: Chef de bataillon Levis
    15/5th Foot Artillery (3/112)(6–6pdrs & 2 How)
    1/3rd Horse Artillery (1/95)(4–6pdrs & 2 How)
    Det. 17th Artillery Artisan Company (0/4)
    1/, 5/3rd Train (bis) Battalion (2/170)

3/3rd Sapper Battalion (2/123)
Gendarmes (1/13)
9th Division: General de division Merle
  1st Brigade: General de brigade Candras
    1st Swiss Line Regiment (2 + artillery co)(57/1,314)
    (2–3pdrs)
    2nd Swiss Line Regiment (3 + artillery co)(80/1,707)
    (2–3pdrs)
  2nd Brigade: General de brigade Amey
    4th Swiss Line Regiment (3 + artillery co)(59/1,513)
    (2–3pdrs)
    3rd Provisional Croatian Regiment (2 + artillery co)
    (41/1,582) (2–3pdrs)
  3rd Brigade: General de brigade Coutard
    3rd Swiss Line Regiment (3 + artillery co)(67/1,233)
    (2–3pdrs)
    123rd Line Regiment (3 + artillery co)(68/1,660)
    (2–3pdrs)
  Artillery: Chef de bataillon Webre
    4/7th Foot Artillery (3/103)(6–6pdrs & 2 How)
    5/2nd Horse Artillery (3/73)(4–6pdrs & 2 How)
    Det. 17th Artillery Artisan Company (0/2)
    3/, 5/8th Train (bis) Battalion (1/165)
    5/1st Sapper Battalion (2/103)
    Gendarmerie (1/11)
Corps Cavalry: General de brigade Corbineau
  5th Light Cavalry Brigade: General de brigade Castex
    23rd Chasseur à Cheval Regiment (2)(30/803)
    24th Chasseur à Cheval Regiment (3)(29/781)
  6th Light Cavalry Brigade: General de brigade Corbineau
    20th Chasseur à Cheval Regiment (2)(219)
    7th Chasseur à Cheval Regiment (2)(26/405)
    8th Chevauléger Regiment (4)(26/589)
  Reserve Artillery: Major Lavoy
    1/1st Foot Artillery (3/113)(6–6pdrs & 2 How)
    15/1st Foot Artillery (3/92)(6–6pdrs & 2 How)
    Det. 17th Artillery Artisan Company (0/4)
    1/8th Train (bis) Battalion (1/119)
    5/8th Train (bis) Battalion (1/78)
  Artillery Park: Colonel Levasseur
    21/9th Foot Artillery (3/99)(6–12pdrs & 2 How)
    22/9th Foot Artillery (2/86)(6–12pdrs & 2 How)

11/1st Pontoonier Battalion (2/83)
1/3rd Train (bis) Battalion (0/11)
3/3rd Train (bis) Battalion (0/28)
1/, 2/, 3/, 4/, 5/, 6/8th Train (bis) Battalion (9/405)
2/, 6/11th Train (bis) Battalion (0/8)
Det. 9th Ambulance Company (2/55)
Gendarmerie (0/34)
4/3rd Sapper Battalion (1/99)
Det. 17th Artillery Artisan Company (4/63)

III CORPS

Commander-in-Chief . . . . . .   Ney . . . .   Maréchal de France
Chief of Staff . . . .   Gouré . . . .   General de brigade
10th Division: General de division Ledru
  1st Brigade: General de brigade Gengoult
    24th Line Regiment (4 + artillery co)(84/3,020)
      (2–3pdrs)
    1st Portuguese Line Regiment (2)(51/500)
  2nd Brigade: General de brigade Morion
    46th Line Regiment (4 + artillery co)(82/2,624)
      (2–3pdrs)
  3rd Brigade: General de brigade Bruny
    72nd Line Regiment (4 + artillery co)(88/2,484)
      (2–3pdrs)
    129th Line Regiment (2 + artillery co)(45/984)
      (2–3pdrs)
  Artillery: Chef d'escadron Ragmey
    12/5th Foot Artillery (6–6pdrs & 2 How)
    5/6th Horse Artillery (4–6pdrs & 2 How)
11th Division: General de division Razout
  1st Brigade: General de brigade Joubert
    4th Line Regiment (4 + artillery co)(94/2,209)
      (2–3pdrs)
    18th Line Regiment (4 + artillery co)(88/2,657)
      (2–3pdrs)
  2nd Brigade: General de brigade Compère
    2nd Portuguese Regiment (2)(49/1,432)
    Illyrian Regiment (4)(65/2,505)(joined later)
  3rd Brigade: General de brigade d'Henin
    93rd Line Regiment (4 + artillery co)(87/2,748)
      (2–3pdrs)

Artillery: Chef de bataillon Bernard
   18/5th Foot Artillery (6–6pdrs & 2 How)
   6/5th Horse Artillery (4–6pdrs & 2 How)
25th Division: Royal Prince of Württemberg
   (later General de division Marchand) (Württemberg)
  1st Brigade: Generalmajor von Hugel
    1st Line Regiment "Prinz Paul" (2)(27/1,173)
    4th Line Regiment (2)(28/1,235)
  2nd Brigade: Generalmajor Koch
    2nd Line Regiment "Herzog Wilhelm" (2)(29/1,309)
    6th Line Regiment "Kronprinz" (2)(27/1,220)
  3rd Brigade: Generalmajor von Bruzelles
    1st Light Infantry Battalion (15/675)
    2nd Light Infantry Battalion (15/674)
    1st Jäger Battalion "König" (15/668)
    2nd Jäger Battalion (14/670)
    7th Württemberg Line Regiment (2)(joined later)
  Artillery: Oberstleutnant Brandt
    1st & 2nd Württemberg Foot Artillery (4/160)
     (4–6pdrs & 2 Howitzers ea)
    1st & 2nd Württemberg Horse Artillery (6/250)
     (3–6pdrs & 1 Howitzer ea)
    12pdr Württemberg Foot Battery (2/171)(6–12pdrs)
Cavalry Corps: Generalmajor Wollwrath
  9th Light Brigade: General de brigade Mouriez
    11th Hussar Regiment (4)(29/607)
    6th Chevauléger Regiment (3)(26/530)
    Jäger zu Pferd Regiment #4 "König" (4)(21/464)
  14th Light Brigade: General de brigade Beurman
    28th Chasseur à Cheval Regiment (2)(10/191)
    4th Chasseur à Cheval Regiment (4)(32/708)
    1st Württemberg Chevauxléger Regiment
     "Prinz Adam" (4)(23/509)
    2nd Württemberg Chevauxléger Regiment "Leib" (4)(22/496)
Artillery Reserve:
  16/, 18/, 21/1st Foot Artillery
    (7/279)(6–12pdrs & 2 How ea)
  2/, 7/9th Foot Artillery (4/182)(6–6pdrs & 2 How ea)
Artillery Train
  1/, 2/, 3/, 4/, 5/6th Principal Train Battalion (5/567)
  2/, 3/, 6/14th Principal Train Battalion (2/194)
  1/, 2/2nd Military Equipage Battalion (3/220)

10th Ambulance Company (2/99)
8/1st Pontoonier Battalion (2/92)
5th Ouvrier Company (3/36)
Reserve Company (4/294)
Engineers:
  3/1st Sapper Battalion (3/104)
  7/, 9/3rd Sapper Battalion (5/248)
  Gendarmerie (3/72)

IV CORPS

Commander-in-Chief . . . . . .   Eugène . . . .   Viceroy of Italy
Chief of Staff . . . .   Duke d'Abrantes . . .   General de division
Italian Royal Guard: General de division Pino
  Brigade: General de brigade Lecchi
    Gardes d'honneur (1 co)(17/274)
    Royal Velites (2 + artillery co)(43/1,105)
    Guard Infantry Regiment (2 + artillery co)(45/1,137)
    Guard Conscript Regiment (2 + artillery co)(40/1,084)
    Guard Dragoon Regiment (2 sqn)(19/392)
    Queen's Dragoon Regiment (4)(37/616)
  Artillery: Captain Clement
    1st & 2nd Italian Foot Artillery (4–6pdrs & 1 how)
    1st & 2nd Italian Horse Artillery (4–6pdrs & 1 how)
    Italian Train
    Det. 2nd Artisan Company
      (total artillery—10/373)
    4/1st Sapper Battalion (3/81)
    1/, 3/1st Military Equipage Battalion (3/239)
    Italian Guard Marines (3/99)
13th Division: General de division Delzons
  Brigade: General de brigade Huard
    8th Légère Regiment (2 + artillery co)(45/1,444)
      (2–3pdrs)
    84th Line Regiment (2 + artillery co)(84/2,708)
      (2–3pdrs)
  Brigade: General de brigade Roussel
    1st Provisional Croatian Regiment (2)(45/1,462)
    92nd Line Regiment (4 + artillery co)(83/2,591)
      (2–3pdrs)

Brigade: General de brigade Guyon (added later)
   106th Line Regiment (4 + artillery co)(80/2,704)
    (2–3pdrs)
Artillery: Chef de bataillon Demay
   9/2nd Foot Artillery (6–6pdrs & 2 How)
   2/4th Horse Artillery (4–6pdrs & 2 How)
   2/, 3/7th Train (bis) Battalion
    Total Artillery (8/350)
   7/1st Sapper Battalion (2/128)
   1/9th Military Equipage Battalion (2/116)
14th Division: General de division Broussier
  Brigade: General de brigade de Sivray
   19th Légère Regiment (2 + artillery co)(36/1,401)
    (2–3pdrs)
   9th Line Regiment (4 + artillery co)(86/2,561)
    (2–3pdrs)
  Brigade: General de brigade
   Joseph Napoleon Croatian Regiment (2)(35/1,294)
   35th Line Regiment (4 + artillery co)(76/2,456)
    (2–3pdrs)
  Brigade: General de brigade Pastol
   53rd Line Regiment (4 + artillery co)(78/2,442)
    (2–3pdrs)
  Artillery: Chef de bataillon Hermann
   7/2nd Foot Artillery (6–6pdrs & 2 How)
   3/4th Horse Artillery (4–6pdrs & 2 How)
   1/, 6/7th Train (bis) Battalion
    Total Artillery (8/357)
   2/1st Sapper Battalion (2/135)
   3/9th Military Equipage Battalion (2/111)
15th Division: General de division Pino
  Brigade: General de brigade Fontana
   1st Italian Light Regiment (1)(22/741)
   2nd Italian Line Regiment (4 + artillery co)(86/2,690)
    (2–3pdrs)
  Brigade: General de brigade Guillaume
   3rd Italian Light Regiment (4 + artillery co)(87/3,309)
    (2–3pdrs)
   Dalmatian Regiment (3 + artillery co)(65/1,681)
    (2–3pdrs)
  Brigade: General de brigade Dembrowski
   3rd Italian Line Regiment (4 + artillery co)(89/2,892)
    (2–3pdrs)

Artillery: Colonel Millo
   14/1st Foot Artillery (6–6pdrs & 2 How)
   2/1st Horse Artillery (4–6pdrs & 2 How)
   3rd & 4th Train Companies
      Total Artillery (13/406)
   6/1st Sapper Battalion (3/101)
   2/1st Military Equipage Battalion (2/152)
Corps Cavalry: General de division Ornano
   12th Light Cavalry Brigade: General de brigade Ferriere
      9th Chasseur à Cheval Regiment (3)(28/513)
      19th Chasseur à Cheval Regiment (3)(23/506)
      7th Polish Uhlan Regiment (joined later)
   13th Light Cavalry Brigade: General de brigade Villata
      2nd Italian Chasseur à Cheval Regiment (3)(39/608)
      3rd Italian Chasseur à Cheval Regiment (3)(33/601)
Reserve Artillery: Colonel Montegnet
   5/, 12/3rd Foot Artillery (6/191)(6–12pdrs & 2 How ea)
   1/, 2/, 6/7th Train (bis) Battalion (1/166)
   Det. Artillery Artisans (0/5)
   2nd & 7th Italian Foot Artillery (8/172)
      (6–12pdrs & 2 How ea)
   5th, 6th, & Det. 9th Italian Train Companies (4/197)
   Det. 2nd Italian Ouvrier Company (0/5)
Artillery Park: Colonel Fiereck
   8/, 10/, 20/2nd Foot Artillery (6/250)
   Det. 6/7th Train (bis) Battalion (176)
   1/2nd Pontoonier Battalion (2/83)
   10th Ouvrier Company (4/53)
   2nd Italian Pontoonier Company (5/72)
   Det. 2nd Italian Artillery Artisan Company (1/14)
   2/1st Italian Sapper Battalion (2/39)
   4/, 5/2nd Italian Transport Battalion (4/137)
   2nd Italian Oxen Transport Battalion (6)(14/334)
   Italian Engineering Train Company (2/95)

V CORPS

Commander-in-Chief . . . . . . Prince Poniatowski . General de division
Chief of Staff . . . . Fiszer . . . . General de division

16th Division: General de division Zayonchek
   Brigade: General de brigade Mielzynski
      3rd Polish Line Regiment (3 + artillery co)(63/2,558)
         (2–3pdrs)

15th Polish Line Regiment (3 + artillery co)(59/2,616)
(2–3pdrs)
Brigade: General de brigade Paszkowski
16th Polish Line Regiment (3 + artillery co)(58/2,313)
(2–3pdrs)
13th Polish Line Regiment (3 + artillery co)(67/2,612)
(2–3pdrs)
Artillery:
3rd Polish Foot Artillery Company (5/139)
(4–6pdrs & 2 How)
12th Polish Foot Artillery Company (4/153)
(4–6pdrs & 2 How)
3/Supplementary Artillery Battalion (1/56)
Det. Polish Sapper Battalion (1/71)
Det. Polish Artillery Artisan Company (0/71)
17th Division: General de division Dombrowski
Brigade: General de brigade Zottowski
1st Polish Line Regiment (3 + artillery co)(60/2,336)
(2–3pdrs)
6th Polish Line Regiment (4 + artillery co)(54/2,489)
(2–3pdrs)
Brigade: General de brigade Krasinski
14th Polish Line Regiment (4 + artillery co)(55/2,489)
(2–3pdrs)
17th Polish Line Regiment (4 + artillery co)(60/2,606)
(2–3pdrs)
Artillery: Chef de bataillon Gugenmus
10th Polish Foot Artillery Company (5/162)
(4–6pdrs & 2 How)
11th Polish Foot Artillery Company (5/170)
(4–6pdrs & 2 How)
1/Supplementary Artillery Battalion (1/55)
Det. Polish Sapper Battalion (2/69)
Det. Polish Artillery Artisan Company (0/7)
18th Division: General de division Kniaziewicz
Brigade: General de brigade Grabowski
2nd Polish Line Regiment (3 + artillery co)(56/2,364)
(2–3pdrs)
8th Polish Line Regiment (3 + artillery co)(60/2,362)
(2–3pdrs)
Brigade: General de brigade Pakosz
12th Polish Line Regiment (3 + artillery co)(33/2,173)
(2–3pdrs)

Artillery:
  4th Polish Foot Artillery Company (5/158)(4–6pdrs & 2 how)
  5th Polish Foot Artillery Company (5/148)1(4–6pdrs & 2 how)
  2/Supplementary Battalion (1/56)
  Det. Polish Sapper Battalion (2/59)
  Det. Polish Artillery Artisan Company (0/7)
Corps Cavalry: General de division Kaminski (later Sebastiani
              & Lefebvre-Desnoettes)
  18th Light Brigade:
    4th Polish Chasseur à Cheval Regiment (4)(38/748)
  19th Light Brigade: General de brigade Tyskiewicz
    1st Polish Chasseur à Cheval Regiment (4)(28/624)
    12th Polish Uhlan Regiment (4)(30/467)
  20th Light Brigade: General de brigade Prince A. Sulkowski
    5th Polish Chasseur à Cheval Regiment (4)(32/759)
    13th Polish Hussar Regiment (4)(33/722)
Reserve Artillery: Colonel Gorski
    2nd Polish Horse Artillery Company (5/147)(6–6pdrs)
    14th Polish Foot Artillery Company (3/152)(6–12pdrs)
    4/Supplementary Battalion (2/119)
    Det. Polish Artillery Artisan Company (0/7)
  Bridging Train: Captain Buialski
    Polish Pontooniers (3/118)
    Det. Supplementary Battalion (1/47)
  General Artillery Park:
    7th Polish Foot Artillery Company (5/164)(no guns)
    8th Polish Foot Artillery Company (1/80)(no guns)
    9th Polish Foot Artillery Company (1/85)(no guns)
    13th Polish Foot Artillery Company (1/74)(no guns)
    15th Polish Foot Artillery Company (2/87)(no guns)
    Det. Polish Artillery Artisan Company (2/27)

VI CORPS

Commander-in-Chief . . . . . .   G. St. Cyr . . . .   Général de division
Chief of Staff . . . .   D'Albignac . . . .   Adjudant commandant

19th Division: Generalleutnant Deroy
  Brigade: Generalmajor von Siebein
    1st Bavarian Light Infantry Battalion (1)(16/581)
    1st Bavarian Line Infantry Regiment (2)(38/1,514)
    9th Bavarian Line Infantry Regiment (2)(41/1,507)

Brigade: Generalmajor von Raglovich
  3rd Bavarian Light Infantry Battalion (1)(19/745)
  4th Bavarian Line Infantry Regiment (2)(39/1,444)
  10th Bavarian Line Infantry Regiment (2)(1,473)
Brigade: Generalmajor Count Rechberg
  6th Bavarian Light Infantry Battalion (1)(20/1,009)
  8th Bavarian Line Infantry Regiment (2)(37/1,272)
Artillery: Major Lamey
  1st Light Battery "Widemann" (3–6pdrs & 1 How)
  3rd Light Battery "Halder" (3–6pdrs & 1 How)
    Total for both batteries (6/153)
  11th Battery "Brack" (6–6pdrs & 2 How)(2/74)
  Battery "Rois" (6–6pdrs & 2 How)(3/84)
  Howitzer Battery (6 How)
  1st Train Company (1/52)
  3rd Train Company (1/49)
  11th Train Company (1/36)
  6th Train Company (1/39)
  Park (1/196)
20th Division: Generalleutnant von Wrede
  Brigade: Generalmajor von Vincenti
    2nd Bavarian Light Infantry Battalion (1)(21/710)
    2nd Bavarian Line Infantry Regiment (2)(41/1,513)
    6th Bavarian Line Infantry Regiment (2)(36/1,528)
  Brigade: Generalmajor Count Beckers
    4th Bavarian Light Infantry Battalion (1)(19/732)
    3rd Bavarian Line Infantry Regiment (2)(37/1,508)
    7th Bavarian Line Infantry Regiment (2)(37/1,481)
  Brigade: Oberst Dalwigk (later Generalmajor Haberman,
    Scherer & Volker)
    5th Bavarian Light Infantry Battalion (1)(13/460)
    5th Bavarian Line Infantry Regiment (2)(39/1,504)
    11th Bavarian Line Infantry Regiment (2)(39/1,528)
  Artillery: Oberstleutnant von Zoller
    2nd Light Battery "Gotthard" (3–6pdrs & 1 How)(4/78)
    4th Light Battery "Gravenreuth" (3–6pdrs & 1 How)(4/76)
    5th Battery "Hoffstetten" (6–6pdrs & 2 How)(3/80)
    8th Battery "Ulmer" (6–6pdrs & 2 How)(4/77)
    4th Battery "Berchem" (4–12pdrs & 2 How)
    2nd Train Company (1/79)
    Det. 4th Train Company (0/47)
    4th Train Company (1/37)

5th Train Company (1/32)
8th Train Company (1/32)
Park (1/239)
Engineers (4/22)
Corps Cavalry:
  20th Light Cavalry Brigade: Generalmajor Seydewitz
    3rd Bavarian Chevauxléger Regiment (4)(19/481)
    6th Bavarian Chevauxléger Regiment (4)(20/494)
  21st Light Cavalry Brigade: Generalmajor Preysing
    4th Bavarian Chevauxléger Regiment (4)(189/442)
    5th Bavarian Chevauxléger Regiment (4)(19/461)
    (The 21st Light Brigade and the 1st Light Battery were detached and
    assigned to the IV Corps)

VII CORPS

Commander-in-Chief . . . . . .   Reynier . . . .   General de division
Chief of Staff . . . .   Goure . . . .   Adjudant Commandant

21st Division: Generallieutenant Le Coq
  Brigade: Generalmajor von Steindel
    Libenau Grenadier Battalion (1)(17/688)
    Prinz Frederick Infantry Regiment (2)(33/1,372)
      (Artillery co—1/62—4–4pdrs)
    Prinz Clemens Infantry Regiment (2)(38/1,393)
      (Artillery co—1/62—4–4pdrs)
  Brigade: Generalmajor von Nostitz
    1st Light Infantry Regiment (2)(34/1,384)
    Prinz Anton Infantry Regiment (2)(38/1,373) ·
      (Artillery co—1/62—4–4pdrs)
  Artillery: Major von Grossman
    4th Foot Battery "Rouvroy" (4–6pdrs & 2 How)(4/115)
    Park (3/110)
    Sapper Company (2/66)
22nd Division: Generallieutenant von Funck
  Brigade: Generalmajor Klengel
    von Brause Grenadier Battalion (1)(17/692)
    König Infantry Regiment (2)(31/1,309)
      (Artillery co—1/62—4–4pdrs)
    Niesmeuschel Infantry Regiment (2)(33/1,300)
      (Artillery co—1/62—4–4pdrs)

Brigade: Generalmajor von Sahr
  von Spiegel Grenadier Battalion (1)(17/647)
  Anger Grenadier Battalion (1)(18/673)
  2nd Light Infantry Regiment (2)(37/1,346)
Corps Cavalry: Generallieutenant von Thielmann
  23rd Light Cavalry Brigade: Generalmajor von Gablenz
  Saxon Hussar Regiment (8)(35/780)
  Polenz Chevauxléger Regiment (4)(26/557)
  Prinz Clemens Uhlan Regiment (4)(31/592)
  1st Horse Battery "von Roth" (4/156)(4–6pdrs & 2 How)
Corps Artillery: Major Auenmuller
  1st Foot Battery "von Brause" (4–12pdrs & 2 How)(1/73)
  2nd Foot Battery "Sontag" (4–12pdrs & 2 How)(3/72)

VIII CORPS

Commander-in-Chief . . . . . .   Junot . . . .   General de division
Chief of staff . . . .   Revest . . . .   Adjudant Commandant
23rd Division: Generallieutenant Tharreau
  Brigade: Generalmajor Damas
    3rd Westphalian Light Battalion (1)(23/733)
    2nd Westphalian Line Regiment (3 + artillery co)
      (67/2,400)(2–3pdrs)
    6th Westphalian Line Regiment (2 + artillery co)
      (44/1,522)(2–3pdrs)
  Brigade: Generalmajor Wickenberg
    2nd Westphalian Light Battalion (1)(23/737)
    3rd Westphalian Line Regiment (2 + artillery co)
      (43/1,634)(2–3pdrs)
    7th Westphalian Line Regiment (3 + artillery co)
      (67/2,252)(2–3pdrs)
  Artillery: Nummers (Major Froede)
    1st Westphalian Foot Battery "Froede" (4/184)(6–6pdrs & 2 how)
24th Division: Generallieutenant Ochs
  Brigade: Generalmajor Legras
    Westphalian Grenadier Guards (1 + artillery co)
      (27/805)
      Guard Foot Artillery Battery "Brunig" (2–6pdrs)
    Westphalian Guard Jägers (1)(26/810)
    Westphalian Jäger Karabiniers (1)(28/644)

Brigade: Generalmajor Borstel
  1st Westphalian Jäger Battalion (1)(19/795)
  5th Westphalian Line Regiment (2)(47/1,716)
Brigade: Generalmajor Danloup Verdun
  2nd Westphalian Line Regiment (2)
Artillery: Captain Volmar
  2nd Westphalian Foot Battery "Lemaître" (6–6pdrs & 2 How)
Corps Cavalry: General de division Chabert
  24th Brigade: Generalmajor Hammerstein
    1st Westphalian Hussar Regiment (4)(38/579)
    2nd Westphalian Hussar Regiment (4)(39/585)
  Guard Brigade: Generalmajor Wolf
    Westphalian Guard Chevauxléger Regiment (4)(624)
    Westphalian Garde du Corps (1 co)(91)
Corps Artillery Reserve:
  1st Westphalian Heavy Foot Battery (3/76)(6–12pdrs & 2 how)
  Westphalian Sappers (2/99)
  Westphalian Artillery Artisans (1/22)
  Westphalian Train (1/132)
  Westphalian Gendarmerie (3/50)

IX CORPS

Commander-in-Chief . . . . . . Victor . . . . Maréchal de France
Chief of staff . . . . Unknown . . . . General de brigade
12th Division: General de division Partoneaux
  Brigade: General de brigade Billard
    4/10th Légère Regiment (1)(22/929)
    44th Line Regiment (2 + artillery co)(39/1,749)
      (2–3pdrs)
  Brigade: General de brigade Blammont
    125th Line Regiment (2 + artillery co)(59/1,417)
      (2–3pdrs)
    126th Line Regiment (2 + artillery co)(84/1,417)
      (2–3pdrs)
  Brigade: General de brigade Camas
    Provisional Regiment (3)(1,911)
      4/36th Line Regiment
      4/51st Line Regiment
      4/55th Line Regiment
    29th Légère Regiment (4 + artillery co)(78/2,663)
      (2–3pdrs)

Artillery: Sibille
  20/5th Foot Artillery (3/113)(4–6pdrs & 2 how)
  5/7th Foot Artillery (3/98)(4–6pdrs & 2 how)
  1/14th Train Battalion (0/23)
  5/14th Train Battalion (1/84)
  Det. Artillery Artisans (0/4)
26th Division: General de division Daendels
  Brigade: General de brigade Damas
    1st Berg Infantry Regiment (2)(41/969)
    2nd Berg Infantry Regiment (2)(43/1,079)
    3rd Berg Infantry Regiment (1)(23/579)
    4th Berg Infantry Regiment (2)(48/926)
  Brigade: Generalmajor Hochberg
    1st Baden Line Regiment (2)(40/1,494)
    3rd Baden Line Regiment (2)(35/1,416)
    Baden Jäger Battalion "Lingg" (1)(18/779)
  Brigade: General Prince Emil of Hesse (formed Nov 1812)
    Hessian Leib Regiment (2)
    Leibgarde Regiment (2)
    Garde Fusilier Regiment (2)
    8th Westphalian Line Regiment (2)
  Artillery: Oberstleutnant Bogaert
    Berg Foot Battery (6/102)(4–6pdrs & 2 how)
    Berg Horse Battery (4/86)(4–6pdrs & 2 how)
    Berg Train Company (3/143)
    Baden Foot Battery (6/64)(4–6pdrs & 2 how)
    Baden Train Company (1/166)
28th Division: General de division Girard
  Brigade: General de brigade Ouviller
    4th Polish Line Regiment (2 + artillery co)
      (37/1,294) (2–3pdrs)
    7th Polish Line Regiment (2 + artillery co)
      (39/928) (2–3pdrs)
    9th Polish Line Regiment (2 + artillery co)
      (44/1,237) (2–3pdrs)
  Brigade: Generalmajor Klengel (joined later)
    Saxon von Low Infantry Regiment (2)
    Saxon von Rechten Infantry Regiment (2)
  Artillery:
    1st Polish Foot Battery (4/63) (4–6pdrs & 2 How)
    2nd Polish Foot Battery (4–6pdrs & 2 How)
    Polish Sappers (4/93)

Corps Cavalry: General de brigade Fourier
  30th Brigade: General de brigade Fourier (later Laroche
    Baden Hussar Regiment (4)(17/382)
    Saxon Prinz Johann Chevauléger Regiment (4)(32/524)
  31st Brigade: General de brigade Delatre
    Hessian Chevauléger Regiment (4)(13/335)
    1st Berg Chevauléger-Lancier Regiment (4)(29/664)

X CORPS

Commander-in-Chief . . . . . . Macdonald . . . . Maréchal de France
Chief of Staff . . . . Terrier . . . . General de brigade
7th Division: General de division Grandjean
  Brigade: General de brigade Ricard
    5th Polish Line Regiment (4 + artillery co)
      (85/2,553)(2–3pdrs)
  Brigade: General de brigade Radziwill
    10th Polish Line Regiment (4 + artillery co)
      (87/2,442)(2–3pdrs)
    11th Polish Line Regiment (4 + artillery co)
      (80/2,324)(2–3pdrs)
  Brigade: General de brigade Bachelu
    13th Bavarian Line Regiment (2)(48/1,275)
    Line Regiment (2 + artillery co)(43/1,439)
      (2–6pdrs)
  Artillery: Farjou
    6/1st Polish Foot Artillery (7/221)(4–6pdrs & 2 How)
    1/1st Polish Horse Artillery (5/161)(4–6pdrs & 2 How)
    4th Polish Sapper Company (4/125)
    2nd Bavarian Foot Battery (detached from IV Corps later)
27th Division (Prussian Corps): General of Infantry Grawart
  Brigade: Generallieutenant von Bulow
    1st Infantry (3)(2/1st, 1/3rd, Fus/1st)(61/2,006)
    2nd Infantry (3)(1/4th, 1/5th, Fus/5th)(65/2,091)
    Fusilier Battalion, 3rd Infantry Regiment (17/559)
  Brigade: Generallieutenant von Yorck
    3rd Infantry (3)(2/2nd, Fus/2nd, 1/10th)
    Leib Regiment (3)(60/1,971)
  Brigade: Generallieutenant vom Raumer
    5th Infantry (3)(1/6th, 1/7th, Fus/7th)(60/2,019)
    6th Infantry (3)(2/11th, 1/12th, Fus/12th)(61/2,047)
    East Prussian Jäger Battalion (1)(L8/464)

Corps Cavalry: Generallieutenant von Massenbach
  26th Light Brigade: Oberst von Hunerbein
    1st Combined Dragoon Regiment (4)(1/4th, 2/4th, 1/5th, 3/5th)(23/574)
    2nd Combined Dragoon Regiment (4)(1/2nd, 3/2nd, 2/5th, 4/5th)(24/586)
  27th Light Brigade: Oberst von Jenneret
    1st Combined Hussar Regiment (4)(3/1st, 4/1st, 2/2nd, 3/2nd)(23/574)
    2nd Combined Hussar Regiment (4)(3/3rd, 4/3rd, 1/5th, 3/5th)(21/504)
  Corps Artillery:
    1st Prussian Foot Battery (6–6pdrs & 2 How)
    2nd Prussian Foot Battery (6–6pdrs & 2 How)
    3rd Prussian Foot Battery (6–6pdrs & 2 How)
    4th Brandenburg Foot Battery (6–6pdrs & 2 How)
      Total 6pdr Foot—16/564
    1/2 Silesian Foot Battery (4–12pdrs)
    1st Prussian Horse Battery (6–6pdrs & 2 How)
    2nd Prussian Horse Battery (6–6pdrs & 2 How)
    3rd Prussian Horse Battery (6–6pdrs & 2 How)
    6/1st Polish Foot Battery (4–6pdrs & 2 How)
    16th Polish Foot Battery (4–6pdrs & 2 How)
    1/1st Polish Horse Battery (4–6pdrs & 2 How)
  Park:
    Prussian Park Columns (5 cos)(6/452)
    Prussian Train Companies (3)
    Bridging Detachment (0/26)
    Pioneer Companies (3)(248)
    4/1st Polish Sappers

XI CORPS

Commander-in-Chief . . . . . .   Augereau . . . .   Maréchal de France
Chief of Staff . . . .   Ménard . . . .   General de brigade

30th Division: General de division d'Heudelet
  Brigade:
    1st Provisional Regiment (3)
  Brigade: General de brigade Breissand
    6th Provisional Regiment (61/2,760)
      4/16th Légère
      4/21st Légère
      4/28th Légère
      5/28th Line
      43rd Line
      65th Line

7th Provisional Regiment (47/2,121)
  4/8th Line
  4/14th Line
  4/94th Line
8th Provisional Regiment (58/2,033)
  4/54th Line
  4/88th Line
  4/95th Line
Brigade: General de brigade Husson
  9th Provisional Regiment (58/1,966)
    4/24th Line
    4/45th Line
    4/59th Line
  17th Provisional Regiment (55/1,051)
    4/6th Légère
    4/25th Légère
    4/39th Légère
Artillery: Oberst Gunkel
  7/7th Foot Artillery (2/103)(6–6pdrs & 2 How)
  17/7th Foot Artillery (3/96)(6–6pdrs & 2 How)
Cavalry:
  Provisional Dragoon Regiment (36/905)
    4/2nd Dragoon Regiment
    4/5th Dragoon Regiment
    4/12th Dragoon Regiment
    4/13th Dragoon Regiment
    4/17th Dragoon Regiment
    4/19th Dragoon Regiment
    4/20th Dragoon Regiment
31st Division: General de division De Lagrange (15 Oct)
  (later Loison)
Brigade: General de brigade Labassée
  10th Provisional Regiment (47/1,752)
    4/27th Line
    4/63rd Line
    4/76th Line
    4/96th Line
  13th Provisional Regiment (48/2,020)
    4/5th Line
    4/11th Line
    4/79th Line
Brigade: General de brigade Schobert

12th Provisional Regiment (71/2,477)
    4/124th Line
    4/123rd Line
    4/125th Line
    4/129th Line
11th Provisional Regiment (38/1,234)
    4/50th Line
    4/27th Légère
Artillery: Major Rouget
   8/8th Foot Artillery (6–6pdrs & 2 How)
   20/8th Foot Artillery (6–6pdrs & 2 How)
32nd Division: General de division Durutte (1 Oct)
  Brigade: General de brigade Devaux (later Anthing)
    Regiment de Belle Isle (3)(62/1,757)
    Regiment de l'Île de Ré (3)(52/2,206)
  Brigade: General de brigade Jarry
    Regiment Île de Walcheren (3)(60/2,278)
    7th Rhinbund Regiment (Wurzburg)(3)
    Wurzburg Chasseur à Cheval Regiment (1)
  Brigade: General de brigade Jalras
    1er Regiment de la Mediterranée (2)(1/681)
    2e Regiment de la Mediterranée (1)(22/967)
  Artillery: Chef de bataillon de Coston
    22/1st Foot Artillery (6–6pdrs & 2 How)
    6/, 17/5th Foot Artillery (6–6pdrs & 2 How ea)
    4/9th Foot Artillery (6–6pdrs & 2 How)
    Wurzburg Foot Battery (6–6pdrs)
33rd Division: General de division Destrees (1 Aug)
  Brigade: General de brigade Rossarol
    Neapolitan Guard Marines (8/176)
    Neapolitan Velites à pied Regiment (2)(46/1,154)
  Brigade: General de brigade Ambrosio
    5th Neapolitan Line Regiment (2)(49/1,594)
    6th Neapolitan Line Regiment (2)(42/1,564)
    7th Neapolitan Line Regiment (2)(41/1,475)
  Brigade: General de brigade Fracheschi
    Neapolitan Velites à Cheval Regiment (2)(22/320)
    Neapolitan Gardes d'Honneur (2)(31/395)
    Neapolitan Horse Battery (6/75)(4–6pdrs & 2 How)
34th Division: General de division Morand
  Brigade: General de brigade Cosson (later Lacroix)
    22nd Légère Regiment (2)

Brigade: General de brigade Schramm
  3rd Line Regiment (1)(7/451)
  29th Line Regiment (2)(30/1,594)
  105th Line Regiment (1)(9/459)
  113th Line Regiment (2)(38/1,469)
Brigade: General de brigade Anthing (later Cavignac)
  Saxon Prinz Maximilian Regiment (2 + artillery co)
    (2–4pdrs)
  4th Westphalian Line Regiment (2 + artillery co)
    (2–4pdrs)(48/1,638)(transferred to IX Corps)
Brigade: General de brigade Osten
  3rd Rhinbund Regiment (Frankfurt)(3)
Brigade: General de brigade Cosson
  4th Rhinbund Regiment (Saxon Ducal Houses)(3)
    (77/2,524)
  5th Rhinbund Regiment (Anhalt/Lippe)(2)(1,702)
  6th Rhinbund Regiment (Schwarzenburg, Waldeck & Reuss)(2)(1,520)
Artillery: Chef de bataillon Marullier
  14 Regimental Batteries assigned to the French Provisional Regiments
    (2–3pdrs ea)
  17/8th Foot Battery (4/70)(6–6pdrs & 2 How)

CAVALRY RESERVE

Commander-in-Chief . . . . . . Joachim Murat . . . . King of Naples
Chief of Staff . . . . Belliard . . . . General de division

I Reserve Cavalry Corps: General de division Nansouty
1st Light Cavalry Division: General de division Bruyere
  3rd Light Brigade: General de brigade Jacquinot
    7th Hussar Regiment (4)(39/914)
    9th Chevauléger Regiment (4)(45/665)
  4th Light Brigade: General de brigade Piré
    16th Chasseur à Cheval Regiment (4)(33/804)
    8th Hussar Regiment (4)(33/902)
  15th Light Brigade: General de brigade Niewiewski
    6th Polish Uhlan Regiment (4)(34/636)
    8th Polish Uhlan Regiment (4)(28/739)
    2nd Combined Prussian Hussars (4)(20/565)
      (1/4th, 3/4th, 1/6th, & 2/6th)

Artillery:
   7/6th Horse Artillery (6pdrs)(3/76)
   1/1st Train (bis) Battalion (0/67)
1st Cuirassier Division: General de division St. Germaine
  Brigade: General de brigade Bessières
   2nd Cuirassier Regiment (4)(33/759)
  Brigade: General de brigade Bruno
   3rd Cuirassier Regiment (4)(34/830)
  Brigade: General de brigade Queunot
   9th Cuirassier Regiment (4)(34/842)
   1st Chevauleger Regiment (1 co)
  Artillery:
   1/5th Horse Artillery (3/86)(4–6pdrs & 2 How)
   3/5th Horse Artillery (3/90)(4–6pdrs & 2 How)
5th Cuirassier Division: General de division Valence
  Brigade: General de brigade Reynaud
   6th Cuirassier Regiment (4)(38/722)
  Brigade: General de brigade Dejean
   11th Cuirassier Regiment (4)(33/653)
  Brigade: General de brigade De Lagrange
   12th Cuirassier Regiment (4)(37/812)
   5th Chevauléger Regiment (1 co)(7/153)
  Artillery:
   4/5th Horse Artillery (4–6pdrs & 2 How)
   6/5th Horse Artillery (4–6pdrs & 2 How)
    Total horse artillery 7/153)
   3/, 6/11th Train (bis) Battalion (1/131)
II Reserve Cavalry Corps: General de division Montburn
  2nd Light Cavalry Division: General de division Sebastiani
    (later Pajol)
   7th Light Brigade: General de brigade St. Genies
    5th Hussar Regiment (4)(34/691)
    9th Hussar Regiment (4)(71/721)
   8th Light Brigade: General de brigade Burthe
    11th Chasseur à Cheval Regiment (3)(27/682)
    12th Chasseur à Cheval Regiment (3)(30/576)
   16th Light Brigade: General de brigade Subervie
    3rd Württemberg Jäger zu Pferd (4)(20/432)
    Prussian Combined Uhlan Regiment (4)(28/653)
     (3/2nd, 4/2nd, 3/4th, 4/4th)
    10th Polish Hussar Regiment (4)(28/653)
   Artillery: Martinot

1/4th Horse Artillery (4–6pdr & 2 How)
2nd Cuirassier Division: General de division Wathier
  Brigade: General de brigade Beaumont (Caulaincourt)
    5th Cuirassier Regiment (4)(36/678)
  Brigade: General de brigade Dornes
    8th Cuirassier Regiment (4)(36/673)
  Brigade: General de brigade Richter
    10th Cuirassier Regiment (4)(37/621)
    2nd Chevauléger Regiment (1 co)(5/113)
  Artillery:
    1/2nd Horse Artillery (4–6pdrs & 2 How)
    4/2nd Horse Artillery (4–6pdrs & 2 How)
      total horse artillery (8/176)
    1/1st Train (bis) Battalion
    5/11th Train (bis) Battalion
      total train (2/155)
4th Cuirassier Division: General de division Defrance
  Brigade: General de brigade Bouvier des Éclats
    (Berkheim & Chouard)
    1st Carabinier Regiment (4)(38/676)
  Brigade: General de brigade Chouard (L'Hertier, Paultre)
    2nd Carabinier Regiment (4)(37/650)
  Brigade: General de brigade Paultre (Ornano & Bouvier des Eclats)
    1st Cuirassier Regiment (4)(37/553)
    4/4th Chevauléger Regiment (1 co)(4/104)

III Reserve Cavalry Corps: General de division Grouchy
3rd Light Cavalry Division: General de division Lahoussaye
  11th Light Brigade: General de brigade Gauthrin
    6th Hussar Regiment (3)(29/596)
    8th Chasseur à Cheval Regiment (3)(32/524)
  10th Light Brigade: General de brigade Gérard
    6th Chasseur à Cheval Regiment (3)(29/561)
    25th Chasseur à Cheval Regiment (3)(25/583)
  17th Light Brigade: General de brigade Dommanget
    1st Bavarian Chevauxléger Regiment (4)(19/489)
    2nd Bavarian Chevauxléger Regiment (4)(22/476)
    Saxon Prinz Albert Chevauxléger Regiment (4)(30/481)
  Artillery:
    6/4th Horse Artillery (3/154)(4–6pdrs & 2 How)
3rd Cuirassier Division: General de division Doumerc
  Brigade: General de brigade Berkheim
    4th Cuirassier Regiment (4)(35/821)

Brigade: General de brigade L'Hértier
  7th Cuirassier Regiment (4)(34/735)
Brigade: General de brigade Doullembourg
  14th Cuirassier Regiment (4)(33/688)
Artillery:
  1/6th Horse Artillery (4–6pdrs & 2 How) (3/95)
  3/6th Horse Artillery (4–6pdrs & 2 How) (3/91)
  1/8th Train (bis) Battalion (0/9)
  2/11th Train (bis) Battalion (1/88)
  6/11th Train (bis) Battalion (1/76)
6th Heavy Division: General de division La Houssaye
  Brigade: General de brigade Thiry
    7th Dragoon Regiment (3)(28/543)
    23rd Dragoon Regiment (3)(23/554)
  Brigade: General de brigade Séron
    28th Dragoon Regiment (3)(24/599)
    30th Dragoon Regiment (3)(578)
  Artillery: Captain Mouillet
    4/, 5/4th Horse Artillery (8/300)(4–6pdrs & 2 How ea)
IV Cavalry Corps: General de division Latour-Maubourg
4th Light Cavalry Division: General de division Rozniecki
  28th Light Brigade: General de brigade Dziemanowski
    7th Polish Uhlan Regiment (3)(33/639)
    2nd Polish Uhlan Regiment (3)(25/571)
    11th Polish Uhlan Regiment (3)(27/524)
  29th Light Brigade: General de brigade Turno
    3rd Polish Uhlan Regiment (3)(26/632)
    11th Polish Uhlan Regiment (3)(31/657)
    16th Polish Uhlan Regiment (3)(31/697)
7th Cuirassier Division: General de division Lorge
  1st Division: Generalmajor Thielemann
    Zastrow Cuirassier Regiment (4)(36/639)
    Saxon Garde du Corps (4)(36/639)
    14th Polish Cuirassier Regiment (4)
  2nd Brigade: General de brigade Lepel
    1st Westphalian Cuirassier Regiment (4)
    2nd Westphalian Cuirassier Regiment (4)
Corps Artillery: Chef d'escadron Schwerin
  2nd Westphalian Horse Battery (3/66)(4–6pdrs & 2 How)
  2nd Westphalian Train Company (1/77)
  2nd Saxon Horse Battery von Hiller (7/169)
    (4–6pdrs & 2 How)

3rd & 4th Polish Horse Artillery Batteries
(11/324)(4–6pdrs & 2 How ea)
Austrian Corps: General Schwarzenburg (4 June 1812)
Cavalry Division: Feldmarschalleutnant Frimont
(Prinz Hohenzollern)
Brigade: Generalmajor Schmelzer
Hohenzollern Chevauxléger Regiment (6)(964)
O'Reilly Chevauxléger Regiment (6)(890)
Reisch Dragoon Regiment (4)(714)
Brigade: Generalmajor Frölich
Kaiser Hussar Regiment (6)(988)
Hesse-Homberg Hussar Regiment (6)(958)
Division: Feldmarschalleutnant Bianchi
Brigade: Generalmajor Hesse-Homberg
Hiller Infantry Regiment (2)(1,822)
Colloredo-Mansfeld Infantry Regiment (2)(1,755)
Brigade: Generalmajor Lilenberg
Simbschen Infantry Regiment (2)(1,710)
Alvinzy Infantry Regiment (2)(1,755)
Brigade: Generalmajor Prinz Phillip
Kirschbetter Grenadier Battalion (1)(673)
Brezinski Grenadier Battalion (1)(673)
Division: Feldmarschalleutnant Siegenthal
Brigade: Generalmajor Mayer (Mohr)
Czatoryski Infantry Regiment (2)(1,009)
Prinz de Ligne Infantry Regiment (2)(1,986)
Brigade: Generalmajor Bolza
Warasdiner Grenz Regiment (2)(1,310)
Jäger Battalion #7 (4 cos)(552)
Brigade: Generalmajor Lichtenstein
Sottulinski Infantry Regiment (2)(1,403)
Davidovich Infantry Regiment (2)(1,721)
Division: Feldmarschalleutnant Trautenberg
Brigade: Generalmajor Pflacher
Jäger Battalion #5 (4 co)(594)
St. Georg Grenz Regiment (1)(1,261)
Brigade: Generalmajor Mayer
Wurzburg Infantry Regiment (4)
Corps Artillery:
Divisional Artillery: 3 Foot Batteries (8–6pdrs ea)
Corps Reserve: 4 Foot Companies (4–6pdrs & 2 How ea)
                        1 Foot Battery (6–3pdrs)

1 Foot Battery (6–12pdrs)
3 Pioneer Companies (578)
1 Pontoonier Company (103)
Artillery Train (609)

Russian I Corps
2 August 1812

Commanding General—Generallieutenant Count Wittgenstein
Chief of Staff   —Generalmajor d'Auvray
Artillery Commander —Generalmajor Jachwill
Quartermaster Chief   —Baron Diebitsch
Chief of Engineers   —Colonel Count Sievers

Advanced Guard: Generalmajor Koulnieff
    Platov #4 Don Cossack Regiment
    Grodno Hussar Regiment (4)
  Brigade:
    23rd Jager Regiment (2)
    24th Jager Regiment (2)
  Artillery:
    Horse Battery #3 (8–6pdrs & 4 Licornes)
Main Battle Line: Generalmajor Berg
    23rd Jager Regiment (2)
    26th Jager Regiment (2)
    Perm Infantry Regiment (2)
    Mohilev Infantry Regiment (2)
    Sievesk Infantry Regiment (2)
    Kalouga Infantry Regiment (2)
    Depot Squadron of Pskof Dragoon Regiment
    Converged Cuirassier Depot Squadrons (4)
    Light Battery #26 (8–6pdrs & 4 Licornes)
    Light Battery #27 (8–6pdrs & 4 Licornes)
    Position Battery #14 (8–12pdrs & 4 Licornes)
2nd Line of Battle: Generallieutenant Kakhoffski
    Reserve Grenadier Battalions
      Leib Grenadiers (1)
      Tauride Grenadiers (1)
      Ekaterinoslav Grenadiers (1)
      Pavlov Grenadiers (1)
      Arakcheyev Grenadiers (1)
      St. Petersburg Grenadiers (1)

Converged Grenadiers of 14th Division (2)
Riga Dragoon Regiment (4)
Horse Battery #1 (8–6pdrs & 4 Licornes)
Position Battery #28 (8–12pdrs & 4 Licornes)
Reserve: Generalmajor Sazonov
    Tenguinsk Infantry Regiment (2)
    Estonia Infantry Regiment (2)
    Toula Infantry Regiment (2)
    Navajinsk Infantry Regiment (2)
    Reserve Battalion of 11th Jagers (1)
    Iambourg Dragoon Regiment (4)
    Light Battery #9 (8–6pdrs & 4 Licornes)
    Position Battery #27 (8–12pdrs & 4 Licornes)

This corps is greatly reduced by numerous detachments on the left bank of the Dvina River.

10 August 1812

Commanding General—Generallieutenant Count Wittgenstein
Chief of Staff   —Generalmajor d'Auvray
Artillery Commander —Generalmajor Jachwill
Quartermaster Chief   —Baron Diebitsch
Chief of Engineers   —Colonel Count Sievers

Advanced Guard: Generalmajor Kastachkowski
    Iambourg Dragoon Regiment (2)
    Horse Battery #1 (9 guns)
    23rd Jager Regiment (2)

Main Battle Line: Generalmajor Berg
    Converged Cuirassier Depot Squadrons (4)
    Perm Infantry Regiment (2)
    Mohilev Infantry Regiment (2)
    Sievesk Infantry Regiment (2)
    Kalouga Infantry Regiment (2)
    Position Battery #28 (8–12pdrs & 4 Licornes)
    Position Battery #5 (8–12pdrs & 4 Licornes)

2nd Line of Battle: Generallieutenant Sasonov
    Tenguinsk Infantry Regiment (2)
    Estonia Infantry Regiment (2)
    Toula Infantry Regiment (2)
    Navajinsk Infantry Regiment (2)

Reserve Battalion of 11th Jagers (1)
Light Battery #27 (8–6pdrs & 4 Licornes)
Position Battery #14 (8–12pdrs & 4 Licornes)

Reserve: Generalmajor Sazonov
Reserve Grenadier Battalions
Leib Grenadiers (1)
Tauride Grenadiers (1)
Ekaterinoslav Grenadiers (1)
Pavlov Grenadiers (1)
Arakcheyev Grenadiers (1)
St. Petersburg Grenadiers (1)
Converged Grenadiers of 14th Division (2)
Iambourg Dragoon Regiment (2)
Horse Battery #3 (8–6pdrs & 4 Licornes)
Position Battery #27 (6 guns)

14 August 1812

Commanding General—Generallieutenant Count Wittgenstein
Chief of Staff   —Generalmajor d'Auvray
Artillery Commander —Generalmajor Jachwill
Quartermaster Chief —Baron Diebitsch
Chief of Engineers   —Colonel Count Sievers

Advanced Guard: Generalmajor Helfreich
Cossacks (100)
Grodno Hussar Regiment (4)
25th Jager Regiment (2)
26th Jager Regiment (2)
Light Battery #26

Main Battle Line
1st Line: Generalmajor Berg
Converged Cuirassier Depot Squadrons (4)
Position Battery #5 (8–12pdrs & 4 Licornes)
23rd Jager Regiment (2)
Brigade: Kozaczkoffski
Sievesk Infantry Regiment (2)
Kalouga Infantry Regiment (2)
Brigade: Prince of Siberia
Perm Infantry Regiment (2)
Mohilev Infantry Regiment (2)
Converged Infantry Regiment

Position Battery #28
Light Battery #9
Iambourg Dragoon Regiment (2)
Converged Guard Depot Squadrons (3)
    (Hussars, Dragoons & Uhlans)
2nd Line: Generalmajor Sazonov
    Riga Dragoon Regiment (4)
    Converged Jager Regiment
        Reserve Battalion of 11th Jagers (1)
        Reserve Battalion of 36th Jagers (1)
    Light Battery #27 (8–6pdrs & 4 Licornes)
  Brigade:
    Tenguinsk Infantry Regiment (2)
    Estonia Infantry Regiment (2)
  Brigade:
    Toula Infantry Regiment (2)
    Navajinsk Infantry Regiment (2)
Reserve: Generalmajor Kakhoffski
    Iambourg Dragoon Regiment (2)
    Converged Grenadiers of 14th Division (2)
    Position Battery #14 (8–12pdrs & 4 Licornes)
    Reserve Grenadier Battalions
        Leib Grenadiers (1)
        Tauride Grenadiers (1)
        Ekaterinoslav Grenadiers (1)
        Pavlov Grenadiers (1)
        Arakcheyev Grenadiers (1)
        St. Petersburg Grenadiers (1)
    2 Converged Infantry Regiments
    Horse Battery #1 (8–6pdrs & 4 Licornes)
    Horse Battery #3 (8–6pdrs & 4 Licornes)
Detachment: Colonel Vlastov
    Grodno Hussar Regiment (4)
    24th Jager Regiment (2)
    Converged Grenadiers of 5th Division (2)
    Cossacks (200)

Grande Armée
15 August 1812

Imperial Guard

Commander-in-Chief .... Mortier .... Maréchal d'Empire

Headquarter Guard:
Neuchâtel Battalion (1 + artillery co) (2–6pdrs)
Guides de la Chef (1 sqn)

Old Guard:

Commander-in-Chief .... Lefebvre .... Maréchal d'Empire

3rd Division: General de division Curial
 Brigade: General de brigade Boyer
  1st Chasseur à Pied (2 + artillery co) (40/1,407)
   (2–3pdrs)
  2nd Chasseur à Pied (2 + artillery co) (30/1,183)
   (2–3pdrs)
 Brigade: General de brigade Michel
  1st Grenadier à Pied (2 + artillery co) (39/1,314)
   (2–3pdrs)
  2nd Grenadier à Pied (2 + artillery co) (39/979)
   (2–3pdrs)
  3rd Grenadier à Pied (2 + artillery co) (39/873)
   (2–3pdrs)
Artillery Reserve:
 Brigade: General de brigade Desvaux
  1st Old Guard Horse Artillery (4–6pdrs & 2 How ea)
  2nd Old Guard Horse Artillery (4–6pdrs & 2 How ea)
  3rd Old Guard Horse Artillery (4-6pdrs & 2 How ea)
  4th Old Guard Horse Artillery (4–6pdrs & 2 How ea)

Young Guard:

Commander-in-Chief .... Mortier .... Maréchal d'Empire
Chief of Staff .... Meinadier ....

1st Division: Général de division Delaborde
 Brigade: General de brigade Berthezène
   (brigade assigned later)
  4th Voltigeur Regiment (2) (33/678)
  4th Tirailleur Regiment (2) (24/557)
  5th Voltigeur Regiment (2) (28/733)
 Brigade: Général de brigade Lanusse
  6th Voltigeur Regiment (2) (27/728)

6th Tirailleur Regiment (2) (30/705)
5th Tirailleur Regiment (2) (28/830)
Artillery: General de brigade Nourry
   4th Company Cannoniers Conscrits (8–3pdrs) (6/94)
   5th Artillery Train Company (1/135)
   2/5th Sapper Battalion
2nd Division: General de division Roguet
  Brigade: General de brigade Boyledieu
   1st Tirailleur Regiment (2) (31/805)
   1st Voltigeur Regiment (2) (22/688)
  Brigade: General de brigade Lanbere
   Fusilier Chasseur Regiment (2) (33/1,164)
   Fusilier Grenadier Regiment (2) (31/1,296)
  Artillery: Colonel Villeneuve
   13/, 14/8th Foot Artillery (5/227)
   6/4th Train Battalion
   2/7th Train Battalion
   Sappers
   Train des equipages
   Administration
Vistula Legion: General de division Claparède
  Brigade: General de brigade Cholpicki
   1st Vistula Regiment (2 + artillery co)
    (2–3pdrs) (26/1,042)
   2nd Vistula Regiment (2 + artillery co)
    (2–3pdrs) (30/882)
  Brigade: General de brigade
   3rd Vistula Regiment (2 + artillery co)
    (2–3pdrs) (29/989)
Attached to the Guard:
  Brigade:
   Portuguese Chasseur à Cheval Regiment (3) (21/367)
   7th Chevauléger Regiment (4)
  Brigade:
   Velites of Turin (1)
   Velites of Florence (1)
   Italian Gardes d'Honneur (1 sqn)
   Spanish Pioneer Battalion
  Artillery: General de division Nourry
   3rd Conscrit Cannonier Company (8–3pdrs)
   1st & 2nd Old Guard Foot Artillery
    (6–12pdrs & 2 How ea)

3rd & 4th Old Guard Foot Artillery
   (6–6pdrs & 2 How)
5th & 6th Old Guard Foot Artillery
   (6–6pdrs & 2 How)
Artillery Artisans
3/2nd Train Battalion
1/, 2/1st Train Battalion
3/, 4/1st Train Battalion
Equipage Train
3rd Division Artillery Artisans
Other Artillery Artisans
Guard Cavalry Maréchal Bessières
Division: General de division Walther
  Brigade: General de brigade St. Sulpice
    Empress Dragoon Regiment (4) (48/800)
    Grenadier à Cheval Regiment (5) (67/959)
  Brigade: General de brigade Guyot
    Chasseur à Cheval Regiment (5) (68/964)
    Mameluke Squadron
  Brigade: General de brigade Krasinski
    1st Chevauléger lancier de la Garde Regiment (Polish)
      (4) (59/557)
  Brigade: General de brigade Colbert
    2nd Chevauléger lancier de la Garde Regiment (Dutch)
      (4) (48/638)
    Gendarmerie d'Elite (2)
  Artillery: General de brigade Devaux
    1/, 2/1st Horse Artillery
    2/, 3/7th Principal Train Battalion
Artillery Reserve: General de division Sorbier
    2/, 3/, 4/Young Guard Horse Artillery
      (4–6pdrs & 2 How ea)
    1/1st Guard Train Battalion
    1/, 5/Young Guard Horse Artillery
      (6–6pdrs & 2 How ea)
    1/, 2/Young Guard Foot Artillery (6–6pdrs & 2 How ea)
    2/, 6/2nd Guard Train
    6/2nd Guard Train Battalion
    5/, 6/1st Horse Artillery
      (6–6pdrs & 2 How ea)
    3/, 4/Young Guard Foot Artillery
    3/, 4/2nd Guard Train Battalion

5/, 6/Young Guard Foot Artillery
1/, 5/2nd Guard Train Battalion
15/, 16/8th Foot Artillery
5/7th Principal Train Battalion
Reserve Artillery Park:
 Det. Conscrit Cannoniers (2–3pdrs)
 Det. Guard Artillery Artisans & Pontooneers
 3/, 6/1st Guard Train Battalion
 Det. Conscrit Cannoniers (2–3pdrs)
 2/1st & 1/, 2/, 3/, 6/2nd Guard Train
 Det. Conscrit Cannoniers (2–3pdrs)
 Det. 16th Artillery Artisans
 6/7th Principal Train Battalion
 1/, 6/4th Principal Train Battalion
 3/1st Pontooneer Battalion
 2/, 3/4th Principal Train Battalion
 1/, 2/, 3/, 5/, 6/13th Train (bis) Battalion
 10/8th Foot Artillery
 12/8th Foot Artillery
 14/8th Foot Artillery
 15/8th Foot Artillery
 16/8th Foot Artillery
 1/8th Horse Artillery (4–6pdrs & 2 How ea)
 2/1st Horse Artillery (4–6pdrs & 2 How ea)
 5/1st Horse Artillery (4–6pdrs & 2 How ea)
 6/8th Horse Artillery (4–6pdrs & 2 How ea)
 Det. 16th Artillery Artisans
Engineer Park: General de brigade Kirgener
 6/5th Sapper Battalion
 1st Cleve-Berg Sapper Company
 Marine Artisan Battalion & 1st Battalion of l'Escaut
 1/, 7/Guard Marine Battalion (8/221)
 Guard Equipage (3 companies)
 1/, 2/, 3/, 4/, 5/, 6/7th Equipage
Equipage of the General Quarters:
 3/, 4/, 5/, 6/2nd Equipage Battalion
 1/, 2/, 3/, 4/, 5/, 6/10th Equipage Battalion
 1/, 2/, 3/6th Equipage Battalion
 4/, 5/, 6/9th Equipage Battalion
 1/, 2/, 3/, 4/, 5/, 6/14th Equipage Battalion
 1/, 2/, 3/, 4/, 5/, 6/15th Equipage Battalion
 1/, 2/, 3/, 4/, 5/, 6/16th Equipage Battalion

1/, 2/, 3/, 4/, 5/, 6/17th Equipage Battalion
1/, 2/, 3/18th Equipage Battalion
1/, 2/, 3/, 4/, 5/, 6/20th Equipage Battalion
1/, 2/, 3/, 4/, 5/, 6/21st Equipage Battalion
1/, 2/, 3/, 4/, 5/, 6/22nd Equipage Battalion
1/, 2/, 3/, 4/, 5/, 6/23rd Equipage Battalion
1st & 2nd Artisans of Military Equipage Companies
1st Ambulance Company
Artillery General Park
    10/1st Foot Artillery
    21/2nd Foot Artillery
    17/, 22/5th Foot Artillery
    8/9th Foot Artillery
    15th & 18th Artillery Artisans Companies
Bridging Train:
    1/, 7/, 9/1st Pontooneer Battalion
    2/, 3/, 4/, 5/, 6/2nd Pontooneer Battalion
    1/, 2/, 3/, 4/, 5/, 6/8th Pontooneer Battalion
    1/, 2/, 3/, 4/, 5/, 6/9th Pontooneer Battalion

I CORPS

Commander-in-Chief . . . . . .   Davout . . . .   Maréchal d'Empire
Chief of Staff . . . .   Baron Romeuf . . . .   General de brigade
1st Division: General de division Morand
    1st Brigade: General de brigade d'Alton
        13th Légère Regiment (5 + artillery co) (88/2,901)
            (4–3pdrs)
    2nd Brigade: General de brigade Gratien
        17th Regiment (5 + artillery co) (85/2,799)
            (4–3pdrs)
    3rd Brigade: General de brigade Bonnamy
        30th Line Regiment (5 + artillery co) (83/3,176)
            (4–3pdrs)
    Artillery: Chef de bataillon Raindre
        1/7th Foot Artillery (6–6pdrs & 2 How) (5/97)
        7/1st Horse Artillery (4–6pdrs & 2 How) (3/87)
        7th Artillery Artisan Company (0/4)
        1/, 2/1st Principal Train Battalion (1/148)
        1/12th Military Equipage Battalion (1/74)
2nd Division: General de division Friant

1st Brigade: General de brigade Dufour
  15th Légère Regiment (5 + artillery co) (114/2,581)
    (4–3pdrs)
2nd Brigade: General de brigade Vandedem
  33rd Line Regiment (5 + artillery co) (106/2,699)
    (4–3pdrs)
3rd Brigade: General de brigade Grandeau
  48th Line Regiment (5 + artillery co) (90/2,536)
    (2–3pdrs)
  Joseph Napoleon Regiment (2 + artillery co) (46/831)
    (2–3pdrs)
Artillery: Chef de bataillon Cabrie
  2/7th Foot Artillery (6–6pdrs & 2 How)
  5/3rd Horse Artillery (4–6pdrs & 2 How)
  Det. Artillery Artisan
  4/, 6/1 Principal Train Battalion
  5/5th Sapper Battalion
    (Total artillery & train 10/323)
  4/12th Military Equipage Battalion (2/11)
3rd Division: General de division Gudin
  1st Brigade: General de brigade Desailly
    7th Légère Regiment (5 + artillery co)
      (4–3pdrs)
    12th Line Regiment (5 + artillery co)
      (4–3pdrs)
  2nd Brigade: General de brigade Leclerc
    127th Line Regiment (2 + artillery co)
      (2–3pdrs)
    21st Line Regiment (5 + artillery co)
      (4–3pdrs)
    8th Rhinbund (Mecklenburg-Strelitz) Battalion
  Artillery: Colonel Pelgrin
    3/7th Foot Artillery (6–6pdrs & 2 How)
    4/3rd Horse Artillery (4–6pdrs & 2 How)
    Det. Artillery Artisan
    1/, 4/1st Principal Train Battalion
    9/5th Sapper Battalion
    1/, 3/12th Military Equipage Battalion
4th Division: General de division Dessaix
  1st Brigade: General de brigade Barbanègre
    33rd Légère Regiment (4 + artillery co)
      (4–3pdrs)

2nd Brigade: General de brigade Frederichs
  85th Line Regiment (5 + artillery co) (95/3,219)
    (4–3pdrs)
3rd Brigade: General de brigade Leguay
  108th Line Regiment (5 + artillery co) (93/3,327)
    (4–3pdrs)
Artillery: Chef de bataillon Thevenot (Total 10/593)
  9/7th Foot Artillery (6–6pdrs & 2 How)
  2/5th Horse Artillery (4–6pdrs & 2 How)
  Det. Artillery Artisans
  3/, 6/Principal Train Battalion
  3/2nd Sapper Battalion
  4/12th Military Equipage Battalion
5th Division: General de division Compans
  1st Brigade: General de brigade Duppelin
    25th Line Regiment (5 + artillery co) (107/2,918)
      (4–3pdrs)
  2nd Brigade: General de brigade Teste
    57th Line Regiment (5 + artillery co) (93/3,056)
      (4–3pdrs)
  3rd Brigade: General de brigade Guyardet
    61st Line Regiment (5 + artillery co) (86/2,643)
      (4–3pdrs)
    111th Line Regiment (5 + artillery co) (83/3,169)
      (2–3pdrs)
  Artillery: Chef de bataillon Klie (Total 11/557)
    2/6th Foot Artillery (6–6pdrs & 2 How)
    16/7th Horse Artillery (4–6pdrs & 2 How)
    Det. Artillery Artisans
    2/, 4/9th Principal Train Battalion
    5/3rd Sapper Battalion
    3/, 5/12th Military Equipage Battalion
Corps Cavalry: General de division Pajol
  1st Light Cavalry Brigade: General de brigade Pajol
    2nd Chasseur à Cheval Regiment (4) (37/662)
    9th Polish Lancer Regiment (4) (28/481)
  2nd Light Cavalry Brigade: General de brigade Bordessoulle
    1st Chasseur à Cheval Regiment (4) (34/695)
    3rd Chasseur à Cheval Regiment (4) (26/470)
  Artillery Reserve:
    Artillery—(31/1,342)
    3/, 17/1st Foot Artillery (6–12pdrs & 2 How)

6/7th Foot Artillery (6–6pdrs & 2 How)
11/, 14/9th Foot Artillery (6–6pdrs & 2 How ea)
7th Artillery Artisan Company
1/, 5/, 6/1st Principal Train Battalion
5/1st Pontooneer Battalion
   Train—(5/167)
1/, 5/, 6/1st Principal Train Battalion
6/3rd Principal Train Battalion
1/, 2/, 3/, 4/, 5/9th Principal Train Battalion
Engineering Park: (11/451)
   8/5th Sapper Battalion
   1st Engineering Train Company
   1/, 3/, 4/, 5/, 6/12th Military Equipage Battalion
Ambulance:
   3rd Ambulance Company (2/100)
Gendarmes:
   Gendarmes à Cheval (3/55)

II CORPS

Commander-in-Chief . . . . . .   Oudinot . . . .   Maréchal de France
Chief of Staff . . . .   De Lorencez . . . . . .   General de brigade

6th Division: General de division Legrand
  1st Brigade: General de brigade Albert
    26th Légère Regiment (4 + artillery do) (60/1,602)
      (2–3pdrs)
  2nd Brigade: General de brigade Maison
    19th Line Regiment (4 + artillery co) (68/1,727)
      (2–3pdrs)
  3rd Brigade: General de brigade Moreau
    56th Line Regiment (4 + artillery co) (54/1,709)
      (2–3pdrs)
  4th Brigade: General de brigade Pamplona
    128th Line Regiment (2 + artillery co) (42/850)
      (2–3pdrs)
    3rd Portuguese Regiment (2 + artillery co) (555/1,025)
  Artillery: Chef de bataillon Bogaert (9/569)
    11/5th Foot Artillery (6–6pdrs & 2 How)
    6/3rd Horse Artillery (4–6pdrs & 2 How)
    Det. 17th Artillery Artisan Company
    3/3rd Train (bis) Battalion

4/3rd Sapper Battalion
Gendarmerie
8th Division: General de division Verdier (Maison)
  1st Brigade: General de brigade Vives (Albert)
    11th Légère Regiment (4 + artillery co) (65/1,025)
    (4–3pdrs)
    2nd Line Regiment (5 + artillery co) (99/2,145)
    (4–3pdrs)
  2nd Brigade: General de brigade Pouget
    37th Line Regiment (4 + artillery co) (55/1,821)
    (4–3pdrs)
    124th Line Regiment (3 + artillery co) (43/537)
    (2–3pdrs)
  Artillery: Chef de bataillon Levis (10/443)
    15/5th Foot Artillery (6–6pdrs & 2 How)
    1/3rd Horse Artillery (4–6pdrs & 2 How)
    Det. 17th Artillery Artisan Company
    3/3rd Sapper Battalion
    Gendarmes
9th Division: General de division Merle
  1st Brigade: General de brigade Candras
    1st Swiss Line Regiment (2 + artillery co) (49/338)
    (2–3pdrs)
    2nd Swiss Line Regiment (3 + artillery co) (75/933)
    (2–3pdrs)
  2nd Brigade: General de brigade Amey
    4th Swiss Line Regiment (3 + artillery co) (52/841)
    (2–3pdrs)
    3rd Provisional Croatian Regiment (2 + artillery co)
    (41/1,454)   (2–3pdrs)
  3rd Brigade: General de brigade Coutard
    3rd Swiss Line Regiment (3 + artillery co) (43/619)
    (2–3pdrs)
    123rd Line Regiment (3 + artillery co) (40/642)
    (2–3pdrs)
  Artillery: Chef de bataillon Webre (6/340)
    4/7th Foot Artillery (6–6pdrs & 2 How)
    5/2nd Horse Artillery (4–6pdrs & 2 How)
    Det. 17th Artillery Artisan Company
    3/, 5/8th Train (bis) Battalion
    5/1st Sapper Battalion
    Gendarmerie

Corps Cavalry: General de brigade Corbineau
  5th Light Cavalry Brigade: General de brigade Castex
    23rd Chasseur à Cheval Regiment (2) (37/685)
    24th Chasseur à Cheval Regiment (3) (33/662)
  6th Light Cavalry Brigade: General de brigade Corbineau
    20th Chasseur à Cheval Regiment (2) (22/165)
    7th Chasseur à Cheval Regiment (2) (24/295)
    8th Chevauléger Regiment (4) (20/394)
  Reserve Artillery: Major Lavoy
    Artillery—(22/952)
    1/1st Foot Artillery (6–6pdrs & 2 How)
    15/1st Foot Artillery (6–6pdrs & 2 How)
    Det. 17th Artillery Artisan Company
      Train—(9/348)
    1/8th Train (bis) Battalion
    5/8th Train (bis) Battalion
  Artillery Park: Colonel Levavasseur
    21/9th Foot Artillery (6–12pdrs & 2 How)
    22/9th Foot Artillery (6–12pdrs & 2 How)
    11/1st Pontooneer Battalion
    1/3rd Train (bis) Battalion
    3/3rd Train (bis) Battalion
    1/, 2/, 3/, 4/, 5/, 6/8th Train (bis) Battalion
    2/, 6/11th Train (bis) Battalion
    Det. 9th Ambulance Company (2/102)
    Gendarmerie (1/20)
    4/3rd Sapper Battalion
    Det. 17th Artillery Artisan Company

III CORPS

Commander-in-Chief . . . . Ney . . . . Maréchal de France
Chief of Staff . . . . Gouré . . . . General de brigade
10th Division: General de division Ledru
  1st Brigade: General de brigade Gengoult
    24th Line Regiment (4 + artillery co) (2,329)
      (2–3pdrs)
    1st Portuguese Line Regiment (2) (580)
  2nd Brigade: General de brigade Morion
    46th Line Regiment (4 + artillery co) (2,467)
      (2–3pdrs)

3rd Brigade: General de brigade Bruny
  72nd Line Regiment (4 + artillery co) (2,144)
    (2–3pdrs)
Artillery: Chef d'escadron Ragmey
  12/5th Foot Artillery (6–6pdrs & 2 How) (111)
  5/6th Horse Artillery (4–6pdrs & 2 How) (61)
11th Division: General de division Razout
  1st Brigade: General de brigade Joubert
    4th Line Regiment (4 + artillery co) (1,853)
      (2–3pdrs)
    18th Line Regiment (4 + artillery co) (2,170) (2–3pdrs)
  2nd Brigade: General de brigade Compère
    2nd Portuguese Regiment (2) (598)
  3rd Brigade: General de brigade d'Henin
    93rd Line Regiment (4 + artillery co) (1,447)
      (2–3 pdrs)
  Artillery: Chef de bataillon Bernard
    18/5th Foot Artillery (6–6pdrs & 2 How) (90)
    6/5th Horse Artillery (4–6pdrs & 2 How) (60)
25th Division: Royal Prince of Württemberg
    (later General de division Marchand) (Wurttemberg)
  1st Brigade: Generalmajor von Hugel
    1st Line Regiment "Prinz Paul" (2) (853)
    4th Line Regiment (2) (593)
  2nd Brigade: Generalmajor Koch
    2nd Line Regiment "Herzog Wilhelm" (2) (654)
    6th Line Regiment "Kronprinz" (2) (419)
  3rd Brigade: Generalmajor von Bruzelles
    1st Light Infantry Battalion
    2nd Light Infantry Battalion
    (combined 805)
    1st Jäger Battalion "König"
    2nd Jäger Battalion
    (combined 683)
  Artillery: Oberstleutnant Brandt
    1st & 2nd Württemberg Foot Artillery (58 & 63)
      (4–6pdrs & 2 Howitzers ea)
    1st Württemberg Horse Artillery (with 14th Light Cavalry Brigade)
      (3–6pdrs & 1 Howitzer ea)
    2nd Württemberg Horse Artillery (99)
      (3–6pdrs & 1 Howitzer ea)
    12pdr Württemberg Foot Battery (6–12pdrs) (151)

Cavalry Corps: Generalmajor Wollwrath
  9th Light Brigade: General de brigade Mouriez
    11th Hussar Regiment (4) (439)
    6th Chevauléger Regiment (3) (459)
    Jäger zu Pferd Regiment #4 "Konig" (4) (417)
  14th Light Brigade: General de brigade Beurman
    28th Chasseur à Cheval Regiment (2) (671)
    1st Württemberg Chevauxlégers Regiment
      "Prinz Adam" (4) (469)
    2nd Württemberg Chevauxléger Regiment "Leib" (4) (481)
Artillery Reserve:
    16/, 18/1st Foot Artillery (6–12pdrs & 2 How ea)
      (detached to reserve in Vilna)
    21/1st Foot Artillery (77)
      (6–12 pdrs & 2 How ea)
    2/9th Foot Artillery (6–6pdrs & 2 How) (64)
    7/9th Foot Artillery (6–6pdrs & 2 How) (82)
Artillery Train
    1/, 2/, 3/6th Principal Train Battalion (318)
    4/, 5/6th Principal Train Battalion (en route)
    2/, 3/, 6/14th Principal Train Battalion (131)
    1/, 2/2nd Military Equipage Battalion
    10th Ambulance Company
    8/1st Pontooneer Battalion (65)
    5th Ouvrier Company (36)
    Reserve Company
Engineers:
    3/1st Sapper Battalion (108)
    7/, 9/3rd Sapper Battalion (103 & 75)
    Gendarmerie

IV CORPS

Commander-in-Chief . . . . Eugène . . . . Viceroy of Italy
Chief of Staff . . . . Duke d'Abrantes. . . . General de division
Italian Royal Guard: General de division Pino
  Brigade: General de brigade Lecchi
    Gardes d'honneur (1 co) (18/202)
    Royal Velites (2 + artillery co) (39/937)
    Guard Infantry Regiment (2 + artillery co) (43/1,046)
    Guard Conscript Regiment (2 + artillery co) (39/937)

Guard Dragoon Regiment (2 sqn) (19/323)
Queen's Dragoon Regiment (4) (37/455)
Artillery: Captain Clement
  1st & 2nd Italian Foot Artillery (4–6pdrs & 1 how)
    (7/115)
  1st & 2nd Italian Horse Artillery (4–6pdrs & 1 how)
    (4/76)
  Italian Train (2/183)
  Det. 2nd Artisan Company
  4/1st Sapper Battalion
  1/, 3/1st Military Equipage Battalion
  Italian Guard Marines (3/99)
13th Division: General de division Delzons
  Brigade: General de brigade Huard
    8th Légère Regiment (2 + artillery co) (35/930)
      (2–3pdrs)
    84th Line Regiment (4 + artillery co) (74/2,180)
      (2–3pdrs)
  Brigade: General de brigade Roussel
    1st Provisional Croatian Regiment (2) (27/773)
    92nd Line Regiment (4 + artillery co) (60/1,935)
      (2–3pdrs)
  Brigade: General de brigade Guyon (added later)
    106th Line Regiment (4 + artillery co) (80/2,136)
      (2–3pdrs)
  Artillery: Chef de bataillon Demay
    9/2nd Foot Artillery (6–6pdrs & 2 How) (3/96)
    2/4th Horse Artillery (4–6pdrs & 2 How) (3/77)
    2/, 3/7th Train (bis) Battalion (1/449)
    Det. 7th Artillery Artisan Company
    7/1st Sapper Battalion (2/108)
    1/9th Military Equipage Battalion
14th Division: General de division Broussier
  Brigade: General de brigade de Sivray
    19th Légère Regiment (2 + artillery co) (30/193)
      (2–3pdrs)
    9th Line Regiment (4 + artillery co) (80/1,805)
      (2–3pdrs)
  Brigade: General de brigade Almeras
    Joseph Napoleon Regiment (2 + artillery co) (30/691)
      (2–3pdrs)
    35th Line Regiment (4 + artillery co) (66/1,874)
      (2–3pdrs)

Brigade: General de brigade Pastol
   53rd Regiment (4 + artillery co) (61/1,458)
    (2–3pdrs)
Artillery: Chef de bataillon Hermann
   7/2nd Foot Artillery (6–6pdrs & 2 How)
   3/4th Horse Artillery (4–6pdrs & 2 How)
    (Artillery—8/305)
   1/, 6/7th Train (bis) Battalion
   2/1st Sapper Battalion (2/104)
   3/9th Military Equipage Battalion
15th Division: General de division Pino
  Brigade: General de brigade Fontana
   1st Italian Légère Regiment (1) (18/480)
   2nd Italian Line Regiment (4 + artillery co) (78/1,053)
    (2–3pdrs)
  Brigade: General de brigade Guillaume
   3rd Italian Légère Regiment (4 + artillery co) (69/953)
    (2–3pdrs)
   Dalmatian Regiment (3 + artillery co) (62/1,134)
    (2–3pdrs)
  Brigade: General de brigade Dembowski
   3rd Italian Line Regiment (4 + artillery co) (77/1,343)
    (2–3pdrs)
  Artillery: Colonel Millo
   14/1st Foot Artillery (6–6pdrs & 2 How) (3/82)
   2/1st Horse Artillery (4–6pdrs & 2 How) (1/50)
   3rd & 4th Train Companies (2/103)
   2nd Artillery Artisan Company
   6/1st Sapper Battalion
   2/1st Military Equipage Battalion
Corps Cavalry: General de division Ornano
  12th Light Cavalry Brigade: General de brigade Ferrière
    (detached to Vitebsk)
   9th Chasseur à Cheval Regiment (3)
   19th Chasseur à Cheval Regiment (3)
  13th Light Cavalry Brigade: General de brigade Villata
   2nd Italian Chasseur à Cheval Regiment (3)
   3rd Italian Chasseur à Cheval Regiment (3)
  Reserve Artillery: Colonel Montegnet
   5/, 12/2nd Foot Artillery (6–12pdrs & 2 How) (229)
   1/, 2/, 6/7th Train (bis) Battalion (1/161)
   2nd & 7th Italian Foot Artillery
    (6–12pdrs & 2 How) (4/91)

5th, 6th, & Det. 9th Italian Train Companies
Det. 2nd Italian Ouvrier Company
Det. Artillery French Artisan Company
   (total artisans 5/166)
Artillery Park: Colonel Fiereck
   8/, 10/, 20/2nd Foot Artillery
Det. 6/7th Train (bis) Battalion
1/2nd Pontooneer Battalion
10th Ouvrier Company
2nd Italian Pontooneer Company (2/81)
7th, 8th, 9th Italian Train Companies
Det. 2nd Italian Artillery Artisan Company
2/1st Italian Sapper Battalion
4/, 5/2nd Italian Transport Battalion
2nd Italian Oxen Transport Battalion (6)
Italian Engineering Train Company

V CORPS

Commander-in-Chief . . . . .   Prince Poniatowski . . . .   General de division
Chief of Staff . . . .   Fiszer . . . .   General de division

16th Division: General de division Zayonchek
   Brigade: General de brigade Mielzynski
      3rd Polish Line Regiment (3 + artillery co) (2,160)
         (2–3pdrs)
      15th Polish Line Regiment (3 + artillery co) (2,238)
         (2–3pdrs)
   Brigade: General de brigade Paszkowski
      16th Polish Line Regiment (3 + artillery co) (1,811)
         (2–3pdrs)
   Artillery: Sowinski (total 361)
      3rd Polish Foot Artillery Company
         (4–6pdrs & 2 How)
      12th Polish Foot Artillery Company
         (4–6pdrs & 2 How)
      3/Supplementary Artillery Battalion
      Det. Polish Sapper Battalion
      Det. Polish Artillery Artisan Company
17th Division: General de division Dombrowski
   Brigade: General de brigade Zottowski
      1st Polish Line Regiment (3 + artillery co) (1,512)
         (2–3pdrs)

6th Polish Line Regiment (4 + artillery co) (1,556)
(2–3pdrs)
Brigade: General de brigade Krasinski
14th Polish Line Regiment (4 + artillery co) (1,120)
(2–3pdrs)
17th Polish Line Regiment (4 + artillery co) (880)
(2–3pdrs)
Artillery: Chef de bataillon Gugenmus (379)
10th Polish Foot Artillery Company
(4–6pdrs & 2 How)
11th Polish Foot Artillery Company
(4–6pdrs & 2 How)
1/Supplementary Battalion
Det. Polish Sapper Battalion
Det. Polish Artillery Artisan Company
18th Division: General de division Kamienicki
Brigade: General de brigade Grabowski
2nd Polish Line Regiment (3 + artillery co) (1,628)
(2–3pdrs)
8th Polish Line Regiment (3 + artillery co) (1,669)
(2–3pdrs)
Brigade: General de brigade Pakosz
12th Polish Line Regiment (3 + artillery co) (1,466)
(2–3pdrs)
Artillery: Chef de bataillon Uszyski (376)
4th Polish Foot Artillery Company (4–6pdrs & 2 How)
5th Polish Foot Artillery Company (4–6pdrs & 2 How)
2/Supplementary Battalion
Det. Polish Sapper Battalion
Det. Polish Artillery Artisan Company
Cavalry Corps: General de division Kaminski (later Sebastiani
& Lefebvre-Desnoettes)
18th Light Brigade: General de brigade
4th Polish Chasseur à Cheval Regiment (4) (696)
19th Light Brigade: General de brigade
1st Polish Chasseur à Cheval Regiment (4) (350)
12th Polish Uhlan Regiment (4) (579)
20th Light Brigade: General de brigade
5th Polish Chasseur à Cheval Regiment (4) (689)
13th Polish Hussar Regiment (4) (645)
Reserve Artillery: Colonel Gorski (total 440)
2nd Polish Horse Artillery Company (6–6pdrs)

14th Polish Foot Artillery Company (6–12 pdrs)
4/Supplementary Battalion
Det. Polish Artillery Artisan Company
Bridging Train: Captain Buialski (135)
Polish Pontooneers
Det. Supplementary Battalion
General Artillery Park: Chef de bataillon Kobylanski
    (Total—1,098)
7th Polish Foot Artillery Company (no guns)
8th Polish Foot Artillery Company (no guns)
9th Polish Foot Artillery Company (no guns)
13th Polish Foot Artillery Company (no guns)
15th Polish Foot Artillery Company (no guns)
Det. Polish Artillery Artisan Company
Engineering Park: (120)
Det. Polish Sapper Battalion
Polish Military Equipage Battalion

VI CORPS

Commander-in-Chief . . . . . .   G. St. Cyr . . . .   General de division
Chief of Staff . . . .   D'Albignac . . . .   Adjudant commandant
19th Division: Generallieutenant Deroy
  Brigade: Generalmajor von Siebein
    1st Bavarian Light Infantry Battalion (1) (14/330)
    1st Bavarian Line Regiment (2) (32/900)
    9th Bavarian Line Regiment (2) (27/822)
  Brigade: Generalmajor von Raglovich
    3rd Bavarian Light Infantry Battalion (1) (16/521)
    4th Bavarian Line Regiment (2) (35/998)
    10th Bavarian Line Regiment (2) (32/880)
  Brigade: Generalmajor Count Rechberg
    6th Bavarian Light Infantry Battalion (1) (18/438)
    8th Bavarian Line Regiment (2) (37/990)
  Artillery: Major Lamey (12/307)
    1st Light Battery Widemann (3–6pdrs & 1 How)
    3rd Light Battery Halder (3–6pdrs & 1 How)
    11th Battery Brack (6–6pdrs & 2 How)
    6th Battery Rois (4–12pdrs & 2 How)
    Howitzer Battery (6 howitzers)

1st Train Company
3rd Train Company
11th Train Company
6th Train Company
  (total train—3/195)
Park (1/190)
20th Division: Generallieutenant von Wrede
  Brigade: Generalmajor von Vincenti
    2nd Bavarian Light Infantry Battalion (1) (19/383)
    2nd Bavarian Line Regiment (2) (39/952)
    6th Bavarian Line Regiment (2) (30/1,103)
  Brigade: Generalmajor Count Beckers
    4th Bavarian Light Infantry Battalion (1) (17/444)
    3rd Bavarian Line Regiment (2) (35/656)
    7th Bavarian Line Regiment (2) (27/894)
  Brigade: Oberst Dalwigk (later Generalmajor Haberman, Scherer & Voller)
    5th Bavarian Light Infantry Battalion (1) (20/604)
    5th Bavarian Line Regiment (2) (37/972)
    11th Bavarian Line Regiment (2) (36/1,118)
  Artillery: Oberstleutnant von Zoller
    2nd Light Battery Gotthard (3–6pdrs & 1 How)
    4th Light Battery Gravenreuth (3–6pdrs & 1 How)
    5th Battery Hoffstetten (6–6pdrs & 2 How)
    8th Battery Ulmer (6–6pdrs & 2 How)
    4th Battery Berchem (4–12pdrs & 2 How)
      (total artillery—17/394)
    2nd Train Company
    Det. 4th Train Company
    4th Train Company
    5th Train Company
    8th Train Company
      (total train—5/475)
  Park (2/73)
  Engineers (4/22)
Corps Cavalry:
  20th Light Cavalry Brigade:
    3rd Bavarian Chevauxléger Regiment (4) (18/398)
    6th Bavarian Chevauxléger Regiment (4) (19/480)
  21st Light Cavalry Brigade:
    4th Bavarian Chevauxléger Regiment (4) (513)
    5th Bavarian Chevauxléger Regiment (4) (509)

CAVALRY RESERVE

Commander-in-Chief . . . . . .   Joachim Murat . . . . . .   King of Naples
Chief of Staff . . . .   Belliard . . . .   General de division

I Reserve Cavalry Corps: General de division Nansouty
1st Light Cavalry Division: General de division Bruyere
   3rd Light Brigade: General de brigade Jacquinot
      7th Hussar Regiment (4) (29/632)
      9th Chevauxléger Regiment (4) (36/335)
   4th Light Brigade: General de brigade Piré
      16th Chasseur à Cheval Regiment (4) (31/507)
      8th Hussar Regiment (4) (30/684)
   15th Light Brigade: General de brigade Niewiewski
      6th Polish Uhlan Regiment (4) (21/340)
      8th Polish Uhlan Regiment (4) (19/378)
      2nd Combined Prussian Hussars (4) (27/412)
        (1/4th, 3/4th, 1/6th, & 2/6th)
   Artillery:
      7/6th Horse Artillery (4–6pdrs & 2 How)
      1/1st Train (bis) Battalion
1st Cuirassier Division: General de division St. Germaine
   Brigade: General de brigade Bessières
      2nd Cuirassier Regiment (4) (32/353)
   Brigade: General de brigade Bruno
      3rd Cuirassier Regiment (4) (30/348)
   Brigade: General de brigade Queunot
      9th Cuirassier Regiment (4) (35/492)
      1st Chevauléger Regiment (1) (14/213)
   Artillery: Chef d'escadron Pons
      1/5th Horse Artillery (4–6pdrs & 2 How)
      3/5th Horse Artillery (4–6pdrs & 2 How)
      1/11th Train (bis) Battalion
      Artillery Artisans
5th Cuirassier Division: General de division Valence
   Brigade: General de brigade Reynaud
      6th Cuirassier Regiment (4) (35/612)
   Brigade: General de brigade Dejean
      11th Cuirassier Regiment (4) (31/511)
   Brigade: General de brigade De Lagrange
      12th Cuirassier Regiment (4) (35/657)
      5th Chevauléger Regiment (1 co) (7/142)

Artillery: Marthez (7/301)
  4/, 6/5th Horse Artillery (4–6pdrs & 2 How ea)
  3/, 6/11th Train (bis) Battalion
II Reserve Cavalry Corps: General de division Montbrun
2nd Light Cavalry Division: General de division Sebastiani
      (Pajol)
  7th Light Brigade: General de brigade St. Genies
    5th Hussar Regiment (4)
    9th Hussar Regiment (4)
  8th Light Brigade: General de brigade Burthe
    11th Chasseur à Cheval Regiment (3)
    12th Chasseur à Cheval Regiment (3)
  16th Light Brigade: General de brigade Subervie
    Prussian Combined Uhlan Regiment (4)
      (3/2nd, 4/2nd, 3/4th, 4/4th)
    3rd Württemberg Jäger zu Pferd Regiment (4)
    10th Polish Hussar Regiment (4)
  Artillery: Martinot
    1/4th Horse Artillery (4–6pdrs & 2 How)
2nd Cuirassier Division: General de division Wathier
  Brigade: General de brigade Beaumont (Caulaincourt)
    5th Cuirassier Regiment (4) (33/520)
  Brigade: General de brigade Dornes
    8th Cuirassier Regiment (4) (32/653)
  Brigade: General de brigade Richter
    10th Cuirassier Regiment (4) (36/554)
    1/2nd Chevauléger Regiment (13/191)
  Artillery: Chef d'escadron Romangin
    1/, 4/2nd Horse Artillery (4–6pdrs & 2 How) (8/175)
    1/1st Train (bis) Battalion (1/80)
    5/11th Train (bis) Battalion (1/36)
4th Cuirassier Division: General de division Defrance
  Brigade: General de brigade Bouvier des Eclats
      (Gerkeim, Chouard)
    1st Carabinier Regiment (4) (32/422)
  Brigade: General de brigade Chouard
      (l'Heriter, Paultre)
    2nd Carabinier Regiment (4) (407)
  Brigade: General de brigade Paultre
      (Ornano, Bouvier des Eclats)
    1st Cuirassier Regiment (4) (37/327)
    4/4th Chevauxléger Regiment (9/196)

Artillery: Parizet
    3/, 4/1st Horse Artillery (4–6pdrs & 2 How) (5/147)
    3/1st Train (bis) Battalion
    5/11th Train (bis) Battalion
      (total train—1/109)
III Reserve Cavalry Corps: General de division Grouchy
3rd Light Cavalry Division: General de division Lahoussaye
  11th Light Brigade: General de brigade Gauthrin
    6th Hussar Regiment (3) (24/499)
    8th Chasseur à Cheval Regiment (3) (32/498)
  10th Light Brigade: General de brigade Gérard
    6th Chasseur à Cheval Regiment (3) (28/432)
    25th Chasseur à Cheval Regiment (3) (24/487)
  17th Light Brigade: General de brigade Dommanget
    1st Bavarian Chevauxléger Regiment (4) (18/378)
    2nd Bavarian Chevauxléger Regiment (4) (18/350)
    Saxon Prinz Albert Chevauxléger Regiment (4) (20/280)
  Artillery:
    6/4th Horse Artillery (4–6pdrs & 2 How) (2/65)
3rd Cuirassier Division: General de division Doumerc
  Brigade: General de brigade Berkheim
    4th Cuirassier Regiment (4) (36/668)
  Brigade: General de brigade L'Heriter
    7th Cuirassier Regiment (4) (34/702)
  Brigade: General de brigade Doullembourg
    14th Cuirassier Regiment (4) (38/561)
    3rd Chevauléger Regiment (1 co) (8/113)
  Artillery: (9/349)
    1/6th Horse Artillery
    3/6th Horse Artillery
    1/8th Train (bis) Battalion
    2/11th Train (bis) Battalion
    6/11th Train (bis) Battalion
6th Heavy Division: General de division La Houssay
  Brigade: General de brigade Thiry
    7th Dragoon Regiment (3) (24/382)
    23rd Dragoon Regiment (3) (25/420)
  Brigade: General de brigade Séron
    28th Dragoon Regiment (3) (33/402)
    30th Dragoon Regiment (3) (30/377)
  Artillery: Captain Mouillet
    4/, 5/4th Horse Artillery (4–6pdrs & 2 How ea) (4/178)

IV Corps: General de division Latour-Maubourg
4th Light Cavalry Division: General de division Rozniecki
    28th Light Brigade: General de brigade Dziemanowski
        7th Polish Uhlan Regiment (3) (407)
        2nd Polish Uhlan Regiment (3) (443)
        11th Polish Uhlan Regiment (3) (501)
    29th Light Brigade: General de brigade Turno
        3rd Polish Uhlan Regiment (3) (329)
        16th Polish Uhlan Regiment (3) (472)
        15th Polish Uhlan Regiment (3) (398)
7th Cuirassier Division
    1st Division: Generalmajor Thielemann
        Zastrow Cuirassier Regiment (4) (421)
        Saxon Garde du Corps (4) (459)
        14th Polish Cuirassier Regiment (4) (264)
    2nd Brigade: General de brigade Lepel
        1st Westphalian Cuirassier Regiment (4) (475)
        2nd Westphalian Cuirassier Regiment (4) (480)
Corps Artillery: Chef d'escadron Schwerin
        2nd Westphalian Horse Battery (4–6pdrs & 2 How)
        2nd Westphalian Train Company
        2nd Saxon Horse Battery von Hiller (4–6pdrs & 2 How)
        3rd & 4th Polish Horse Artillery Batteries
            (4–6pdrs & 2 How ea)
        (total artillery—571)

Battle of Smolensk
17 August 1812

French Forces at Smolensk

Imperial Guard:
    1st Division
    2nd Division
    3rd Division
    Vistula Legion
    Guard Cavalry
    Guard Artillery
I Corps:
    1st Division
    2nd Division

3rd Division
Corps Artillery
Corps Cavalry
III Corps:
  10th Division
  11th Division
  25th Division
  Corps Artillery
  Corps Cavalry
V Corps:
  16th Division
  17th Division
  18th Division
  Corps Artillery
  Corps Cavalry
VIII Corps:
  23rd Division
  24th Division
  Corps Artillery
  Corps Cavalry
I Reserve Cavalry Corps
  1st Light Division
  1st Cuirassier Division
  5th Cuirassier Division
II Reserve Cavalry Corps
  2nd Light Division
  2nd Cuirassier Division
  4th Cuirassier Division
Actual Artillery Strength
        12pdrs—57
         6pdrs—267
         4pdrs—32
         3pdrs—2
     6" Mortars—16
   5.5" Howitzers—122

Russian Forces at Smolensk

On the Left Bank:
7th Corps: Raevsky
  One Jager Regiment

6th Corps: Docturov
  7th Division (8,400)
  24th Division (8,400)
3rd Corps: Tuchkov
  3rd Division (8,400)
2nd Corps: Baggovout
  4th Division (7,500)
  One Line Regiment from 17th Division (2,800)

Reserve on Right Bank: Barclay de Tolly
3rd Corps: Tuchkov
  1st Grendier Division (8,400)
2nd Corps: Baggovout
  17th Division (less 1 regiment) (5,600)
4th Corps: Ostermann (9,500)
  11th Division
  23rd Division
5th Corps: Grand Duke Constantine
  1st Converged Grenadier Division
  1st Cuirassier Division
Army Cavalry:
  1st Reserve Cavalry Corps
  2nd Reserve Cavalry Corps
  3rd Reserve Cavalry Corps
  Cossack Corps

On the Road to Moscow: General Bagration
7th Corps: Raevsky (11,500)
  26th Division
  12th Division
  (One Jager Regiment Detached)
8th Corps: Borosdin (9,500)
  2nd Grenadier Division
  2nd Converged Grenadier Division
  27th Division
Corps Cavalry:
  2nd Cuirassier Division
  4th Cavalry Corps
  Cossack Corps

French VIII Corps
23 August 1812

Commander-in-Chief . . . .   Vandamme . . . . . .   General de division
Chief of Staff . . . .   Revest . . . .   Adjudant commandant

23rd Division: Generallieutenant Tharreau
 Brigade: Generalmajor Damas
  3rd Westphalian Light Battalion (1) (19/569)
  2nd Westphalian Line Regiment (3 + artillery co)
   (59/1,568) (2–6pdrs)
  6th Westphalian Line Regiment (2 + artillery co)
   (41/1,241) (2–6pdrs)
 Brigade: Generalmajor Wickenberg
  2nd Westphalian Light Battalion (1) (20/583)
  3rd Westphalian Line Regiment (2 + artillery co)
   (37/1,138) (2–6pdrs)
  7th Westphalian Line Regiment (3 + artillery co)
   (58/1,417) (2–6pdrs)
 Artillery: Nummers (Major Frode)
  1st Westphalian Foot Battery Froede (4–6pdrs & 2 How)
   (4/208)
24th Division: Generallieutenant Ochs
 Brigade: Generalmajor Legras
  Westphalian Grenadier Guards (1 + artillery co)
   (25/628) Guard Foot Artillery Battery Brunig (2–6pdrs)
  Westphalian Guard Jägers (1) (25/628)
  Westphalian Jäger Karabiniers (1) (23/452)
 Brigade: Generalmajor Borstel
  1st Westphalian Light Battalion (1) (19/569)
  5th Westphalian Line Regiment (2) (37/1,172)
 Artillery: Captain Volmar
  1st Westphalian Horse Battery (5/167)
  2nd Westphalian Foot Battery Lemaître (6–6pdrs & 2 How)
   (3/178)
Corps Cavalry: Generalmajor Hammerstein
  (General de division Chabert)
 24th Brigade: Generalmajor Hammerstein
  1st Westphalian Hussar Regiment (4) (30/408)
  2nd Westphalian Hussar Regiment (4) (28/428)
 Guard Brigade: Generalmajor Wolf
  Westphalian Guard Chevauléger Regiment (4) (31/397)

Corps Artillery Reserve: General de division Allix
    1st Westphalian Heavy Foot Battery (6–12pdrs & 4 How)
    Westphalian Sappers
    Westphalian Artillery Artisans
    Westphalian Train
    Westphalian Gendarmerie

French VI Corps
29 August 1812

Commander-in-Chief . . . . . .   G. St. Cyr . . . .   Général de division
19th Division: Generallieutenant Deroy
    Brigade: Generalmajor von Siebein
        1st Bavarian Light Infantry Battalion (1) (5/24/15)
        1st Bavarian Line Regiment (2) (27/56/482)
        9th Bavarian Line Regiment (2) (18/48/288)
    Brigade: Generalmajor von Raglovich
        3rd Bavarian Light Infantry Battalion (1) (10/23/194)
        4th Bavarian Line Regiment (2) (22/57/455)
        10th Bavarian Line Regiment (2) I12/52/399)
    Brigade: Generalmajor Count Rechberg
        6th Bavarian Light Infantry Battalion (1) (14/35/255)
        8th Bavarian Line Regiment (2)
    Artillery: Major Lamey
        1st Light Battery Widemann (3–6pdrs & 1 How)
        3rd Light Battery Halder (3–6pdrs & 1 How)
        11th Battery Brack (6–6pdrs & 2 How)
        6th Battery Rois (4–12pdrs & 2 How)
        Howitzer Battery (6 howitzers)
        1st Train Company
        3rd Train Company
        11th Train Company
        6th Train Company
        Park
20th Division: Generallieutenant von Wrede
    Brigade: Generalmajor von Vincenti
        2nd Bavarian Light Infantry Battalion (1) (18/40/190)
        2nd Bavarian Line Regiment (2) (25/53/359)
        6th Bavarian Line Regiment (2) (12/55/532)
    Brigade: Generalmajor Count Beckers
        4th Bavarian Light Infantry Battalion (1) (7/30/165)

3rd Bavarian Line Regiment (2) (25/55/382)
7th Bavarian Line Regiment (2) (18/49/312)
Brigade:
  5th Bavarian Light Infantry Battalion (1) (15/32/225)
  5th Bavarian Line Regiment (2) (32/54/463)
  11th Bavarian Line Regiment (2) (30/60/505)
Artillery: Oberstleutnant von Zoller
  2nd Light Battery Gotthard (3–6pdrs & 1 How)
  4th Light Battery Gravenreuth (3–6pdrs & 1 How)
  5th Battery Hoffstetten (6–6pdrs & 2 How)
  8th Battery Ulmer (6–6pdrs & 2 How)
  4th Battery Berchem (4–12pdrs & 2 How)
  2nd Train Company
  Det. 4th Train Company
  4th Train Company
  5th Train Company
  8th Train Company
  Park
  Engineers

French Grande Armée at the Battle of Borodino
7 September 1812

Commander-in-Chief: Emperor Napoleon Bonaparte

Headquarters Escort:
  2/2nd Hessian Leib Regiment
  1/2nd Baden Erbgrossherzog Regiment
  Portuguese Legion Chasseur à Cheval Regiment (4)
  28th Chasseur à Cheval Regiment (1) (detached from III Corps)

General Park:
  10/1st Foot Artillery
  21/2nd Foot Artillery
  5/, 7/, 22/8th Foot Artillery
  15/, 19/7th Foot Artillery
  8/, 16/, 17/9th Foot Artillery

Left Wing: Prince Eugène de Beauharnais
IV CORPS

Commander-in-Chief . . . .   Eugène . . . .   Viceroy of Italy

Italian Royal Guard: General de division Pino
  Brigade: General de brigade Lecchi
    Royal Velites (2)
    Guard Infantry Regiment (2)
    Guard Conscript Regiment (2)
  Guard Cavalry: General de brigade Triaire
    Gardes d'honneur (5 coys)
    Guard Dragoon Regiment (2 sqn)
    Queen's Dragoon Regiment (4)
  Artillery:
    1st & 2nd Italian Foot Artillery (6pdrs)
    1st & 2nd Italian Horse Artillery (6pdrs)
    2/, 7/1st Italian Foot Artillery (12pdrs)

13th Division: General de division Delzons
  Brigade: General de brigade Huard
    8th Légère Regiment (2)
    84th Line Regiment (4)
    1st Provisional Croatian Regiment (2)
  Brigade:
    92nd Line Regiment (4)
    106th Line Regiment (4)
  Artillery:
    9/2nd Foot Artillery (6–6pdrs & 2 How)
    2/4th Horse Artillery (4–6pdrs & 2 How)

14th Division: General de division Broussier
  Brigade:
    19th Légère Regiment
    Joseph Napoleon Regiment
    53rd Line Regiment
  Brigade:
    35th Line Regiment
    9th Line Regiment
  Artillery:
    7/2nd Foot Artillery
    3/4th Horse Artillery

1st Division: General de division Morand (Detached from
    I Corps)

1st Brigade: General de brigade d'Alton
   13th Légère Regiment (5)
2nd Brigade: General de brigade Gratien
   17th Regiment (5)
3rd Brigade: General de brigade Bonamy
   30th Line Regiment (5)
Artillery:
   1/7th Foot Artillery (6pdrs)
   7/1st Horse Artillery (6pdrs)
3rd Division: General de division Gerard (Detached from I Corps)
   1st Brigade: General de brigade Desailly
     7th Légère Regiment (5)
     12th Line Regiment (5)
   2nd Brigade: General de brigade Leclerc
     127th Line Regiment (2)
     21st Line Regiment (5)
     1/, 2/Mecklenburg-Strelitz Battalion
   Artillery:
     3/7th Foot Artillery (6pdrs)
     4/3rd Horse Artillery (6pdrs)
Corps Artillery:
Reserve
   5/, 12/2nd Foot Artillery
Park
   8/, 16/, 20/2nd Foot Artillery
Corps Cavalry: General de division Ornano
   12th Light Cavalry Brigade: General de brigade Guyon
     9th Chasseur à Cheval Regiment (3)
     19th Chasseur à Cheval Regiment (3)
   13th Light Cavalry Brigade: General de brigade Villata
     2nd Italian Chasseur à Cheval Regiment (3)
     3rd Italian Chasseur à Cheval Regiment (3)
VI Corps Cavalry:
   20th Light Cavalry Brigade: Generalmajor Seydewitz
     3rd Bavarian Chevauxléger Regiment
     6th Bavarian Chevauxléger Regiment
   21st Light Cavalry Brigade: Generalmajor Preysing
     4th Bavarian Chevauxléger Regiment
     5th Bavarian Chevauxléger Regiment
III Reserve Cavalry Corps: General de division Grouchy
3rd Light Cavalry Division: General de division Chastel
   11th Light Brigade: General de brigade Gauthrin

6th Hussar Regiment (3)
8th Chasseur à Cheval Regiment (3)
10th Light Brigade: General de brigade Gerard
  6th Chasseur à Cheval Regiment (3)
  25th Chasseur à Cheval Regiment (3)
17th Light Brigade: General de brigade Dommanget
  1st Bavarian Chevauxléger Regiment (4)
  2nd Bavarian Chevauxléger Regiment (4)
  Saxon Prinz Albert Chevauxléger Regiment (4)
Artillery:
  6/4th Horse Artillery
6th Heavy Division: General de division La Houssaye
Brigade: General de brigade Thiry
  7th Dragoon Regiment (3)
  23rd Dragoon Regiment (3)
Brigade: General de brigade Seron
  28th Dragoon Regiment (3)
  30th Dragoon Regiment (3)
Artillery:
  4/, 5/4th Horse Artillery

French Center: Napoleon I
III CORPS

Commander-in-Chief . . . .   Ney   . . . .   Maréchal de France

10th Division: General de division Ledru
1st Brigade: General de brigade Gengoult
  24th Line Regiment (4)
  1st Portuguese Line Regiment (2)
2nd Brigade: General de brigade Morion
  46th Line Regiment (4)
3rd Brigade: General de brigade Bruny
  72nd Line Regiment (4)
  129th Line Regiment (2)
Artillery:
  12/5th Foot Battery (6pdrs)
  5/6th Horse Battery (6pdrs)
11th Division: General de division Razout
1st Brigade: General de brigade Joubert
  4th Line Regiment (4)
2nd Brigade
  18th Line Regiment (4)

3rd Brigade: General de brigade d'Henin
  93rd Line Regiment (4)
Artillery:
  18/5th Foot Artillery (6pdrs)
  6/5th Horse Artillery (6pdrs)
25th Division: Generallieutenant Scheler
  1st Brigade: Generalmajor von Hugel (Total strength
    1 Battalion)
    1st Line Regiment "Prinz Paul"
    4th Line Regiment
  2nd Brigade: Generalmajor Koch (Total strength 1 Battalion)
    2nd Line Regiment "Herzog Wilhelm"
    6th Line Regiment "Kronprinz"
  3rd Brigade: Generalmajor von Bruxelles
    1st Light Infantry Battalion
    2nd Light Infantry Battalion
    1st Jäger Battalion "König"
    2nd Jäger Battalion
      (Total strength 1 Battalion)
Artillery:
  1st & 2nd Württemberg Foot Artillery (6pdrs)
  1st & 2nd Württemberg Horse Artillery (6pdrs)
Calvary Corps: Generalmajor Wollwrath
  9th Light Brigade: General de brigade Mouriez
    11th Hussar Regiment (4)
    6th Chevauléger Regiment (3)
    Jäger zu Pferd Regiment #4 "König" (4)
  14th Light Brigade: General de brigade Beurman
    28th Chasseur à Cheval Regiment (2)
    4th Chasseur à Cheval Regiment (4)
    1st Württemberg Chevauléger Regiment
      "Prinz Adam" (4)
    2nd Württemberg Chevauléger Regiment "Leib" (4)
Artillery Reserve:
  12pdr Württemberg Foot Battery
  16/, 21/1st Foot Artillery (12pdrs)

VIII CORPS

Commander-in-Chief . . . . Junot . . . . General de division
23rd Division: Generallieutenant Tharreau
  Brigade: Generalmajor Damas
    3rd Westphalian Light Battalion (1)
    2nd Westphalian Line Regiment (2)
    6th Westphalian Line Regiment (2)
  Brigade: Generalmajor Wickenberg
    2nd Westphalian Light Battalion (1)
    3rd Westphalian Line Regiment (2)
    7th Westphalian Line Regiment (3)
  Artillery:
    1st Westphalian Foot Battery Froede (6pdrs)
24th Division: Generallieutenant Ochs
  Brigade: Generalmajor Legras
    Westphalian Grenadier Guards (1)
      Guard Foot Artillery Battery Brunig (2–6pdrs)
    Westphalian Guard Jägers (1)
    Westphalian Jäger Karabiniers (1)
    1st Westphalian Jäger Battalion (1)
  Artillery:
    2nd Westphalian Foot Battery Lemaître (6pdrs)
Corps Cavalry: General de division Chabert
  24th Brigade: Generalmajor Hammerstein
    1st Westphalian Hussar Regiment (4)
    2nd Westphalian Hussar Regiment (4)
    Westphalian Guard Chevauxléger Regiment (4)
    (Two unknown squadrons were detached from this
      brigade)
Corps Artillery Reserve:
    1st Westphalian Heavy Foot Battery (12pdrs)
    Westphalian Guard Horse Battery (6pdrs)
IV Corps: General de division Latour-Maubourg
4th Light Cavalry Division: General de division Rozniecki
  29th Light Brigade: General de brigade Turno
    3rd Polish Uhlan Regiment (3)
    11th Polish Uhlan Regiment (3)
    16th Polish Uhlan Regiment (3)
7th Cuirassier Division: General de division Lorge
  1st Division: Generalmajor Thielemann
    Zastrow Cuirassier Regiment (4)

Saxon Garde du Corps (4)
14th Polish Cuirassier Regiment
2nd Brigade: General de brigade Lepel
  1st Westphalian Cuirassier Regiment (4)
  2nd Westphalian Cuirassier Regiment (4)
Corps Artillery: Chef d'escadron Schwerin
  2nd Westphalian Horse Battery (6pdrs)
  2nd Saxon Horse Battery von Hiller (6pdrs)

I CORPS

Commander-in-Chief . . . . Davout . . . . Maréchal d'Empire
2nd Division: General de division Friant
  1st Brigade: General de brigade Dufour
    48th Line Regiment (5)
  2nd Brigade: General de brigade Vandedem
    33rd Line Regiment (5)
  3rd Brigade: General de brigade Grandeau
    15th Légère Regiment (5)
    Joseph Napoleon Regiment (2)
  Artillery:
    2/7th Foot Artillery (6pdrs)
    5/3rd Horse Artillery (6pdrs)
4th Division: General de division Dessaix
  2nd Brigade: General de brigade Frederichs
    85th Line Regiment (5)
  3rd Brigade: General de brigade Frederichs
    85th Line Regiment (5)
  3rd Brigade: General de brigade Leguay
    108th Line Regiment (5)
  Artillery:
    9/7th Foot Artillery (6pdrs)
    2/5th Horse Artillery (6pdrs)
5th Division: General de division Compans
  1st Brigade: General de brigade Duppelin
    25th Line Regiment (5)
  2nd Brigade: General de brigade Teste
    57th Line Regiment (5)
  3rd Brigade: General de brigade Guyardet
    61st Line Regiment (5)
  4th Brigade: General de brigade Louchamp
    111th Line Regiment (5)

Artillery:
  2/6th Foot Artillery (6pdrs)
  16/7th Horse Artillery (6pdrs)
Corps Cavalry: General de division Girardin
  1st Light Cavalry Brigade:
    2nd Chasseur à Cheval Regiment (4)
    9th Polish Lancer Regiment (4)
  2nd Light Cavalry Brigade: General de brigade Bordessoulle
    1st Chasseur à Cheval Regiment (4)
    3rd Chasseur à Cheval Regiment (4)
  Artillery Reserve:
    3/, 17/1st Foot Artillery (12pdrs)
  Park:
    6/7th Foot Artillery (6pdrs)
    11/, 14/9th Foot Artillery (6pdrs)
I Reserve Cavalry Corps: General de division Nansouty
1st Light Cavalry Division: General de division Bruyere
  3rd Light Brigade: General de brigade Jacquinot
    7th Hussar Regiment (4)
    9th Chevauléger Regiment (4)
  4th Light Brigade: General de brigade Piré
    16th Chasseur à Cheval Regiment (4)
    8th Hussar Regiment (4)
  15th Light Brigade: General de brigade Roussel d'Hureal
    6th Polish Uhlan Regiment (4)
    8th Polish Uhlan Regiment (4)
    2nd Combined Prussian Hussars (4)
      (1/4th, 3/4th, 1/6th, & 2/6th)
  Artillery:
    7/6th Horse Artillery (6pdrs)
1st Cuirassier Division: General de division St. Germaine
  Brigade: General de brigade Bessieres
    2nd Cuirassier Regiment (4)
  Brigade: General de brigade Bruno
    3rd Cuirassier Regiment (4)
  Brigade: General de brigade Queunot
    9th Cuirassier Regiment (4)
    1st Chevauléger Regiment (1 co)
  Artillery:
    1/5th Horse Artillery (6pdrs)
    3/5th Horse Artillery (6pdrs)
5th Cuirassier Division: General de division Valence

Brigade: General de brigade Reynaud
  6th Cuirassier Regiment (4)
Brigade: General de brigade Dejean
  11th Cuirassier Regiment (4)
Brigade: General de brigade De Lagrange
  12th Cuirassier Regiment (4)
  5th Chevauléger Regiment (1 co)
Artillery:
  4/5th Horse Artillery (6pdrs)
  6/5th Horse Artillery (6pdrs)
II Reserve Cavalry Corps: General de division Montburn
2nd Light Cavalry Division: General de division Pajol
  7th Light Brigade: Genéral de brigade Desirad
    11th Chasseur à Cheval Regiment (3)
    12th Chasseur à Cheval Regiment (3)
  8th Light Brigade: General de brigade Burthe
    5th Hussar Regiment (4)
    9th Hussar Regiment (4)
  16th Light Brigade: General de brigade Subervie
    3rd Württemberg Jäger zu Pferd (4)
    Prussian Combined Uhlan Regiment (4)
    10th Polish Hussar Regiment (4)
1st Cuirassier Division: General de division Wathier
  Brigade: General de brigade Beaumont
    5th Cuirassier Regiment (4)
  Brigade: General de brigade Richter
    8th Cuirassier Regiment (4)
  Brigade: General de brigade Dornes
    10th Cuirassier Regiment (4)
    2nd Chevauléger Regiment (1 co)
  Artillery:
    1/2nd Horse Artillery (6pdrs)
    4/2nd Horse Artillery (6pdrs)
4th Cuirassier Division: General de division Defrance
  Brigade: General de brigade Chouard
    1st Carabinier Regiment (4)
  Brigade: General de brigade Paultre
    2nd Carabinier Regiment (4)
  Brigade: General de brigade Bouvier des Eclats
    1st Cuirassier Regiment (4)
    4/4th Chevauléger Regiment (1 co)

Right Wing: Prince Poniatowski
V CORPS

Commander-in-Chief . . . . Prince Poniatowski . . . General de division
16th Division: General de division Zayonchek
  Brigade: General de brigade Mielzynski
   3rd Polish Line Regiment (3)
   15th Polish Line Regiment (3)
  Brigade: General de brigade Paszkowski
   16th Polish Line Regiment (3)
  Artillery:
   3rd Polish Foot Artillery Company (6pdrs)
   12th Polish Foot Artillery Company (6pdrs)
18th Division: General de division Kniaziewicz
  Brigade: General de brigade Grabowski
   2nd Polish Line Regiment (3)
   8th Polish Line Regiment (3)
  Brigade: General de brigade Pakosz
   12th Polish Line Regiment (3)
  Artillery:
   4th Polish Foot Artillery Company (6pdrs)
   5th Polish Foot Artillery Company (6pdrs)
   3/Supplementary Battalion
Reserve Artillery:
   2nd Polish Horse Artillery Company (6pdrs)
   14th Polish Foot Artillery Company (6pdrs)
   4/Supplementary Battalion
  Park:
   7th Polish Horse Artillery Company
   8th Polish Horse Artillery Company
Cavalry Corps:
  19th Light Brigade: General de brigade Tyskiewicz
   12th Polish Uhlan Regiment (4)
  20th Light Brigade: Prince A. Sulkowski
   5th Polish Chasseur à Cheval Regiment (4)
   13th Polish Hussar Regiment (4)

RESERVE—Imperial Guard

Commander-in-Chief . . . . . . Mortier . . . . Maréchal d'Empire

2nd Division: General de division Roguet
  Brigade: General de brigade Lanabere
    1st Tirailleur Regiment (2)
    1st Voltigeur Regiment (2)
  Brigade: General de brigade Boyledieu
    Fusilier Chasseur Regiment (2)
    Fusilier Grenadier Regiment (2)
  Artillery:
    3/Old Guard Foot Artillery
    3/Young Guard Foot Artillery
    5th Prussian Foot Artillery
    7th Prussian Foot Artillery
3rd Division: General de division Curial
  Brigade: General de brigade Boyer
    1st Chasseur à Pied (2)
    2nd Chasseur à Pied (2)
  Brigade: General de division Curial
    1st Grenadier à Pied (2)
    2nd Grenadier à Pied (2)
    3rd Grenadier à Pied (2)
    2/Old Guard Foot Artillery
    1/Young Guard Foot Artillery
Vistula Legion: General de division Claparéde
  Brigade: General de brigade Cholpicki
    1st Vistula Regiment (2)
    2nd Vistula Regiment (2)
  Brigade:
    3rd Vistula Regiment (2)
Guard Cavalry Marechal Bessières
Division: General de division Walther
  Brigade: General de brigade St. Sulpice
    Empress Dragoon Regiment (5)
    Grenadier à Cheval Regiment (5)
  Brigade: General de brigade Guyot
    Chasseur à Cheval Regiment (5)
    Mameluke Squadron
  Brigade: General de brigade Colbert
    1st Chevauléger lancier de la Garde Regiment (4)

2nd Chevauléger lancier de la Garde Regiment (4)
Gendarmerie d'Elite (2)
Artillery:
    1/Old Guard Horse Artillery
    3/Old Guard Horse Artillery
Reserve Artillery:
    2/Old Guard Horse Artillery
    4/Old Guard Horse Artillery
    4/Old Guard Foot Artillery
    5/Old Guard Foot Artillery
    6/Old Guard Foot Artillery
Park:
    10/, 16/8th Foot Artillery

Other French forces detached from the main body at Borodino

IV Corps:
    3rd Division:
        3rd & 4th Companies Mecklenburg-Strelitz Battalion in garrison at Viday
    15th Division: (En route to Borodino after an antipartisan sweep)
        4/1st Italian Legere
        2nd Italian Line Regiment
        3rd Italian Line
        3rd Italian Légère
        Dalmatian Regiment

VIII Corps

3/2nd Westphalian Line Infantry	—At Gzhatsk
1/5th Westphalian Line Infantry	—At Viasma
2/5th Westphalian Line Infantry	—At Dorogobuzm
1st Westphalian Line Infantry (2)	—With 7th Division, X Corps
8th Westphalian Line Infantry (2)	—At Vilna

IV Reserve Cavalry Corps:

28th Light Brigade: Dziewanoljsk	—With Dombrowski's around Mstislavl
2nd Polish Uhlans	
7th Polish Uhlans	
15th Polish Uhlans	

I Corps:
    5th Division:
        1st & 2nd Companies Mecklenburg-Strelitz Battalion in garrison at Vilna

4th Division:
    1/2nd Hessian Leib Regiment — At Vitebsk
    2/2nd Hessian Leib Regiment — With HQ escort
    33rd Légère (2) — At Minsk
    33rd Légère (2) — At Smolensk

II Reserve Cavalry Corps:
    16th Light Brigade:
        1st Polish Chasseur à Cheval Regiment — At Smolensk

V Corps:
    16th Division:
        13th Polish Line Regiment — Garrison of Zamosc
    17th Division: — Detached and operating
        1st Polish Line Regiment   around Mstislavl
        6th Polish Line Regiment
        14th Polish Line Regiment
        17th Polish Line Regiment

Imperial Guard:
    2nd Division: — At Vitebsk
        Flanquer-Chasseur Regiment
        Flanquer-Grenadier Regiment
    Vistula Legion: — At Smolensk
        3/1st Vistula Regiment
        3/2nd Vistula Regiment
        3/3rd Vistula Regiment

III Corps:
    11th Division:
        Illyrian Infantry Regiment (3) — At Minsk
    25th Division:
        7th Württemberg Line Infantry Regiment — Garrison in Danzig
VIII Corps:
    Westphalian Garde du Corps — Returned to Westphalia

Other Major Detachments:
II & VI Corps — At Polotsk
3rd Cuirassier Division — At Polotsk
VII Corps — Around Pripet Marshes
Austrian Hilfkorps — Around Pripet Marshes
X Corps — In Courland
XI Corps — En route from Tilsit to
   Smolensk

3rd Chevaulégers de la Garde — Forming in Slonim

29th Division
  1st, 2nd, 3rd, 4th   —En route to Smolensk
  Demibrigades de Marche
Polish Army
  18th, 19th, 20th, 21st, & 22nd Polish Line   —Forming in Lithuania
  17th, 18th, 19th, & 20th Polish Uhlans   —Forming in Lithuania
  21st Polish Chasseurs   —Forming in Lithuania

Russian Order of Battle for Borodino
5–7 September 1812

Commanding Officer:	General of Infantry Kutusov
Chief of Staff:	General of Cavalry Bennigsen
Quartermaster General:	Major General Vistitzki II
Adjutant:	Colonel Toll
Chief of Artillery:	Major General Count Kutaisov
General's Aide du Jour:	Colonel Kaisarov
Chief of Engineers:	Major General Ivachev
Chief of Gendarmes:	Major General Levtizki
Adjutant:	Colonel Choulguin
Chief of Revictualling:	Senator Lanskoi
Health Inspector:	Villiers

Headquarters Escort
  2nd Combined Grenadier Battalion, 11th Division
  Selenguinsk Infantry Regiment (1 bn)
  Kargopol Dragoon Regiment (4 sqns)
  Ingermanland Dragoon Regiment (4 sqns)
  2nd Bug Cossack Regiment
  1st Engineer Regiment (3 cos)
  2nd Engineer Regiment (1 co)
  Equipage of the Marines of the Guard Police

1ST ARMY OF THE WEST

Commanding General	—Barclay de Tolly
Chief of Staff	—Tormolov
Quartermaster General	—Colonel Toll
Service Chief	—Colonel Kikin
Chief of Artillery	—General Koutaissof
Chief of Engineers	—General Trousson

Right Wing: General Miloradovitch
Right Flank Guard Detachment: Lt. Colonel Vlasov III
  Vlasov III Don Cossack Regiment
  Ataman Cossack Regiment (5 sotnias)
  Illowaiski #4 Cossack Regiment
  Illowaiski #8 Cossack Regiment

2nd Corps: Generallieutenant Baggovout
4th Division: Prince Eugène of Württemberg
  Brigade: Pyshnitskoi
    Krementchug Infantry Regiment (2)
    Minsk Infantry Regiment (2)
  Brigade: Rossi
    Tobolsk Infantry Regiment (2)
    Volhynie Infantry Regiment (2)
  Brigade: Pillar
    4th Jager Regiment (2)
    34th Jager Regiment (2)
  Artillery: Wojeitov
    Position Battery #4 (8–12pdrs & 4 Licornes)
    Light Batteries #7 & #8 (8–6pdrs & 4 Licornes ea)
17th Division: Olsoufieff
  Brigade: Tehoubarov
    Riazan Infantry Regiment (2)
    Bieloserk Infantry Regiment (2)
  Brigade: Tuchkov II
    Wilmanstrand Infantry Regiment (2)
    Brest Infantry Regiment (2)
  Brigade: Potemkin
    3rd Jager Regiment (2)
    48th Jager Regiment (2)
  Brigade:
    Elisabethgrad Hussar Regiment (8)(detached to 1st Cavalry Corps)
  Artillery Brigade: Walewacz
    Position Battery #17 (8–12pdrs & 4 Licornes)
    Light Batteries #32 & #33 (8–6pdrs & 4 Licornes ea)
11th Division: Bakhmetieff II
  Brigade: Philissov
    Polotsk Infantry Regiment (2)
    Jeletz Infantry Regiment (2)
  Brigade: Tchoglokov
    Kexholm Infantry Regiment (2)
    Pernov Infantry Regiment (2)

Brigade: Bistrom
  1st Jager Regiment (2)
  33rd Jager Regiment (2)
Artillery Brigade: Cotliarev
  Position Battery #2 (8–12pdrs & 4 Licornes)
  Light Batteries #3 & #4 (8–6pdrs & 4 Licornes ea)
23rd Division: Bakhmetieff I
Brigade: Okoulov
  Rilsk Infantry Regiment (2)
  Ekaterinburg Infantry Regiment (2)
Brigade: Alcksapol (Detached to 3rd Division)
  Seleguinsk Infantry Regiment (2)
  18th Jager Regiment (2)
Artillery Brigade: Goulewicz (Detached to Artillery Reserve)
  Position Battery #23 (8–12pdrs & 4 Licornes)
  Light Battery #44 (8–6pdrs & 4 Licornes)
Brigade:
  2nd Combined Grenadier Battalion (11th & 23rd Division)
  Karporsk Infantry Regiment (2)

I Cavalry Corps: Generallieutenant Ouvarov
Guard Cavalry Division
Brigade: Tchalikov
  Guard Dragoon Regiment (5)(detached to 1st Cuirassier Division)
  Guard Uhlan Regiment (4)
Brigade
  Guard Hussar Regiment (4)
  Guard Cossacks
Brigade: Tchernich
  Niejine Dragoon Regiment (4)
  Elisabethgrad Hussar Regiment (8) (Detached from 17th Division)
Artillery:
  Horse Battery #2 (8–6pdrs & 4 Licornes)
2nd Cavalry Division: Generalmajor Baron Korff
6th Brigade: Davydov
  Pskof Dragoon Regiment (4)
  Moscow Dragoon Regiment (4)
8th Brigade:
  Isoum Hussar Regiment (8)
  Polish Uhlan Regiment (8)
9th Brigade: Klebev
  Orenburg Dragoon Regiment (4)
  Kourland Dragoon Regiment (4)

10th Brigade: Skalon
  Siberian Dragoon Regiment (4)
  Irkhoutsk Dragoon Regiment (4)
11th Brigade:
  Soum Hussar Regiment (8)
  Marioupol Hussar Regiment (4)
Artillery:
  Horse Battery #6 (8–6pdrs & 4 Licornes)

6th Corps: General of Infantry Docturov
7th Division: Generallieutenant Kapsevitch
  Brigade: Liapounov
    Moscow Infantry Regiment (2)
    Pakof Infantry Regiment (2)
  Brigade: Balem
    Libau Infantry Regiment (2)
    Sofia Infantry Regiment (2)
  Brigade: Balla
    11th Jager Regiment (Detached to III Corps)
    36th Jager Regiment
  Artillery: Demel
    Position Battery #7 (8–12pdrs & 4 Licornes)
    Light Batteries #12 & #13 (8–6pdrs & 4 Licornes ea)
24th Division: Generalmajor Lichatcheff
  Brigade: Tschoulski
    Oufa Infantry Regiment (2)
    Chirvan Infantry Regiment (2)
  Brigade: Denissieff
    Tomsk Infantry Regiment (2)
    Bourtirki Infantry Regiment (2)
  Brigade: Vouitch
    19th Jager Regiment (2)
    40th Jager Regiment (2)
  Artillery: Iesremov
    Position Battery #24 (8–12pdrs & 4 Licornes)
    Light Batteries #45 & #46 (8–6pdrs & 4 Licornes ea)

3rd Cavalry Corps: Kreutz
  Brigade:
    Siberia Uhlan Regiment (4)
    Alexandria Hussar Regiment (8)
  Brigade
    Smolensk Dragoon Regiment (4)
  Artillery
    Horse Battery #7 (8–6pdrs & 4 Licornes)

5th Corps: Grand Duke Constantin
Guard Division: Generallieutenant Lavrov
  1st Brigade: Baron Rosen
    Preobragenski Guard Infantry Regiment (3)
    Semenovski Guard Infantry Regiment (3)
  2nd Brigade: Udom
    Ismailov Guard Infantry Regiment (3)
    Lithuanian Guard Infantry Regiment (3)
  3rd Brigade: Bistrom
    Guard Jager Infantry Regiment (3)
    Finland Guard Infantry Regiment (3)
  Artillery:
    1st & 2nd Guard Position Batteries
      (8–12pdrs & 4 Licornes ea)
    1st & 2nd Guard Light Batteries (8–6pdrs & 4 Licornes)
    Guard Equipage Battery (2–6pdrs) (in Borodino with another battery)
1st Converged Grenadier Division:
  Brigade:
    Guard Marine Equipage Battalion (1)
  Brigade:
    Converged Grenadiers of the 17th Division (2)
    Converged Grenadiers of the 4th Division (2)
  Brigade:
    Pioneer Companies (2)
1st Cavalry Division: Depreradovitch
  Brigade: Borosdin II
    Emperor Cuirassier Regiment (5)
    Empress Cuirassier Regiment (5)
  Brigade: Generalmajor Cheviez
    Chevalier Guard Regiment (5)
    Guard Dragoon Regiment (5)(detached from 1st Cavalry Division)
  Artillery:
    Guard Horse Batteries #1 & #2 (8 guns each)
2nd Cuirassier Division: Detached to 2nd Army of the West)

1st Army of the West Artillery Reserve: Kutaisov
  Position Battery #29 (8–12pdrs & 4 Licornes) (in the reserve)
  Position Battery #30 (8–12pdrs & 4 Licornes) (in the reserve)
  Light Battery #1 (8–6pdrs & 4 Licornes) (in the reserve)
  Light Battery #2 (8–6pdrs & 4 Licornes) (in the reserve)
  Light Battery #5 (8–6pdrs & 4 Licornes) (in the reserve)
  Horse Battery #4 (8–6pdrs & 4 Licornes) (in the reserve)
  Horse Battery #5 (8–6pdrs & 4 Licornes) (in the reserve)
  Horse Battery #9 (8–6pdrs & 4 Licornes) (in the reserve)

Horse Battery #10 (8–6pdrs & 4 Licornes) (in the reserve)
Horse Battery #22 (8–6pdrs & 4 Licornes) (in the reserve)
Cossacks: General of Cavalry Platov
  2nd Don Horse Batteries (12 guns)
  Ataman Don Cossack Regiment (5 sotnias)
  Illowaiski #5 Cossack Regiment
  Kharitonov Don Cossack Regiment
  Denissov #7 Don Cossack Regiment
  Grekov #18 Cossack Regiment
  Zhirov Cossack Regiment

2ND ARMY OF THE WEST

Commanding General —Prince Bagration
Chief of Staff   —Generalmajor Count St. Preist
Quartermaster General—Generalmajor Vistitski II
Service General   —Colonel Marin
Chief of Artillery   —Generalmajor Lowenstern
Chief of Engineers   —Generalmajor Forster

Commander of the Left Wing: Gorchakov II

7th Corps: Generallieutenant Raevsky
12th Division: Generalmajor Vasil'chikov
  Brigade: Ryleieff
    Smolensk Infantry Regiment (2)
    Narva Infantry Regiment (2)
  Brigade: Pantzerbieter
    New Ingremannland Infantry Regiment (2)
    Alexopol Infantry Regiment (2)
  Brigade: Palitzin
    6th Jager Regiment (2)
    41st Jager Regiment (2) (Detached to III Corps)
  Artillery Brigade: Sablin (Detached to Artillery Reserve)
    Position Battery #12 (8–12pdrs & 4 Licornes)
    Light Battery #23 (8–6pdrs & 4 Licornes ea)
26th Division: Generalmajor Paskevitch
  Brigade: Liebert
    Ladoga Infantry Regiment (2)
    Poltava Infantry Regiment (2)
  Brigade: Samoini
    Orel Infantry Regiment (2)
    Nivegorod Infantry Regiment (2)

Brigade: Gogel
  5th Jager Regiment (2)
  42nd Jager Regiment (2)
Artillery Brigade: Schoulmann
  Position Battery #26 (8–12pdrs & 4 Licornes)
  (In Raevsky Redoubt)
  Light Batteries #47 & #48 (8–6pdrs & 4 Licornes ea)
  (#48 detached to Artillery Reserve)
27th Division: Generalmajor Neverovski
  Brigade: Kniajnin
    Vilna Infantry Regiment (2)
    Simbrisk Infantry Regiment (2)
  Brigade: Stavitski
    Odessa Infantry Regiment (2)
    Tarnopol Infantry Regiment (2)
  Brigade: Woiekov
    49th Jager Regiment (2)
    50th Jager Regiment (2)
2nd (7th) Converged Grenadier Division: Generalmajor Voronzov
  Brigade:
    Converged Grenadiers of the 2nd Division (2)
    Converged Grenadiers of the 12th Division (2)
    Converged Grenadiers of the 26th Division (2)
  Artillery:
    Position Batteries #31 & #32 (8–12pdrs & 4 Licornes ea)

4th Cavalry Corps: Generalmajor Sievers
4th Cavalry Division: Generalmajor Sievers
  12th Brigade: Generalmajor Pantchaulidseff
    Karkov Dragoon Regiment (4)(dismounted)
    Tchernigov Dragoon Regiment (4)(dismounted)
  13th Brigade: Emmanuel
    Kiev Dragoon Regiment (4)
    New Russia Dragoon Regiment (4)
  Brigade:
    Akhtyrsk Hussar Regiment (Detached from 12th Division)
    Lithuanian Uhlan Regiment (8)
  Artillery:
    Horse Battery #8 (8–6pdrs & 4 Licornes)
    Pontooneer Company #4
    Pioneer Companies (4)
2nd Grenadier Division: Generalmajor Prince Charles of Mecklenburg
  Brigade: Chatilov

Kiev Grenadier Regiment (2)
Moscow Grenadier Regiment (2)
Brigade: Buxhowden
Astrakhan Grenadier Regiment (2)
Fangoria Grenadier Regiment (2)
Brigade: Hesse
Siberia Grenadier Regiment (2)
Little Russia Grenadier Regiment (2)
Artillery Brigade: Bogoslavski (Detached to Artillery Reserve)
Position Battery #11 (8–12pdrs & 4 Licornes)
Light Artillery Batteries #20 & #21
(8–6pdrs & 4 Licornes ea)
2nd Cuirassier Division: Generalmajor Knorring
2nd Brigade: Kretov
Military Order Cuirassier Regiment
Ekaterinoslav Cuirassier Regiment
3rd Brigade: Duka
Gluchov Cuirassier Regiment
Novgorod Cuirassier Regiment
Little Russia Cuirassier Regiment

3rd Corps: Generallieutenant Tuchkov I
3rd Division: Konovnitzin
Brigade: Tuchkov III
Mourmonsk Infantry Regiment (2)
Revel Infantry Regiment (2)
Brigade: Voeikov
Tchernigov Infantry Regiment (2)
Seleguinsk Infantry Regiment (2) (Detached from 23rd Division)
Brigade: Prince Chakoffski
20th Jager Regiment (2)
21st Jager Regiment (2)
Artillery: Tornov (Detached to Artillery Reserve)
Position Battery #3 (8–12pdrs & 4 Licornes)
Light Batteries #5 & #6 (8–6pdrs & 4 Licornes)
1st Grenadier Division: Generallieutenant Strogonoff
Brigade: Tsvilenev
Pavlov Grenadier Regiment (2)
Ekaterinoslav Grenadier Regiment (2)
Brigade: Geltoukhin
Count Arakcheyev Grenadier Regiment (2)
Leib Grenadier Regiment (2)
Brigade: Pock I

St. Petersburg Grenadier Regiment (2)e
Tauride Grenadier Regiment (2)
Artillery: Gluchov (Detached to Artillery Reserve)
   Position Battery #1 (8–12pdrs & 4 Licornes)
   Light Batteries #1 & #2 (8–6pdrs & 4 Licornes ea)
Brigade: Generalmajor Karpov
   Guard Cossack Regiment (4)
   North Sea Cossack Sotnia (1)
   Teptiarsk Cossacks (4)
Brigade:
   11th Jager Regiment (2)
   41st Jager Regiment (2)
Other Attached:
   Converged Grenadier of 1st Grenadier Division (1)
   Converged Grenadier of 3rd Division (1)
Other: Generallieutenant Count Markov
   1st, 2nd, & 3rd Moscow Opolochenie Divisions
Other: Generallieutenant Lebedev
   Smolensk Opolochenie
Left Flank Guard Detachment: Karpov II
   Karpov #2 Cossack Regiment
   Illowaiski #11 Cossack Regiment
   Krasnov #1 Cossack Regiment
   Gordeev #1 Cossack Regiment
   1st & 3rd Bug Cossack Regiments
   Perekop Tartars
   Feodosiiski Tartars

2nd Army of the West Artillery Reserve: Lowenstern

Position Battery #1 (4–12pdrs & 2 Licornes) (Semenovskaya Redoubt)
Position Battery #3 (8–12pdrs & 4 Licornes) (Flèches)
Position Battery #11 (8–12pdrs & 4 Licornes) (Flèches)
Position Battery #12 (8–12pdrs & 4 Licornes) (Reserve)
Position Battery #23 (8–12pdrs & 4 Licornes) (Reserve)
Position Battery #31 (8–12pdrs & 4 Licornes) (Semenovskaya Redoubt)
Position Battery #32 (8–12pdrs & 4 Licornes) (Flèches)
Light Battery #6 (8–6pdrs & 4 Licornes) (Reserve)
Light Battery #20 (8–6pdrs & 4 Licornes) (Reserve)
Light Battery #21 (8–6pdrs & 4 Licornes) (Reserve)
Light Battery #22 (8–6pdrs & 4 Licornes) (Reserve)
Light Battery #23 (8–6pdrs & 4 Licornes) (Reserve)
Light Battery #48 (8–6pdrs & 4 Licornes) (Reserve)

Russian Armies of Volhynie and Danube
8 September 1812

Commanding General—Admiral Tchichagov

1st Corps: Generalmajor Count Lambert
  Alexandria Hussar Regiment (8)
  White Russia Hussar Regiment (8)
  Tartar Uhlan Regiment (8)
  Grekov #4 Don Cossack Regiment
  Tchikeleff Cossack Regiment
  Bashkirs
  Barbantchikov #2 Cossack Regiment
  Koslov Infantry Regiment (2)
  Riajsk Infantry Regiment (2)
  Iakout Infantry Regiment (2)
  Kolyvan Infantry Regiment (2)
  Apcheron Infantry Regiment (2)
  10th Jager Regiment (2)
  13th Jager Regiment (2)
  38th Jager Regiment (2)

2nd Corps: Generalmajor Prince Tchervatov
  Tver Dragoon Regiment (2)
  Starodoub Dragoon Regiment (4)
  Pavlovgrad Hussar Regiment (8)
  Vladimir Dragoon Regiment (4)
  Taganrog Dragoon Regiment (4)
  Diatchkin Cossack Regiment
  2nd Kalmuck Regiment
  Nacheburg Infantry Regiment (2)
  Vitebsk Infantry Regiment (2)
  Kourin Infantry Regiment (2)
  Vladimir Infantry Regiment (2)
  Dnieper Infantry Regiment (2)
  Kostroma Infantry Regiment (2)
  14th Jager Regiment (2)
  28th Jager Regiment (2)
  32nd Jager Regiment (2)

3rd Corps: General of Infantry Count Langeron
  Saint Petersburg Dragoon Regiment (4)
  Lithuania Dragoon Regiment (4)
  Serpuchov Dragoon Regiment (4)

Arasmass Dragoon Regiment (4)
Loubny Hussar Regiment (8)
Grekov #8 Don Cossack Regiment
4th Orel Cossack Regiment
Saratov Infantry Regiment (2)
Viborg Regiment (2)
Viatka Infantry Regiment (2)

4th Corps: Generallieutenant Essen
Sieversk Dragoon Regiment (4)
Jitomir Dragoon Regiment (2)
Smolensk Dragoon Regiment (4)
Vlassov #2 Don Cossack Regiment
Kalmucks
Eupatorie Tartar Regiment
Archangle Infantry Regiment (2)
Ukraine Infantry Regiment (2)
3rd Jager Regiment (2)
Converged Grenadier Battalions (6)

Corps: Generallieutenant Voinov
Kinbourn Dragoon Regiment (4)
Dorpat Dragoon Regiment (4)
3rd Orel Cossack Regiment
Kireiev Cossack Regiment
Panteliev #2 Cossack Regiment
Kursk Infantry Regiment (2)
Crimea Infantry Regiment (2)
Bieloserk Infantry Regiment (2)
Saratov Infantry Regiment (2)
Jaroslav Infantry Regiment (2)
8th Jager Regiment (2)
39th Jager Regiment (2)

Corps: Generalmajor Boulatov
Tchougouiev Uhlan Regiment (8)
Pereiaslav Dragoon Regiment (4)
Tiraspol Dragoon Regiment (4)
Melnikov #3 Cossack Regiment
Okhotski Infantry Regiment (2)
Kamchatka Infantry Regiment (2)
Mingrelia Infantry Regiment (2)
27th Jager Regiment (2)
43rd Jager Regiment (2)

Detachment: Generalmajor Engelhardt
  Jitomir Dragoon Regiment (2)
  Tver Dragoon Regiment (2)
  Melinkov #5 Cossack Regiment
  Schusselburg Infantry Regiment (2)
  Old Ingremanland Infantry Regiment (2)

Reserve Corps: Generallieutenant Sabaneiev
  Olviopol Hussar Regiment (8)
  Loukoffkin Cossack Regiment
  Olonetz Infantry Regiment
  7th Jager Regiment (2)
  12th Jager Regiment (2)

French II Corps
15 September 1812

II CORPS

Commander-in-Chief . . . . Oudinot . . . . Maréchal de France

6th Division: General de division Legrand
  1st Brigade: General de brigade Albert
    26th Légère Regiment (4 + artillery co)(1,353)
      (2–3pdrs)
  2nd Brigade: General de brigade Moreau
    19th Line Regiment (4 + artillery co)(986)
      (2–3pdrs)
    56th Line Regiment (4 + artillery co)(1,266)
      (2–3pdrs)
  4th Brigade: General de brigade Pamplona
    128th Line Regiment (2 + artillery co)(1,345)
      (2–3pdrs)
  Artillery: (Total 659)
    11/5th Foot Artillery (6–6pdrs & 2 How)
    6/3rd Horse Artillery (4–6pdrs & 2 How)
    Det. 17th Artillery Artisan Company
    3/3rd Train (bis) Battalion
    4/3rd Sapper Battalion
    Gendarmerie
8th Division: General de division Maison
  1st Brigade: General de brigade Vives

11th Légère Regiment (4 + artillery co)(1,252)
(4–3pdrs)
2nd Line Regiment (5 + artillery co)(1,497)
(4–3pdrs)
2nd Brigade: General de brigade Pouget
37th Line Regiment (4 + artillery co)(1,113)
(4–3pdrs)
124th Line Regiment (3 + artillery co)(325)
(2–3pdrs)
Artillery: (Total 299)
15/5th Foot Artillery (6–6pdrs & 2 How)
1/3rd Horse Artillery (4–6pdrs & 2 How)
Det. 17th Artillery Artisan Company
1/, 5/3rd Train (bis) Battalion
3/3rd Sapper Battalion
Gendarmes
9th Division: General de division Merle
1st Brigade: General de brigade Candras
1st Swiss Line Regiment (2 + artillery co)(864)
(2–3pdrs)
2nd Swiss Line Regiment (3 + artillery co)(983)
(2–3pdrs)
2nd Brigade: General de brigade Amey
4th Swiss Line Regiment (3 + artillery co)(664)
(2–3pdrs)
3rd Provisional Croatian Regiment (2 + artillery co)
(1,330) (2–3pdrs)
3rd Brigade: General de brigade Coutard
3rd Swiss Line Regiment (3 + artillery co) (314)
(2–3pdrs)
123rd Line Regiment (3 + artillery co) (1,045)
(2–3pdrs)
Artillery: (Total 369)
4/7th Foot Artillery (6–6pdrs & 2 How)
5/2nd Horse Artillery (4–6pdrs & 2 How)
Det. 17th Artillery Artisan Company
3/, 5/8th Train (bis) Battalion
5/1st Sapper Battalion
Gendarmerie
Corps Cavalry: General de brigade Corbineau
5th Light Cavalry Brigade: General de brigade Castex
23rd Chasseur à Cheval Regiment (4) (404)

24th Chasseur à Cheval Regiment (4) (462)
6th Light Cavalry Brigade: General de brigade Corbineau
   20th Chasseur à Cheval Regiment (4) (395)
   7th Chasseur à Cheval Regiment (4) (327)
   8th Chevauléger Regiment (3) (207)
Reserve Artillery: Major Lavoy (Total 365)
   1/1st Foot Artillery (6–6pdrs & 2 How)
   15/1st Foot Artillery (6–6pdrs & 2 How)
   Det. 17th Artillery Artisan Company
   1/8th Train (bis) Battalion
   5/8th Train (bis) Battalion
Artillery Park: Colonel Levasseur (Total 895)
   21/9th Foot Artillery (6–12pdrs & 2 How)
   22/9th Foot Artillery (6–12pdrs & 2 How)
   11/1st Pontooneer Battalion
   1/3rd Train (bis) Battalion
   3/3rd Train (bis) Battalion
   1/,2/,3/,4/,5/,6/8th Train (bis) Battalion
   2/,6/11th Train (bis) Battalion
   Det. 9th Ambulance Company
   Gendarmerie
   4/3rd Sapper Battalion
   Det. 17th Artillery Artisan Company
Detachment from III Cavalry Corps: General de division Doumerc
3rd Cuirassier Division: General de division Doumerc
   Brigade: General de brigade Berkheim
      4th Cuirassier Regiment (4) (535)
   Brigade: General de brigade L'Hériter
      7th Cuirassier Regiment (4) (321)
   Brigade: General de brigade Doullembourg
      14th Cuirassier Regiment (4) (528)
   Artillery: (Total 583)
      3rd Chevaulégers (3)
      1/6th Horse Artillery
      3/6th Horse Artillery
      1/8th Train (bis) Battalion
      2/11th Train (bis) Battalion
      6/11th Train (bis) Battalion

Russian Army of Occupation of Finland
22 September 1812

Finland: Commanding Officer—Steingell
  27th Brigade:
    Finland Dragoon Regiment (3)(278)
    Lotchilin Cossack Regiment (3)(316)
    Azov Infantry Regiment (2)(883)
    Nisov Infantry Regiment (2)(1,264)
    3rd Jager Regiment (2)(731)
    Neva Infantry Regiment (2)(1,130)
    Petrovsk Infantry Regiment (2)(1,114)
    Lithuania Infantry Regiment (2)(1,308)
    Position Battery #21 (6 guns)(130)
    Light Battery #11 (192)
    Pioneers (46)

French Left Wing
September 1812

II CORPS

Commander-in-Chief . . . . . . Oudinot . . . . Maréchal de France
Chief of Staff . . . . De Lorencez . . . . . . General de brigade
6th Division: General de division Legrand
  1st Brigade: General de brigade Albert
    26th Légère Regiment (4 + artillery co)
    (2–3pdrs)
  2nd Brigade: General de brigade Maison
    19th Line Regiment (4 + artillery co)
    (2–3pdrs)
  3rd Brigade: General de brigade Moreau
    56th Line Regiment (4 + artillery co)
    (2–3pdrs)
  4th Brigade: General de brigade Pamplona
    128th Line Regiment (2 + artillery co)
    (2–3pdrs)
    3rd Portuguese Regiment (2 + artillery co)
  Artillery: Chef de bataillon Bogaert
    11/5th Foot Artillery (6–6pdrs & 2 How)
    6/3rd Horse Artillery (4–6pdrs & 2 How)
    Det. 17th Artillery Artisan Company

3/3rd Train (bis) Battalion
4/3rd Sapper Battalion
Gendarmerie
8th Division: General de division Verdier (Maison)
  1st Brigade: General de brigade Vives (Albert)
    11th Légère Regiment (4 + artillery co)
      (4–3pdrs)
    2nd Line Regiment (5 + artillery co)
      (4–3pdrs)
  2nd Brigade: General de brigade Pouget
    37th Line Regiment (4 + artillery co)
      (4–3pdrs)
    124th Line Regiment (3 + artillery co)
      (2–3pdrs)
  Artillery: Chef de bataillon Levis
    15/5th Foot Artillery (6–6pdrs & 2 How)
    1/3rd Horse Artillery (4–6pdrs & 2 How)
    Det. 17th Artillery Artisan Company
    1/, 5/3rd Train (bis) Battalion
    3/3rd Sapper Battalion
    Gendarmes
9th Division: General de division Merle
  1st Brigade: General de brigade Candras
    1st Swiss Line Regiment (2 + artillery co)
      (2–3pdrs)
    2nd Swiss Line Regiment (3 + artillery co)
      (2–3pdrs)
  2nd Brigade: General de brigade Amey
    4th Swiss Line Regiment (3 + artillery co)
      (2–3pdrs)
    3rd Provisional Croatian Regiment (2 + artillery co)
      (2–3pdrs)
  3rd Brigade: General de brigade Coutard
    3rd Swiss Line Regiment (3 + artillery co)
      (2–3pdrs)
    123rd Line Regiment (3 + artillery co)
      (2–3pdrs)
  Artillery: Chef de bataillon Webre
    4/7th Foot Artillery (6–6pdrs & 2 How)
    5/2nd Horse Artillery (4–6pdrs & 2 How)
    Det. 17th Artillery Artisan Company
    3/, 5/8th Train (bis) Battalion

5/1st Sapper Battalion
Gendarmerie
Corps Cavalry: General de brigade Corbineau
  5th Light Cavalry Brigade: General de brigade Castex
    23rd Chasseur à Cheval Regiment (4)
    24th Chasseur à Cheval Regiment (4)
  6th Light Cavalry Brigade: General de brigade Corbineau
    20th Chasseur à Cheval Regiment (4)
    7th Chasseur à Cheval Regiment (4)
    8th Chevauléger Regiment (3)
Reserve Artillery: Major Lavoy
  1/1st Foot Artillery (6–6pdrs & 2 How)
  15/1st Foot Artillery (6–6pdrs & 2 How)
  Det. 17th Artillery Artisan Company
  1/8th Train (bis) Battalion
  5/8th Train (bis) Battalion
Artillery Park: Colonel Levavasseur
  21/9th Foot Artillery (6–12pdrs & 2 How)
  22/9th Foot Artillery (6–12pdrs & 2 How)
  11/1st Pontooneer Battalion
  1/3rd Train (bis) Battalion
  3/3rd Train (bis) Battalion
  1/, 2/, 3/, 4/, 5/, 6/8th Train (bis) Battalion
  2/, 6/11th Train (bis) Battalion
  Det. 9th Ambulance Company
  Gendarmerie
  4/3rd Sapper Battalion
  Det. 17th Artillery Artisan Company

VI CORPS

Commander-in-Chief	G. St. Cyr	General de division
Chief of Staff	D'Albignac	Adjudant commandant

19th Division: Generallieutenant Deroy
  Brigade: Generalmajor von Siebein
    1st Bavarian Light Infantry Battalion (1)
    1st Bavarian Line Regiment (2)
    9th Bavarian Line Regiment (2)
  Brigade: Generalmajor von Raglovich
    3rd Bavarian Light Infantry Battalion (1)
    4th Bavarian Line Regiment (2)
    10th Bavarian Line Regiment (2)

Brigade: Generalmajor Count Rechberg
  6th Bavarian Light Infantry Battalion (1)
  8th Bavarian Line Regiment (2)
Artillery: Major Lamey
  1st Light Battery Widemann (3–6pdrs & 1 How)
  3rd Light Battery Halder (3–6pdrs & 1 How)
  11th Battery Brack (6–6pdrs & 2 How)
  6th Battery Rois (4–12pdrs & 2 How)
  Howitzer Battery (6 howitzers)
  1st Train Company
  3rd Train Company
  11th Train Company
  6th Train Company
  Park
20th Division: Generallieutenant von Wrede
  Brigade: Generalmajor von Vincenti
    2nd Bavarian Light Infantry Battalion (1)
    2nd Bavarian Line Regiment (2)
    6th Bavarian Line Regiment (2)
  Brigade: Generalmajor Count Beckers
    4th Bavarian Light Infantry Battalion
    3rd Bavarian Line Regiment (2)
    7th Bavarian Line Regiment (2)
  Brigade: Oberst Dalwigk (later Generalmajor Haberman, Scherer & Voller)
    5th Bavarian Light Infantry Battalion (1)
    5th Bavarian Line Regiment (2)
    11th Bavarian Line Regiment (2)
  Artillery: Oberstleutnant von Zoller
    2nd Light Battery Gotthard (3–6pdrs & 1 How)
    4th Light Battery Gravenreuth (3–6pdrs & 1 How)
    5th Battery Hoffstetten (6–6pdrs & 2 How)
    8th Battery Ulmer (6–6pdrs & 2 How)
    4th Battery Berchem (4–12pdrs & 2 How)
    2nd Train Company
    Det. 4th Train Company
    4th Train Company
    5th Train Company
    8th Train Company
    Park
    Engineers

X CORPS

Commander-in-Chief . . . . . . Macdonald . . . . Maréchal de France
Chief of Staff . . . . Terrier . . . . General de brigade
7th Division: General de division Grandjean
  Brigade: General de brigade Ricard
    5th Polish Line Regiment (4 + artillery co)
      (2–3pdrs)
  Brigade: General de brigade Radziwill
    10th Polish Line Regiment (4 + artillery co)
      (2–3pdrs)
    11th Polish Line Regiment (4 + artillery co)
      (2–3pdrs)
  Brigade: General de brigade Bachelu
    13th Bavarian Line Regiment (2)
    1st Westphalian Line Regiment (2 + artillery co)
      (2–6pdrs)
  Artillery: Farjou
    6/1st Polish Foot Artillery (4–6pdrs & 2 How)
    1/1st Polish Horse Artillery (4–6pdrs & 2 How)
    4th Polish Sapper Company
    2nd Bavarian Foot Battery (detached from IV Corps later)
27th Division (Prussian Corps): General of Infantry Grawert
  Brigade: Generallieutenant von Bulow
    1st Infantry (3)(2/1st, 1/3rd, Fus/1st)
    2nd Infantry (3)(1/4th, 1/5th, Fus/5th)
    Fusilier Battalion 3rd Infantry Regiment
  Brigade: Generallieutenant von Yorck
    3rd Infantry (3)(2/2nd, Fus/2nd, 1/10th)
    Leib Infantry (2 Musketeer & 1 Fusilier)
  Brigade: Generallieutenant von Raumer
    5th Infantry (3)(1/6th, 1/7th, Fus/7th)
    6th Infantry (3)(2/11th, 1/12th, Fus/12th)
    East Prussian Jäger Battalion (1)
Corps Cavalry: Generallieutenant von Massenbach
  26th Light Brigade: Oberst von Hunerbein
    1st Combined Dragoon Regiment (4)(1/4th, 2/4th, 1/5th, 3/5th)
    2nd Combined Dragoon Regiment (4)(1/2nd, 3/2nd, 2/5th, 4/5th)
  27th Light Brigade: Oberst von Jeanneret
    1st Combined Hussar Regiment (4)(3/1st, 4/1st, 2/2nd, 3/2nd)
    3rd Combined Hussar Regiment (4)(3/3rd, 4/3rd, 1/5th, 3/5th)

Corps Artillery:
    1st Prussian Foot Battery (6–6pdrs & 2 How)
    2nd Prussian Foot Battery (6–6pdrs & 2 How)
    3rd Prussian Foot Battery (6–6pdrs & 2 How)
    4th Brandenburg Foot Battery (6–6pdrs & 2 How)
    1/2nd Silesian Artillery Battery (4–12pdrs)
    1st Prussian Horse Battery (6–6pdrs & 2 How)
    2nd Prussian Horse Battery (6–6pdrs & 2 How)
    3rd Prussian Horse Battery (6–6pdrs & 2 How)
    6/1st Polish Foot Battery (4–6pdrs & 2 How)
    16th Polish Foot Battery (4–6pdrs & 2 How)(in Danzig)
    1/1st Polish Horse Artillery (4–6pdrs & 2 How)
Park
    Prussian Park Columns (5 companies)
    Prussian Train Companies (3)
    Bridging Detachment
    Pioneer Companies (3)
    4/1st Polish Sappers
Detachment from III Cavalry Corps: General de division Doumerc
3rd Cuirassier Division: General de division Doumerc
    Brigade: General de brigade Berkheim
        4th Cuirassier Regiment (4)
    Brigade: General de brigade L'Heriter
        7th Cuirassier Regiment (4)
    Brigade: General de brigade Doullembourg
        14th Cuirassier Regiment (4)
    Artillery:
        1/6th Horse Artillery
        3/6th Horse Artillery
        1/8th Train (bis) Battalion
        2/11th Train (bis) Battalion
        6/11th Train (bis) Battalion

Russian I Corps after
Joined by the Finland Corps
16/28 October 1812

1st Corps: Generallieutenant Count Wittgenstein

Advanced Guard: Generallieutenant Prince Jachwill
    Grodno Hussar Regiment (8)
    Converged Hussar Regiment (4)
    Converged Dragoon Regiment (3)

Rodinov #2 Don Cossack Regiment
Platov Don Cossack Regiment
2nd, 3rd, 24th & 25th Jager Regiments (7)
Mohilev & Podolsk Infantry Regiments (5)
Navajinsk Infantry Regiment (3)
Position Battery #14 (6 guns)
Light Batteries #26
Horse Batteries #1 (10 guns)
Right Wing: Generallieutenant Count Steingell
  1st Line: Generallieutenant
    Mitau Dragoon Regiment (4)
    26th Jager Regiment (2)
    Tenguinsk Infantry Regiment (3)
    Toula Infantry Regiment (3)
    Estonia Infantry Regiment (2)
    Navajinsk Infantry Regiment (2)
    Position Battery #6
    Position Battery #28 (4 guns)
  2nd Line: Generalmajor Adadourov
    Riga Dragoon Regiment (4)
    Petrovsk Infantry Regiment (2)
    Lithuania Infantry Regiment (2)
    Light Battery #11
Left Wing: Generallieutenant Berg
  1st Line: Bibikov
    Converged Guard Cavalry (5)
    Converged Jager Regiment (3)
    Perm Infantry Regiment (2)
    Sievesk Infantry Regiment (2)
    Position Battery #5
    Light Battery #7 (7 guns)
  2nd Line: Generallieutenant Koulneff
    Kalouga & Azov Infantry Regiments (5)
    Iambourg Dragoon Regiment (4)
Reserve Corps: Generalmajor Fock
  Right Reserve: Generalmajor Rachmanoff
    Nisov Infantry Regiment (2)
    1st Reserve Grenadier Regiment (2)
    Converged Grenadiers of 5th & 14th Divisions (4)
    Position Battery #21
    Horse Battery #23 (4 guns)
  Left Reserve: Generalmajor Prince of Siberia

    Converged Cuirassiers (4)
    1st Marine Infantry Regiment (2)
    2nd Reserve Grenadier Regiment (2)
    3rd Reserve Grenadier Regiment (2)
    Position Battery #14 (6 guns)
    Horse Battery #3
Detachment: Generalmajor Vlastov
    23rd & 24th Jager Regiments (5)
    1st & 2nd Converged Infantry (8)
    Finland Dragoon Regiment (3)
    Lotchilin Cossack Regiment
    Position Battery #28 (4 guns)
    Horse Battery #23 (8 guns)

4 October 1812

1st Corps: Generallieutenant Count Wittgenstein
  Advanced Guard: Generallieutenant Berg
    Rodinov #2 Don Cossack Regiment (330)
    Grodno Hussar Regiment (4)(527)
    Horse Batteries #3 (6 guns)(119)
    25th & 26th Jager Regiment (4)(1,888)
    Kexholm Regiment Depot Battalion (1)(358)
  Main Body
    Converged Guard Regiment & 2 Sqn's of Polish Uhlan Regiment (5)(696)
    Horse Battery #3 (6 guns)(118)
    Mohilev & Kalouga Infantry Regiments (2,107)
    Perm & Sievesk Infantry Regiments (4)(1,483)
    Light Battery #27 (103)
  Reserve: Generalmajor Kakhoffski
    Riga Dragoon Regiment (3)(392)
    Converged Cuirassier Regiment (4)(448)
    Horse Battery #1 (149)(8 guns)
    Depot Battalions of 1st Grenadier Division (3)(1,887)
    Guard Depot Battalions (2)(926)
    Position Battery #14 (220)
2nd Column: Generalmajor Beguiczeff
  Advanced Guard: Generalmajor Diebitsch
    Cossacks (100)
    Riga & Iambourg Dragoon Regiments (3)(367)
    Ingremannland Dragoon Regiment (1)(97)

Horse Battery #23 (149)(8 guns)
Converged Grenadiers of 5th & 14th Divisions (4)
Light Battery #45 (100)(6 guns)
Converged Jager Regiment (3)(620)
Main Body:
  Light Battery #35 (220)
  Polotsk Infantry Regiment Depot Battalion (1)(236)
  St. Petersburg Opolochenie (6 cohorts)(4,310)
Reserve:
  St. Petersburg Opolochenie (2 cohorts)(1,507)

Corps: Generallieutenant Jachwill

Advanced Guard: Generalmajor Vlastov
  Grodno Hussar Regiment (4)(526)
  23rd & 24th Jager Regiments (4)(2,181)
  Horse Battery #1 (91) (6 guns)
  St. Petersburg Opolochenie (2 cohorts)(909)
  Platov #4 Don Cossack Regiment (341)

Main Body:
  Tenguinsk & Toula Infantry Regiment (4)(1,520)
  Navajinsk & Estonia Infantry Regiments (4)(1,556)
  St. Petersburg Opolochenie (4 cohorts)(1,825)
  Voronege Opolochenie (2 cohorts) (1,186)
  Converged Dragoon Regiment (3)
  Position Battery #27 (106)(6 guns)
  Position Battery #28 (210)(12 guns)
  Light Battery #9 (79)
  Light Batteries #26, #50, & #57 (416)
  Horse Battery #1 (61)(4 guns)
Detachment: Generalmajor Alekseieff
  Mitau Dragoon Regiment (4)(569)
  Light Battery #45 (106)(6 guns)
  1st Marine Regiment (2)(1,178)
  St. Petersburg Opolochenie (1 cohort)(1,468)
Detachment: Lt. Colonel Bedraigua
  Cossacks (75)
  Converged Hussar Regiment (4)(557)
Detachment: Major Bellingshausen
  Horse Battery #23 (142)(4 guns)
  1st & 2nd Converged Infantry (8)(1,726)

Austrian Hilfkorps
27 October 1812

Commanding General—General Schwarzenberg
Advanced Guard: Generalmajor Frolich
   Kaiser Hussar Regiment (6)
   Blankenstein Hussar Regiment (6)
   Liechtenstein Hussar Regiment (6)
Right Wing: Fieldmarshal Lieutenant Trautenberg (Generalmajor Pflacher)
  Brigade: Suden
   Hesse-Homberg Hussar Regiment (1)
   Jager Battalion #5 (4 co)
   St. Georg Grenz Regiment (1)
   Beaulieu Infantry Regiment (1)
  Brigade: Winzian
   Duka Infantry Regiment (2)
   Liechtenstein Infantry Regiment (2)
Center: Fieldmarshal Lieutenant Bianchi
  Brigade: Generalmajor Hesse-Homberg
   Hiller Infantry Regiment (2)
   Colloredo-Mansfeld Infantry Regiment (2)
  Brigade: Marissay
   Simbschen Infantry Regiment (2)(Hungarian)
   Hesse-Homberg Infantry Regiment (2)
  Brigade: Liechtenstein
   Kirchbetter Grenadier Battalion (1)
   Brezinski Grenadier Battalion (1)
   Davidovich Infantry Regiment (2)
   Esterhazy Infantry Regiment (2)
Left Wing: Fieldmarshal Lieutenant Siegenthal
  Brigade: Mackelliot
   Hesse-Homberg Hussar Regiment (1)
   Jager Battalion #7 (4 co)
   Warasdiner Kreutzer Grenz Regiment (1)
   Czartoryski Infantry Regiment (2)
  Brigade: Andrassy
   Sottulinski Infantry Regiment (2)
   Kaiser Infantry Regiment (2)
Reserve: Fieldmarshal Lieutenant Frimont
  Brigade: Zechmeister
   Hohenzollern Dragoon Regiment (6)
   O'Reilly Chevauxléger Regiment (6)

Brigade:
  Riesch Dragoon Regiment (4)
  Levenehr Dragoon Regiment (4)
  Kienmayer Hussar Regiment (6)
Corps: Mohr
  Brigade:
    Prinz de Ligne Infantry Regiment (2)
    Hesse-Homburg Hussar Regiment (4)

Russian Order of Battle
Battle of the Berezina
Army of the Danube
15/27 October 1812

Commanding General—Admiral Tchichagov

Detachment: Generalmajor Tchlapitz
  28th Jager Regiment (2)
  32nd Jager Regiment (2)
  Tver Dragoon Regiment (3)
  Pavlovgrad Hussar Regiment (8)
  Diatchkin Cossack Regiment
  2nd Kalmuck Regiment
  Bashkirs
  Horse Battery #13
Advanced Guard: Generalmajor Count Lambert
  Grekov #4 Don Cossack Regiment
  Grekov #8 Don Cossack Regiment
  Melinkov #5 Cossack Regiment
  Barbantchikov #2 Cossack Regiment
  Eupatorie Tartar Regiment
  Alexandria Hussar Regiment (8)
  Tartar Uhlan Regiment (8)
  Starodoub Dragoon Regiment (4)
  Arasmass Dragoon Regiment (4)
  Jitomir Dragoon Regiment (4)
  14th, 27th, & 38th Jager Regiments (7)
  Horse Batteries #11 & #12

Corps: Generallieutenant Voinov
  Kireiev Cossack Regiment
  3rd Orel Cossack Regiment
  White Russia Hussar Regiment (8)
  Saint Petersburg Dragoon Regiment (4)

Lithuania Dragoon Regiment (4)
Sieversk Dragoon Regiment (4)
Vladamir Infantry Regiment (2)
Tambov Infantry Regiment (2)
Dnieper Infantry Regiment (2)
Kostroma Infantry Regiment (2)
Nacheburg Infantry Regiment (2)
Apcheron Infantry Regiment (2)
Riajsk Infantry Regiment (2)
Iakout Infantry Regiment (2)
10th Jager Regiment (2)
Position Batteries #9 & #18
Light Batteries #16, #17, #34, & #35
Reserve Corps: Generallieutenant Sabaneiev
Loukoffkin Cossack Regiment
Panteliev #2 Cossack Regiment
Melnikov #3 Cossack Regiment (2)
Olviopol Hussar Regiment (8)
Dorpat Dragoon Regiment (4)
Kinbourn Dragoon Regiment (4)
Kolyvan Infantry Regiment (2)
Kourin Infantry Regiment (2)
Vitebsk Infantry Regiment (2)
Koslov Infantry Regiment (2)
Converged Grenadiers (6)
7th, 12th, & 13th Jager Regiments (7)
Position Batteries #38, #39, & #34
Light Batteries #25 & #50

Russian Army of Volhynie
15 October 1812

Advanced guard: Generallieutenant Sacken
Smolensk Dragoon Regiment (4)
4th Ural Cossack Regiment

Corps: Generalmajor Boulatov
Vlassov #2 Don Cossack Regiment
2nd Kalmucks
Pereiaslav Dragoon Regiment (4)
Tchougouiev Uhlan Regiment (8)
Viborg, Viatka, & Galitz Infantry Regiment (7)
Kamchatka Infantry Regiment (2)

Staroskol Infantry Regiment (2)
Okhotski Infantry Regiment (2)
Mingrelia Infantry Regiment (2)
29th & 45th Jager Regiment (5)
Position Battery #22
Light Battery #41

Reserve Corps: Generalmajor Count Lieven
   Bieloserk, Jaroslav, & Crimea Infantry Regiment (8)
   8th & 39th Jager Regiment (5)
   Position Battery #10
   Light Battery #18

Corps: Generallieutenant Essen
   Tver, Vladimir, & Serpuchov Dragoon Regiments (8)
   Loubny Hussar Regiment (8)
   Old Ingremanland Infantry Regiment (2)
   Ukraine, Archangle, & Olonetz Infantry Regiment (7)
   37th Jager Regiment (3)
   Position Battery #8
   Light Batteries #14 & #15
   Horse Battery #15

Russian I Corps
December 1812

Corps: Generallieutenant Lewis
   1st Brigade: Generalmajor Veliaminov
      Detachment Grodny Hussar Regiment
      Detachment Selivanov #2 Don Cossack Regiment
      Jakhontov Cossack Regiment (4)
      1st Combined Infantry Regiment
      2nd Combined Infantry Regiment
      3rd Combined Infantry Regiment
      Light Battery #10
      Light Battery #57
   2nd Brigade: Generalmajor Gorbuntsov
      Depot Squadron Riga Dragoon Regiment
      Depot Squadron Kazan Dragoon Regiment
      Depot Squadron Finland Dragoon Regiment
      Detachment Selivanov #2 Don Cossack Regiment
      Detachment of an Opolochenie Corps
      44th Jager Regiment
      4th Combined Infantry Regiment

Briansk Infantry Regiment
Light Battery #40

1st Corps: General of Cavalry Wittgenstein
  Advanced Guard: Generalmajor Vlastov
    Finland Dragoon Regiment
    Combined Hussar Regiment
    Platov #4 Cossack Regiment
    Loshchilin Cossack Regiment
    Lithuania Infantry Regiment
    23rd Jager Regiment
    24th Jager Regiment
    1st & 9th Cohort St. Petersburg Opolochenie
    Position Battery #28 (6 guns)
    Light Battery #11 (6 guns)

Corps: Generallieutenant Steingell
    Combined Guard Cavalry Regiment
    Mitau Dragoon Regiment
    Toula Infantry Regiment
    Tenguinsk Infantry Regiment
    Navajinsk Infantry Regiment
    Estonia Infantry Regiment
    2nd Jager Regiment
    3rd Jager Regiment
    25th Jager Regiment
    2nd, 7th, & 8th Cohort St. Petersburg Opolochenie
    Position Batteries #6 & #21
    Light Battery #26
    Horse Battery #3

Corps: Generallieutenant Berg
    Combined Dragoon Regiment
    Iambourg Dragoon Regiment
    Perm Infantry Regiment
    Sievesk Infantry Regiment
    Kalouga Infantry Regiment
    Petrovsk Infantry Regiment
    Azov Infantry Regiment
    1st Marine Infantry Regiment
    5th, 10th, 11th, & 15th Cohort St. Petersburg Opolochenie
    Novgorod Opolochenie
    Position Batteries #5 & #14
    Light Battery #27
    Horse Battery #1 (10 guns)

Reserve Corps: Generalmajor Fock
   Mohilev Infantry Regiment
   Nisov Infantry Regiment
   Vorohenz Infantry Regiment
   Depot Battalion of Leib Grenadiers
   Depot Battalion of Pavlov Grenadiers
   Depot Battalion of Ekaterinoslav Grenadiers
   Depot Battalion of Count Arakcheyev Grenadiers
   Depot Battalion of Tauride Grenadiers
   Depot Battalion of St. Petersburg Grenadiers
   4th, 6th, 13th, & 14th Cohort St. Petersburg Opolochenie
   Position Battery #28 (4 guns)
   Light Battery #11 (6 guns)
   Horse Battery #3

Detachment: Generalmajor Diebitsch
   Grodno Hussars
   Rodniov #2 Cossack Regiment
   Chernozubov Cossack Regiment
   1/23rd Jager Regiment

Detachment: Generallieutenant Golenischev-Kutusov
   Kazan Dragoon Regiment
   Isoum Hussar Regiment

Detachment: Generalmajor Svechin
   5th Bashkirs
   Podolsk Infantry Regiment
   3rd Cohort St. Petersburg Opolochenie

Detachment: Baron von der Pahlen
   Riga Dragoon Regiment (2)
   Cossack Detachment
   26th Jager Regiment
   Horse Battery #1 (2 guns)

Detachment: Colonel Nikolajev
   Riga Dragoon Regiment (2)
   Guard Infantry Reserve Battalion #1
   Guard Infantry Reserve Battalion #2
   12th Cohort St. Petersburg Opolochenie
   Novgorod Opolochenie Infantry (2 cohorts)
   Novgorod Opolochenie Cavalry (2 sotnias)

Artillery:
   Position Batteries #27 & #50
   Light Batteries #9, #35, & #49

1st Pioneer Regiment—Company of Lt. Col. Miller
—Company of Captain Gerout

In Volhynie:
  Detachment Vorohenz Infantry Regiment
  Novgorod Opolochenie Cavalry (2 sotnias)
  Novgorod Opolochenie Infantry (1 cohort)
  Riga Dragoons (2)

Russian Army of the Danube
December 1812

Commanding General—Admiral Tchichagov

Advanced Guard: Generalmajor Tchlapitz
  Kinbourn Dragoon Regiment
  3/Twer Dragoon Regiment
  Taganrog Dragoon Regiment
  Volhynie Uhlan Regiment
  Diatchkin Cossack Regiment
  Melnikov #5 Cossack Regiment
  Grekov #4 Don Cossack Regiment
  Kireieff #2 Cossack Regiment
  7th Jager Regiment
  10th Jager Regiment
  14th Jager Regiment
  27th Jager Regiment
  28th Jager Regiment
  32nd Jager Regiment
  38th Jager Regiment
  Netchlot Infantry Regiment
  Converged Horse Battery (4 guns each from the 11th, 12th, & 13th Horse
    Batteries)

Corps: Generallieutenant Voinov
  Sieversk Dragoon Regiment
  Starodoub Dragoon Regiment
  Apcheron Infantry Regiment
  Vladimir Infantry Regiment
  Tambov Infantry Regiment
  Dnieper Infantry Regiment
  Iakout Infantry Regiment
  Kostroma Infantry Regiment

Position Batteries #9 & #18
Light Battery #16 (6 guns)
Light Battery #17 (6 guns)
Light Battery #34 (6 guns)
Light Battery #35
Corps: General of Infantry Langeron
    Saint Petersburg Dragoon Regiment
    Vitebsk Infantry Regiment
    Koslov Infantry Regiment
    Kolyvan Infantry Regiment
    Kourin Infantry Regiment
    13th Jager Regiment
    Position Battery #15
    Light Batteries #28 & #29
Reserve of Langeron's Corps:
    Dorpat Dragoon Regiment
    Panteleieff Cossack Regiment
    12th Jager Regiment
    22nd Jager Regiment
    Converged Grenadier Battalions (6)
    Position Battery #34
    Light Battery #25
Detachment: Generalmajor Lanskij
    Alexandria Olviopol Hussar Regiment
    White Russia Hussar Regiment
    Lithuania Dragoon Regiment
    3rd Orel Cossack Regiment
    Horse Artillery Company of Buschujev

Russian 2nd Army of the West
December 1812

Commanding General—General of Infantry Docturov

Corps: Colonel Knorring
    Tartar Uhlan Regiment
    Eupatoria Tartar Regiment
    Melentiva #3 Cossack Regiment
    Light Artillery Battery #16

Detachment: Generalmajor Tuchkov II
    Depot Squadrons of the 10th Division
    Kourland Dragoon Regiment

Orenburg Dragoon Regiment
Irkhoutsk Dragoon Regiment
Siberia Uhlan Regiment
Lithuania Uhlan Regiment (2)
Akhtyrsk Hussar Regiment (2)
Soumy Hussar Regiment (2)
Ekaterinoslav Cuirassier Regiment
Gluchov Cuirassier Regiment
Little Russia Cuirassier Regiment
12th Brigade:
  Karkov Dragoon Regiment
  Tchernigov Dragoon Regiment
13th Brigade:
  Kiev Dragoon Regiment
  New Russia Dragoon Regiment
Cossacks:
  Isajeva #2 Don Cossack Regiment
  Grekov #9 Don Cossack Regiment
  Semenchikov Don Cossack Regiment
  Chernigov #2 Little Russian Cossack Regiment
  Chernigov #5 Little Russian Cossack Regiment
  Various other Little Russian Cossacks (501)
Infantry
  Gamekeeper Skirmishers (217)
  Depot Battalions of the 12th Division
    Smolensk Infantry Regiment
    Narva Infantry Regiment
    New Ingremannland Infantry Regiment
    Alexopol Infantry Regiment
  Depot Battalions of the 15th Division
    Kourin Infantry Regiment
    Kolyvan Infantry Regiment
    Kozlov Infantry Regiment
    Vitebsk Infantry Regiment
    13th Jager Regiment
    14th Jager Regiment
  Depot Battalions of the 18th Division
    Tambov Infantry Regiment
    Vladimir Infantry Regiment
    Dnieper Infantry Regiment
    Kostroma Infantry Regiment

28th Jager Regiment
32nd Jager Regiment
Position Battery #33
Light Battery #4
1/2 3pdr Artillery Company from Bobruisk
Detachment: Generallieutenant Ratt
  Depot Battalions of the 24th Division
    Bourtirki Infantry Regiment
    Tomsk Infantry Regiment
    Oufa Infantry Regiment
    Chirvan Infantry Regiment
    19th Jager Regiment
    40th Jager Regiment
  Depot Battalions of the 27th Division
    Tarnopol Infantry Regiment
    Vilna Infantry Regiment
    49th Jager Regiment
Detachment: Generallieutenant Essen
    Serpuchov Dragoon Regiment (4)
    Vladimir Dragoon Regiment (4)
    Tver Dragoon Regiment (4)
    Loubny Hussar Regiment (8)
    Chevelev Cossack Regiment
    1st Kalmucks
    2nd Bashkirs
  8th Division
    Ukraine Infantry Regiment (2)
    New Ingremannland Infantry Regiment (2)
    Schusselburg Infantry Regiment (2)
    Archangle Infantry Regiment (2)
  22nd Division:
    Olonetz Infantry Regiment (2)
  Artillery:
    Position Battery #8
    Light Batteries #14 & #15
    Horse Battery #15
Corps: Generallieutenant Sacken
    Pereiaslav Dragoon Regiment (4)
    Tchougouiev Uhlan Regiment
    Smolensk Dragoon Regiment (4)
    Vlassov #2 Cossack Regiment

Melenteva #3 Cossack Regiment
4 Ukranian Cossack Regiments under Count Witt
10th Division:
  Bieloserk Infantry Regiment (3)
  Crimea Infantry Regiment (2)
  Jaroslav Infantry Regiment (2)
  8th Jager Regiment (3)
  39th Jager Regiment (2)
13th Division:
  Galitz Infantry Regiment (2)
  Saratov Infantry Regiment (2)
16th Division:
  Kamchatka Infantry Regiment (2)
  Mingrelia Infantry Regiment (2)
  Okhotsk Infantry Regiment (2)
22nd Division:
  Staroskol Infantry Regiment (3)
  Viborg Infantry Regiment (2)
  Viatka Infantry Regiment (3)
  29th Jager Regiment (3)
  45th Jager Regiment (3)
Artillery:
  Position Batteries #10, #16, & #22
  Light Batteries #18, #19, #31, #41, & #42
  Pioneer Company of Kutsevch
Detachment: Generalmajor Musin-Pushkin
  Turchaninov #1 Cossack Regiment
  Tiraspol Dragoon Regiment
13th Division:
  Pensa Infantry Regiment (2)
  Saratov Infantry Regiment (3 companies)
16th Division:
  43rd Jager Regiment (3)
  Mingrelia Infantry Regiment (1)
  Okhotsk Infantry Regiment (1)
  Neutchlot Infantry Regiment (3)
Artillery:
  Position Battery #38
  Light Batteries #19, #24, & #31
  Horse Battery #18

Russian Main Army
December 1812

Advance Detachment: General Count Platov
  All of the army's Cossack Regiments
  Jitomir Dragoon Regiment
  Arasmass Dragoon Regiment
  Olivopol Hussar Regiment

Advanced Guard: General Miloradovich

4th Corps: Generallieutenant Count Ostermann-Tolstoy
11th Division:
  Brigade:
    Polotsk Infantry Regiment
    Jeletz Infantry Regiment
  Brigade:
    Kexholm Infantry Regiment
    Pernov Infantry Regiment
  Brigade:
    1st Jager Regiment
  Artillery Brigade:
    Position Battery #2
    Light Batteries #3 & #4
23rd Division:
  Brigade:
    Rilsk Infantry Regiment
    Ekaterinburg Infantry Regiment
  Brigade:
    Kaporsk Infantry Regiment
  Artillery Brigade:
    Position Battery #23
    Light Batteries #43 & #44

2nd Corps: Prince Eugène of Württemberg
4th Division:
  Brigade:
    Krementchug Infantry Regiment
    Minsk Infantry Regiment
  Brigade:
    Tobolsk Infantry Regiment
    Volhynie Infantry Regiment
  Brigade:
    4th Jager Regiment
    34th Jager Regiment

Artillery:
  Position Battery #4
  Light Batteries #7 & #8
3rd Division:
  Brigade:
    Mourmonsk Infantry Regiment
    Revel Infantry Regiment
  Brigade:
    Tchernigov Infantry Regiment
    Korporsk Infantry Regiment
  Brigade:
    20th Jager Regiment
  Artillery:
    Light Batteries #5 & #6
    Position Battery #3
2nd Cavalry Division: Generalmajor Baron Korff
  Pskof Dragoon Regiment
  Kargopol Dragoon Regiment
  Moscow Dragoon Regiment
  Siberia Dragoon Regiment
  Orenburg Dragoon Regiment
  Kourland Dragoon Regiment
  Soum Hussar Regiment
  Marioupol Hussar Regiment
  Polish Uhlan Regiment
  Lithuanian Uhlan Regiment
  Horse Battery #7 Nikitin
  Horse Battery #8 Shusherin
  Horse Battery #6 Zakharzhevskij
  1/2 Horse Battery #4 Merlin
  1/2 Horse Battery #5 Kandybn
Don Cassacks
  Karpov #2 Cossack Regiment
  Grekov #3 Cossack Regiment
  Chernozubov Cossack Regiment
  Sliusarev Cossack Regiment
  Popov Cossack Regiment
  Danilov Cossack Regiment
  Koshkin Cossack Regiment
  Starzhin Zhirov Cossack Regiment
Corps: General of Cavalry Tormassov

6th Corps: General of Infantry Docturov

7th Division:
  Brigade:
    Moscow Infantry Regiment
    Pskof Infantry Regiment
  Brigade:
    Libau Infantry Regiment
    Sofia Infantry Regiment
  Brigade:
    11th Jager Regiment
  Artillery Brigade:
    Position Battery #7
    Light Batteries #12 & #13
24th Division:
  Brigade:
    Oufa Infantry Regiment
    Chirvan Infantry Regiment
  Brigade:
    Tomsk Infantry Regiment
    Bourtirki Infantry Regiment
  Artillery Brigade:
    Position Battery #24
    Light Batteries #45 & #46

7th Corps: Generallieutenant Raevsky
12th Division:
  Brigade:
    Smolensk Infantry Regiment
    Narva Infantry Regiment
  Brigade:
    New Ingremannland Infantry Regiment
    Alexopol Infantry Regiment
  Brigade:
    6th Jager Regiment
  Artillery Brigade:
    Position Battery #12
    Light Batteries #22 & #23
26th Division:
  Brigade:
    Ladoga Infantry Regiment
    Poltava Infantry Regiment
  Brigade:
    Orel Infantry Regiment
    Nivegorod Infantry Regiment

Brigade:
    5th Jager Regiment (2)
Artillery Brigade:
    Position Battery #26
    Light Batteries #47 & #48
Reserve: Grand Duke Constantin
5th Corps: Generallieutenant Lavrov
    Brigade:
        Preobragenski Guard Infantry Regiment
        Semenovski Guard Infantry Regiment
    Brigade:
        Ismailov Guard Infantry Regiment
        Lithuanian Guard Infantry Regiment
    Brigade:
        Guard Jager Infantry Regiment
        Finland Guard Infantry Regiment
    Brigade:
        Guard Marine Equipage Battalion
    Artillery:
        Guard Position Battery (8–12pdrs & 4 Licornes)
        Count Arakcheyev Position Battery (8–12pdrs & 4 Licornes)
        1st & 2nd Guard Light Batteries (8–6pdrs & 4 Licornes)
        Guard Horse Battery (8–6pdrs & 4 Licornes)

3rd Corps: Generallieutenant Konovnitzin
1st Grenadier Division:
    Brigade: Tsvilenev
        Pavlov Grenadier Regiment
        Ekaterinoslav Grenadier Regiment
    Brigade:
        Count Arakcheyev Grenadier Regiment
        Leib Grenadier Regiment
    Brigade:
        St. Petersburg Grenadier Regiment
        Tauride Grenadier Regiment
    Artillery Brigade:
        Position Battery #1
        Light Batteries #1 & #2
2nd Grenadier Division:
    Brigade:
        Kiev Grenadier Regiment
        Moscow Grenadier Regiment
    Brigade:

Astrakhan Grenadier Regiment
Fangoria Grenadier Regiment
Brigade:
    Siberia Grenadier Regiment
    Little Russia Grenadier Regiment
Artillery Brigade:
    Position Battery #11
    Light Artillery Batteries #20 & #21
Brigade:
    Guard Cossack Regiment
1st Cavalry Division:
    Brigade:
        Emperor Cuirassier Regiment
        Empress Cuirassier Regiment
        Astrakhan Cuirassier Regiment
    Brigade:
        Chevalier Guard Regiment
        Horse Guard Regiment
2nd Cuirassier Division:
    2nd Brigade:
        Military Order Cuirassier Regiment
        Ekaterinoslav Cuirassier Regiment
    3rd Brigade:
        Gluchov Cuirassier Regiment
        Novgorod Cuirassier Regiment
        Little Russia Cuirassier Regiment

8th Corps: Generallieutenant Prince Dolgorukov
17th Division:
    Brigade:
        Riazan Infantry Regiment
        Bieloserk Infantry Regiment
    Brigade:
        Wilmanstrand Infantry Regiment
        Brest Infantry Regiment
    Brigade:
        3rd Jager Regiment
        48th Jager Regiment
    Artillery Brigade:
        Position Battery #17
        Light Batteries #32 & #33
27th Division:
    Brigade:

Vilna Infantry Regiment
Simbrisk Infantry Regiment
Brigade:
49th Jager Regiment
Detachment: Lt. Colonel Davydov
2 Don Cossack Regiments
1 Bug Cossack Regiment
Detachment of Akhtyrsk Hussar Regiment
Detachment: Adjudant General Vasil'chikov
Karlov Dragoon Regiment
Tchernigov Dragoon Regiment
Kiev Dragoon Regiment
New Russia Dragoon Regiment
Akhtyrsk Hussar Regiment
33rd Jager Regiment
6 Horse Guns
4 Don Cossack Regiments
Detachment: Count Orlov-Denisov
Niejine Dragoon Regiment
6 Don Cossack Regiments
Horse Battery #4 (4 guns)
1st Pioneer Regiment (3 companies)
2nd Pioneer Regiment (3 companies)
Pontooneer Companies

Various other Detachments:

In Orsha	1st Jagers (en route to army)
In Viazma	Ekaterinburg Infantry Regiment (1)
In Krasnoe	Tarnopol Infantry Regiment
	Odessa Infantry Regiment
In Smolensk	20th Jager Regiment (en route to army)
In Mohilev	Guard Dragoon Regiment
In Shkolv	Guard Hussar Regiment
In Belynich	Guard Uhlan Regiment

Acting as Headquarters Provost Guard—New Ingremanland
   Dragoon Regiment
Acting as Headquarters Convoy Escort—Irkhoutsk Dragoon Regiment
Reserve Artillery:
Position Batteries #12, #17, #23, & #24
Light Batteries #1, #20, #21, & #35
Horse Battery #2
Horse Battery #9 (6 guns)
Pontooneer Companies #1 & #2

Appendix IV

Russian Replacements and Casualties

Assignment and Dispatching of Forces for the Rebuilding of the 1st Army of the West

Arrived on 30 and 31 August:

Infantry Regiments:	Commander:	Assigned to:
1st Reserve Regiment	Col. Krechetnikov	2nd Corps
2nd Reserve Regiment	Col. Rehbinder	2nd Army
3rd Reserve Regiment	Col. Sakozen	4th Corps
4th Reserve Regiment	Cpt. Jakovlev	6th Corps
5th Reserve Regiment	Sr. Cpt. Dempfer	2nd Army
Jeletz Bataillon de Marche	Maj. Masekin	Jeletz Infantry
Jeletz 4th Recruit Regiment	Lt. Shigorin	6th Corps
Jager Regiments		
1st Reserve Regiment	Maj. Bobrujka	2nd Army
2nd Reserve Regiment	Cpt. Muntiakov	2nd & 4th Corps for Jager Regts
Recruit Battalions of the 28th & 32nd Jagers	Cpt. Novoselov	28th Jager Regt 32nd Jager Regt

Arrived on 4 and 5 September:

Depot Squadrons		
Courland Dragoons	Cpt. Erdman	Parent Unit
Orenburg Dragoons		Parent Unit
Soumy Hussars		Parent Unit
Pavlograd Hussars (2)		Mariapoul Hussars

Assignment and Dispatching of Forces for the Rebuilding of the 2nd Army of the West

The two depot squadrons of the Akhtyrsk Hussars, as well as the depot squadrons of the Karkov, Tchernigov, New Russia, and Kiev Dragoons, under the command of Lieutenant Colonel Semek, were dispatched to their parent units. In addition, on 5 September, Lieutenant Colonel Pavlischchev escorted two depot squadrons from the Isoum and Elisabethgrad Hussar Regiments, and the Pskof, Moscow, Ingremanland, and Kargopol Dragoon Regiments.

Allocation of Moscow Opolochenie
4 and 5 September 1812

Regiment:	Commander:	Assigned to:
1/, 4/1st Jager Regiment	Major Matskoj	2nd Corps
2/, 3/3rd Jager Regiment	Major Posnikov	6th Corps
1/, 3/3rd Jager Regiment		3rd Corps
3/, 4/4th Jager Regiment	Colonel Obolenskij	4th Corps

In addition to these men from the Moscow Opolochenie, Lieutenant Kul'man took 730 men from the Moscow Garrison Regiment to Volokolmansko. Lieutenant Chubenkov took a further 216 men from the Moscow Garrison Regiment to Vera. Both forces were assigned to the 6th Corps.

Borodi 7 Sept.

Initially these men were distributed amongst the various battalions to fill out the third ranks, but with the distribution of draftees to the regiments, the opolochenie found itself in the regiments and divisions with the reserve regiments, formed under the command of Generalmajor Miller.

12th Reserve Regiment	Major Kuszmin	2nd Army
13th Reserve Regiment	Major Kulikov	3rd Division
1/, 2/14th Reserve Regiment	Major Lukhanov	23rd Division
3/14th Reserve Regiment		2nd Army

The cadres of the following regiments were sent to Nizhni-Novgorod in mid-September under Generalmajor Ushakov:

1/6th Reserve Regiment	4th Corps
2/, 3/6th Reserve Regiment	2nd Corps
1/, 2/7th Reserve Regiment	6th Corps
3/7th Reserve Regiment	3rd Division
1st Jager Battalion (1st & 2nd Cos)	2nd Corps
1st Jager Battalion (3rd & 4th Cos)	3rd Division
2nd Jager Battalion (1st & 2nd Cos)	4th Corps
2nd Jager Battalion (3rd & 4th Cos)	6th Corps

The cadres of the 6th and 7th Reserve Regiments and the two jager battalions were sent to Nizhni-Novgorod on 25 September.

The following cavalry depots were distributed as follows. In these cases the men were drafted as indicated, but cadres were preserved for the training of more raw recruits. The cadres were sent to Nizhni-Novgorod:

Lithuanian Uhlans (1 sqn)	2nd Army
Tartar Uhlans (2 sqns)	1st Army
Alexandria Hussars (1 sqn)	1st Army

Starodoub Dragoons (1 sqn)	1st Army
Tver Dragoons (1 sqn)	1st Army
Jitomir Dragoons (1 sqn)	1st Army
Arazamas Dragoons (1 sqn)	1st Army

The Riazan brigade, under the command of Lieutenant Colonel Demidov, was distributed to the 1st and 2nd Armies on 30 September:

1/, 2/5th Reserve Regiment	8th Corps
3/5th Reserve Regiment	7th Corps
1/6th Reserve Regiment	7th Corps
2 /6th Reserve Regiment	2nd Corps
3/6th Reserve Regiment	6th Corps

A portion of these reserve regiments were distributed amongst the Guard Regiments by the order of Colonel Nabokov, of the Semenovski Guard Infantry Regiment.

Brigades under Generalmajor Rusanov, with the exception of those distributed to the Guard and grenadier regiments, were distributed on 9 October as follows:

1/, 2/7th Tambov Regiment	2nd Corps
3/7th Tambov Regiment	6th Corps
1/6th Tambov Regiment	8th Corps
2/6th Tambov Regiment	4th Corps
3/6th Tambov Regiment	6th Corps
1/3rd Voronezh Jager Regiment	4th Corps
2/3rd Voronezh Jager Regiment	7th Corps
3/3rd Voronezh Jager Regiment	2nd Corps
1/4th Voronezh Jager Regiment (2 coys)	3rd Division
1/4th Voronezh Jager Regiment (2 coys)	6th Corps
2/4th Voronezh Jager Regiment	8th Corps
3/4th Voronezh Jager Regiment	6th Corps

Again, cadres were preserved and concentrated in Nizhni-Novgorod.

Strength of Moscow Opolochenie Presented to Barclay de Tolly 29 August 1812

1st Jager Regiment: Generalmajor Demidov
  Staff Officers   3
  Senior Officers   28
  Under Officers   131
  Rank and File   1,748
                      ‾‾‾‾‾
                      1,910

2nd Jager Regiment: Generalmajor Talizin
  Staff Officers   1
  Senior Officers   13
  Under Officers   88
  Rank and File   1,167
                      ‾‾‾‾‾
                      1,269

3rd Jager Regiment: Generalmajor Talizin
  Staff Officers   3
  Senior Officers   4
  Under Officers   20
  Rank and File   270
                       ‾‾‾‾
                        297

1st Infantry Regiment: Generalmajor Gagarin
  Staff Officers   4
  Senior Officers   24
  Rank and File   1,471
                      ‾‾‾‾‾
                      1,499

2nd Infantry Regiment: Generalmajor Odoevskoi
  Staff Officers   4
  Senior Officers   17
  Under Officers   176
  Rank and File   2,143
                      ‾‾‾‾‾
                      2,340

3rd Infantry Regiment: Generalmajor Svecin
  Staff Officers   2
  Senior Officers   9
  Under Officers   10
  Rank and File   803
                       ‾‾‾‾
                        824

6th Infantry Regiment:	Generalmajor Lopukhin
Staff Officers	4
Senior Officers	34
Under Officers	50
Rank and File	2,050
	2,138

7th Infantry Regiment:	Generalmajor Arsenbev
Staff Officers	2
Senior Officers	16
Under Officers	102
Rank and File	1,783
	1,903

8th Infantry Regiment:	Generalmajor Potulov
Staff Officers	4
Senior Officers	—
Under Officers	—
Rank and File	—

Moscow Opolochenie Defending Moscow
September 1812

1st Cavalry Regiment

Location	Moscow
Commanding Colonels	1
Staff Officers	6
Under Officers	40
Noncommissioned Officers	47
Lower Officers	—
Soldiers	126
Division Assignment	None

1st Jager Regiment

Location	Rozye
Commanding Colonels	1
Staff Officers	6
Under Officers	38
Noncommissioned Officers	76
Lower Officers	—
Soldiers	2,400
Division Assignment	1st Division

2nd Jager Regiment
  Location   Mozhaizk
  Commanding Colonels   1
  Staff Officers   5
  Under Officers   38
  Noncommissioned Officers   —
  Lower Officers   120
  Soldiers   2,049
  Division Assignment   3rd Division

3rd Jager Regiment
  Location   Mozhaizk
  Commanding Colonels   1
  Staff Officers   5
  Under Officers   48
  Noncommissioned Officers   17
  Lower Officers   5
  Soldiers   2,557
  Division Assignment   3rd Division

1st Infantry Regiment
  Location   Mozhaizk
  Commanding Colonels   1
  Staff Officers   4
  Under Officers   36
  Noncommissioned Officers   67
  Lower Officers   —
  Soldiers   2,400
  Division Assignment   3rd Division

2nd Infantry Regiment
  Location   Rozye
  Commanding Colonels   1
  Staff Officers   4
  Under Officers   24
  Noncommissioned Officers   60
  Lower Officers   —
  Soldiers   2,007
  Division Assignment   1st Division

3rd Infantry Regiment
  Location   Mozhaizk
  Commanding Colonels   1
  Staff Officers   4
  Under Officers   19

Noncommissioned Officers   —
Lower Officers   15
Soldiers   2,100
Division Assignment   3rd Division

4th Infantry Regiment
Location   Rozye
Commanding Colonels   1
Staff Officers   4
Under Officers   32
Noncommissioned Officers   1
Lower Officers   9
Soldiers   2,400
Division Assignment   1st Division

5th Infantry Regiment
Location   Veree
Commanding Colonels   1
Staff Officers   5
Under Officers   20
Noncommissioned Officers   —
Lower Officers   12
Soldiers   2,602
Division Assignment   2nd Division

6th Infantry Regiment
Location   Rozye
Commanding Colonels   1
Staff Officers   4
Under Officers   38
Noncommissioned Officers   —
Lower Officers   9
Soldiers   1,850
Division Assignment   1st Division

7th Infantry Regiment
Location   Veree
Commanding Colonels   1
Staff Officers   4
Under Officers   27
Noncommissioned Officers   15
Lower Officers   —
Soldiers   2,400
Division Assignment   2nd Division

8th Infantry Regiment
Location	Veree
Commanding Colonels	1
Staff Officers	5
Under Officers	39
Noncommissioned Officers	26
Lower Officers	74
Soldiers	1,944
Division Assignment	2nd Division

Opolochenie Raised in Vladimir
7 August 1812

Unit	District of Origin	Soldiers
1st Vladimir Cohort (Generalmajor Merkhlova)		
	Vyaznikov	982
	Gorokhov	1,091
	Shchue	442
		2,515
2nd Vladimir Cohort (Cavalier Sourudiva)		
	Vladimir	1,154
	Sudogod	684
	Melenkov	677
		2,515
3rd Vladimir Cohort (Cavalier Zubova)		
	Kovrov	1,272
	Alexandrov	1,801
	Pereyaslav	162
		3,235
4th Vladimir Cohort (Cavalier Polivahova)		
	Pokrov	1,292
	Alexandrov	687
	Pereyaslav	535
		2,514

5th Vladimir Cohort
(Cavalier Cherepanova)

Ur'ev	1,528
Suzdal	576
Pereyaslav	410
	2,514

6th Vladimir Court
(Cavalier Nefed'eva)

Murmon	1,570
Melenkov	542
Gorokhov	402
	2,514

Moscow Opolochenie Reinforcements Assigned to the Regiments of the 2nd Army of the West 7 September 1812

Borodino Sept. 7

7th Infantry Corps

	Opolochenie Reinforcements
12th Division:	
Smolensk Infantry Regiment	339
Narva Infantry Regiment	292
Alexopol Infantry Regiment	294
New Ingermannland Infantry Regiment	284
6th Jager Regiment	290
41st Jager Regiment	250
Total	1,749
26th Division:	
Nivegorod Infantry Regiment	233
Ladoga Infantry Regiment	295
Poltava Infantry Regiment	227
Orel Infantry Regiment	335
5th Jager Regiment	250
42nd Jager Regiment	295
Total	1,635

	Opolochenie Reinforcements
8th Infantry Corps:	
27th Division:	
Vilna Infantry Regiment	153
Odessa Infantry Regiment	198
Tarnopol Infantry Regiment	198
Simbrisk Infantry Regiment	144
49th Jager Regiment	180
50th Jager Regiment	152
Total	1,025
To artillery brigades of the 2nd Army:	500

Opolochenie Raised in Tver
12 September 1812

	1st	2nd	3rd	4th	5th	Horse Cossacks
Regimental Commander	1	1	1	1	1	1
Staff	4	4	4	4	4	3
Senior Officers	46	37	35	40	43	19
Brevet Officers	3	20	12	19	5	3
Veterans Sergeants	70	114	103	74	57	21
Cossack Sergeants	132	88	99	128	145	39
Cossacks from Tver	2,417	2,363	2,305	2,352	2,317	607
Cossacks from Province	120	77	120	120	121	—
Horses	—	—	—	—	—	609
Deficit Officers	8	—	9	—	9	—
Deficit Cossacks	—	64	111	35	53	74
Deficit Horses	—	—	—	—	—	56

St. Petersburg Opolochenie
4 October 1812

	1st Brigade	2nd Brigade	3rd Brigade	4th Brigade	5th Brigade	Total
Staff Officers	7	10	7	9	10	43
Senior Officers	53	65	46	62	67	293
Under Officers	18	23	21	20	20	102
Sergeants	69	146	103	154	132	604
Musicians	5	4	5	3	5	22
Privates	64	59	54	55	59	291
Soldiers	1,462	1,834	1,861	1,873	1,974	9,004
Total	1,678	2,141	2,097	2,176	2,267	10,359

Status of the 2nd Novgorod Opolochenie Cohort
25 September 1812

	1st Troop	2nd Troop	3rd Troop	Total
Assigned Personnel				
Staff Officers	2	1	3	6
Senior Officers	19	14	15	48
Under Officers	60	40	48	148
Drummers	9	18	—	27
Soldiers	695	710	728	2,133
Civilians	27	27	27	81
Hospitalized in Novgorod				
Under Officers	—	—	—	—
Drummers	—	—	—	—
Soldiers	4	8	5	17
Starorus				
Under Officers	—	—	—	—
Drummers	—	—	—	—
Soldiers	3	—	—	3
Elsewhere				
Under Officers	—	—	—	—
Drummers	—	—	—	—
Soldiers	—	—	1	1

	1st Troop	2nd Troop	3rd Troop	Total
Deserters				
Under Officers	—	—	—	—
Drummers	—	—	—	—
Soldiers	4	1	7	12
Detached				
Staff Officers	—	—	—	—
Senior Officers	4	—	—	4
Under Officers	—	—	—	—
Drummers	9	18	—	27
Soldiers	—	—	—	—
Civilians	12	27	36	75
Present Under Arms				
Staff Officers	2	1	3	6
Senior Officers	15	14	15	44
Under Officers	60	40	48	148
Drummers	—	—	—	
Soldiers	684	701	710	2,095
Civilians	15	—	—	15
Draft Horses	12	12	12	36

Status Report of the Ukrainian Cossack Corps
6 October 1812

	1st Pulk	2nd Pulk	3rd Pulk	4th Pulk	Total
Assigned					
Staff Officers	3	3	2	1	9
Senior Officers	25	20	36	19	100
Under Officers	88	88	88	88	352
Artisans	17	17	17	17	68
Cossacks	1,168	1,158	1,162	1,139	4,627
Mounts	1,304	1,304	1,304	1,304	5,216
Draft Horses	—	—	—	—	—
Reserve Command					
Staff Officers	—	—	—	—	—
Senior Officers	1	1	1	1	4

	1st Pulk	2nd Pulk	3rd Pulk	4th Pulk	Total
Under Officers	8	3	7	8	26
Artisans	—	—	—	—	—
Cossacks	127	126	124	134	511
Mounts	61	82	75	96	314
Draft Horses	—	—	—	—	—
Present					
Staff Officers	3	3	2	1	9
Senior Officers	24	19	30	18	91
Under Officers	79	85	80	80	324
Artisans	17	17	17	17	68
Cossacks	1,030	1,023	1,030	993	4,076
Mounts	1,234	1,215	1,221	1,203	4,873
Draft Horses	—	—	—	—	—
Detachments					
Staff Officers	—	—	—	—	—
Senior Officers	—	—	2	—	2
Under Officers	—	—	1	—	1
Artisans	—	—	—	—	—
Cossacks	—	—	2	—	2
Mounts	—	—	—	—	—
Draft Horses	—	—	—	—	—
Deficiency to Complement					
Staff Officers	1	—	1	2	4
Senior Officers	11	16	—	17	44
Under Officers	—	—	—	—	—
Artisans	—	—	—	—	—
Cossacks	32	42	38	61	173
Mounts	—	—	—	—	—
Draft Horses	—	—	—	—	—

Note: There was a shortage of cossacks because some had been assigned to serve as under officers or buglers.

Breakdown of Russian Units and
Distribution of Moscow Opolochenie
10 October 1812

Borodino 7 Sept

2nd Corps
4th Infantry Division:

	Tobolsk Infantry	Volhynie Infantry	Krementchug Infantry	Minsk Infantry	46th Jager
Staff Officers	4	2	4	2	4
Senior Officers	24	22	33	12	33
NCOs	42	38	53	35	62
Musicians	22	24	24	25	39
Veterans	459	457	425	436	785
Opolochenie	211	221	174	203	33
Recruits	198	198	221	199	338
Total Privates	862	876	820	838	1,156

17th Infantry Division:

	Riazan Infantry	Bieloserk Infantry	Brest Infantry	48th Jager
Staff Officers	—	5	3	4
Senior Officers	26	20	17	43
NCOs	54	71	31	62
Musicians	27	28	36	44
Veterans	508	581	454	767
Opolochenie	188	201	126	—
Recruits	181	121	221	373
Total Privates	877	903	801	1,140

17th Artillery Brigade

	Position Battery #17	Light Battery #32	Light Battery #33
Staff Officers	1	1	1
Senior Officers	4	4	5
NCOs	16	13	18
Musicians	17	2	2
Veterans	199	109	109
Opolochenie	—	5	—
Recruits	—	—	—
Total Privates	199	114	135

3rd Corps
1st Artillery Brigade

	Position Battery #3	Light Battery #1	Light Battery #2
Staff Officers	1	—	—
Senior Officers	4	8	6
NCOs	16	15	16
Musicians	10	2	2
Veterans	164	104	118
Opolochenie	45	20	20
Recruits	—	—	—
Total Privates	209	124	138

3rd Artillery Brigade

	Position Battery #1	Light Battery #5	Light Battery #6	Horse Battery #4
Staff Officers	—	—	—	1
Senior Officers	5	5	5	7
NCOs	15	12	15	24
Musicians	12	2	1	2
Veterans	164	107	126	181
Opolochenie	32	10	14	—
Recruits	—	—	—	—
Total Privates	196	177	140	181

4th Corps
11th Infantry Division

	Kexholm Infantry	Pernov Infantry	Jeletz Infantry	1st Jager
Staff Officers	4	3	1	4
Senior Officers	29	24	37	34
NCOs	39	38	31	52
Musicians	—	—	—	—
Veterans	407	443	406	599
Opolochenie	217	164	161	96
Recruits	284	331	401	228
Total Privates	908	938	968	923

23rd Division

	Rilsk Infantry	Ekaterinburg Infantry	Kaporsk Infantry	33rd Jager
Staff Officers	4	4	1	4
Senior Officers	24	28	37	34
NCOs	42	38	31	52
Musicians	—	—	—	—
Veterans	323	113	406	599
Opolochenie	177	160	161	96
Recruits	590	650	401	228
Total Privates	1,090	923	968	923

11th Artillery Brigade

	Position Battery #2	Light Battery #3	Light Battery #4
Staff Officers	—	1	1
Senior Officers	5	5	2
NCOs	19	15	7
Musicians	—	—	—
Veterans	146	80	49
Opolochenie	31	3	10
Recruits	26	27	18
Total Privates	203	110	77

23rd Artillery Brigade

	Position Battery #23	Light Battery #44
Staff Officers	1	—
Senior Officers	6	6
NCOs	19	21
Musicians	—	—
Veterans	157	123
Opolochenie	60	—
Recruits	12	—
Total Privates	229	123

Moscow
Opolochenie

Staff Officers	—
Senior Officers	9
NCOs	2
Musicians	—
Veterans	47
Opolochenie	714
Recruits	—
Total Privates	761

2nd Reserve Artillery Brigade:

	Position Battery #29	Position Battery #30
Staff Officers	1	1
Senior Officers	8	7
NCOs	17	16
Musicians	1	1
Veterans	199	168
Opolochenie	9	20
Recruits	—	—
Total Privates	208	188

6th Corps
7th Division

	Pskof Infantry	Moscow Infantry	Libau Infantry	Sofia Infantry	11th Jager
Staff Officers	3	2	4	4	4
Senior Officers	22	21	22	32	34
NCOs	46	42	36	25	71
Musicians	28	30	23	25	44
Veterans	495	517	307	240	727
Opolochenie	27	36	31	36	14
Recruits	219	216	359	409	550
Total Privates	741	769	697	685	1,291

24th Division:

	Chirvan Infantry	Bourtirki Infantry	Oufa Infantry	Tomsk Infantry	3/19th Jager
Staff Officers	4	5	5	2	1
Senior Officers	24	30	21	27	19
NCOs	31	29	29	32	12
Musicians	28	29	28	28	18
Veterans	162	293	227	184	275
Opolochenie	399	327	299	276	124
Recruits	355	277	306	343	420
Total Privates	916	897	832	803	819

7th Artillery Brigade:

	Position Battery #7	Light Battery #12	Light Battery #14
Staff Officers	—	—	1
Senior Officers	6	5	7
NCOs	15	12	16
Musicians	13	1	2
Veterans	215	96	113
Opolochenie	—	17	20
Recruits	13	9	10
Total Privates	228	122	143

24th Artillery Brigade

	Position Battery #24	Light Battery #45	Light Battery #46	Horse Battery #5
Staff Officers	1	—	—	—
Senior Officers	6	5	7	3
NCOs	14	20	16	8
Musicians	1	1	1	—
Veterans	168	146	105	67
Opolochenie	19	18	24	—
Recruits	—	—	—	52
Total Privates	187	164	129	119

7th Corps
12th Infantry Division:

	Smolensk Infantry	Narva Infantry	Alexopol Infantry	New Ingermannland Infantry	6th Jager
Staff Officers	2	2	2	2	4
Senior Officers	16	22	18	11	36
NCOs	42	48	29	64	66
Musicians	26	34	30	29	33
Veterans	192	410	342	309	477
Opolochenie	247	251	237	243	292
Recruits	413	309	301	296	383
Total Privates	852	970	880	848	1,152

26th Infantry Division

	Nivegorod Infantry	Ladoga Infantry	Poltava Infantry	Orel Infantry	5th Jager
Staff Officers	1	1	2	1	3
Senior Officers	14	12	17	14	20
NCOs	34	44	50	44	47
Musicians	26	25	28	32	23
Veterans	340	469	328	285	563
Opolochenie	209	240	131	305	348
Recruits	412	297	440	405	381
Total Privates	961	1,006	899	995	1,292

12th Artillery Brigade

	Position Battery #12	Light Battery #22	Light Battery #23
Staff Officers	1	—	—
Senior Officers	3	3	3
NCOs	11	14	17
Musicians	5	1	1
Veterans	128	117	132
Opolochenie	18	48	21
Recruits	—	—	—
Total Privates	146	165	153

26th Artillery Brigade:

	Position Battery #26	Light Battery #47	Light Battery #48
Staff Officers	1	—	—
Senior Officers	4	5	3
NCOs	22	12	17
Musicians	3	1	1
Veterans	226	112	132
Opolochenie	12	15	21
Recruits	—	—	—
Total Privates	238	127	153

8th Corps
27th Infantry Division:

	Odessa Infantry	Tarnopol Infantry	Vilna Infantry	Simbrisk Infantry	49th Jager
Staff Officers	1	1	2	1	1
Senior Officers	15	11	15	19	18
NCOs	16	34	35	30	16
Musicians	20	25	27	15	27
Veterans	153	189	174	148	254
Opolochenie	59	93	65	103	140
Recruits	580	548	535	546	435
Total Privates	792	830	774	797	829

2nd Artillery Brigade:

	Position Battery #49	Light Battery #53	Light Battery #54
Staff Officers	1	—	—
Senior Officers	3	5	4
NCOs	12	8	16
Musicians	8	—	2
Veterans	169	114	102
Opolochenie	22	28	23
Recruits	—	—	—
Total Privates	191	142	125

3rd Reserve Artillery Brigade

	Position Battery #31	Position Battery #32	Horse Battery #8	Horse Battery #9	Horse Battery #10
Staff Officers	1	1	1	1	1
Senior Officers	4	3	4	3	3
NCOs	14	13	15	13	16
Musicians	1	1	2	—	2
Veterans	253	196	250	156	142
Opolochenie	—	—	—	—	—
Recruits	—	—	—	—	—
Total Privates	253	196	250	156	142

Example of French Regimental Strengths
15 December 1812

	4th Voltiguer Regiment Colonel Clary	5th Tirailleur Regiment Colonel Hennequin
Forces in Smolensk		
Officers	32	27
Men	427	470
Killed in Battle		
Officers	3	—
Men	26	5
Wounded or Captured		
Officers	—	—
Men	65	12
Frozen to Death		
Officers	—	—
Men	103	1
Left in Hospital		
Officers	1	10
Men	204	422
Total Losses		
Officers	4	10
Men	398	440
Present Under Arms		
Officers	10	9
Men	29	5

	4th Tirailleur Regiment Colonel Robert	6th Tirailleur Regiment Colonel Falte
Forces in Smolensk		
Officers	29	31
Men	252	300
Killed in Battle		
Officers	—	—
Men	6	13
Wounded or Captured		
Officers	—	4
Men	4	52
Frozen to Death		
Officers	—	—
Men	58	24
Left in Hospital		
Officers	17	13
Men	174	201
Total Losses		
Officers	17	17
Men	242	290
Present Under Arms		
Officers	12	14
Men	10	10

Extract from the Roll Call of 24 December 1812
V Corps of Eugène

Royal Guard	Officers	Men
Guard Grenadiers	28	47
Guard Chasseurs	11	2
Guard Velites	27	15
15th Division		
2nd Italian Line Regiment	14	4
3rd Italian Line Regiment	14	8
1st Italian Legere Regiment	7	6
3rd Italian Legere Regiment	5	12
Dalmation Regiment	7	11
Horse Artillery	3	4
Foot Artillery	3	3
1st Train Battalion	2	—
	121	112

Russian Casualties at Borodino

1st Cavalry Corps

	Guard Hussar	Guard Uhlan	Guard Cossack	Nijine Dragoon	Elisabethgrad Hussar
KILLED					
NCOs	1	—	—	—	1
Rank & File	11	—	3	—	4
Noncombatant	—	—	—	—	—
Cavalry Horses	15	—	—	7	17
WOUNDED					
NCOs	2	—	8	—	2
Rank & File	15	—	20	—	12
Noncombatant	—	—	2	—	—
Cavalry Horses	28	—	—	—	40
MISSING					
NCOs	—	—	—	—	—
Rank & File	—	—	—	—	20
Noncombatant	—	20	—	—	—
Cavalry Horses	—	18	—	—	18
TOTAL	30	20	33	7	39
FULL STRENGTH	629	629		644	1,811
% LOSSES	4.8%	3.2%		0.7%	2.2%

Note: These strength figures are based on the number of battalions or squadrons known to be in the battle and the normal full strength organization. It should be realized that the Russian regiments were tremendously under strength by the time they reached Borodino. These figures are presented solely to provide an idea of the type of punishment the Russians received during this battle.

2nd Cavalry Corps

	Moscow Dragoon	Pskof Dragoon	Isoum Hussar	Polish Uhlan	Kourland Dragoon	Orenburg Dragoon	Siberian Dragoon	Irkhoutsk Dragoon	Marioupol Hussar	Soum Hussar
KILLED										
NCOs	4	2	2	—	2	—	—	2	8	1
Rank & File	19	20	9	16	15	8	28	24	155	28
Noncombatant	1	79	1	—	—	—	—	3	—	1
Cavalry Horses	90	79	102	19	138	32	35	74	198	146
WOUNDED										
NCOs	3	2	8	—	6	2	4	7	9	9
Rank & File	43	49	99	20	49	22	82	65	26	44
Noncombatant	—	—	—	1	—	—	—	—	—	1
Cavalry Horses	43	30	35	—	—	23	43	38	31	27
MISSING										
NCOs	—	—	—	1	—	—	1	1	—	—
Rank & File	20	32	18	15	7	16	42	21	—	33
Noncombatant	—	—	—	—	—	—	—	—	—	—
Cavalry Horses	18	66	13	13	8	13	42	15	—	15
TOTAL	90	184	137	52	79	48	157	123	198	117
FULL STRENGTH	644	644	1,811	1,811	644	644	644	644	1,811	1,811
% LOSSES	14.0%	28.6%	7.6%	6.8%	12.3%	7.5%	24.4%	19.1%	10.9%	6.5%

2nd Corps
4th Division

	Tobolsk Infantry	Minsk Infantry	Volhynie Infantry	Krementchug Infantry	4th Jager	34th Jager
KILLED						
NCOs	10	3	3	2	—	1
Rank & File	236	38	235	23	79	43
Noncombatant	2	—	2	2	1	1
WOUNDED						
NCOs	5	11	10	5	7	9
Rank & File	125	160	95	141	183	204
Noncombatant	3	2	4	5	1	—
MISSING						
NCOs	2	1	1	—	—	—
Rank & File	32	128	147	57	19	24
Noncombatant	—	—	3	—	—	1
TOTAL	415	343	500	235	290	283
FULL STRENGTH	2,591	2,591	2,591	2,591	2,591	2,591
% LOSSES	16.0%	13.2%	19.3%	9.1%	11.2%	11.3%

17th Division

	Riazan Infantry	Brest Infantry	Bieloserk Infantry	Wilmanstrand Infantry	3rd Jager	48th Jager
KILLED						
NCOs	1	1	1	2	1	3
Rank & File	12	1	69	85	29	41
Noncombatant	1	—	—	1	1	1
WOUNDED						
NCOs	8	7	11	22	10	22
Rank & File	79	138	118	154	145	134
Noncombatant	4	—	3	3	2	1
MISSING						
NCOs	1	—	1	1	—	4
Rank & File	80	181	60	60	79	118
Noncombatant	—	—	1	1	2	—
TOTAL	186	328	261	329	270	324
FULL STRENGTH	2,591	2,591	2,591	2,591	2,591	2,591
% LOSSES	7.2%	12.7%	10.1%	12.7%	10.4%	12.5%

3rd Corps
1st Grenadier Division

	Leib Grenadier	Count Arakcheyev Grenadier	Ekaterinoslav Grenadier	St. Petersburg Grenadier	Tauride Grenadier	Pavlov Grenadier
KILLED						
NCOs	2	41	—	2	1	—
Rank & File	41	9	8	23	62	21
Noncombatant	—	—	—	—	1	—
WOUNDED						
NCOs	12	16	6	7	11	9
Rank & File	120	191	81	104	151	216
Noncombatant	4	4	2	1	3	—
MISSING						
NCOs	4	1	1	—	1	—
Rank & File	67	41	74	125	159	58
Noncombatant	1	1	3	—	1	2
TOTAL	251	555	175	262	390	306
FULL STRENGTH	2,591	2,591	2,591	2,591	2,591	2,591
% LOSSES	9.7%	21.4%	6.8%	10.1%	15.1%	11.8%

3rd Corps
3rd Division

	Tchernigov Infantry	Mourmonsk Infantry	Revel Infantry	Seleguinsk Infantry	20th Jager	21st Jager
KILLED						
NCOs	3	2	2	3	2	1
Rank & File	68	42	11	12	27	20
Noncombatant	1	3	2	1	1	1
WOUNDED						
NCOs	7	6	12	1	7	11
Rank & File	218	96	150	73	113	23
Noncombatant	1	7	3	4	1	4
MISSING						
NCOs	3	2	3	1	—	1
Rank & File	132	30	86	61	55	38
Noncombatant	—	3	1	—	—	—
TOTAL	433	191	270	156	206	99
FULL STRENGTH	2,591	2,591	2,591	2,591	2,591	2,591
% LOSSES	16.7%	7.4%	10.4%	6.0%	8.0%	3.8%

	1st Converged Grenadier Battalion	2nd Converged Grenadier Battalion
KILLED		
NCOs	—	1
Rank & File	3	11
Noncombatant	—	2
WOUNDED		
NCOs	5	7
Rank & File	78	73
Noncombatant	—	2
MISSING		
NCOs	—	—
Rank & File	23	25
Noncombatant	—	—
TOTAL	106	122
FULL STRENGTH	549	549
% LOSSES	19.3%	22.2%

4th Corps
11th Division

	Kexholm Infantry	Pernov Infantry	Polotsk Infantry	Jeletz Infantry	1st Jager	33rd Jager
Killed						
NCOs	2	3	1	3	9	—
Rank & File	69	68	33	70	188	10
Noncombatant	2	—	2	—	—	1
WOUNDED						
NCOs	14	13	6	25	7	—
Rank & File	273	243	199	435	258	17
Noncombatant	5	—	1	4	1	—
MISSING						
NCOs	—	—	—	—	—	—
Rank & File	49	45	99	254	—	2
Noncombatant	—	—	—	1	—	
TOTAL	414	372	341	792	463	30
FULL STRENGTH	2,591	2,591	2,591	2,591	2,591	2,591
% LOSSES	16.0%	14.4%	13.2%	30.6%	17.9%	1.2%

4th Corps
23rd Division

	Rilsk Infantry	Ekaterinburg Infantry	Kaporsk Infantry	18th Jager	1st Converged Grenadier Battalion	2nd Converged Grenadier Battalion
KILLED						
NCOs	2	2	6	—	—	—
Rank & File	16	50	110	110	3	1
Noncombatant	—	—	1	1	—	—
WOUNDED						
NCOs	4	10	12	6	1	—
Rank & File	55	148	250	111	6	4
Noncombatant	1	4	1	4	—	—
MISSING						
NCOs	—	—	2	4	—	—
Rank & File	36	238	118	30	—	—
Noncombatant	—	3	—	1	—	—
TOTAL	114	455	500	267	10	5
FULL STRENGTH	2,591	2,591	2,591	2,591	549	549
% LOSSES	4.4%	17.6%	19.3%	10.3%	1.8%	0.9%

5th Corps
1st Cavalry Division

	Chevalier Guard	Guard Dragoon	Emperor Cuirassier	Astrakhan Cuirassier	Empress Cuirassier
KILLED					
NCOs	1	2	—	4	2
Rank & File	9	17	28	52	19
Noncombatant	—	—	—	—	—
Cavalry Horses	88	120	166	229	99
WOUNDED					
NCOs	5	6	3	6	3
Rank & File	63	48	52	73	54
Noncombatant	—	—	1	—	1
Cavalry Horses	48	26	21	81	68
MISSING					
NCOs	—	—	—	9	1
Rank & File	—	15	26	87	4
Noncombatant	—	—	1	—	—
Cavalry Horses	—	—	1	26	6
TOTAL	78	88	111	231	84
FULL STRENGTH	784	814	784	784	784
% LOSSES	9.9%	10.8%	14.2%	29.4%	10.7%

Guard Division

	Preobragenski Guard	Semenovski Guard	Ismailov Guard	Lithuanian Guard	Guard Jager	Finland Guard
KILLED						
NCOs	4	1	16	30	3	5
Rank & File	22	18	153	400	43	51
Noncombatant	—	—	7	5	1	—
WOUNDED						
NCOs	12	9	20	35	54	23
Rank & File	90	503	503	143	473	308
Noncombatant	3	5	5	5	16	5
MISSING						
NCOs	—	—	5	13	5	—
Rank & File	—	—	67	100	96	62
Noncombatant	—	—	1	—	2	—
TOTAL	131	536	772	731	693	454
FULL STRENGTH	1,858	1,858	1,858	1,858	1,858	1,858
% LOSSES	7.1%	28.8%	41.6%	39.3%	27.3%	24.4%

6th Corps
7th Division

	Moscow Infantry	Pskof Infantry	Libau Infantry	Sofia Infantry	11th Jager	36th Jager
KILLED						
NCOs	3	—	3	2	—	—
Rank & File	6	6	47	27	19	31
Noncombatant	—	—	1	1	1	1
WOUNDED						
NCOs	3	2	13	9	6	4
Rank & File	90	31	182	131	79	72
Noncombatant	1	—	1	4	—	1
MISSING						
NCOs	—	—	2	1	1	3
Rank & File	23	35	60	111	42	62
Noncombatant	—	—	1	—	—	—
TOTAL	123	74	310	286	148	174
FULL STRENGTH	2,591	2,591	2,591	2,591	2,591	2,591
% LOSSES	4.7%	2.9%	12.0%	11.0%	5.7%	6.7%

24th Division

	Tomsk Infantry	Chirvan Infantry	Oufa Infantry	Bourtirki Infantry	19th Jager	40th Jager
KILLED						
NCOs	1	5	10	2	1	17
Rank & File	6	174	208	29	129	267
Noncombatant	—	2	—	—	1	2
WOUNDED						
NCOs	10	14	10	11	11	7
Rank & File	91	283	160	113	81	12
Noncombatant	1	4	3	2	1	1
MISSING						
NCOs	9	—	12	1	1	—
Rank & File	345	41	179	184	49	—
Noncombatant	1	—	6	—	—	—
TOTAL	464	523	588	352	274	306
FULL STRENGTH	2,591	2,591	2,591	2,591	2,591	2,591
% LOSSES	17.9%	20.2%	22.6%	13.6%	10.6%	11.8%

4th Cavalry Corps
4th Cavalry Division

	Karkov Dragoon	Tchernigov Dragoon	Kiev Dragoon	New Russia Dragoon	Akhtyrsk Hussar	Lithuanian Uhlan
KILLED						
NCOs	—	1	1	—	2	—
Rank & File	—	20	8	—	27	—
Noncombatant	—	—	—	—	—	—
Cavalry Horses	—	—	72	—	—	—
WOUNDED						
NCOs	—	4	1	—	8	—
Rank & File	—	41	37	—	98	—
Noncombatant	—	—	1	—	4	—
Cavalry Horses	—	—	37	—	—	—
MISSING						
NCOs	—	3	—	—	1	—
Rank & File	—	44	1	—	19	—
Noncombatant	—	1	1	—	1	—
Cavalry Horses	—	—	—	—	—	—
TOTAL	—	114	50	—	160	—
FULL STRENGTH	644	644	644	644	1,811	1,811
% LOSSES		17.7%	7.8%		8.8%	

2nd Cuirassier Division

	Military Order Cuirassier	Ekaterinoslav Cuirassier	Gluchov Cuirassier	Novgorod Cuirassier	Little Russia Cuirassier
KILLED					
NCOs	2	2	2	2	—
Rank & File	10	16	37	23	7
Noncombatant	—	—	—	—	—
Cavalry Horses	23	23	140	188	25
WOUNDED					
NCOs	2	8	6	4	6
Rank & File	26	62	71	53	44
Noncombatant	—	—	—	—	—
Cavalry Horses	24	45	87	39	90
MISSING					
NCOs	1	—	4	—	4
Rank & File	38	29	30	62	79
Noncombatant	—	—	—	—	—
Cavalry Horses	33	27	10	—	103
TOTAL	79	117	150	144	140
FULL STRENGTH	784	784	784	784	784
% LOSSES	10.1%	14.9%	19.1%	18.4%	17.9%

7th Corps
12th Division

	Smolensk Infantry	Narva Infantry	New Ingremannland Infantry	Alexopol Infantry	6th Jager	41st Jager
KILLED						
NCOs	3	6	12	1	8	3
Rank & File	—	234	248	66	364	105
Noncombatant	—	—	—	—	—	—
WOUNDED						
NCOs	9	17	4	16	28	19
Rank & File	215	205	109	148	510	155
Noncombatant	—	—	—	—	—	—
MISSING						
NCOs	1	5	—	3	—	1
Rank & File	100	30	—	207	—	198
Noncombatant	—	—	—	—	—	—
TOTAL	328	497	373	409	810	481
FULL STRENGTH	2,591	2,591	2,591	2,591	2,591	2,591
% LOSSES	12.7%	19.2%	14.4%	15.8%	31.3%	18.6%

26th Division

	Ladoga Infantry	Poltava Infantry	Orel Infantry	Nivegorod Infantry	5th Jager	42nd Jager
KILLED						
NCOs	5	3	—	2	3	—
Rank & File	35	49	41	85	53	24
Noncombatant	—	—	—	—	—	—
WOUNDED						
NCOs	13	15	15	12	21	15
Rank & File	202	155	159	148	438	164
Noncombatant	—	—	—	—	—	—
MISSING						
NCOs	—	2	1	2	3	1
Rank & File	156	208	217	198	141	283
Noncombatant	—	—	—	—	—	—
TOTAL	411	432	433	447	659	511
FULL STRENGTH	2,591	2,591	2,591	2,591	2,591	2,591
% LOSSES	15.8%	16.7%	16.7%	17.3%	25.4%	19.7%

8th Corps
2nd Grenadier Division

	Kiev Grenadier	Moscow Grenadier	Astrakhan Grenadier	Fangoria Grenadier	Siberia Grenadier	Little Russia Grenadier
KILLED						
NCOs	5	6	8	9	6	10
Rank & File	152	99	167	75	157	48
Noncombatant	—	—	—	—	—	—
WOUNDED						
NCOs	20	23	16	22	11	17
Rank & File	338	430	422	147	103	149
Noncombatant	—	—	—	—	—	—
MISSING						
NCOs	3	5	—	4	5	6
Rank & File	92	80	61	236	196	200
Noncombatant	—	—	—	—	—	—
TOTAL	610	616	674	493	478	403
FULL STRENGTH	2,591	2,591	591	22,591	2,591	2,591
% LOSSES	23.5%	23.8%	26.1%	19.3%	18.4%	16.6%

2nd Converged Grenadier Division

11 Battalions from 2nd, 7th, 12th, 24th,
& 26th Divisions

KILLED
  NCOs   45
  Rank & File   481
  Noncombatant   —
WOUNDED
  NCOs   74
  Rank & File   1,159
  Noncombatant   —

MISSING
  NCOs   19
  Rank & File   231
  Noncombatant   —
TOTAL   2,009
FULL STRENGTH   6,039
% LOSSES   33.2%

27th Division

	Vilna Infantry	Simbrisk Infantry	Odessa Infantry	Tarnopol Infantry	49th Jager	50th Jager
KILLED						
NCOs	23	13	5	—	—	2
Rank & File	372	278	63	79	43	158
Noncombatant	—	—	—	—	—	—
WOUNDED						
NCOs	19	14	22	22	11	12
Rank & File	301	252	182	182	91	177
Noncombatant	—	—	—	—	—	—
MISSING						
NCOs	—	9	5	2	5	11
Rank & File	155	126	231	242	89	126
Noncombatant	—	—	—	—	—	—
TOTAL	870	692	508	527	239	486
FULL STRENGTH	2,591	2,591	2,591	2,591	2,591	2,591
% LOSSES	33.6%	26.7%	19.6%	20.3%	9.2%	18.6%

| | 11th Artillery Brigade | | | 12th Artillery Brigade |
	Position Battery #11	Light Battery #20	Light Battery #21	Position Battery #12 / Light Battery #22 / Light Battery #24
KILLED				
NCOs	1	—	4	3
Rank & File	18	7	7	17
Noncombatant	1	—	—	—
Artillery Horses	—	—	—	—
WOUNDED				
NCOs	3	4	5	7
Rank & File	60	20	25	77
Noncombatant	1	—	—	2
Artillery Horses	—	—	—	—
MISSING				
NCOs	—	—	—	1
Rank & File	6	7	—	22
Noncombatant	—	—	—	1
Artillery Horses	—	—	—	—
TOTAL	95	38	41	130
FULL STRENGTH	231	231	231	693
% LOSSES	41.1%	16.4%	17.1%	18.8%

| | 26th Artillery Brigade | | | 27th Artillery Brigade | | |
	Position Battery #26	Light Battery #47	Light Battery #48	Position Battery #49	Light Battery #53	Light Battery #54
KILLED						
NCOs	1	2	1	—	—	—
Rank & File	14	5	—	—	—	—
Noncombatant	1	—	—	—	—	—
Artillery Horses	—	—	—	—	—	—
WOUNDED						
NCOs	1	—	—	—	—	—
Rank & File	28	34	15	—	—	—
Noncombatant	—	—	—	—	—	—
Artillery Horses	—	—	—	—	—	—
MISSING						
NCOs	2	—	—	—	—	—
Rank & File	11	—	3	—	—	—
Noncombatant	—	—	—	—	—	—
Artillery Horses	—	—	—	—	—	—
TOTAL	50	41	19	—	—	—
FULL STRENGTH	231	231	231	231	231	231
% LOSSES	21.6%	17.7%	8.2%			

| | 3rd Reserve Artillery Brigade | | Horse Battery #8 |
| | Position | Position | Horse Battery #9 |
	Battery #31	Battery #32	Horse Battery #10
KILLED			
NCOs	2	—	14
Rank & File	24	11	103
Noncombatant	—	1	3
Artillery Horses	—	40	40
WOUNDED			
NCOs	5	2	27
Rank & File	26	16	309
Noncombatant	—	—	3
Artillery Horses	—	15	15
MISSING			
NCOs	6	1	10
Rank & File	107	12	168
Noncombatant	13	—	14
Artillery Horses	88	—	88
TOTAL	183	43	651
FULL STRENGTH	231	231	675
% LOSSES	79.2%	18.6%	96.4%

	Moscow Militia	1st Converged Grenadier Brigade
	1st Jager (2 bns)	(from 5th Corps)
	2nd Jager (2 bns)	Converged Grenadiers from
	Det. 3rd Jager	4th & 17th Divisions (4 Bns)
KILLED		
NCOs	4	20
Rank & File	24	417
Noncombatant	15	—
WOUNDED		
NCOs	61	41
Rank & File	2,824	605
Noncombatant	—	23
MISSING		
NCOs	—	—
Rank & File	2,885	250
Noncombatant	—	—
TOTAL		1,356
FULL STRENGTH		2,196
% LOSSES		61.7%

Listing of Artillery Personnel and Equipment Lost and Damaged at Borodino 1st Army of the West

	Leib-Guard Brigade					Count Arakcheyev Battery				
	Captured	Dead	Wounded	Missing	Damaged	Captured	Dead	Wounded	Missing	Damaged
Staff Officers	—	—	—	—	—	—	—	1	—	—
Senior Officers	—	1	3	—	—	—	1	5	—	—
Artillerists	—	—	5	—	—	—	3	6	—	—
Musicians	—	—	—	—	—	—	—	—	—	—
Privates	—	11	51	—	—	—	39	46	—	—
Foreigners	—	—	—	—	—	—	—	—	—	—
Mounts (Horses)	—	—	—	—	—	—	—	—	—	—
Draft Horses	—	52	16	—	—	—	74	15	—	—
20pdr Licornes	—	—	—	—	—	—	—	—	—	—
Medium 12pdr	—	—	—	—	—	—	—	—	—	1
Short 12pdr	—	—	—	—	—	—	—	—	—	—
10pdr Licorne	—	—	—	—	—	—	—	—	—	—
6pdr Cannon	—	—	—	—	—	—	—	—	—	—
20pdr Caisson	—	—	—	1	1	—	—	—	3	—
12pdr Caisson	—	—	—	2	1	—	—	—	10	2
10pdr Caisson	—	—	—	—	—	—	—	—	—	—
6pdr Caisson	—	—	—	—	—	—	—	—	—	—
Service Saddles	—	—	—	—	—	—	—	—	—	—
Artillery Saddles	—	—	—	24	—	—	—	—	35	—
Horse Collars	—	—	—	52	—	—	—	—	74	—
Bridles	—	—	—	52	—	—	—	—	74	—
Halters	—	—	—	52	—	—	—	—	74	—

	Generalmajor Kasperskogo Battery					Captain Gogelya Battery				
	Captured	Dead	Wounded	Missing	Damaged	Captured	Dead	Wounded	Missing	Damaged
Staff Officers	—	—	—	—	—	—	—	—	—	—
Senior Officers	—	1	5	—	—	—	—	2	—	—
Artillerists	—	3	3	—	—	—	—	—	—	—
Musicians	—	—	9	—	—	—	—	2	—	—
Privates	—	10	25	—	—	—	5	18	—	—
Foreigners	—	—	—	—	—	—	—	—	—	—
Mounts (Horses)	—	—	—	—	—	—	—	—	—	—
Draft Horses	—	29	—	—	—	—	27	8	—	—
20pdr Licornes	—	—	5	—	—	—	—	—	—	—
Medium 12pdr	—	—	—	—	—	—	—	—	—	—
Short 12pdr	—	—	—	—	—	—	—	—	—	—
10pdr Licorne	—	—	—	—	—	—	—	—	—	—
6pdr Cannon	—	—	—	—	—	—	—	—	—	—
20pdr Caisson	—	—	—	—	—	—	—	—	—	—
12pdr Caisson	—	—	—	—	—	—	—	—	—	—
10pdr Caisson	—	—	—	—	1	—	—	—	—	1
6pdr Caisson	—	—	—	2	1	—	—	—	—	1
Service Saddles	—	—	—	—	—	—	—	—	—	—
Artillery Saddles	—	—	—	14	—	—	—	—	13	—
Horse Collars	—	—	—	29	—	—	—	—	27	—
Bridles	—	—	—	29	—	—	—	—	27	—
Halters	—	—	—	29	—	—	—	—	27	—

1st Artillery Brigade

	3rd Position Battery					1st Light Battery				
	Captured	Dead	Wounded	Missing	Damaged	Captured	Dead	Wounded	Missing	Damaged
Staff Officers	—	2	1	—	—	—	—	—	—	—
Senior Officers	—	2	1	—	—	—	—	—	—	—
Artillerists	—	—	2	1	—	—	1	—	—	—
Musicians	—	—	1	1	—	—	—	—	—	—
Privates	—	16	42	4	—	—	6	6	8	—
Foreigners	—	—	1	1	—	—	—	—	—	—
Mounts (Horses)	—	—	—	—	—	—	—	—	—	—
Draft Horses	—	57	17	3	—	—	22	—	—	—
20pdr Licornes	—	—	—	—	—	—	—	—	—	—
Medium 12pdr	—	—	—	—	—	—	—	—	—	—
Short 12pdr	—	—	—	—	—	—	—	—	—	—
10pdr Licorne	—	—	—	—	—	—	—	—	—	—
6pdr Cannon	—	—	—	—	—	—	—	—	—	—
20pdr Caisson	—	—	—	—	—	—	—	—	—	—
12pdr Caisson	—	—	—	1	3	—	—	—	—	—
10pdr Caisson	—	—	—	—	—	—	—	—	—	—
6pdr Caisson	—	—	—	—	—	—	—	—	—	—
Service Saddles	—	—	—	—	—	—	—	—	—	—
Artillery Saddles	—	—	—	14	—	—	—	—	9	—
Horse Collars	—	—	—	60	—	—	—	—	22	—
Bridles	—	—	—	60	—	—	—	—	22	—
Halters	—	—	—	60	—	—	—	—	22	—

	2nd Light Battery				
	Captured	Dead	Wounded	Missing	Damaged
Staff Officers	—	—	—	—	—
Senior Officers	—	—	1	—	—
Artillerists	—	2	1	—	—
Musicians	—	—	—	—	—
Privates	—	6	5	6	—
Foreigners	—	—	—	—	—
Mounts (Horses)	—	—	—	—	—
Draft Horses	—	18	9	—	—
20pdr Licornes	—	—	—	—	—
Medium 12pdr	—	—	—	—	—
Short 12pdr	—	—	—	—	—
10pdr Licorne	—	—	—	—	—
6pdr Cannon	—	—	—	—	—
20pdr Caisson	—	—	—	—	—
12pdr Caisson	—	—	—	—	—
10pdr Caisson	—	—	—	—	1
6pdr Caisson	—	—	—	—	1
Service Saddles	—	—	—	—	—
Artillery Saddles	—	—	—	10	—
Horse Collars	—	—	—	18	—
Bridles	—	—	—	18	—
Halters	—	—	—	18	—

3rd Artillery Brigade

	1st Position Battery					5th Light Battery				
	Captured	Dead	Wounded	Missing	Damaged	Captured	Dead	Wounded	Missing	Damaged
Staff Officers	—	—	1	—	—	—	—	1	—	—
Senior Officers	—	1	1	—	—	—	—	3	1	—
Artillerists	—	—	—	—	—	—	1	3	1	—
Musicians	—	—	—	—	—	—	—	—	—	—
Privates	—	16	43	3	—	—	6	35	16	—
Foreigners	—	—	—	—	—	—	—	—	—	—
Mounts (Horses)	—	—	—	—	—	—	—	—	—	—
Draft Horses	—	37	17	—	—	—	—	50	—	—
20pdr Licornes	—	—	—	—	—	—	—	—	—	—
Medium 12pdr	—	—	—	—	1	—	—	—	—	—
Short 12pdr	—	—	—	—	—	—	—	—	—	—
10pdr Licorne	—	—	—	—	—	—	—	—	1	1
6pdr Cannon	—	—	—	—	—	—	—	—	1	1
20pdr Caisson	—	—	—	—	—	—	—	—	—	—
12pdr Caisson	—	—	—	—	2	—	—	—	—	—
10pdr Caisson	—	—	—	—	—	—	—	—	2	—
6pdr Caisson	—	—	—	—	—	—	—	—	3	—
Service Saddles	—	—	—	—	—	—	—	—	—	—
Artillery Saddles	—	—	—	20	—	—	—	—	11	—
Horse Collars	—	—	—	37	—	—	—	—	50	—
Bridles	—	—	—	37	—	—	—	—	50	—
Halters	—	—	—	37	—	—	—	—	50	—

| | 6th Light Battery | | | | |
	Captured	Dead	Wounded	Missing	Damaged
Staff Officers	—	—	—	—	—
Senior Officers	—	—	—	—	—
Artillerists	—	—	—	—	—
Musicians	—	—	1	—	—
Privates	—	2	2	5	—
Foreigners	—	—	—	—	—
Mounts (Horses)	—	—	—	—	—
Draft Horses	—	5	2	—	—
20pdr Licornes	—	—	—	—	—
Medium 12pdr	—	—	—	—	—
Short 12pdr	—	—	—	—	—
10pdr Licorne	—	—	—	—	—
6pdr Cannon	—	—	—	—	—
20pdr Caisson	—	—	—	—	—
12pdr Caisson	—	—	—	—	—
10pdr Caisson	—	—	—	—	—
6pdr Caisson	—	—	—	—	2
Service Saddles	—	—	—	—	1
Artillery Saddles	—	—	—	—	—
Horse Collars	—	—	—	—	—
Bridles	—	—	—	—	—
Halters	—	—	—	—	—

4th Artillery Brigade

	4th Position Battery					7th Light Battery				
	Captured	Dead	Wounded	Missing	Damaged	Captured	Dead	Wounded	Missing	Damaged
Staff Officers	—	1	—	—	—	—	—	—	—	—
Senior Officers	—	—	1	—	—	—	—	—	—	—
Artillerists	—	1	—	—	—	—	—	—	1	—
Musicians	—	—	—	—	—	—	—	—	—	—
Privates	—	4	2	9	—	—	3	—	1	—
Foreigners	—	—	—	1	—	—	—	—	1	—
Mounts (Horses)	—	—	—	—	—	—	—	—	—	—
Draft Horses	—	22	—	—	—	—	4	—	—	—
20pdr Licornes	—	—	—	—	—	—	—	—	—	—
Medium 12pdr	—	—	—	—	—	—	—	—	—	—
Short 12pdr	—	—	—	—	—	—	—	—	—	—
10pdr Licorne	—	—	—	—	—	—	—	—	—	—
6pdr Cannon	—	—	—	—	—	—	—	—			
20pdr Caisson	—	—	—	—	—	—	—	—	—	—
12pdr Caisson	—	—	—	—	—	—	—	—	—	—
10pdr Caisson	—	—	—	—	—	—	—	—	—	—
6pdr Caisson	—	—	—	—	—	—	—	—	—	—
Service Saddles	—	—	—	—	—	—	—	—	—	—
Artillery Saddles	—	—	—	—	—	—	—	—	—	—
Horse Collars	—	—	—	—	—	—	—	—	—	—
Bridles	—	—	—	—	—	—	—	—	—	—
Halters	—	—	—	—	—	—	—	—	1	—

| | 8th Light Battery | | | | |
	Captured	Dead	Wounded	Missing	Damaged
Staff Officers	—	—	—	—	—
Senior Officers	—	—	—	—	—
Artillerists	—	—	—	—	—
Musicians	—	—	—	—	—
Privates	—	—	—	2	—
Foreigners	—	—	—	1	—
Mounts (Horses)	—	—	—	—	—
Draft Horses	—	—	—	—	—
20pdr Licornes	—	—	—	—	—
Medium 12pdr	—	—	—	—	—
Short 12pdr	—	—	—	—	—
10pdr Licorne	—	—	—	—	—
6pdr Cannon	—	—	—	—	—
20pdr Caisson	—	—	—	—	—
12pdr Caisson	—	—	—	—	—
10pdr Caisson	—	—	—	—	—
6pdr Caisson	—	—	—	—	—
Service Saddles	—	—	—	—	—
Artillery Saddles	—	—	—	—	—
Horse Collars	—	—	—	—	—
Bridles	—	—	—	—	—
Halters	—	—	—	—	—

7th Artillery Brigade

	7th Position Battery					12th Light Battery				
	Captured	Dead	Wounded	Missing	Damaged	Captured	Dead	Wounded	Missing	Damaged
Staff Officers	—	—	1	—	—	—	—	1	—	—
Senior Officers	—	—	—	—	—	—	—	3	—	—
Artillerists	—	—	2	—	—	—	1	3	—	—
Musicians	—	—	—	—	—	—	—	—	—	—
Privates	—	2	7	—	—	—	5	25	7	—
Foreigners	—	—	—	—	—	—	—	—	—	—
Mounts (Horses)	—	—	—	—	—	—	—	—	—	—
Draft Horses	—	9	4	—	—	—	25	6	10	—
20pdr Licornes	—	—	—	—	—	—	—	—	—	—
Medium 12pdr	—	—	—	—	—	—	—	—	—	—
Short 12pdr	—	—	—	—	—	—	—	—	—	—
10pdr Licorne	—	—	—	—	—	—	—	—	2	—
6pdr Cannon	—	—	—	—	—	—	—	—	2	—
20pdr Caisson	—	—	—	—	—	—	—	—	—	—
12pdr Caisson	—	—	—	—	—	—	—	—	—	—
10pdr Caisson	—	—	—	—	—	—	—	—	1	—
6pdr Caisson	—	—	—	—	—	—	—	—	2	—
Service Saddles	—	—	—	—	—	—	—	—	—	—
Artillery Saddles	—	—	—	—	—	—	—	—	10	—
Horse Collars	—	—	—	—	—	—	—	—	35	—
Bridles	—	—	—	—	—	—	—	—	35	—
Halters	—	—	—	—	—	—	—	—	35	—

	Captured	Dead	13th Light Battery Wounded	Missing	Damaged
Staff Officers	—	—	—	—	—
Senior Officers	—	—	—	—	—
Artillerists	—	—	4	—	—
Musicians	—	—	—	—	—
Privates	—	1	14	1	—
Foreigners	—	—	—	—	—
Mounts (Horses)	—	—	—	—	—
Draft Horses	—	12	5	—	—
20pdr Licornes	—	—	—	—	—
Medium 12pdr	—	—	—	—	—
Short 12pdr	—	—	—	—	—
10pdr Licorne	—	—	—	—	—
6pdr Cannon	—	—	—	—	—
20pdr Caisson	—	—	—	—	—
12pdr Caisson	—	—	—	—	—
10pdr Caisson	—	—	—	—	—
6pdr Caisson	—	—	—	2	—
Service Saddles	—	—	—	—	—
Artillery Saddles	—	—	—	8	—
Horse Collars	—	—	—	17	—
Bridles	—	—	—	17	—
Halters	—	—	—	17	—

	2nd Position Battery					3rd Light Battery				
	Captured	Dead	Wounded	Missing	Damaged	Captured	Dead	Wounded	Missing	Damaged
Staff Officers	—	—	—	—	—	—	—	—	—	—
Senior Officers	—	1	—	—	—	—	—	—	—	—
Artillerists	—	—	—	—	—	—	—	—	—	—
Musicians	—	—	—	—	—	—	2	1	—	—
Privates	—	8	21	2	—	—	—	—	—	—
Foreigners	—	—	—	—	—	—	—	—	—	—
Mounts (Horses)	—	32	7	—	—	—	11	—	—	—
Draft Horses	—	—	—	—	—	—	—	—	—	—
20pdr Licornes	—	—	—	—	—	—	—	—	—	—
Medium 12pdr	—	—	—	—	—	—	—	—	—	—
Short 12pdr	—	—	—	—	—	—	—	—	—	—
10pdr Licorne	—	—	—	—	—	—	—	—	—	—
6pdr Cannon	—	—	—	—	—	—	—	—	—	—
20pdr Caisson	—	—	—	—	—	—	—	—	—	—
12pdr Caisson	—	—	—	—	—	—	—	—	—	—
10pdr Caisson	—	—	—	—	—	—	—	—	—	—
6pdr Caisson	—	—	—	—	—	—	—	—	—	2
Service Saddles	—	—	—	7	—	—	—	—	—	—
Artillery Saddles	—	—	—	23	—	—	—	—	5	—
Horse Collars	—	—	—	23	—	—	—	—	11	—
Bridles	—	—	—	23	—	—	—	—	11	—
Halters	—	—	—	23	—	—	—	—	11	—

| | 4th Light Battery | | | | |
	Captured	Dead	Wounded	Missing	Damaged
Staff Officers	—	—	—	—	—
Senior Officers	—	—	—	—	—
Artillerists	—	—	3	—	—
Musicians	—	—	—	—	—
Privates	—	3	3	—	—
Foreigners	—	—	—	—	—
Mounts (Horses)	—	—	—	—	—
Draft Horses	—	15	—	—	—
20pdr Licornes	—	—	—	—	—
Medium 12pdr	—	—	—	—	—
Short 12pdr	—	—	—	—	—
10pdr Licorne	—	—	—	—	—
6pdr Cannon	—	—	—	—	—
20pdr Caisson	—	—	—	—	—
12pdr Caisson	—	—	—	—	—
10pdr Caisson	—	—	—	—	—
6pdr Caisson	—	—	—	—	—
Service Saddles	—	—	—	—	—
Artillery Saddles	—	—	—	6	—
Horse Collars	—	—	—	15	—
Bridles	—	—	—	15	—
Halters	—	—	—	15	—

	17th Position Battery					32nd Light Battery				
	Captured	Dead	Wounded	Missing	Damaged	Captured	Dead	Wounded	Missing	Damaged
Staff Officers	—	—	—	—	—	—	—	—	—	—
Senior Officers	—	1	1	—	—	—	—	—	—	—
Artillerists	—	1	1	—	—	—	—	—	—	—
Musicians	—	—	—	—	—	—	—	—	2	—
Privates	—	8	21	—	—	—	2	4	—	—
Foreigners	—	—	—	—	—	—	—	—	—	—
Mounts (Horses)	—	—	—	—	—	—	—	—	—	—
Draft Horses	—	20	10	—	—	—	4	2	—	—
20pdr Licornes	—	—	—	—	—	—	—	—	—	—
Medium 12pdr	—	—	—	—	—	—	—	—	—	—
Short 12pdr	—	—	—	—	—	—	—	—	—	—
10pdr Licorne	—	—	—	—	—	—	—	—	—	—
6pdr Cannon	—	—	—	1	—	—	—	—	—	—
20pdr Caisson	—	—	—	—	2	—	—	—	—	—
12pdr Caisson	—	—	—	—	3	—	—	—	—	—
10pdr Caisson	—	—	—	—	—	—	—	—	—	—
6pdr Caisson	—	—	—	—	—	—	—	—	—	—
Service Saddles	—	—	—	12	—	—	—	—	3	—
Artillery Saddles	—	—	—	18	—	—	—	—	3	—
Horse Collars	—	—	—	18	—	—	—	—	3	—
Bridles	—	—	—	18	—	—	—	—	3	—
Halters	—	—	—	—	—	—	—	—	—	—

	Captured	Dead	33rd Light Battery Wounded	Missing	Damaged
Staff Officers	—	—	—	—	—
Senior Officers	—	—	1	—	—
Artillerists	—	—	3	—	—
Musicians	—	—	—	—	—
Privates	—	8	17	1	—
Foreigners	—	—	—	—	—
Mounts (Horses)	—	—	—	—	—
Draft Horses	—	11	13	—	—
20pdr Licornes	—	—	—	—	—
Medium 12pdr	—	—	—	—	—
Short 12pdr	—	—	—	—	—
10pdr Licorne	—	—	—	—	—
6pdr Cannon	—	—	—	—	—
20pdr Caisson	—	—	—	—	—
12pdr Caisson	—	—	—	—	—
10pdr Caisson	—	—	—	—	—
6pdr Caisson	—	—	—	—	—
Service Saddles	—	—	—	—	—
Artillery Saddles	—	—	—	10	—
Horse Collars	—	—	—	32	—
Bridles	—	—	—	32	—
Halters	—	—	—	32	—

| | 23rd Artillery Brigade | | | | | | | | | |
| | 23rd Position Battery | | | | | 44th Light Battery | | | | |
	Captured	Dead	Wounded	Missing	Damaged	Captured	Dead	Wounded	Missing	Damaged
Staff Officers	—	—	—	—	—	—	—	—	—	—
Senior Officers	—	—	—	—	—	—	—	—	1	—
Artillerists	—	—	—	—	—	—	—	—	—	—
Musicians	—	—	—	—	—	—	—	—	—	—
Privates	—	4	10	—	—	—	5	2	—	—
Foreigners	—	—	—	—	—	—	—	—	—	—
Mounts (Horses)	—	—	—	—	—	—	—	—	—	—
Draft Horses	—	—	—	—	—	—	—	—	—	—
20pdr Licornes	—	—	—	—	—	—	—	—	—	—
Medium 12pdr	—	—	—	1	—	—	—	—	—	—
Short 12pdr	—	—	—	—	—	—	—	—	—	—
10pdr Licorne	—	—	—	—	—	—	—	—	—	—
6pdr Cannon	—	—	—	—	—	—	—	—	—	—
20pdr Caisson	—	—	—	—	5	—	—	—	—	—
12pdr Caisson	—	—	—	—	5	—	—	—	—	—
10pdr Caisson	—	—	—	—	—	—	—	—	—	1
6pdr Caisson	—	—	—	—	—	—	—	—	—	1
Service Saddles	—	—	—	—	—	—	—	—	—	—
Artillery Saddles	—	—	8	—	—	—	—	—	5	—
Horse Collars	—	—	24	—	—	—	—	—	25	—
Bridles	—	—	24	—	—	—	—	—	25	—
Halters	—	—	24	—	—	—	—	—	25	—

| | 24th Artillery Brigade | | | | | | | | | |
| | 24th Position Battery | | | | | 45th Light Battery | | | | |
	Captured	Dead	Wounded	Missing	Damaged	Captured	Dead	Wounded	Missing	Damaged
Staff Officers	—	1	—	—	—	—	—	—	—	—
Senior Officers	—	—	3	—	—	—	—	2	—	—
Artillerists	—	—	1	—	—	—	—	3	—	—
Musicians	—	—	—	—	—	—	—	1	—	—
Privates	—	5	15	4	—	—	8	24	9	—
Foreigners	—	—	—	—	—	—	—	—	—	—
Mounts (Horses)	—	—	—	—	—	—	—	—	—	—
Draft Horses	—	51	—	—	1	—	30	10	—	—
20pdr Licornes	—	—	—	—	—	—	—	—	—	—
Medium 12pdr	—	—	—	—	—	—	—	—	—	—
Short 12pdr	—	—	—	—	—	—	—	—	—	—
10pdr Licorne	—	—	—	—	—	—	—	—	—	1
6pdr Cannon	—	—	—	—	—	—	—	—	—	—
20pdr Caisson	—	—	—	—	—	—	—	—	—	—
12pdr Caisson	—	—	—	3	—	—	—	—	—	—
10pdr Caisson	—	—	—	—	—	—	—	—	—	3
6pdr Caisson	—	—	—	—	—	—	—	—	1	3
Service Saddles	—	—	—	—	—	—	—	—	—	—
Artillery Saddles	—	—	—	13	—	—	—	—	10	—
Horse Collars	—	—	—	33	—	—	—	—	30	—
Bridles	—	—	—	33	—	—	—	—	23	—
Halters	—	—	—	33	—	—	—	—	23	—

	46th Light Brigade					5th Horse Battery				
	Captured	Dead	Wounded	Missing	Damaged	Captured	Dead	Wounded	Missing	Damaged
Staff Officers	—	—	1	—	—	—	—	1	—	—
Senior Officers	—	—	4	—	—	—	—	6	—	—
Artillerists	—	—	5	—	—	—	2	4	—	—
Musicians	—	1	1	—	—	—	—	—	—	—
Privates	—	—	34	2	—	—	32	50	15	—
Foreigners	—	—	1	—	—	—	—	—	—	—
Mounts (Horses)	—	—	—	—	—	—	110	34	—	—
Draft Horses	—	22	14	—	—	—	92	22	—	—
20pdr Licornes	—	—	—	—	—	—	—	—	—	—
Medium 12pdr	—	—	—	—	—	—	—	—	—	—
Short 12pdr	—	—	—	—	—	—	—	—	—	—
10pdr Licorne	—	—	—	—	—	—	—	1	3	1
6pdr Cannon	—	—	—	—	—	—	—	—	3	—
20pdr Caisson	—	—	—	—	—	—	—	—	—	—
12pdr Caisson	—	—	—	—	—	—	—	—	1	—
10pdr Caisson	—	—	—	—	—	—	—	—	2	—
6pdr Caisson	—	—	—	—	1	—	—	—	2	—
Service Saddles	—	—	—	—	—	—	—	—	114	—
Artillery Saddles	—	—	—	4	—	—	—	—	33	—
Horse Collars	—	—	—	12	—	—	—	—	92	—
Bridles	—	—	—	12	—	—	—	—	92	—
Halters	—	—	—	12	—	—	—	—	206	—

	6th Horse Battery					29th Position Battery				
	Captured	Dead	Wounded	Missing	Damaged	Captured	Dead	Wounded	Missing	Damaged
Staff Officers	—	—	1	—	—	—	—	—	—	—
Senior Officers	—	—	2	—	—	—	—	2	—	—
Artillerists	—	—	3	—	—	—	—	—	—	—
Musicians	—	—	1	—	—	—	—	—	—	—
Privates	—	9	28	12	—	—	7	15	1	—
Foreigners	—	—	—	2	—	—	—	—	—	—
Mounts (Horses)	—	36	6	—	—	—	—	—	—	—
Draft Horses	—	38	3	—	—	—	15	10	—	—
20pdr Licornes	—	—	—	—	—	—	—	—	—	—
Medium 12pdr	—	—	—	—	—	—	—	—	—	1
Short 12pdr	—	—	—	5*	—	—	—	—	—	—
10pdr Licorne	—	—	—	2*	6	—	—	—	—	—
6pdr Cannon	—	—	—	—	6	—	—	—	—	—
20pdr Caisson	—	—	—	—	—	—	—	—	2	—
12pdr Cassion	—	—	—	—	—	—	—	—	—	—
10pdr Caisson	—	—	—	1	—	—	—	—	—	—
6pdr Caisson	—	—	—	1	—	—	—	—	—	—
Service Saddles	—	—	—	28	—	—	—	—	—	—
Artillery Saddles	—	—	—	11	—	—	—	—	8	—
Horse Collars	—	—	—	16	—	—	—	—	15	—
Bridles	—	—	—	17	—	—	—	—	15	—
Halters	—	—	—	45	—	—	—	—	15	—

* Carriages

	Captured	Dead	Wounded	Missing	Damaged
		30th Position Battery			
Staff Officers	—	—	—	—	—
Senior Officers	—	—	—	—	—
Artillerists	—	2	3	—	—
Musicians	—	—	—	—	—
Privates	—	18	22	2	—
Foreigners	—	—	—	—	—
Mounts (Horses)	—	—	—	—	—
Draft Horses	—	—	52	—	—
20pdr Licornes	—	—	—	—	1
Medium 12pdr	—	—	—	—	—
Short 12pdr	—	—	—	—	—
10pdr Licorne	—	—	—	—	—
6pdr Cannon	—	—	—	—	—
20pdr Caisson	—	—	—	1	—
12pdr Caisson	—	—	—	1	—
10pdr Caisson	—	—	—	—	3
6pdr Caisson	—	—	—	—	—
Service Saddles	—	—	—	—	—
Artillery Saddles	—	—	—	14	—
Horse Collars	—	—	—	36	—
Bridles	—	—	—	36	—
Halters	—	—	—	36	—

	1st Reserve Brigade 2nd Horse Battery					2nd Reserve Battery 4th Horse Battery				
	Captured	Dead	Wounded	Missing	Damaged	Captured	Dead	Wounded	Missing	Damaged
Staff Officers	—	—	—	—	—	—	—	1	—	—
Senior Officers	—	—	—	—	—	—	—	1	—	—
Artillerists	—	—	2	—	—	—	3	3	—	—
Musicians	—	1	10	1	—	—	—	—	—	—
Privates	—	1	10	15	—	—	2	20	—	—
Foreigners	—	—	—	1	—	—	—	—	—	—
Mounts (Horses)	—	19	6	—	—	—	35	—	—	—
Draft Horses	—	17	4	—	—	—	34	—	—	—
20pdr Licornes	—	—	—	—	—	—	—	—	—	—
Medium 12pdr	—	—	—	—	—	—	—	—	—	—
Short 12pdr	—	—	—	—	—	—	—	—	—	—
10pdr Licorne	—	—	—	—	1	—	—	—	—	1
6pdr Cannon	—	—	—	—	—	—	—	—	—	1
20pdr Caisson	—	—	—	—	—	—	—	—	—	—
12pdr Caisson	—	—	—	—	—	—	—	—	—	—
10pdr Caisson	—	—	—	—	—	—	—	—	—	—
6pdr Caisson	—	—	—	—	1	—	—	—	—	3
Service Saddles	—	—	—	13	—	—	—	—	23	1
Artillery Saddles	—	—	—	2	—	—	—	—	10	—
Horse Collars	—	—	—	13	—	—	—	—	11	—
Bridles	—	—	—	13	—	—	—	—	11	—
Halters	—	—	—	13	—	—	—	—	35	—

	3rd Reserve Battery 7th Horse Battery					4th Reserve Battery 22nd Horse Battery				
	Captured	Dead	Wounded	Missing	Damaged	Captured	Dead	Wounded	Missing	Damaged
Staff Officers	—	—	1	—	1	—	—	—	—	—
Senior Officers	—	—	8	—	—	—	—	1	1	—
Artillerists	—	—	—	—	—	—	—	1	—	—
Musicians	—	—	—	—	—	—	—	—	—	—
Privates	—	10	33	—	—	—	6	8	7	—
Foreigners	—	—	—	—	—	—	—	—	—	—
Mounts (Horses)	—	—	—	—	—	—	—	30	3	—
Draft Horses	—	—	—	—	—	—	—	12	3	—
20pdr Licornes	—	—	—	—	—	—	—	—	—	—
Medium 12pdr	—	—	—	—	—	—	—	—	—	—
Short 12pdr	—	—	—	—	—	—	—	—	—	—
10pdr Licorne	—	—	—	—	—	—	—	—	—	—
6pdr Cannon	—	—	—	—	—	—	—	—	—	—
20pdr Caisson	—	—	—	—	—	—	—	—	—	—
12pdr Caisson	—	—	—	—	—	—	—	—	—	—
10pdr Caisson	—	—	—	—	—	—	—	—	1	—
6pdr Caisson	—	—	—	—	—	—	—	—	2	3
Service Saddles	—	—	—	—	—	—	—	—	27	—
Artillery Saddles	—	—	—	—	—	—	—	—	5	—
Horse Collars	—	—	—	—	—	—	—	—	12	—
Bridles	—	—	—	—	—	—	—	—	12	—
Halters	—	—	—	—	—	—	—	—	12	—

Note: The artillery material losses are from contemporary Russian source documents. The losses they indicate are not always consistent. Various listings will show fewer horse collars, bridles, and halters missing than draft horses lost. It would seemingly imply that the Russian soldiers scrambled about gathering up the equipment from the dead horses rather than fighting the French. In other instances it shows more horse equipment lost than horses, which would seemingly indicate that horses were stripped of their halters, etc., and led out of the battle. In addition, the casualties do not seem high enough in view of the various commentaries made by contemporaries, unless the Russians suffered a tremendous desertion-under-fire rate and, after the battle, all these men returned to their colors. It is more likely that these records are not as accurate as one might wish.

Select Bibliography

Alombert, P., and Colin, J., *La Campagne de 1805 en Allemagne*, Librairie Militaire R. Chapelot, Paris, 1904.

Alt, Lt., *Geschichte der Königl. Preussischen Kurassiere und Dragooner seit 1619 resp 1631–1870*, Herre der Vegangenheit J. Olmes, Krefeld, 1970.

Armeemuseums Karlsruhe, *1808–1814, Badischen Truppen in Spainen*, Karlsruhe, 1939.

Armeemuseums Karlsruhe, *1812 Badischen Truppen in Russland*, Karlsruhe, 1937.

Atteridge, A. H., *Joachim Murat*, Brentano's, New York, 1911.

Arvers, P., *Historique du 82e Régiment d'Infanterie de Ligne et du 7e Régiment d'Infanterie Légère, 1684–1876*, Typographie Lahure, Paris, 1876.

Baden-Hochberg, Margraf Wilhelm von, *Denkwurdigkeiten, bearbeitet von Karl Obser*, Heidelberg, 1906.

Beck, F., *Geschichte des l. Grossherzoglich Hessen Infanterie- (Leibgarde-) Regiments Nr. 115, 1621–1899*, Berlin, 1899.

Beck, F., *Geschichte des Grossherzoglichen Artilleriekorps l. Grossherzoglich Hessischen Feldartillerie Regiments Nr. 25 und seiner Staemme 1460–1912*, Berlin, 1912.

Belhomme, Lt. Col., *Histoire de l'Infanterie en France*, Charles-Lavauzelle, Paris, 1898.

Beitzke, H., *Geschichte des Russischen Krieges im Jahre 1812*, Berlin, 1856.

Belloc, H., *Napoleon's Campaign of 1812 and the Retreat from Moscow*, Harper & Brothers, New York, 1926.

Bertin, G., *La Campagne de 1812*, ed. Ernest Flammarion, Paris, 1895.

Blankenhorn, E., *1812, Badischen truppen in Russland*, Karlsruhe, 1937.

Bleibtreu, C., *Maschalle, Generale, Soldaten, Napoleons I*, A. Schall, Berlin, unknown.

_____, *Der rusische Feldzuge 1812*, Jena, 1897.

Blond, G., *La Grande Armée*, R. Laffont, Paris, 1979.

Bogdanovitch, M., *Geschichte des Feldzuges im Jahre 1812*, Leipzig, 1863.

Bonaparte, N., *Correspondance de Napoleon 1er*, Paris, 1861.

Bonin, U. von, *Geschichte des Ingenieurkorps und der Pioniere in Preussen*, LTR Verlag, Wiesbaden, 1981.

Bonnal, H., *La Manoeuvre de Vilna*, Librairie Militaire R. Chapelot, Paris, 1905.

Boppe, A., *Les Espagnols dans la Grande Armée; Le Division Romana (1808–1809); Le Régiment Joseph Napoleon (1809–1813)*, Berger-Levrault & Co., Paris, 1899.

————, *La Légion Portuguese* (*1808–1813*), Berger-Levrault & Co., Paris, 1897.

Bouchard, S., *Historique du 28e Régiment de Dragons*, Berger-Levrault & Co., Paris, 1893.

Brett, James, *1812—Eyewitness Accounts of Napoleon's Defeat in Russia*, R. Clay Ltd., Bungay, Suffolk, England, 1966.

Brissac, R., *Historique du 7e Régiment de Dragons* (*1673–1909*), Ed. Leroy, Paris, 1909.

Bujac, E., *L'Armée Russe—son histoire, son organization actuelle*, Paris, 1894.

Buturlin, D., *Atlas des Plans et Legendes etc., de l'histoire militaire de la campagne de Russie*, Paris, date unknown.

————, *Histoire Militaire de la campagne de 1812*, Paris, 1824.

Capello, G., *Gli italiani in Russia nel 1812*, Cita di Castello, 1912.

Cathcart, G., *Commentaries on the War in Russia and Germany in 1812 and 1813*, John Murray, London, 1850.

Caulaincourt, A., *With Napoleon in Russia*, W. Morrow & Co., New York, 1937.

Cerrini di Monte Varchi, C. F. X., *Die Feldzuge der Sachsen in den Jahren 1812 und 1813 aus den bewahrtesten Quellen gezogen*, Dresden, 1821.

de Chambray, M., *Histoire de l'Expedition de Russie*, Paris, 1825.

Chandler, D., *Dictionary of the Napoleonic Wars*, Macmillan, New York, 1979.

————, *The Campaigns of Napoleon*, Macmillan, New York, 1966.

Chapuis, Col., *Observations sur la Retraite du Prince Bagration*, Paris, 1856.

Chichagov, *Memoires de l'Amiral Tchichagoff* (*1767–1849*), Leipzig, 1862.

Chleminski, J., von, *L'Armée du Duche de Varsovie, 1807–1815*, Paris, 1910.

Chuquet, A., *Lettres de 1812*, Paris, 1911.

————, *La Campagne de 1812, Memoires du Margrave de Bade*, Fontemoing Co., Paris, 1912.

Clausewitz, C. von, *The Campaign of 1812 in Russia*, Greenwood Press, Westport, Connecticut, 1979.

Corda, H., *Le Régiment de la Fère et le 1er Régiment d'Artillerie*, Berger-Levrault & Co., Paris, 1906.

Creveld, M. von, *Supplying War, Logistics from Wallenstein to Patton*, Cambridge Univ. Press, New York, 1977.

Czernczitz, G. R. H. von, *Geschichte des K.u.K. Infanterie-Regiments Graf von Lacy, No. 22*, Verlag des Regiments, Zara, 1902.

von Decker, H., *Geschichtliche Ruckblicke auf die Formation der Preussischen Artillerie seit dem Jahre 1809*, Berlin, 1866.

Dodge, T. A., *Napoleon*, Houghton, Mifflin & Co., Cambridge, Mass., 1904.

Duffy, C., *Borodino, Napoleon against Russia, 1812*, C. Scribner's & Sons, New York, 1973.

Duhesme, *Essai sur l'infanterie légère ou Traite des Petits Operations de la Guerre*, Librairie Militaire J. Dumaine, Paris, 1864.

Dundulis, B., *Napoleon et la Lithuanie en 1813*, France, 1940.

Erzherzog, Johann, *Geschichte des K.u.K. Infanterie-Regiments Erzherzog Wilhelm No. 12*, Druck und Verlag von L. Seidel & Sohn, Vienna, 1880.

Esposito, Gen., *A Military History and Atlas of the Napoleonic Wars*, AMS Press, New York, 1978.

Exerzir-Reglement für die Artillerie der Königlich-Preussischen Armee, George Decker, Berlin, 1812.

Exerzir-Reglement für die Infanterie der Königlich-Preussischen Armee, George Decker, Berlin, 1812.

Exerzir-Reglement für die Kavalerie der Königlich-Preussischen Armee, George Decker, Berlin, 1812.

Fabry, G., *Campagne de Russie*, Librairie Militaire R. Chapelot, Paris, 1900–1903.

_____, *Campagne de 1812; documents relatifs à l'aile droit, 20 août–4 decembre*, Librairie Militaire R. Chapelot, Paris, 1912.

_____, *Campagne de 1812; documents relatifs à l'aile gauche, 20 août–4 decembre, IIe, VIe, et IXe Corps*, Librairie Militaire R. Chapelot, Paris, 1912.

Fain, Baron, *Manuscript de Mil Huit Cent Treize*, Delauny, Paris, 1824.

_____, *Manuscript de Mil Huit Cent Douze*, Delauny, Paris, 1827.

Ferber, *Geschichte des l. Badischen Feldartillerie-Regiments Nr. 14 mit Zustimmung des Regiments zum 50jahrigen Chef-Jubilamn*, Karlsruhe, 1906.

_____, *Geschichte des l. Badischen Feldartillerie-Regiments Nr. 14 mit Zustimmung des Regiments zum 50jahrigen Chef-Jubilamn*, Karlsruhe, 1906.

Fezensac, M. de, *The Russian Campaign, 1812*, Athens, 1970.

Foord, E., *Napoleon's Russian Campaign of 1812*, Little, Brown & Co., Boston, 1913.

Forst, *Geschichte des Königlich Preussischen Thuringischen Feldartillerie-Regiments Nr.l und seiner Stamm-Truppentheile*, Berlin, 1897.

French General Staff, *Réglement concernant l'Excercice et les Manoeuvres de l'Infanterie du Premier août 1791*, Chez Magimel, Paris, 1811.

_____, *Manuel d'Infanterie ou Resumé de tous les Réglements, Decrets, Usages, et Renseignements propres aux Sous-Officiers de cette Armée*, Chez Magimel, Paris, 1813.

Freiherr von Welden, C., *Der Feldzug der Oesterreichen gegen Russland im Jahr 1812*, Vienna, 1870.

Funck, F. von, *In Russland und Sachsen 1812–1815*, Dresden, 1930.

_____, *In the Wake of Napoleon: Being the Memoirs (1807–1809) of Ferdinand von Funck, Lieutenant General in the Saxon Army and Adjutant General to the King of Saxony*, John Lane, the Bodley Head Ltd., London, 1931.

Gayda, M., and Krijitsky, A., *L'Armée Russe sous le Tsar Alexandre 1er de 1805 à 1815*, Editions Sabretache, Paris, 1955.

George, H., *Napoleon's Invasion of Russia*, New Amsterdam Book Co., New York, 1899.

Geschichte des 3. Württ. Infanterie-Regiments No. 121, 1716–1891, Stuttgart, 1891.

Gessler and Tognarelli, *Geschichte des 2. Württembergischen Feldartillerie-Regiments Nr. 29, Prinzregent Lutipold von Bayern*, Stuttgart, 1892.

Giesse, K., *Kassel-Moskau-Küstrin 1812–1813*, Leipzig, 1912.

Gouvion Saint-Cyr, Laurent, *Memoires pour Servir à l'Histoire sous le Directoire, Le Consulate et l'Empire*, Paris, 1851.

Gleich, *Die ersten 100 Jahren des Uhlanen-Regiments König Wilhelm (2 Württemberger) Nr. 20*, Uhland'schen Buchdruckerei, G.m.b.h., Stuttgart, unknown.

Gourgaud, Gen. *Napoleon and the Grande Armee in Russia; or Critical Examinations of Count Philip de Segeur's Work*, Anthony Finley, Philadelphia, 1825.

Griefinger, *Geschichte des Uhlanen Regiments "König Karl,"* Stuttgart, 1883.

Grossen Generalstab, *Urkundliche Beitrage und Forschungen zur Geschichte des Preussischen Heeres*, LTR-Verlag, Wiesbaden, 1982.

————, *Die Reorganization der Preussischen Armee nach dem Tilsiter Frieden*, Berlin, date unknown.

————, *Geschichte der Bekleidung, Bewaffnung und Ausrüstung des Königlich Preussischen Heeres, die leichte infanterie oder die Fusilier-Bataillone 1787–1809 und die Jäger 1744–1809*, Vol. III, Weimar, 1912.

Guesdon, A., *Histoire de la Guerre de Russie en 1812*, Paris, 1829.

Guye, A., *Le Bataillon de Neuchâtel, dit les Canaris au service de Napoleon*, à la Baconnière, Neuchâtel, 1964.

Hansch, Pr. Lt., *Geschichte des Königlich Saechsischen Ingenieur- und Pionier-Korps, Pionier-Batallons Nr. 12*, Dresden, 1898.

Has, W., *Geschichte des l. Kurhessischen Feldartillerie-Regiments Nr. 11 und seiner Stamtruppen*, Marburg, 1913.

Hellmüller, R., *Die Schlacht an der Berezina und die Schweizer*, Bern, date unknown.

Hemingway, J., *The Northern Campaigns and History of the War, from the Invasion of Russia, in 1812*, Manchester, 1815.

Heuman, Lt. Col., *Historique du 148e Régiment d'Infanterie*, Henri Charles-Lavauzelle, Paris, unknown.

Holleben, Gen. Maj. von, *Geschichte des Fruhjahrsfeldzuges 1813 und Vorgeschichte*, E. S. Mittler & Sohn, Berlin, 1904.

Holtzhauzen, P. *Ein Verwandter Goethes im russischen Feldzuge, 1812*, Morawe & Schaffelt Verlag, Berlin, 1912.

_____, *Die Deutschen in Russland, 1812*, Morawe & Schaffelt Verlag, Berlin, 1912.

von Horsetzky, A., *Der Feldzug 1812 in Russland*, Vienna, 1889.

Hughes, Maj. Gen. B. P., *La Puissance de Feu*, T. & A. Constable, Ltd., Edinborough, 1976.

Jomini, Gen. Baron, *Histoire Critique et Militaire des Campagnes de la Revolution Paisant suit au Traite des Grandes Operations militaires*, Chez Magimel, Anselin & Pouchard, Paris, 1816.

Kaisenberg, M. von, *König Jérôme Napoleon Ein Zeit- und Lebensbild*, Verlag von H. Schmidt & C. Gunther, Leipzig, 1899.

Kandelsdorfer, K., *Geschichte des K.u.K. Feld-Jäger Bataillons Nr. 7*, Bruck A. D. Mur, Vienna, 1896.

Kattrein, L., *Ein Jahrhundert deutscher Truppengeschichte dargestellt an derjenigen des Grosse Hessischen Kontingents 1806–1906*, Darmstadt, 1907.

Keegan, J., *The Face of War*, Viking Press, New York, 1976.

Kersten, F., and Ortenburg, G., *Die Sachsische Armee von 1763 bis 1862*, Bekum, 1982.

Kiem, A., *Geschichte des Infanterie-Leibregiments Grossherzogin (3. Grossherzog. Hessisches Nr. 117) und seiner stamme 1677–1902*, Berlin, 1903.

Kiesling, *Geschichte der Organization und Bekleidung des Trains der Königlich Preussischen Armee 1740 bis 1888*, Berlin, 1889.

Kraft, *Die Württemberger in den Napoleonischen Kriegen*, Stuttgart, 1953.

Kretschmer, A. von, *Geschichte K.u.K. Sachsischen Feld Artillerie von 1620–1820*, Berlin, 1914.

Labaume, E., *Relation complète de la campagne de Russie*, Rey & Gravier, Paris, 1816.

de Labeaudorière, J. P., *La Campagne de Russie de 1812*, Paris, 1902.

Lachouque, H., *The Anatomy of Glory*, Providence, R.I., 1962.

Langeron, *Memoires de Langeron*, Brown University, Paris, 1902.

Lantz, G., *Geschichte der Stammtruppen des 6. Thuringischen Infanterie-Regiments No. 95 als Deutsche Bundes-Kontingente von 1814–1867*, Braunschweig, 1897.

Laumera, M., *L'Artillerie de Campagne Française pendant les Guerres de la Revolution. Evolutions de l'Organization et de la tactique*, Helsinki, 1956.

Lesage, C., *Napoleon 1er, Greancier de la Prusse*, Librairie Hachette, Paris, 1924.

von Lindenau, *Der Beresina-Uebergang des Kaisers Napoleon*, Berlin, 1896.

Linnebach, K., *Geschichte der Badischen Pioniere*, Leipzig.

Lucas-Dubreton, J., *Soldats de Napoleon*, Librairie Jules Tallandier, Paris, 1977.

Lunsman, F., *Die Armee des Königreichs Westfalen 1807–1813*, C. Leddihn Verlag, Berlin, 1935.

Maag, Dr. A., *Geschichte der Schweizer truppen in Französischen Dienst vom Ruckzug aus Russland bis zum zweiten Pariser Freiden*, E. Kuhn, Viel, 1894.

_____, *Die Shicksal der Schweizer Regiment in Napoleons 1. Feldzug nach Russland 1812*, E. Kuhn, Beil, 1854.

Macdonald, Marshal, *Memorien des Marschalls Macdonald*, Verlag von R. Lutz, Stuttgart, 1903.

Maciage, *Geschichte des K.u.K. galizischen Infanterie-Regiments Feldmarschall Friederich Josias Prinz zu Sachsen-Colburg-Saafeld, Nr. 57*, Kreisel & Groger, Vienna, 1898.

Margueron, L. J., *Campagne de Russie*, H. Charles-Lavauzelle, Paris, 1897–1906.

McQueen, J., *The Campaigns of 1812, 1813, and 1814*, E. Khull & Co., Glasgow, 1815.

Meneval, C. F., *Memoirs of Napoleon Bonaparte*, P. F. Collier & Son, New York, 1910.

Meyer, K., *Geschichte des Infanterie-Regiments Fürst Leopold von Anhalt-Dessau (1. Magdeburgischen) Nr. 26 1813–1913*, Magdeburg, 1913.

Muller, H., *Die Entwicklung der Feld-Artillerie in Bezug auf Material, Organization und Taktik, von 1815 bis 1870*, Berlin, 1873.

Muller, H., *Geschichte des 4. Württembergischen Infanterie-Regiments No. 122 Kaiser Franz Joseph von Oestereich, König von Ungarn, 1806–1906*, Heilbronn, 1906.

Munich, F., *Geschichte der Entwicklung der Bayerischen Armee seit zwei Jahrhunderten (1618–1870)*, Meisenheim, 1972.

Nash, D., *The Prussian Army 1808–1815*, Almark Publishing Co., Ltd., Great Britain, 1972.

von Neubronner, *Geschichte des Dragoner Regiment König*, Stuttgart, date unknown.

Ney, Marshal, *Memoirs of Marshal Ney*, Bull & Churton, London, 1833.

Nuebling, *Geschichte des Grenadier Regiment König Karl*, Berlin, 1911.

Ochwicz, G., *Rok 1809*, Poznan, 1925.

Osten, S., *Der Feldzuge von 1812*, Berlin, 1901.

Palmer, A., *Napoleon in Russia, The 1812 Campaign*, Simon & Schuster, New York, 1967.

Paret, P., *Yorck and the Era of Prussian Reform 1807–1815*, Princeton, N.J., 1966.

Parkinson, R., *The Fox of the North*, David McKay & Co., New York, 1976.

Parquin, Cpt, *Souvenirs du Capitaine Parquin 1803–1814*, Boussod, Valadon & Cie, Paris, 1892.

Pawlowski, B., *Historja Wojyn Polsko-Austrejackiej 1809 Roku*, Warsaw, 1935.

Persy, N., *Elementary Treatise on the Forms of Cannon and Various Systems of Artillery*, Bloomfield, Ontario, Canada, 1979.

von Pfannenberg, L., *Geschichte des Infanterie-Regiments Grossherzog von Sachsen (5. Thuringisches) Nr. 94 und seiner Stammtruppen 1702–1912*, Berlin, 1912.

Pfister, A., *Aus dem lager des Rheinbunds 1812 und 1813*, Deutsche Verlags-Anstalt, Leipzig, 1897.

Pietsch, P. von, *Die Formations- und Uniformierungs Geschichte des Preussischen Heeres 1808–1914*, Verlag H. G. Schulz, Hamburg, 1963.

Pichard and Tuety, *Unpublished Correspondance of Napoleon I*, Duffield & Co., New York, 1913.

Pitot, Lt., *Historique du 83e Régiment d'Infanterie 1684–1891*, Privately Published, Toulouse, date unknown.

Poniatowski, J., *Correspondance du Prince Joseph Poniatowski avec la France*, Poznan, 1929.

Porter, Sir R. K., *A Narrative of the Campaign in Russia during the Year 1812*, Longhan, Hurst, Rees, Orme & Brown, London, 1815.

Prussian Grosser Generalstab, *Exerzir-Regelment für die Kavallerie der Königlich Preussische Armee*, G. Decker, Berlin, 1812.

————, *Exerzir Regelment für artillerie der Königl. Preussische Armee*, G. Decker, Berlin, 1812.

————, *Exerzir Regelment für die infanterie*, G. Decker, Berlin, 1812.

Quimby, R. S., *The Background of Napoleonic Warfare*, AMS Press, N.Y., date unknown.

Rau, F., *Geschichte des l. Badischen Leib-Dragoner-Regiments Nr. 20 und dessen Stamm-Regiments des Badischen Dragoner-Regiments von Freystedt von 1803 bis zur Gegenwart*, Berlin, 1878.

von Ravelsberg, F. S. E., *Geschichte des K.u.K. 12 Dragoner-Regiments*, R. Brzezowsky & Sohne, Vienna, 1890.

Roeder, H., *The Ordeal of Captain Roeder*, Methuen & Co., Ltd., London, 1960.

Rothenberg, *The Art of Warfare in the Age of Napoleon*, Indiana Univ. Press, Bloomington, Indiana, 1978.

Roulin, Lt. Col., *125e Régiment d'Infanterie*, G. Jacob, Orlèans, 1890.

Rouquerol, G., *L'Artillerie au debut des Guerres de la Revolution*, Paris, 1898.

Saint-Hilaire, *Histoire de la Campagne de Russie pendant l'année 1812 et de la captivité des Prisonniers Français en Sibérie et dans les autres Provinces de l'Empire précédée d'une resumé de l'Histoire de Russie*, Ed. E. & V. Penaud Frères, Paris, date unknown.

Sarrazin, M., *Histoire de la Guerre de Russie et d'Allemagne, Depuis le passage du Niemen, June 1812, jusqu'au passage du Rhin, Novembre 1813*, Paris, 1815.

Sauzey, Cpt., *Les Allemands sous les Aigles Françaises*

_____, *Le Contingent Badois*, Librairie Militaire R. Chapelot, Paris, 1904.

_____, *Les Saxons dans nos rangs*, Librairie Militaire R. Chapelot, Paris, 1907.

_____, *Le Régiment des Duches de Saxe*, Librairie Militaire R. Chapelot, Paris, 1908.

_____, *Nos Allies les Bavarois*, Librairie Militaire R. Chapelot, Paris, 1910.

Saxon Army, *Stamm und Rang Listes der Königlich Sachsischen Armee auf das Jahr 1810*, Dresden, 1810.

Saxon General Staff, *Exercir-Reglement für die Königlich Sachsische Cavalerie*, Dresden, 1810.

Schauroth, *Im Rheinbund-Regiment der Herzoglich Sachsischen Kontingente Koburg-Hildburghausen-Gotha-Weimar während der Feldzuge in Tirol, Spanien und Russland, zusammengestellt von A. von Schauroth*, Berlin, 1905.

Schehl, C., *Vom Rhein bis Moskwa 1812*, Krefeld, 1957.

Schmidt, C. Dr., *Le Grand-Duche de Berg (1806–1813)*, Paris, 1905.

Schmitt, Lt., *151e Régiment d'Infanterie*, Paris, 1901.

Schnitzler, *La Russie en 1812*, Paris, 1899.

Schreiber, *Geschichte des Brandenburgischen Train-Bataillons Nr. 3*, Berlin, 1903.

Schuster, O. and Franck, F. A., *Geschichte der Sachsischen Armee*, Vol. II, Leipzig, 1885.

Schwarzbach and Wieser, *Geschichte des K.u.K. Siebenten Dragoner-Regiments Herzog Wilhelm von Braunschweig von seiner errichtung 1663 bis Ende Mai 1879*, Vienna, 1879.

von Seebach, L. *Geschichte des herzoglichen Sachsen Scharfschützenbataillons in Jahre 1806 und des Infanterieregiments der herzoge von Sachsen in den Jahren 1807, 1809, 1810, und 1811*, Weimar, 1838.

Seeliger, E., *Geschichte des K.u.K. Infanterie-Regiments Nr. 32 für immerwahrende Zeiten: K.u.K. Maria Theresia von seiner Errichtung 1741 bis 1900*, Pester Buchdruckerei-Actien-Gesellschaft, Budapest, 1900.

de Segur, P., *History of the Expedition to Russia Undertaken by the Emperor Napoleon in the Year 1812*, Truettel & Wurtz, Treuttel, Jun. & Richter, London, 1825.

du Seruzier, Baron, *Memoires Militaires du Baron Seruzier, Colonel d'Artillerie Légère*, Librairie Militaire de L. Baudoin, Paris, unknown.

von Seydlitz, Generalmajor, *Tagebuch des Königlich Preussischen Armeekorps unter Befehl des General-Lieutenants von York im Feldzuge von 1812*, Berlin, 1823.

Shanahan, W. O., *Prussian Military Reforms 1786–1813*, Columbia Univ. Press, New York, 1945.

Simond, E., *Le 28e de Ligne, Historique du Régiment*, Megard & Co., Rouen, 1889.

Soltyk, R., *Relation des Operations de l'Armée*, Paris, 1841.

Stiegler, E., *Le Maréchal Oudinot Duc de Reggio*, Paris, 1894.

Strack von Weissenbach, *Geschichte der Königlich Württembergischen Artillerie*, Stuttgart, 1882.

Starkof, *Geschichte des K. Württembergischen 2. Reiter Regiment*, Darmstadt, 1862.

Strotha, von, *Die Königlich Preussische Reitende Artillerie von Jahre 1759 bis 1816*, LTR Verlag, Wiesbaden, 1981.

Tchuykevitch, Col., *Reflection on the War of 1812 with Tables*, Boston, 1813.

Thiry, Baron J., *La Campagne de Russie*, Berger-Levrault, Paris, 1969.

Treuenfest, G. R. A., *Geschichte des K.u.K. Infanterie-regiments Nr. 46*, Verlag des Regiments, Vienna, 1890.

U.S. War Department (Cpt. G. McClellan), *Report to the Secretary of War, Communicating the Report of Captain George B. McClellan*, A. O. P. Nicholson, Washington, D.C., 1857.

Vallotton, G., *Les Suisses à la Berezina*, A La Baconnière, Neuchâtel, 1942.

de Vaudoncourt, General, *Memoires pour servir a l'Histoire de la Guerre entre la France et la Russie en 1812*, Paris, 1817.

Viger, Count, *Davout, Maréchal d'Empire*, Ed. P. Ollendorff, Paris, 1898.

Vogel, *Theilnahme der König. Preuss. Artillerie an dem Kampf des Befreiungskriege*, LTR Verlag, Wiesbaden, 1981.

Vossler, Lt. H. A., *With Napoleon in Russia 1812*, The Folio Society, London, 1969.

Wust, G., *Geschichte des K.u.K. 34 Linien-Infanterie-Regiments Prinz Regent von Preussen*, K. K. Hoff & Staatsdruckerei, Vienna, 1860.

Young, P., *Napoleon's Marshals*, Hippocrene Books, Inc., New York, 1973.

von Zech and von Porbeck, *Geschichte der Badischen Truppen 1809 im Feldzuge der Französischen Hauptarmee gegen Österreich*, Heidelberg, 1909.

Zimmerman, *Geschichte des Grossherzoglich Hessischen Dragoner-Regiments (Garde-Dragoner-Regiments) Nr. 23*, Darmstadt, 1878.

Zweguintov, *L'Armee Russie*, unpublished manuscript.

Index

Croatian p 175-6
mtd carbine fire on cossacks p 178
Cavalry into giant square p 184
Polish converged voltigeurs p
6 & 12 pdrs can't batter hole in walls p 192
converged howitzers p 192, 194, 229
whole rank killed w/one cannon ball p 193
cossack pichets, p 198
Lithuanian Light Infantry p 210
  "   Tartars p 211
Russian tactics in contrast to Wellington p 218-9
Destroyed redoubt p 222, Page 246
Prolonged cannon p 233
Square broken p 241, 248, p 311
Infantry bayonets charging cavalry p 242
cavalry melee losses Due to lack of cuirasses p 242
Cavalry over breast work p 246
Danish p 448
Opolochenie fills out third rank p 575, 582, 587, 27
  Also grenadier 273
  Italian Guard Conscripts p 471